Tennessee
in the Civil War

Tennessee in the Civil War

Selected Contemporary Accounts of Military and Other Events, Month by Month

Compiled by
JAMES B. JONES, JR.

McFarland & Company, Inc., Publishers
Jefferson, North Carolina, and London

LIBRARY OF CONGRESS CATALOGUING-IN-PUBLICATION DATA

Tennessee in the Civil War : selected contemporary accounts
of military and other events, month by month /
compiled by James B. Jones, Jr.
p.   cm.

ISBN 978-0-7864-6129-5
softcover : 50# alkaline paper ∞

1. Tennessee — History — Civil War, 1861–1865 — Campaigns.
2. Tennessee — History — Civil War, 1861–1865 — Sources.
3. United States — History — Civil War, 1861–1865 — Campaigns.
4. United States — History — Civil War, 1861–1865 — Sources.
I. Jones, James B., 1947–
E470.4.T46   2011
976.8'04 — dc22   2011006772

BRITISH LIBRARY CATALOGUING DATA ARE AVAILABLE

© 2011 James B. Jones, Jr. All rights reserved

*No part of this book may be reproduced or transmitted in any form
or by any means, electronic or mechanical, including photocopying
or recording, or by any information storage and retrieval system,
without permission in writing from the publisher.*

Front cover: Wood engraving, Chattanooga, 1894
(Library of Congress); flag (Civil War Press).

Manufactured in the United States of America

*McFarland & Company, Inc., Publishers
Box 611, Jefferson, North Carolina 28640
www.mcfarlandpub.com*

Table of Contents

Introduction
1

Tennessee and the Civil War
3

The Days of the War
9

Bibliography
271

Index
283

Introduction

This book aims at introducing the idea that the Civil War was not just a series of big battles "fought" by famous generals. It is a new way for learning about the discord in Tennessee, one that offers the reader only primary source information about the struggle in the Volunteer State and its impact on its people. This book's target is to give the reader a better way to learn about the Civil War in Tennessee, the only state designated by Congress as a Civil War National Heritage Area. The book offers rare glimpses of the Civil War as it unfolded in Tennessee.

Entries are transcriptions of primary sources with citations, but without comment from the author or other historians. Readers will not be advised as to what to take into account, but can judge for themselves the value of the documents. In this way the reader can gain an enhanced understanding of the war based upon materials seen usually only by professional historians.

Entries are arranged monthly from April 1861 to April 1865, for a total of 49 months. In each month citations provide tales frozen in time. Those documents that focus on martial features are not about big battles, but may tell about their aftermath or a number of lesser combat actions, including skirmishes, engagements, reconnaissances, scouting and guerrilla warfare. Other topics rarely addressed in Civil War books are included, such as public health issues, juvenile delinquency, urban history, politics, illegal cotton trading, anti–Semitism, train wrecks, inflation, welfare, commodities speculation, charity, refugees, African Americans, Native Americans and the role of women. The sources utilized include the *Official Records of the War of the Rebellion* as well as a broad range of diaries, journals, gunboat logs, letters and newspaper stories. The war was many things to many people, not just an experience shared by uniformed white males. Within the borders of Tennessee the war touched the lives of literally millions of people, whether soldiers or civilians, men, women or children. This book is a source for some absorbing and exciting narrative evaluation. After each document entry there is a citation, indicating the source from which the account was taken.

A list composed by the author shows that skirmishes, numbering 1,255, account for 39 percent of total combat events, while battles account for .04 percent. There is little doubt the numbers are larger, but reference to them has not yet been discovered. Here is the breakdown of types of combat incidents in Civil War Tennessee: actions, 100; affairs, 69; artillery duels, 4; attacks, 134; charges, 16; combat, 9; battles, 10; bombardments, 17; conscript sweeps, 42; demonstrations, 27; descents, 6; engagements, 36; expeditions, 238; guerrilla incidents, 402; pursuits, 35; reconnaissances, 186; retreats, 24; mass murders, 2; murder, 57; naval operations, 48; raids, 89; sacks, 4; scouts, 394; skirmishes, 1,255; surrender, 28; withdrawal, 12; for a total of 3,245.

Not all of these are found in the pages of this book, but the list is presented to show how wide the kinds of combat operations were during the war in Tennessee. As may be seen, greater weight is given to the smaller kinds of combat action than to big battles. This is in part because the famous battles fought in Civil War Tennessee have been examined in detail by many historians and to duplicate those efforts here would be, at best, gilding the lily. It also directs the focus of this book to the common soldier. This is best epitomized in an excerpt from an April 1863 Confederate newspaper article on the Army of Tennessee. It identifies the ordinary casualty and his usual level of combat:

> The wounded are supported away on horseback; so is the limber man, whose placid face proves that he died very suddenly. After a while a widow weeps somewhere, but the world never hears anything about it — it was only "a skirmish up at the front." And so of lesser skirmishes, where small scouting parties meet. Many of the noblest and bravest spirits of this war have thus fallen; but no halo of battle glory brightens their names — they fell "skirmishing up at the front."

It isn't entirely a story of how they died in the war — in fact, far more died of disease than resulting from actual combat — it is also a story of how they lived in the war, both civilian and soldier, in the country and in the cities. Life was adversely affected, but it went on nonetheless. We know how the war turned out, but the people swept up in it had no idea it would take nearly four years to realize its outcome. This book undertakes to address the civilian side of the Civil War to reveal the sense of the chaos and confusion that are among the offspring of war.

One further note may be advisable: Spelling and grammar in the nineteenth century were not as uniform as they are today. It is sometimes considered best, when confronted with an unusual spelling, to use the literary device "[*sic*]," Latin meaning "thus; so." Herein, however, its use has been all but removed as cumbersome, and misspellings in the original documents are preserved without comment.

Tennessee and the Civil War

Tennessee, at the end of the 1850s, had prospered from the agricultural wealth that dominated economic life. Most of this prosperity was created by producing cotton and made possible by slave labor. Tennessee was in sympathy with her sister states, those that would form the Confederacy, in this regard. Manufacturing was not a major source of this prosperity. Regardless of a number of economic setbacks in the 1850s, Tennessee and the nation were on the road to recovery. But there was more dividing the nation than economic models.

Beginning in the 1830s a sentiment grew in the South that states could nullify, or veto, laws passed by Congress should they be thought to work against Southern interests. Nullification emphatically meant a state could and should secede from the Union should its leaders think it necessary to protect states' rights. In 1831 South Carolina attempted to secede. Only the vigorous opposition of President Andrew Jackson, a Southerner himself, who proclaimed "Disunion by armed force is treason," quelled the unrest. Nevertheless, the philosophical underpinnings for the Civil War were recognizable. The idea of secession did not rest, and in reaction to federal limits placed on the expansion of slavery in 1850, Southern advocates of a separatist agenda took steps to consider their position on the question of Southern rights, or secession. Delegates from nine slave states met in Nashville, Tennessee, on June 3, 1850. Extremists saw an opportunity to broaden their support for secession but moderates were in control. In the end the convention adopted a resolution calling for the extension of the Missouri Compromise line of 1828 to the Pacific: north of the line being free, and to the south, slavery. The notion of secession had once again been broached, but in Tennessee, the idea was still more theoretical than indisputable.

Another issue was the abolition of slavery. A newly rejuvenated abolitionist movement had developed in the New England states at about the same time as the nullification movement in the South. While all abolitionists called for the end of slavery, they were not united on how or when this should be done. Regardless, the more radical abolitionists attacked the southern slave holders as evil malcontents whose use of chattel slavery was immoral, inhuman and debased. Slave owners, while a distinct minority of the Southern white male population, resented these attacks and claimed slavery was a positive good. Their control of the media of the day (newspapers, public speaking and political debate) allowed them to dominate thought on the subject. The underlying message, both obvious and subtle, was that freed male slaves would attack white families, and that slaves were mere children who needed guidance only the blessings of white civilization could provide. The abolition movement also manifested itself in national politics and was indeed a divisive force in national debate. Northerners remained undecided on the question.

Thus, political, economic and moral differences caused friction between the two sections that erupted into Civil War.

Soon after the election of Abraham Lincoln (characterized in the South along with his party as "Black Republicans"), the South Carolina legislature unanimously passed an "ordinance to dissolve the Union between the State of South Carolina and other States united with her under the compact entitled the Constitution of the United States of America," on December 20. The die was cast. In quick succession Mississippi, Florida, Alabama, Georgia, Louisiana and Texas had followed suit by February. The war started with the bombardment of Fort Sumter in Charleston, South Carolina, setting off a popular wave of secessionist excitement in the region. Arkansas and Virginia were prompted to leave the Union in May. After an initial failure to win a secession vote in February 1861 (62,282 against, 59,449 for), Tennessee did opt to join the Confederacy on June 8, 1861 (104,913 for, 47,238 against). The Volunteer State had the distinction of being the last state to secede. Kentucky, Delaware, Maryland and Missouri remained loyal to the Union but not without major internal opposition. Still, political sentiments in many areas were strongly pro–Union. After Tennessee seceded from the Union, a convention held in Greeneville determined that East Tennessee should secede from the state and stay in the Union. All but one of the counties participating voted in favor of staying in the Union. Confederate authorities, however, demurred.

Tennessee was long on spirit and rhetoric but short on the materiel with which to fight a war. In fact it was difficult for the state to provide its volunteers with uniforms, blankets and firearms. The state's attempt to modify its armory of flintlock muskets into more modern rifles was not adequate to equip the volunteers. At one point Governor Isham G. Harris, recognizing the inability of the state to provide rifles to its soldiers, was forced to make a statewide appeal for civilians to turn in their personal rifles to the state to help arm its soldiers. He likewise experienced opposition to the state draft he instituted after the initially spirited reaction to his call for volunteers lost steam.

In spite of this, recognizing that the Tennessee and Cumberland rivers were highways directly into South Tennessee, the Confederate government built forts Henry and Donelson on the Tennessee and the Cumberland. Fort Henry was poorly built in low ground which made it impossible to defend when winter rains flooded it. Fort Donelson, while a more resilient stronghold, was hastily built with levies of slave labor and soldiers; some masters refused to let their slaves work on the fort.

On February 6, 1862, a joint Federal naval and army attack successfully captured Fort Henry, however, most of its garrison had already redeployed to Fort Donelson. The Confederate commander, Albert Sidney Johnston, rightly regarded Donelson as the major defense for Nashville. He had established a defensive line stretching from the Mississippi River through Kentucky and Tennessee. Fort Donelson was the fortress that would keep Federal forces from taking Nashville and splitting the upper South. While Confederate forces amassed at their defensive haven at Fort Donelson, a Union army led by Brigadier General U.S. Grant and a brown-water flotilla of gunboats, led by Commodore A. H. Foote, soon arrived and laid siege to the fort. After four days of fighting the Confederate forces were surrendered on February 16, setting off the retreat of Johnston's army to Mississippi. When Confederate generals asked for the conditions of surrender Grant replied "unconditional surrender" thus earning his nickname. On February 22, General U.S. Grant proclaimed martial law over all of West Tennessee. The Confederate army's retreat through the City of Rocks initiated the "Panic of Nashville" in which a majority of Confederate sympathizers hurried to leave the capital city for fear the advancing Federal forces would burn the city and kill its citizens. Governor Isham G. Harris and the legislature were among the first to flee. Nashville fell on February 25, but there was no sacking of the city, only an orderly and subdued occupation. It was the first of a series of major losses for the Confederacy in Tennessee.

One objective of the Union was to control the Mississippi River. One obstacle preventing this objective was Island No. 10, located at the extreme northwest of Tennessee. Accordingly, General John Pope's forces, supported by Commodore Foote, followed Grant's winning strategy at Fort Donelson, and besieged the island from March 16 to April 7, 1862. Some of the Confederate forces surrendered and some retreated and regrouped with their counterparts in Corinth, Mississippi, led by A. S. Johnston and P. G. T. Beauregard.

Johnston planned an attack upon Grant's army which had previously arrived by steamboat from Fort Donelson at Pittsburg Landing by way of the Tennessee River. A Confederate attack burst out against Grant at Shiloh on April 6. After a day of heavy, chaotic combat in which General Johnston was killed, Federal forces were on the brink of defeat. Yet, during the stormy night of April 6–7 reinforcements from the Army of the Ohio, led by General Don Carlos Buell and General Lew Wallace's division, arrived. As the battle resumed on April 7 Federal forces reversed the Confederate offensive and by the evening the Confederates withdrew to Corinth, Mississippi. The Union army was too bruised and bloodied to pursue. Both sides sustained heavy losses; an estimated 13,000 out of 63,000 Union troops fell and 11,000 out of 40,000 Confederates were killed, giving the contest the sobriquet "Bloody Shiloh." Casualties totaled 23,746: the U.S., 13,047; the Confederate states, 10,699.

Things did not improve for the Confederacy in the next two months. The U.S. Navy, after a loss to the Confederate River fleet at Plum Run Bend on the Mississippi River in early May, approached Fort Pillow. After initial resistance Confederate forces evacuated in the middle of the night of June 4, 1862, leaving behind all they could not take or destroy. Two days later the naval battle of Memphis took place in which the Confederate fleet protecting the city and the upper Mississippi was vanquished. The Bluff City was taken without a musket shot being fired. In slightly less than a year since declaring secession, and in a period of less than five months, Confederate forces in Tennessee had lost three major forts, control of two rivers, two major cities, a strategic island in the Mississippi River and had withdrawn badly battered, if not defeated, in two major battles.

General Braxton Bragg, now commander of the Army of Tennessee, launched an offensive from Chattanooga with the intent of taking Louisville, Kentucky. His army and that of General Buell met at the village of Perryville, Kentucky, where Bragg's initiative was thwarted on October 8, 1862. Yet Bragg continued to dominate Middle Tennessee after the fight. The costly battle of Murfreesboro (Stones River), from December 31, 1862, to January 3, 1863, which pitted the Army of the Cumberland, led by William Rosecrans, against the Army of Tennessee, forced Bragg to continue his withdrawal southward in Middle Tennessee. The battle's casualties totaled 23,515 killed and wounded (U.S., 13,249; Confederate states, 10,266). The two armies regrouped, resupplied and reinforced.

On June 24, 1863, the Federal Army of the Cumberland began its offensive against Bragg's forces centered in Tullahoma, Tennessee. The initiative was hampered by heavy and constant rain, yet by July 3, 1864, Bragg had been outmaneuvered from Middle Tennessee to Chattanooga, which in turn was occupied in force by the Army of the Cumberland on September 9. Rosecrans had accomplished his goal without one major challenge from the Confederates. President of the Confederacy Jefferson C. Davis, astounded at the loss of the city to the Union, hurried General James Longstreet with 11,000 reinforcements by railroad to Bragg. The armies clashed from September 18 to 20, 1863, on the battlefield of Chickamauga, Georgia, south of Chattanooga. The Union line broke, resulting in a stinging and shameful loss to the Federals. Chattanooga might well have been retaken but for the leadership of Major General George H. Thomas, whose successful opposition to the Confederate onslaught earned him the nickname of "the Rock of Chickamauga." Union troops retreated to Chattanooga, and Bragg assaulted the city from the heights of Lookout Mountain and Missionary Ridge. A constant contest of artillery between the two forces resolved nothing. Union forces had a plethora of supplies at Bridgeport, Alabama, yet could not deliver them because of the presence of Confederate forces. Grant, having replaced Rosecrans, determined a shorter route, one that would require an amphibious attack across the Tennessee River at Brown's Ferry. The attack was successful and soon the "cracker line" opened, and Federal troops received foodstuffs and additional ammunition in late October. Reinforcements arrived.

On November 23 the armies began fighting. Union forces pushed Confederate defenders off Lookout Mountain and the knolls south of Chattanooga. Bragg concentrated his forces on Missionary Ridge. On November 25 Union forces routed the Confederates from the ridge. Union casualties for these two engagements were surprisingly low for the Union, 753 killed, and about 5,000 wounded and missing; Confederacy, 361 killed, about 6,000 wounded and missing. As a result of the battles Chattanooga remained under Union control, allowing for future aggression against the Confederacy in the lower South.

Yet another field of contention was the East Tennessee Campaign, from August 16 to October, 19, 1863. After all plans had been completed on August 17, Major-General Ambrose Burnside began his advance to East Tennessee. He met little opposition and managed to occupy Knoxville on September 1 and 2. Thereafter, on September 9, he trapped Confederate forces at Cumberland Gap. Burnside's command was reinforced in late September. The U.S. Army established dominion over the lion's share of territory in East Tennessee. The last serious attempt by the Confederacy to retake East Tennessee took place during the Knoxville Campaign of November 4, 1863, to December 23, 1863. The Confederate army, led by General Longstreet, made spirited attacks and laid siege to the city, but could not take it. Longstreet's army was forced to withdraw to Virginia on December 3, a relocation that required 20 days.

A significant amount of foraging took place in East Tennessee in order to feed the growing demands of the two armies. In addition, pillaging by poorly disciplined troops added to the hardships of civilians in the region. It has been said that Federal forces stationed in East Tennessee were responsible for more property damage than was caused by genuine combat.

The long Atlanta Campaign which resulted in the capture of the city in the summer of 1864 propelled the new commander of the Army of Tennessee, John Bell Hood, to formulate a campaign to strike at the heart of the Federal forces, in Nashville. If successful he could not just take Nashville, but lessen the pressure upon the rest of the Confederacy, especially in the Deep South. The plan was impracticable, to say the least, and romantic at best. The confidence of the Rebel soldiers was outstanding as they crossed the Tennessee River from Northern Alabama in October. Hood sought glory and while minor conflicts arose on his way to Nashville, he had his chance to win laurels by picking a quarrel with General John M. Schofield at Franklin, Tennessee, on the last day of November 1864. The five-hour battle at Franklin was a catastrophe for the Army of Tennessee. Hood daringly ordered a force of 20,000 infantry men to make a full frontal assault across an open field against a Federal enemy entrenched on the high ground. There were 6,250 Confederate soldiers killed, along with fifteen out of twenty-eight generals. Union deaths amounted to 2,330. The glory Hood sought, while escaping his grasp in Franklin, could now only be found at Nashville. For the next two weeks the weakened Army of Tennessee slowly moved toward Tennessee's capital. On December 15 and 16, 1864, the Battle of Nashville resulted in what was an inevitable conclusion, the unqualified defeat of the Army of Tennessee. Hood's army retreated while being harassed by Federal cavalry.

In four months the war would end.

Another feature of the war in Tennessee was that of the "contrabands," or self-freed slaves. Whenever Union armies came within walking distance of a middling farm or a plantation, large numbers of slaves left their masters, seeking freedom. Previous to the presence of the Union army patrols, slave patrols kept the African Americans in bondage, returning any runaways to their masters. Where Union support and Federal armies were strongest, slave patrols diminished. Federal commanders organized "contraband" camps to accommodate the ever-increasing number of African Americans escaping bondage. From their number the army hired skilled blacksmiths, brick masons, and laborers to build forts, levees, canals and military railroads. Sympathetic northern missionaries and teachers established schools. Marriages were made legal. The contraband camps provided a segue for unpaid blacks to become wage earners and eventually freedmen. Additionally, contrabands joined regiments formed by the Federals, United States Colored Troops (USCT), some of which eventually fought in Tennessee, most dramatically at the Battle of Nashville.

In the major cities there were difficulties with crime, juvenile delinquency, public health, public education, smuggling, prohibition, trading with the enemy and prostitution. Curiously, the theater prospered as well. The role of women, from that of spies to maintaining households in an atmosphere of guerrilla warfare, is noted. Some disguised themselves as men and served with military units. Many stayed home to maintain their farms and houses in the face of dangerous irregular forces. Guerrilla or partisan warfare proliferated throughout the state and posed a major problem for the military and citizenry. At times guerrilla activity would appear as "conscript sweeps," or the dragooning of civilian boys and men into the Rebel and Yankee armies. Railroad and wagon trains and civilian homes were often their targets. On other occasions Federal "foraging" was no more than outright theft. Infrequently was partisan warfare legitimate, with sometimes successful attacks on Union forces. In the main, however, guerrilla warfare was triggered by personal vendettas and was a business for thugs and thieves whose loyalty was to their pocketbook, not to either cause. Perhaps two of the most fierce guerrilla leaders were Champ Ferguson, a rebel, and "Tinker" Dave Beatty, a Union supporter, who plundered and killed in a territory stretching from the Cumberland Plateau into Kentucky. In West Tennessee, Richard V. Richardson's Confederate Partisan Rangers were a power with which Union forces reckoned.

It cannot be said that the Civil War in the Volunteer State was a series of big battles fought between "blue-belly yanks and grey-back rebs." It was multidimensional, a characteristic this book is aimed at demonstrating.

As Harry S. Truman said: "The only thing new in the world is the history you don't know."

The Days of the War

1861

◆ APRIL ◆

1 "A Wife whipper"
A Wife Whipper.— For distinguished bravery in whipping his wife, Hugh Gilmore was yesterday admitted by the recorder into the employment of the city, an honor for which many respectable gentlemen are earnest candidates. He will be boarded and lodged at the city's expense for over three weeks. Brave Hugh!
   Memphis *Daily Appeal*, April 2, 1861.

4 Another Murder.— Susan Striker, who was shot in the bosom on Saturday night by Charles Burton, died yesterday [4th]. Her real name was Julianna Johnson.... The gem that makes a woman loftier than a throne, she had lost, but she had not parted with *all* that makes a woman noble. This man, Burton, was abusing and ill-treating his wife. Poor Julianna — poor Magdalen, who not only with the frowns of those who were of her sex — stood up for the ill-used wife, and the *man* shot her, *killed* her because she said a word for an oppressed, injured sister.... God bless her memory.
   Memphis *Daily Appeal*, April 5, 1861.

5 Assault with intent to kill Rabbi Peres in Memphis
Rabbinical.— Rabbi Peres, late pastor of the synagogue in this city, has been giving some of his flock — not gehenna exactly, but law, and that is about as bad. For assaulting the Rev. J. J. Peres, with intent to kill him, L. Helman was yesterday condemned, by the ... court, to pay a fine of two hundred dollars, and ... three months imprisonment....
   Memphis *Daily Appeal*, April 5, 1861.

6 Secessionist fever in Jackson
Jackson, Tenn., April 6, 1861.
Editors *Appeal*: The "Independent Southern Guards" raised a new flag of the Confederate States here to-day, in place of the one which was first raised, as it was only a temporary one....
The "Independent Southern Guards" were out on parade ... to the sound of martial music.
   Memphis *Daily Appeal*, April 9, 1861.

9 Shameful Outrages.— On two or three occasions lately, outrages of a scandalous character have been committed on premises occupied by branches of the public schools. On one occasion during the night, a considerable number of books were taken from a school room and thrown down the privy vault, and the ink was poured over the floor. On another occasion, filth was daubed on doors and forced into locks.
   Memphis *Daily Appeal*, April 9, 1861.

10 A Connecticut-Tennessean offers support to the Confederacy
New Haven, Conn., April 10, 1861.
Hon. Jefferson Davis:
...I am a native of Tennessee, the stepson of the Hon. John Bell.... I can, without the slightest

difficulty, raise and equip from this city two companies of 100 men each to serve under your command, every man a Democrat, upon whom you can rely.... I am a lawyer ... a graduate of Yale College, served in the Mexican war, was present at the siege of Vera Cruz and the battle of Cerro Gordo....
THOMAS YEATMAN.

OR, Ser. IV, Vol. 1, p. 216.

12 Fort Sumter fired upon

12 The Tennessee Cadets.—This is a new company of lads from eleven to seventeen years of age, formed for the purpose of drill and future service *under a southern flag* ...The uniform is a ... dark green coat, with red pants and blue stripe, and cap with long brim.

Memphis *Daily Appeal*, April 12, 1861.

15 Governor Isham G. Harris' reply to President Lincoln's request for Tennessee militia to support the Union

Sir:

...

Tennessee will not furnish a single man for purposes of coercion but 50,000 if necessary for the defense of our rights and those of our southern brothers.

Isahm G. Harris, Governor of Tennessee

Messages of the Governors of Tennessee, Vol. 5.

17 Talk of secession and war in Jackson

...a good deal of excitement there a large crowd were at the Court house. Speaking going on. War is inevitabel Lincoln ... says he has reason to expect an attack on Washington City. Fort Sumpter [*sic*] has been taken by the Confederate troops.... Civil War is too horrible to even think of. It might be avoided but I fear [it] will not.

Robert H. Cartmell Diary.

17 The Ladies of Memphis.

In all the great revolutions which history records, woman has initiated the movement and led the van of public opinion....

...

The following note ... expresses the patriotic sentiment which fills the hearts of all:

Memphis, April 16, 1861.

...We, the young ladies of Memphis, cannot bear arms in our country's cause, but our hearts are with you and our hands at your service, for making clothes, flags, or anything that a patriotic woman can do, for the southern men and southern independence.

Memphis *Daily Appeal*, April 17, 1861.

18 Secessionist activity Memphis

Southern Flags.—Messrs. Whitmore & Bro., of the *Appeal* job office, have issued a beautiful flag of the Confederate States, about three feet long and in graceful proportions ... which they will furnish in any quantity at $1.50 singly, or at a reduction if taken in large numbers.

A Methodist Military Company.—The *Argus* says that they are informed by the Rev. Mr. Harris, that a military company is being formed among the members of his church; it is to be called "Gideon's Band."

Maynard Rifle Company.—Forty-five men joined this company on Tuesday night. Their weapon is a tremendous one, and if an opportunity ever offers, they will be found murderously efficient.

Memphis *Daily Appeal*, April 18, 1861.

19 Some notes fleshing out secessionist *Zeitgeist* in Memphis

Military.—The members of the German Turner Society have organized a military corps for the protection of the city of Memphis. The company may be used in some cases better than others, as they are all active gymnasts....

...

Memphis, April 18, 1861.

Editors Appeal: We ask a place in your columns to suggest to the merchants and business men generally, the propriety of closing our places of business at an early hour—say, seven and a half o'clock ... so as to afford opportunity to the employes, as well as employers, to attend meetings ... of the military ... organizations to which they severally belong.

Memphis *Daily Appeal*, April 19, 1861.

19 Memphis Blue Jackets, the Committee of Public Safety and enlistment in the army

...

I stepped upon the landing; meaning to look over the state of things in the city, and see if I could get out of it in the direction of the *Nashville*....

But I had not left the wharf, when a "blue jacket," the sobriquet of the military policeman that then guarded the city, stepped up and said, "I see you are a stranger.... You answer the description very well, sir. The Committee of Public Safety wish to see you, come along."

They questioned me as to my ... political opinion ... they were unable to establish any crime, and ... they told me I could retire. I was ... followed by the policeman, who handed me a letter written by the chairman, suggesting that I would do well to go directly to a certain recruiting office, where young men were enlisting ... where I would find it to my interest to volunteer, adding: "Several members of the committee think if you do not see fit to follow this advice, you will probably stretch hemp instead of leaving Memphis" ... I now saw ... that the military power in the city had resoled to *compel* me to *volunteer*, and in my friendlessness I could think of no way to escape....

...I walked on ... and soon reached the recruiting station. I saw ... that the only door was guarded by bayonets, crossed in the hands of determined men ... the recruiting officer ... when turning to me ... said ... "Well young man, I learn you have come to volunteer; glad to see you-good company," &c.

...

"No need of time, sir — no time to be lost; here is the roll — enter your name, put on the uniform, and then you can passout," with a glance of his eye at the policeman and the crossed bayonets, which meant ... "*You do not go out before.*"

...

I wrote my name and thus I *volunteered!*

...

Stevenson, *Thirteen Months in the Rebel Army*, pp. 31–33.

19 Good Out of Nazareth
How they talk in Knoxville
We have the following extract from a letter written at Knoxville, East Tennessee, the 15th. "To-day the news reached us of Lincoln's proclamation calling for 75,000 militia to reposes the Forts. It electrifies every body here. The glorious news from Fort Sumter, last Friday, had silenced the mouths of almost all the abolitionists or tories here, but the news, to-day, raises, in this place even, a perfect storm of Southern feeling. The future of Tennessee is not longer doubtful. *She will go head-long into the Southern Confederacy*, and her soldiers will be among the most willing to charge the cohorts of negro equality.... The thorough and sudden homogeneity of feeling is amazing.
The Macon *Daily Telegraph*; April 19, 1861.

19 Mass Exodus Reported in Memphis
A letter from Memphis, dated on the 19th inst., to a gentleman in St. Louis, who communicates it to the Missouri *Democrat*, says:

"Yesterday, over two thousand persons left for the North and as many will leave this evening. This drain will be much felt in the coming conflict. I have no idea of leaving, but will stick it out as long as possible.

...

This one fact is a volume of itself, and it is an argument that damps the cause of Secession. Already is a bounty offered in the South for enlistments, already are the traitors pressing men into service, already are the peaceful inhabitants who can get away, fleeing with their treasure and their children to the North....
Daily Cleveland Herald, April 27, 1861.

19 Proclamation of the Memphis Committee of Safety; a Coup in the Bluff City.
To the Public.
The committee of safety of the city of Memphis ... deem it necessary to make the following proclamation:

That all and every question that has or may arise, where vigilance is necessary, either at home or abroad, will receive their constant attention and prompt action. This committee have access to all telegraphic dispatches ... that bear upon the peace and stability of this city in any and every shape.

The military force of the city, as well as its municipal police, are all at their command ... everything will be done that can be for their protection and safety. This committee will meet daily, at ten in the morning and four o'clock in the evening....
Memphis Daily Appeal, April 19, 1861

20 Murfreesboro before Tennessee's secession from the Union
...volunteers are gathering all over the country and our town.... A company was raised by Stephen White ... [and] left for Virginia on their own account....

...

Guns and ammunitions was about to prove a difficult matter to procure. So men citizens put to work. Salt peter cans was searched for in fact, the whole country ransached for materials in the way of ammunition.

A small gun establishment was started at Murfreesboro.... They ... could turn eight or ten very good rifles per day. They had a large number of barrels forged out by the smiths. Also had an agent Stephen Singleton, whose business was to collect all the old rifle guns that was of any size or such as would make a Mississippi Rifle. In this way great many guns was furnished. They had got in the way of making a neat finished gun. Soldiers were supplyed with this arm.

Other branches of business was also carrying on the making of catridge boxes, straps, and belts.
...

John C. Spence, *A Diary of the Civil War*.

20 Secessionist Obsession in Memphis
FEELING IN TENNESSEE.

...Last Saturday evening buildings were illuminated, fire works exploded, speeches made, and the secession flag hoisted on the public buildings....

...

About fifteen companies of Riflemen Infantry and Cavalry, have been formed during the present week–Cannon have been sent to them from St. Louis....

Batteries are already begun ... to protect them from Federal troops.... All the spare guns have been bought up.... The Vigilance Committee are out with a proclamation printed in *Red*, requiring all who do not sympathize with them to leave the city, and some of their own citizens have also been ordered to go in twenty-four hours.... Terror reigns....

The Daily Cleveland Herald, April 20, 1861.

21 Garibaldi Guards.—A company of our Italian fellow-citizens organized some time ago under this name, and have reached a high degree of perfection in their drill, but have thus far been unable to procure arms. As soon as the necessary accoutrements can be procured, they hold themselves in readiness to do active and valiant service for their adopted country.

Memphis *Daily Appeal*, April 21, 1861.

21 Sharpe's Rifles.—The Home Guard of the sixth ward yesterday dispatched Mr. Galbreath, of the firm of Meacham & Galbreath, to New Orleans, as their agent, to purchase a hundred and fifty Sharpe's rifles for the use of the company. There are at present a hundred and six men in the company.

Memphis *Daily Appeal*, April 21, 1861.

21 To the Ladies of the Eighth Ward. The undersigned would call the attention of ladies of the eighth ward to the necessity of the early formation of a society to make uniforms, flags, etc., for the military company recently formed in said ward. We can do something in this emergency, and suggest the propriety of a meeting of the ladies at the house of B. D. Nabers, on Alabama street, on Monday, 22d inst., at 4 o'clock P.M., for the purpose of organizing.

Memphis *Daily Appeal*, April 21, 1861.

23 The Ladies Patriotic Association of South Memphis organized

South Memphis Ladies' Patriotic Association.—A number of the ladies of South Memphis met at Grace church, on Monday evening, to arrange for the making up of military uniforms.... Thirty ladies enroled ... and it was resolved to take the name of "The Ladies' Patriotic Association of South Memphis." They will make uniforms for the Young Guards, the Shelby Greys, and the companies of the home guard of South Memphis....

Memphis *Daily Appeal*, April 23, 1861.

24 Nashville Mayor R. B. Cheatham issues proclamation banning vigilantism

WHEREAS, it is understood that self-constituted Committees, or Individuals on their own responsibility, have notified one or more of our Northern-born Citizens to leave Nashville; and whereas it is the determination of the City Authorities to preserve and sustain the peace and quiet of the City: This is ... to notify all Persons that any complaints or suspicions against Persons of Northern birth can be lodged with me for investigation ... all Persons implicated can be assured that they will be protected from unfounded rumors and stories, until properly investigated by the proper Authorities.

AND all good Citizens are earnestly requested ... to quiet the public mind in the present state of excitement, and to aid the Authorities in preserving the peace of the City.

Broadside Collection, TSL&A.

24 Tennessee Rifles.— The Tennessee Rifles will continue their drill at the hours before mentioned, commencing at 10 A.M., and 8 P.M., daily. the company is equipping and getting ready for immediate service, and is rapidly progressing; recruits are earnestly desired, as Maynard rifles have been obtained. Armory and drill room, Adams' block, on Second street, between Adams and Jefferson.

Memphis *Daily Appeal*, April 24, 1861.

24 Free Negroes and the Committee of Safety in Memphis

The Danger of Insurrection.

The Memphis *Avalanche* perceives signs of trouble from the negroes in that city. Speaking especially of the free blacks, it says:—

...

The free negro is the natural and necessary conduit, conveying intelligence from the Abolitionist to the slaves. Through their agency all mischievous plots are arranged. Through their intelligence the slave becomes an assassin, and guilty of the bloodiest deed. The ignorant negro cannot forsee the evils which must befall him for his folly and crimes. The negro can only harm an individual or a family; the consequence is, that negroes are slaughtered like wild beasts. To avoid such contingencies, it has occurred to us that the necessities of the public demand and removal of free negroes from this city. They can, in the midst of the impending struggle, do *no conceivable good*, and accomplish *nothing but harm*. Many of our citizens have already suggested to us the fact that their slaves are under the malign influence of the free negroes. Insubordination is even now recognized, and house servants are constantly informing their mistresses of the sayings of the "freed men." Under such circumstance we are glad to learn that Alderman Kirby has, as chairman of the vigilance committee, instituted the strictest surveillance over the colored gentry, and we would only suggest that we may soon find the proposed policy ... a matter of absolute necessity — at least in times like these.

Philadelphia *Inquirer*, April 24, 1861.

24 A Religious and Humanitarian Justification for Slavery by an East Tennessee Southerner: An Extract from the Diary of Eliza Rhea Anderson Fain

...

O could our Christian friends [up] North come and live with us for a few months I do think it would greatly change their feelings toward us. Let a Northern woman come into one of our black peoples homes and see stretched on a bed of sickness one of our servants — man, woman or child and see us in tender solicitude bending over the sufferer doing all that we can to relieve their sufferings and then know the great anxiety we are often suffering in regard to their spiritual well being methinks you would turn from the spot and if this is slavery so let it continue unmolested by me until the great head of the church sees fit to change it if it is his will. Our happy land that which has been the song and pride of so many hearts will never, while we live, be looked on as it has been. The world will soon know we do not love one another. O how sad how sad.

Diary of Eliza Rhea Anderson Fain.

25 Excerpts from Governor Isham Harris' Legislative Message advocating secession

...I have convened you again at the seat of Government, for the purpose of enabling you to take such action as will most likely contribute to the defense of our rights, the preservation of our liberties, the sovereignty of the State, and the safety of our people; all of which are now in imminent peril by the usurpations of authorities at Washington, and the unscrupulous fanaticism which runs riot through the Northern States.

...

The present administration, elected upon avowed purposed of hostility to the South —.... I have been called upon, as their governor, to furnish a portion of these troops. I have answered that demand as in my judgment became the honor of the State, and leave the people to pass upon my action.

...

I trust that a few days will be amply sufficient to dispose of the business which I have laid before you. Your presence may soon be needed in the field....

Messages of the Governors, Vol. 5, pp. 279–287.

25 Mr. Elwell's and Mr. Kelly's Hegira from Nashville

A Western Reserve Man Thinks the Weather Rather Warm in Nashville, Tenn.

Mr. William H. H. Elwell, a young journeyman

printer, who left Cleveland two years ago, and well known here, has just returned from Nashville, where he has been for the last year. We have gathered from him the following reliable statement.

Being a Northern man, and expressing himself firmly for the Union under all circumstances ... he was warned that such sentiments ... would not be tolerated in the South. Though he had many personal friends ... they had no power whatever to protect him against the mob.... No Northern man is safe ... unless he avows himself a secessionist, and declares himself ready to go the full length of the Southern bloody programme. Mr. Kelley, editor of the Nashville *Democrat* ... was threatened by the Vigilance Committee ... if he continued his treasonable *Union* paper, and the mob gathered for the purpose of the destruction of himself and press.

The office was put in a state of defence, and the American flag ran up. Finally, however, the friends of the editor persuaded him to let them take down the flag, and ... he came North ... Senator Johnson is in Washington and his friends dare not have him return to the State — his life would be taken.... The idle masses and demagogues completely crush out the Union men ... the people seem to be insane on the subject of Southern rights.... They think ... one Southern man can whip a dozen Northern men....

The Daily Cleveland Herald, April 25, 1861.

28 Families of Volunteers.— In most cities a generous patriotism has liberally provided for the families of those whose devotion to the southern cause leads them away from wife and children. This subject must not be lost sight of in Memphis. Men who pour out their blood in our defense must not have the ardor of the battle damped with a fear that their loved ones are a prey to want. What say our city council on this subject, and what say our citizens generally. Let us have appropriations, and subscriptions.

Memphis *Daily Appeal*, April 28, 1861.

29 Excerpt from a letter by Robert D. Jamison of Murfreesborough relative to excitement surrounding secession crisis in Middle Tennessee

...Uncle Atha is the most excited man I ever saw. He can talk about nothing else but the state of our country. Companies of soldiers are mustering at every point. They have two companies at Franklin, two at Columbia, one at Spring Hill, and one at Thompson Station. All of the schools have broken up....

...

I never saw such excitement in my life. Everyone is trying to see who can do the most for his country.... The cry is heard on every side, "to arms, to arms."

Robert D. Jamison Papers, TSL&A.

30 Sallie Gannaway Jamison to Camilla Jamison in Murfreesborough

War with all its horrors, is upon us. I hear and think of but little else. 'This the greatest calamity that could befall us. Who dreamed that we would ever come to this? The United States! The star country! The model government — by which other nations endeavored to frame theirs,— but I fear the star has sunk,— her glory has departed.... All is confusion,— no telling what the future will be.... The ladies are highly excited in some places, quite patriotic. I expect we are all intensely southern in feeling about now, believe in withdrawing our patronage from the North and encouraging home manufactory exclusively.... There are two military companies preparing for service. Mr. Donnell [a school master] is Capt. of one, and has almost given up his place in the school; doesn't pay much attention to it.... The excitement has gotten into the school, and the girls are making make the military clothes....

Robert D. Jamison Papers, TSL&A

30 Special rates on the Nashville & Chattanooga Railroad

N. & C. Railroad Company
Superintendent's Office
Nashville, Apr. 30, '61
To Whom this may Concern:—
The Nashville & Chattanooga Railroad Company will transport FREE OF CHARGE against the company, all volunteer companies, supplies and munitions of war, intended for the defence of the South. The commanding officer will be required to furnish the forwarding agent with a certificate showing them number of men and tonnage of freight so transported.

This proposition will not apply to individuals, but is confined to organized companies.

Nashville *Daily Gazette*, December 12, 1861.

♦ MAY ♦

1 Resolution of Tennessee General Assembly to explore joining the Confederate States in a military league

...

Resolved by the Gen. Assembly of the State of Tennessee, That the Governor be, and he is hereby, authorized and requested to appoint three commissioners on the part of Tennessee to enter into a military league with the authorities of the Confederate States and with the authorities of such other slave holding States as may wish to enter into it, having in view the protection and defense of the entire South against the war that is now being carried on against it.

Adopted May 1, 1861.

OR, Ser. I, Vol. 52, pt. II, pp. 83-84.

1 Conditions in and around Murfreesboro on the eve of the secession of Tennessee

...There is quite a commotion over the country. Volunteers are being raised, but all independant, individual enterprises. They all important question with Tenn. has not come up. She has been once tryed and the question will have to come again. There is a heavy influence working in the mind of the people. Still, a distant hope that something may turn up that will stop blood shed.... The Subject of War is not being thought. More of the people begin to look at the matter. Volunteers are now being raised by different persons....

Spence Diary.

1 The Ascendancy of Fear and Apprehension in Memphis, Jackson and West Tennessee

The Cairo correspondent of the *Chicago Post* furnishes some late [news]....

I have just returned from an interview with a lady who arrived from Jackson, Tennessee, this morning. Being suspected of loyalty to the government, her husband was waited upon by the "vigilance committee" and *warned* of the necessity of his enlisting in the motley army of Jeff. Davis. He resolved to fly, and with all diligence put his family on board the train for Columbus, KY. The mob heard of it, and with knives and revolvers pursued him, searching through the cars to kill him. By the aid of the baggage master he succeeded in escaping to the woods and made his way on foot through swamps and bayous to Columbus where he rejoined his wife ... there are a large number of loyal citizens, but they are overawed by the drunken rabble, and dare not utter their real sentiments. The best citizens of the place held a meeting and protested the unlawful and outrageous proceedings of the "vigilance committee," but their voices were powerless against men inflamed with bad passion and bad liquor.

...

Milwaukee Daily Sentinel, May 1, 1861.

3 Allaying concerns of class prejudice

The great body of yeomanry and laborers of Tennessee may be poor, but they are brave, honest, patriotic and true-hearted. Some who do not know them, may doubt their patriotism and valor to defend their rights when invaded, but this is a great mistake.... When it becomes necessary to defend our rights against the foul power of Black Republican domination, the yeomanry of the mountains and the valleys, of very portion of Tennessee, will swarm around her standard, with a resolution that will strike terror into abolition cohorts ... wealthy men may cry for peace ... for fear they may lose their money; but the honest laborers of Tennessee can never consent to see slavery abolished, and submit to the ... low wages and ... degradation that must follow. They will never consent to be reduced to an equality with the negro, or to take his place: God forbid.

...demagogues have attempted to deceive non-slaveholders by appealing to their prejudices.... The rights and interests of ... the rich and the poor ... are reciprocal, homogeneous and identical....

...

SOUTHERN WATCHMAN

Clarksville *Chronicle*, May 3, 1861.

3 SECESSION

We have a round-about despatch from Richmond, announcing the passage of a Secession Ordinance by the Tennessee Legislature — to be submitted to the people, as a matter of course. A verbal count from a gentleman lately arrived from Nashville, says the act asessed by a vote of *ninety-five* to *five!* ... But the indications of events are so clear and unmistakable that no man, with a Southern heart in his bosom, can longer doubt or hesitate. The opponent of Secession now, is only he who prefers Northern institutions — Northern

dictation—Northern supremacy. The people of Tennessee will sustain the ordinance by ten to one.
...

    Macon *Daily Telegraph*, May 3, 1861.

4 Thoughts on the secession crisis
...

Little though have I had that I should ever live to see civil war in this, our goodly land, but so it is! The Southerners are so hot they can stand it no longer, and have already made the break. There will be many a divided family in this once happy Union. There will be father against son, and brother against brother. O, God! that such things should be in a Christian land....
...

I do not feel well....

    Diary of Amanda McDowell.

6 Fear of abolitionists in White County, an excerpt from the journal of Amanda McDowell....

The news is flying around that they are going to hang a man by the name of Barger tomorrow at Sparta.... They say he expressed Abolition principles most too freely....

    Diary of Amanda McDowell.

7 Tennessee General Assembly passes resolutions in favor of secession and admission of Tennessee into the Confederacy subject to popular vote on June 8, 1861

NASHVILLE, TENN., May 7, 1861.

Hon. ROBERT TOOMBS, Secretary of State, &c.:

Sir: I have the honor to inform you that the two ordinances to which I referred in my last dispatch—the one for secession and the other providing for the admission of Tennessee into our Confederacy—have passed the legislature by a large majority in both Houses. They are subject to ratification by the people, the vote to be taken on the 8th day of June next....
...

    OR, Ser. I, Vol. 52, pt. II, p. 88.

7 Panhandling in Memphis

Street Begging.—A system that has long been a curse to northern cities has lately been inaugurated here—we mean the practice of sending little girls out into the streets to beg. As soon as one of these young swindlers—for that is what they are in reality—sees two or three gentlemen conversing together in the streets, she thrusts herself in among them and by pertinacious importunity she interrupts them until she is paid to go away. Rarely, if ever, we have good reason to believe, are these girls—or rather those who compel them to pursue their vicious occupation—really objects of charity. The poor child who is sent out on this soul-destroying business is indeed an object of compassion; but to give her the money she solicits, is to pay those who ill use her to persist in their cruelty. Instead of giving money to these children, the children should be given into custody to the nearest policeman that inquiry may reveal the actual position of those to whom they belong. Yesterday a girl twelve years old, named Mary Anne Moray, was thus placed in custody. It proved that she had a father, who is a shoemaker. Her sister took her from the station house, putting down twenty-five dollars as security for her appearance for examination this morning. In taking the money from her purse she showed not less than fifty to sixty dollars. Do the credulous now see what need there was for the five and ten cent pieces they have kept from the really poor, to give to imposters?

    Memphis *Daily Appeal*, May 7, 1861.

7 Civil Disturbance in Knoxville
...

The following extract from a letter to a gentleman in Connecticut, from his friend in Knoxville, Tennessee, illustrates the influences at work to drive that State into rebellion:

Knoxville, May 9, 1861

Dear____: I am writing at the office.... There are about 800 soldiers here now ... of the most worthless, desperate class of men, and frenzied by liquor. Among them is one Wash Morgan, who is part Indian, and is captain of a company of spirits of the same class, but if possible more wicked than himself.

Day before yesterday [7th] the Stars and Stripes were floating from the Union pole, and ____ was making a few remarks to a crowd of Union men. Among them was Charles Douglass ... a strong Union man and is not ... prudent about denouncing Secessionists ... on this occasion, Morgan and two of his men were near him, and taking offence at what he said, fired their pistols at him.... Nine shots were fired in all, but Douglass escaped.... He was near his store at the time, and as soon as he could get his gun they were off like "quarter horses." Morgan ran to Sackey's stable, jumped on a horse, and ran him to the Fair Grounds, where his men were quartered. As soon as possible back the cowardly rascal came, with 400 men to kill *one man*. The citizens commenced arriving ... and succeeded in stopping his men ... thereby preventing a general fight.

...Yesterday Morgan ... came round by the back way to the Lamar House, and, in at the "Ladies' Entrance," ... shot Douglas ... the ball passing through his breast. He is still alive, but thought to be mortally wounded.

No arrests have been ... and Morgan is to-day in high favor with the Secessionists.

...

Milwaukee Morning Sentinel, May 21, 1861.

8 Confederate stationery for sale in Memphis
Confederate Flag Envelopes.—We have received from our friend R. C. Hite, a pack of the "latest style" envelopes. They contain a beautiful colored engraving of the Confederate flag, with *nine* stars in a circle, and one in the center, crossed with the letter T, to represent Tennessee. Mr. Hite has also on hand ribbon badges ... with the following mottoes—"For Our Rights We Fight!" and "Death to the Invader!"

Memphis *Daily Appeal*, May 8, 1861.

8 Report on the secessionist climate of opinion in the Volunteer State
Tennessee

Fraud, tyranny and terror are as rampant in Tennessee as they have been, and are, in most of the Southern States. There, as elsewhere, the oligarchs and anarchists suppress free speech and free action, take the management of their affairs from the hands of the people, and rule everything with a rod of iron.... A week or two since, so we find it stated, seven hundred free citizens were driven from Memphis, and afterwards eight hundred more in a single day

...

A reign of terror almost as fierce and merciless is inaugurated at Nashville, and almost everywhere in the western half of the State.

...

The Philadelphia *Inquirer*, May 8, 1861.

12 Defending the South. An Extract from the Diary of Eliza Rhea Anderson Fain

...

I have felt this morning, have Christian mothers [in the] North laid their sons with the same loyalty of feeling upon their country altar that we mothers of the South have done. I feel it can hardly be possible. Our homes are here, they have been endangered by the intemperance of those who know nothing of us—only by misrepresentation.... The name traitor, rebel and other odious epithets are heaped upon us and for what—because we have dared to resist an oppression threatening the extinction of the whole Southern population. I do feel so troubled at the thought of such tyranny and feel will a righteous God give us up to such utter desolation. I feel he will not.

Fain Diary.

12 Anxieties about weaponry expressed in pre–Confederate Tennessee
HEADQUARTERS, Nashville, May 12, 1861, Hon. L.P. Walker, Secretary of War

...We can do literally nothing without arms from you. We have at Memphis about 5,000 percussion muskets in good order. We have here, say, 3,000 muskets, 1,000 of them rifled, fit for use. Besides these there are in the armory some 4,000 muskets (flints) ... entirely unfit for use ... they are being repaired, but it will be several months before we can rely upon them. We have nothing for the cavalry service ... we are ruined unless we have arms furnished us....

OR, Ser. I, Vol. 52, pt. II, pp. 96–97.

13 Prospects for Enfield rifle manufacturing in Nashville
Nashville, May 13, 1861

To Irby Morgan, Esq., care of Hon. W. P. Chilton, Montgomery, Ala.

Dear Sir: Since writing you yesterday, I have received by express, without any advices, an Enfield rifle, which, I presume, has been sent me by Judge Chilton. It is the most superior arm for a soldier. I do not think it can be improved. It is simple, strong, and light. I can have them made here just as good as the sample.... Every piece of machinery necessary can be contracted for here also....

In haste,
S. D. Morgan

How It Was, pp. 168–169.

14 Anxieties about free Negroes in Memphis
Our Free Colored Men—What Shall Be Done With Them?—Editors *Appeal*: The proposition of the committee of safety, to enlist companies of our free colored men, is not relished by our citizens gen-

erally; and the question comes up, "what must be done with them?" Let me suggest to that committee that they confer with Major-General Pillow as to the policy of placing four or five of our free negroes in each company from Memphis, for cooking, washing, etc. That is their post, one of inferiority, not of citizen soldiers. They understand that sort of work better than any boys who are called to do battle. Let them be made useful in that way.

Common Sense.

Memphis *Daily Appeal*, May 14, 1861.

14 Excerpts from School Master Milford Clark Butler's Letter to His Sister on Conditions in Knoxville

...

Parties in this city are nearly equally divided, hence we have many street fights & much angry contention. About 1000 troops are encamped near the city, much to the annoyance of our ... inflammatory speeches were made at the depot, amid the wildest excitement; all class of our people & both sexes turning out en masse. Some of our students have left to join the CSA army and the most have formed themselves into a military company for drill for recreation....

You may wish to know if we Yankees are safe here; thus far we are, though ... the vigilance committee have decided that some of them must leave....

Letter of Milford Clark Butler, May 14, 1861.

15 Tennessee takes another step towards joining the Confederacy

A RESOLUTION to ratify the agreement and convention entered into between the Commonwealth of Tennessee and the Confederate States of America.

Resolved by the Congress of the Confederate States of America.... That the Congress advise and consent to the ratification of the convention and agreement entered into on the 7th day of May, 1861, at Nashville, Tenn., between the Commonwealth of Tennessee, by her commissioners, and the Confederate States of America, by their commissioner, the Hon. Henry W. Hilliard.

CONGRESS, May 15, 1861.

I, Johnson J. Hooper, Secretary of the Congress of the Confederate States of America, do hereby certify that the foregoing is a true and correct copy ... this 15th day of May 1861.

OR, Ser IV, Vol. 1, p. 320.

16 A brief report on army life at camp Randolph, near Memphis

The first two or three days after we came here were very inclement, rendering it impossible to keep dry or comfortable in marching, or on guard, or even in our tents. They are open at one end; plank or straw are placed upon the ground, to lay our blankets on.... Six men are allotted to each tent, and eight to each mess. Every mess has its head man, who, every day at 10 o'clock, draws rations for it, and is supplied with an iron kettle, oven wash pan, tin bucket, wooden bucket and coffee pot. Each member of the mess has his tin plate, cup, spoon and knife and fork. We have our own cooking, washing, etc., to do, which seems quite funny....

Memphis *Daily Appeal*, May 16, 1861.

18 Dwindling population.

...

It is estimated that from four to five thousand have thus left Memphis, many of them under circumstances of imminent peril. A Committee of safety ... cause any they choose to be brought before them, and after a nasty *ex parte* examination, they give a decision from which there is no appeal....

...

Philadelphia *Inquirer*, May 18, 1861.

19 Letter from G. Wharton to his Uncle describing life at a Confederate camp of instruction in Middle Tennessee

May 19, 1861

Uncle Daniel,

...We arrived at this camp on the railroad ... pitched our tents among two or three thousand volunteers and are now spending a real soldiers life. We see nothing scarcely but volunteers and hear nothing but the sounds of drums and fifes and the usual noises of camp life.

...

I will now tell you something about our fare. We are divided into messes of 8 men and our provisions are issued out to us. We have bacon, meal or flour, a little rice, potatoes, sugar, coffee & salt and then we can cook to suit ourselves.

You would have laughed to see me cooking supper this evening.... We have no spoons, knives, nor forks, but use our fingers, pocket knives & sharp sticks.

...
G. W. Wharton
W. P. A. Civil War Records, Vol. 3, p. 9.

20 Enthusiasm for war in Middle Tennessee, excerpt from the diary of John C. Spence

The Confederate army are still increasing. At Camp Trousdale, from the best information, are all in good health and spirits are kept close at drill every day — the friends of the boys are making visits every week to them, taking them clothing and boxes of something to eat. So, war is not such a bad thing after all? They have no fears, are satisfied they can whip two Yankees to one and would not wish to engage a less number. Being in a war camp has a tendency to make men courageous and defiant and may add somewhat devilish.

Spence Diary.

22 Mrs. McEwin's Union Sentiment in Nashville

In Nashville, Tenn., while secession banners wave from every other building, both public and private, one heroic lady (Mrs. McEwin) has placed the National Flag on her house, and says she will shoot whoever attempts to tear down the glorious old Stars and Stripes. Let her name be engraved on the hearts of all loyal Americans.

Louisville *Journal*, May 22, 1861.

22 Unionism in East Tennessee
Union Feeling in East Tennessee
ADMISSION BY A REBEL

A Secession soldier, writing to the New Orleans *Crescent,* makes the following confessions in regard to the Union feeling in East Tennessee:— We crossed the Cumberland mountains in a dark, rainy night ... we remarked a decided abatement of the enthusiasm which had hitherto greeted our progress. Those who did salute us did it with a vim and furor seemed intended to assure us that we had friends there as well as enemies, but a class almost as numerous stood and gazed upon us in sullen silence as we passed, making no reply to the demonstrations of our rollicking soldiers, and evidently not daring to express their real feeling, their hostility to Southern independence, in any other than a passive way.

This phenomenon was explained to my satisfaction.... Few persons in the South have and adequate idea of the extent to which Abolitionism has ... in the Border States. The eastern part of Tennessee east of the Cumberland mountains, is afflicted with a colony of this kind, and its pernicious influence upon the simple-minded mountain men of that region is painfully evident. Owning no slaves, the latter know nothing of the institution of slavery, nor do they care to know ... their abolition neighbors tell them that the Government is still the Government of WASHINGTON, JEFERSON, and JACKSON, and they quite normally hold as one enemy the men who would destroy it or replace it by another.

Philadelphia *Inquirer*, May 22, 1861.

26 Aid to the Poor.— Mr. Underwood, city almoner, had several applications at his office on Second street near Madison yesterday, for assistance. Nine persons received articles of food for which they appeared very grateful. Three were refused, having revealed that they were not in necessitous circumstances. One woman, on being offered a piece of bacon, turned up her nose with the remark that she did not eat the article. She was informed that she might call again when real necessity had made her less delicate. Mr. Underwood will evidently make a good almoner. He is kind without credulity, and firm without harshness.

Memphis *Daily Appeal*, May 26, 1861.

28 Convict war production in Nashville
A Good Work Going On.

The Nashville *Union* speaks encouragingly of the manner in which military work is being forwarded in the penitentiary. On visiting that institution on Friday last, the editor found sixty-five men employed alone in making cartridges, turning them out at the rate of 20,000 per diem. A little practice will greatly increase the result of their labors. Thirty men are employed in repairing and cleaning muskets, who finish up, as bright and perfect as when new, about one hundred daily. The manufacture of cap boxes, cartridge belts, haversacks, camp chairs, stools, cots, military chests, etc., etc., is also being vigorously prosecuted. Of course all these preparations are being made at a very trifling expense to the State.

Memphis *Daily Appeal*, May 28, 1861.

29 Women drill in Confederate military camps in Jackson
Letter from Jackson.

Jackson, Tenn., May 29, 1861.

Editors Appeal: According to promise, I write you this letter to let you know how times are with us, and something about times in camp since our arrival here. The most interesting circumstance ... since our arrival this place was a large company of ladies out on drill at the camp on yesterday....

The camps are filled daily with ladies and gentlemen from the vicinity of Jackson....

Memphis *Daily Appeal*, May 31, 1861.

29 Editorial opinion on the indecency of young women giving daguerreotypes to soldiers

Advice to Girls.— There is a practice, quite prevalent among young ladies of the present day, which we are old fashioned enough to consider very improper. We allude to giving daguerreotypes of themselves to young men who are merely acquaintances. We consider it indelicate in the highest degree. We are astonished that any young girl should hold herself as cheap as this....

...we give this advice to anybody's sister who needs it, most anxiously desiring that she should at all times preserve her dignity and respect.

Memphis *Daily Appeal*, May 29, 1861.

30 Excerpt from a letter by Davidson Countian Edward Bradford, at Camp Trousdale

We are getting plenty to eat and plenty of exercise. We drill two hours twice a day. They carry us about two miles from Camp to drill us and when we get back we have to stay on our own ground, about an acre.... I enjoy everything but the way we sleep. We have not got any straw in our tents and have to sleep on the ground with one blanket.... We have a dance every night. We have more music than we want. There is about a dozen fiddlers to every camp. John [Edward's brother] and I both had to stand guard last night from eleven until one. We all keep our health so far....

Frederick Bradford Papers, TSL&A.

31 Assisting the poor in Memphis

The City Poor.— We are happy to observe that the measure introduced at the last meeting of the board of aldermen for aiding the poor of the city is working well. The efficient city almoner, Mr. Underwood, deserves great credit for his management, and is no doubt held in grateful remembrance by those whose wants he has alleviated....
...

Memphis *Daily Appeal*, May 31, 1861.

♦ JUNE ♦

1 Decaying vegetables for the poor

Vegetables for the Poor.— Those who attend market with vegetables frequently have some left over, which are spoiled and thrown away before next morning; the city almoner desires us to state that if market people will leave such vegetables at his office, on Second street, east side, four doors north of Madison, he will each day distribute them to the widowed and other poor.

Memphis *Daily Appeal*, June 1, 1861.

ca. 2 General P. G. T. Beauregard vs. the Memphis Vigilance Committee

A gentleman from Memphis informs us that Gen. Beauregard arrived there a few days since, and used great endeavors to keep his movements secret. Being a stranger and somewhat observant he attracted the attention of the Vigilance Committee, who arrested him as a spy.... The generalissimo of the Confederate forces had to send for Gen. Pillow to identify him, and the hero of Camargo soon convinced the vigilants that they had dug their ditch on the wrong side of the rampart of Memphian defence, whereupon Beauregard was discharged with apologies.

Louisville *Daily Journal*, June 4, 1861.

3 Provocation and reply, a battle of words

The Pillow Guards of Memphis, challenged the bodyguard of Federal General Benjamin Prentiss, the Prentiss Guards of Cairo, Illinois, to deadly combat. According to the challenge:

"We have enlisted under the stars and bars of the Confederate States for the purpose of defending Southern rights and vindicating Southern honor. But more especially we have been selected and sworn in for the purpose of guarding the person of our gallant Gen. Pillow. Understanding that you occupy a like position with reference to Prentiss, the commandant at Cairo, we challenge you to meet us at any time, at any place, in any number, and with any arms or equipment which you may select. We wish to meet no others till we have met and conquered you and your General. Make your own terms, only let us know when and where, and be certain you will meet the bravest guard the world has ever known."

An answer came on June 17:

The Prentiss Guards responded to the braggadocio of a challenge issued to them on June 3 by the Pillow Guards. According to Captain Joseph D. Walker of the Prentiss Guards:

'We accept no challenges from traitors, but hang them. If we ever meet, you shall suffer the fate of traitors.'"

Anecdotes, Poetry and Incidents of the War, p. 160.

3 Report on Voter Intimidation in Nashville on the Eve of the June 8 Secession Vote and Tennessee's Interference with Kentucky's Commerce

Tennessee.—A short time ago a gentleman of Davidson county addressed two written questions, anonymously, to the *Union & American*, the leading disunion organ at Nashville. The questions, in substance, were: First, Will the Union men be allowed to discuss publicly the issues in this canvass?, and, Secondly, Will they be allowed to vote in the election? The editor published the questions, and, with considerable circumlocution, gave the author of them and the community distinctly to under stand that *both privileges would be refused*....

That it was the determination of the Vigilance Committee and the armed and organized troops at their command to crush out Union speaking and Union voting, and he didn't think it worth while to attempt to disguise the notorious fact. The Union speaker would be shot upon the stand in Nashville, and a Union voter, if such a one there be, will be shot at the polls.... It would really seem as if, when innumerable Vigilance Committees are daily and nightly at work throughout Tennessee expelling Union men and their families from the State, they might venture to permit such as shall be left on the 8th of June to exercise the right of free suffrage, but no, they are afraid, that, notwithstanding the driving of thousands into exile and the turning of the whole artillery of the late Union press of the State against the Union party, secession would still be voted down unless the polls should be girt with secession bayonets...

Louisville *Daily Journal*, June 3, 1861.

5 Large Unionist meeting disrupted by weapons' fire from pro-Confederate soldiers at Strawberry Plains

Cowardly and Inhuman Conduct
AN ASSEMBLY OF LADIES AND GENTLEMEN FIRED INTO BY SECESSION TROOPS

We find in the Knoxville (Tenn.) *Whig.*, [Tuesday June 11th], the particulars of a most wanton and unprovoked assault by Southern troops upon a meeting of Unionists at Strawberry Plains, Tennessee. The *Whig* says:—

We have never witnessed such a scene as we beheld on Wednesday, the 5th instant, at Strawberry Plains, and we hope never to see the like again. The procession of Union men on horseback, about four deep, was half a mile long.... At the head of each division the Stars and Stripes were floating to the number of six banners. Marching by the Plains, and passing the depot, there was a train of cars having on board some Alabama troops, who, strange to say, remained there with steam up for three hours.

After our procession had passed into the gap of Mr. Meek's ... grove, where the stand and seats were erected, and where ... several hundred ladies and children, were seated awaiting the arrival of the procession ... the train started towards us at a very slow rate....

...There were two men in uniform on the top of one of the cars, each had a revolver in his hand, one of them a stone, which he threw at me with great force and precision, and I barely dodged it. This was followed up by one of them deliberately firing at me....

...It looks like a *premeditated* attack.

The bullets actually whistled over the heads of our crowd around the stand, cutting off leaves and sprigs.... The fire was returned by the Union men, who fired some thirty to forty rifles, besides revolvers ... but ... the train passed on without halting.

But a wild and terrific scene occurred instantly, by the rush of one thousand men ... with threats to tear up the track, and to burn the bridge over the Holston.... With difficulty they were quieted....

...

Philadelphia *Inquirer*, June 13, 1861.

5 "There is some sickness in the camp." James I. Hall's letter home from his camp of instruction near Union City
(Mr. & Mrs. J. D. Hall
Mountain, Tipton County, Tenn.)

Union City, June 5 [1861]
Dear Parents,
When I wrote to you last we were at Jackson. Our company came here last Saturday [June 1]. I remained in Jackson till Monday on business for the company. It was quite a treat to spend the Sabbath in quiet. While in Jackson, I have spent most of the time in camp slept in the tents at night, have been doing the same since I came here, we are very conformably fixed [and] have a good tent, got cotton mattress, chairs, etc., We have provisions in abundance and of good quality. We were however glad to see the nice box of provisions [illegible] anything from home tastes good. There is some sickness in the camp. [O]ne or two cases of mumps, one case of pneumonia and some bowel complaints.

Dumpy Daniel has had a mild attack of the flux, is now well, the three boys from the neighborhood are well. There are five Regiments here, composed of between 5 & 6 Thousand men. We are encamped within a mile of Union City & forty miles a place Wilson Mathews lives near there, was in camp yesterday. We have received our guns-percussion muskets since we came here and are drilling with them....
Jas I Hall

Ninth Tennessee, p. 130.

ca. 6 Excerpts from a Secessionist poster in Memphis on the eve of the vote on secession

"TRUE MEN OF THE SOUTH TO THE RESCUE"

Whereas, Abraham Lincoln, President of the Northern States, has seen fit to make a call upon the States of the Union for 75,000 men, for the declared purpose of subjugating the States of the Southern Confederacy, and make them subservient to his will....

We, loyal citizens of the South, who have pledged our lives, our property, and our sacred honors, in support of the Government of the Confederate States ... urge immediate arming of all our able-bodied men who are willing to resist the cohorts of the North.... Our safety requires that those living in our midst, who do not wish to abandon their allegiance to Lincoln's Government, who are in favor of negro equality and the degradation of the white race should leave as soon as possible....

...

Let the proprietors of business houses, machine, carpenter, and cabinet shops, foundries, printing-offices, paint and tailor ships, hotel and boarding houses, report ... those who they know cannot be trusted as friends to the South.... Our gallant sons, who are anxious to march ... wish to carry with them the consoling thought that they have not left behind them the lurking enemy who ... would incite our negroes to ... bring the worst calamities upon our wives, our mothers, and our daughters.
...

Rebellion Record, Vol. 2, p. 58.

7 Tennessee bullets and rifles; experimental ballistics in Nashville

Experiments with the Minnie Ball.

Experiments, says the Nashville *Banner*, conducted for several days by direction of the military and financial board, demonstrate that the Minnie ball in the Tennessee rifle, with the same charge of powder used with the round ball, has a range and force of three-fold that of the round ball.

A rifle carrying 100 balls to the pound, used with the ordinary sight is, at 300 yards, a most deadly weapon, projecting the ball with greater accuracy and force than the rifled musket. The rifle of larger calibre has greater range and force.

The ball should be of less diameter than the round ball, so as to admit of grater rapidity in loading. The cartridges should be dipped ... in a compound of beeswax and tallow, and a patch should not be used. A rifle thus used may be fired one hundred times without cleaning.
...

Memphis *Daily Appeal*, June 7, 1861.

8 TENNESSEE SECEDES FROM THE UNION

8 Tennessee voters select secession over union

Tennessee voted 102,172 to 47,238 (69% to 31%) to ratify the "Declaration of Independence" adopted by the General Assembly, and so to secede from the union.

Messages of the Governors, Vol. 5, pp. 304–306.

8 Voting for secession in Jackson

I rode into town and voted for Tennessee being separated from the United States & to be represented in the Congress of the Confederate States. Tennessee now makes 11 states now seceded. It matters not how the future historians may record events now transpiring, & I don't [think] there can be any doubt as to how the impartial historians will record it. *I feel that I have done right.* If the majority have the right to violate the constitution & encroach upon the rights of the minority, then the South is *clearly in the wrong*....

Robert H. Cartmell Diary.

9 James I. Hall's letter home describing facets of life at the Confederate camp of instruction near Union City

Union City June 9th [1861]

Dear Parents,

It is Sunday night, There is preaching in the camp to night but as I have two sermons today & feel tired I will write home instead of attending preaching I have been quite well since I came here with the exception of one spell of headache. I think that camp life will agree with me. The boys from the neighborhood are all well. There is some sickness in the camp but not severe so far. We have had a quiet day drilling or work have a delightful encampment in a shady grove. Are rather scarce of water but are digging wells and soon have plenty.... We shall expect some of you up soon. The camp is crowded with visitors from all parts of the district. We are making arrangements to have a tent made for the accommodation of our friends.

Some of the boys were up today to the Miss. troops about half a mile above us. Saw Ed Stitt & Joe Ross who was in my school have a pleasant time. Cousin Wilson M. came to the camp frequently, had his wife with him today she is an agreeable woman busy preparing our grounds. Do not know how long we will stay here.... My love to the children

Ninth Tennessee, p. 130.

13 Letter to the Memphis *Appeal* commenting on apparent lack of patriotism displayed by a majority of Memphis men

I was in common with many ladies of Memphis, greatly gratified at witnessing the parade of the Home Guards Tuesday evening; and while witnessing it, I was told that there were in the ranks about six hundred soldiers. I then wondered where the remainder of the five thousand voters were; but on looking around I discovered some hundreds of young, healthy looking men congregated on the bluff to witness the scene, and were all apparently complacent and happy-doubtless satisfied that the military array there would be able to protect and defend them in the hour of danger and peril.

Memphis *Appeal*, June 13, 1861.

15 Preparations for home defense in Jackson

The minute men from this district organized this evening ... according to the law passed by the last called session of the Legislature. Minute men are appointed by the county court for each civil district making in all for the county 25,000 or 30,000 men or more. I was appointed for this District. It was impossible for me to join a Volunteer Company as my family were very sick at the time the companies were formed and now more are tendered than can be received.... I have been in hopes all the time & have believed that our troubles would be settled without a great loss of blood but the prospects for so desireable an event grows encouraging each day. The north are moving determined it would seem to punish the traitors and from what has transpired it is easy to see what that punishment will be — death, confiscation of property. Men, women children are to suffer....

Robert H. Cartmell Diary.

17 A British war correspondent's observations of Memphis, Gideon J. Pillow and the Southern army

It was 1:40 P.M. when the train arrived at Memphis. I was speedily on my way to the Gayoso House....

...the Gayoso House ... is the headquarters of General Gideon J. Pillow....

...

...General Pillow sent his aid-de-camp to inform me that he was about starting in a steamer up the river, to make an inspection of the works and garrison at Fort Randolph.... Before the Mexican War General Pillow was a flourishing solicitor, connected in business with President Polk, and commanding so much influence that when the expedition was formed he received the nomination of brigadier-general of volunteers. He served with distinction and was severely wounded at the battle of Chapultepec....

...[the] General ... made himself ludicrously celebrated in Mexico for having undertaken to throw up a battery which, when completed, was found to face the wrong way.... General Pillow is a small, compact, clear-complexioned man, with short gray whiskers ... and a pompous manner of speech.... He wore a round black hat, plain blue frock-coat, dark trousers, and brass spurs on his boots; but no sign of military rank ... we went to see the batteries on the bluff.... A parapet of cotton bales, covered with tarpaulin, has been erected close to the edge of the bank.... This parapet could offer no cover against vertical fire, and is so placed that well-directed shell into the bank below it would tumble it all into the water....

...

William Howard Russell,
My Diary, North and South.

18 A British war correspondent's experiences at Fort Pillow

General Pillow proceeded on shore after breakfast, and we mounted the coarse cart-horse chargers which were in waiting at the jetty to receive us. It is ... worthwhile to transcribe ... a description of the works ... a more extraordinary maze could not be conceived, even in the dreams of a sick engineer — a number of mad beavers might possibly construct such dams....

The General ordered some practice to be made with round shot down the river.... The General and his staff took their posts on the parapet to leeward, and I ventured to say, "I think General, the smoke will prevent your seeing the shot." ...the General replied, "No, sir," in a tone which indicated, "I beg you to understand I have been wounded in Mexico, and know all about this kind of thing." "Fire!" The string was pulled, and out of the touch-hole popped a piece of metal with a little chirrup. "Darn these friction tubes! I prefer the linstock and match ... but General Pillow will have to use friction tubes made at Memphis, that aren't worth a cuss." Tube No. 2, however, did explode, but where the ball went no one could say, as the smoke drifted right into our eyes.

...

The volunteers were mostly engaged at drill in distinct companies ... by order of the General some ... 800 ... were formed into line for inspection.... These men have been only five weeks enrolled....

...

...the General addressed them in a harangue in which he expatiated on their patriotism, on their courage.... But the only matter which appeared to interest them much was ... that they would be released from work ... and that negroes would be sent to perform all that was required.... And when General Pillow wound up ... assuring them, "When the hour of danger comes I will be with you...." The men did not seem to care much whether General Pillow was with them ... one of the officers called out, "Boys, three cheers for General Pillow."

William Howard Russell,
My Diary, North and South.

19 William Howard Russell's observations on the Confederate army while traveling to Columbus, Kentucky, via Troy and Union City, Tennessee

...

By the time I had arrived at the [train].... I was obliged to take my place in a carriage full of Confederate officers and soldiers who had a large supply of whiskey, which at that early hour they were consuming ... to get as nearly drunk as possible. Whiskey, by-the-by, is also a sovereign specific against the bites of rattle-snakes. All the dews of the Mississippi and the rattle-snakes of the prairie might have spent their force or venom in vain on my companions before we had got as far as Union City.

...

There is no appearance of military order or discipline.... Some of the sentinels carried their firelocks under their arms like umbrellas, others carried the butt over the shoulder and the muzzle downwards, and one for his greater ease had stuck the bayonet of his firelock into the ground, and was leaning his elbow on the stock with his chin on his hand ... [others] had simply deposited their muskets against the trees, and were lying down reading newspapers. Their arms and uniforms were of different descriptions ... but the men, nevertheless, were undoubtedly material for excellent soldiers....

...

William Howard Russell,
My Diary, North and South.

20 East Tennessee Unionist resolutions to secede from Tennessee and remain in the Union

KNOXVILLE, TENN., June 20, 1861.

...

Resolved, First. "That we do earnestly desire the restoration of peace to our whole country, and most especially that our own section of the State of Tennessee shall not be involved in civil war."

Second. "That the action of the State Legislature in passing the so called 'declaration of independence' and in forming the 'military league' with the Confederate States and in adopting other acts looking to a separation of Tennessee from the

Government of the United States, is unconstitutional and illegal, and therefore not binding upon us as loyal citizens."

...

OR, Ser. I, Vol. 52, pt. I, pp. 178–179.

22 The ammunition factory in Memphis
Manufactory of Ammunition.—... we were yesterday admitted within the Confederate Government saber manufactory.... On mounting to the immense room up stairs, we found four large tables ranged from end to end of the room, and ... two hundred and fifty women and girls, principally young girls, were busily engaged in the labor of preparing cartridges. The paper is rapidly passed round a stick, giving the required shape and size, then three buck shot and a bullet are placed at the bottom of it and held in their place by threads neatly and quickly tied round them. These are passed to others, who, placing a small funnel into the top of the paper tube deposit within, from a small measure, the required quantity of gunpowder. Others folded up the end of the paper and the cartridge was completed. Ten cartridges are next tied together in a package, and a given number of them are packed in a box, marked and certified as inspected, when they are ready for army use ... as many as seventy-five thousand cartridges have been turned out in one day.... Smoking is prohibited, matches are excluded ... and the men ... wear slippers. Beside cartridges, fixed ammunition...fuses for bombshells, rockets, signal lights, friction tubes for cannon, and other combustibles and implements are manufactured....

Memphis *Daily Appeal*, June 22, 1861.

27 The care of the indigent insane Confederate soldier or his family members
CHAPTER 5, An Act for the benefit of Insane Members of the Families of Volunteers
Section 1. Be it enacted by the General Assembly of the State of Tennessee, That the wives or other members of the families of volunteers who are citizens of this State, and who have enlisted, or who may hereafter enlist in the service of the State, or of the Confederate States, who have been, or who may hereafter be placed in the Tennessee Asylum for the Insane, as pay patients, shall, during the time of their enlistment, or which such volunteers are in actual service, be supported by the State, upon the written certificate of the Chairman of the County Court from the county of residence of said volunteers, setting forth that he or they are unable, from indigent circumstances, to support such patient in the asylum.

Sec. 2 That any one of the Tennessee volunteers who may become deranged while in the service, and who has not the pecuniary means to enter the asylum as a pay patient, shall be received and treated as a pauper patient....

...

Passed June 27, 1861.

Public Acts of the State of Tennessee, passed at the extra session of the Thirty-third General Assembly, April, 1861, (Nashville: J. G. Griffith & Co.: 1861.), pp. 34–35.

29 General Pillow's Order and Proclamation
Major-General Pillow, having given order that whisky and tobacco should be supplied to the soldiers under his command, has issued a proclamation recalling the order. He says that he had no doubt the military board would ratify his action, as he knew the soldiers to be gentlemen and used to plenty of whisky and tobacco. The board disagree with the general.

Boston Daily Advertiser, June 29, 1861.

30 Chickasaw Pikemen
TENNESSEE
Interesting from Memphis. Strength of the Military Forces in West Tennessee.
[From the Indianapolis *Journal*, June 22]

...

The Memphis *Appeal* says the Mayor of Memphis is about to form a company of men for the protection of the city, to be called the Chickasaw Pikemen. For this company sixty-four formidable Irish pikes have already been made. They are ten feet in length, and at the butts there is a spike. The pike resembles a bayonet in size and appearances, and at the point where it joins the staff a hooked blade projects. The pike will cut with a thrust, the hook with a pull. On the approach of cavalry the butts are set on the ground and the pikes presented to the enemy....

...

New York Herald, June 30, 1861.

♦ JULY ♦

1 Excerpt from Moses Nichols' letter to his grandmother in Cookeville

...

July 1, 1861
Dear Grandmother,
...

There are fifty eight sick in the Hospital with the measles and many other cantageous diseases. One man died last Saturday in Numan's regiment, and they buried him yesterday in honor of war.... I went to the burying ... when we got there we found a camp ground surrounded with tombs. The Funeral was preached by a very able minister, who is the Chaplain of that regiment, the harbor under which the sermon was preached was about 50 yards from the grave of the warrior and during the sermon I (being tired) layed down to sleep and when I awoke I found myself alone, but ran up to the graveyard and they were just putting him in the grave, they covered the body slightly with dirt and then fired twenty four guns over the grave. I would not like to be buried here if I were to die, but would want to be brought home....
...

W. P. A. Civil War Records, Vol. 3, p. 120.

2 Governor Isham G. Harris reports to Confederate authorities relative to the strength of the provisional army of Tennessee
EXECUTIVE DEPARTMENT, Nashville, July 2, 1861.
SIR:
...

The provisional army of Tennessee is composed of twenty-two regiments of infantry, two regiments of cavalry, ten companies of artillery, engineer corps, ordnance bureau, &c., commanded by Maj. Gen. Gid. J. Pillow, Maj.-Gen. Anderson, Brig.-Gen.'s Zollicoffer, Cheatham, Foster, Caswell, and Sneed. The infantry fully armed and equipped ready for the field; part of the cavalry armed with revolvers and sabers, the balance with double-barrel shotguns, and all well mounted. No field batteries completed yet....
Very respectfully,
ISHAM G. HARRIS.

OR, Ser. IV, Vol. 1, p. 417.

2 Memphis Presbyterians secede from the Northern church
Proceedings of the Presbytery.-The Presbytery of Memphis, Tenn., have unanimously adopted an ordinance of Secession from the General Assembly of the Old School Presbyterian Church of the United States, and it is said that the Presbyteries of the other Rebel States will take action....
...

Philadelphia *Inquirer*, July 2, 1861

2 Artillery shells and hand grenades
A New Shell.— ... Quinby & Robinson's foundry, is completing a new shell.... The shell is conical, two thin pieces of metal, each about three and a half inches long, are let into slits cast in the sides of the shell ... obliquely. Behind them are springs which, when the shell has left the gun, will pitch them forward sufficiently to make their width project from its sides. As these wings will present an angle to the air, the latter impinging against them is expected to give the shell a rotary motion after it leaves the gun....

Hand Grenade.—A brass hand grenade will be cast at the foundry ... to-day. The cannon that have been cast from brass, made of Tennessee copper, when put in the lathe, turn out to be beautiful specimens of workmanship....

Memphis *Daily Appeal*, July 2, 1861.

4 The Fourth of July in Confederate Memphis
The Fourth of July.—This is the "glorious Fourth," the day of music, banners, orations, bonfires, and fireworks. We saw few indications yesterday of an approaching festival; two or three banks gave notice of closing, and the criminal court concluded not to sit; but the juvenile and the patriotic portions of the community showed no sign of observing the time honored customs of the day. Should the day of national independence rank as a mere Yankee institution?

Memphis *Daily Appeal*, July 4, 1861.

8 Memphis Defenses
There are three fortified posts in Memphis, Tenn....

A. Breastwork, two hundred yards long, on a high bank commanding the river, composed of cotton bales, two bales in height. It is simply a row of bales running parallel with the river, with no side or rear defenses.

B. A three gun battery, open in the rear.

C. Four gun battery, made of sand, open in the rear, and very roughly made.

...the principal streets leading to the levee are barricades with cotton bales and sand bags, which has created considerable dissatisfaction and petitions have been presented to the Common

Council to have a carriage way made through them.
...

New York Herald, July 8, 1861.

11 Alarm about secret societies and loyalty to the Confederacy in the Tennessee/Georgia border counties
...July 11, 1861.
President DAVIS.
SIR: The startling state of the public mind in this country lying as it does upon the Georgia boundary impels me to again importune your early attention in some effective manner to this section of the South. It is fortunate that we are not now left to conjecture the purposes of the Union men in East Tennessee who are in arms, or the probable number of them in this county. On a Sunday, July 7, an alarm was given that a troop of secessionists had entered the county to disarm the Union men. By some means unknown to our friends here in twelve hours near 1,000 Union men were in arms at different rendezvous and disclosed a most complete organization, secret hitherto in its character and numbers....

...

...take action to avert disaster now ... threatening not only to the true men in East Tennessee but so demoralizing to the great movement of the South!...
WILLIAM G. SWAN, Knoxville, Tenn.
OR, Ser. II, Vol. I, p. 828.

12 Selection from Edward Bradford's letter to his mother
We have the best drilled company in Camp Trousdale, do more work and have less sickness than any company in our Regiment. We have had two or three deaths here in the last few [days] but only one in our regiment.... There has been two run away, but they caught one of them and drummed him out of the camp. They had one side of his head shaved and a pair of horns on him, his breeches rolled up to his knees, barefooted with his shoes in his hand, his budget on his back and a board across his back on which was marked ["]Deserter.["] He made tracks for Kentucky as soon as he was turned loose.

Frederick Bradford Papers, TSL&A.

12 Reduction of Memphis' city school budget
Public Schools.—We learn from the secretary of the board of visitors that the board is now organized and propose to open the schools at the usual time in September next. They will reduce the expenses of the schools for the year about $1200. They intend to reduce the number of teachers and school houses and the amount of salaries. The salary of the superintendent will be reduced from $2500 to $1200 a year. There will be one senior teacher at $800; the junior and primary teachers will be paid $750 each per annum. In city scrip, this will be a very moderate salary.

Memphis *Daily Appeal*, July 12, 1861.

15 A Description of Chattanooga
...
Your readers will be gratified, doubtless, to learn that there is in the vicinity of this town one of the largest tanneries in the South. It is now in active operation, and turning our fro 8000 to 10,000 sides of well tanned leather every four months, giving an aggregate of 30,000 sides of leather per annum.... It is the design of the new firm to go largely into the manufacture of shoes, at this point, at an early period.

The advantages of Chattanooga over other places for the tanning business are numerous. The abundance of the very best quality of tan bark, and the lowest prices; the facilities for procuring hides of every variety, and being located in the centre of our great Southern market, are some of the advantages....

The great scarcity of pig iron at the South, at this time, will certainly induce those competent to the work to look towards this point. We visited the large smelting furnace erected a few years ago, which we regretted to find entirely idle....

During the few days which we have been anchored at this place, between 2500 and 3000 soldiers have arrived and departed for the seat of war. There are now ... at the depot about 600.... About 2000 soldiers are expected to arrive here this afternoon and to-night ... 200 Texans passed here yesterday.

More than 40,000 soldiers have passed through this city.... The eagerness of the people for the latest news from the "seat of war," is the cry. At every station, on any road you pass, squads of from 10 to 20 men may be seen standing around while one reads the last paper procured of some newsboy.... Citizens and soldiers ... ask at once for news....
...

Charleston Mercury, October 19, 1861.

18 Anxieties in Memphis about food shortages and blankets for Tennessee's soldiers

We desire to call the attention of planters to the importance of an early subscription in flour and corn-meal for the use of our army. The Confederate Government purchases in May last an immense quantity of flour, and stored it as this place, but the supply is now nearly exhausted.... Let each planter indicate ... what quantity he is willing to sell to the Government ... send it forward immediately. There are five mills in operation ... to which the planters ... can send their wheat and have it ground and barreled, ready for transportation.

...

The supply of blankets in store is exhausted, and the possibility of supply from the North is cut ... while the blockading of our seaports cuts us off from all hopes of a reasonable supply.... How, then, it may be asked, are the wants of our soldiers to be supplied: It can only be done by every family giving up a portion of the blankets they have ... to the soldiers ... and our people are expected to ... send their blankets to the soldiers. There is no time to be lost in doing it either....

Memphis *Appeal*, July 18, 1861.

21 FIRST BATTLE OF MANASSAS (BULL RUN), VIRGINIA

22 Death and burial of the slave "Old Aunt Lucy" in Maury County

Old Aunt Lucy died of dropsy. Sick a long time[, and she was] buried [at] Francis burying ground. She was a faithful servant. All the family white and black war greatly attached to her. She had the care of the family white and black for forty years. She died much regretted.

Diary of Nimrod Porter

24 The Memphis Vigilance Committee

The *Philadelphia Inquirer* of the 22nd publishes the statement of John McLean Collins.... He was arrested by a vigilance committee and incarcerated in a Memphis prison on the 27th of April for writing a letter published in the *New York Tribune*.... Mr. Collins, who represents himself "a Southern man by birth, education, and feeling," says:

...I never dreamed that in any moment of excitement there could be found, in any portion of this land, one single man, who could be base enough and fiend enough, to lay the lash upon the back of an innocent and defenceless *woman*. Incredible as it may appear, *it was done in the city of Memphis on the 19th of May*. The victim was a young beautiful, refined, and accomplished lady.... Her offence was being from Maine, and expressing too loudly her wishes for the success our of arms.

She purchased a ticket for Cairo, and was congratulating herself upon soon reaching a land of liberty, when an officer ... [a]rrested her and brought her to the jail.— She was confined all night, and in the morning she was brought in front of the rear door of the jail ... [where] three men had been whipped with the *knout*, and their heads shaved, *she was stripped to the waist and thirteen lashes given her with a strap, and the right side of her head shaved!*....

...I shall never forget her appearance while suffering.... Not one word escaped her lips: not a groan came up from her breast. But the livid hue of her face, the compressed lips, the quivering of every muscle, attest how ... keenly she felt the impious wrong....

Daily Cleveland Herald, July 24, 1861.

24–25 The saga of Dan Edson

The Livery Stable Clerk.— A livery stable in this city has, for a week or ten days, been under the management of a sprightly fellow, who told a good story ... and handled the ribbons with an off-hand skill that never failed to draw admiration.... Dan Edson, for that was the young fellow's name, kept the books, fingered the money, managed the stable boys, let out horses and buggies, and discussed the points of a horse and the achievements of a racer ... and all with the ... decided style that he exhibited in everything he said or did. Dan ... was becoming a favorite.... The young "bloods" about town ... were fond of dealing with Dan ... Dan was knowing; he had a jaunty air ... about him.... Of course the few ladies who had enjoyed the pleasure of Dan's ready aid, as they mounted or left the steps of their carriages, were admirers of his.... They were sure he was "the very devil among the girls." In fact Dan was on the way to greatness.... The stable was feeling the benefit of his popularity.... We must now take a graver tone. Man is mortal, and mortality is changeable, and a change came over Dan's expanding fortunes.... A whisper was muttered that expanded into a rumor, and the rumor grew into a downright assertion that Dan, the polite, roguish, smart, industrious Dan, was a *woman!* ...

yesterday, the chief of police and officer Winters waited upon Dan with an invitation to accompany them to jail. But Dan ... laughed in the faces of his visitors ... he had not time just then to attend to their jokes. Capt. Garrett ... assured the young scapegrace that it was a very serious matter. "Can't attend to you now, gentlemen, that's flat," said Dan. "I let one of our horses to a gentleman yesterday, and he's gone and killed it.... The fellow has to pay us for our horse, and I expect him every minute. I'm fond of fun, gentlemen; but we'll settle the jail subject when you call again. We can then take a laugh and a sherry cobbler together. Good day, gentlemen," and Dan was retiring into ... the stable, with one of his ... laughing nods, when a few more words from the police convinced *her* that the play was ended.... Dan. Edson was placed on the charge of being, properly, a tenant not of pants but of petticoats, and entitled to the name of Mrs. Ray.... What may come to light, at the investigation that will take place before the recorder this morning, we cannot tell.

Memphis *Daily Appeal*, July 24, 1861.

The Livery Stable Clerk.—Daniel Edson, the livery clerk ... was before the recorder yesterday morning on the charge of being a woman ... in man's clothes. A large crowd filled the courtroom.... The lady appeared to answer the charge in the manly garb which she has chosen instead of crinoline.... She was fined ten dollars, which she paid.

Can a Woman Legally Wear Pants?... It ... appeared to the court ... that employing or retaining a female in man's attire in service, was not an offense known to the law, however liable the female might be herself for thus being in a man's attire....

Memphis *Daily Appeal*, July 25, 1861.

26 Tobacco for the troops
General Order No. 29.
Headquarters Army of Tennessee, Memphis, July 24, 1861.

The use of tobacco having become so fixed a habit with a very large proportion of our troops that the deprivation of it is to them a very severe inconvenience, and it being impossible for them to procure it at many of the encampments ... the Governor of the State, directs the various Commissary Staffs throughout the State to purchase by wholesale ... such amounts of good tobacco as may be necessary, and resell it to the soldiers of the Army of Tennessee at the cost price.

Memphis *Daily Appeal*, July 26, 1861.

27 Letter from R. J. C. Gailbreath [C. S. A.] in Bristol, Tennessee, to his wife Mariah Gailbreath, near Gainesborough, relative to railroad transportation, the first battle of Bull Run, and righteousness of the Southern cause

Bristol, Sullivan County, Tennessee
July 27th, 1861.
Dear Wife and Children—

I again embrace the pleasure of writing to you & as Ink is scares amongst us, you will pardon me for making this impression with pencil.

...I am in excellent health, as well as the other boys from your neighborhood.

We left Camp Trousdale on Sunday the 21st. Inst. and arrived her on Thursday the 25, making 4 days and nights travel by Railroad, passing through Nashville, Chattanooga, Knoxville, Greenville, Jonesboro, and other places....

Crossing the Tennessee and other smaller Rivers, on Bridges, passing the Cumberland Mountains through a gap and tunnel and running under ... the Iron Mountains hundreds of Miles amid the most delightful and Majestic like Cenery the Eye of Man ever beheld.... Could it have been that our thoughts had not occasionally strayed from the cenery around us and found a resting place, The Hearth at Home, where our wives and Children...

...

No accident of a serious nature occurred until we were leaving Knoxville, when one of our Company, a son of Joseph Law, by the name of Don. F. in attempting to jump the Train, fell under the Train, cutting his leg smooth into, just below the left knee. We carried him into the warehouse where the Seargant cut it off again just above the knee. I carried his foot and leg in my hand ... with a shoe and a sock and a part of the Breeches leg on it-We left him there and his brother to wait on him, but learned this Morning that he has since died.

...

R. J. C. Gailbreath
W. P. A. Civil War Records, Vol. 3, pp. 64–65.

28 A member of the 16th Mississippi comments on Knoxville and East Tennessee

Knoxville, Tennessee, July 28th, 1861.

The 16th Mississippi Regiment arrived at this place this morning (Sunday) about 1 o'clock A.M. We left Corinth at 1 o'clock P.M., Friday, in one train.... We are now in the disaffected part of Tennessee, and occasionally find a man who is still for the Union.—At all points heretofore, the ladies have turned out to cheer us. Old and young, rich and poor, those dressed in silk and those dressed in homespun, have waved handkerchiefs and banners to welcome our approach. In looking at some of the fair faces ... I have thought I could see anxiety depicted for the fate of a brother or a husband who was far away from the endearments of home in the ranks of the patriot army....

I think there is a gradual change going on among the people here ... yet ... there is a majority in East Tennessee who are strongly disposed to resist ... secession.... The country people are generally very poor, and ignorant. Grain and stock raising occupy the farmers. There are many coal mines here, and considerable manufactories, while the people are more like the Northern people....

...Knoxville is said to have 7000 inhabitants, but where they are I can't imagine. The town ... does not appear to ... have over 2500 inhabitants.

Eastern *Clarion* [PAULDING, MS], August 9, 1861.

29 Fayetteville Committee of Correspondence offers to furnish Confederate soldiers with winter clothing

Fayetteville, Tenn., July 29, 1861

...

Secretary of War, Richmond, VA:

DEAR SIR:

The undersigned have the honor to inform you that at and by a meeting of a portion of the citizens of the county of Lincoln on this day they were appointed a committee to correspond with you touching the matters embodied in the following resolution....

Resolved....

Can the said Department furnish all of our soldiers now in the field with shoes, socks, coats, pants, blankets, shirts, and every article necessary to constitute a soldier's winter dress? If not all of them can be so furnished, what proportion can be so supplied by the Department, and to what extent, with each of the articles making a complete soldier's dress? The object of our citizens being, if the Department cannot furnish all of said necessary winter clothing, shoeing, &c., to inaugurate a plan by which the deficit, if there should be a deficit, may be partially supplied.

...

Our citizens solicitude about our soldiers and their comfort during the approaching winter, and knowing that our ports were under a blockade.... We therefore desired to know whether the Government wants aid and cooperation.... From our wool we can make blankets, clothing, and socks, and clothe every man we have in the field (about 900) if necessary ... the Government has to rely upon private contribution, that some plan may be adopted at Richmond ... looking to the unity and cooperation of the people of every county ... we are all animated by the one high and holy purpose of achieving and maintaining our independence....

OR, Ser. IV, Vol. 1, pp. 506–507.

29 A Madison County farmer justifies secession

...It must pass into history that the Southern People withdrew themselves from this Union unwilling longer to live with a people continually agitating & harping on the sin of slavery.... Abe Lincoln declaring... "A House divided against itself cannot stand, that the Union could not continue half slave, half free.".. In less than 3 months from the time he took his seat he userped powers no former President dared.... Let History give impartial record of the Revolution & the *South must stand justified before the world.*

Robert H. Cartmell Diary

ca. 31 Report on the strength of the Provisional Army of Tennessee

MIDDLE TENNESSEE

Infantry at Camp Trousdale.—Colonel Fulton's regiment, 889 men, percussion muskets; Colonel Palmer's regiment, 883 men, flint-lock muskets; Colonel Savage's regiment, 952 men, flint-lock muskets; Colonel Newman's regiment, 914 men, flint-lock muskets; Colonel Battle's regiment, 880 men, flint-lock muskets.

Infantry at Camp Cheatham.—Colonel Rains' regiment, 880 men, 710 flint-locks, 175 minie rifles; Colonel Brown's regiment, 885 men, percussion muskets. Considerable sickness in last named regiment, mostly measles; it might well take place of Colonel Maney's regiment in East Tennessee, although not now in good condition for active, efficient services.

At Fort Henry.—Colonel Heiman's regiment,

720 men, flint-lock muskets. Erecting fortifications at mouth of Big Sandy.

Cavalry at Camp Cheatham. — One company, Captain Woodward, fully armed.

Camp Jackson. — Battalion, five companies, Lieutenant-Colonel McNairy, fully armed.

Camp Lee. — Battalion, five companies, fully armed. Our cavalry is armed with sabers, Colt navy pistols, and double-barrel shotguns, English twist.

FORCES IN EAST TENNESSEE

Infantry. — Col. George Maney, 944 men, rifle muskets; Colonel Hatton, 856 men, rifles; Colonel Forbes, 860 men, percussion muskets; Colonel Cumming, 877 men, flint-lock muskets. Field officers not chosen; ten companies strong.

Cavalry. — Eight companies, about 653 men.

Artillery. — Captain Rutledge's company, 110 men, four 6-pounders, two howitzers.

FORCES IN WEST TENNESSEE.

Infantry at Union City. — Colonel Travis' regiment, 860 men, flint-lock muskets; Colonel Stephens' regiment, 851 men, flint-lock muskets; Colonel Douglass' regiment, 838 men, flint-lock muskets; Colonel Russel's regiment, 737 men, flint-lock muskets; Colonel Pickett's regiment, 744 men, flint-lock muskets.

At Fort Wright. — Colonel Smith's Regiment, 802 men, percussion muskets; Colonel Walker's regiment, 541 men, flint-lock muskets.

Cavalry. — Five hundred and fourteen men, flint-lock muskets.

Artillery. — Colonel McCown, 140 men, flint lock muskets; Captain Polk, 67 men, flint-lock muskets; sappers and miners, Captain Pickett, 44 men, flint-lock muskets; riflemen, 493, flint-lock muskets.

The governor called for 2,000 riflemen, each man to bring his gun, to be taken by the State at valuation and converted into minie rifles, shooting sixty balls to pound. In response to this call ten companies are in camp at Murfreesborough, Middle Tennessee, and their guns are being converted into minie rifle[s] at the rate of 300 per week. Other companies more than sufficient to fill the call have tendered themselves and are marching or preparing to march into encampment. It is believed that from 4,000 to 5,000 men armed in this way can be raised in the State as twelve-months' volunteers.

Total infantry, about 19,400; total cavalry, 2,079; total artillery, 558; sappers and miners, 44.

The State is making good sabers at the rate of thirty per day, casting cannon, making powder, and will soon be doing so on a considerable scale, as well as making guns in considerable numbers of superior quality; making caps in large quantities.

OR, Ser 1, 52 pt. II, pp. 122–123.

♦ AUGUST ♦

2 Grand Junction Insurrection

"The riot at Grand Junction on Friday [August 2] was a serious affair, and might have been still more disastrous but for the firmness and bravery of the commander of the brigade, Col. Soulakowski, who, we are informed, shot down some of the men who refused to submit to his authority. We learn that when at Holly Springs the men, by some means got access to a barrel of whisky. They knocked out the head and drank immoderately.... The men, who were traveling in box cars, indulged in the worst extravagances-even it is stated going so far as to throw their bayonets at each other. One man was thrown from the platform and killed by the train passing over him, cutting off an arm and a leg. On leaving the cars at Grand Junction, open mutiny broke out, and the men turned against each other with perfect ferocity, entirely disregarding the authority of their officers, until the determined conduct of Col. Soulakowski compelled a return to military rule....

One citizen of Grand Junction wrote the following eye-witness account which was published in the *Appeal*:

"About 12 o'clock yesterday [August 2] there arrived here from Camp Pulaski a regiment of Louisiana volunteers commanded by C.L. Soulakowski, on their way to Virginia. About six o'clock in the evening, after imbibing pretty freely of "bust head" a row was commenced between the Frank Guards and some of the other companies which resulted in a general fight of about one hour's duration.... It seemed to be growing general when some of the men took shelter in the Percey Hotel, the doors ... were immediately assailed ... whatever could else could be found to answer the purpose of a battering-ram. They soon succeeded in smashing in all the doors, blinds and sash, when they rushed in like a mob of infuriated devils, and commenced an indiscriminate destruction of the hotel furniture and everything they could lay their hand on....

About this time the efforts of the officers of the

day and the guard proving unavailing to quell the mob, the officers, led by the colonel, commenced firing on them, which resulted in the death of two on the spot and the mortally wounding of some five or six others, and some six more dangerously wounded.... The majority of the wounded were from pistol shots, some were bayonet wounds and broken heads from the clubbed muskets-the men not having any ammunition.

The hotel looks ... like a hospital after a hard fought battle. The dead and wounded are strewn all over the second floor and the groans of the suffering are terrible.

After destroying the furniture and breaking all that they could about the house, two unsuccessful attempts were made to fire it."

...

Memphis *Appeal*, August 4, 1861.

2 Description of the Confederate camp at Union City

At Union City there were about 6000 men there, it was said-rude, big rough fellows, with sprinklings of old companies, composed of gentlemen of fortune exclusively. The soldiers who were only entitled to the name is [by] virtue of their carrying arms, their duty, and possibly their fighting qualities, lay under the trees playing cards, cooking, smoking, or reading the paper, but the camp was guarded by sentries some of whom carried their firelocks [sic] under their arms like umbrellas, others by the muzzle with the butt over the shoulder; one, for ease, had struck his, with the bayonet upright in the ground before him; others laid their arms against the trees, and preferred a sitting to an upright posture. In front of one camp there were two brass field pieces, seemingly in good order. Many of the men had sporting rifles or plain muskets. There were several boys of fifteen and sixteen years of age among the men, who could scarcely carry their arms for a long day's march; but the Tennessee and Mississippi infantry were generally the materials of good soldiers. The camps were not regularly pitched, with one exception, the tents were too close together; the water is bad, and the result was that a good deal of measles, fever, diarrhea and dysentery prevailed.

Memphis *Appeal*, August 2, 1861.

3 The Parable of the Patriotic, Self-sacrificing Tennessee Plantation Mistress

A Noble Woman.

We overheard a conversation some few weeks since, which threw light upon the character of our fair countrywomen. A lady, young and beautiful, a graduate of one of our most popular Female Colleges, married the choice of her heart. They have a large plantation and a strong force to work it. He felt it to be his duty to lead a company of his neighbors and friends to the field of war to meet the invaders of our homes. But she was in such a condition that he hesitated to go from home, and for a time she was not quite willing that he should leave her.

After some deliberation and consultation with friends, however, she said she earnestly desired him to go. ["]But who will take care of the plantation?"

"I can do it myself."

"You will need at least an overseer?"

"No, I can manage better than any overseer we are likely to procure."

"You must not be left alone."

"No, I will get some sensible woman for a companion. That is all I need or wish."

"What if you are disturbed or insulted?"

"I can shoot as well as my husband."

"What if your servants rebel against your authority?"

"There is no danger. They love me too well, and if need be I can make them fear me."

"Then you really wish your husband to go?"

"I do not like to be separated from him. It is a terrible trial, but some must go. And between submission to the North and the short separation from my husband it is easy to choose. I can't go and fight but I can stay and take his place on the plantation while he is gone. Let him go and do his duty. I will stay and do mine."

Tennessee and all the South is full of just such women. They can and will, to a great extent, take upon themselves the cares and labors of the loved ones who have gone to the camp, so far at least as business is concerned. Why will not our sisters in the churches do the same, so far as practicable, in the labors of the church and the Sabbath School? Much or most that is to be done in the school they can do as well or better than anybody else. Try it sisters. Try it at once. Don't let your school disband or if it has done so, don't let another Sabbath pass till you gather it again. Don't wait for some one else to begin. Begin yourself, by going at once to the others who will help you, and secure the hearty co-operation of all. These times of trouble and distress are no time to neglect the duties of religion. When the dampness of death broods over the land the light of religion is more needful than ever. Take your places, then, at once, my sisters in the Lord. Fill up, at once, the ranks left vacant by our brethren who have gone to defend you and the "other loved ones at home" from horrors worse than death. Don't let the cause of God, at home, suffer from their absence any more than the good lady referred to above intends to let the interest of her noble husband suffer in his absence.

A. C. D.

Tennessee Baptist, August 3, 1861.

4 The "Huyett Battery."

No people whose country is invaded and whose homes are threatened with all the evils of a desolating war, hail with pleasure every new and formidable means presented of overcoming and destroying their enemy. The more destructive the means, the more welcome the announcement of their availability. We have just learned that an engine of war, terrible in the work it will do, but simple and easy in construction and management, has been invented by Col. D. H. Huyett of this city. It may not be prudent to state thus publicly the precise *modus operandi* of this new weapon, but according to the judgment of well known military gentlemen, it is entire feasible, and will supply a want long felt in the army and naval service. After the close of the war it may not be imprudent to give a full description of the instrument.

We have seen a drawing of this battery, and if certainly promises to be a very powerful engine either of defense or attack.

Chattanooga *Gazette*, August 4, 1861.

6 Prominent Memphis capitalists seek immunity from Confederate draft

MEMPHIS, TENN., August 6, 1861.

Gen. L. POLK, Cmdg.:

SIR: The undersigned, officers of the Memphis Legion, beg leave to represent that since the war proclamation of President Lincoln in April last, nearly 4,000 citizens of Memphis and vicinity have gone into the Army of the Southern Confederacy, leaving at home only the heads of families and business men, who cannot go into regular service until compelled by dire necessity. Of this class about 700 have formed a military organization, known as the Memphis Legion, many members of which are men of prominence and influence, who have large amounts invested in the commercial and manufacturing interests of this place and cannot leave without great pecuniary sacrifice, and, as we believe, without great inconvenience to the public.... it is, we think, important that as many of our enterprising merchants and manufacturers should remain at home.... to give a considerable portion of their time to business operations.... our organization contemplated no other object than the protection of our families and our homes. It is thought, however, that we can make our legion more effective for this purpose and more useful to the public by placing ourselves under your command.... to be detailed for duty mainly for the defense of Memphis and immediate vicinity (with the understanding that when not on duty our members may be allowed the privilege of attending to their ordinary business). We are led to believe that there are duties required here which can be performed by us under this arrangement. The subject of pay and ... uniforms and arms, we leave to be settled by yourself and the Department, but would remark that we are poorly armed and equipped....

OR, Ser. I, Vol. 52, pt. II, pp. 127–128.

6 Bawdy House Police Ordinance in Memphis

Be it Ordained &c That the Mayor is hereby empowered and authorized and by and with the consent of the Board of Aldermen [to] appoint and employ as addition to the police force of the city one policeman for each and every bawdy house in the city of Memphis.

Be it further ordained That the Mayor and Committee on Police be authorized to prescribe the districts in which each of Said Policemen shall serve

Be it further Ordained That a tax shall be levied on the several bawdy houses of the city for the security and protection of which said policemen are appointed of an amount sufficient to pay the salaries of the policemen to be appointed under the provisions of this Ordinance — the said tax to be paid monthly and in advance to the City tax Collector and in the event of the failure or refusal of the property of any such bawdy house to pay the said monthly installment promptly in advance as herein before provided for the house kept by such recusant shall be suppressed in such manner as the Mayor and Police Committee Shall direct.

...

Memphis City Council Meeting Minutes, Meeting of August 6, 1861, p. 510.

9 "The reign of terror exists to a frightful extent in Tennessee, and men are hung every day for the expression of sentiments that do tally precisely with the ideas of the slave oligarchy." News from recently seceded Tennessee

From the Cincinnati Gazette, July 7th.
News from the South.

We conversed yesterday with a gentleman direct from the infected district of Tennessee, and ascertained from him some facts in relation to the true condition of things in Secessia. Our informant left Randolph, about a week ago, under pretense of going to Missouri to join the Rebel army. He represents a most deplorable state of affairs in Memphis and Nashville-a want of employment and among all classes but the military, and a want of food among a great many. Merchants and businessmen are becoming heartily tired of the war, and do not hesitate to say to the military chieftains that they must whip the North very soon, or else give up the idea. Planters, too, are less enthusiastic in the Davis cause, and grumbles both loud and deep are uttered at the slowness with which it progresses. The removal of the blockade will be demanded of the Southern Government before long-so our informant says.

The reign of terror exists to a frightful extent in Tennessee, and men are hung every day for the expression of sentiments that do tally precisely with the ideas of the slave oligarchy. A couple of weeks since a meeting was held near Randolph to take into consideration the case of a miller, from Hamilton, in this State, who was guilty of the high crime of being a subscriber to the Cincinnati *Gazette* and *Commercial*. He was assured that nothing but the fact that men of his occupation are very scarce in Tennessee saved him from the halter.

The troops have nearly all been withdrawn from Fort Randall and sent to New Madrid, Missouri. Great efforts are being made in the interior of the State to raise volunteers for the Rebel army in Missouri.

...

Philadelphia *Inquirer*, August 9, 1861.

10 "To the Clerks of the County Courts of the State of Tennessee."

You are hereby requested to issue each constable in your respective counties, an order requiring him to make diligent enquiry at each house in his civil district for all muskets, bayonets, rifles, swords and pistols, belonging to the State of Tennessee, to take them into possession and deliver them to you.

A reward of one dollar will be paid to the constable for each musket and bayonet or rifle, and of fifty cents for each sword or pistol thus reclaimed.

You will forward the arms thus obtained, at public expense, to the military authorities at Nashville, Knoxville and Memphis ... and will inform the Military and Financial Board ... of the result of you actions and the expenses incurred. A check for the amount will be promptly forwarded.

It is hoped that every officer will exert himself to have this order promptly executed.

ISHAM G. HARRIS, Gov. &c.
Nashville, Aug. 10, 1861

Clarksville *Chronicle,* August 23, 1861.

13 Nashville Vigilance Committee Forces Judge John Catron from his Home

Judge Catron-His Expulsion from Tennessee.

Five or six weeks ago, more or less, Judge Catron of Nashville, one of the Judges of the Supreme Court of the United States, made a charge to the Grand Jury in St. Louis, in which he gave his views as to what constitutes treason. The publication of the charge, it was understood, created a good deal of excitement among the disunionists of Tennessee, and the question off the Judge's expulsion from the State was much agitated.

...

One day last week, the Vigilance Committee of Nashville waited upon Judge Catron, informed him that he must either resign his office of Judge or leave the State, and asked him which he would do. The Judge was not prepared to render an answer. The Committee gave him twenty-four hours to decide upon his course, letting him understand that if, at the end of that time, he should neither have resigned nor left Tennessee, they would take his affairs into their own hands-meaning they would eject him by whatever force might be found necessary. Within the twenty-four hours, the old man took his departure from Tennessee, leaving his aged wife behind him, as she was too sick and feeble to be removed. We heard of him in this city on Friday or Saturday, but did not see him. We presume that he is still in this vicinity.

...

Louisville *Daily Journal*, August 13, 1861.

15 Shortage of black powder complicates Confederate needs in West Tennessee

MILITARY AND FINANCIAL BOARD, Nashville, Tenn., August 15, 1861.

Maj. Gen. LEONIDAS POLK, Memphis:

SIR: Your letter of the 13th to Governor Harris requesting him to send you gunpowder of every description has been sent to this department. We have but 11,000 pounds of blasting and 35,000 pounds of rifle powder, and are using from 600 to 700 pounds daily in making cartridges and field ammunition. Having sent a great part of our cartridges, &c., to Virginia and East Tennessee, we have scarcely any on hand. We have as yet but little saltpeter on hand, and but faint hope of getting it for some time in any considerable quantities. Under the circumstances, we feel reluctant to part with any part of our stock, unless there is a necessity for it. If your command requires it, of course we will send it to the last ounce, but we suppose from the last report of the ordnance department at Memphis that you must have double the quantity that we possess here. If you are compelled to have it, let us know.

With respect,

J. E. BAILEY, For the Board.

OR, Ser. I, Vol. 52, pt. II, p. 130.

23 Animosity between Major-General Leonidas Polk and Major-General Gideon J. Pillow

MEMPHIS, August 23, 1861.

Hon. D. M. CURRIN, Richmond, Va.:

DEAR SIR: Our army matters here are in a terrible condition.... Polk and Pillow are at loggerheads—Polk giving a command and Pillow countermanding it by the same messenger. Something must be done, and that quickly. Pillow, I learn, is acting on his own hook; will not give up his position as a senior general; denies Polk's authority to give him orders. Pillow has ordered his forces (only 6,000 to 7,000 men) into the interior of Missouri, against the advice of Cheatham, Stephens.... This state of things will produce mutiny and revolt, and our people, whose sons, brothers, and husbands are in the army, will rise up in revolution at such conduct.

Your friend, SAM. TATE.

...

OR, Ser. I, Vol. 4, p. 396.

23 Governor Harris' appeal to Tennessee's patriotic mothers, wives and daughters

Isham G. Harris, Governor of the State of Tennessee, to the patriotic Mothers, Wives, and Daughters of said State:

Whereas, The approach of winter admonishes us of the necessity and importance of providing warm and comfortable clothing, blankets ... and a state of war renders it difficult, if not impossible, to draw our usual supply of winter clothing from other markets, we must therefore rely upon our own resources....

I, therefore, appeal to the patriotic women of Tennessee to set about the work at once, of manufacturing all the jeans, linseys, socks, blankets, comforts, and all other articles which will contribute to the relief, health, and comfort of the soldier in the field.

...

ISHAM G. HARRIS

Rebellion Record, Vol. 3, p. 2.

24 Memphis Mayor John Park's Proclamation on Activities of the Vigilance Committee

"To the Citizens of Memphis-Applications have repeatedly been made to me, as executive officer of the city, for protection against indiscreet parties who are sent out to impress citizens into the service against their will on steamboats. Many of these men have been dragged from their beds, wives and children, but never has there been a man taken who had on a clean shirt. I hereby notify any citizens who may wish to pass within the city of Memphis to call on me, and I will furnish the same, and will see he will be protected. One poor man being shot yesterday by one of these outlaws, as they may be called, causes me to give the above notice.

August 24, 1861

JOHN PARK, Mayor."

Frank Leslie's Illustrated Newspaper, September 14, 1861.

28 Newspaper report on forced deportation of northern printers from the Southern Methodist

Publication House in Nashville and conditions in Nashville

Interesting from Tennessee.

Yesterday morning we had an interview with two Philadelphians, who left Nashville, Tennessee, on Wednesday last [21st]. Some six or seven year ago they left this city for Nashville, and have been employed in the Southern Methodist Publication House in that city. They enjoyed the respect and friendship, for many years, of many of the principal citizens, all of whom expressed regret at their departure, but the recent proclamation of Jeff Davis, requiring all Northern men to leave within a prescribed time, compelled them to vacate their positions and come home....

On the night before their departure, they made a friendly call upon Mr. Jas. T. Bell, the local and commercial editor of the *Daily Gazette*, to bid him a kind good bye. They had a ... pleasant conversation with him, and he told them that he couldn't blame him for leaving.... He shook hands with them all round, and the farewell was spoken, and, the next morning, the following appeared in Mr. Bell's department of the *Gazette*: —

"Stampede Among the Printers. — We understand that a number of Northern printers engaged at the Southern Methodist Publishing House ... leave today for the other side of Mason & Dixon's line. The proclamation of President Davis has shown them up in their true light. Since its publication they have been seen in groups upon our street corners, evidently consulting in regard to sudden movements. They have been holding a good situation for several years past, continuing no doubt lately a portion of their wages to assist in subjugating the people who have fed them, acting too, probably, as spies in our midst communicating such intelligence as has recently been seen in the Northern papers under the head of 'Nashville Correspondence.' They would have been perfectly willing to have continued at work, and given us the befit of their *amiable* presence, had it not been for the proclamation and the 'forty days' notice. Let us feel thankful that the proper means have been adopted to rid the cities of the South of such vampires."

...

Philadelphia *Inquirer*, August 28, 1861.

29 Memphis prostitutes arrested for refusing to pay monthly municipal tax

Persons of Ill-Fame. — The police are arresting women, having received directions to do so, on the charge of being inhabitants of houses of ill-fame. Several women will be brought before the Recorder this morning on that charge. It is believed that there is a connection between these arrests and the refusal of this class of this population to pay a monthly tax of fifty dollars, each house, to the city, as they are required to do by an ordinance recently passed by the Council. That ordinance is entirely illegal, and is not worth the paper it is written upon, and no outside proceeding can make it binding, or give its provisions the force of law.

Memphis *Daily Appeal*, August 29, 1861.

31 Camp Meetings Decline in East Tennessee as a Consequence of War

Camp Meetings.

But a few Camp Meetings are being held this season, in our country, and the few that have been held have been failures.... The state of feeling in the country is by no means favorable to religious meetings of any sort. The people are arrayed against each other, and all are on one side or the other.... But, as a general thing, the Preachers have acted so badly, as to destroy confidence in them, or kill off all respect for them. No class of Church members have been as intemperate, as proscriptive as those Preachers who have entered into this contest. The result is, that in all the congregations of the country, there is a division in sentiment, and a portion of the congregation are unwilling to hear these men preach. Others ... have aspired to be Chaplains in the army, and whether the people are just or unjust in their reflections upon them or not they nevertheless incline to the opinion that it is the eighty or ninety dollars per month that they are after. Believing this, though it may be uncharitable, these men can't preach profitably to the people. Upon the whole, we think it most advisable to hold as few camp meetings as possible this season.

...

This is a sad picture of affairs, but it is nevertheless a true one!

Brownlow's Knoxville Whig, August 31, 1861.

♦ SEPTEMBER ♦

2 Negro workers march through Memphis

A procession of several hundred stout negro men, members of the "domestic institution," marched through the streets of Memphis, under the command of Confederate officers. They were armed and equipped with shovels, axes, blankets, etc. A merrier set never were seen. They were brimful of patriotism, shouting for Jeff. Davis and singing war-songs, and each looked as if he only wanted the privilege of shooting an abolitionist. The arms of these colored warriors were rather mysterious. Could it be that those gleaming axes were intended to drive into the thick skulls of abolitionist the truth, to which they are willfully blind, that their interference in behalf of Southern slaves is neither appreciated nor desired; or that these shovels were intended to dig trenches for the interment of their carcasses: It may be that the shovels are used in digging ditches, throwing up breastworks, or the construction of masked batteries, those abominations to every abolition Paul Pry who is so unlucky as to stumble upon them.

Memphis *Avalanche*, September 2, 1861.

3 "Mammoth Apples."

Mr. I. T. Chilton who has a farm on the Nolensville turnpike, about two miles from the city, left in this office yesterday, the largest apple perhaps, ever grown in the State. We have seem the fine mountain apple exhibited at our State Fairs, but in size this eclipses anything that has yet made its appearance. The one in our possession measures 4½ inches in diameter and weighs 18 ounces. It is a regular whale and no mistake. We learn from Mr. C. that it was grown on a remarkably small tree.

Nashville *Daily Gazette*, September 3, 1861.

3 Southern Mothers swamped

Sick Soldiers.—The Southern Mothers' house is overflowing with sick soldiers, and citizens willing to take any of the sufferers in their own house are earnestly requested to inform the association.

Memphis *Daily Appeal*, September 3, 1861.

4 "The Ladies Helping."

...Like Joan of Arc, they may not, through the smoke and carnage of battle, bear their country's standard to victory, yet their efforts are no less patriotic and honorable, and no less essential to the success of the glorious cause. Emulating the great example of Spartan mothers and Roman matrons, the women of the South encourage and sustain the valor of their sons and husbands, and will have their full share in the glory of the achievement of Southern independence. God bless them.

Nashville *Daily Gazette*, September 4, 1861.

4 The Miscreant Horace Maynard

The Traitor Horace Maynard.

The Knoxville *Register*, of the 4th inst., says:

A distinguished southern gentleman and his son returned a few days since from a visit of several months through the Northern States. One of the party heard a speech delivered by Maynard, which for its atrocity is unparalleled. We fully indorse the gentleman for truthfulness, as we have known him for several years. This atrocious miscreant said-"We, the Union people of East Tennessee, will burn every house, village and city, and kill every woman and child within her borders, but we will maintain her loyalty to the Union." These murderous sentiments, however, will create no sensation in the breasts of the "conciliators." In two months form this time we doubt not that Maynard will walk the streets of Knoxville with the highest magnates in the land. We unhesitatingly say that any person who will shout down this monster, after uttering such sentiments as he has, will deserve a monument....

Memphis *Daily Appeal*, September 6, 1861.

6 "Cutting It Fat."

Some of our merchants, not greatly troubled with some conscientious scruples, are now reaping a golden harvest. It may be reasonably expected that those of them receiving their goods by way of a short [cut] across the line dividing Dixie from Nod, would increase their prices to suit the nature of the case, but our citizens were hardly prepared to see them demanding a profit of 200 per cent. Whenever the margin of profit gets to be wider than Broad street, it has ceased to be reasonable, and does not deserve to be very liberally encouraged. The spirit of extortion will soon be crushed out, if ... consumers ... buy no article whatever until absolutely compelled to do so. Wear patched garment, take additional care of your old hats, bonnets, boots and shoes, live on cheaper food, do anything within the bounds of decency to obviate the necessity of buying a dime's worth from any one you have reason to regard as an extortioner.

Nashville is not altogether ... of that class of heartless individuals, who would wickedly mock at the calamity of their neighbors, if it but enables them to pour gold in their purses. Or people know them, and should now and forever avoid them, as they would a house on fire or a city visited by the plague.

Nashville Daily Gazette, September 6, 1861.

7 Suggestion to use female prisoners as washerwomen for the Southern Mothers' hospital

WOMEN CONVICTS. — Men convicted of offenses against the city ordinances are set to work in the streets; women so convicted are kept within the walls of the city prison and no especial labor is provided for them, but they are set to do various jobs of washing.... It appears to us that the city might ... send them all the women convicts, these might be overlooked in the grounds where they wash, iron, and hang out clothes.... The hospital would pay for the work done, thus indemnifying the city for expenses incurred, and the city would have an excellent way of disposing of the female convicts....

Memphis Daily Appeal, September 7, 1861.

9 Fighting near Cedar Creek, Greene County

We learn from a stage passenger from Asheville to Greenville, on Monday [9th], that a difficulty occurred near Cedar Creek, in Green County, between some Confederate troops stationed there, and a portion of a company of Home Guards, in which one of the Confederate troops named *Henegar* was shot, and instantly killed. The particulars could not be had by any, further than there was great excitement and confusion. From another source we learn that the difficulty grew out of an order to arrest a man by the mane of Fry, a captain of a Union company.....

Brownlow's Knoxville Whig, September 14, 1861.

9 Citizens of Sneedville request protection from Unionists in Hancock and Hawkins counties

SNEEDVILLE, September 9, 1861.

Brig. Gen. F. K. ZOLLICOFFER, Cmdg., Knoxville, Tenn.

DEAR SIR: We ... are threatened with immediate invasion from the Union party of Hancock and.... We have the proof showing these facts from men who have heretofore belonged to and acted with the Union party of our own county ... the sheriff of our county, revealed the following facts ... that in a few days there would be a strong force from Kentucky escorted here through the mountains by a force of union men from this county and Hawkins who have lately gone from here to Kentucky ... 500 men who we understand are determined to bring back with them from Kentucky a sufficient force to overrun Southern men in Hancock ... thence to the railroad with a view to tear it up so as to stop any transportation upon the East Tennessee and Virginia Railroad. We have abundant proof.... We do not feel that the lives of ourselves and our families are by any means safe.

...

OR, Ser. II, Vol. 1, p. 833.

9 A Nashville Trade Union Local Secedes from its National Organization

At a meeting of the Nashville Typographical Union, on the 9th inst. An ordinance dissolving all connection with the National Union was adopted by a unanimous vote.

Daily Picayune, September 12, 1861.

10 Gender confusion in Memphis

IN PANTS. — Yesterday, the police arrested Ellen Bosquis, a fine, tall woman of five feet ten inches, on the charge of being in man's clothing. She had on pants that were full made and tied at the ankle, and a handsome uniform of the Confederate army. It proved that she was a vivandiere* of the army, and had accompanied her regiment from New Orleans to Richmond, Va., at which place she obtained a furlough to come and see her friends in this city. Of course she was set at liberty.

Memphis Daily Appeal, September 10, 1861.

10 Corks, Bottles and Mineral Water in Nashville

...

Everything is scarce down South. The Nashville (Tenn.) *Gazette* contains the following advertisement of a manufacturer of mineral water in that city.—

"notice. I hope my customers in the city of Nashville will be good enough to save all the mineral water corks for me as I cannot obtain a further supply, in consequence of the Lincoln blockade.

---

*A female sutler.

Your attention to the above will oblige me very much, as corks are as essential to me now as the bottles."
...

Boston Herald, September 10, 1861.

12 Evolution of the Southern Mothers' hospital

Mothers' Hospital.—This institution, now located in the Irving block, has grown from a little effort, with thirty beds to start on, to the dignity of a Confederate States hospital, whose walls on Sunday last, inclosed no less than 497 patients.... Of the above patients 181 were allowed furloughs to go to their friends; 75 were taken into private families; 2 died, one of them from the effects of an overdose of opium administered to him in camp. In the hospital there are now 300 beds, and room for 150 more. No money from the Confederate States has hitherto been used; volunteer efforts having, so far, met all demands.... It is fortunate for the sick soldier that such care is ready for him in his need. The unselfish philanthropy of those good women ... is ... worthy of all praise.

Memphis *Daily Appeal*, September 12, 1861.

12 Greene County Unionist Uprising

The Knoxville *Register*, of the 10th instant says: Blood has been spilled in Greene county, the home of Andy Johnson The Lincolnites have been keeping up the excitement there—drilling companies under the stars and stripes of the United States, and threatening death to southern rights men. Among the leaders of these rebellionists was Capt. David Fry. An order was issued for his arrest, and a detachment of Capt. Jas. Fry's company, stationed at Midway, under his command, went to make the arrest.

The Greene county Lincolnites connived at Dave Fry's escape. Capt. Jas. Fry arrested several men.... In retaliation, a party of near fifty Lincolnites attacked a force of twelve or fifteen Confederates soldiers stationed at Cedar Creek, killing one of them name James Henegar, after which they retreated to the bushes, and after several rounds, escaped.

Memphis *Daily Appeal*, September 9, 1861

13 "Confederate School Books"

Dr. J. B. McFerrin, Agent of the Southern Methodist Publishing House, has placed upon our table several specimens of school books now being printed at that establishment. They are entitled "The Confederate Primer," "The First Confederate Speller," and "The Second Confederate Speller." The matter was arranged by an association of Southern Teachers, and the casual examination we have been able to give it, impresses us with the opinion that the work could not have been better done. The printing is clear, near and precise.

It affords us much pleasure to chronicle the fact that an effort is now being made in this city to supply a want long felt in Southern schools, and we hope to see the enterprise meet with the proper kind of encouragement.

Nashville *Daily Gazette*, September 13, 1861.

14 "Whiskey Drinking in Knoxville"

We dislike to make any suggestions to the Military authorities here, in regard to the intemperate use of ardent spirits, lest we be viewed in the light of a *dictator*, but seeing a complaint against the Doggeries of Knoxville.... Whisky is the *main spring* of all the machinery of ungodliness in motion in Knoxville. It is only when men are drunk that they are lost to all sense of honor and shame. Those troops who blackguard and insult the inmates of private houses, only do so when in a state of intoxication. These troops who ride upon the side-walks and yell like savages would not commit such an outrage if they were sober. And the private of a cavalry company, who, *galloped over* Mr. Formault's little daughter only five years old, without even looking back to see what injury he had done, would never have been guilty of the like if he had not been drunk.... We again, say, let every liquor house in Knoxville be closed and made to stay closed while so many troops are here who will drink to excess.

Brownlow's Knoxville Whig, September 14, 1861.

14 High cost of housing in Confederate Knoxville

High Rents

In view of the times, the war, and the suspension of business, tenants are required to pay too high rents in this city, and its surroundings, and there should at once be a reduction. The laboring classes, dependent upon their daily labor for money to meet their unavoidable expenses, cannot make enough to pay the high rents demanded of them, these dull and trying times. The impossibility of making collections-the utter impossibility of getting new and additional stocks of goods, forbid that merchants should be required to pay their former high rents.... The owners of property should have a meeting, and agree upon a reduction in rents. To exact extravagant rents, and take the advantage of men's necessities, at this time, is swindling under a pretense of renting out property!

Brownlow's Knoxville Whig, September 14, 1861.

14 "Coffee! Coffee!! Coffee!!!"

In these days of blockades, when coffee is scarce, prices high, and in many places none to be had at any price, many substitutes are tried.

I am glad to have it in my power to recommend a substitute.... Take the common *Red Garden Beet*, pulled fresh from the ground, wash clean, cut into small squares the size of as coffee grain or a little larger, toast till thoroughly parched, but not burned, transfer to the mill and grind.—The mill should be clean. Put from one pint to one and a half, to a gallon of water, and settle within an egg as in common coffee, make and bring to the table hot-with nice, fresh *cream* (not milk) and sugar. I will defy you or anybody else to tell the difference between it and the best Java.

Brownlow's Knoxville Whig, September 14, 1861.

14 A Plea to East Tennessee Unionists for Accommodation to the Confederacy

...

When the alternative is presented to us of choosing between a *Northern* or a *Southern* Government, but few we imagine will experience any difficulty in making a decision. The universal response well be "*Let us live among our own people.*" Indeed, the people of East Tennessee could not do otherwise. Here they were born, and there they expect to live and die, and, whether they prefer it otherwise or not, the people must yield to the Government that has jurisdiction over their territory. To be a citizen of one Government and owe allegiance to another is an impossibility, and upon the assumption we had made,—that the old Government can not reclaim the seceded States—we must submit to the Government of the Confederate States, or remove from its limits ultimately.

...

...Let the people in each Congressional District in East Tennessee see to it that they elect a man who will properly represent the feeling of his district.... Such a man can be found in each of the three districts without much search. If we must live under the Confederate Government, we must be represented....

...We may be mistaken, but ... we beg our friends to bear in mind that we are now subject to the Confederate Government ... and ... it is our ... duty to make ourselves as comfortable under it as possible.... Should the Confederate Government be finally overthrown, we will have lost nothing....

...

Brownlow's Whig, September 14, 1861

19 Knitting Socks for Confederate Soldiers at the Franklin Female College

The Franklin (Tenn.) *Review* says that the young ladies of the Tennessee female college, in that place, knit socks for the soldiers one hour in each day. This is done at the suggestion of the esteemed President, C. W. Callender, than whom, the Review adds, there is not a more accomplished gentleman and efficient educator in the Southern Confederacy.

Daily *Chronicle & Sentinel* [Augusta, Georgia], September 19, 1861,

19 Diminution of soap manufacturing in the Bluff City

...Mr. Prescott, soap maker, informs us that manufacturers are obliged to decline large orders of soap, owing to the scarcity of a chemical ingredient necessary to its composition. He suggests that country people would do a good work to manufacture for home consumption and also for camp use for which country made soap is well adapted. In districts where wood is plenty the manufacture of potash would now prove very profitable.

Memphis *Daily Appeal*, September 19, 1861.

20 "A Brave Woman."

A friend has communicated to us the following particulars, showing the heroism of a lady (Mrs. Julia H. Waugh) in Johnson county, East Tennessee, which entitles her to a place among the bravest of the brave:

About the 10th of August a mob of about 150 men ... commenced their depredations and insults in the county above named ... hunting down friends of the Confederate Government, and forcing the weak and defenseless to take the oath of allegiance to Lincoln.

A portion of this mob ... fifty or sixty in number, visited the ... storehouse of Wm. R. Waugh, who was absent at the time. Their Captain ... surrounded the house and demanded of Mrs. Waugh all the arms and ammunition which her husband had. She told them her husband was absent, and had left her to take care of the store and defend the family.

They assured her that if she would quietly surrender the arms, she and the family would not be hurt. She refused ... and gathering an axe, placed herself on the door of the building, and told them she would split the head of the first man who attempted to enter. She had with her stepson, about 14 years of age, armed with a double-barreled gun and pistol-her daughter, about 18, armed with a repeater and a knife, and a young man who had volunteered to defend the building, was also armed. They could and would have killed a dozen or so of the mob if the attack had been made.

...the crowd, chagrined and mortified ... slowly retired, and soon afterward disbanded. The iron nerve of one woman-on other occasions tender and gentle as a child-had met and turned back from their purpose some fifty or sixty desperate men.

Nashville *Daily Gazette*, September 20, 1861.

22 Meeting of the Hebrew Ladies' Association of Memphis

Jewish Liberality.—On the 22d inst., a meeting of the Israelite ladies of this city was held at the home of Mr. Strauss, dry goods merchant, where a society was formed under the name of "The Hebrew Ladies' Association for the aid of the Volunteers," for the purpose of giving aid and comfort to the Confederate army. Mesdames Simon and Strauss were appointed a committee to call upon the Hebrew ladies of this city and solicit contributions. The Rev. S. Tuska was elected secretary. The donations will be sent to the regiment serving under General Jeff. Thompson. All ladies who have not been called upon and have subscribed, are asked to send their donations to the houses of Mrs. Strauss or of Mrs. Simons, and those ladies of the Hebrew faith whose residences are not known, wishing to contribute will please do the same. Blankets, drawers, socks, etc., will be gladly accepted....

Memphis *Daily Appeal*, October 1, 1861.

24 Arming soldiers in Knoxville with reworked country rifles

Gen. Wm. H. Carroll.—This gentleman, whose rifle regiment is at Camp Ramsey, has so rapidly filled up, returned yesterday from a brief visit to Memphis. He brings with him the arms for the regiment here a specimen of which has been submitted for our inspection. It is the ordinary country rifle, altered to carry the minnie ball. The pieces have all been cut down to a uniform length, and provided with the saber bayonet, making them at once the lightest, most effective and beautiful weapon ... our Tennessee troops have been furnished. The regiment here has been actively drilling for some weeks past, under competent drill-masters.—Knoxville *Register*.

Memphis *Daily Appeal*, September 24, 1861.

26 Isham Harris' Proclamation for 30,000 Volunteers

THE PROCLAMATION OF GOV. HARRIS TO THE TENNESSEEANS.

Whereas, the Government of the Confederate States having called upon me ... for thirty thousand troops, for immediate service ... it becomes my duty to proclaim to the gallant citizens of Tennessee that their country demands their services.

...

Let our gallant citizen soldiery assemble in such numbers, and press forward with such spirit upon the hireling invaders, as will hurl them back upon those who sent them! Let us call together an army sufficient, not only to repel invasion, but to punish the aggressor.

The Weekly Raleigh Register, October 9, 1861.

29 Affair at Travisville, Pickett County. (First Civil War Combat Incident in Tennessee.)

Report of Col. William A. Hoskins, Twelfth Kentucky Cavalry.

CAMP AT ALBANY, September 29, 1861.

SIR:

...

This morning I received information that the Confederate forces were forming another encampment at Travisville, distant from us 13 miles. Accordingly I ordered Capt. Morrison to take the effective force under his command and proceed to that point, and after reconnoitering sufficiently to satisfy himself that the number was not too great to justify an attack, to take them by surprise, order a surrender, which, should they refuse, to fire upon them.

In obedience to my orders he proceeded to that point as directed. In about two hours after Capt. Morrison left camp Lieut. Adams joined us, as also the Home Guards of Hustonville Cavalry. I ordered a detail of 15 men from the company under command of Lieut. Adams and 30 from the Hustonville Home Guards, which were placed under command of Maj. Brunets, and he ordered to proceed to Travisville, to support Capt. Morrison in the event he was repulsed; but before reaching that point Capt. Morrison had surprised the camp, finding about 100 troops, which, being ordered to surrender, fled, when they were fired upon and 4 killed, the balance effecting their escape by fleeing to the hills.
...

OR, Ser. I. Vol. 4, p. 205.

30 Cannon Foundry Burns

Fire Last Night.—A fire broke out last night, at half-past eight o'clock, in the engine room, which is entirely of brick, of Messrs. Quinby & Robinson, machinists and founders, on Poplar street, below Front Row. The flames could readily have been got under, but there was no water at hand. The seam fire engine succeeded at last in getting a stream from a pond at a considerable distance, near the navy yard. Notwithstanding every effort, the delay in getting water proved fatal to the building....

Above this was the machine shop containing twelve lathes, a planing machine and three drill presses.... The firm have for some time been turning out several cannon each week, which were much prized for their superiority. All the finished cannon were got out except one which was there for re-boring.
...

The various fire companies were present, and worked with praiseworthy diligence....

It is a loss to the Confederacy as well as to the proprietors, for the cannon made at this establishment was the best work of the kind turned out in the South....

Memphis *Daily Appeal*, October 1, 1861.

◆ OCTOBER ◆

1 Rotten Beef and Pork Kill Tennessee Confederate Soldiers

The Chattanooga *Rebel* calls attention to the fraudulent and outrageous manner in which beef and pork were put up for the army last year by the governmental agents in East Tennessee. It says many of the deaths in the army were caused by this unwholesome food, and premises to keep a sharp look out for such criminal remissness the present winter.

Memphis *Daily Appeal*, October 1, 1861.

3 Knoxville paper mill

Home Made Letter Paper.—We have seen a fine specimen of letter paper made at the new paper mill established at Knoxville, Tenn., which is very creditable to the manufacturers. Whatever may be the great detriment to our country in the way of commerce, occasioned by the present war, there is no denying that so far as manufactures are concerned, it is doing more to call forth the enterprise and energy of our people than whole years would have done under the system of dependence upon the North, which had already made us too subservient and dependant upon their people.

Daily Constitutionalist [AUGUSTA, GA], October 3, 1861.

7 Shelby County Court appropriates $20,000 for the relief of soldiers' families

Soldiers' Families.—The County Court met at Raleigh on Monday, when an appropriation was made of $20,000, to be applied from the 1st of October, 1861, to the 1st of January, 1862, to the relief of the destitute wives and children of soldiers absent in the field. It was provided that a committee should be appointed in each ward of the city to dispense the relief only to those who needed it, at the rate of seven dollars a month for the wife, three dollars for each child from one to six years old, and four dollars for each child from six to twelve years old, for each month....

Memphis *Daily Appeal*, October 9, 1861.

8 Excerpt from a letter to Mrs. U. G. Owen
...
Oct. 8th 1861.
...

We are at the roughest place in the world, camped on the mountain at the Gap. It is so cold that I can scarcely write this evening. We are not fixed here yet don't know how long we will stay here. We are building forts breastworks &c of every sort going to stick the mountain full of cannons to prevent the Lincolnites from crossing. We have one hundred at work every day, building fortifications. I have my tent up on the side of the mountain plenty of straw on the floor plenty of cover to keep me warm at night. I also have a cot to sleep on — brought from Knoxville — did not cost me anything....

...

Dr. U. G. Owen to Laura, October 8, 1861.

8 Texas Rangers in Nashville
The Texas Rangers.
On Thursday morning, the first division of a Texas regiment, under the command of Col. B. F. Terry, arrived in our city. They have come from the far off South, and, altogether, we regard them as one of the finest regiments we yet have seen. It is their purpose to provide themselves with horses at this point, and then to await orders for service in Kentucky. Some of the finest horsemen in the world are in this regiment. The son of Col. Terry, who, undoubtedly, is the best rider we have ever seen, can pick up from the ground, any small object while his horse shall be going at full speed — a feat peculiar to Texas horsemen.

...

There are, at present, four companies encamped at the fair grounds ... each containing one hundred and sixteen men — all armed with six-shooters, double barreled shot-guns, and bowie-knives....

When such a regiment as this ... shall enter the field, the unprincipled myrmidons of Abraham Lincoln will fall like grain before the reaper's scythe.... Nashville *Banner*.

Memphis Daily Appeal, October 8, 1861.

12 "Vampires."
So outrageous and grasping have speculations recently become in the country among tradesmen and adventurers, that the Executive of our State has been forced to recommend stringent legislation on the subject to the General Assembly.... The laws of trade ... supply and demand, are so simple, that in ordinary times tampering with them by legislation would be ... indefensible. But at a crisis like the present ... and hungry vampires, unmoved by an instinct of patriotism and bent ... on the satisfaction of their own rapacious appetites are sapping the very life-blood of the government ... the question assumes an entirely different aspect.

If public opinion cannot put down this infamous system ... it is time for the strong arm of Government to be brought to bear upon it ... be careful to keep one distinction constantly in mind. A difference ... between mercantile transactions where *bona fide* sales take place at market prices, and cases where professional speculators are holding large stores of goods.... waiting for an advance in price, and refusing absolutely to make any sales at present whatever.

We constantly hear of these Shylocks every day hiding away under lock and key such necessary articles of food as coffee, pork, salt, etc., used daily by our army, with the expectation of realizing on them ten times their original cost.... This class of gentry ... should receive the ... attention of the Legislature. They are as insensible to the mortification of popular odium as a rhinoceros hide to a stroke from an ordinary horsewhip, and ... cannot be influenced in the slightest degree by a mere exposition of their infamy at the hands of a journalist.... Missiles of a heavier character must be used.

...When the army shall stand in want of these necessaries, and find it impossible to obtain them elsewhere, government can order them to be seized and appropriated to its own use, paying the owners a reasonable price ... grasping monopolists ... had better take warning in time, and "save their bacon."

...there is a limit beyond which this forbearance will cease to be a virtue ... no dishonest schemes of speculators and extortionists can be allowed ... to circumvent ... this great and glorious consummation.

Memphis *Daily Appeal*, October 12, 1861.

15 Judge Selby's son, Harmon, murders Hettie Rogers
Murder of a Woman.— A thrill of horror ran through the community yesterday by the rumor that a woman had been shot dead as she was lying, in bed, by the son of a well know and respected citizen. On making inquiries at the place where the horrid deed was perpetrated, a house of illfame ... we ascertained that in the afternoon Hettie Rogers, who was twenty-two years old.... was lying sick in bed, being under medical attendance.... Between three and four o'clock the woman was roused from sleep by hearing somebody asking Hettie why she wrote that letter about him to Dr. Dickinson? The speaker was Harmon Selby, son of Judge Selby.... he immediately added a threat to shoot her. In great alarm the girl shrieked "I did not do it." And sprung up in bed to make her

escape, immediately a pistol was fire by Selby, the ball entered Hettie's back ... then came out below the left breast.... The girl fell dead. Selby ... escaped. The deceased was a very pretty girl ... remarkable for the beauty of her curling hair. Selby is a mere boy of nineteen.... His vicious courses have long been a source of grief to his gray-headed father.

Memphis *Daily Appeal*, October 15, 1861.

15 Repeal of Bawdy House Police ordinance in Memphis

Be it ordained &c. That the ordinance passed by the Board on the 6th of August last entitled "Bawdy Houses" ... is hereby repealed.

Passed 1st reading and referred to the Ordinance Committee.

Memphis City Council Meeting Minutes, Meeting of October 15, 1861, p. 604.

15 A Mississippi Mistake in Knoxville

In former times, when peace and prayer meetings prevailed in the South, the good people of Knoxville, of various denominations, were wont to assemble together in one place to worship God, and over the door ... they placed high, in neat gilt letters, "Union Prayer Meetings." The other day two of the ignorant soldiery ... the "flower of the youth" of Mississippi, tore down the sign and broke it in pieces. Being remonstrated with by a minister who happened to be passing, they swore vehemently that "no d — — d union sign" should stay up in their presence....

Lowell Daily Citizen and News (Lowell, MA) October 15, 1861.

18 Price inflation in Jackson

Times are if anything *tighter* ... the North seems more determined to subjugate the South.... One must live in such times to fully appreciate the conditions of everything. Revolutions are terrible things. Every day approaches nearer a state of DESPERATION ... everything is becoming scarce & enormously high. Bacon 25 cts per pound, Coffee 50 cts, Axes $2.75, cotton and woolen cards usually worth 50 cts now $1.75.... When there will be a change & what that change will be no mortal can see....

Robert H. Cartmell Diary.

18 "VAMPIRES AGAIN."

...our articles, denouncing the intolerable avarice and extortion of adventurous tradesmen have created a considerable fluttering among some of this class, induces us to continue.... The "army worms," who are eating into the very vitals of the South by ... speculation and monopoly, can be influenced in no other possible manner. They are mere vampires that maintain life only by phlebotomizing the Confederacy.... Patriotism and honesty constitute no part of their moral system ... so *they* can reap profit....

...We, of course, allude particularly to those scoundrels who have bought up such necessaries of life, as are needed by our soldiers and keep them hoarded under lock and key ... refusing to sell until they can realize at least six or eight hundred per cent profit.... These libels on humanity ... have their ... agents prowling about in every little country town and village, buying every ... barrel of pork down to a paper of plus [pius?]; and ... represent themselves as the commissioned agents of the Government.

We can see only one or two proper and feasible modes of remedying this evil.... Government can take possession of the hoarded stores of these huckstering harpies, allowing them a reasonable profit on their investments, and a proper remuneration for the trouble and labor of having so long carried the keys of their locked up warehouses....

...The amount of provisions, pork, flour, salt, etc., in the South is amply sufficient to last until another year.... The laws of supply and demand, which usually regulate the matter, are silent amid arms...

...we again advise the vampires that ... necessity ... may extend to circle of its persuasive influence over some of their own outrageous transactions.

Memphis *Appeal*, October 18, 1861.

18 "LETTER FROM GEN. PILLOW."
Headquarters Division
Columbus, KY, Oct. 14, 1861
To the Conductors of the Memphis Press

I inclose you for publication a letter.... From this letter you will see that the families of the brave men composing the army are suffering for the necessaries of life.

...

GID. J. PILLOW, Brigadier-General

...

CHELSEA, September 28, 1861
My Dearest Charlie:

I will write again to you, and perhaps you may get this one, but I do not know. I have written several letters to you, and get no answers.... Here I might starve and die, and you never would hear of it. I think it very hard that I should be almost destitute of the necessaries of life and the one I have on earth has been taken from me to go off and fight for the property of others that stay at home, *and* see the poor women suffer for the mere want of bread; they care not for that, self is all they care for.... Oh, Charlie, please come, for I need your presence at home to make some provision for me and the baby.... I am sick ... for my sake come home and let me see you once more. I really need your assistance at home. The baby is well. I shall look for you, if not, write soon. I do not get one cent from the county, and what am I to do? Write soon.

...

Mollie

Memphis *Appeal*, October 18, 1861.

19 Captain Thomas R. Mason's Report
[Robertson County]

Return of the strength and condition of the Company of Infantry commanded by Thos. R. Mason, and attached to the 89th. Regiment, Tennessee Militia, for the year 1861.

1 Captain, 2 lieutenants, 1 ensign, 3 sargents, 3 corporals, 2 musicians, 75 privates, 3 swords, 39 rifles, 6 double barrel shotguns, 17 single barrel shotguns, 17 pouches, 37 powder horns, 1 drum, 1 fife.

...

Given under hand this 19th day of October, 1861.

T. R. Mason, Captain

W. P. A. Civil War Records, Vol. 3, p. 180.

19 The *Tennessee Baptist's* Advice on Firearm Cleansing

How to Clean a Gun.

No one should put away a gun without cleaning, not even if it has fired but one shot — that one barrel should be cleaned. First take the barrels off the stock, and immerse them in cold water about four inches deep.— Then wrap some stout cloth ... about the cleaning rod, so thick that you will have to press rather hard to get it into the barrels; then pump up and down, changing the cloth till the water comes out clear; then pour hot water in them, stopping up the nipples, and turn the muzzles downward. Then put on dry cloth and work till you can feel the heat through the barrels, and the cloth comes out without a particle of moisture on it. Then put a few drops of clarified oil ... on the cloth and rub the insides; rub the outsides all over and then put the gun away.

Tennessee Baptist, October 19, 1861.*

19 Appeal for Boards to Bind Bibles and Testaments for Confederate Soldiers

An Especial Appeal to Our Sisters.

Who Will Help At Once?

The late movement upon the line of the Louisville Rail Road unfortunately cut off a large stock of boards purchased in Louisville with which to bind Bibles and Testaments for our soldiers....

...

Now the aid we want is this: That some one or two sisters in each town ... also at each post office of the Southern Confederacy will visit each store, and each family and solicit the donation of every piece of.... Paste ... board as large as a book cover for ... binding Testaments and Bibles. These can then ... sent to this Office by Express....

...Sisters go to work at once and help us to work for the soldiers.

Tennessee Baptist, October 19, 1861.

20 Report on bridge burning in East Tennessee

[Knoxville *Register*, of the 17th]

...So far as we can learn, there are but two sections of this division of the State where rebellion is making any head. From the Jonesborough *Express* we learn that some 800 of the citizens of Carter and Johnson ... armed with rifles have assembled in Carter county, and are organizing for the purpose ... of resisting an attempt to arrest the party who burned the Union bridge.... The Southern men have all left Carter county, the fear of arrest, and considerable excitement prevails in East Tennessee.

...

Savannah (Ga.) *Daily Morning News*, November 20, 1861.

22 "Arrest of Selby."

It will be remembered that Armand Selby, who, on Tuesday last, killed Hattie Rogers, by shooting

*As cited in: http://www.uttyl.edu/vbetts.

her in the back as she lay sick in bed, ran off.... Since that time Captain Klink and others of the police.... sent officers ... to Grenada, Mississippi.... On Saturday the two officers met him in the town. He knew them and endeavored to run. Morgan got near him, when he drew two pistols ... and told Selby if he made a move he would shoot him. Selby ... was taken. He had about him the portrait of his victim, he loved.... He was brought to this city and placed in jail.... Yesterday the grand jury returned a bill of indictment against him with the crime of murder.

Memphis *Appeal*, October 22, 1861.

22 Miscegenation in Memphis

At a boarding house on Beal street, between Main and Mulberry, soon after nine o'clock last evening, officers Mahoney and Ryan discovered a white man in a room with a negro woman. On finding the police on his track, the visitor jumped out of the window and ran off. In his hurry he left ... coat behind him....

Memphis *Appeal*, October 22, 1861.

23 Bobbed Hair in Clarksville

The Clarksville (Tenn.) *Chronicle* says that quite a rage for closely cropped hair has seized the young ladies of that city. It was suggested that as the war may last, and the boys be gone a long time, the girls want to be able to say when they come back and find them a little antiquated: "Why, when you went away I was a little bit of a thing with short hair!" A pretty good dodge.

Daily Chronicle & Sentinel [Augusta, Georgia], October 23, 1861.

24 Old apparel in Nashville

We have been gratified at the number of calico dresses, ... number of old coats, hats, and pantaloons, we have seen in the street lately. Sons and daughters seem to know that their fathers can not do as they wish to and would do under other circumstances. All praise to them ... Ben Franklin says that "he who buys what he does not want, will soon want what he can not buy."

Nashville *Daily Gazette*, October 24, 1861.

25 AWOL Shelby county soldiers families barred from receiving aid

Families of Soldiers.—Esquire Richards ... went last week to Columbus to have the blanks filled with the names of those soldiers from this county whose families are entitled to aid. He visited personally twenty-seven companies ... obtained the lists, properly signed, of twenty-eight companies ... it appears ... that there are instances in which families have received their allowance, the heads of which have been entered as "absent without leave." If this be so, caution should be exercised; for those fully entitled to claim aid will require all that can be done for them....

Memphis *Daily Appeal*, October 25, 1861.

26 "Suffering Women and Children"

There are in and near Nashville about thirty families of the members of the *Burns Artillery*, all in the most destitute circumstances. The husbands and fathers of these wanting ... have now been in the service more than three months.... their families are now suffering from the want of food, fuel and clothing.... Dr. Morton ... was mainly instrumental in getting up the company, ... It is well known that Dr. Morton is not a man of wealth, and he cannot be expected to continue this drain upon his limited means....

Nashville Daily Gazette, October 26, 1861.

27 William Blount Carter reports on conditions faced by Union loyalists in East Tennessee and prospects for a military raid

NEAR KINGSTON, ROANE COUNTY, TENN., October 27, 1861

Gen. THOMAS.

...

This whole country is in a wretched condition; a perfect despotism reigns here. The Union men of East Tennessee are longing and praying for the hour when they can break their fetters. The loyalty of our people increases with the oppressions they have to bear. Men and women weep for joy.... I have not seen a secession flag since I entered the State....

...

WM. BLOUNT CARTER.

OR, Ser. II, Vol. 1, p. 890.

27 Noting Nostradamus in Memphis

...

...many of the predictions made by Nostradamus ... have been completely verified, they are generally discredited in our times. But in the *Prophecies of Vaticinations*, of that great man, vol. 2d, (edition of 1609,) we find the following:

"About that time (1861) a great quarrel and contest will arise in a country beyond the seas (America). Many poor devils will be hung, and many poor wretches killed.... The war will not cease for four years, at which none should be astonished or surprised, for there will be no want of hatred and obstinacy in it. At the end of that time, prostrate and almost ruined, the people will embrace each other in great joy and love."

The period of four years ... comprises the exact term of Lincoln's administration. At the close, a new era, it seems, will commence of harmony and peace. Well, if we are to go through this fiery ordeal we must make up our minds to bear up manfully through the conflict, and acquit ourselves like men....

Memphis *Daily Appeal*, October 27, 1861.

28 Nashville as a War Material Manufacturing Center

Affairs at Nashville, Tenn.

Mr. Q. C. DeGrove, late Revenue collector of Nashville, Tenn. ... furnishes the following facts to the correspondent of the New York *Times*:

In Nashville the Southern intolerants have organized and put into operation a society which is miscalled "The Committee of Safety." It is the business of these men to spy out and denounce every man or woman suspected of Union proclivities, where upon follows an edict of banishment.... Nashville ... bids fair to become one of the greatest ... commercial and manufacturing emporiums of the South, from which the wants of the Confederate armies are to be supplied.... They are well supplied with material and manufactures of tents and army clothing of every description.... All the Northern sewing machine companies have agents in Nashville, but since the breaking of the war ... they offered their services to the Confederate Government.... All the tailors in the city are likewise engaged in making clothing for the army, so that Nashville is the grand ready-made military clothing store....

The leather dealers and shoe manufacturers of Nashville are also doing a big business....

There are two large manufactories which turn out immense quantities of saddles, harness, and cartridge boxes....

...

As to munitions of war, the resources of Nashville, in this particular, are very superior.

There is a powder mill on Sycamore Creek ... now in successful operation. Also, a manufactory ... for percussion caps ... made at the rate of two thousand five hundred per day. Rifles and muskets are also manufactured, and ... bowie knives and swords.

One hundred men are employed day and night at the manufactory for cannon shot and shell.

...

...The loss of ... Nashville would be a paralyzing blow ... to the interest of the Southern Confederacy....

Louisville *Daily Journal*, October 28, 1861.

30 An Act to amend the law respecting Bowie Knives and other weapons

SECTION 1. Be it enacted by the General Assembly of the State of Tennessee, That all laws forbidding the importation, manufacture, selling or giving away of Bowie Knives or other weapons and all laws prohibiting the carrying of pistols, Bowie knives, or other weapons, openly or unconcealed, be suspended during the ... war.

...

Passed October 30, 1861.

Public Acts of the State of Tennessee for 1861–1862, p. 26.

30 Memphis as seen by "The Rambler."

...Everybody is in a hurry. No one walks except the aged and infirm. Everybody runs. Hurry is the work; On, on is everybody's motto. Truly this is a fast age. People live fast, they travel fast, they come rich or poor fast, and they die fast.

Why is that tall man, who is engaged in leading that dray, so profane! He interlards every sentence he utters with some horrid imprecation. He swears as if he had notes before him.... I am told that profanity is by no means uncommon.... the little boys ... are imitating their seniors, cursing and swearing almost before they can articulate words.... Is this a characteristic for Memphis ... the expected capital of the Confederate States.... Then, why is it so profane? Why is the disgusting habit tolerated by the city authorities?...

There is a female in tattered rags, leading a sickly looking child along the pavement ... she is weeping. Some sorrow is brooding over her.... Many a man looks with horror upon one that will steal a loaf of bread to keep his wife and children from starving. His wife rolls in her carriage, or moves like a queen, in her comfortable mansion. Wealth has poured upon her its abundant stores.... She worships at fashion's shrine, ... Might not a change in her circumstances, bring about a change in her husband's standard of morals! Let down that braided hair; exchange that costly silk for the coarsest of epparedy ... those delicate little fingers of the jewels that now sparked upon them; let that little hand ... be stained with exposure to cold, let that ... wife want for bread, and might not her ... husband ... feel strongly tempted to take by force what he could not otherwise obtain?

Here come several men in uniform ... soldiers ... camped near the city.... Two of the four are intoxicated, and can scarcely move along the street. The other two are striving to get them away from the drinkshops, and ... to their camp. How disgustingly noisy they are! They are in a sad condition to meet the Yankees....

...

Memphis, October 26, 1861
        Memphis *Appeal*, October 30, 1861.

◆ NOVEMBER ◆

3 "To the People of Nashville"
Sewanee Coal Mines,
November 2, 1861

Some trouble has occurred in filling our orders for coal, mainly on account of transportation, it being impossible to get our cars returned. While we are dependent upon the ordinary freight trains.... But next week we are to have a regular coal train, to be continued. Under this new arrangement we can reassure the people of Nashville henceforth more than 100 tons of coal shall be delivered to Nashville everyday, without a change in price, and that everything shall be done that can be done to deliver it.

A. S. Colyar
        Nashville *Daily Gazette*, November 3, 1861.

7 ENGAGEMENT AT BELMONT, MISSOURI

8 Skirmish at Strawberry Plains Bridge
"The Hero of Strawberry Plains"

A correspondent of the Knoxville *Register* thus describes a visit he lately made to James Keelan, the man who so nobly defended the bridge at Strawberry Plains against an attack upon the property of Union men: ".... He was shot in three places-the back, thigh and elbow. His hand was severed at the wrist. Many gashes are found upon his person.... twenty attempts were made to cut his throat. When I saw him he was perfectly calm and sensible, bearing his pains with patience and fortitude. He will probably recover. He is a poor man, with a large family depending upon his labor for the subsistence of life. He fought sixteen men, probably killing their leader. whilst in the act of firing the bridge, and finally drove the enemy away without their accomplishing their fiendish purpose. He done all that [a] human could...: 'They have killed me, but I saved the bridge.' He is a hero, and has physically done more for the welfare of his country than any man in the Confederacy."

Nashville *Daily Gazette*, November 17, 1861

8–18 Revolt of East Tennessee Unionists
KNOXVILLE, November 11, 1861. Adjutant-Gen. COOPER:

Three bridges burned between Bristol and Chattanooga, two on Georgia road. Five hundred Union men now threatening Strawberry Plains; fifteen hundred assembling in Hamilton County; and a general uprising in all the counties. I have about 1,000 men under my command.

W. B. WOOD, Col.

KNOXVILLE, November 11, 1861.
Gen. S. COOPER, Adjutant and Inspector Gen.

SIR: My fears expressed to you by letters and dispatches of 4th and 5th instant have been realized by the destruction of no less than five railroad bridges — two on the East Tennessee and Virginia road, one on the East Tennessee and Georgia road an two on the Western and Atlantic road.... The whole country is now in a state of rebellion. A thousand men are within six miles of Strawberry Plains bridge and an attack is contemplated tomorrow. I have sent Col. Powel there with 200 infantry, one company cavalry and about 100 citizens armed with shotguns and country rifles. Five hundred Unionists left Hamilton County to-day we suppose to attack Loudon bridge.... An attack was made on Watauga yesterday.... A few regiments and vigorous means would have a powerful effect in putting it down. A mild or conciliating policy will do no good....

...I have arrested six of the men who were engaged in burning the Lick Creek bridge.... The slow course of civil law in punishing such incendiaries ... will not have the salutary effect which is desirable ... another camp is being formed about ten miles from here in Sevier County and already 300 are in camp.... I need not say that great alarm is felt by the few Southern men. They ... would gladly enlist if we had arms to furnish them. I have had all the arms in this City seized.... I felt it to be my duty to place this City under martial law ... a large majority of the people sympathizing with the enemy....

W. B. WOOD, Col., Commanding Post.

OR, Ser. II, Vol. 1, pp. 840–841.

9 Old Abe's U. F. O. spotted over Knoxville

The Knoxville *Register*, of the 10th, has the following:

Yesterday afternoon a balloon was seen, by a number of persons, passing over this city, coming from the direction of a little North of West, and continuing its course South of East. Some of those who saw it declare that a car was attached to it containing men. Conjecture was rife as to whence this strange visitant came. We think it probable that some of Old Abe's scouts have been up reconnoitering in Kentucky, and struck a current in the storm of yesterday, which carried them Southward. If they land anywhere in Dixie they will probably get more information of our strength and resources than they bargained for.

The Daily Dispatch, November 21, 1861.

11 Blackface entertainment for sick Confederate soldiers

Tennessee Minstrels.—On Monday night [11th], banjo and bones, breakdown and melody, black faces and fun, will, after a long interval, make their appearance at Odd-Fellows' Hall. The proceeds will be devoted to the wounded soldiers at the Overton Hospital. There must be a big crowd on hand—the occasion demands it. For once the people must go and laugh for charity. The band intend having a season, giving three or four concerts a week.

Memphis *Daily Appeal*, November 17, 1861.

11–25 Energetic efforts by C. S. A. authorities to suppress East Tennessee insurrection

KNOXVILLE, TENN., November 25, 1861.

...

...Every Union man in the county either took up arms or was fully advised of the intention of his party to do so, so they are all principals or accessories before the fact. If they are all prosecuted every citizen of East Tennessee must be arraigned before the court or brought up as witnesses. Nearly every rebel in my county could be convicted if all the Southern-rights citizens were brought up as witnesses; but this perhaps would look too much like political prosecutions.

Martial law ought to be enforced in every county in East Tennessee.... If we are invaded every Southern man will be taken a prisoner or else murdered in the night time. Our very existence depends on Mr. Lincoln's ability to invade the state.

...

MADISON T. PEOPLES.

OR, Ser. II, Vol. 1, pp. 846–848.

12 "To the People of Tennessee.... If you fail to respond to this appeal, I shall be compelled ... to disband these regiments of brave soldiers and call you who have arms into service as militia."

...

Prompted by the noblest impulses of patriotism, these brave men are ready ... to prevent the theater of this cruel and vindictive war being brought within our borders. They appeal to you, who quietly remain at home, to place arms in their hands, that they may give you protection and security.

If you fail to respond to this appeal, I shall be compelled by the sternest convictions of duty, charged as I am with the responsibility of seeing that the State is defended, to disband these regiments of brave soldiers and call you who have arms into service as militia.

I earnestly entreat that the people will bring forward ... every effective double-barrel shot gun and sporting rifle which they have, to be immediately shipped to the Arsenal at Nashville, Knoxville or Memphis, where the same will be valued ... and the value paid to the owner by the Confederate Government.

I urge you to give me your aid in the important work of arming our troops ... if you refuse, prepare to take the field, for I am resolved to exhaust all resources before the foot of the invader shall pollute the soil of Tennessee.

...

ISHAM G. HARRIS
Nashville, Nov. 12, 1861

Clarksville *Chronicle*, November 22, 1861.

13 Jewish support for the Confederacy in Memphis

Meeting of the Israelites—Subscription for the Wounded.

Since the breaking out of the war there is no class of our citizens who have been more liberal in their contributions. When arms, equipments or other things have been wanted, they have readily given their assistance. The Hebrew Ladies' Society have made liberal gifts of socks, blankets, and other warm woolen articles for the soldiers in the field.

...

Memphis *Daily Appeal*, November 14, 1861.

14 "To the Owners of Guns"
There are today hundreds of guns.... in and around Nashville. The State is threatened with invasion by a strong hostile army, richly and abundantly provided with the most formidable weapons of warfare ... thousands of our gallant citizens are enlisting to drive back the coming hordes of despoilers, but the State has no arms to place in their hands, and is ... forced to the necessity of appealing to such persons as are fortunate enough to have guns in their possession, to give, loan, or sell them for the use of our unarmed soldiery. What patriot who owns a gun, and is not actively in the service of his country, can reasonably turn a deaf ear to this appeal?... Who that is able, is not willing to make this trifling sacrifice in behalf of the common defence? Let every man worthy [of] the glorious name of Tennesseean, promptly respond to the call of our Governor for arms, and in less than two weeks ... enough good guns to arm every man in the service. If you have a gun ... no matter what kind, no matter who fine or how indifferent, give it now.... It will not do to delay, it will not do to wait on others, it will not do to depend on shipments of arms from Europe. The emergency is upon us.... *We must depend upon ourselves*, and what we do, must be done NOW.

Nashville *Daily Gazette*, November 14, 1861.

14 Report of fighting between Confederates and Unionist Insurgents on the South Fork of the Hoslton River and near Elizabethon
From Lynchburg.
The Skirmishes in Carter County, Tennessee....
[Special Correspondence]
Lynchburg, Nov. 12.
Since writing this morning, I have gathered the following particulars in relation to the skirmish which took place in Carter county, Tennessee, on Sunday night last between the bridge burners and a reconnoitering parting sent out by Col. Clarkson. The party of Confederates engaged consisted of 21 men under the Capt. Miller, of the Vicksburg Sharp-Shooters, whose company is now stationed from Manassas. The captain obtained a furlough some few days ago and was on his way home when he was detained at Bristol by the burning of the bridge. A party of citizens of Bristol armed themselves and requested Capt. Miller to take command of them for the purposes of aiding in the arrest of the traitors who had burned the bridge, which he did.

It appears that Gen or Col. Clarkson, with about 150 men, had previously gone in search of the scoundrels. The Captain and his party left Bristol about 9 o'clock Sunday evening, and marched in the direction of Elizabethtown, the county seat of Carter county; he had not proceeded very far before he fell in with Col. Clarkson, under orders he subsequently acted, and was detailed, with twenty-one men, to reconnoiter in the neighborhood of Elizabethtown, with orders that in case he should find the enemy posted in any strength to fall back and report. Capt. Miller proceeded some two or three miles to the South fork of the Holston river, which runs near Elizabethtown, when with one man he forded the river, which was about three fee deep and 150 yards wide. Soon after reaching the opposite shore he was hailed by a party of men not more than twenty paces off. Satisfying himself that they were traitors, he replied by firing upon them, dropping one at the first shot. His companion also fired both barrels of a double-barrel shot-gun in their midst. The enemy responded by firing a whole volley at the party, but none of their shots took effect. The Captain immediately recrossed the river, being met when about half way across by his men, who were coming too his assistance. While crossing volley after volley was fired at the party, two shots of which struck Captain M., one on the back of his left hand, inflicting a very slight wound, the other in his back, also a flesh wound, and, though painful, is of no serious importance His horse was also badly wounded that he died after reaching the shore. One of his men was also slightly wounded.

After this little affair a reconnaissance was made opposite Elizabethtown, when a smart skirmish took place, the parties firing across the river at each other. Capt. Miller, from whom my information is derived, states that the enemy were posted along the river bank for about three hundred yards, and estimates the number engaged in firing at not less than three hundred. He could distinctly hear them give orders order in up their different companies, and state it as his impression that there were not less than seven, or eight companies at this point. Having effected the object for which they were detailed, the partly fell back to the main body, and while on the way back captured two of the traitors, scouts who had been sent this side of the river. The prisoners stated that two of their party were killed in the first encounter and seven wounded.

...

Daily Dispatch (Richmond, Va.)
November 14, 1861.

15 Federal prisoners taken at the Engagement at Belmont arrive in Memphis

Arrival of Prisoners.— The bluff was lined all yesterday afternoon with crowds anxious to witness the arrival of prisoners taken at the battle of Belmont.... As they appeared, shouts and yells went up from a portion of the crowd.... These noisy demonstrations were made at intervals as the men were marched along the street. Some coarse attempts at witticisms were occasionally heard, but the expression that most carried the day was "Here's your mule!" An Irishman ... as if agreeably surprised, "Be jabers, they're all Dutchmen; there's not a rale reg'lar Paddy among the whole on 'em." Then turning toward the prisoners, "Byes, we've got no sour krout here for you." The proportion of Germans was large among the prisoners; the whole of them appeared to be men of very ordinary condition. As they went along amid the staring crowd, most of them had a dull, unexpressive look of absolute indifference. Here and there, however, among the brown visaged backwoodsmen..., showed the indignant and defiant feelings that were pent up within....

Memphis *Daily Appeal*, November 16, 1861.

17 Governor Isham G. Harris' call for civilians' sporting arms and serious thoughts as to the meaning of war by one Madison County farmer

The Governor has called for all shot guns & rifles to arm soldiers now organized into companies. Says he is determined to exhaust the resources of the State before the invader shall pollute the soil of Tennessee.

...

...We cannot tell what a day may bring forth. Providence alone knows the end and what the end will be. Numbers, resources, a powerful navy &c are against the South but under a Just God with a good cause, she is determined to conquer or die. The country may be laid to waste, her cities burned, her people butchered, a merciless insurrection aroused, & there is no doubt as to arms, is a deplorable state of affairs but the invader of our soil must be driven back, NO MATTER what comes. To be overcome and reduced to worse than dependants will never do. Affairs are fast approaching a crisis or perhaps a turning point. Winter will soon stop all movements by land & the rebels will be no nearer conquered next spring than last spring. In the meantime, Europe may become very hungry for cotton.

Robert H. Cartmell Diary.

20 Costume ball announced in Memphis

Ball Masque.— We understand that a grand Masquerade Ball will be given at Odd Fellows' Hall, on Tuesday evening next. It is intended to be a *recherche* affair, and every assurance is given that nothing offensive or indecorous will be permitted.... They afford room for display of taste in costuming, and of sustaining character. So many of the young and gay people of Memphis have been engaged in the various tableaux, they must be quite well provided with the necessary paraphernalia, and suitable masks may easily be procured or made.

Memphis *Daily Appeal*, November 20, 1861.

24 Chattanooga and the Tory Menace

Stampede Among the Tories.

From the Chattanooga *Gazette*, November 21.

Our town has been placed under martial law and our streets thronged with soldiers for nearly two weeks past, which has had quite a salutary influence on the Lincolnites in the upper end of this county. Col. Clift,* the tory leader of Soddy, who had marshaled his motley clan to the tune of some five or six hundred ragamuffins and outlaws, with the avowed purpose of joining ... East Tennessee renegades at Jamestown, and marching from thence upon Chattanooga, after covering himself

Correctly spelled: Cliff.

with glory in many *prospective* battles, upon hearing of the near approach of a detachment of an Alabama regiment, thought it prudent to disband his gallant followers and go home....

Six or eight arrests have been made in Chattanooga, but all having been soundly convicted are not enjoying their liberty....

Memphis *Daily Appeal*, November 24, 1861.

26 Tales of Brave Spouses in Knoxville
The Noble Wives of Knoxville.

The Chicago *Journal* says that after Parson's Brownlow's paper was suppressed by the rebels, he still persisted in defending the flag of the Union, until at length it became ... that he was jeopardizing the life of all his family, and finally prevailed on him to take it down. His wife ... forbade him. "No," said Mrs. Brownlow, "your hand shall never strike the American flag. If it must come down, I will take it down myself. That act shall never be written of Parson Brownlow"-and she then reluctantly drew down the flag.

When Parson Brownlow's Stars and Stripes no longer tossed ... to the breeze, there still waved another American flag at Knoxville ... that of Mr. Williams ... a bold, brave, true man ... had quietly but firmly attached and defended the flag on ... his house-top. His premises were closely watched by the rebels. They saw him depart one day for a fair two or three miles distant, and immediately prepared for their work. Some horsemen were detailed to take the flag down. Mrs. Williams saw them coming and stepped to the door with a loaded rifle in her hand. When within hearing, "Halt" she exclaimed with the firm voice of a sentry" Halt!" and pointed the rifle into their midst.... One by one they turned and rode away. Up to a late date that flag remained unfurled.

The Scioto Gazette, (Chillicothe, OH)
November 26, 1861.

28 "Tennessee Patriotism"

Wearing justly the proud title of the "Volunteer State," and every citizen of hers feeling that in the future as in the past, Tennessee will still deserve and bear the high distinction won by her chivalric and patriotic sons in former wars, in the number and character of troops she sends.... The number of enlistments required can be obtained in good time, probably before arms are ready to be placed in their hands, and we regard it as peculiarly unfortunate, both for the character of the State and the cause we are we are struggling to sustain, that any portion of our people should be threatened with the compulsory process indicated by that hated and infamous term *drafting*.

The mere suggestion that such a resort would be made in a certain contingency was ... in bad taste, but will prove, we fear, the source of such harm to cause it was designed to aid. Tennesseans needed no such threats to make them sensible of their duties as patriots in this hour of their country's peril. Needless alarm in high places, misapprehension of the temper of our people, or probably an inordinate desire upon the part of certain little men to wear big honors, has had a good deal to do with the indelicate haste and bad judgment displayed in this matter, and it is especially desirable that the patriotic spirit being evinced by the people of the State to enter the service as volunteers, should no longer [be] dampened by threats of compulsion.

Nashville *Daily Gazette*, November 28, 1861.

30 "Why Must Tennessee be Disgraced?"

...The Executive of no other Southern State has yet found it necessary to say to his people that he would resort to forcible means to get them into the military service of the Southern Confederacy, or that he even thought such a necessity would arise in the future. No page of history of either of the Southern States, either in their relation to the old or new government, is blackened with the disgraceful chronicle, telling posterity that, in a time of war, its citizens were dragged, and thus dragged, forced, *nolens volens*, into military service.

In no Southern State did such dire necessity ever occur-in no Southern State will a resort so disgraceful and humiliating to freemen ever be necessary.... Why, then, should Tennessee be disgraced with a draft upon ... those of her citizens, who for ... good and sufficient reason, are not at present disposed to volunteer for a term lasting through a series of years—but are, nevertheless, perfectly willing to offer their services for a shorter term.

There is reason in all things, even in panics and revolutions, but there is not reason in all men, not even in all men who wear Gubernatorial robes and military feathers. In this matter ... there is either a miserable trick and conspiracy ... to make the disgrace of the State complete, or an inexcusable incompetency upon ... those most immediately charged with the keeping of the State's fair fame.... The truism "Eternal vigilance is the price of liberty," is sometimes quite as applicable to tyranny at home as to despotism from abroad.

Nashville *Daily Gazette*, November 30, 1861.

30 "Attention, Militia."

...Judging from all that I can see and hear, I think there is a great injustice in regard to the non-drafting of those working for the State. I am confidently informed from some militia men who are working for the State, and who earn from twelve to thirty dollars per week.... would rather for eleven dollars per month, with rations (soldier's pay,) than to lay out in camp during the wet and frosty, winter months.

To put the whole population on an equal footing, there ought to be no exception. Let them be all drafted alike and give those who work for the State if drafted, the choice either to go to the field, or work for soldier's pay at home for the Government, and only excuse such men who cannot be spared or replaced by others in the different branches of Government work.

Another injustice is done by a great many doctors in this city, by giving certificates to a great many individuals certifying their unfitness for active service. Such certificates, some of which were bought with money, should not be accepted, and those men unfit for service if drafted, should be compelled to wait on the sick soldiers, if they are any way fit for that service, for the same pay as soldiers in active service.

...

A Militia Man

Nashville *Daily Gazette*, November 30, 1861.

♦ DECEMBER ♦

1 Tribute to James Keelan

The Watchman of Strawberry Plain-We have had few examples of heroism to compare with that exhibited by James Keelan, who guarded the bridge at Strawberry Plain, in East Tennessee, and repulsed the incendiaries, single-handed, though he came near losing his life in the effort. His remark, when he considered his wounds mortal-"They have killed me, but I have saved the bridge"-will live in history, and posterity will listen with almost breathless interest to the narrative of Keenan's courage and devotion. We are gratified to observe that the people of the South are bestowing substantial testimonial upon him, such as his circumstances require; and among other contributions for his benefit, the sum of $100 has been given by the Richmond, Fredericksburg and Potomac Railroad Company. We are assured that pecuniary favors will not be unworthily bestowed upon the watchman of Strawberry Plain.

Daily Dispatch, December 2, 1861.

2 President of the East Tennessee and Virginia Railroad, George R. Branner, protests the Confederate military's disruption of his railroad's schedule

Morristown, December 2, 1861.

J. P. Benjamin, Secretary of War:

I must inform you that in several instances the military authorities who are in command of troops and volunteers along the line of our road have taken possession of our road and trains and forced our engines and cars out of the face of regular schedules. This I will not submit to...

If this course is persisted in by the military authorities any more, I shall on my part stop all of our engines and cars immediately.

...

OR, Ser. I, Vol. 7, p. 733.

4 Presidents of the East Tennessee and Georgia Railroad Company, C. Wallace, and the East Tennessee and Virginia Railroad Company, George R. Branner, threaten to cease railroad traffic in East Tennessee

Knoxville, East Tenn., December 4, 1861.

Hon. J. P. Benjamin Secretary of War, Richmond:

Dear Sir: With ... an earnest desire to serve the Confederate States ... we notify you that unless certain unbearable evils are at once corrected we shall cease to run any trains on the roads of which we are the presidents on and after the 15th instant.... The military, influenced by no more patriotism than ourselves, have for days past, and without the least necessity for so doing taken possession of the running of our trains.... Our men ... feel ... that their lives are constantly in the hands of an inconsiderate and reckless soldiery.

...

OR, Ser. I, Vol. 52, pp. 227–228.

4 A call to raise the "black flag" in Memphis; the rhetoric and logic of war

We unhesitatingly say that the cause of justice and the cause of humanity itself, demands that the black flag shall be unfurled on every battlefield-that extermination and death shall be proclaimed against the hellish miscreants who persist in polluting our soil with their crimes. We will stop the effusion of blood, we will arrest the horrors of war, by terrific slaughter of the foe, by examples of overwhelming and unsparing vengeance. When Olive Cromwell massacred the garrison at Drogheda, suffering not a man to escape, he justified it on the ground that his object was to bring the war to a close-to stop the effusion of blood-and, that it was, therefore, a merciful act on his part. The South can afford no longer to trifle-she must strike the most fearful blows-the war-cry of extermination must be raised.

Memphis *Appeal*, December 4, 1861

5 Love, Marriage and Suicide in Civil War Memphis

The End of a Lucky Marriage.— Some six or seven months ago we gave an account of the marriage of a beautiful courtesan from a house of ill fame in this city. Her husband was a very wealth planter in Arkansas. We state in that account that the woman had declared that on her part the man who had chosen her should have no reason to complain of the future, whatever might be the events of the past. She was taken to her husband's home. Her life was far from stain. She appeared to be in the way to recover the position in society she had lost, when an individual arrived in the neighborhood that knew her. Her previous history was then exposed. Her efforts to escape the consequences of past guild were in vain. She committed the sin for which there is no earthly pardon. For her that world could offer no hope. He who had power to say, "Let him who is without sin cast the first stone," was not there to repeat them. Her new acquaintances avoided her; her now friends upbraided her; her new relatives denounced her and demanded of the husband that she should be driven like Hagar to the desert — to a desert where there was no angel to open the weeping wanderer's eyes and discover to her the well flowing with healing waters. The months of her purity counted as nothing in her favor; her husband brought her to this city and left her to misery and crime. She lately resided on Vance street, near the first bayou, passing by the name her husband first knew her by—Alice Simpson. She had been plunged into her early wrong course on her first return to the city, but had lately been industriously engaged in sewing for a living, and ... was striving hard to lay aside finally the slough of her past life, and to maintain herself by honest labor. But that banishment from the brief paradise in which she had enjoyed the society of the pure and the respect of the good, she could not forget. Ceaselessly she turned her eyes back to those doors eternally closed to her, and saw no more the brightness that was within, only the fierce glittering of the flaming sword that tuned every was repelling her from hope. That brief interval of pure wifehood had awakened within the knowing consciousness of what she lost when her honor was robbed from by the honey-tongued seducer in her girlish, thoughtless days. This brief sojourn with good had been the fruit communicating to her a knowledge of good and evil too bitter to be borne. Despairing, she sought the sad fatal refuge of despair. On Thursday night [November 28] she took a large dose of morphine; yesterday Alice Simpson was a corpse and a suicide. How sad must be that sin whose anguish is increased by communion with virtue.

Memphis *Daily Appeal*, December 5, 1861.

6 Poor Folks' Prices in Clarksville

Encouraging to Poor Folks.— Pork is selling at ten to twelve cents per pound; flour at ten dollars per bbl; bacon at twenty-seven cents; butter at forty cents; goods and groceries at just what a man has the face to ask — and other things in proportion. Truly the poor man, with a wife and children depending on him, has many incentives to join the volunteers and leave his family to the tender mercies of the community.— Clarksville (Tenn.) *Chronicle*, Nov. 29th.

Daily Chronicle & Sentinel [Augusta, Georgia], December 6, 1861

11 Martial law declared in Knoxville

PROCLAMATION

HDQRS., Rifle Brigade

Knoxville, Tenn.

December 11, 1861

The exigencies of the time requiring ... the adoption of the sternest measures of military policy, the commanding general feels called upon to suspend ... the function of the evil tribunals.

Now ... I William H. Carroll ... commander of the post at Knoxville do ... proclaim martial law to exist in Knoxville and the surrounding county to the distance of 1 mile ... by order of Brig. Gen. William H. Carroll

OR, Ser. 1. Vol. 7, p. 761.

12 "Cow Wanted."
The Ladies of the South Nashville Hospital are in want of a large quantity of milk for the sick under their care ... some one of the many farmers in the county should send a cow to the Hospital, to be kept there ... who will be the first to respond? There is a fine lot attached to the building by which ... the animal would be well taken care of and when no longer wanted could be returned in as good condition as when received.

Nashville *Daily Gazette*, December 12, 1861.

12 Report of negative reactions to the Confederate draft in Nashville

I have news from Nashville to the sixth [Dec. 6th]. Indignation of Gov. Harris' orders to raise troops by draft from the militia was intense, even among the secessionists.... In South-Nashville ... a mob of more than one hundred men rushed upon the Governor's officers, and broke up the boxes used in drafting. A fight ensued between the Confederate officers and the people, in which two persons were killed and ten or twelve wounded.

"Gov. Harris was compelled to keep his room at the St. Cloud ... for fear of assassination by the incensed people. He had received many anonymous letters threatening his life....

...

Cincinnati *Gazette*, December 12, 1861.

14 Counterfeiter Arrested

The counterfeit money that has been brought to Memphis from time to time was of northern manufacture, and it seems to have struck the northern genius we are about to speak of that it would be a good speculation to make the article on the spot. A few weeks ago circumstances led officers Klink, Dyer and Causey to suspect there was something wrong about a man named W.R. Markham, who came here from Vicksburg, but was originally from Massachusetts. Klink watched him attentively, and at length found that he was making overtures to a German employee at the jewelry store of A.J. Warren & Co. The workman communicated to the police what was the nature of the man's business with him, and at their desire he constructed for Markham the apparatus he required. Yesterday Markham was arrested, and a receipt for rent he had about him showed that he had a room over Holst & Sons, undertakers, on Main street. On searching this room the man's tools and apparatus were found. Other articles were also discovered at his residence — for he had a wife and child — on Market street, between Third and Fourth. The principal articles seized are a galvanic battery and two dies of each of the two faces of a $20 gold piece. These were of course in reverse, that is, the parts that are raised on the coin were sunk in; the execution was as true and accurate as in the original. It was intended by means of the apparatus and dies to produce a thin shell of gold of each face of the coin. Within this was to be enclosed a piece of metal of the weight and ring of gold. When the whole was finished, it would have stood all the usual tests. In making the arrest, the officers have saved many persons from being victimized by severe losses. Beside this apparatus were many tools, steel dies for two and half dollar pieces, an outsider used for opening doors when locked, an instrument for cutting cards in a certain manner for cheating at play, and sheets often used in counterfeiting. Markham was committed by Recorder Moore for trial. He was a lawyer by profession, but is an excellent practical mechanic. He informed the workman whom, he thought, he had made his accomplice, that he knew a man who would give ten negroes for good counterfeit gold coins.

Memphis *Appeal*, December 14, 1861.

14 "Strike."

The Typographical Society of this city have struck for a large advance of wages, which the Publishers have decided they are not able to pay, as they are paying more for paper and ink now than ever before, and the subscription price of their papers being the same. Will our friends make enquiries for us and send us four type setters, at the regular prices 3 1/3 cents per thousand ems. — Come on old type setters — come on and brighten up and help out. Fifty printers are wanted in the city now.

Tennessee Baptist, December 14, 1861

15 A call to rich planters to furnish slave labor to help poor white soldiers stationed at Fort Donelson to bring in their crops

...

The Governor of Tennessee has coerced the

poor whites into the army till there are not enough left to gather the crops and chop wood for the families....

FORT DONELSON, Dec. 15, 1861.

TO THE FRIENDS OF THE SOLDIERS OF THE THIRTIETH REGIMENT TENNESSEE VOLUNTEERS: Letters are daily received by many of the brave men of my command, stating that their crops are wasting in the field, and their families unprovided for. This should not be. These soldiers are depriving themselves of the comforts of home, and enduring the hardships and privations of camp life to protect and defend a common interest. Their pay is not sufficient to furnish their families.... it is your ... solemn duty to see that the little they have left.... is not sacrificed — that their wives and children are supplied with the necessaries of life.

...

Many of you have a large negro force, whose labor should, in part, be used for the benefit of these men. By timely cooperation much can be done to aid and relieve them and their families.

J.W. HEAD,
Colonel Commanding Thirtieth Regiment.
New York Times, January 4, 1862.

17 Confederate soldiers die from disease in Jackson environs
...Some 17 of the soldiers have died lately, typhoid or camp fever and measles.
Robert H. Cartmell Diary.

17 "Wanted"
Immediately, 10,000 bushels of Corn delivered at Race Track, or at our Pork House, to feed Government cattle and hogs, for which we will pay the highest market price in cash.
E. M Bruce & Co.
Nashville *Daily Gazette*, December 17, 1861.

18 "Another Portrait."
Mr. William Cooper, the Artist, has recently executed another portrait of President Davis, which he has placed at the disposal of the ladies of the Tennessee Hospital Association. We understand the picture will be raffled off at an early day, the proceeds to be applied to comforting the sick soldiers. Those who desire to take chances can leave their names at Calhoun's jewelry store, where the picture can be seen.
Nashville *Daily Gazette*, December 18, 1861.

20 "Selling Fire Crackers."
A law of the cooperation of Nashville attaches a heavy and just penalty to selling fire crackers. The law is violated now quite extensively, for it really seems that every boy in town has for the past few days carried his hat, picket and boots crammed full of these abominable little red babywakers and throw them around without regard to consequences. Officers of the city inform us that they will today begin the rigid reinforcement of the law against fire cracker vending. Look out.
Nashville *Daily Gazette*, December 20, 1861.

20 "Pork."
This article, we have heard, has still an advancing tendency in our market. Ten dollars gross has been paid for some weeks past, but we saw it refused by one of our farmers for hogs in the pen. We are told that one reason for the upward tendency (if not actual advance) is in Government agents bidding against each other. They are paid a commission on all they buy, and hence are anxious to buy all they can. Such competition should not exist, it is injurious both to private consumers and the Government.

...

Clarksville *Chronicle*, December 20, 1861.

20 Afflicted Confederate soldiers arrive in Murfreesboro, excerpt from the diary of John C. Spence
About the twentieth of the month, a large number of sick *soldiers* was sent forward from Nashville and other places to this hospital. This being the first introduction of hospital services at this place. All ever on the go and anxious to see who could render the most aid to the sick, having quite a store room of clothing. As fast as the soldiers would come they were washed and a suit of clean clothes were put on them. A comfortable bunk assigned them, and upon the whole, a hospital did not appear so bad after all.

The meal times were regular and of the best that was to be had. A long table was spread with a clean cloth, plates, knives, and forks, and other necessary things to set off, and a plenty to attend the wants of the soldiers. In fact, it was not far behind a second rate Hotel, and all felt a patriotic feeling for the comforts of the soldiers. If there was a chance for a man to get well, he had it there.
Spence Diary.

26 Christmas for the Cartmell slaves in Madison County

...*Taking Christmas*, suits negroes exactly, [they get to] laze around. Their natural occupation if not interfered with....

Robert H. Cartmell Diary.

27 Letter from Henry Yarbrough, Big Bottom, Humphreys County, to his son-in-law, Christopher Corlew Cooke, relative to deaths, cheating the government out of slave labor and a hunting trip

Big Bottom, Tenn.
Paid 5 c[ents]
Dec. 27
C. C. Cocke
Pleasant Mound, Tenn.,
Dec. 27/61
Chris,

Our family is tolerable well. The boys (our negroes) have had chills, but I have missed them.

I wrote you ... but have not received your answer.

Our soldiers are at Fort Donaldson. Mike Hunt died at Fort Donalson on the 24th and was buried today at *L. C. M. Lewis* Esq. Patterson died at the fort the same day Mr. Hunt died.

Mrs. Reid Booker died Saturday before last, and today they buried Mrs. Jerrell. All died with pneumonia.

I expect Sally to come to Montgomery, so our place will be to let out.

I have just finished gathering corn, made the rise of 500 barrels by actual measurement.

I have not killed my hogs yet. Will kill next week if we have a spell to suit.

We have had a draft among the negroes here to go to Fort Donaldson to ditch. They made a call for 130 from this County, and when they were counted up, there was but 146 in the County. Esq. C. E. Harris detailed every negro in the County, leaving one at every place where they have negroes. So there was 3 of mine detailed to go. I was a little too sharp for them. I called in Dr. Wilkerson, gave them some physic, and then gave me a certificate. I enclosed it to Gen. Tillman and kept my sick negroes at home, so you understand how that trick was worked off. There are some that begrudged us our negroes and would be glad they were all taken to the fort to die.

I think it will be about 2 weeks before Horace and Pleas come up, on account of shoes and clothing. Bryant has been making boots all the fall for soldiers, and our family with the rest of the neighbors is barefooted.

Billy Poyner is expected to die at the fort. Brother Sam is there now waiting on him. Harriet is but very little better, if any. Josia expects to come up in January. Hook is well, and got a bad case on hand, a woman in child-bed. She is so bad he has not been over this Christmas. He was to have been over on Christmas Day to go deer hunting. As it was, me and Billy drove the Gumpond drive and I went to the foot of Cyprus pond with my double barrell shot gun loaded with turkey shot, wadded with a rifle ball. He drove out 3, a 4 point buck, a doe, and a spy. They failed to run the gap, but came down the side next [to] the *design*. I saw them coming.... I was in about 50 or 60 yds. I cocked both barrells, leveled on the buck and fired both barrells at once. Nobody could distinguish but one gun at the crack. I turned him over, shot 1 rifle ball and 3 shots through the lights, one shot through the spine. The other ball broke the fore leg bone through the knee. Charles had killed one turkey with her and Bob Dickson his dog.

H. Yarbrough

W. P. A. Civil War Records, Vol. 3, pp. 206–207.

28 Desperate need for weapons at Fort Donelson

HDQRS., Fort Donelson December 28, 1861.
His Excellency President DAVIS,
Richmond, Va.;

SIR; The exposed position of this command and the impossibility of obtaining arms here has induced us both to make an effort to secure them at Richmond. Knowing the difficulties we all labor under on this score, permit me simply to state that I feel deeply solicitous about our condition on the Tennessee and Cumberland, and believe that no one point in the Southern Confederacy needs more the aid of the Government than [these] points.

With every assurance of the highest consideration, and the hope that a complete restoration to health will enable you to meet the heavy demands on your time....

LLOYD TILGHMAN, Brig.-Gen., C. S. Army, Cmdg. Defenses Cumberland and Tennessee Rivers.

OR, Ser. I, Vol. 52, pt. II, pp. 245–246.

29 "The Careless Handling of Fire-Arms."

Warning instances of the careless handling and use of fire-arms have not of late been unfrequent in this community. And yet another must be added to the terrible list. This calm Sabbath morning, while the sacred tones of Church bells invite our people to the worship of God, the spirit of an esteemed and loved citizen of Nashville has gone to test the realities of the world beyond the shores of time, or his body yet writhes in the physical pain incident to an accidental pistol shot, which seems to baffle the skill of physicians, and to set at naught the prayful solicitations of devoted friends. This instance, whether our unfortunate friend be this morning no more, or still lingering in pain upon the shores of time, is another solemn warning to those in the habit of carrying fire-arms, and we earnestly hope that the costly admonition may not be unheeded, especially by the people of Nashville.

Nashville *Daily Gazette,* December 29, 1861.

1862

♦ JANUARY ♦

3–4 The *Pink Varble* Affair

Returned from Nashville.—Messrs. Dan'l Richards, Barney Seales, Dan'l McLaughlin, Wm. Varble, Geo. Dickinson, and Wm. Brown, together with five deck-hands, the party who took the *Pink Varble* up the Cumberland river some time ago, returned to this city on Wednesday by the steamer *Sunny Side.* We learn from then that the *Varble* has been detained by the authorities at Nashville, and that the owner, in this city (Louisville), will be paid to the amount of her value. The crew of the *Varble*, after having been kept under guard in Nashville for several weeks, obtained passes through the rebel lines from Gen. Johnston. They left Nashville on Christmas day, and had rather a tough experience on their journey to this city. They were detained at Dover, Tenn., in jail, for twenty-seven hours, and was regarded everywhere with suspicion. Benj. Miller, who was a passenger for Nashville by the *Varble*, went to Bayou Sara, La., as an agent of Mr. I. I. Hatton this city, for the sale of coal. Some of the men inform us that they were well treated while in Nashville and others complain bitterly of the treatment they received at the hands of their old acquaintances....

Louisville Daily Journal, January 3, 1862.

The *Pink Varble* Affair.—We learn in reference to the return of the crew of the *Pink Varble,* from Nashville, that they came back in consequence of the fact that they were unable to bring the boat back through the blockade. They left Nashville under an order from Gen. A. S. Johnson, that they should be escorted beyond the rebel lines at the expense of the government, and that the rebel government would remunerate Captain Varble for the loss of the boat....

Louisville Daily Journal, January 4, 1862.

7 Clandestine loyalty to the Union in Nashville

The Union Feeling in Nashville.—The following letter was found in Fort Henry after the battle:

Nashville, Tenn., Jan. 7, 1862.

Dear Son:—I received your always welcome letter yesterday, and I am going to answer it speedily. I received your package containing $300 of C. S. scrip, for which I am very grateful. I am glad that you are doing well and that you are well, but I tremble when I think of you being engaged in this torrid war. Henry, my son, I can but feel the South is in the wrong. We may console ourselves with whatever belief we chose, the U.S. is bound to subdue us. General McClellan has and is exercising great generalship. I fear that soon a movement will be made that will crush us out. Henry, I know you must think as I do. I wish you would resign, and we will move North. No one here suspects my Union proclivities. I am obliged, for the sake of your mother and sisters, to talk and be a secessionist; but I say to you, what I said when you were at home, I do not believe that Northern men desire the ruin of the South. A great interest is felt here as regards your position (Fort Henry); if that is taken, the South is surely conquered. You can see this as well as others.

Destroy this letter, as it may get you into trouble.

Hartford *Courant,* February 28, 1862.

7 Fayetteville Negroes Support Confederate Soldiers' Relief Society

...

The President of the Soldiers' Relief Society, at Nashville, has acknowledged the receipt of a liberal contribution from the negroes of Fayetteville, the money being raised from a tableaux exhibition gotten up for the purpose.

...

Louisville Journal, January 7, 1862.

8 A Confederate flag presentation
Letter from Dover. The Flag Presentation.
Dover, January 10, 1862
Mr. Chronicle:—
Thinking that probably your readers have never heard the particulars of the entertainment at Fort Donelson, on the 8th inst., I have taken upon myself the liberty of picking up the "scraps" and telling them.

At about 11 o'clock A.M., your *homely* servant reached the camp, where a neat little platform had been constructed by the "gallants" of the 30th, which was covered, and surmounted by "fair women and brave men."

Yours *tremendously* secured a position to see and hear, but what was most attractive to sight, was the noble, commanding form of Col. Head, who, I will venture, is as brave an officer as ever bore a commission. The members of the 30th were drawn up in the form of a square around the platform, and presented quite a fine appearance. When the banner which was to be presented to them was unfurled to the breeze the soldiers fixed their eyes upon it, and prepared to look inspiring-the ladies do, bewitching; and all was *beginning* to go "merry as a marriage bell," when-alas! for moral grandeur-the "sweet baptismal fount from Heaven," which had commenced "sprinkling" the BRIGHT BANNER, became rather ungentle, in fact boisterous; a general engagement ensued, in which our forces were used rather roughly. Col. Head endeavored to rally his troops, but was compelled to "sound a retreat," which was excused in as "masterly" a manner as the "Grand Army" from Manassas. We took up the "line of march" for *Gen Anderson's* "headquarters."

...the presentation would take place on the steamer *Gen. Anderson;* whither we all repaired, with all possible expedition.

We were then entertained by an eloquent, graceful, and truthful address by Miss Winchester, who presented the beautiful colors, which were received by Lieut. Nichols with suitable remarks. We were afterwards addressed by Messrs. Winchester, Bidwell, Lockhart, Turner, and "last, but not least," Maj. Chenoweth, a Kentuckian, whose remarks touched a chord in every heart, which vibrated in unison with his own....

One of our "dandies in militaire" being called upon to speak, in his eagerness to escape, precipitated himself into an open state-room. He was surveying his surroundings with evident complacency, when he discovered to his discomfiture, that he had intruded upon a lady, reclining upon her couch in *undress.*

...

Au revoir,
Ella.

Clarksville *Chronicle,* January 24, 1862.

10 Anti-Confederate-draft demonstrations and riots in West Tennessee

We regret to say that considerable evidence has been manifested in some of the counties in West Tennessee since the call upon the militia was made; one county (Carroll) having gone so far, we learn, as positively to refuse to submit to the detail. In Weakly county, also, we learn there was trouble on Monday last [January 6th], which led to the fear that serious difficulties would occur there; but we understand that matters were settled peaceably and without bloodshed.... In McNairy county, however, the disaffection seems to have reached its highest point, as we see from the West-Tennessee *Whig* that it was ... necessary to send troops ... to arrest some of the authorities, and to send detachments of soldiers into ... other counties for the same purpose.

Trenton *Standard,* January 10, 1862.

10 Confederate postal policy and postage rates
The Post-office laws require that all letters be placed in the Post office for the mail or delivery,

should be prepaid, except letters from soldiers in the Confederate service, and they must be endorsed with the name of the writer, the name of his Company and Regiment, and his official position in the same. Postage on single letters, for over 500 miles, 10 cents; under 500 miles, 5 cents, drop letters, 2 cents.

Clarksville *Chronicle*, January 10, 1862.

15-25 Reconnaissance from Paducah to Fort Henry

JANUARY 15-25, 1862.—Reconnaissance from Paducah, Ky., to Fort Henry, Tennessee.

REPORTS.

No. 1.—Brig. Gen. Charles F. Smith, U.S. Army.

No. 2.—Brig. Gen. Lloyd Tilghman, C. S. Army.

No. 1.

Reports of Brig. Gen. Charles F. Smith, U.S. Army.

HDQRS. UNITED STATES FORCES, Paducah, Ky., January 27, 1862.

SIR: On the 25th instant I briefly reported my return on that day. The distance from Callaway to Aurora is by water about 3 miles, by land 6. From the latter place to this it is 40 miles; a good road even at this period of the year, but destitute of water, except in the rainy season. We accomplished the march (46 miles) in three days, an average of 15 miles per day. This is the State road, but is not marked on any map I have seen. It is generally on a ridge of clay and gravel, and is called the Ridge road. Its course is nearly straight from Aurora to Paducah, at no point farther than 10 miles from the river.

My reports ... will give all the necessary information about the march, except on one point, outrages committed by the men in killing hogs and poultry; this, despite every precaution taken by myself and brigade and regimental commanders. Horses even were attempted to be carried off. Some men are in arrest for such offenses, whom I shall bring before a proper tribunal for trial. The reason for this is, in my belief, that the company officers have not done their duty. They will not see, if they do not in fact encourage, this misconduct.

The general will pardon me if I venture to make a suggestion in reference to the future. I know nothing about the course of operations to be pursued, but if Union City (which I have always thought to be a strong strategic point) is to be occupied, the most feasible means of supplying our troops there at this period of the year is from here by rail to the State line. Place good engines and wood cars on our road, repair the road as we go, and guard the whole line with a strong force. The distance from the end of the railway to the Columbus road is but 8 miles to be marched, or we can march the 35 miles to Union City from the terminus of the road. I speak of this on account of the extreme difficulty of sending wagon trains for a large force at this period of the year.

I send herewith a rather meager infantry of the march.

...

C. F. SMITH, Brig.-Gen., Cmdg.
HDQRS. UNITED STATES FORCES,
Paducah, Ky., January 28, 1862.

SIR: I transmit herewith an itinerary of the recent march of this command, which ought to have accompanied my report of yesterday. I spoke of the march from Fulton-the terminus of the railway from this place to the State line-to Union City as 35 miles. It is only 11 miles. From Fulton to the Mobile and Ohio railway by the State line is 8 miles. It is the same distance from Fulton to the Nashville and Northwestern Railway.

Very respectfully, your obedient servant,

C. F. SMITH, Brig.-Gen., Cmdg.

[Inclosure.]

Journal of the march of the First and Second Brigades of the United States forces from Paducah, Ky., to Callaway, on the Tennessee River, and back.

...

January 21.—Road towards Callaway bad; Callaway-a small place of three or four houses and one mill, not running now-has got a poor landing place. We found here the gunboat *Lexington* and the steamer *Wilson*, with forage and provision. The gunboat *Lexington* went up river towards Fort Henry; chased a small rebel gunboat with two 12-pounder rifled guns, but the rebel escaped; then threw twelve shells into Fort Henry. During the night, frost. Four miles north is Aurora, a small place, with a landing and ferry on the Tennessee River.

January 22.—Brig.-general commanding, C. F. Smith, Brigade Surgeon Dr. Hewitt, and Capt. John Rizha went up the river on the gunboat *Lexington* to reconnoiter Fort Henry. When our gunboat reached the south point of the island, next to Fort Henry, we could see two rebel steamers depart in great haste. We shelled Fort Henry, and the fort returned our fire with one shot, which must have been a 32-pounder rifled gun. The north side of the fort is a cremaillere line, mounting four 32-pounders. The three other sides are rectangular, mounting two 64 and two 24 pounders. In front cremaillere line is, I should judge, a redan commenced. South of the fort is a large camp. East of the fort is one regiment encamped. From Fort Henry to Fort Donelson, on the Cumberland River, 12 miles; connected by a good road. On the west side of the Tennessee River, opposite the fort, two hills, about 90 feet above river. Fort Henry is strongly built, and I believe well garrisoned. All around the fort abatis, from head of island to the fort, two miles and a half.

...

Very respectfully, your obedient servant,
JOHN RZIHA, Capt., Nineteenth Infantry, U.S. Army.
No. 2.
Reports of Brig. Gen. Lloyd Tilghman, C. S. Army.
FORT DONELSON, January 18, 1862 — 8 A.M.

All quiet this morning; 2,000 infantry and 200 cavalry have landed at Eggner's Ferry and encamped 6 miles out on road to Murray. Have 15 wagons. Their object, I think, is our railroad at Paris.

Gunboats below us have retired again, with transports. All quiet at Dover.
TILGHMAN.

OR, Ser. I, Vol. 7, pp. 73–74

18 Letter of S. T. Williams, at Fort Donelson, to his Cousin

I take the present opportunity to write you a few lines to let you know that I have not forgotten you. I am well at present and hope when these few lines come to hand they find you enjoying the same blessing. Most of the boys are well. We have quite a muddy time here. It is raining now and has been all the morning. The river is rising very fast, very fast. We have taken charge of a battery on the river bank. We have one 128 pounder. I think we would shake an old gunboat right smartly if she was to vinture up. It is rumored that they were fighting at Fort Henry yesterday and would attack us today, but it is twelve 0-clock and no Yankees yet. We are all sitting back in our house as safely as pigs. They have made little house for the guards to stand in. I don't think they will be exposed, so know they can stand in them when it is raining and not get wet. I want you to tell me John Williams is getting to the present and if him and Mr. H. has been down to raise the blockade yet. We have plenty to eat here. Frank bought us three or four boxes of cakes, pies, chickens, butter, and such things. We have been living high on them. Well, it is dinner and I must close. Tell all the girls howdy for me and give them my best respects. Tell them to write me....

...

Winds of Change, pp. 24–25.

21 Warnings of residual pro–Union sentiment in East Tennessee
HDQRS., Knoxville, Tenn.
January 21, 1862.
Gen. S. COOPER, Adjutant and Inspector-Gen., Richmond, Va.
SIR:
...

Outwardly the country remains sufficiently quiet but it is filled with Union men who continue to talk sedition and who are evidently waiting only for a safe opportunity to act out their rebellious sentiments. If such men are arrested by the military the Confederate State courts take them by writ of habeas corpus and they are released under bond to keep the peace; all which is satisfactory in a theoretical point of view but practically fatal to the influence of military authority and to the peace of the country. It seems not unlikely that every prisoner now in our hands might or will be thus released by the Confederate court even after being condemned by court-martial to be held as prisoners of war.

It is reported to-day that several fragmentary companies recruiting in different counties ostensibly for the service of the Confederate States have suddenly disappeared; gone to Kentucky.

It is confidently hoped that the bridge over the Holston at Union will be completed in the current month.

Very respectfully, sir, your obedient servant,
D. LEADBETTER, Col., Cmdg.

OR, Ser. II, Vol. 1, p. 877.

21, 25 Reports on construction of Confederate forts on the Cumberland, Tennessee and Red Rivers

CLARKSVILLE, January 21, 1862.

Maj. Gen. W. J. HARDEE, Bowling Green:

MY DEAR SIR: Our forts are still in an unfinished condition, and will remain so, unless the 2,000 men who are now here are ordered to work on them immediately if necessary, night and day. As yet no work has been done by the soldiers, and if half we hear is true we have no time to lose. There is a great deal of work done on the forts, but they are unfinished, and in the present condition do no earthly good, and are no more effective for defense than if they were in their original condition before a spade of dirt was removed. More energy must be infused into the work of preparation here for defense, or we will be unprepared, if the enemy should pass Fort Donelson and march around it. We hear the enemy are in force 6,000 strong at Murray, about 25 miles north of Paris. We don't know the truth of this report, but the people of Paris are in a great state of excitement about it. They believe the report to be true.

I understand the authorities here have again sent out over the country to collect in the negroes to finish these. This will necessarily produce delay, though none could be finished before the negro force can be assembled if the soldiers were detailed for the work. Last night twelve companies arrived here from Nashville, and we have now here two regiments....

I need not apologize for my urgency, for I cannot and ought not, in the position I occupy, to stand still in such a moment as this.

Ever your friend and obedient servant,

GUS. A. HENRY.

[Indorsement.]

ENGINEER'S OFFICE,

January 25, 1862.

I have just received a telegraphic report from Mr. Edward B. Sayer, assistant engineer at Clarksville, in which he says "work progressing very well now; 200 slaves and 50 soldiers at work; 24-pounders mounted; one 12-pounder also mounted."

I have directed him to mount the 32s in the water battery at mouth of Red River.

[J. F. GILMER,]

Maj., and Chief Engineer
Western Department.

OR, Ser. I, Vol. 7, pp. 841–842.

23 Newspaper Report on Pork Production in Tennessee

...

The Knoxville *Register* has some information as to the number of hogs the Government has purchased, and is having slaughtered and packed, in Tennessee, and gives the following approximate estimate: At Bristol, about 12,000, Morristown and vicinity, 20,000; Knoxville, 10,000; Loudon and Sweetwater, 12,000; Chattanooga, 20,000; Shelbyville, 50,000; Nashville, 20,000; Clarksville, 10,000; Other places about 16,000-making in all, 200,000. From these hogs the Government will net about twenty four million pounds of Bacon.

...

Charleston *Mercury*, January 23, 1862.

25 "From Fort Henry."

Fort Henry, Jan. 25, 1862

Dear *Chronicle*:— Since my last letter we ... are now camping in our tents again, and as the weather has been very cold ... we miss our comfortable cabins very much. Our company (A) of Col. Bailey's Regiment, and one from Col. Sugg's ... Regiment are now encamped here together.—

PADDIES TICKTACKS: Since our arrival we have been furnished with side arms-*spades and shovels*.... Our boys were greatly disappointed at not meeting the enemy here, and now feel that they have been badly sold, or taken in-*to the ditches* -instead of among the enemy.

The day after our arrival, the gunboat "*Conestoga*" chased the steamer *Dunbar* 14 miles up the river until within sight of the Fort, and then fired her seventh shot and ran up behind the Island, two miles below the Fort. She afterwards fired three shots at the Fort and meeting no response, she retired with a white flag flying to the breeze. No damage was done by her shots as they all fell short. However, she again made her appearance with the stars and stripes flying and opened fire on the Fort. As soon as the first shot was fired by her the Confederate flag was raised in the Fort, and we all expected to have a brush with the "Feds," but as soon as we fired one shot, she responded with a shell (which burst some yards below the Fort,) and retired behind the Island. Nobody hurt.

...

The enemy are reported to be 15,000 strong ...

35 miles below here. They were 16 miles from here a few days ago, but are now falling back. Little prospect of a *squirmish*

Clarksville *Chronicle*,
January 31, 1862.

25 Concerns expressed in Confederate-occupied Chattanooga about speculators in a newspaper editorial titled "The Extortioner."

[The Extortioner] is not a *thief* because all his transactions square with the law. He is not a murderer or highway robber ... yet he is a villain, possessing the will to rob, or steal, or murder, or do what not for money.... He is in time of war, not only the spoiler of the poor, but traitor to his country. The conduct of Judas Iscariot squared with the maxim of commerce ... [but] there is a day of revolution. He will be an outcast from the new order of society.... He will them be marked with scorn and hunted from the ease of his riches and the peace of mind, and will transmit the brand of infamy to his posterity."*

Chattanooga *Gazette and Advertiser*,
January 25, 1862.

28 Excerpt from a letter by Edward Bradford, at a Confederate camp of instruction in Gainesboro, to his father in Tank, Tennessee

...There was a great many gentlemen from Nashville up here to see their boys. The most of them expected to find them dead or badly wounded.... John Porch ... was wounded in the hand and one of his fingers had to be taken off.... I am in hopes we will be transferred to the Bowling Green service as I never want to go into a fight under Gen. Crittenden again. I don't think he is of the right stripe. He was in camp two hours before anybody else and one of the first that crossed the river. If he had stayed with us and carried on things right, I don't think we would have lost more than half we did. I believe we could have saved every one of our cannons and all of our wagons and mules....

Frederick Bradford Papers, TSL&A

29 Report on Widespread Alarm in Paris
...
PANIC AT PARIS-NEGROES MOVED TO MEMPHIS.

The greatest excitement prevails at Paris, and the inhabitants are fleeing from certain destruction of Henry county in which Pairs is situated, is perfectly bare of military force, having sent two regiments into the field. Besides, the adjoining county is said to contain a large number of Union men.

Colonels J. Cook and Cummins, together with their families, and several hundred negroes, all from the neighborhood of Paris, arrived in the city last night, and represent that the greatest apprehensions exist in that vicinity. The prudent people are all moving their negroes off as there is said to be nothing in the way, except their cowardice, to prevent the Federals from coming over and possessing the railroad and the country in the vicinity. We cannot believe, however, that such an impression is correct, for as Generals are too sagacious to permit so valuable an artery as the Memphis and Ohio railroad to remain in an exposed condition.

...

Paris was in a perfect ferment of excitement yesterday, and many, anticipating an immediate descent of the army which they deemed themselves utterly powerless to resist, were preparing to leave with negroes and other property for various points southward. Mr. Wise informs us that one gentleman alone endeavored to obtain transportation on the train for seventy negroes fearing they would fall into the hands of the Federals.

...

Philadelphia *Inquirer*, January 29, 1862

♦ FEBRUARY ♦

12–16 Siege & capture of Fort Donelson
Report of Col. A. Heiman, Tenth Tennessee Infantry, commanding brigade.

RICHMOND, VA., August 9, 1862.

SIR: My imprisonment since the surrender of the troops at Fort Donelson has prevented me from reporting the operations of the brigade under my command during the action at Fort Donelson before now. In the absence of Gen. Pillow, who commanded the division to which my brigade was attached, it becomes my duty, and I have the honor, to submit to you the following report:

After the battle of Fort Henry, on February 6

---

*There followed a biblical quotation: "Amos 8, 4–16," yet there are but 14 verses in this citation.

last, I was directed by Gen. Tilghman, then in command of the defenses of the Tennessee and Cumberland Rivers, to retreat with the garrison of the fort by the upper road to Fort Donelson. The garrison consisted, besides the company of artillery which was surrendered with the fort, of two, the first commanded by myself and the second by Col. Drake, consisting of an aggregate of about 2,600 men. After a very tedious march we reached Fort Donelson at 12 o'clock at night, where Col. Head, of the Thirtieth Tennessee, was in command during the absence of Gen. Tilghman. Expecting the arrival of Gen. B. R. Johnson and other general officers in a few days I did not assume command, which would have been my duty, being next in command to Gen. Tilghman.

Gen. Johnson arrived on the 8th, Gen. Pillow on the 9th, Gen. Buckner on the 12th, and Gen. Floyd on the 13th of February.

The brigade assigned to my command consisted of the Tenth Tennessee, Lieut.-Col. MacGavock; Forty-second Tennessee, Col. Quarles; Forty-eight Tennessee, Col. Voorhies; Fifty-third Tennessee, Col. Abernathy; Twenty-seventh Alabama, Col. Hughes, and Capt. Maney's light battery, amounting in all to an aggregate of about 1,600 men.

This brigade formed the right of Gen. Pillow's division, and was in line on the left of the division of Gen. Buckner, who commanded the right wing.

The ground I occupied in line of defense was a hill somewhat in the shape of a V, with the apex at the angle, which was the advance point as well as the center of my command, and nearly the center of the whole line of defense. From this point the ground descended abruptly on each side to a valley. The valley on my right was about 500 yards in width, and divided my command from Gen. Buckner's left wing. The one on my left was about half that width, and ran between my left wing and the brigade commanded by Col. Drake. These two valleys united about half a mile in the rear. The ground in front of my line (2,600 feet in length) was sloping down to a ravine and was heavily timbered.

We commenced digging rifle pits and felling *abatis* on the 11th, and continued this work during the following night, under the directions of Maj. Gilmer and Lieut. Morris, engineers, the latter belonging to Gen. Tilghman's staff. The pits were occupied by Lieut.-Col. MacGavock's regiment on the right, Col. Voorhies' regiment on the left, Col.'s Abernathy's and Hughes' regiments and Maney's battery in the center. Col. Quarles' regiment I held in reserve, but several of his companies also had to occupy the pits, the other regiments not being sufficient to cover the whole line. Col. Head, of the Thirtieth Tennessee Regiment, occupied the valley between my command and Col. Drake's brigade. I was afterward informed that this regiment was also placed under my command, but, the colonel not having reported to me, I did not know it.

In the mean time the enemy commenced forming his line by investment and his pickets were seen in every direction. Early on the morning of the 12th he had two batteries placed in range of my position, one on my left and front, and the other on the other side of the valley, on my right. Both were in the edge of the woods and under cover, while Capt. Maney's battery, on the summit of the hill, was entirely exposed not only to the enemy's artillery, but also to their sharpshooters. No time could yet have been spared to protect his guns by a parapet; besides, we were ill-provided with tools for that purpose. However, our battery had some advantage over the battery on my left in altitude, and had also a full range of a large and nearly level field to the left, which the enemy had to cross to attack Col. Drake's position or my own from that direction. In that respect and some other points the position of my battery was superb.

The enemy's battery on my right had only range of part of my right wing, but was in a better position to operate on Gen. Buckner's left wing. Both batteries opened fire at 7 o'clock in the morning and kept it up until 5 o'clock in the evening, firing at any position on our line within their range. Their fire was returned by Maney's battery, Graves' battery of Col. Brown's command, and a battery at Col. Drake's position. The enemy's guns were nearly all rifled, which gave them a great advantage in range and otherwise. However, with the exception of the loss of two artillery horses, my command met with no other serious casualties on that day.

At night I strengthened my pickets and directed Lieut.-Col. MacGavock to throw a strong picket across the valley on my right. There were no rifle pits or any other defenses in that valley, although a road leading from Dover to Paris Landing, on the Tennessee River, runs through it Col. Cook, of Col. Brown's brigade, co-operate with Lieut.-Col. MacGavock in guarding this point afterwards. Strong parties were kept at work during the whole night in improving the rifle pits and felling *abatis*.

Daylight next morning (13th) showed that the enemy was not idle either. During the night he placed another battery in position on my left, and the one on my right and center and on Capt. Graves' battery. He had also thrown across the main valley two lines of infantry (advance and rear), about three-quarters of a mile from our line, and the firing of all his batteries was resumed early in the morning and was promptly answered by our batteries. One of the gunners had both his hands shot off while in the act of inserting the friction primer.

At about 11 o'clock my pickets came in, informing me of the advance of a large column of the enemy. Having myself been convinced of that fact, and finding that they were deploying their columns in the woods in front of my right and center, I directed Capt. Maney to shell the woods, and use grape and canister when they came within the proper range, which was promptly executed. Capt. Graves, seeing the enemy advancing upon my line, with excellent judgment opened his battery upon them across the valley. In the mean time their sharpshooters had approached my line through the woods, fired their rifles from behind the trees, killing and wounding Maney's gunners in quick succession. First Lieut. Burns was one of the first who fell. Second Lieut. Massie was also mortally wounded; but the gallant Maney, with the balance of his men, stood by their guns like true horses, and kept firing into their lines, which steadily advanced within 40 yards of our rifle pits, determined to force my right wing and center. Now the firing commenced from the whole line of rifle pits in quick succession. This constant roar of musketry from both lines was kept up for about fifteen minutes, when the enemy were repulsed; but they were rallied, and vigorously attacked us the second and third time, but with the same result, and they finally retired. They could not stand our galling fire. The dry leaves on the ground were set on fire by our batteries, and, I regret to state, several of their wounded perished in the flames. The pickets I sent out after their retreat brought in about 60 muskets and other equipments they had left behind. I learned from two prisoners who were brought in that the attack was made by the Seventeenth, Forty-eighth, and Forty-ninth Illinois Regiments, and have since learned from their own report that they lost in that attack 40 killed and 200 wounded.

Our loss I cannot accurately state, nor am I able to give the names of killed and wounded, as subsequent events prevented me from getting reports of the different commanders; but I am sure that my loss is not over 10 killed and about 30 wounded, nearly all belonging to Capt. Maney's artillery and Col. Abernathy's regiment, which was at that time under the command of Lieut.-Col. Winston. The firing from their batteries continued all day.

Late in the evening Gen. Pillow re-enforced me with section of a light battery, under Capt. Parker. The night was unusually cold and disagreeable. Snow and sleet fell during the whole night; nevertheless we constructed a formidable parapet in front of the battery, in which I was actively assisted by Maj. Grace, of the Tenth Tennessee. This hard and most unpleasant labor was chiefly performed by Col. Quarles' regiment. It was a horrible night, and the troops suffered dreadfully, being without blankets.

Next day (14th), finding the enemy again in line across the valley, and believing that he would attempt to force my line on my right, I directed Capt. Maney to move a section of his battery down the hill, in range of the valley. The advance of the enemy towards this direction would then have been checked by Graves' and Maney's batteries, and the fires of MacGavock's and Cook's regiments from the right and left; but no demonstration was made in that direction, although I considered it the weakest point in our line. During the whole day my command was exposed to a cross-fire of the enemy's batteries and were much annoyed by their sharpshooters.

At 11 o'clock at night I was summoned to attend a consultation of general officers at Gen. Floyd's headquarters. The general opinion prevailed that the place could not be held against at least treble the number of our forces, besides their gunboats, and that they could cut off our communication at any time and force a surrender; therefore it was agreed to attack the enemy's right wing in force at 4 o'clock in the morning, and then to act according to circumstances, either to continue the fight or to cut through their lines and retreat towards Nashville. Gen. Buckner was to move a little later and attack the enemy's flank at the moment he gave way to our forces in his front. I was directed to hold my position. Col. Bailey was to remain in the fort (near the river), and Head's regiment was to occupy the vacated rifle pits of Gen. Buckner's command. I doubted very much that these positions, isolated as they were from each other, could be held if attacked, and I stated my fears to Gen. Floyd, who replied, if I was pressed to fall back on the fort or act as circumstances would dictate.

At the appointed hour on the 15th the different brigades moved to their assigned positions. Maj. Rice, aide-de-camp to Gen. Pillow, brought an order to me from Gen. Buckner to send a regiment forward and hold the Wynn's Ferry road until the arrival of Gen. Buckner's division. This duty I assigned to Col. Quarles' regiment, which returned after the fulfillment of this order. Maj. Cunningham, chief of artillery (directed by Gen. Floyd), reported to me that two light batteries were at my disposal. Having more guns than I could use to an advantage, and not a sufficient number of gunners to work them, I respectfully declined the offer, but requested him to send me efficient gunners for at least one battery. This was done. Maj. Cunningham came with them and remained with me for some time. During the day my guns were used to the best advantage, and at one time with excellent effect, against the enemy's cavalry, who immediately after were pursued by Forrest's cavalry.

About noon I was directed by an aide-de-camp of Gen. Buckner to guard the fire of my battery, as he intended to send a column to charge one of the enemy's batteries. Seeing these regiments pass my left in the open field, and being aware that my left wing could not be attacked at that time, I sent two regiments from my left (Col. Voorhies' and Col. Hughes') to their support; but before they reach the ground the three attacking regiments were withdrawn. The battery was not taken, and my regiments returned. Early in the evening the different troops were ordered back to their respective rifle pits, but the fighting continued at different points until night.

At 2 o'clock on the morning of the 16th Lieut. Moorman, aide-de-camp to Gen. Johnson, brought the order to vacate the rifle pits without the least noise and to follow the movement of the troops on my left, stating at the same time that it was the intention to fight through their lines before the break of day. All the forces were concentrated near Dover, under the command of Gen. Johnston. In the mean time white flags were placed on the works of our former lines, and by the time the sun rose above the horizon our forces were surrendered.

Much credit is due to Capt.'s Maney and Parker, of the artillery, for their gallant conduct during the action, as well as to many other officers and men, whom, in the absence of reports from their respective commanders, I am unable to particularize; but it gives me great pleasure to state that, with very few exceptions, they all have done their duty like brave and gallant soldiers.

To Capt. Leslie Ellis, acting assistant adjutant-general, and my aide-de-camp, Capt. Bolen, I am particularly indebted for their untiring exertions in assisting me in the performance of my duties. Very respectfully, your obedient servant,

A. HEIMAN, Col., Cmdg. Brigade.

OR, Ser. I, Vol. 7, pp. 366–370.

ca. 16 Elvira J. Powers records a slave's feelings at the fall of Nashville

Aunt Nanny, the former housekeeper of the rebel banker who owned this residence, has just been giving me a highly interesting account of the scenes here when it became known that our forces were coming towards Nashville. It was on Sunday morning the news reached the citizens, when they were on their way to church. And the streets were soon filled with half-crazed people flying here and there, women and children and even men running out of breath, and screaming, "The Yankees are coming," while the less excited ones were securing every possible conveyance to use for flight.

"We colored folks," said Nanny, "knew it in the night, and all de mornin' while de white ones was so quiet a putin' on dere finery for church, we knew it wouldn't last long. An' we was all so full wid de great joy, dat we'se a sayin' in our hearts all de time "Bless de Lord," "Thank de good God," for de "day of jubilee has come!"

"But we was mighty hush, an' put on just as long faces as we could, and was might 'sprized when they told us of it. An' missus she come runnin' back from the street wid' her bonnet on her neck, an' the strings a flyin,' and she come to the kitchen and put up both arms and she said:—

"'Oh, Aunty Nanny, we'll all be killed! The Yankees are coming! They'll hang or cut the throat of every nigger that's left here!'

"An' after that she tried to have me go south with her, but I told her I'd risk the Yankees a killin' us, and I wouldn't go."

Powers, Pencillings, pp. 70–71.

16 Change of venue for the state Confederate government

EXECUTIVE DEPARTMENT, Nashville, Tenn., February 16, 1862

The Members of the General Assembly of the State of Tennessee will assemble at Memphis, Tennessee, on Thursday next, the 20th instant, for the dispatch and transaction of such business as may be submitted to them.

House Journal, p. 423.

ca. 18 The Fall of Nashville as witnessed by Maggie Lindsley

Rejoice with me dear grandma! The glorious Star-spangled Banner of the United States is again floating above us! O, how we have hoped for, longed for, prayed for this joyous day! I am wild, crazed almost, with delight....

...The morning that Fort Donelson surrendered, there seemed to be such an intense feeling of bitterness here against the Union men! The papers ... came out on that Sunday morning with ... threats ... saying that if such a *fiendish villain* remained in our midst, he must and should be dealt with instantly as a traitor....

...Can you wonder that, in the state of feeling I was in that Sunday morning ... when Tom knocked at the door, and called out to me that Fort Donelson was surrendered and the Federal army would soon be in Nashville, I became perfectly frantic with joy?

I ran screaming over the house, knocking down chairs and tables, clapping my hands, and shouting for the 'Union' until the children were terrified, and ma and pa thought I was delirious! I rushed to the parlor and thundered 'Yankee Doodle' on the piano in such a manner as I had never done before. I caught little Johnny up in my army, and held him over the porch railing upstairs until he hurrahed for the Star-Spangled Banner, Seward, Lincoln, and McClellan! The little fellow thought his sister was going to kill him, she looked so wild, and would not come near me again for several days.

...

The [Confederate] army did not stop in Nashville *one day*, but went on as swiftly as possible. The citizens here were mortified and exasperated to the quick by this surrender. Floyd remained in Nashville a few days after his *brave* escape from Fort Donelson....

...

...on the 16th.... Away flew the citizens without stopping for anything! The brave city regiments who on the 15th took their stand on the square.... vowed to die there, fighting ... against ... the 'barbarians,' should they ever reach Nashville, heard ... of the surrender of Donelson, and at eight o'clock in the evening of that same day, not one ... was to be found within miles of Nashville....

This town is almost deserted, so many families have left their homes, and fled, panic-stricken, away.... The Governor and Legislature left the very day Donelson surrendered. May they never return!

"MAGGIE!" Maggie Lindsley's Journal, pp. 5–9.

19 Excerpts from Governor Isham G. Harris' proclamation to the people of Tennessee upon his arrival in Memphis after abandoning the capitol at Nashville

As Governor of your State, and commander in chief of its army, I call upon every able bodied man of the State, without regard to age to enlist in its service....

...

To those who have not enlisted for the war I appeal, go cheer your brethren already there. Your native land now calls upon you, you have only waited until you were needed. The Confederate government calls upon me to raise thirty regiments....

Let not a day pass until you are enrolled...

Memphis Appeal, February 20, 1862.

22 The report of Brig. Gen. John B. Floyd, C. S. Army:

KNOXVILLE, TENN., March 22, 1862.

SIR:

...

I arrived at Nashville on a steamboat, together with a portion of the command rescued from Fort Donelson, consisting of parts if the various regiments from Virginia, Texas, Arkansas, Kentucky, and Tennessee, at 7 o'clock on the morning of the 17th of February. Immediately on coming within view of the landing at the City I beheld a sight which is worthy of notice. The rabble on the wharf were in possession of boats loaded with Government bacon, and were pitching it from these boats to the shore, and carrying what did not fall into the water by hand and carts away to various places in the City. The persons engaged in this reprehensible conduct avowed that the meat had been given to them by the City council. ... I was placed in command of the City, and immediately took steps to arrest the panic that pervaded all classes and to restore order and quiet. One regiment, the First Missouri, Lieut.-Col. Rich, together with a portion of Col. Forrest's and Capt. Morgan's cavalry, were added to my command, and these were principally occupied in guarding public warehouses and the streets of the City....

I immediately stopped the indiscriminate distribution of public stores by placing guards over them, and, having thus secured them from the gaps of the populace, I commenced the work of saving the stores that were in the City. Day and night the work was continued, being only temporarily stopped at times for the purpose of feeding the teams that were at work transporting articles of Government property from the wharves and store-houses to the railroad depot. My men worked.... Owing to the exhausted condition of the men thus engaged, it became absolutely necessary to force the able-bodied men who were strolling about the City unoccupied to assist.... During the interval between the morning of the 17th and the evening of the 20th of February trains were loaded and dispatched as fast as they arrived. Much more could have been saved had there been more system and regularity in the disposition of the transportation by rail. Several trains were occupied in carrying off sick and wounded soldiers ... there was an excessively heavy rain on the 19th of February.

As the moment for destroying the bridges had been left to my discretion up to a certain period, I allowed them to stand until.... 10 o'clock on the evening of the 19th the destruction of the suspension bridge was commenced.... At 3 o'clock on the morning of the 20th the railroad bridge was destroyed....

During the period embraced by this report Col. Forrest and Capt. Morgan, with their cavalry, rendered ... service in dispersing the mobs ... which often had to be scattered at the point of the saber....

...

JOHN B. FLOYD, Brig.-Gen.

OR, Ser. I, Vol. 7, pp. 427–429.

27 William Driver, "Old Glory," at Nashville before & after

A letter from a Salem Shipmaster at Nashville. Rejoicings of a Staunch Union Man.

The following letter from an old Salem shipmaster to his daughter in that city:

Nashville, Tenn., Feb. 27, 1862.

Dear M.— Thank God! The flag of the Union now floats over our proud, deluded Capital. On Tuesday, the 25th, Brig. General Nelson's wing of the army, in fifteen transports, escorted by one gunboat came up to town without firing a gun. The Ohio 6th, the first to land, hoisted their beautiful flag on our State House. A few moments, or about an hour later, I carried my flag, "Old Glory" as we have been used to call it, to the Capitol, presented it to the Ohio 6th, and hoisted it with my own hands on the capitol, over this proud city, amid the Heaven shaking cheers of thousands-over this proud city, where, for the last eight months, I have been treated with scorn and shunned as one infected with the leprous spot.

...How shall I tell you all my sorrows during that fearful period? My soul filled with scorn while insult upon insult poured upon me. God of my Fathers.... I always hoped, although against hope, that this hour would come. Again and again have I told these deluded men, in the hour of madness, "Gentlemen, I will yet hoist my flag, 'Old Glory' over your proud, fallen Capitol.... " That hour has come! With my own hands, in the presence of thousands, I hoisted that flag where it now floats, on the staff which has trembled with the flattering of Treason's hated banner....

For the last ten days I have scarcely slept at all. The Texan Rangers had been told I had a flag and intended to hoist it, and they swore to burn me in my house if I did not give it up: but a bunch of Union friends.... saved my house and flag. The later I had made into a comfort early in the insurrections, and have kept it on or under my bed ever since, no child of mine knowing where to find it.

...In all this vast city of 27,000 souls, but one Union flag waves. That is my own, "Old Glory."
... Sullen silence and looks of hate are seen on almost every face. Our women are worse than the men. As I passed Zollicoffer's house, with a guard of the Ohio 6th, and my flag, one woman, a wealthy one, called out "look at Old D., the traitor," and then went up a hiss and yell from a dozen more. I tell you ... the Union men of the South

are slaves without arms, and palsied with long oppression. The Government has no hope of help from them, as far as Middle Tennessee is concerned.

...

New Hampshire *Sentinel*, March 20, 1862.

♦ MARCH ♦

1 Engagement at Pittsburg, Tenn.
Report of Brig. Gen. George W. Cullum, U.S. Army.

CAIRO, ILL., March 3, 1862.

Am quite sick, but at office. Made demonstration yesterday afternoon. Too foggy to see much. Will try it again to-morrow in force. Saturday gunboats *Tyler* and *Lexington* attacked rebel battery of six guns, supported by two regiments of infantry and one of cavalry, at Pittsburg River. Under cover of the grape and shell of gunboats, some sailors, and two companies of Illinois sharpshooters landed and destroyed house where battery had been placed. The enemy being re-enforced, our men returned to gunboats. Loss, 2 killed, 3 missing, and 6 wounded. Enemy's much greater.

G. W. CULLUM, Brig.-Gen.

Congratulatory order of Brig. Gen. Daniel Ruggles, C. S. Army.

GEN. ORDERS, No. 7. HDQRS. FIRST DIV. C. S. TROOPS, SECOND GRAND DIV. ARMY MISS. VALLEY, Corinth, Miss., March 8, 1862.

...

II. The brigadier-general commanding the First Corps of the Second Grand Division of the Army of the Mississippi Valley has been requested by Gen. G. T. Beauregard, commanding the forces, to express to Col. [A.] Mouton, and his Eighteenth Regt. Louisiana Volunteers, his "thanks for their brilliant success on their first encounter with the enemy at Pittsburg, Tenn.... and the hope that it is only the forerunner of still more gallant deeds on the part of the regiment...."

...

By command of Brig.-Gen. Ruggles:

OR, Ser. I, Vol. 7, p. 435.

4 General Bushrod Johnson's Coat
The Coat of General Bushrod Johnston [sic].— In the panic incidental to the evacuation of Nashville, one of the merchants tailors of that city despatched a large quantity of goods to Messrs. Edgerton, Richard & Co, of this city. Among the goods is a magnificently finished military coat for General Bushrod W. Johnston [sic]. The collar is beautifully worked (by a lady of Nashville), and the coat is otherwise elegantly gotten up. It was to have been delivered to General Johnston [sic] the 17th ult. [February]-the day after the surrender took place.

Charleston *Mercury*, March 4, 1862.

11 Mrs. Piquet fined for wearing pants
A Feminine in Pants.— Mrs. Piquet was found parading the streets on Sunday night in masculine habiliments. Nelson Warsaw was in company with her. The Recorder fined them six dollars each.

Memphis *Daily Appeal*, March 11, 1862.

15 D. C. Donnohue, Special Agent of the U.S. Department of the Interior writes to the Secretary of the Interior relative to the acquisition of cotton seeds

On board Steam Boat
Near Savanna, Tenn.
March 15, 1862
Hon. C. B. Smith
Secty Interior
Dear Sir,

I am with Genl. Smith's army at this place- have found cotton seed plenty — & will buy them after a battle is fought — I cannot have them brought into the boats until the rebels are either driven off or captured.

Cotton is plenty at from 8 to 10 cents per pound in some instances — they burn it on the approach of our army — The men from this section of the state are principally in the southern army — I will report from Paducah at the earliest possible day.

Yours Respectfully,
D. C. Donnohue

Letters of D. C. Donnohue.

16 D. C. Donnohue to Secretary of the Interior C. B. Smith on progress in acquiring cotton seed

Savana, Tenn.
March 16, 1862
Hon. C. B. Smith
Secretary of the Interior
Washington City, D.C.

I can procure cotton seed — in great abundance — So soon as the country is occupied by our troops — cotton plenty and cheap. Dispatch to me care of Genl. Smith

D .C. Donnohue

Letters of D. C. Donnohue.

22 Juvenile crime in Memphis

Juvenile Stealing.— A system of stealing from packages about the bluff and in other parts of the city, by children sent out by their parents with bags in their hands daily for the purpose, has of late been persistently pursued in this city. This proceeding is not only causing heavy loss to our merchants, but it is breeding up thieves and prostitutes in our midst. In order to do something to check the evil, officers O'Brien, Brannan and Hickey, furnished with search warrants, yesterday entered a number of houses from which they recovered a considerable quantity of hams, bacon, and sugar, which the owner can obtain by applying at the station house. They were taken from the homes of the following children, which children were arrested: J. O. Day, Maryam Magione, also Mrs. Brown, of the Navy Yard, and J. D. Spain, R. Sheean, and Maggie Coveny, residing on the corner of Main and Jackson streets. The night police deserve credit for their activity in this matter.

Memphis *Daily Appeal*, March 22, 1862.

22 Memphis Crime Rate Associated with the Influx of the Confederate Army

...

Memphis, just now, is overrun by gamblers, garrotters and murderers-the foul birds of prey who follow in the wake of an army. An old man, a cigar dealer, doing business in one of the most public streets of the city, was strangled last night during a thunder storm, and robbed of about $15,000 in specie, the hard earnings of a life of labor and economy. His dead body was not discovered until this morning. Not a day or night passes that someone is not dirked, knocked down, or robbed. In a single street it is reported there are no less than fourteen gambling halls.

...

Daily Dispatch, March 22, 1862.

24 General Ormsby MacKnight Mitchel reprimands Mrs. Polk

The Nashville correspondent of the Cincinnati *Gazette* tells these incidents:

"The following interesting scrap of news is told by an eye-witness to the scene: One day last week General Buell and the Brigadiers of the Department, who were present, went in a body to call upon Mrs. James K. Polk and her niece, daughter of Ex.-Rev. Gen. Leonidas. Mrs. Polk seemed determined that no doubt should be entertained as to her sentiments in regard to our unhappy difficulties. The gentlemen present, as they were severally addressed, simply bowed in silence, until Gen. Mitchel who was standing somewhat away from the party, was singled out. To him Mrs. P. remarked: "General, I trust this war will speedily terminate by the acknowledgment of Southern Independence." The remark was the signal for a lull in the conversation, and all eyes were turned upon the General to hear his reply.

He stood with his lips firmly compressed, and his eyes looking fully into those of Mrs. Polk, as long as she spoke. He then said: Madam, the man whose name you bear was once the President of the United States; he was an honest man and a true patriot, he administered the laws of this Government with equal justice to all. We know no independence of one section of our country which does not belong to all others, and judging by the past, of the mute lips of the honored dead, who lies so near us, could speak, they would express the hope that this war may never cease if that cessation was purchased by the dissolution of the Union of States over which he once presided." Needless to say that remark was, in a calm dignified tone, apt with that earnestness for which the General is noted, no offence could be taken.

Southern independence was not mention again during the interview.

New York *Times*, March 24, 1862.

27 Federal capture of Confederate pork

HDQRS. DISTRICT OF WEST TENNESSEE, Savannah, Tenn. March 27, 1862.

Capt. N. H. MCLEAN, Saint Louis, Mo.:

The steamer *John Raine*, sent with two companies of infantry and 40 cavalry to Nichols' Landing after the balance of Confederate pork left there, has returned, bringing in with them from 100,000 to 120,000 pounds that was found. The pork is in good order, and has been distributed between the different division commissaries, with directions to issue it on the first returns sent in.

...

U. S. GRANT, Maj.-Gen.

OR, Ser. I, Vol. 10, pt. II, p. 70.

30 The trouble with Green Pork

Whose business is it to see that the government supplies of army stores, and especially green pork, are kept in a proper and safe condition?

Green pork just taken from the pickle will suffer deterioration if shipped and warehoused in large masses without being hung up and smoked till it becomes hard and dry: much of it may even be lost without this precaution. Let somebody look into this matter. The government daily loses by carelessness and unfaithfulness of its agents.—Knoxville *Register*.

Memphis *Daily Appeal*, March 30, 1862.

29 Civil War Fiction set in Tennessee

THE TENNESSEE BLACKSMITH.

Near the cross-roads, not far from the Cumberland mountains, stood the village forge. The smith was a sturdy man of fifty. He was respected wherever known for his stern integrity. He served God, and did not fear man—and, it might be safely added, nor the devil either. His courage was proverbial in the neighborhood, and it was a common remark, when wishing to pay any one a high compliment, to say, "He is a brave as old Bradley."

One night toward the close of September, as he stood alone by the anvil, "plying his vocation" his countenance evinced a peculiar satisfaction as he brought his hammer down with a gorgeous stroke on the heated iron. While blowing the bellows he would occasionally pause and shake his head, as if communication with himself He was evidently meditating upon something of a serious nature. It was during one of these pauses that the door was thrown open, and a pale trembling figure staggered into the shop, and sinking at the smith's feet, faintly ejaculated:

"In the name of Jesus, protect me!"

As Bradley stooped to raise the prostrate form, three men entered-the foremost one exclaiming:

"We've treed him at last! There he is—seize him!" and, as he spoke, he pointed at the crouching figure.

The others advanced to obey the order, but Bradley suddenly arose, seized the sledge hammer, and, brandishing it about his head as if it were a sword, exclaimed:

"Back! Touch him not, or, by the grace of God I'll brain ye!"

They hesitated and stepped backward, not wishing to encounter the sturdy smith, for his countenance plainly told them that he meant what he said.

"Do you give shelter to an abolitionist?" fiercely shouted the leader.

"I give shelter to a weak, defenceless man," replied the smith.

"He is an enemy!" vociferated the leader.

"Of the devil!" ejaculated Bradley.

"He is a spy! And abolitionist hound" exclaimed the leader, with increased vehemence "and we must have him. So I tell you, Bradley, you had better not interfere. You know that you are already suspected, and to insist on sheltering him will certainly confirm it."

"Suspected? Suspected of what?" exclaimed the smith, in a firm tone, riveting his gaze upon the speaker.

"Why, of adhering to the North," was the reply.

"Adhering to the North?" as he cast his defiant glances at the speaker.

"I adhere to no North!" he continued, "I adhere to my country—my whole country—and will do so, so help me God! As long as I have breath," he added, as he brought the ponderous sledge-hammer to the ground with great force.

"You had much better let us have him, Bradley, without any further trouble. You are only risking your life by your interference."

"Not so long as I have life to defend him!" was the answer. Then, pointing towards the door, he again raised his sledge hammer.

They hesitated a moment, but the firm demeanor of the smith awed them in compliance with the order.

"You'll regret this in the morning, Bradley" said the leader as he retreated.

"Go!" was the reply of the smith, as he pointed to the door.

Bradley followed them menacingly to the entrance to the shop, and watched them until they disappeared from sight down the road. When he turned to go back into the shop, he was met by the fugitive, who grasping his hand, exclaimed:

"Oh! How shall I ever be able to thank you Mr. Bradley?"

"There is no time for thanks, Mr. Peters, unless it is to the Lord: you must fly to the country at once."

"But my wife and children?"

"Mattie and I will attend to them, but you must go tonight."

"Tonight?"

"Yes, in the morning — if not sooner — they will return with a large force and carry you off, and probably hang you on the first tree. You must leave to night."

"But how?"

"Mattie will conduct you to the rendezvous of our friends. There is already a party made up who intend to cross the mountains and join the Union forces in Kentucky. They were to start to night. They have provisions for the journey, and will gladly share with you."

At this moment a young girl entered the shop, and hurriedly said:

"Dear father, what is the trouble to night? Her eye resting on the fugitive, she approached him, and in a sympathizing look continued: "Ah, Mr. Peters, has your turn come, then, so soon?"

This was Mattie. She was a fine rosy girl, just past her eighteenth birthday, and the sole daughter of Bradley's home and heart. She was his all — his wife had been dead five years. He turned toward her, and is a mild but firm tone said:

"Mattie, you must conduct Mr. Peters to the rendezvous immediately — then we will call at the parsonage to cheer his family — Quick! — no time is to be lost. The bloodhounds are upon the track. They have scented their prey, and will not rest until they have secured him. They may return much sooner than we expect. So hasten, daughter, and God bless ye!"

This was not the first time that Mattie had been called upon to perform such an office. She had safely conducted several Union men, who had been hunted from their homes and sought shelter with her father, to the place designated, from whence the made their escape across the mountains into Kentucky. Turning to the fugitive, she said:

"Come, Mr. Peters — do not stand upon ceremony, but follow me."

She left the shop and proceeded but a short distance up the road, and there turned off in a bridle through a strip of woods closely followed by the fugitive.

A brisk walk of half an hour brought them to a small house that stood alone in a secluded spot. Here Mattie was received with a warm welcome by several men, some of whom were engaged in running bullets, while others were cleaning their rifles and fowling-pieces. The lady of the house — a hale woman of forty — was busy stuffing the wallets of the men with biscuits. She greeted Mattie very kindly. The fugitive, who was known by two of three of the party, was received in a bluff spirit of kindness by all, saying that they would make him chaplain of the Tennessee regiment when they got to Kentucky.

When Mattie was about to return home, two of the party prepared to accompany her, but she protested-warning them of the danger, as the enemy was doubtless abroad in search of the minister. But, notwithstanding, they insisted and accompanied her until she reached to road a short distance to her father's shop.

Mattie hurried on, but was somewhat surprised, upon reaching the shop, to find it vacant. She hastened into the house but her father was not there. As she returned to the shop she thought she could hear the noise of horses' hoofs clattering down the road. She listened, but the sound died away. Going into the shop she blew the fire into a blaze-then beheld that the things were in great confusion and that spots of blood were on the ground.

She was now convinced that her father had been seized and carried off but not without a desperate struggle on his part.

As Mattie stood gazing at the pools of blood, a wagon, containing two persons, drove on-one of whom, as athletic young man of five and twenty years, got out and entered the shop.

"Good evening, Mattie! Where is your father?" he said.

Then, observing the demeanor of the girl, he continued:

"Why, Mattie, what ails you? What has happened?"

The young girl's heart was too full for her tongue to give utterance, and, throwing herself upon the shoulder of the young man, she sobbed bitterly [and] exclaimed:

"They have carried him off. Don't you see the blood?"

"Have they dared to lay hands upon your father? The infernal wretches!"

Mattie recovered herself sufficiently to narrate

the events of the evening. When she had finished he exclaimed:

"Oh that I have lived to see the day old Tennessee was to be thus disgraced." "Here, Joe!"

At this, the other person in the wagon alighted and entered the shop. He was a stalwart negro.

"Joe," said the young man, "you would like your freedom?"

"Well, Massa John, I wouldn't like very much to leabe you; but den I'se like to be a free man."

"Joe, the white race have maintained their liberty by their valor. Are you willing to fight for yours?—aye, fight to the death?"

"I'se fight hard for youns any time, Massa John."

"I believe you, Joe. But I have desperate work on hand to-night, and I do not want you to engage in it without at least a prospect of reward. If I succeed, I will make you a free man. It is a matter of life and death—-will you go?

"I will Massa."

"Then kneel down and swear before the everliving God that, if you falter or shrink [from] the danger you may hereafter be assigned to eternal fire!"

"I swear, Massa!" said the negro kneeling. "An' I hopes that der A'mighty may strike me dead if I don't go wid you through fire and water, and everything."

"I am satisfied, Joe," said the master.

Then turning to the young girl, who had been a mute spectator of this singular scene he continued:

"Now, Mattie, you get in the wagon, and I'll drive down to the parsonage, and remain there with Mrs. Peters and the children until I bring you some intelligence of your father."

While the sturdy blacksmith was awaiting the return of his daughter, the party that he had repulsed returned with increased numbers and demanded the minister.—A fierce quarrel ensued, which resulted in their seizing the smith and carrying him off. They conveyed him to a tavern half a mile distant from the shop, and he was arraigned before what was termed a vigilance committee. The committee met in a long room on the ground floor, dimly lighted by a lamp which stood upon a small table in front of the chairman. In about half an hour after Bradley's arrival, he was placed before the chairman for examination. The old man's arms were pinioned but nevertheless he cast a defiant look upon those around him.

"Bradley, this is a grave charge against you. What have you to say?" said the chairman.

"What authority have you to ask?" demanded the blacksmith fiercely, eyeing his interrogator.

"The authority of the people of Tennessee," was the reply.

"I deny it."

"Your denials amount to nothing. You are accused of harboring an abolitionist, and the penalty of that act you know is death. What have you to say to the charge?"

"I say that it is a base lie, and that he who utters such charges against me is an infamous scoundrel!"

"Simpson," said the chairman to the leader of the band that had captured Bradley, and who now appeared with a large bandage about his head, to bind up a wound which was the result of a blow from the fist of Bradley, "Simpson," continued the chairman, "what have you to say?"

The leader then stated that he had tracked the preacher in the blacksmith's shop, and that the prisoner refused to give any information concerning him.

"Do you hear that, Mr. Bradley?" said the chairman.

"I do—what of it?" was the reply.

"Is it true?"

"Yes."

"Where is the preacher?"

"That is none of your business."

"Mr. Bradley, this tribunal of the people is not to be insulted with impunity. I again demand to know where Mr. Peters is. Will you tell?"

"No."

"Mr. Bradley, it is well known that you are a member in Mr. Peters' church, and therefore some little excuse is to be made for your zeal in defending him. He is from the North, and has been suspected, and is now accused of being an abolitionist and a dangerous man. You do not deny sheltering him, and refusing to give him up. If you persist in this, you must take the consequences. I ask you, for the last time, if you will inform us of his whereabouts?"

"And again I answer—No!"

"Mr. Bradley, there is also another serious charge against you, and your conduct in the present instance fully confirms it. You are accused of giving aid and comfort to the enemies of your country. What have you to say to that?"

"I say it is false, and he who makes it is a villain!"

"I accuse him of being a traitor, aiding the cause of the Union," said Simpson.

"If my adherences to the Union merits for me the name of traitor, then I am proud of it. I have been for the Union, am still for the Union, and will be for the Union so long as life lasts!"

At these words the chairman clutched a pistol that lay upon the table before him; and the bright blade of Simpson's bowie knife glittered near Bradley's breast, but before he could make the fatal plunge a swift-winged messenger of death laid him dead at the feet of his intended victim; while, at the same instant, another plunged into the heart of the chairman, and he fell forward over the table, extinguishing the light and leaving all in darkness.

Confusion reigned. The inmates of the room were panic stricken.

In the midst of the consternation, a firm hand rested upon Bradley's shoulder-his bonds were severed, and he hurried out of the open window. He was again a free man but hastened toward the woods at the back of the tavern, and through them to a road of a quarter of a mile distant-then into a wagon, as was driven off. In half an hour the smith made one of the party at the rendezvous, that was to start at midnight across the mountains.

"John," said the patriotic smith, as he grasped the hand of his rescuer, while his eyes glistened and a tear coursed down his furrowed cheek, "I should much like to see Mattie before I go."

"You shall," was the reply.

In another hour the blacksmith clasped his daughter to his bosom.

It was an affecting scene-there, in that lone house in the wilderness, surrounded by men who had been driven from their house for their attachment to the principles for which the patriot fathers fought, bled and died — the sturdy old smith, a type of the heroes of other days, pressing his daughter to his breast, while the tears coursed down his furrowed cheeks.

He felt that perhaps it was to be his last embrace, for his resolute heart had resolved to sacrifice all upon the alter of his country, and he could no longer watch over the safety of his only child. Was she to be left to the mercy of the parricidal wretches who were attempting to destroy the country that had given them birth, nursed their infancy and opened a wide field for them wherein to display the abilities with which nature had endowed them?

"Mr. Bradley," said his rescuer, after a short pause, "as you leave the State it will be necessary, in these troublous time, for Mattie to have a protector, and I have thought that our marriage had better take place tonight."

"Well, John," he said, as he relinquished his embrace and gazed with a fond, look at her who was so dear to him, "I shall not object, if Mattie is willing."

"Oh, we arranged that as we came along," replied the young man.

Mattie blushed but said nothing.

In a short time the hunted down minister was called upon to perform a marriage service in that lost house.

It was an impressive scene. Yet no diamonds glittered upon the neck of the bride-no pearls looped upon her tresses, but a pure love glowed within her heart as she gave utterances to a vow which was registered in heaven.

Bradley, soon after the ceremony, bade his daughter and her husband an affectionate farewell, and set out with his friends to join others who had been driven from their houses, and were now rallying under the old flag, to fight for the Union, and as they said, "Redeem old Tennessee!"

Harper's Weekly Magazine, March 29, 1862, p. 202.

✦ APRIL ✦

1 Tennessee Brigadier-General William H. Carroll and Major General George B. Crittenden arrested for drunkenness

HDQRS. THIRD ARMY CORPS, ARMY OF THE MISS., Corinth, April 1, 1862.

Maj.-Gen. BRAGG, Chief of Staff:

GEN.: I have the honor to report that in obedience to your orders I visited the command at Iuka yesterday, and made as thorough an investigation of the reports against Maj.-Gen. Crittenden and Brig.-Gen. Carroll as opportunity afforded. I found sufficient evidence against them to require their arrest. I accordingly arrested Brig.-Gen. Carroll last night, and this morning ordered Brig.-Gen. Wood to relieve Maj.-Gen. Crittenden of the command of that place. The latter was ordered to consider himself in arrest for drunkenness, after turning over his command. I arrested Brig.-Gen. Carroll for drunkenness, incompetency, and neglect of his command.

I caused an inspection of the guards of three regiments to be made by Maj. Shoup, of my staff, and his report shows a most wretched state of discipline and instruction.

I have the honor to be, very respectfully, your most obedient servant,

W. J. HARDEE, Maj.-Gen.

OR, Ser. I, Vol. 10, pt. II, p. 379.

2 News from the City of Rocks
Late News from Nashville.

...

"We have exciting times here, the Yankees being as numerous as flies in summer time; the river is perfectly alive with boats and ferry boats, and the Yankees pushing everything with desperate energy. The troops that have passed through here could hardly be counted, and there seems to be no end to the trains of artillery and canon. Even while I am writing four cannon are passing with ten horses to each one. Army wagons are also passing continually, and there are hundreds of sick soldiers coming in every day. All other business except that in which the Yankees are engaged is at a perfect stand still. They are busily employed in repairing the Chattanooga railroad, and have an engine running on it.

"A good many deserters are coming every day, and have taken the oath of allegiance....

"The enemy has been encamped about three miles from the city but have advanced to Murfreesboro. Skirmishing is going on to a considerable event every night, but with what results I cannot tell...

...

All the churches are closed. We have heard that the southerners are pressing men into service, but I hope you may not be compelled to go....

Your affectionate mother." Atlanta *Commonwealth*.

Memphis *Daily Appeal*, April 2, 1862.

6-7 Battle of Shiloh

8 Cavalry Engagement near Shiloh

We have to record another brilliant victory for the Confederate arms, which occurred on Tuesday [8th] last, and was achieved by a small force of our cavalry, composed of a detachment of Col. Forrest's regiment and a party of Texas Rangers under Maj. Thos. Harrison. The whole force was about nine hundred, and was under command of Col. Forrest.

When our army commenced retiring from Shiloh on Monday [7th] evening, Gen. BRECKINRIDGE'S brigade, with the cavalry, was ordered to bring up the rear, and prevent the enemy from cutting off an of our trains. On Tuesday afternoon the cavalry mentioned were attacked by a Federal force of two regiments of infantry and one of cavalry, the latter being in the advance. After receiving the enemy's fire, which killed and wounded ten, Col. Forrest, in a few spirited words, called upon his men to advance upon the enemy, which they did in the most gallant style.

At the first fire the cavalry of the enemy turned and fled, actually breaking the ranks of their own infantry in endeavoring to escape the missiles of the Confederates. The result of this dashing affair was — Federal loss, killed and wounded, two hundred and fifty, and forty-eight prisoners; Confederates, ten killed and wounded.

In this affair Col. Forrest received a painful, though not dangerous wound. Just as he had brought down the colonel of the Federal cavalry, one of the enemy fired at him with effect. The next instant a bullet from the colonel's pistol revenged the personal injury have had received. The colonel will be with his command in a few days.

Memphis *Appeal*, April 11, 1862

8 Assistant Secretary of War, Thomas A. Scott, to Secretary of War, E. M. Stanton relative to the fall of Island No. 10

[Telegram]

NEW MADRID, April 8, 1862.

Just returned from Tennessee. General Pope's movement has been a glorious success. Captured the rebel general, and nearly all his forces are prisoners. They will number about 5,000. Over 100 pieces of heavy artillery at Island No. 10, and along the river shore a large amount of arms and property of every description. The rebels sunk six steamers. Will endeavor to have five of them raised. If transportation arrives to-morrow or next day we shall have Memphis within ten days, and General Pope can cooperate with General Grant at Corinth in wiping out secession. Captain Walke, of the gunboat Carondelet, is entitled to great credit for his efficient cooperation with General Pope to effect the crossing of the river.

THOMAS A. SCOTT, Assistant Secretary of War.

Hon. E. M. STANTON, Secretary of War.

Navy OR, Ser. I, Vol. 22, p. 722.

8 An Iowa soldier's observations on the mass burial of Confederate soldiers at Shiloh battlefield
...

Where the retreat commenced on Monday afternoon are hundreds and thousands of wounded rebels. They had fallen in heaps and the woods had taken fire and burned all the clothing off them and the naked and blackened corpses are still lying there unburried[.] On the hillside near a deep hollow our men were hauling them down and throwing them into the deep gulley [.] *One hundred and eighty* had been thrown in when I was there. Men were in on top of the *dead* straightening out their legs and arms and *tramping* them down so as to make the hole contain as many as possible[.] Other man on the hillside had ropes with a noose on one end and they would attach this to a mans foot or his head and haul him down to the hollow and roll him in[.] Where the ground was level it was so full of water that the excavation filled up as fast as dug and the corpse was just rolled in and the earth just thrown over it and left.

War is *hell* broke and benumbs all the tender feeling of men and makes them brutes[.] I do not want to see any more such scenes and yet I would not have missed this day for any consideration[.]

Boyd Diary

9 The Courageous Governor
Gov. Harris in the Field.

Governor Harris was present on the field during the terrible struggle at Shiloah and while there he played a brave and active part. We learn that, in the course of the action on Sunday [6th]. A Tennessee regiment, on being ordered to the charge, showed some symptoms of wavering. Gen. Johnston called the attention of the Governor to the fact. That gentleman at once rode up to the regiment, addressed to them a few stirring, thrilling words, and placing himself at their head, ordered the charge. The charge was made — it proved unsuccessful. Again he led them, and, the second time the enemy stood the shock. A third time he brought them to the contest, and with a vigor so determined, that the foe gave way and retreated, leaving a considerable number of prisoners on the hands of the Tennessee boys and their gallant Governor.

Memphis *Appeal*, April 9, 1862.

9 Triumph at Shiloh
The Victorious on the Field of Shiloh.

It is our proud privilege this morning, to congratulate our fellow citizens throughout the Confederacy, on the success that has crowned our arms on the corpse-heaped plain of Shiloah. For two days have the brave soldiers of the South, stood the utmost efforts the finest troops the North could make against them. Men well drilled, armed with the most perfect weapons, modern skill can produce, and in possession of those numerous advantages which the expenditure of unstinted millions, and free access to the workshops of Europe impart, were driven before them in ignominious flight. Breast to breast our gallant boys stood before the confident foe; but unawed by their swelling cohorts, their proud array their pompous panoply, they charged them with a weapon no art can produce no money buy — the chivalrous attribute of Southern COURAGE. With sparkling eye, cheek unblenched, eager step, and unfailing soul, they marched on the opposing ranks — they baffled their mightiest efforts, they subdued their loftiest rage, they drove back their seried files, and taught the vaunting legions that brave hearts and iron wills, sting by a sense of wrong, and fired with the ardor of patriotism, cannot be conquered. In the pages of history the hard-won field of Shiloah will have a name among the great battle-grounds of the world.

Memphis *Appeal*, April 9, 1862.

11 Skirmish at Wartrace
Report of Maj. Gen. E. Kirby Smith, C. S. Army.

HDQRS. DEPARTMENT OF EAST TENNESSEE, Knoxville, Tenn., April 28, 1862.

GEN.: I have the honor to report that on the 10th instant a detachment of the Eighth Tennessee Cavalry, under Lieut.-Col. Starnes, was sent out from Hillsborough, in this State, by order of Brig.-Gen. Maxey, for the purpose of scouring the country lying near the western slope of the Cumberland Mountains.

This force, consisting of about 200 men, came upon a body of the enemy, 600 strong, at Wartrace, in Bedford County, and immediately attacked them in their camp.

After a short engagement our men were withdrawn, with a loss of 3 killed and 8 wounded.... Lieut.-Col. Starnes reports killing a considerable number of the enemy, but owing to the fact that they fought from their tents, their exact loss could not be ascertained. A good effect was, however, produced, as it was a surprise to the enemy, and so alarmed him as to stop for some time the running of trains on the Nashville and Chattanooga Railroad.

The officer commanding the expedition reports that the officers and men of his command behaved themselves with great gallantry.

Respectfully, your obedient servant,
E. KIRBY SMITH, Maj.-Gen., Cmdg.
OR, Ser. I, Vol. 10, pt. I, p. 644.

14 Special Agent D. C. Donnohue to U.S. Secretary of the Interior, C. B. Smith, relative to problems encountered in obtaining cotton seed.

Pittsburg Landing, Tennessee
April 14, 1862
Hon. C. B. Smith
Secretary of the Interior
Washington City, D.C.
Dear Sir,

I arrived at this place on the 6th Inst. Just as the fight commenced — have not been able to get the cotton seed aboard the boats on account of the confusion occasioned by the fight and unless our army moves at an early day I will have to change my location and look for more peaceful regions I have an awful supply in this neighborhood if they can only be gotten—

I forwarded the first shipment according to your directions — I fear they will all be planted to [sic] soon — and be lost as cold spring weather destroys the growth of the cotton — Cotton is seldom planted here before the first of May — I will write you again in a few days — I have written some of the incidents of the fight as I witnessed the most of it—

Yours,
D. C. Donnohue
Letters of D. C. Donnohue.

15 Campbell County Confederate Bloodhounds

The Dogs of War.

Among the astounding developments of the last few months is the following advertisement taken from the Memphis *Appeal*. Its brands and earmarks are well known in this community who have had a chance to read it in papers nearer home:

"Bloodhounds Wanted.

"We, the undersigned, will pay five dollars per pair for fifty pairs of well bred hounds, and fifty dollars for one pair of thoroughbred bloodhounds that that will take the track of a man. The purpose for which these dogs are wanted is to chase the infernal, cowardly Lincoln bushwhackers of East Tennessee and Kentucky (who have the advantage of the bush to kill and cripple many good soldiers) to their tents and capture them. The said hounds must be delivered by the 10th of December next, where a mustering officer will be present to muster and inspect them.

"F. N. McNairy,
"F. H. Harris
"Camp Grinfort, Campbell co., Tenn., Nov. 16. [1861]

"P.O. — Twenty dollars per month will also be paid for a man who is competent to train and take charge of the above named dogs."

...

Nashville Daily Union,
April 15, 1862.

17 Skirmish with and capture of Union Loyalists near Woodson's Gap, East Tennessee

KNOXVILLE, TENN., April 26, 1862.

SIR: According to your order of the 16th I left Knoxville at 4 P.M., with about 40 men from my company and the same number of Capt. Bradley's, and proceeded to Clinton, where I was joined by 40 men of Capt. Gillespie's company, under Lieut. King. I marched all night, reaching Jacksborough about sunrise next morning. [17th]

Five miles above Jacksborough, at Big Creek Gap, I left Capt. Bradley, with his command, to reconnoiter the country between that point and Fincastle, 5 miles above Big Creek Gap, there to await further orders. With the remainder of my command I pressed on to Woodson's Gap, 6 miles beyond Fincastle, where I detached Lieut. Gibbs, of my company, with 10 men, to guard the road coming into Woodson's Gap from the direction of Clinch River. I then pressed forward with the remnant of my command to watch some passes a few miles above.

In a short time a courier from Lieut. Gibbs informed me that he had captured the advance guard of the tories, when I immediately changed direction and returned to Woodson's Gap. The tories had by this time come in full view, with an apparent force of from 700 to 800 men. I at once ordered Lieut.'s Owens and Gibbs, of my company, to attack them in the rear with 25 men, while I charged them in front, thereby preventing their crossing to Cumberland Mountains. After an hour's fight I succeeded in capturing 423 prisoners, killing about 30 and wounding the same number.

...

OR, Ser. I, Vol. 10, pt, I, pp. 649–650.

19 Authorities ordered to repress Union resistance to Confederate conscription in East Tennessee

HDQRS. DEPARTMENT OF EAST TENNESSEE, Knoxville, April 19, 1862.

Maj. W. L. EAKIN, Cmdg., &c., Morristown, Tenn.:

MAJ.: The major-general commanding directs me to inform you, in response to your communication of 18th instant, that you will arrest all Union leaders who circulate exaggerated reports of the military draft, and thereby induce ignorant men to fly their homes and go to Kentucky.

...

H. L. CLAY, Assistant Adjutant-Gen.

OR, Ser. I, Vol. 10, pt. II, pp. 429–430.

19 Nashville's female teachers and the oath

Some of the female teachers in the city are highly enraged at the *Union* because it advocates administering the oath of loyalty to them. We can't help it. We are not only in favor of administering the oath to all ladies who are employed in the public schools in training up our children, but to make the business certain we would like to administer the oath ourselves to all the pretty ones. We have a way of clinching it and making it stick. It softens the tempers of the angelic creatures. When they are done taking our version of the oath, they look as placid, as contented and as blissful as if they had been saying their prayers. Come along, girls, and hold up our hands!

Nashville *Daily Union*, April 19, 1862.

20 "'SECESH,' CHRINOLINE IN CLARKSVILLE."

Notwithstanding the presence of the Lincoln soldiery in Clarksville, they have been unable to *squeeze* out the patriotism of the ladies of that city. A correspondent writes us as follows:

'Secesh girls in Clarksville, Tenn., are conquered but not subdued; for they have, right under the very noses of their Yankee oppressors, formed themselves into a *bona fide* company, well drilled, which they call, very appropriately, and doubtless in derision of the well-known feats of said oppressors, "The Rebel Masked Battery." They appear on the street frequently in complete Confederate uniform, which consists of rather a short grey dress, blue stripes down the sides, coat sleeves, blue cuffs, tight waists, with blue lapels, standing collars, secession cravats, and the whole profusely trimmed with gold lace and brass buttons, *ad infinitum*. Turned up black hats with a long black feather in front, with a gold star and white buckskin gauntlets. Complete the dress: deadly pistol and dagger; there are about seventy-five in the company. The Federals are on the *qui vive* to find out where the young ladies drill, but that they manage to conceal with woman's usual strategy. Hurrah, for the Clarksville girls.

We suggested that the Feds at Clarksville had "Better let the girls alone."

Memphis *Appeal*, April 20, 1862

20 Observation on the Confederate flag

We saw a young lady on the streets recently with a Confederate flag pinned across her bosom. We guess it was a rebel flag floating over *cotton breastworks*.

Nashville *Daily Union*, April 20, 1862.

22 Life in the Midst of Death; the Birth of Baby Empress

The *Empress* ... left Pittsburg Tuesday noon, with three hundred and fifty-seven patients.... On board was also a party of nurses and other assistants from St. Louis. During the passage a number of amputations were performed, and ten of the patients died.

In the midst of the scene of suffering and death, a woman on board, the wife of a missing soldier who was in the fight at Pittsburg, gave birth to a female infant. The woman accompanied or closely followed her husband to Pittsburg, and, on the second day of the fight, while the conflict was raging around here, was engaged in searching for him on the battle-field. While thus employed she received a gunshot wound — a flesh wound only — in the breast. Failing, at last, to find her husband, in despair she took passage on the *Empress*. Her child received the name of the steamer.

The missing father is said to be a Polander or Norwegian, with a long name, which our informants find it impossible to remember.

Chicago *Times*, April 22, 1862.

24 Aftermath at Shiloh Battlefield
The Horrors of the Battle-field of Pittsburg.
...

The most curious feature is a sort of neutral hospital just this side of their lines. In it are wounded from both parties, attended by the physicians of whichever side at the time has possession. To their comrades the rebels seem inhumanly inattentive. Not a day passes but numbers are brought in from the woods.... Half a dozen were carried by us this morning.... They are generally dressed in homespun, or "butternut" — not showily, but comfortably ... we yesterday passed again over the grounds. The terrible stench from its putrefying bodies is daily becoming more sickening, so shallow being the graves that poisonous gases escape easily from the mass of corruption and nestle down near the earth, seeming loath as those lately living to leave it. Mile after mile we met the same graveyard atmosphere, and occasionally a head peered from some rude mound, or a limb, rigid and slightly corrupted, was thrust into view. For ages to come, the battle-field of Pittsburg, or, as Beauregard aptly terms it, Shiloh, will be a scene of melancholy interest. Five thousand died there, and other thousands will go through life disfigured, or linger out an existence upon sick beds....
— Cor. St. Louis *Republican*.
Chicago *Times*, April 24, 1862.

26 Confederate authorities give Mrs. Andrew Johnson more time to prepare for exile
HDQRS. DEPARTMENT OF EAST TENNESSEE, OFFICE PROVOST-MARSHAL,
April 26, 1862.
Mrs. ANDREW JOHNSON.
MADAM: Your note to Maj. Gen. E. Kirby Smith has been referred to this office and I am directed respectfully to reply in order to give you more time to make your arrangements for leaving. The time is extended thirty-six hours from the delivery of this second note when the major-general hopes you will be ready to comply with his request. You can go by way of Norfolk, Va., north, or by Kingston to Nashville.
Passports and an escort will be furnished for your protection.
Very respectfully,
[W. M. CHURCHWELL,] Col. and Provost-Marshal.
OR, Ser. II, Vol. I, p. 885.

26 Bottles for business; recycling in Civil War Nashville
Notice.— Having lost a large amount of bottles the last year, I am necessarily compelled to call the attention of my customers to the fact that unless each and every customer returns to my drivers the full number of bottles, or their equivalent in cash, and also the corks, I will cease to supply such customers. Every business man in this city is aware that if an article is sold at 40 cents, and that customer destroys 10, 15, or 20 cents worth of bottles out of the 40 cents that is paid for a dozen of spruce beer, it is better not to supply such customers. I am aware there are many who save all my bottles, while there are others who wantonly destroy or give them away. I hope all will take this into consideration, and comply with the above in saving my bottles and corks.
M. McCormack.
Nashville *Dispatch*, April 26, 1862.

28 A. J. Campbell's failed mission to force Mrs. Andrew Johnson into exile
JONESBOROUGH, TENN., April 28, 1862.
Col. W. M. CHURCHWELL, Provost-Marshal.
SIR: My mission to Mrs. Johnson was unsatisfactory. She said she would not go North but Judge Patterson and her son Charles have assured me that she would go. You will please state what goods and chattels she will be allowed to take with her; also how much money and if you are willing that her son Charles shall accompany her. He is a young unmarried gentleman and I think should go with his mamma. Mrs. Carter will go unhesitatingly but has a sick child just now but can go in a few days. She says she has not the funds. She is in bad health and must take a nurse with her, a slave. You will answer by 12 o'clock.
A. J. CAMPBELL.
OR, Ser. I, Vol. 1, p. 887.

28 Pikes and the Methodist Publishing House
Publishing House — The Nashville Book Concern. — Our Nashville correspondent gives a sadly graphic account of the doings of the Methodist Publishing House at Nashville in its efforts to add fuel to the flame of rebellion. Under the pretext of serving that God whose son was given to the world as the harbinger of "peace on earth and good will toward man," its officers have converted its rooms into armories, and we have now in our office one of the *tracts* which they were preparing

to send out, in the shape of a pike, which was seized, with five hundred others of the same sort, on its premises. The exposure of our correspondent is crushing, and the effrontery of the Concern, in asking facilities from the Government they have abused and imperiled, exceeds anything which ever came under our observation.

Louisville *Daily Journal*, April 28, 1862.

29 Female entrepreneurs in Nashville
New Southern, Straw Hat and Bonnet Manufactory.

The People of Nashville and vicinity are informed that they can be supplied with Hats and Bonnets from the production of their own soil — no way inferior, if not surpassing any English importation or any handicraft of the Northern States. Also, that their old Hats and Bonnets, however much soiled and out of modern style, can be made to compete with new ones, in shape and finish, at very short notice, and on reasonable terms. Hats and Bonnets are colored and finished in superior style.

Black lace Veils, &c., although reduced to an apparently worthless condition, may be restored to their primitive beauty in color and finish. Feathers colored white and red, and finished to equal new. All those who wish to see "old things pass away and all things become new" in the way of Hats, Bonnets, Lace, &c., will please call at No. 15½ Kirkman's Block, Summer street.

Mrs. Lloyd,
Mrs. C. C. Dow.

Nashville *Dispatch*, April 29, 1862.

♦ MAY ♦

1 Contemplating the fall of Memphis
"IF THE ENEMY SHALL REACH MEMPHIS — WHAT THEN?"

A correspondent this morning, in a few well-timed observations, calls attention to the fact that Memphis may very soon be placed in a similar attitude with New Orleans, and asks what shall be the course pursued by its authorities. This is no ordinary or trivial inquiry, but is one fraught with consequences of the most vital and important character, and it is proper that it should be decided in advance, when discretion and judgment may direct our counsels, and the disgrace incident to a senseless panic and trepidation be avoided.

We believe that the position assumed by the Mayor of New Orleans, in his response to Flag Officer FARRAGUT, is not less logical and proper in itself than it is commendable and patriotic. The surrender of a city by is *municipal* offers to an invading foe, as he truly characterizes it, "an idle and unmeaning ceremony."

War is properly a conflict between the opposing armies of the belligerents, and the municipal authorities of a city have no more right to negotiate for the terms of surrender to the foe than a resident custom house officer or postmaster. Indeed it is questionable as to whether such a procedure ought not to be absolutely forbidden by our commanding generals.

Should Memphis be sooner or later confronted by the enemy, we believe that we reflect the unanimous opinion of every respectable citizen within its limits when we enjoin upon the Mayor the duty of refusing to engage in the humiliating ceremony of a surrender. Let his language be that of the gallant, true and intrepid MONROE.

"The city is yours by power and brutal force, not by choice or consent of its inhabitants. It is for you to determine what be the fate that awaits her. As to hoisting any other flag than that of our own adoption and allegiance, let me say to you, sir, that the man lives not in our midst whose hand and heart would not be palsied at the mere thought of such an act; nor could I find in my entire constituency so wretched and desperate a renegade as would dare to profane with his hands the sacred emblem of our aspirations."

This glorious sentiment which will go down in history to render illustrious it author, has struck the proper chord in our young nation's heart. It has produced a moral effect as cheering in its character and important in its results as the winning of a great battle. Now let Memphis add another verse to this chapter of our war for independence that will illustrate the intrepidity of southern heroism and the ardor of southern patriotism. Woe be to the dastard, in the day of future retribution, who shall by his official short coming disgrace her by a cowardly and ignominious capitulation.

Memphis *Appeal*, May 1, 1862.

2 Report on Union prisoners of war from Shiloh pass through Memphis and news from Fort Pillow

On Wednesday succeeding the battle of Pittsburg, General Prentiss and two thousand three hundred and eight-six Union prisoners passed through Memphis. The men were in good spirits, and kindly treated by the inhabitants, particularly the Irish and German women. The citizens contented themselves with waving handkerchiefs and looking the interest they dare not openly express.

Prentiss made a Union speech to his men, and the citizens cheered him. Provost Marshal E.D. McKissock bade him to remain silent. Prentiss told him that he had four to one more friends in Memphis than he (McKissock), and said to the citizens, keep quiet for a few weeks, and you will have an opportunity to cheer the old flag to your hearts' content. Our soldiers sand "The Star Spangled Banner," "Red, White and Blue," "Happily land of Canaan," and "Old John Brown," as they were starting on the cars for Tuscaloosa, Ala., where they are at present confined. There were one hundred and fourteen Union officer among the prisoners. Beauregard claims to have taken three thousand prisoners.

The Memphis and Ohio, and Memphis and Charleston, and Mississippi and Tennessee Railroads, are connected by union track to give greater facilities for moving rolling stock and prisoners in case of a Union attack. All the old iron and brass was being concealed and forwarded below. The Confederate loss, all told, at Pittsburgh Landing, was about four thousand. One thousand two hundred Rebel soldiers are here in Memphis. Government machinery, Commissary and Quartermaster's stores are removed. It is thought the fate of the Confederacy hangs upon the Corinth battle.

Four deserters from Fort Pillow arrived at the flotilla Sunday morning, and reported twenty-five more in the swamps opposite. A tug was sent for them. They say the Confederate army at the fort is greatly demoralized, whole companies refusing to do ordinary military duty. A large number of soldiers are in irons. Their term of enlistment had expired, and officers wish to compel them to serve two years longer. At the fort one man had been killed and a dozen wounded by the explosion of our shells.

Philadelphia *Inquirer*, May 2, 1862.

3 A session of the Nashville Police Court
...
Mary Brown was accused of disorderly conduct. Mr. George German swore that she cursed steadily, without any hold up, for three or four hours, and that, among other things, she said "she wouldn't give a d__n for any one who would not *hooray* for Jeff. Davis." One of the Federal soldiers said "she was a raarin an' pitchin' and cavortin' around about." Miss Alice Write said German was as bad as Mary, and Mrs. Wright corroborated her statement, naming to the Court some of the language used by German, which Miss Alice could not be prevailed upon to repeat, and which we cannot soil our pen to record. The defendant stated that the soldiers frequently tantalized and mocked her, and that a German encouraged them in so doing, causing her to lose her temper, and to use language which she knew was improper. The Recorder took a very sensible view of the matter, and imposed a fine upon both, adding $30 to the city finances.

Nashville *Dispatch*, May 6, 1862

5 Action at Lebanon
Report of Brig. Gen. Ebenezer Dumont, U.S. Army.
LEBANON, TENN., May 5, 1862.
I surprised and attacked the enemy under Col.'s Morgan and Wood this morning at 4 o'clock at this place, and after a hard-fought battle of one and a half hours and a running fight of 15 miles in pursuit achieved a complete and substantial victory. My force was about 600, composed of detachments from Col. Wynkoop, G. Clay Smith, and Wolford; that of the enemy, as stated by himself, upward of 800, besides which the disloyal inhabitants not in the army opened a murderous fire on our soldiers from their houses and kept it up until all the organized forces of the enemy had fled or been slain or captured. The loyal inhabitants-not a few, but having no arms-could render us no assistance. Forces on either side were exclusively mounted troops. I captured, say, 150 prisoners, among whom is one Col. Wood, 3 captains, and 4 lieutenants; upward of 150 horses and upward of 100 stand of arms, I would think. Our killed will not exceed, as now advised, 6, and our wounded 25. Among the latter is Col. G. Clay Smith, Fourth Kentucky Cavalry, in the abdomen, dangerously. I am not as yet advised that we lost any prisoners except Maj. Given, Seventh Pennsylvania Cavalry, who fell into the hands of the enemy during the street fight by mistaking the enemy for our own troops.

I will make a detailed report as soon as I can get returns which will enable me to make it strictly accurate; they are not yet in. The detailed report can make little change or in any way affect the substantial value of the victory that was and is complete and overwhelming.

Never did men behave better. It will be may duty in my detailed report to mention meritorious conduct, a duty which justice to the meritorious requires and which I shall execute with exceeding delight, for in this little affair intrepidity, personal daring, and heroic courage were conspicuous from the firing of the first to the last gun. Battles of more import, measured by the number of troops engaged or results, might afford less to commend than does the battle of Lebanon of May 5.

I have the honor to be, your obedient servant, E. DUMONT, Brig.-Gen.

OR, Ser. I, Vol. 10, pt. I, pp. 884–886.

5 Lydia in trousers

In Pants.—Among the parties introduced in court yesterday to the Recorder was Miss Lydia Angela, who, having become disgusted with crinoline, and especially with the frightful staring, outspreading, skyscraping, flower-bed-containing fashionable bonnet, had put on a neat coat and pants, a tidy white stand up collar and a felt hat, and was parading the town unencumbered by flowing garments or head covering monstrosity. For thus indulging her dislikes, and entering her practical protest against the fashionable bonnet she repudiates, as more fit for the ample front of a cow than for the head of a woman, Lydia was compelled to pay six dollars to the city treasury.

Memphis *Daily Appeal*, May 6, 1862.

6 Renewing police surveillance of free Negroes in Nashville

To Free Colored Persons.—Almost every day one or more colored persons are brought before the Recorder, charged with being out without a certificate, and fined. Most of them are aware that the law requires them to have their certificate always with them; but the old police being acquainted with all those doing business in town, they were never molested, and the consequence is, they left their certificates at home. A new set of policemen having been appointed, colored persons must comply with the law.

Nashville *Dispatch*, May 6, 1862.

9 Newspaper report on the death of a true son of the South and hero of the Confederacy from Memphis

A Boy Hero.—We this morning announce the death of Charles H. Jackson, son of Capt. D. F. Jackson, of this city. He boy was only fifteen years and eight months old, yet one year ago he entered as a private in his father's company. Young as were his years, his actions showed a many heart. His fearless bravery won for him the admiration, and his amiable traits attracted the affection of all who knew him.

We have been permitted to see the leave of absence granted him by the surgeon of his regiment, of which the following is a copy:-"Charles H. Jackson, private in company K, 2d Confederate regiment, had his right thigh fractured in the battle of Shiloh while gallantly fighting by the side of his father, Capt. R. F. Jackson. This gallant boy is hereby granted an indefinite furlough." During his agonizing sufferings he always expressed the deepest regret, because, as he said, he could not help his father to raise enough men to take the place of those who fell with him in battle. He bore the suffering from his wound with a hero's patience, and frequently he asked of his physician, Dr. Keller, who paid every possible attention, "Urge my father to hurry back to camp and be ready to fight again; I do not want him to mind my sufferings and lose time here." The boy is dead. Though but a child, there severer was a braver heart or a truer soldier.

Memphis *Appeal*.

Georgia *Weekly Telegraph*, May 9, 1862.

10 Juvenile delinquency in Memphis; a social consequence of war

Juvenile Criminals.—The introduction into Council of an ordnance establishing a poor house—an institution greatly wanted in this city—gives opportunity to suggest that some special provision should be made in that institution for juvenile criminals. This class of unfortunates abound in this city to an extent we never suspected until recent events made the fact public. Since the changes caused by the war have crowded our bluff and empty spaces about the city with merchandise, especially sugar, a swarm of young children of both sexes, from four to fourteen years of age, have been habitually stealing all kinds of articles, even navy pistols, from chests at the government landing. Provided with a bag hung around the neck with a string, they will lie down beside a sugar hogshead, coffee sack or box of goods, and availing themselves of holes or cracks, which they will enlarge and sometimes make for themselves, they rapidly fill their bag, take the stolen property home and return and renew their cunning depredations. In some cases the children, when arrested and interrogated, have stated that their parents had sent them out with orders to "go and get something." If these children are brought before the Recorder what can be done with them? That officer has power only to fine, if the fine is not paid, as of course in these instances it is not likely to be, the prisoner is sent to the chain gang. There the boys are put into the company of the worst miscreants in the city and become hardened in guilt by the very mode adopted to punish their errors, and the girls must mingle with the lowest of these outcast females, who are the great blot on our civilization. This is evidently to damn yet deeper the already polluted soul. If this be not done, the young culprit escapes punishment altogether, and finding guilt can be indulged in with impunity, evil practices are pursued until all sense of purity, honesty and self-respect is destroyed, and the juvenile criminal grows up to be a curse to society. Society has neglected him, and he punishes society by preying upon it. The young sugar and coffee stealer becomes a pickpocket, a garroter or a housebreaker. After much injury has been inflicted and property lost, the criminal is arrested. Then the public has to pay magistrate's fees, jailor's fees, lawyers' fees, witness' fees, and all the multiplied expenses that accumulate from the arrest to the trial. If, after all the expenses, a verdict of guilty is found, the criminal must go to the penitentiary and be maintained there. Take into consideration the injury and loss one of these criminals inflicts upon society, and it will be evident that if society had taken the juvenile criminal, given him an education, then put him out where he would have been instructed in honest labor, the expense would be much less than is required in the case of a convicted criminal, while the honest man would spend his life in contributing to the possessions of society instead of taking away from them. It is manifestly our interest, to say nothing of higher motives when we find children raised by their parents or guardians in criminal habits, or when we find them homeless and friendless, exposed to every evil influence, take possession of them, put them where they will be taught to fear God, to live uprightly, and to labor industriously. There should be a department in the poorhouse for such children of bitter misfortune, where they can be taught to read, write, and work. We earnestly hope this subject will receive attention, and that a provision will be made to receive from the horrible fate that impends over them, such young people as now come before our magistrates charged with guilt into which they have been driven by vicious parents, or into which they have fallen because they are without home and without friends.

Memphis *Daily Appeal*, May 10, 1862.

16 Law and Order; complaints about skinny-dippers in Nashville

The following comes to us anonymously. Its publication will direct the attention of the proper officers to the nuisance, and they will doubtless abate it. The writers says:

"Boys, young and old, can be seen bathing, particularly in the afternoon, in Brown's creek, near the Fair Grounds and Nolensville Pike. If there is any law against it, whose duty is it to enforce it? By answering these questions in your valuable paper, you will much oblige some females who are compelled to pass daily those who try to insult ladies."

We hear similar complaints in regard to boys bathing in the river at points along the city. Such offences against public decency are punishable under the city laws, by a fine of not less than one nor more than twenty dollars, for each offence.

Nashville *Dispatch*, May 16, 1862.

20 "'Blood Hound' Harris"

Another of the Lebanon prisoners [May 5] is Captain W. H. Harris of the 1st Tennessee rebel cavalry. This man has acquired an unenviable reputation as a brutal and inhuman persecutor of Union men throughout the state, and it will afford gratification to not a few who have been the victim of his beastly passion to know that he is on the high road to retribution. During the rebel reign of terror, this Harris was employed to hunt down Union men, drive them and their families from their doors and desecrate or destroy their homesteads and property. Some of the men thus hunted, unable to cope with him in strength, took the redress of their wrongs into their own hands and visited it upon his plundering and murderous followers. Unwilling to brave the danger he had incurred manfully, he resorted to a mode of warfare which even a Comanche would scorn, and with brazen impudence promulgated the following notice in the public newspapers; (Cut from the Nashville *Gazette* of Dec. 1st, 1861.)

NOTICE EXTRAORDINARY

We, the undersigned, will pay Five dollars per pair for fifty pairs of well bread *Hounds*, and Fifty Dollars for one pair of thorough-bred Blood Hounds that will take the track of a man. The purposes for which these dogs are wanted is to chase the infernal cowardly Lincoln bushwhackers of East Tennessee and Kentucky (who have taken the advantage of the bush to kill and cripple many good soldiers) to their dens and capture them. The said Hounds must be delivered at Capt. Hanner's Livery Stable by the 10th of December next, where a mustering officer will be present to muster and inspect them.

E.W. .McNairy, W. H. Harris

Camp Comfort, Campbell Co. Tenn. Nov. 16

And yet this cowardly man hunting with bloodhounds, Harris, is one of the [illegible] of Tennessee! What would be their verdict upon a Union Officer who should advertise for blood hounds to hunt up the male and female traitors and "bushwhackers" of Murfreesboro? Truly, their lamentations would out vie poor old Jeremiah, and their indignation turn into red hot wrath. But they can lionize and cheer, throw boquets and kissed to "Blood Hound" Harris with a sanctimony and grace which [they] deem irresistible. What an astonishing degree of *chivalry* this rebellion is developing among the people of Tennessee!! Kisses and tears for "Bull Dog and Blood Hound" Harris-May kind heaven avert the deserved retribution for such crimes against humanity.

Murfreesboro *Union Volunteer*, May 20, 1862.

20 Account of Major Morgan's company of Cherokee Warriors visit to Knoxville

Cherokee Warriors in Knoxville.

From the *Knoxville Register*.

Our streets were enlivened yesterday by the arrival of a large company of Cherokee warriors, from the mountainous regions of North Carolina. These "children of the forest" have been enlisted in the Confederate service my Major Morgan, third Tennessee Regiment. The company already here numbers about one hundred and thirty, and we learn that Major Morgan expects to raise a battalion composed partly of these Indians, who, we predict, will do good service with their unerring rifles, under the lead of their gallant major. This officer, we must say, deserves the highest praise for his indefatigable zeal and energy, as displayed in the enlistment of so many valuable recruits from the aboriginal population.

The battalion has gone into camp at Flint Hill, and have name their ground "Camp Oe-con-os-to-ta," in honor of the distinguished Cherokee chief of that name, whose remains lie buried on Major Morgan's farm, at Citico, in Monroe county. Other companies of whites and Indians are desired to fill up the battalion to six companies. They will go into immediate active service.

Philadelphia *Inquirer*, May 20, 1862.

25 "He was one of our soldiers that had escaped jail, just half an hour ago...." Assisting an escaped Confederate prisoner of war in Murfreesboro

This afternoon we were lying down, when we saw Ma come tipping upstairs with mysterious air which I could not make out. I rushed out on the back porch, (as I was undressed) and saw Ma pass through with a (what proved afterwards a confederate) soldier. She seemed greatly excited. He was one of our soldiers that had escaped jail, just half an hour ago & Ma was trying to disguise him so as to let him escape. He changed his clothes [and] shaved off his whiskers, (Ma giving him some of Pa's clothes) making him look like quite a different man. Ma carried him up something to eat, he would not eat much said he had been to dinner, & would not take any more money, he had plenty. I hope he will get safely back to Starn's Cavalry. He said we had 5,000 men just above here, had had a fight, & we killed 30 or 40 Yankees, & it was that night he was taken prisoner. That was the first time we had heard of the engagement. They always keep a defeat such a secret. This soldier came very near being discovered. There were three Yanks in the front hall who said they had come up to make Ma's acquaintance, as they heard Ma fed their prisoners when Morgan captured them, & when our escaped prisoner asked for the master of the house, the servant asked him in to the front hall, & lo! & behold there sat the man that had captured him a few nights before, and not having any suspicions, they took no notice of him, & he asked Ma for some water and then told his story, so Ma had to play a double game, make herself agreeable to the Yankees whilst getting our soldier off, & I felt vastly relieved when he got off safe. Ma went up town this evening & Kate Avent returned with her home. Cousin William Tilford, wife & daughter stopped by & made a visit awhile this afternoon. An old sick Yankee came here this evening late, & Pa had his sympathies aroused [and] consented to let him stay all night, made me so angry I cried until bedtime & would not eat any supper. He was put into poor Legrand's room to sleep, just to think, he may be lying out on the wet ground, wet hungry and sick & then for his enemy enjoying his room. I didn't like [it] one bit.

Kate Carney Diary.

28 Descent on bagnios in Confederate Memphis

Last night the police made a descent on several bagnios, from which quite a number of persons of both sexes were removed to the calaboose to appear for trial this morning in police court. Many were fined in sums ranging from five to twenty five dollars.

Memphis *Argus*, May 29, 1862.

31–June 9 Negley's Raid into East Tennessee
SHELBYVILLE, TENN., June 12, 1862.

Our expedition into East Tennessee has proved successful. We are returning with 80 prisoners, including a number of prominent officers. Also captured a drove of cattle and a large quantity of horses intended Sweeden's Cove was much more complete than reported. He [Col. Adams] escaped without sword, hat, or horse. We silenced the enemy's batteries at Chattanooga on the evening of the 7th after a fierce cannonading of three hours.

We opened on the 8th at 9 A.M. and continued six hours upon the town and rifle pits, driving the enemy out and forcing him to abandon his works and evacuate the City. They burned several railroad bridges to prevent pursuit. The Union people in East Tennessee are wild with joy. They meet us along the roads by hundreds. I shall send you a number of their principal persecutors from Sequatchie Valley.

Yours, very truly,
JAS. S. NEGLEY, Brig.-Gen.
Governor ANDREW JOHNSON.

OR, Ser. I, Vol. 10, pt. I, p. 910.

◆ JUNE ◆

1 Dragging the flag in Murfreesboro

...It appears on the return of Col. P.[arkhurst], he captured a confederate flag on the road that some playful boys had placed on their mammas hen house for their own amusement. This was a rare Trophy, but cost little to make the capture. The boys of course made objections. It availed nothing; had to submit to the loss. It was brought to Murfreesboro. A novel scene takes place on the arrival of the union men, a display that rivals anything in the annals of history.

The men are formed on horseback. The Col. places himself at the head of the column. The Confederate Flag has a long string attached to it, the other end of string is fastened to his horse's tail so it will drag along on the ground. All things being ready to make the start from the R. Depot. The word March! is given. The whole column moves off. The Col. in the lead with the flag wallowing in the dust fastened to his horse tail. They make their way to the public square, and pass round in this dignified manner, cheering as they go, assisted by the little boys and negros. Genl. Jackson would say "Glory enough for one day."

Spence Diary.

3–5 Fort Pillow evacuated by Confederate States Army & occupied by United States Army
MEMPHIS, June 3, 1862
Gen. RUGGLES, Grenada:

Fort Pillow is evacuated. I left the fort this morning myself. The remainder of the ammunition and 600 troops were taken by steamer *Golden Age* this morning to Vicksburg. The remainder of the troops, with Gen. Villepigue, are coming by land. There is neither arms nor powder here.

In view of the importance of holding Memphis, public meetings have been held and addressed by Gen. Thompson, Col. Rosser, and Capt. Baird, with the most discouraging results. Col. Foute will leave on the evening train for Grenada, and will explain to you the true condition of things here. Capt. Baird will accompany him.

CHARLES JONES.

OR, Ser. I, Vol. 10, pt. II, p. 579.

4 Complaints about nude bathers
"A Nuisance."

While we will ever advocate that among the most wholesome sports that youth and manhood can indulge in that swimming is far superior to all the rest, we maintain that with a proper regard for the rights of others, that there are some localities not altogether suited to its use. For instance, of late we have heard many complaints from ladies, whom business or pleasure compels to cross the river from the upper wharf Ferry, that they are frequently shocked by the sight of a man or half-grown boy squirming around in the water in the neighborhood of the Ferry crossing like a Mississippi cat-fish. If the guilty parties do not seek some more secluded spot to bathe, they will probably find its indulgence, in day time, conducive to trouble. We respectfully refer the subject to the City Marshal for further consideration, and earnestly ask his attention to the matter, that this nuisance may be speedily and effectually halted.

Citizens of Edgefield.

Nashville *Daily Union*, June 4, 1862.

6 Preparing the citizenry of Memphis for the city's occupation on the day of the battle for Memphis

The Peace of the City.—At a time like the present it is necessary that our citizens hold themselves prepared to preserve the public peace, and to protect life and property, during a period in which we shall be under no other protection than that of our city government. We have no fears of the occurrence of those lawless scenes that were witnessed in New Orleans and elsewhere, in circumstances similar to those in which we are now placed; but disorders that have happened the last day or two show that, though there is no reason to dread wholesale violence, it will be necessary to be on our guard against stray deserters and other unknown intruders who are ready to seize opportunity to pillage and do mischief. We have the example of other cities to guide us, and we know that the disorders that have broken out there have been the doings of a few wild-minded persons. When at such a time as this a man talks of burning property, and of committing outrages upon individuals he may choose to consider on the wrong side in politics, that man requires watching. He will be found to be some worthless individual who has nothing to lose himself, and who would like to make something by a dishonest investment in the property of others. We are glad to learn from the Mayor that he has ample arrangements made for the crisis, and that he can quickly put down any tendency to disorder. The Home Guards are now patrolling the streets night and day, and will continue to do so until other authority introduces the regular operation of the laws. The police will continue zealously to perform their functions. It will be the duty of the good, order-loving citizen to hold himself in readiness to promptly give his aid and his countenance to those who are watching over the safety of the city, on any occasion in which any attempt at disorder may prevail. It is the law in some places, during times of public difficulty, to prevent the collection of crowds in the streets, by requiring any little knot of persons who congregate for conversation, to "move on," and arrest them if they refuse. This explanation of the preparations made, and the watchfulness exercised, will convince the helpless and the timid that their safety is cared for, and that they will be unremittingly and amply protected.

Memphis *Daily Appeal*, June 6, 1862.

6 Battle for Memphis on the Mississippi River and occupation of the city by Federal forces

Report of C. H. Davis, Flag Officer, U.S. Navy, on the Battle of Memphis, June 6, 1862.

U.S.S. *BENTON*

Sir: I arrived here last evening at 9 o'clock, accompanied by the mortar fleet under Captain Maynadier, the ordnance steam storeships, etc., and anchored a mile and a half above the City. This morning I discovered the rebel fleet, which had been reinforced, and not consisted of eight rams and gunboats, lying at the levee.

The engagement which commenced at 5.30 A.M. and ended at 7, terminated in a running fight. I was ably supported by the ram fleet, under command of Colonel Ellet, who was conspicuous for his gallantry, and is seriously but not dangerously wounded.

The result of the action was the capture or destruction of seven vessels of the rebel fleet, as follows: *General Beauregard*, blown up and burned; *General Sterling Price*, one wheel carried away; *Jeff Thompson*, set on fire by shell, burned, and magazine blown up; [*General*] *Sumter*, badly cut up by shot, but will be repaired; *Little Rebel*, boiler exploded by shot and otherwise injured, but will be repaired. Besides this, one of the rebel boats was sunk in the beginning of the action: her name is not known. A boat, supposed to be the *Van Dorn*, escaped from the flotilla by her superior speed. Two rams are in pursuit. The officers and crews of the rebel boat endeavored to make the shore; many of their wounded and prisoners are now in our hands. The mayor surrendered the City to me after the engagement. Colonel Fitch came down at 11 o'clock and has taken military possession.

Navy OR, Ser. I, Vol. 23, pp. 118–119.

7 Capture of Jackson

Report of Maj.-Gen. John A. McClernand, U.S. Army.

BETHEL, June 8, 1862.

The detachment from my command, consisting of the Thirtieth Illinois, Col. Dennis, Gen. Logan's division, and part of the Seventy-eighth Ohio, Col. Leggett, Gen. Wallace's division, seized Jackson yesterday at 3.15 o'clock P.M., putting a rebel force to flight, taking their dinner, a number of animals, and a quantity of commissary and quartermaster's stores. The detachment is also in possession of both depots and telegraph office.

JOHN A. MCCLERNAND, Maj.-Gen.

OR, Ser. I, Vol. 10, pt. I, p. 918.

11 Altercation in a Memphis bagnio

[W]hile in one of the parlors at Pirse Perry's bagnio on Main street, [a U.S. naval officer] was shot by John Forrest. Both had been in the parlor some time, and those who witnessed.... say the parties had had a difficulty. Forrest was intoxicated. The name of the officer was Gilmore. The police and a Federal guard soon entered the room and arrested Forrest, who was taken to the fleet.

Memphis *Argus,* June 12, 1862.

12 A refugee's dream; an excerpt from the diary of Sarah Estes

...after falling asleep I dreamed that we concluded to remain here and one day when we were in the front hall Aunt Nannie looked down the lane and said there is Cavalry and they have on blue coats, my husband rushed to the door and said, no I suppose not. I saw they were Yankees and caught my brother and beckoned him to run. He ran around the house but they rushed up and saw him trying to escape them and took him and my husband prisoners. My distress was very great, the scene changed. I thought they were already north and I followed them that I was very miserable and the Yankee women laughed at my misery saying they felt no sympathy for a Southerner. I was so unhappy that I woke. I felt as if I had this dream to comfort me and make me willing to go....

...

Estes Diary, June 12, 1862.

13 Shiloh Souvenirs

All the movable framework, roof, &c., of the church at Shiloh, near Pittsburg Landing, have been carried away as trophies, and nothing remains but the logs, which are already being cut up in pieces to be removed by seekers after mementos from the most famous battle-field of the rebellion.

Chicago *Times,* June 13, 1862.

17 Military orders relative to prohibition of liquor sales, protection of Union flag, possession of firearms, restrictions upon lewd women and theft in Memphis

"NOTICE."

Office Provost Marshal

Memphis, Tenn., June 17, 1862

For the purpose of better preserving the peace and good order of the city of Memphis, the following orders are announced for the information of all parties concerned; and it is made the duty of the Provost Guard to see that they are obeyed:

I. The guard stationed in the various parts of the city will use the utmost vigilance to discover the parties who are in the habit of selling intoxicating liquors in defiance of orders. Persons found guilty of a violation of the order relating to the sale of liquors, will be at once arrested, his liquors confiscated, his place of business closed, and the offenders reported to headquarters and punished to the extent of military authority. This order applies on steamboats as well as in the city.

II. The practice too often indulged in by evil disposed persons of insulting and using violence toward loyal citizens will no longer be tolerated under any circumstances. Union citizens who have placed the American flag over their houses will be protected in this manifestation of their loyalty to the Government; and hereafter the Provost Guard are instructed to shoot down any one who may attempt to remove the flag or molest the owner of his premises.

III. No citizen, except the Police force of the city, will hereafter be allowed to carry any firearms or other weapons, and when so found they will be promptly arrested and placed in close confinement upon bread and water. The members of the Police are required to report themselves immediately at this office, and register their names, stating the number of the ward where they perform police duty.

IV. Lewd women are prohibited from conversing with soldiers while on duty nor will they be allowed to walk the streets after sunset. Any one of the class indicated who shall violate this order will be conveyed across the river, and will not be allowed to return within the limits of the city.

V. Some unknown person representing himself as "Capt. J. K. Lindsey, Co. K. 43d Ill. Vol.," has committed several depredations by entering private houses and taking private property, giving a receipt for the same, under the pretense that he is acting by authority of the Provost Marshal. No such officer is in this army. No orders are issued to take private property from the citizens, and on a repetition of these outrages it is hoped the fact will be speedily reported to our office, that justice may be done and the guilty punished.

John H. Gould

Captain and Provost Marshal, J.R. Slack, Col. Commanding

Memphis *Union Appeal*, July 7, 1862.

18 Occupation of Cumberland Gap by Union forces

Excerpt from the Report of Brigadier General George W. Morgan relative to the Federal occupation of Cumberland Gap

...

Well, the Gap is ours, and without the loss of a single life. I have since carefully examined the works, and I believe that the place could have been taken in a ten days' struggle from the front, but to have done so I should have left the bones of two-thirds of my gallant comrades to bleach upon the mountain-side, and, after all, this fastness, all stained with heroic blood, would only have been what it now is, a fortress of the Union, from whose highest peak floats the Stars and Stripes. The result secured by strategy is less brilliant than a victory obtained amid the storm and hurricane of battle, but humanity has gained all that glory has lost, and I am satisfied.

OR, Ser. I, Vol. 10, pt. p. 61.

18 The psychological impact of the war upon Mrs. Sarah Estes

My heart was almost broken today. Words cannot express my wretchedness. Oh! Will we be crushed and starved out by such a mean race as the Yankees? The thought is like tearing my heart out, to seem my husband ruined and suffer so much after struggling so hard, and all our poor soldiers suffering for nothing, worse than nothing. All the precious blood shed for naught. Merciful Father is this our wretched fate? It seems more than I can bear.

Estes Diary, June 18, 1862.

ca. June 18–ca. August 27 Federal presence at Battle Creek prior to the skirmish at Fort McCook on Battle Creek, August 27, 1862

Soon after the arrival of General Buell.... Colonel Sill was near the mouth of Battle Creek, not far from Jasper, Tenn.

General McCook's troops were ordered to that point and soon quite an army was congregated there and we were temporarily placed in his command. It was not long, however, until Colonel Sill, having been promoted to a brigadier generalship, was transferred to another command and Colonel Len A. Harris, 2d O. V. I., took charge of the old ninth brigade.

The road leading to our camps from Jasper ran along the bank of Battle Creek, a small sluggish stream which flowed at the foot of the mountains until it emerged into a cove and emptied into the Tennessee. This road had to be picketed and our regiment was thrown out on it a mile or more from the general camp and went into regular quarters, where we established quite a trade with citizens in blackberries, roasting ears, etc. We had numerous false alarms and I have a painful recollection of a lively game of poker being broken up one morning about 2 A.M. by information from head quarters that the enemy was advancing on us and we were ordered to fall back immediately on the main force. In the hurry and confusion which followed a pocketbook which had frequently been called upon in the progress of the game, but still containing some forty dollars, which was being held as a reserve, was lost. The alarm proved false, but a thorough search of the camp on the next morning failed to recover the missing property, in all probability it having fallen into the hands of the citizens who were busily searching the camp almost as soon as we had left it. After that we remained with the man force and enjoyed ourselves as best we might in the hot summer weather which was then upon us. It was not too hot though for a proper observance of the 4th of July and a full supply of patriotism in bottles and kegs being received about that time by the sutler of the 24th Illinois and through the kind hospitality of the gallant Colonel Mihalotzy ... the privilege of sharing it being extended to a favored few, the forenoon of that day was most patriotically celebrated. As to the afternoon my recollection is not so distinct.

But it was not all play there and the troops were kept busily at work in building a fort, which was afterward to prove of doubtful benefit. It was built on the side of the mountain, not far from the Tennessee river and named for our commander "Fort McCook."

About that time a force of the enemy established a camp on the south bank of the river, but by mutual understanding there were no hostilities, and the men of both sides mingled in the most friendly manner. They bathed on the opposite sides of the river at the same hours and frequently some daring spirit would swim across and enjoy the society of his enemies for a short time and was always allowed to return without injury or opposition. But this friendly spirit was not always to continue — mischief was brewing and, although we of the rank and file were kept in ignorance, there was no mistaking that important movements were in progress. One command after another was ordered away until the old brigade was all that was left of the large force which had been congregated there. Soon ... the only Union troops on the ground were Colonels Harris with his staff, a small detachment of the 4th Ohio cavalry and the 33d regiment O. V. I.

Our friends on the opposite side of the river were no longer to be seen in force and the swimming frolics were entirely broken up. We remained there for a week or more foraging on the country and having, as we thought, quite a picnic. To be sure there was not quite enough of the *lady* element to make it a very enjoyable one, yet we were not entirely unprovided for in that line, for the daughter of a family living almost in the camp soon became a great favorite and her society was quite a solace for the lonely soldier boys.

A true type of the native Tennesseean, her blond locks and strawberry complexion added to the grace in which she handled a snuff stick, would have attracted attention anywhere, but in a community like ours in which there were no rivals and where her charms alone held sway, it was little wonder that she was the "Belle of Battle Creek," and that every soldier from the stern commander to the most bashful private, was her devoted admirer. So long as the main army was there her lot, in a feminine point of view, was a most enviable one, for all sought to gain favor in her eyes and the strongest coffee, sweetest roasting ears and choices bits of bacon were always at her command. But the old experience of "I never loved a tree nor flower" was soon to be hers and as her lovers were marched off by platoons, companies and regiments, she must have felt miserable indeed and the snapping of heart strings was no doubt terrible.

But she adapted herself to circumstances. When the number of her lovers was reduced to four or five hundred she smiled on them just as pleasantly as when they were that many thousands. Her ideas of rank could not have been very distinct for the company cook and company commander were alike favored and the captain, with his glittering shoulder straps, as he proudly marched at the head of his company, was no more to her than the corporal, with his modest chevrons, who brought up the rear.

Love and war are closely allied. We were having lots of one but very little of the other, and soon there was to be an *evening* up. It so happened that our foraging party one day ran across a few rebel cavalrymen on our side of the river, who soon make known that their intentions were not as friendly as in the swimming days, and a brisk skirmish was the result, during which the enemy returned to their own territory with the loss of one man. The mere fact of their being on the north side of the river showed that they were growing bolder and more confident and arrangements were quickly made for our protection in case of attack. The regiment was sent out in companies to picket the various roads and fords, while the regimental field and staff, with "A" company remained in the camp immediately without the fort. Although a night attack was expected it passed without incident and we slept undisturbed except by the voices of the sentinels as they announced the hour and proclaimed that "All's well." At early dawn the various pickets were visited, who reported all quiet on their front with the exception of the one at the ford of Battle Creek, where Captain Minshal was in command. Movements of the enemy had been heard in his front during the night and it was thought that an attack if made at all, would commence at that point. The morning, which was bright and hot, passed without incident, until about the noon hour, when while seated in the open air at my mess chest, eating dinner, I chanced to look across the river and saw some persons pulling the bushes aside and peering through them. The cook's attention was drawn to it, but we decided it was of no special moment and went on with the meal. Had we known then what we knew afterward, that we had been left there as a corps of observation, while the entire army was being withdrawn from that section of the country, we might have been a little more uneasy. Such was really the case and we were the only Union troops on the south side of the Cumberland mountains, while on the other side everything was in confusion and doubt as to where General Bragg was to make his first appearance. But of all this we were ignorant and in the calm mood in which one usually feels after a hearty dinner, I sauntered slowly to the headquarters tent in which the colonel and chaplain said busily engaged in writing. But this serenity was short lived, for before I reached there b-a-n-g went a gun and w-h-i-z-z came a shell.

Waddle, *Three Years*, pp. 20-23.

19 GENERAL ORDERS, No. 7, relative to prohibition of beer sales in Memphis

Drunkenness upon the streets has become so common that it is a disgrace to the army now occupying the city.

Hereafter the sale of ale and larger beer is prohibited, and the Provost Guard is instructed to arrest all persons guilty of a violation of this order.

James R. Slack, Provost Marshal

Memphis *Daily Union Appeal*, July 4, 1862.

20 SPECIAL ORDERS, No. 5, requiring Memphis city police to report to Provost Marshal and take the oath of allegiance

The officers of the Police of the city of Memphis are hereby required, within three days, to come before the Provost Marshal and take the oath of allegiance as prescribed by said Marshal for those asking passes.

All police officers refusing to comply with this order will be arrested and detained for trial.

James R. Slack, Provost Marshal

Memphis *Daily Union Appeal*, July 7, 1862.

• JULY •

1 Federal clampdown of the press in Memphis The Memphis *Avalanche* under Ban.

The Avalanche of Wednesday contains the following, which explains itself:

Headquarters Dis't West Tennessee,
Office Provost Marshal General,
Memphis, Tenn., July 1, 1862.

Messrs. Willis, Bingham & Co., Proprietors of the Memphis *Avalanche*:

You will suspend the further publication of your paper. The spirit of which it is conducted is regarded as both incendiary and treasonable, and its issue cannot be longer tolerated.

This order will be strictly observed from the time of its reception

By command of Mag. Gen. U.S. Grant.

Wm. S. Hillyer, Provost Marshal General.

Memphis July 1, 1862.

The *Avalanche* can continue, by the withdrawal of the author of the obnoxious article under the caption of "Mischief Makers," and the editorial allusion to the same.

U.S. Grant, Maj. General

To our patrons-For reason apparent from the foregoing order, I withdraw from the editorial management of the *Avalanche*. Self-respect, and the spirit of true journalism, forbid any longer attempt to edit a paper. I approved and indorse the article in question. Prudence forbids my saying more, and duty less, to the public.

Jeptea Fowlkes.

Macon *Daily Telegraph*, July 11, 1862.

2 Special Orders, No. 9

It having been made known to these headquarters that bills posted up in the city by Federal officers, advertising for recruits to join the United States army, have been torn down by some unmitigated vandals; it is hereby ordered that all such persons guilty of said offense upon detection, shall be arrested and most severely punished by the military authorities, and the Provost Guard is required to be vigilant and watchful in detecting the perpetrators.

Col. James R. Slack, Provost Marshall

Memphis *Union Appeal*, July 2, 1862.

2 SPECIAL ORDERS, NO. 10, from the Office of the Provost Marshal General, District of West

Tennessee requiring oath of allegiance to United States for newspaper editors

No newspaper will be permitted to be published within this District, unless the Editors and Proprietors thereof, shall first take an oath that they will bear true allegiance to the Government of the United States of America, and that they will support the Constitution and Laws thereof, and disclaim or renounce all allegiance to the so-called Confederate States. Local Provost Marshals will see that this order is strictly enforced.

[signed] William S. Hillyer, Colonel and Provost Marshal General.

Memphis Union Appeal, August 27, 1862.

2 Oath of Allegiance to the U.S., as employed in Nashville

I solemnly swear that I will bear true allegiance to the Government of the United States of America, that I will support and obey the constitution and laws thereof-and I hereby renounce all fealty and allegiance to the so-called "Confederate States" of America.

Memphis Union and Appeal, July 2, 1862.

3 Report on the fate of some of Nashville's clerics

THE NASHVILLE MINISTERS.

A second special conference of the Nashville clergymen on Saturday, before Gov. Johnson, all declined to take the oath of allegiance. Most of them were sent to the penitentiary, prior to their removal to Gen. Halleck for the purpose of being exchanged for Tennessee prisoners. Many Nashville churches were without pastors on Sunday. Among those sent to durance vile were Rev. Doctors Baldwin, Sehon, and Sawnie, Methodists, and Ford and Howell, Baptists. Rev. Dr. Wharton was allowed some days grace on account of illness. The Rev, Mr. Elliot did not appear. The Rev. Mr. Hendricks is expected to take the oath. Catholic divine services, being loyal, were not disturbed.

New Hampshire *Sentinel*, July 3, 1862.

3 Report on Confederate Martial Law in Knoxville

Knoxville, Tenn., is under martial law. The editor who holds Brownlow's spectre, having experiences its delights in a midnight arrest and a lodging in the guard house, soliloquizes thus upon the order of things:

"We have got martial law, and we feel disposed to return thanks for it-just as Cuffy did. He was a pious negro, and always returned thanks for what he had on his table, but always mentioned his wants also. Some wags who knew that he was short of potatoes, provided themselves with a basketful, and when Cuffy returned thanks for what was on the table, and added, "Mighty good dinner, Mass' Lord, if I only had a few pertaters,' down came a shower of the coveted tubers, playing smash with cuff's scant delf-ware The pious negro, without changing his attitude, unhesitatingly continued his prayer—'Dem's 'em, Mass' Lord-only just luff 'em down a little easier next time."

We are very thankful to our government for martial law, but hope they will 'luff down a little easier' next time."

Milwaukee *Morning Sentinel*, July 3, 1862.

4 A Protest Against Feminine Taunting of Federal Pickets

POLITENESS.

It costs but very little to be polite and affable. The effort, intellectual and physical, neither exhausts the constitution nor impoverishes the mind.

Gentlemen of refinement.... Furnish indubitable evidence of being well bred ... which contrasts strongly with the course, vulgar, uncultivated booby.... The ... always blundering and stammering, sitting on his hat ... or falls sprawling on the door steps....

...

We are led to make these remarks on what is expected from every well-bred person, in consequence of the insulting course pursued by a well-known pseudo poetess of a bevy of goslin[g]s green on Madison street, towards our soldiers.

All that an envenomed, vile tongued, virago, aided by hissing adders could do, has been done, to insult our pickets, as they come in from and to out on duty.

...Her demonstrations are eloquent of her early training, her associations were evidently coarse, unrefined and far removed from that retiring modesty, which so embellishes and ennobles woman.

Crack-brained, dreamy and visionary secessionists, whose head is crammed with rickety, disjointed poetical twaddle, which would get any school girl a sound thrashing for writing, and very apt to fancy themselves buoyed up with a divine afflatus, which is really excessively offensive and gassy. Such vagaries, however, we can tolerate, and by great exertion endure, but we cannot, and will not, endure their silly taunts and indignities to our men. We therefore strongly urge our military authorities to arrest all such offenders and send them South.

Secessia is precisely the place for them, they should yearn to reach their beloved Dixie.

We don't want them.

CHESTERFIELD.

Memphis *Union Appeal*, July 4, 1862.

4 Special Orders, No. 12, Memphis, relative to display of Confederate symbols

If any proprietor or occupant of any building in any town or city within this District, in the occupancy of the Federal army, shall display or suffer to be displayed, from his or her house any treasonable flag or other emblem intended to insult the Federal army or loyal citizens, it shall be the duty of the Local Provost Marshal to take immediate possession of such building and remove the occupants, and convert the same to hospital or other Government use.

[Signed] William S. Hillyer, Provost Marshal General, District of west Tennessee

Memphis *Union Appeal* August 27, 1862.

4 General Orders, No. 61, Federal soldiers forbidden from selling government issue arms, clothing and ammunition, Memphis

GENERAL ORDERS, No. 61. HDQRS. DIST. OF WEST TENNESSEE, Memphis, July 4, 1862.

I. Officers and soldiers are hereby prohibited under severe penalties from selling military clothing, arms, or ammunition, whether the same be public or private property, to citizens. In cases where such sales have been heretofore made the citizens who purchased the same will at once return the property so purchased to the commanding officer of the company or regiment to which the soldier belongs of whom the articles were obtained, or to the post quartermaster, under penalty of being arrested and placed in confinement.

II. It is made the duty of all officers to see that this order is strictly enforced, and that all officers, soldiers, or citizens violating the same, by either selling or purchasing, are arrested.

By order of Maj.-Gen. Grant:

OR, Ser. I, Vol. 17, pt. II, p. 70.

4 Burning the flag on the Fourth of July in Murfreesboro

Vulgarity

A gentleman of Murfreesboro writes to us that several girls of respectable families in that place, on passing his residence on the 4th, threw rocks and dirt at a Union flag flying in his yard. On coming out, they hurried away; but, after a while, the she rebels again sneaked up, stole the flag, and burned it in the presence of several rebel ladies whom they had assembled in their yard. What a dirty set of strops those girls must be; a negro kitchen wench would have better manners. Within the last day or two the flags on the dwellings of at least three Union families of this city, have been pelted with rocks and sticks by the children of rebel families. No boy or girl would dare to do such an outrage did he not know that it would be winked at, if not openly approved, by older ones at home. It is a little thing, a contemptible thing, we admit; in ordinary times too insignificant to be noticed, but at a time like the present the parents of such vulgar, dirty little ruffians should be kept on bread and water in the work house for at least a week. When they got out they perhaps might teach their children something about common decency and civility. Public safety demands that every symptom of treason be punished.

Nashville *Daily Union,* July 9, 1862.

7 SPECIAL ORDERS, No. 21, directing the arrest and confinement of any Tennessean refusing to take the oath of allegiance

SPECIAL ORDERS, No. 21. HDQRS. CENTRAL DIVISION OF THE MISS., Trenton, Tenn., July 7, 1862.

The provost-marshal will arrest and hold in confinement any person refusing to take the oath. He will arrest all soldiers and officers returning from the rebel army who do not come forward voluntarily and take the oath. He will ascertain what property if any that can be used by the U.S. forces any persons who are now in the rebel army may own and report the same from time to time to these headquarters.

By order of Brig. Gen. G. M. Dodge

OR, Ser. II, Vol. 4, p. 146.

7 Skirmish with guerrillas near Pierce's Mill on the Lebanon Pike

Another Guerrilla Raid — Two Federal Soldiers Killed and three Wounded!

We learn from Adjutant Blakely, of the 2d Minnesota Brigade, Col. Lester, that five pickets of this Brigade were sent out yesterday, from Murfreesboro to Pierce's Mill, eight miles distant on the Lebanon pike. While at their post they were attacked by a party of men, supposed to be citizens of the neighborhood, and two were killed and three wounded. The attacking party had no horses, and are supposed to belong to the neighborhood. Seventy-five soldiers were immediately sent out in search of the assassins, who, we hope will be treated as common murderers, and not as prisoners of war. No man who joins these bodies of murderers, who do not carry on regular warfare, has any right to claim the treatment due a soldier. It is assassination to kill men as these pickets were killed and the perpetrators should be treated as such when taken. Self-preservation imperiously demands it. If vengeance be not inflicted, men will refuse to come as soldiers to a State where murderers are treated as their equals, and receive the courtesy extended to prisoners of war.

Nashville *Daily Union*, July 8, 1862.

8 A Cumberland Plateau woman's view of Confederate conscription law

...I wish that the mean cowardly wretches who made the law had to stand in the places of the poor honest fellow whom they have beguiled into this unhappy war, and kept there by such low-lifed tyranny. I believe that if the boys knew all that we know, they would rise "en masse" and come home at the peril of their lives; as it is there will be some tracks made with the heel toward the camps, and many a soldier who is put on guard will be "found missing" when his time is out.

Diary of Amanda McDowell.

8 "I hope it will make the last one of them sick."

This morning Ma & sister Amanda went down to see Bro. Jno. carrying his provisions &clothes. Jose Turner came in William's barouche and is staying with Rosa. Mr. Watterson, a Confederate prisoner who had taken the oath came up on the cars, said he thought Bro. Jno. would be paroled & come up tomorrow. He ate dinner with us, seems very polite, & quite intelligent & if he hadn't taken the oath, I would think him quite nice. I must confess to be crowded into the filthy jail, filled with vermine, with little air, scarcely food to sustain life, & then threatened if they did not take it they would be forced in their cells, or else lose their life. It is awful to think of those low born Yankees (Andy Johnson at the head of them) acting towards our men so cruelly. The Yankees did not succeed in taking a single one of our men prisoners last night; but bringing 19 citizens, old & young, making no exceptions, & when the ladies sent the poor men their dinners, the Yankees ate it up & sent word it was very nice, that they enjoyed it. I hope it will make the last one of them sick. Mr. Joe Ewing is among the number of prisoners. Our little army outside of town* numbers 75, but the Yankees did not get to see them. Prisy seems intensely gratified whenever she hears any bad news for our army & quite angry when we rejoice over bad news over the Yankees. I understand the Union men are getting considerably frightened.

Kate Carney Diary, July 8, 1862.

10 Guerrilla attack at Holly Tree Gap, near Franklin

Nashville *Daily Union*, July 12, 1862.

Franklin, Tenn., July 10, 1862.

Editor of Nashville *Union*:

Sir: As Mr. Barnett, wagon-master of the 69th Regt. O. V. I., and Capt. T. H. Reynolds, sutler of 78th Pennsylvania Regt., were returning from Nashville in an open buggy, last evening, about 8½ o'clock, they were fired upon at a point distance five miles from here, known as the Holly-tree Gap, by a number of guerrillas in ambush. Mr. Barnett, though severely wounded, will doubtless recover. Capt. Reynolds was killed instantly, being struck by as many as a dozen shot, several of them ranging towards the heart. Mr. B. having made good his escape by hard driving, informed the military authorities here of what occurred, who immediately ordered out all the available force of cavalry, with a wagon, to recover the body of Reynolds, and to find out the cowardly assassins.

They returned about 1 o'clock. A.M., without having obtained any clue to the perpetrators. Has it come to this, that a person dare not travel on the public highway for fear of being murdered by parties of white-livered scoundrels in cold blood, and in 13 miles of the Capital.

---

*Most likely a reference to a local Confederate guerrilla unit.

Such an act, as atrocious and so cowardly, demands a prompt and severe punishment inflicted upon guilty parties when found.

Yours, &c.,

X.

Nashville *Daily Union*, July 12, 1862.

11 Federal patrols initiated to stop Confederate cotton smuggling in Middle Tennessee

HDQRS., Huntsville, July 11, 1862.

Gen. NEGLEY, Columbia, Col. LESTER, Murfreesborough,

Col. HAMBRIGHT, Shelbyville or Wartrace,

COMDG. OFFICER, Tullahoma,

COMDG. OFFICER, Elk River Bridge, Chattanooga Road:

A party of about 200 Starnes' cavalry captured a cotton and sutler's train at 12 last night, about 16 miles north of Huntsville, on Fayetteville road. Half of the party, with the wagons, went toward Winchesters and the other half toward Shelbyville. Be on the alert and try and intercept them. The cavalry along the line south of Murfreesborough should watch the roads and scour the country for this purpose, and infantry posted on the thoroughfares over which the rebels with their prize could escape. This information is sent to commanding officers at Columbia, Murfreesborough, Wartrace, Shelbyville, Tullahoma, and Elk River. The cavalry should be notified by the officer nearest to them who gets this dispatch. Commanding officer at Elk River will communicate this information to the troops south of him and act in concert with them.

JAMES B. FRY, Chief of Staff

OR, Ser. I, Vol. 16, pt. II, p. 123.

13 Confederate attack on Murfreesboro

Report of Maj. Gen. J. P. McCown, C. S. Army.

CHATTANOOGA, TENN., July 17, 1862.

Col. Forrest dispatched me as follows:

Attacked Murfreesborough 5 A.M. last Sunday morning; captured two brigadier-generals, staff and field officers, and 1,200 men; burnt $200,000 worth of stores; captured sufficient stores with those burned to amount to $500,000 and brigade of 60 wagons; 300 mules, 150 or 200 horses, and field battery of four pieces; destroyed the railroad and depot at Murfreesborough. Had to retreat to McMinnville, owing to large number of prisoners to be guarded. Our loss 16 or 18 killed; 25 or 30 wounded. Enemy's loss 200 or 300.

Leaves to-day for re-enforcements coming from Kingston.

J. P. MCCOWN.

Gen. BRAXTON BRAGG

OR, Ser. I, Vol. 16, pt. I, p. 808.

16 Nashville's Rabble

"There go the rabble," said a rebel dressed in slick broadcloth, yesterday morning, and the long procession of citizen volunteers passed along the streets with the Stars and Stripes floating at their head. Rabble, indeed! And what have the working men and mechanics of this city done to these new made noblemen of ours that they should be reproached as a rabble? Have they not made these very purse-proud creatures rich, and ministered continually to their comfort? Have not the poor laboring men been the benefactors of this and all other countries? Ah, men whose hardened hands have never counted the gains of extortion and heartless oppression, hold up your heads like true men, and be not abashed by the insulting jeers of those who are living witnesses that wealth and principle do not always go together. "*There go the rabble!*" Rabble! Rabble masons, rabble carpenters, rabble smiths, rabble printers and rabble tailors. We think we saw some rabble lawyers, doctors and merchants also in the procession; men whose hearts are open to all honest men, and who have brains and principle as well as wealth, and who scorn to affiliate with traitors. Loyal men of Nashville, tell your brainless villifiers that you have weapons for the defence of your wives and children, and that while you scorn to bandy words with a would be aristocrat, you have strength to put twice your number to inglorious flight, if they are of such material as your former masters.... If *you* are "rabble," so was Patrick Henry, the penniless grocer; so was Henry Clay, the mill boy of the Slashes; so was ... Andrew Jackson, the orphan and a child of poverty. All that the world cares of the useful, the sublime and the beautiful in human intellect has been the offspring of the "rabble." ...aristocracy is the chattering jackdaw which struts in borrowed feathers. Jackdaws, beware, lest you be stripped of your plumage?

Nashville *Daily Union*, July 16, 1862.

17–22 Effect of Confederate guerrilla attacks and rain upon Federal railroad communications in Middle Tennessee

...

On July 17 the guerrillas were so bad between Nashville and Huntsville that the sending of the mails was suspended. On July 21, eight days after the capture of Murfreesborough, the rebels destroyed an important railroad bridge at Antioch, 12 miles south of Nashville, on the Chattanooga road, also several small bridges on the Decatur and Nashville road between Reynolds' Station and Columbia, besides attacking and driving in our forage trains. About the same time, July 21 or 22, there were heavy rains; a flood on the Duck River washed away part of the bridge across Duck river at Columbia.

...

JOHN P. HAWKINS, Capt., Commissary of Subsistence.

OR, Ser. I, Vol. 16, pt. I, p, 608.

19 Disarming civilians in Murfreesborough and federal situation report for Middle Tennessee after Forrest's raid

NASHVILLE, July 19, 1862.

Maj.-Gen. BUELL:

I came up to-night to communicate. The enemy are in the neighborhood of McMinnville, from 2,000 strong to any given amount above that; the line from Lebanon is open to Nashville; part of my force is detained still at Columbia by accident to the Duck River Bridge. I found here your orders to move on McMinnville. The cavalry I found at Nashville, 300 strong, I ordered to march to Lebanon and join me at Murfreesborough, where they arrived at 10 A.M. to-day. I will make them patrol both approaches to Nashville. Some 400 stand of arms taken from our troops were distributed by Forrest to disloyal citizens in and about Murfreesborough. I issued a proclamation threatening arrest of any one found with them in possession. Some 200 were sent in to-day. Your directions as to posting the troops at Murfreesborough will be strictly attended to. You can rely upon my being found at the place ordered and the time ordered on all occasions. Boyle telegraphs me to death. I think he has lost his senses.

W. NELSON, Gen.

OR, Ser. I, Vol. 16, pt. II, p. 183.

20 Federals initiate counter attack on guerrilla uprising on Obion and Hatchie Rivers

HDQRS. CENTRAL DIVISION OF THE MISSISSIPPI, Trenton, Tenn., July 20, 1862.

Capt. M. ROCHESTER, Asst. Adjt. Gen., Columbus, Ky.:

There appears to be a general uprising among the guerrillas along the Obion and Hatchie Rivers. The force that threatened Humboldt has been driven south toward Gordonsville, and Brig.-Gen. Logan has sent his forces after them. The force at Key Corners I have sent five companies of cavalry after, and the force 15 miles west of Troy I have sent three companies of cavalry after. None of the bands had rendezvoused over twenty-four hours before I was aware of their movements, and I immediately sent out my cavalry from all points with instructions to attack, no matter where found or in what force, knowing that quick movements and bold attacks is the most efficient method of breaking them up.

I informed Gen. Logan of the position of those south of us and ordered Col. Bryant to march on them. They fled the moment Col. Bryant moved, to escape Gen. Logan's forces. They report that band as a portion of Jackson's cavalry.

I telegraphed in relation to horseshoes. It is almost impossible for me to get along without them.

I am, very respectfully, your obedient servant,

G. M. DODGE, Brig.-Gen.

OR, Ser. I, Vol. 17, pt. II, p. 107.

30 Confederate newspaper report on thwarted cotton brokers in the Memphis environs

Cotton Speculators Frustrated.—Another effort of the Yankee speculators that infest Memphis, to speculate in the staple of the country, was frustrated by a squad of Porter's cavalry on Friday last, at a point some eighteen miles north-east of Memphis. The small party overhauled some twenty-five drays, loaded with sixty-four bales of cotton, en route for the city. The drivers were ordered to unload and pile up the bales in the road, which was done in a workmanlike manner, when the pile was fired and the coveted Yankee prize destroyed. Those accompanying the contraband train were then dismissed, with the injunction that if they were caught engaged in the business again, they would be held personally responsible.—The Yankees find "Jordan a hard road to travel" in the vicinity of Memphis....

Macon *Daily Telegraph*, July 30, 1862.

31 Remarks by a private in the 15th Iowa Infantry relative to the greetings slaves made in Hardeman County, on the way to Bolivar

Hundreds of Negroes flock after us and don't seem to be afraid of the soldiers. They yelled and shouted and said "day was glad to see Uncle Sams boys" With all their ignorance they seem to have pretty good ideas as to what is going on and I think it will not be many months until their influence will be felt in the scale.

About 10 o'clock we came to Bolivar a beautiful town and surrounded by a splendid country. My feet were worn out when we halted and we were all very tired upon this our really first march. Dan and I put up our little tent and will sleep in it tonight. I think our tramp has been as useless as there is no enemy here in arms.

Boyd Diary

✦ AUGUST ✦

1 Confederate General E. Kirby Smith decries Federal policies toward civilians and threatens reprisals

HDQRS. DEPARTMENT OF EAST TENNESSEE, Knoxville, August 1, 1862.

Brig. Gen. GEORGE W. MORGAN, Cmdg. United States Forces, Cumberland Gap:

GEN.: It has been reported to me that by your orders peaceable citizens without your lines have been arrested on account of their political opinions and are now held as prisoners.

Since assuming command in this department I have arrested but 7 persons for political offenses and of these 6 have been released.

By my intercession many who before my taking charge of the department had been sent South and confined have been released. I have ever given to the citizens of East Tennessee protection to persons and property regardless of their political tenets.

Six hundred and sixty-four citizens escaping to Kentucky, most of them with arms in their hands and belonging to military organizations in open hostility to the Confederate States, have been taken prisoners. All of these have been released excepting 76, who previously had voluntarily taken the oath of allegiance to the Confederate States Government, and are now held as prisoners of war.

This policy has been pursued with an earnest desire to allay the horrors of war and to conduct the campaign with as little severity as is consistent with the interests of my Government. It is therefore, general, with deep regret that I hear of your arresting peaceable citizens without your lines, thereby inaugurating a policy which must bring great additional suffering on the two contending peoples. I cannot but hope that this course has resulted from a misapprehension of my policy and a want of knowledge of my treatment of the Union element in East Tennessee. I have constantly had it in my power to arrest numbers of citizens disloyal to the Confederate States, but have heretofore refrained from so doing for the reasons above stated, and hoping all the while that the clemency thus extended would be appreciated and responded to by the authorities of the United States.

It is perhaps needless for me to state that if you arrest and continue citizens from without your lines whom the usages of war among civilized nations exempt from molestation I shall be compelled in retaliation to pursue a similar course toward the disloyal citizens of my department, and shall arrest and confine the prominent Union men in each community.

I hope, however, that this explanation may correct any misapprehension on your part regarding my policy, and thereby obviate the necessity of my pursuing a course which is, to say the least, a disagreeable duty.

This communication will be delivered to you by Mr. Kincaid, who hopes to be able to effect the release of his father, now held as a prisoner.

Inclosed is a list of political prisoners arrested by me since assuming command in this department.

I am, general, your obedient servant,

E. KIRBY SMITH, Maj.-Gen., Cmdg.

OR, Ser. I, Vol. 16, pt. II, pp. 244–245.

2, 14 Communications between C. S. Brigadier-General Gideon J. Pillow and Major-General William T. Sherman relative to protection of Pillow's property in Arkansas

...

...I enclose a copy of a letter from Gen. Pillow, addressed to S. P. Walker, esq., of this City, and designed for Gen. Grant and myself. It did not come under a flag of truce, but by one of the secret mails which I have not yet succeeded in breaking up. I also inclose a copy of my answer, which I will hand to Mr. Walker and allow him to send as he best may. I do not consider my answer as strictly official, as the matters inquired about are as to the situation of his private property. I have published Gen. Grant's order, based on the one from Hdqrs. of the Army, annulling all restrictions on the purchases of cotton and payment of gold therefore. I cannot see how Gen. Halleck can allow gold, which is universally contraband, thus to pass into possession of an enemy, but I hope his reasons, as usual, are based on a far-seeing policy. I shall of course obey the order and facilitate the trade in cotton and its shipment, but it seems against the grain.

Yours,
W. T. SHERMAN, Maj.-Gen., Comdg.

[Inclosure No. 1.]
OXFORD, MISS.,
August 2, 1862.
SAMUEL P. WALKER, Esq.:

DEAR SIR: The Federal army at Helena have taken off by bodies of armed men all my negroes -men, women, and children — some 400 in number. They have taken off and destroyed everything else I had. They killed one of my overseers and had the other three in jail. I have been informed that many of the women and children are wandering about Memphis suffering for food. I also understand that there are 85 young men and women in a cotton-warehouse or negro-mart in Memphis who are also neglected and are suffering for food. It is difficult for me to realize that such conduct is done by the sanction of the Federal officers of rank; but yet the wholesale robbery which has been carried on below would seem to admit of no other conclusion. My object in this communication is to request of you the favor of ascertaining if the reports I have heard are true, viz.,: if any of my negroes — men, women, or children — are in Memphis, and to inform me of their condition and if any of them will be restored to me or to my agent. Please see if any gang of the negroes are confined in the warehouse or negro-mart. If cannot imagine what the Federals want with the women and children.

If you can have access to Gen.'s Grant or Sherman please ascertain if these proceedings have been ordered by them or meet with their approval. The law of confiscation does not take effect for some time to come, and my negroes were in no legal sense liable to seizure. If the Federals intend to seize all the negroes and other property within their power we can only say that the time may come for proper reprisals. My brother James' negroes and L. Long's and Thomas Brown's have all been carried off. Please see if any of these negroes are in Memphis and what is their condition.

I have uniformly in Missouri and Kentucky protected the property of Union men as well as their persons from violence. Gen. Crittenden has a plantation and negroes 25 miles below Columbus, on the river, which I declined allowing to be interrupted, when in command at Columbus, though applied to for the purpose.

If you cannot have a personal interview either with Gen.'s Grant or Sherman you will please transmit my letter to them. Your attention to this matter will be gratefully remembered. Please send me through same channel an answer.

Your friend,
GID. J. PILLOW,

If any of my negroes are in Helena will you ascertain if Gen.'s Grant or Sherman will have them restored to me, and all such information as you can get?

[Inclosure No. 2.]
HDQRS., Memphis,
August 14, 1862.
Gen. GIDEON J. PILLOW, Oxford, Miss.:

SIR: I have received your letter of August 2, 1862, at the hands of Samuel P. Walker, esq. It is not proper in war thus to communicate or to pass letters, but I am willing to admit the extreme difficulty of applying the harsh rules of war when but a few days ago all was peace, plenty, and free intercourse, and on this ground, not Officially, I am willing that you should know the truth of the matter concerning which you inquire. It so happens that Gen. Curtis was here yesterday, and I inquired of him the truth concerning the allegations in the first part of your letter touching the seizure and confiscation, the killing of one overseer, the imprisonment of three others, and generally the devastation of your entire estate in that quarter. Gen. Curtis answered no slave was taken by armed men from your or any other plantation unless he had proof that such slaves had been used in war against him; no overseer had been killed or none imprisoned, and the damage to plantation was only such as will attend the Armies, such as marked the progress of your and A. Sidney Johnston's columns a year ago in Kentucky.

I understand Gen. Curtis has given letters of manumission to negro applicants who satisfied him they had been used as property to carry on war. I grant no such papers, as my opinion is it is the provision of a court to pass on the title to all kinds of property. I simply claim that I have a right to the present labor of slaves who are fugitives, and such labor is regulated and controlled that it may ultimately be paid for to the master or slave, according to the case. I have no control over Gen. Curtis, who is my superior, but I take it for granted some just and uniform rule will soon be established by our common superior to all cases alike.

I certainly never have known, nor do I believe it possible, that your slaves or those of any other person have wandered about the streets of Memphis in want and destitution. We have abundance of provisions, and no person shall suffer from want here. When we can provide labor it will be done, and thereby they (laborers or slaves) earn their provisions, clothing, and necessaries; but wages are always held in reserve to answer the order of the rightful party. The worst you have to apprehend in case you claim the sixty days under the confiscation law is that your slaves may become scattered. None are allowed to pass up the river save with written passes, and I understand your negroes are either at your plantation or near Helena. I know of none of them here.

Gen. Curtis expressed great surprise at your solicitude for these negroes and at your application that Gen. Grant and myself would have them restored to you or your agent. He says you had sold them all or had transferred them by some instrument of writing for a record to a gentleman near the plantation, who is loyal citizen of the United States.

I will refer your letter to Gen. Grant, with a copy of this, and have already given a copy to Gen. Curtis, now at Helena. If Mr. Walker can find any of your negroes here the men will be put to work; but Mr. Walker can keep a watch on them and of the women till such times as rules are established for ascertaining and determining the right and title to such kind of property. At present I know of none of your negroes in or near Memphis; certainly none are in the negro-pen or any cottonseed here.

I am, respectfully, your obedient servant,
W. T. SHERMAN, Maj.-Gen.

OR, Ser. I, Vol. 17, pt. II, pp. 169–172.

18 Surrender of Clarksville to Confederates
The Clarksville Surrender.

When we recorded the Murfreesboro' surprise and surrender, we felt that we were deeply humiliated, but it has been reserved for Col. Mason to humiliate us still more deeply, by what seems to have been almost cowardly surrender to the guerrillas. We are told that his troops were on a hill very strongly entrenched behind a stockade, guarded by a ditch, with two pieces of artillery and loopholes for musketry. The position was one of a thousand. And yet, with all these advantages, instead of fighting — instead of sweeping his assailants to instant destruction — instead of fighting with the courage of a patriot soldier for the honor of his flag, he basely, ignominiously surrendered, like a poltroon, to a squad of lousy guerrillas, led by a drunken Yankee, and actually numbering less than his own command. Was ever any act more mean and contemptible? Why doesn't he go ahead and hang or drown himself immediately. How can he ever again look a decent man in the face; after proving so false to all his boastful promises, and so infamously treacherous and cruel to the men who reposed confidence in him, and looked to him for direction in the hour of danger? We are told that the guerrillas sent him word that they would give him two hours to consider their demand for a surrender, but he very politely told them that he didn't want two hours to make up his mind, for he had already ordered his troops to stack their arms! And so were surrendered to a miserable rabble, armed with shot-guns, a strong garrison, two cannons, guns, ammunition, army wagons, and a large amount of stores. Shame on such unmitigated, unparalleled cowardice. It is no pleasure for us to dwell on these things, but stern duty requires that we should hold up to universal scorn and abhorrence such disgraceful actions on the part of our officers. It is high time that such crimes were punished with the severest penalty known to a Court Martial. A few cases of hanging or shooting would put a stop to these immediate surrenders.

In contrast with this shameful affair we take pride in mentioning the gallant and brilliant resistance of Capt. Atkinson and his twenty men, in the stockade at Edgefield Junction, to an immensely superior force. Desperately and heroically did they withstand the rebels thrice repulsing them, and scattering them to confusion and dismay, until finally they drove them to a precipitate retreat. The deeds of this gallant little band of heroes will live forever in the hearts of their countrymen. They showed true courage and the real pluck of soldiers. We know of nothing more brilliant in American history. Let our troops all profit by this example.

Nashville Daily Union, August 22, 1862.

21 "DEATH TO DOGS!"

Weary citizens, overcome with heat, hard work, the last official war report, the weak tea drunk just before going to bed, find their hopes of sleep are vain. Open windows give entrance to the cooling night breeze; closed lace curtain keep from intrusion the musical mosquito bent on wounds and blood — but what shutters, bolts, locks, or designs of ingenious man can shout out the ceaseless bow-wow-wow, the howls the yells, the sleep destroying cries of countless dogs? "Soon as the evening shades prevail" the din begins. Barks no druggist's skill can resolve into healing tinctures or sublimate to strong but silent emences — yells in every key, your shrieking contralto to the growling bars making it hideous. Crying babies sometimes sleep, and scolding wives in the course of passing hours cease their curtain themes, but the dogs, the baying yelping babel — bawling dogs, never give up. While stars look out and night's dark curtain veils the scene, with voice vociferous and unwearying lungs the canine quadruped's curse drives from the couch life's gentle solace — sleep. In vain are pistols fired, and missiles thrown with curses deep and dire! The skulking herd, with drooping tail and cunning crawl, are off— off where no pebble, stick, or shot can reach, but not off to silence-still the bow-wow-wow goes on unending When comes the calm, no more is heard the angry dash the roaring of unchained winds, not deafening crash of fear-inspiring thunder — the echoing peal of the fading avalanche hurdling down the mountain side — the bellowing fury of the volcanoes' wrath have limit and an end; but the row, the racket, the fierce, sleep-destroying howl and yell and bark of Memphian dogs, for nights unending, unmarked by stoppage or interval, banish balmy sleep. Not more constant was sweet Philomel, "who all night long her amorous descant sung" than is the canine curse. A flaming sword that every way showed its glittering edge, kept man from paradise, so noisy, deafening dogs keep Memphis citizens from the heaven of speed. Death to the dogs-that is the slogan of the coming war upon the nightly enemy. By shot or poisoning arsenic, quick death must be the fate of our relentless foes. Death to the dogs, death to the brute destroyers of our nightly rest. Death! death! no less will satiate our ... revenge or curse the canine crowd we're cursed with.

Memphis *Bulletin*, August 21, 1862.

22 Guerrilla recruitment and methods in West Tennessee

New Southern Mode of Enlistment.

In Shelby and other counties of Tennessee, the rebel authorities have hit upon the honorable plan of enlisting men for home duty, giving the following interpretation and definition of that duty. The recruit is regularly sworn but not uniformed, mustered into service, but detailed to special duty on his own farm to act in concert with his neighbors similarly enrolled and detailed. When these bucolic legionnaires see a chance to shoot a picket, burn a bridge or run out a Union man, they remember they are soldiers of the Confederate States Army, or Confederate Stealing Association and do the job. When a Federal detachment comes along to hunt the rebels, the "soldiers" remember they are farmers, and come to the office with demands for protection or answer all inquiries with — "don't know a thing about it." Now this may be a very convenient thing for the framers, but it is rather exasperating to the detachment of undisguised solders of the nation; and gives them a clear and palpable right to treat such men as their crimes deserve. Our troops are fast discovering the guile and seeing through the flimsy veil; and for the sake of humanity and justice we do trust they will treat such men as their duplicity, cowardice and crimes deserve.

Where lurk guerrillas long, there the people are their coadjutors and deserve the punishment due to all accessories to crime.

Memphis *Union Appeal*, August 22, 1862.

23 Military occupation of a farm in Madison County

Last night the Federals started an encampment of cavalry in [my] front woods lot. I had hoped there would be no more encampment there on account of scarcity of water, but they come after night and such a running about in the yard looking for a well, wanting supper &c. These men have been in the habit of calling at houses & by threats making citizens furnish them with what they wished. I declined, putting myself to the trouble of having cooking done for them. Dogs barking and sabres rattling was the order of the night & through today. They have nearly used the cistern dry. An order came out this evening from the Colonel to stop using out of the cistern & to use out of the well. The well being farther off, of course they prefer the cistern. These same men have committed all kinds of depredations upon the citizens. My father has a negro man & some of his horses are in their possession. They or some others plundered his house at the farm carrying off what they saw proper, just such a set of impudent negroes as have gone to them or they have taken is enough to make one sick. We have to submit as well as we can to our fate. These fellows curse & swear that we brought them down here & ought to suffer for it. They pretend to look upon us as traitors and everything we have as of right belonging to them....

Robert H. Cartmell Diary, August 24, 1862.

29 Defeat of Forrest: The Skirmish at Short Mountain Cross-Roads, near McMinnville, Tennessee

SHORT MOUNTAIN CROSS-ROADS, TENN., August 30, 1862.

COL.: On Friday, August 29, the troops under my command, numbering 100 effective men, of Company A, Eighteenth Ohio Volunteers; Company I, Eighteenth Ohio Volunteers, Capt. Charles C. Ross, and Company D, Ninth Michigan Volunteers, Lieut. Wallace, had just completed the inclosure of a stockade at this place 30 by 40 feet square, of round timber, 12 feet high. The men were eating dinner at about 1 o'clock P.M. in a grove, distant from the stockade about 100 yards, and in which also we had the ammunition belonging to the command, except such as was in boxes, when the enemy, 1,500 strong, made his appearance, formed in line of battle along the skirt of woods extending from the railroad along the south side of the stockade at the distance of about 200 yards, and rapidly extended his line on east and west sides. My men ran rapidly to the stockade, and at the same time the enemy, with a terrific yell, fired a volley and rushed to cut us off from the stockade. The attacking force consisted of 900 dismounted cavalry, commanded by Gen. Forrest, and led to the charge by him. My men kept up a sharp running fire on the way to the stockade, checking the impetuosity of the enemy, and all but some 10 of Company I and the men on picket got inside the fort before the enemy. The men cut off kept up a constant fire from the railroad and woods during the engagement and got in safety. The race to the stockade was a desperate one. On getting within the stockade I at once sent three parties of 6 men each, one from each company, to bring in the ammunition. These squads were commanded by Sergeant [Edward] McLaren, Company A; Sergeant [James K.] Williams, Company I, and I regret that I do not know who from Ninth Michigan company. They ran to the thicket under a terrible fire from the enemy's skirmishers and succeeded in bringing in the ammunition.

The enemy now made an attack from three directions with great desperation, approaching within 50 feet of the stockade. I kept up a constant and well-directed fire upon him for ten minutes, when, finding it impossible to dislodge us or seriously injure our men and his own falling rapidly around, he made a rapid retreat to the woods in great confusion. His men ran in every direction before our fire, throwing down their arms, and immediately fell back out of range. Soon after an attempt was made to destroy the railroad above us. I went out with a party and drove then away.

I at once sent messengers to Manchester and McMinnville on foot through the enemy's lines with information. To do this dangerous duty I called for volunteers, and from those offering to go I sent Clinton L. Lee, private Company A, to McMinnville, and Henry F. Thayer, private Company D, Ninth Michigan, to Manchester. They both got safely through and gave information of our situation.

The enemy's forces consisted of Col. Wharton's Texas Rangers; one battalion Alabama Cavalry, Capt. Bacot's; one battalion Tennessee Cavalry, Maj. Smith, and one battalion Kentucky Cavalry, numbering, as I learn from Dr. Houston, surgeon Texas Cavalry, 1,500 strong. I have also the same information from Lieut. Butler and other prisoners.

We buried 12 of the enemy left dead and dying on the field, and have 41 of his wounded in our hands and scattered among the houses of citizens in the vicinity. Among the dead are Capt. W. Y. Houston and Lieut. Butler, Texas Rangers. Our loss is 9 wounded, to wit: Seven of Company I, Eighteenth Ohio Volunteers; 1 of Company A, Eighteenth Ohio Volunteers, and 1 of Company D, Ninth Michigan Volunteers. Two are wounded dangerously and the others slightly. I send list of wounded.

Drs. Johnson and Mills, surgeons Eighteenth Ohio Volunteers, arrived at midnight and at once proceeded to give all possible attention to the wounded. At daylight Drs. Stimmel and Sabine, Twenty-sixth Ohio Volunteers, arrived from McMinnville, and assisted in attentions to the wounded and suffering. To all the gentlemen my thanks are due for their promptness, industry, and skill in ministering to the wounded.

We captured 8 horses, 3 saddles, and 30 guns.

The conduct of all the officers and men of the command was such as to compel my admiration. They fought from the first with great coolness, bravery, and determination. The enemy outnumbered us as nine to one.

I have the honor to be, your obedient servant,

H. R. MILLER, Capt. Eighteenth Ohio Volunteers, Cmdg.

...

OR, Ser. I. Vol. 16, pt. I, pp. 901–906.

HDQRS FIRST DIVISION, ARMY OF THE OHIO
McMinnville, August 31, 1862

Thursday Forrest was whipped by Colonel Grose's men near Woodbury. Friday [August 29] he attacked the stockade on the McMinnville Railroad 8 miles from and was whipped again.... Started yesterday [30th] for Bragg's camp by Altamont; was met by McCook's advance and again whipped. He then returned toward Woodbury again, but was pursued by one of Wood's regiments, overtaken, and attacked at the crossing of the road from Manchester to Smithville and the road from here to Murfreesborough, and again badly whipped and dispersed.

GEO. H. THOMAS, Maj.-Gen., U.S. Volunteers.
OR, Ser. I, Vol. 16, pt. II, 462.

♦ SEPTEMBER ♦

5 Initiation of Confederate draft in Tennessee by Bragg, Special Orders No. 1
SPECIAL ORDERS, No. 1. HDQRS. DEPARTMENT NO. 2, Sparta, Tenn., September 5, 1862.

The President having authorized the enforcement of the conscript law in the State of Tennessee, officers are now engaged in the preparatory steps for its execution. All persons liable to its terms will be allowed to volunteer in such companies as they may select in thirty days. This indulgence will not exempt them, however, from conscription at any moment. It is hoped the ranks of our noble Tennessee regiments will soon be filled by volunteer enlistments. No new companies or regiments will be received until the ranks of those now in service are full.

By command of Gen. Bragg
OR, Ser. I, Vol. 16, pt. II, pp. 797–798.

5 Skirmish near Humboldt at Burned Bridge
Fight at "the Burned Bridge."

Last Friday week [September 5], the rebels made another attack upon the railroad, at what is known as "the burned bridge," where the fight occurred July 28 near Beadles. The rebels first fired on the pickets killing one and wounding two, then attacked the camp at the bridge, and after a fight of nearly thirty minutes, drive off our boys, wounding 7 more. They captured the tents and baggage of the boys, burning what they did not want, and then retreated back to the Hatchie, crossing the Forked-Deer Creek near Poplar Corners. The boys claim that 10 rebels were killed and many wounded, they claim three wounded men, and one officer and none killed. The troops attacked were two companies of the 31st Ills. Under command of Capt. Casey. Shortly after the fight our mounted infantry under Capt. Maxon arrived and gave chase to the retreating scamps, capturing Col. Borough at Widow Cruse's where he had been left, dangerously wounded in the head with a mine ball. The rebels had made too good time in their "strategic movements" and were not overtaken. Col. Borough was taken possession of from Capt. Maxon by the Col. 31st Ills, who took him to Jackson on the cars where it is reported he has since died of his wounds. The Col. has been a minister of the Cumberland Presbyterian persuasion, and a wholesale shoe dealer at Evansville, Indiana, until last fall he joined his friends and has been in active service until the present time. He was acting in this attack under the orders of Brig. Gen. Armstrong, and had one battalion, 130 men with him.

Soldier's Budget, September 15, 1862.

9 Union refugees arrive in Nashville

The Exodus.

Yesterday morning we saw a train of wagons filled with women and children and a few articles of household goods. These people are native Tennesseans, driven by guerrillas from their farms and shops on account of their loyalty. They have sacrificed the honest accumulations of years of hard labor on the altar of loyalty, and are now winding their way to a land where the rebel flag is not tolerated. The story related by these unhappy people is most lamentable. They tell of respectable, law-abiding men being tied up and whipped until they are streaming with blood; of houses plundered and sacked; of crops destroyed, and of every species of outrage. Companies of outlaws belonging to neither side, taking advantage of the anarchy which prevails in the country, roam about for the sole purpose of plunder. These bandits prey on secessionists and loyalists alike. A man named Anderson, we are told, leads one of these parties in Bedford county. When he plunders the house of a Confederate, and the inmates plead that they are for the Southern Confederacy, he replies, "Damn the Southern Confederacy!" Unless the people come as one man into the Federal ranks, and utterly destroy these land-corsairs, an awful future awaits this afflicted commonwealth. The friends of the Confederacy will be certain to find the "ingredients of their poisoned chalice" of rebellion commended to their own lips by the very men whom they now encourage in robbery and lawlessness. Justice is often slow, but she is "even handed," and her blows will fall with fearful effect at last upon obdurate offenders.

Nashville *Daily Union*, September 10, 1862.

9 Attack on Federal column in Pulaski; an entry from the diary of John Hill Fergusson, 10th Illinois Volunteer Infantry

Tusday 9th — we marched 15 miles that day we passed through Linville in the morning it is a small neglected looking place in rather a poor part of country. Yet whare a planters dwelling is to be seen it is of a splendid appearance the houses have lots and gardens shoes that the[y] have welth and pride and a tast[e] for buty and the comforts of Life in the evening we reached Columbia we marched through in good order we formed in fives and timed to yankee dodle the town is of a splendid and welthy appearance rather a large town the girls and Ladies of the city seemed glad to see the union troops some waved whith handkerchiefs from the windows. [In] some places the girls were gathered in groups of 10 or 12 holding up union collors the city was full of citizens there was not lest than 3 or 4 hundred going around and standing about the sidewalks and corners in white linen and canes in there hands we crossed a long narrow bridge without siding and prepared for camping the regts had all passed crossed and the [wagon] train was coming through town when a volley of musketry was heard at the other side of town then another and another directly the musketry became quick and sharp our regt was formed and led into town on the double quick but we soon got to learn that the fiaring was all from our side the rebels had only fiared a few rounds when our rear gard opened on them and made them skidaddle from what we could learn of that town it was a perfect Secesch hole and we believed those that fiared on the rear gard were the same men that seemed to be good citizens as we passed through our regiment returned without fiaring a gun our rear guard never left the road to see whither the[y] had killed any of the trators but we soon had the train all cross the bridge and the pickets were sent out So we went to rest for the night expecting from what we could learn a hot time in the morning

John Hill Fergusson Diary, 1862

10 Confederates surprised by Federals in Columbia

The Columbia Panic.

We are told that when a body of Federal troops entered Columbia on Wednesday [10th], there was a tremendous trepidative panic, terror and skedaddle among the rebels. Some ran away in their drawers, some in their shirt and breeches, some bare-headed, and two or three fellows, who had been blustering loudly and largely for the Southern Butternuteracy, in *puris naturabilus*. They fled through cabbage-patches, through cornfields, through jimson-weed thickets, through dog-fennel meadows, and through brier-patches, with streaming hair and dilated eyes, and gaping mouths, and panting breasts. Good heavens! How the blatant, white-livered, black-hearted tatterdemalions were horrified. They ran like a puppy with a kettle on his tail, like a colt with a thousand yellow jackets on his hide, like a cow with a million buffalo-gnats buzzing around here, like a mouse pursued by a fierce tom-cat, like a miserable drunkard chased by the devils, witches and serpents of a raging delirium tremens. Rebel flags were hastily jerked down from chimney-tops and committed to the flames, and general dismay pervaded the entire rebel portion of the village. Several persons who had taken the oath of allegiance to the Federal Government, whilst General Negley was there, and after his foes had thrown off the mask and showed themselves bitter rebels, hid themselves in sink-holes, in garrets, in straw-piles, and under beds. Instead of enjoying a triumphant entry with the guerrillas into evacuated Nashville, they were only doomed to behold the country swarming with Union troops, while private news from Louisville warned them that "three hundred thousand more" were marching down in Dixie, to punish false and treacherous traitors like themselves.

Nashville *Daily Union*, September 12, 1862.

12 "The recovery of Cumberland Gap is a necessity to the peace and quiet of this deluded region."

HDQRS. DEPARTMENT OF EAST TENNESSEE, Knoxville, Tenn, September 12, 1862.

Gen. S. COOPER, Richmond, Va.:

GEN.: The Federal forces at Cumberland Gap have taken advantage of the advance of Gen. Smith's command into Kentucky to blockade the passes through mountains [through] which Gen. Smith entered Kentucky. A detachment of Kentucky cavalry left a few days since without orders to join Gen. Smith and were captured near Pine Mountain. Gen. Smith is calling on me for re-enforcements. Gen. Bragg has ordered a portion of my small command to join Gen. Smith. I shall obey the order. With the force at my command at present I can only invest the Gap on this side, guard the various mountain passes and the railroad bridges. I am unpleasantly situated, taking in view the necessity of recovering Cumberland Gap, the key to East Tennessee, and the requisitions for re-enforcements for Kentucky. The recovery of Cumberland Gap is a necessity to the peace and quiet of this deluded region. It cannot be recovered unless it can be reinvested on the north side. I cannot do this and send off the forces to Kentucky called for unless in his confusion Gen. Morgan may abandon it. I am now organizing a force to re-enforce Gen. Smith and escort funds. I shall push it forward as soon as it is of sufficient strength to certainly protect these funds.

Respectfully, your obedient servant,

J. P. MCCOWN, Maj.-Gen., Cmdg.

OR, Ser. I, Vol. 16, pt. II, p. 814.

14 Free Negroes meet to consider mass exodus from Nashville

Meeting of Free Colored Men.—A circular was lately received by one of our free colored men from James Mitchell, Commissioner of the Colonization Society, addressed to the free colored people of Nashville, and requesting their opinions on the propriety of emigrating to some country where they could live entirely among people of their own color. A meeting was held on Sunday [14th] evening to take the matter into consideration, when the circular was read, and referred to a committee, who were instructed to report suitable resolutions at a subsequent meeting to be held on Thursday [18th] evening. The meeting of Sunday was only a preliminary one, and but little was done more than above noted. In our paper of Friday, we will give a full report of all that transpires.

Nashville *Dispatch*, September 16, 1862.

16 Kate Cumming, Confederate nurse, arrives in Chattanooga

I arrived at Chattanooga this morning, about 5 o'clock....

...

We have a good many patients. One man, by the name of Hughes, died in my ward this morning. He was a member of the Sixteenth Louisiana Regiment. I hope this not ominous.

We have nothing to cook on but one small stove, and that a smoky one. It cooks for the whole of this side of the hospital. We have nothing to give the men to eat but wheat bread ... fresh beef, rice, tea, and coffee.

...

Cumming, *A Journal of Hospital Life*, pp. 45–46.

25 A disappointed Maury County Confederate father throws his reluctant son out, excerpt from the diary of Nimrod Porter

I loaned George Martin $5.00

George Martin (son of Judge Martin) came to town today, said his father had told him if he did not start off to the army of the Southern Confederacy on the next day he should leave his house he could not stay here he had not one dollar in the

World but few clothes and no bridle, and was trying H. Bradshaw and a few others to get him a bridle said his father would do nothing for him.

Diary of Nimrod Porter, September 25 1862.

26 "I do not want further to make an ass of myself in trying to do that which cannot be done." Confederate conscription troubles in Greeneville

The New Regiments and the Conscription.

We alluded yesterday to the rumored action of the Government in refusing to receive new regiments from East Tennessee. We have good reason to believe that the policy will not be insisted upon in regard to those already authorized to be raised. To show how it would operate, if adhered to, we publish the following extract of a letter from a gentleman in Green county, who has not enrolled a company of one hundred men, the most of them "good fighting material." This is but one among many similar cases in upper East Tennessee:

I see an order from Col. Blake that seems to conflict very seriously with my permission from Gen. McCown. I scarcely know what to do, but I shall go on the organize under my authority, and hope to be treated in good faith but the authorities and their promises to me, that my company when obtained, would be put into one of the regiments now (for then forming) with as much respect to the desire of myself and company as would be consistent with the public service. My men have volunteered with these assurances by me-much upon the authority and assurances given me at the A. A. General's office; and now, I cannot but think, I shall be dealt with in good faith accordingly. Please ascertain if possible, what will be done; for I have gone to considerable expense and trouble already, and I do not want further to make an ass of myself in trying to do that which cannot be done-viz., raising a company as volunteers when the same cannot be done. The majority of my company are good Southern men-yes, I say as good Southern men as can be found in the Confederacy not in the service heretofore, because their affairs were such at home that they could not leave them; men who have sustained this war with as much zeal and patriotism as any in the South, and that too often with the danger of having the torch applied to their dwellings: and now such men are to be taken and treated as Conscript Tories, nor will I believe it.

Knoxville *Daily Register*, September 26, 1862.

28 Conditions inside the Confederate hospital in Chattanooga; an entry from the diary of Kate Cumming

Have been very busy all week, too much so to write in my journal. Three men died in the course of the week.

...

Diarrhea is the prevailing disease among the patients. I have been so busy that I have not taken time to visit Mrs. M's ward. She has many sick men, as has also Mrs. W. They both have a great deal of trouble. The stove smokes as badly ever. I have the use of one that belongs to the surgeons. (They all mess together; their kitchen and dining-room are near my ward.) It answered for what little I have to cook-beef-tea, toast, sago, and arrow-root. I have a nice little distributing room in the ward, which the head nurse, George Bean, has fixed up very neatly.

The great cry of our sick is for milk. We could buy plenty, but have no money. We get a little every day for the worst cases, at our own expense. I intend letting the folks at home know how many are suffering for want of nourishment, for I feel confident that if they knew of it they would lend us means.

Last week, in despair, I went to Dr. Young, the medical purveyor, and begged him to give me some wine; in fact, any little thing, I told him, would be acceptable. I did not come away empty-handed. He gave me arrow-root, sago, wine and several kinds of spices, and many things in the way of clothing.

In every hospital there is invariable a fund, there is not at present in this [one]. The reason, we have been told, is because the hospitals at this point are in debt to the government, by drawing more money from it than their due, and until it is paid we will get no more. The fund consists so money drawn instead of the soldiers rations, as the sick men are unable to eat the rations.

Mrs. W. and myself went to the Episcopal Church this morning. There were very few present. The pastor's, Rev. Mr. Denniston, sermon was a political one.

I went to give my sick men their dinners, and found that the food I had cooked for them was spoiled. I asked Huldah, the negro woman who cooks for the surgeons, who had ruined everything. She told me the steward's wife had been over there and put handfuls of salt into the beef-tea and other things. She had done the same before, but I did not know who did it. My poor men had to go that day dinnerless. I do not know when I have felt so badly about any thing. I am afraid the next thing she does will be to attempt my life. We had made up our minds, if Dr. Hunter did not put an end to these persecutions, it would be impossible for us to remain here. One of the assistant surgeons came to me, and told me that if Dr. Hunter did not put a stop to them, he and the other assistant surgeons would do so. But I have been informed that Dr. H. has told the steward, that if his wife comes over to this side of the hospital he will then her out altogether. It seems we will never get rid of troubles of this sort.

When we first came here Dr. H. told us that there was another lady coming to assist us; we found out who she was, and concluded if she came we would not remain. We told Dr. H. what we knew of her, and he said that was strange, as he had certificates from our first surgeons. I told him there were some of them whose certificates I did not value as much as the paper they were written on. He said on no account would he have her come.

...

We have a good deal of trouble about servants; the soldiers do the cooking, in fact all the domestic work. We have a few free Negroes, and they give us no little trouble. For this reason the slaves here are not near so respectful as they are with us; although they seem to have great contempt for the free Negroes. The other day I heard the doctor's servant indignantly say that some one had spoken to her as if she was free, and had no master to care for her.

There are quite number of soldiers in the place who can not get on to their commands, as the country is filled with bushwhackers, and it is dangerous for them to go through it unless in very large bodies.

I am a good deal worried about my brother, as I have not heard from him since the army went into Kentucky.

Cumming, *A Journal of Hospital Life*, pp. 46–47.

28 Sparta's women, according to a Confederate war correspondent

Hoops Ignored.—A correspondent of the Columbus (Ga.) *Sun*, attached to Gen. Bragg's army, writing from Sparta, Tenn., says: The land here is fertile, and the people look more like folks. The ladies in the neat little village of Sparta, as we passed through waved us on amid vociferous cheers, which made the welkin ring. Most of the citizens in that portion of Tennessee, thro' which we have passed belong to the mediocrity, and are ignorant and disaffected. The women, *horrible dictu*, go barefooted, and look like a piece of calico tied around a lamp post.

Southern Confederacy [Atlanta, Georgia], September 28, 1862.

30 Lysistrata at Powell's River, East Tennessee Tennessee Female Tories.

The editor of the Henderson (N.C.) *Times* has recently made a visit through East Tennessee to Cumberland Gap. Upon his return, he fixed up the following story for the edification of his readers.

At Powell's river, I stopped and engaged for more milk, at an old Lincolnite jade, keen as a brier, and mother of three (and I don't know how many more,) rather nice looking gals. She complained to me of having been rudely treated by a North Carolina officer, the morning previous. Arriving at camp, I informed the officer of the old lady's story, and he told me that knowing their political status, he had placed a guard around the house, to keep any of the family from going to the Gap, while our army was crossing the river, and in the meantime, the following conversation took place:

Officer.—(Entering the house,) Good morning ma'am. No answer. "Where is your husband, ma'am?"

Old Woman.—None of your business, you rebel you.

Officer.—I know. He is in the Yankee army.

Old Woman.—Well he is. What are you going to do about it? He is in the 1st Tennessee Federal regiment at Cumberland Gap, and will take off your rebel head, if you go up there.

Officer.—Yes. But we have him and your General Morgan's whole command completely surrounded—hemmed in—with an army on both sides of the Gap, and in a few days they will be starved out, and have to surrender on our own terms.

Old Woman.—We know all that, and are easy. But Lincoln will send an army through Kentucky, which will wipe out your General Smith, just like a dog would lick out a plate, and then you and your army of barefooted, roasting ear stealers, will have to leave here in the dark again, and badly scared at that. Besides this —

Officer. — That's your opinion, but you are deluded. Where were you born?

Old Woman. — Born! Why I was born and raised in Tennessee. I am an Old Hickory Tennessean — dead out against Nullification, and its bastard offspring, Secession. But where are you from?

Officer. — I am from North Carolina, but a native of South Carolina.

Old Woman. — A South Carolinian — scion of nullification — double rebel, double devil.

Old Jackson made your little turnip patch of a State walk the chalk once, and Old Abe Lincoln will give you rebels hell before Spring.

Officer. — (Quitting the old lady, and turning to the eldest daughter, whom he recognized as a mother) Madam, where is your husband?

Young Woman. — That is none of your business.

Officer. — But it is my business. Where is he?

Young Woman. — Where I hope I'll never see him again. Where I hope you will soon be.

Officer. — Where is that?

Young Woman. — Why, a prisoner in the hands of the army at the Gap.

Officer. — What is that for?

Young Woman. — For being what you are, an infernal rebel.

Officer. — Oh, if that's all, I will send him back to you as soon as we take the Gap.

Young Woman. — No you need'nt. Cust if ever he sleeps in my bed again. I intend to get some Union man to father this child. Here, Bet, (calling a nurse,) take this little rebel and give him Union milk. Let us try and get the "secesh" out of him.

Officer. — (Turning to a Miss.) Did you find a beau among the Yankee officers?

Miss. — Yes, I did; a nice, sweet, gallant fellow. One who stepped like a prince. When you become his prisoner, give him my love, and tell him for my sake to put a trace chain around your infernal neck.

Officer. — When do you expect to see him again?

Miss. — Just after your General takes the next "big scare," which will be in ten days from this time.

Daylight having broken, and the army having crossed the river, the conversation I have given terminated.

Weekly Columbus [Georgia] *Enquirer*, September 30, 1862.

◆ OCTOBER ◆

1 Life and death in the Confederate hospital in Chattanooga; an entry from the journal of Kate Cumming

One of Mrs. May's patients died a few days ago. His name was Huntley, was a lieutenant in the Twenty-seventh Mississippi Regiment. He was sick for some time, and died perfectly resigned, in the full hope of a blessed resurrection. He spoke a good deal about his family, and would like to have seen them before his departure from this world. Mrs. W. conversed and prayed with him, and was much gratified at the frame of mind in which he died. His father came to see him, but too late, as he was dead and buried. A few days before his death he told me that my friend Lieutenant Booth, a member of the same regiment, was here sick. Dr. Hunter has sent a messenger around to all the hospitals in search of him, but he is not to be found.

In a letter received a few days ago from home, was a notice of the death of Charles Farrow.... He was confined at Camp Douglas; was taken sick while on the transport, coming down ... died on the 21st or 22d of September. Poor fellow! He was one of my brother's school-mates.

Cumming, *A Journal of Hospital Life*, pp. 48.

16 Aquariums, statuary, the penitentiary, Polk's monument and sulphur water in Nashville: an entry in the diary of John Hill Fergusson, 10th Illinois Volunteer Infantry

Thursday 16th N. Francer Elgin Rock & Decherty & myself get a pass after brackfast and went through the most important parts of the town we visited a old gentleman house got to see his gold and silver fish: the first thing that drawed our attention was 2 lions they ware cast iron and looked as natural as if alive one stay[ing] on each side of his front door or porch then along by the side of a graveled walk stood a large new found land dog of full sice and looked as natural as life a little further along was a very fancy gray hound laying down on his hind leggs with his fore leggs streatched out in front of him he had his neck streatched up and his head fixed as if he was looking at some thing while we ware taking particler notice of these things the old gentleman came out he was a very frendly old he told us to come along and see his fish the first we seen ware in a large free stone bason about 12 feet wide and 4 or 5 feet deep it was suplyed with water from the rizzervoy on pipe leeding the watter in and another letting it out the baisen first go so full and no fuller then he took us to another fixing he had for fish it was a large glass box about 4 feet long and 3 feet wide and 3 height with an iron bottom with gravel stones and some oyster shells laying in the bottom this box stood about 3 or 3½ feet from the ground the top of the box was covered with fine wiar: worked like the bottom of a riddle the pipe suplying the box with watter forced the watter up into a glass globe on top of the box then the water run sick back into the box another larger pipe stood up within 2 inches of the top the water wrise that high and no higher the fish ware shaped like a sun fish only the gold fish more yellow and glistened when they would move around in the clear water the silver fish ware off the same shape and size only they ware off the coller and glistened like silver they ware from the size of a minney up to half a lb whare this box was placed was in side of a nice lates worked summer house with seats all around it at each side of the door on the inside ware a woman cut out of marble there hair hanging down over there sholders there sholders and breasts was apearently bair with the form of a white sheet rapped around these lady on the outside of the door stood a little darky holding a kee out in his hand he resembled the works of natur as much as any thing I ever saw: from that we went to the States prison the clark in the office took us all through whare the prisoners ware to work the States prisen occupies a hole block there is a stone wall all around in three sides about 15 feet high in side of this wall there is a 2 story bilding extends all around three side upon the upper story wood work of all kinds was carried on also tailering and stone making in the lower story blacksmithing and hewing and dressing free stone and marble was carried and a variety of other imployments every one seemed to be hard to work the front side was the jail 3 stories high with large iron doors and dark scells that was wharre murderers was kept in cloce confinement it is mostly filled at the preset time with Secesh prisoners after having a good view of this place we went back uptown and visited the grave of James K Polk he is berried inside of a house sat in front of a large house I suppose the house he live in when he died the monument over his grave was small but very nice it was supported on pillars the ingraving on the monument read as follows: James Knox Polk 10th president of the United State born November 2nd 1795 dies June 15, 1849 the mortle remains of James Knox Polk are resting in the vault benieth he was born in Mackleburg county NorthCarlina and imagrated with his Father Samuel Polk to Tennessee in 1806 the beauty of virtue was illustrated in his life the excellence of Christianity was exemplifed in his death: his life was devoted to the public service he was elected successfuy to the fist places in the State or federal governments a member of the general assembly a member of congress and chairman of the most important congressional comities speaker of the house of representitives governor of Tennessee 7 President of the United States by his public policy: his definit established [the] extended boundaries of his country he planted the laws of American union on the shores of the Picific his influnce and his counsels tended to organize the national treasury on the principles of the constitution and to apply the rule of freedom to Navigation trade & industry.

This the 16th day of October 1862 in the town of Nash Vill Tennessee I like to forget I visited the sulferey spring citizens pays 5 cts per glass Soldiers drinks free I drank only one glass that was all I wanted I would sooner drink sals Some are very fond of it.

John Hill Fergusson Diary.

7 Skirmish near LaVergne
BATTLE ON THE MURFREESBORO' PIKE.
40 or 50 Confederates Killed and wounded
240 Prisoners Captured
The city was thrown into an unusual state of excitement yesterday morning by the current rumor that a number of Confederate prisoners had been brought into town. It was generally known that a large force had left about midnight on Monday, taking the Murfreesboro pike, and as it was supposed the Confederates were in force at Lavergne , a fight was of course expected. From what one can hear from parties who are likely to know the truth, the following statement is prob-

ably mainly correct: The force which left here about midnight was so divided and disposed of as to get around the Confederate pickets, whom they made prisoners this side of the Lunatic Asylum, say about five miles from town. Sending to the rear, the Federal troops proceeded slowly and quietly as possible, until they reached a Confederate camp, which they speedily surrounded, and captured the entire force. They went on to within half a mile of Lavergne, where they encountered about 2,000 Confederates. Without loss of time a shell was thrown into the Confederate army, which penetrated the magazine and caused its explosion, killing and wounding a large number of Confederates. A brisk fight ensued which ended in the complete rout of Gen. Anderson's command, he himself escaping, it is said, on a locomotive. Between forty and fifty Confederates were killed and wounded, and 240 taken prisoner, including some citizens.

The Federals captured all the rebel camp equipage, and a large lot of guns and ammunition; also a number of horses and other articles. Three cars were captured, and after the contents were secured, they were burned.

All the prisoners have arrived in town, and are located in the Penitentiary, and the work-house. The Federal loss was twenty-five or thirty killed and wounded.

Several of the soldiers brought in trophies from the battle field, among them a very handsome regimental flag.

Nashville *Dispatch*, October 8, 1862.

8 Horatio Alger in Confederate Chattanooga
"Honesty Its Own Reward."

A lady from Mississippi who is on a mission of mercy to our city, was so unfortunate yesterday as to lose her purse, containing nearly three hundred dollars. An honest little boy—an orphan—who assists in supporting his widowed mother by selling newspapers and fruit, picked the purse up on the street, and, in obedience to his honest impulses, brought it immediately to this office with a request that we would advertise it and keep it until claimed by the owner. In less than ten minutes after he left our office, the lady who had lost the purse called to advertise its loss, and describing the purse and its content accurately, we had the pleasure of returning it to her. The little boy was sent for and received, as the reward of his honesty, thirty dollars, and the thanks of the excellent lady. The name of the youth is Jas. Flora.

Chattanooga *Daily Rebel*, October 8, 1862.

9 Juvenile Crime in Memphis

We earnestly call attention to the amount of crime among the young of our city. It is rapidly increasing. We this morning counted at the landing, congregated opposite the stern of the St. Louis wharfboat, eleven boys and six girls of from six to twelve years of age. Several of them had sacks with them; these are used for the reception of coffee, cotton or any other goods which they can steal from boxes, bales, and bags on the landing. We stood near the crowd of little ones for some time. The girls were mostly playing some game with pebbles, which they threw up and caught in their hands. Their conversations was in too low a tone for us to hear, but the wharf master informs us that they sometimes use language of the most horribly vicious character. The boys, as we stood by, were in loud and somewhat angry discussion, about some point that interested them, and from their mouths, even from the least of them, came oaths of the most savage and brutal import, and which nearly always commenced with the sacred name of God. The boys and girls are already criminals. The value of property they steal from the merchandise deposited at the landing, is far beyond what anyone, who is not conversant with their proceedings, would think, *This petty* is the juvenile school in which the boys are trained for burglary and all degrees of crime. And those girls-who can regard them without a shudder! Some of them only want clean faces, well arranged hair, and neat garments, to be pretty and attractive. But who can hope for them the fascinations of maiden innocence, the purity of virgin love, the virtues of wifely affection, the devotion of motherly care? The work of sin and death and hell is going on daily at our landing with those "little ones" whom the Redeemer has commanded should be suffered to come to him and "no man layeth it to heart." The police, we think, ought to receive instructions to keep these young thieves from the landing altogether, if not for their own at least for the sake of the property lying at the wharf. Can nothing be done to save them from the sad future that hangs dark and threatening over their young heads? Can nothing be done to turn their steps to the school houses instead of along the paths of crime? The sight of youthful transgression exhibited on our wharf day by day is a mournful comment on our religion. How vain are prayers. How useless are churches unless the inspire compassion for such little wanderers from the paths of holiness as those that daily frequent our landing.

Memphis *Bulletin*, October 9, 1862.

17 Skirmish at Island No. 10

Report of Maj. Quincy McNeil, Second Illinois Cavalry.

HDQRS. U.S. FORCES, Island No. 10, October [1]7, 1862.

SIR: This camp was attacked at 4 o'clock this morning. At daylight I sent Capt. Moore, Company L, Second Illinois Cavalry, in pursuit. He overtook a body of cavalry about 20 miles from here, gave battle, taking Col. Faulkner, Capt. Meriwether, Capt. Blakemore, Lieut. Johnson, and 11 privates, from whom he found the enemy to consist of 300 men. After fighting an hour Capt. Moore finding himself outnumbered (he having but 40 men) fell back to camp, the rebels declining to follow.

The loss on our side is 3 men supposed to be killed; that of the rebels is unknown so far as the battle, but 7 were wounded and many supposed to be killed. From the prisoners we learn that they came from Mississippi, traveling three days and nights to take this post, and then move on Hickman, take that place, and leave immediately for the south.

To an overruling Providence do we owe our safety. With citizens for guides and traveling from the Obion between moonrise and 4 o'clock in the morning they evaded all the scouting parties and approached to within a hundred yards of the camp. They were about forming into line of battle when the sentinel fired upon the advancing column; the rear of the rebel band fired into the front, when the front (thinking they were attacked from the rear) defended themselves from that quarter. The fight between the rebel front and rear lasted about three minutes, wounding several of their number and creating the impression that they were ambushed by the forces from this camp. This caused a panic and they fled to their horses, stationed a mile distant. They immediately mounted and gave up the capture of either this place or Hickman. Had they come as they intended they would have given us much trouble, as they had a perfect plan of this camp; had their men selected, three to catch officers, whom they intended to capture in bed; but finding the guards drawn in toward the camp led them to think that we had been apprised of their approach and that we were prepared for them. They could not have taken the camp, but might have killed and wounded many before they could have been repulsed.

...I intend to cut off the retreat of the rebels by taking the fords of the lake near the Obion River.

I am, sir, your obedient servant,

QUINCY MCNEIL, Maj. Second Illinois Cavalry, Comdg.

OR, Ser. I, Vol. 17, pt. I, pp. 460–461.

19 Sherman's reply to Miss P. A. Fraser relative to policy of retribution following guerrilla attacks on the steamboats *Catahoula* and *Gladiator*

MEMPHIS, October 22, 1862.

Miss P. A. FRASER, Memphis:

DEAR LADY:

...

If from silence or a positive answer from their commanders I am led to believe such fiendish acts are to be tolerated or allowed it would be weakness and foolish in me to listen to appeals to feelings that are scorned by our enemies. They must know and feel that not only will we meet them in arms, but that their people shall experience their full measure of the necessary consequences of such barbarity.

The Confederate generals claim the Partisan Rangers as a part of their army. They cannot then disavow their acts, but all their adherents must suffer the penalty. They shall not live with us in peace. God himself has obliterated whole races from the face of the earth for sins less heinous than such as characterized the attacks on the *Catahoula* and *Gladiator*. All I say is if such acts were done by the direct or implied concert of the Confederate authorities we are not going to chase through the canebrakes and swamps the individuals who did the deeds, but will visit punishment upon the adherents of that cause which employs such agents. We will insist on a positive separation; they cannot live with us. Further than that I have not yet ordered, and when the time comes to settle the account we will see which is most cruel-for your partisans to fire cannon and musket-balls through steamboats with women and children on board, set them on fire with women and children sleeping in their berths, and shoot down the passengers and engineers, with the curses of hell on their tongues, or for us to say the families of men engaged in such hellish deeds shall not live in peace where the flag of the United States floats.

I know you will say these poor women and children abhor such acts as much as I do, and that their husbands and brothers in the Confederate service also would not be concerned in such acts. Then let the Confederate authorities say so, and not employ their tools in such deeds of blood and darkness. We will now wait and see who are the cruel and heartless men of this war. We will see whether the firing on the *Catahoula* or *Gladiator* is sanctioned or disapproved, and if it was done by the positive command of ... the Confederate Government, you will then appreciate how rapidly Civil War corrupts the best feelings of the human heart.

Would to God ladies better acted their mission on earth; that instead of inflaming the minds of their husbands and brothers to lift their hands against the Government of their birth and stain them in blood, had prayed them to forbear, to exhaust all the remedies afforded them by our glorious Constitution, and thereby avoid "horrid war," the last remedy on earth.

Your appeals to me shall ever receive respectful attention, but it will be vain in this case if Gen. Holmes does not promptly disavow these acts, for I will not permit the families and adherents of secessionists to live here in peace whilst their husbands and brothers are aiming the rifle and gun at our families on the free Mississippi.

Your friend,

W. T. SHERMAN, Maj.-Gen., Comdg.

OR, Ser. I, Vol. 17, pt, II, p. 288.

22 "A Pretty Minx."

The people in the neighborhood of the Navy Yard had their attention attraction yesterday afternoon by seeing a lady gracefully riding through the streets, attended by a youth on another horse. The elegant appearance of the couple was much admired and the young misses were warm in their expressions of admiration of the boy who so gallantly squired the lady. His white hat sat graceful upon flowing hair; a faultlessly white collar was tied with a beautiful colored neckerchief, a round jacket, and a very neatly made pair of pants. The foot set off with a handsome half boot, made up as exquisite a toilette as fancy could well devise. Among the admiring eyes attracted to the graceful couple were those of policeman Parker. His experienced eye detected that the exquisiteness was too exquisite. It was no male hand that had arranged all with such accurate taste, such harmonious faultless elegance — the boy was a woman! The woman was two quick not to know when she was recognized. She at once put her horse to a gallop and a soon as she thought she had eluded the search of the officer, she threw the girdle of her horse to her companion, who rode off, while she darted into a house, strange enough she was; and seeing a lady seated, she commenced at once in her confusion to divest herself of the *inexpressible* cause of her difficulties. The sudden appearance of a pretty, saucy looking strange boy, who was about to be guilty of so gross an outrage on all boyish politeness naturally alarmed the lady, who was about to scream for help, when the intruder assured her that she was a woman. A hurried council was held which ended in a hack being sent for and the saucy young fellow being sent home sheltered by its friendly roof. It was too late, however — Parker had detected the whole movement. The boy-girl was arrested. She gave the name of Frank Gordon, and deposited a sum of money as security for her appearance before Recorder Tighe this morning.

Memphis *Bulletin*, October 23, 1862.

25 One Tennessean's recollections of the battle of Perryville, Ky, an excerpt from a brother's letter home to his sisters in White County

Camp near Knoxville, Tenn.

Oct. 25th 1862

Dear Sisters:

I have not had chances to send many letters and sometimes not time to write. I will start a letter anyhow. I have a great many interesting things to say if I had time and my fingers did not get so cold. I had a pleasant time until we got up the main army. We lived as well as we could ask, We just got to our brigade in time for the great battle at Perryville, which [was] fought on the 8th inst. and a great victory for us. I have [never] seen such a wholesale manslaughter as we made of them. Not many of our side were killed. I think they lost as many killed as we lost in killed and wounded. I have heard of many victories and doubted them but I saw this and know something about it. There were [more] dead men on their part of the field than you ever saw at one time in live ones. I hope I never again shall see such a wholesale slaughter of humans. But it is now the morn of the 26th and "cold as Hannah's heel" and I have not a tent, but, thanks to Aunt Rachel for a good blanket and to my purse for a great shirt just purchased last night, I slept warm last night for the first time in two weeks. I now have a blanket stretched over a stick behind me to shelter to snow off my paper but my fingers are very cold and have two passes to write every four lines I write for myself. Well all goes in a lifetime. As I live and do well, that is all I expect. My horse had nothing to eat since yesterday morning.

...

Yours etc.,
L. L. McDowell

Diary of Amanda McDowell.

29 Mademoiselle Urso.

Go and Hear the Wonderful Violinist

We hope none will deny themselves the pleasure of listening to M'M'lle Urso's astonishing performances on the violin this afternoon, at the Theatre. She was a pupil of the renowned Norwegian Minstrel, Ole Bull, and the great Wizard of the North never had a disciple so worthy of him, as M'm'lle Urso. One may listen to fine violin playing a year, and then fancy himself listening to a new instrument while attending her performances, so wonderful are the power, variety and sweetness of the notes which evokes from her violin. She is not only a most accomplished artist, but she touches the hearts of all her auditors by the soul which she throws into her art. Her "Dream" is one of the strangest, wildest, and sweetest of pieces of music, that ever entranced the ear, and the hearer might close his eyes, and imagine himself revelling in a luxurious Opium dream, in some balmy garden of the Orient. In addition to her own performances, she will be assisted by the finest vocal talent in the city. Such a musical entertainment rarely presents itself in the west, and we are sure that the Concert room will be thronged this afternoon by hundreds and hundreds.

Nashville *Daily Union*, October 29, 1862.

♦ NOVEMBER ♦

1 Excerpt from Special Order No. 4, relative to Confederate conscripting on the Cumberland Plateau

Head Quarters Army of Middle Tennessee
Murfreesboro, Nov. 1, 1862

...

VI. Brig. Gen. Forrest will furnish the requisite number of men to Gen. Jones on demand, for the purpose of enforcing the Conscript Act in the counties of Jackson, Macon, Overton, Putnam & White.

...

William B. Bate collection

7 Major-General William T. Sherman explains to Mrs. Valeria Hurlbut his policy of sending certain Memphis families south of Union lines as a consequence of supporting Partisan attacks on ships HEADQUARTERS DISTRICT OF MEMPHIS

Memphis, November 7, 1862

Mrs. VALERIA HURLBUT, Memphis:

Your letter of October*— was duly received. I did not answer it at that time, as I had already instructed Colonel Anthony, provost-marshal, to suspend the execution of the order expelling certain families from Memphis for fifteen days, to enable them to confer with the Confederate authorities upon the cause of that order, viz.,: the firing from ambush on our boats carrying passengers and merchandise by bands of guerrillas in the service of the enemy.

In war it is impossible to hunt up the actual perpetrators of a crime. Those who are banded together in any cause are held responsible for all the acts of their associates. The Confederate Government, in resisting what we claim to be the rightful prerogative and authority of our Government, by armies in the field and bands of armed men called guerrillas or partisan rangers, claims for these latter all the right of war, which means that the Confederate Government assumes the full responsibility of the acts of these Partisan Rangers. These men have, as you know, fired on steamboats navigating on the Mississippi River, taking the lives and endangering the safety of peaceful citizens who travel in an accustomed way, in no wise engaged in the operations of war. We regard

---

*Mrs. Valeria Hurlbut's letter to Sherman is not known to be extant.

this as inhuman and barbarous, and if the Confederate authorities do not disavow them, it amounts to a sanction and encouragement of the practice. We must stop this, and no measures would be too severe. The absolute destruction of Memphis, New Orleans, and every city, town and hamlet of the South would not be too severe a punishment to people for attempting to interfere with the navigation of the Mississippi. I have commenced mildly by requiring the families of men engaged in this barbarous practice to leave and to their own people. Certainly there can be no hardship for the wife and children going to their own husbands and families. They ought to be glad of the opportunity, and the measure, instead of being severe, is very mild. How would they like it if they were to fire through the houses of their wives and families. If any person will look at this question who feels for our people, he or she will perceive that the measure of retaliation is mild, and I do not promise by any means that in future cases I will be so easy. Misplaced kindness to these guerrillas, their families, and adherents is cruelty to our people. Were you to travel on a boat and have the bullets whistle and hear the demon yells of these Confederate partisans, you would not feel so kindly disposed to those who approve the act.

I have given them time to disavow the attack on the *Gladiator*; they will have not done it. They therefore approve, and I say not only shall the families go away, but all the Confederate allies and adherents shall feel the power of an indignant Government.

OR, Ser. I, Vol. 17, pt. II, p. 860.

8 Advertisements for Confederate conscription substitutes and guaranteed exemption from the draft in Knoxville

$1500 for a substitute — Any one not liable to conscription and fit for military duty can get Fifteen Hundred Dollars to go as a substitute, by applying at this office.

Substitutes Wanted — The Undersigned will give Fifteen Hundred Dollars for a substitute who is in every way qualified, if one will present himself within ten days. Apply at Co. B, 29th Mississippi Regiment, Gen. Chalmers Brigade, Withers Division, for J. M. H.

Laborers Wanted at the Embreville Iron Works, in Washington county, E. Tennessee, whose liberal wages will be given to axemen, teamsters, laborers and others engaged in making iron for the Government. The persons thus employed will not be subject to conscription.

Duf. Green.

Knoxville *Daily Register*, November 8, 1862.

9 Guerrilla blockade of Nolensville pike thwarts mother-daughter visit

A respectable widow left Huntsville, Ala., recently on a visit to a married daughter in Nashville. She arrived at the residence of Capt. B. D. Harris, a few miles from town, on the Nolensville turnpike, where she was stopped by Confederate guerrillas and forbidden to come any farther. Sad and sorrowful she yesterday started on her return to Alabama. This excellent lady has three sons in the Confederate army — her last, having been torn from her by the Conscript law, leaving her almost without the means of subsistence. Unfortunately her daughter is the wife of a Union man — for this the rebel guerrillas punished her, even though their hellish cause had taken all her sons from here. When she started back home, a couple of rebel women started from the same point for Nashville. The latter met with no obstacle. They came into the city safely, and without question by either rebel or Federal pickets. How long is this state of things to continue? Is there no remedy? Is no consideration to be extended to any but rebels?

Nashville *Daily Union*, November 9, 1862.

10 Major-General U.S. Grant forbids the use of railroads to Jews in West Tennessee

LAGRANGE, November 10, 1862.

Gen. WEBSTER, Jackson, Tenn.:

Give orders to all the conductors on the road that no Jews are to be permitted to travel on the railroad southward from any point. They may go north and be encouraged in it; but they are such an intolerable nuisance that the department must be purged of them.

U.S. GRANT, Maj.-Gen.

OR, Ser. I, Vol. 17, pt. II, p. 337.

10 A Battlefield Orphan

A Baby Found on the Battle Field of the Hatchie.*

---

*Most likely the Engagement at Hatchie (or Davis') Bridge, Big Hatchie River, near Metamora, October 5, 1862.

Extract from a letter from a private soldier in the 14th Illinois Reg[iment]'t.:

Bolivar, Tenn., Nov. 10.

Let me relate to you a touching little incident, that will doubtless strike you a little strange. I thought it strange when I witnessed it; my comrades thought it "passing strange," if not wonderful. At the battle of Hatchie, when the conflict was waging fiercest, upon advancing midway between the contending forces, we found, what do you think? Not a masked battery — not an insidious trap, inviting but to destroy — not any visible engine of death — but a sweet little blue eyed baby, fresh from the womb of the mother that groaned and gave it birth. Sweet little thing, as I saw it there, hugging the cold earth, its only bed — the little tear on its cheek,

"That nature bade it weep, turned
An icedrop sparkling in the morning beam"

Unalarmed mid the awful confusion of that tearful battle, with the missiles of death lying thick about it, and crowding close upon existence, yet unhurt, it seemed a wonderful verification of the declaration, "Out of the mouth of babes and sucklings I will ordain wisdom." That little "child of war," as it lay in its miraculous safety, seemed to say to me those words of profound instruction, "My helplessness and innocence appealed to God, and he preserved me in the midst of this wrecking carnage. If you will make your plaint to Heaven, God will preserve your poor bleeding country."

Little child of destiny, born amid the flash of musketry, the thunder of cannon, and clash of arms, I will watch your course through life, and witness whether an existence so auspiciously begun, will pass by the masses unnoticed, and end without leaving a name "damned to everlasting fame!" Who would suppose that in the wild fierce battle of the Hatchie, where the field was strewn with the dead, and the shrieks and groans of the wounded rent the heavens with agony, a great army would pause in the thickest of the conflict to save harmless a helpless child? Yet the brave 14th that never yet has quailed in battle, did pause, and the officer of the regiment ordered our "little baby" to be carried to headquarters and tenderly cared for.

I remember of having read somewhere in Grecian history a story something like the one I have related. A little child was found on the battle field, and by an infuriated soldiery trampled in the dust. After the battle the victorious general said: "But for the blood of the little child that mars it, our victory would be complete." Thank God, the blood of no little child mars our victory.

The next day after the battle "our babe" was brought before the 14th, and unanimously adopted "child of the regiment." Three or four days later, strange as it may seem, a poor heart stricken, poverty pinched mother, came searching the battle field in quest of her child. My dear _____, imagine if you can the wild exclamation of thanksgiving that burst from that poor woman's heart, when informed that her child had been rescued, and with a mother's tenderness cared for. I saw the mother receive her child, heard her brief prayer for the soldiers who saved it, and, with the blessings of a thousand men following her and hers, she took away

"Our little baby —
Little blue eyed, laughing baby."

Soldier's Budget [Humboldt], January 22, 1862

12 Hog collection regulations in East Tennessee

Headquarters, Department E. Tenn.
Knoxville, Nov. 12th, 1862

The Government having made arrangements to purchase all the fattened hogs in the counties of East Tennessee, the shipment of the same to other States is prohibited, unless permission is obtained from these Headquarters.

By command of Lieut. Gen. E. Kirby Smith

Knoxville *Daily Register*, December 14, 1862.

14 A civilian's impression of the Confederate reoccupation of Murfreesboro

From Murfreesboro.

From the first number of the *Daily Rebel Banner*, a new publication at Murfreesboro, Tennessee, we clip the following:

A jolly time this, for Murfreesboro. On every side the eye meets nothing but the pomp and circumstance, the soul-stirring din and picturesque tumult of glorious war — the steady tramp of veteran infantry, with banners streaming in the wind — the heavy roll of artillery, whose bright field pieces shine like mirrors in the sun, and anon the dashing charge of the cavalry, passing like phantoms in a cloud of dust. Every avenue leading to the city discloses the pleasant spectacle of arriving multitudes of men, women and children, with joyful faces, once more permitted to "go at large," to greet and be greeted, and to enjoy the blessed privileges of freedom. No more shackled hands; no more manacles; no more Yankees. The old times loom up again, out of the hazy terrors of an oppression of six months, which already begin to wear away, like the remembrance of some hideous nightmare.

Murfreesboro' presents quite a military appearance, and everything indicates a forward movement....

Quite a *cortege* of goods was overhauled near Murfreesboro' yesterday afternoon, containing hats, boots, shoes, and other supplies much needed by the army.

American Citizen [CANTON, MS], November 14, 1862.

14 Report on Confederate draft dodging in East Tennessee

How Conscription Operates in East Tennessee.

The Greenville (Tenn.) *Banner* of the 17th [of October] has the following on the way Conscription works in East Tennessee:

It really is amusing to hear the enrolling officers tell how the conscripts talk and act, when they call on them for their names, age, etc. Many of the Union men have fled to the hills and caves, thinking to avoid being sent to the army, others are claiming to be manufacturers of saltpeter, shoes, etc. There are more Government agents and mechanics than were ever known before. Some men have bought or leased worn out iron works, calculating thereby to be exempt. The move from cave to cave, under the pretense of manufacturing saltpeter, and never made any that any one knows of.

The female portion of our community who are connected with Union men have the hardest cheeks imaginable; they can outlie the devil. They never know where their husbands and sons are; but when the enrolling officers take the contrary course to what they direct, they are certain to find the conscript.

There are more hip-shot, string-halted, broken-legged, knock-kneed, and rheumatic-stricken young men through our country than were ever know to infest any country before.

Nashville *Daily Union*, November 14, 1862.

15 Excerpt from the letter of Henry Albert Potter, Fourth Michigan Cavalry, to his sister
Saturday November 15th 1862
In Camp near Nashville, Tenn.

My dear Sister

Having time this afternoon, I thought I would write a line home and tell you of my whereabouts ... have just been eating dinner. Had some fried shoulder, sweet potatoes, cold beans, bread and coffee. So you can see we don't live so bad here. It is only when we are on a scout or march that we have hard feed. Then we take it as we can catch it.... We are camped just across the river from Nashville, the capital of Tenn. I have been through the city, it is a pretty place, about half as large as Detroit. The State House is a splendid building built upon a hill. You can see it 3 or 4 miles from the city in any direction. The country around here is very fine. Nice farm houses with their little cabins in the rear for the darkies. They have no barns in this country of any account. A great many houses have been burnt along the road. The chimnies stand as a bleak monument of the desolation of war.... The regiment is not here nor has it been. They are scouting around after Morgan. We expect them in now every day. There was fighting night before last about 17 miles from here. We think the 4th was engaged, but have heard no particulars....

From your brother, Albert

Henry Albert Potter Correspondence.

ca. 15 C.S.A. Lieutenant A. J. Lacy, Eighth Tennessee cavalry, to his wife in Jackson County

Elisabeth here is a case for my likeness that I sent to you when I was at Salem. My horse was valled at $200 and my riging at $25 dollars .

Here is a flag that I will send to you that was given to me in Murfreesborough 3 weeks ago to day by a verry nice lady. I want you to save it untill I get home if I ever do. This letter will be taken to Cookeville by Mr. Hamp More. He says that they went an awful report up about Cookvill of our fight in Elys Bend. They was I expect 20 bawls passed in 3 ft. of my head. I rode out towards the enemy to try to rally our co when I rode out towards them they made the bullets whistle all around me.

I must close and go to church.

When this you see, remember me tho many miles apart we may be. Round is the ring that has no end so is my love to you.

A J Lacy 3 Lieutenant in Capt Woolsy s Co
To Miss M. E. Lacy 1862

Lacy Correspondence.

17 East Tennessee saltpetre miners unlawfully drafted into the Confederate army

ATTENTION!
Confederate States of America,
War Dep't. N. & M. Bureau
Knoxville, Nov. 17, 1862.

It having frequently occurred, in the past few days, that men have been taken from the works under my charge, notwithstanding the order of Col. Blake, of the 10 instant, and as it would be too troublesome to Lieut. Gen. E. Kirby Smith, who has promptly acted when cases have been brought to his notice, I publish, for general information the following order from Adjutant General Cooper. I request the return of all men who have been taken from their work that they may continue their duty; and if this request is not promptly complied with, the parties making the arrests of such men, may, in their turn, be arrested for Gen Cooper's order expressly forbids any interference with the workmen or employees at the Nitre, Lead, or Copper [mines] without the consent of the superintendent of such works, and I, as superintendent of the Nitre and Lead works in East Tennessee, have not given my consent to any such proceedings, and those who have so interfered will see the necessity of returning the men they have arrested in violation of this order, which is as follows:

"Enrolling or recruiting officers, in the discharge of their duties, under the conscription or other acts, are enjoined not to remove or interfere with workmen or employees at the Nitre, Lead or Copper works or mines worked by Government officers or by contractors for the Ordinance Department, without first apprising and obtaining the consent of the superintendent officers in charge, who will be held strictly responsible for any abuse or evasion of the law.
S. Cooper, Adjutant and Inspector General."

All persons who have been taken from the Nitre works or Lead mines, are ordered to return to duty, and I will protect them in so doing, no mater who has taken them from their work, but I do not protect pretenders or shirkers from duty.
T. J. Finnie, Captain and Sup't. N. & M. Bureau
Knoxville *Daily Register*, December 14, 1862.

22 Fritters' options in Jackson
Twinkley Twinkle.
A war correspondent writes thus from Jackson, in this State:

An officer of my acquaintance, who is inordinately fond of "fritters," just dropped into a dwelling in Jackson, a day or two since, where this delicacy was smoking hot upon the table, and very politely asked to share the meal with the landlady. She graciously complied, and asked him to be seated. "Will you take these 'twinkley twinkle,' or on the 'dab?'" My friend was entirely ignorant of the meaning of these terms, but at a venture chose the former. He was soon enlightened. The ancient female dipped her not-over-clean fingers into a tumbler of molasses standing beside here, and allowing the drippings to fall upon the delicacy, presented it to him as "twinkley twinkle." "On the dab," was a spoonful of treacle upon the center of the "fritter." In some hotels sheets and tableclothes are convertible terms, and the former do double duty.

Nashville *Daily Union*, November 22, 1862.

25 "Why can you not use cotton for money? It has a very convenient price — 50 cents a pound."
Sherman sanctions "shinplasters" in Memphis

HDQRS. DISTRICT OF MEMPHIS, Memphis, November 25, 1862.

The Mayor and Council, City of Memphis:

GENTLEMAN: I regret to notice that you propose to issue a species of currency of denomination as low as 10 cents ("shinplasters") to swell the amount of bad money with which your community is already sufficiency afflicted.

The issuing of bills of credit by way of money is, in my judgment, in direct violation of the Constitution of the United States, and I think Congress at the last session passed a bill prohibiting all issues below $1, and provided a species of currency called the "post-office currency," which will soon gradually supplant the worthless trash which now is a disgrace to the name of money. As soon as possible, enough of this post-office money will come here and suffice for the wants of the people.

Inasmuch as we seem to be imitating the example of Mexico, rather than those high models of ancient and modern times that we were wont to do in times past, I would suggest a simpler and better currency for the times. In Mexico soap is money, and the people do their marketing through the medium of cakes of soap.

Why can you not use cotton for money? It has a very convenient price — 50 cents a pound. Put it up in pounds and fractions and it will form a far better currency than the miserable shinplasters you propose to issue. If cotton is king, it has the genuine stamp and makes money, is money; therefore I suggest that, instead of little bits of paper, you set to work and put up cotton in little parcels of 5, 10, 25, and 50 cents.

If it be my last act, I wish to spare the people of Memphis from the curse of any more bad money.

I am, &c.,
W. T. SHERMAN, Maj.-Gen.

OR, Ser. I, Vol. 17, pt. II, p. 875.

26 "Substitute Wanted

A substitute over forty-five years of age is wanted for three years or during the war. A liberal price will be paid. For further information apply at this office.

Chattanooga *Daily Rebel*, November 26, 1862.

30 Cupid and Confederate conscription confusion near Knoxville

MALICIOUS CONDUCT OF MAJOR RUCKER.

Some days ago Major Rucker was in conversation with a fair, fat and forty buxom widow of an adjoining county where by accident she mentioned the age of one of her admirers, saying that he was not quite thirty-nine. The Major made a mental note of the fact, and soon departed. He went straightway in pursuit of this juvenile admirer of the attractive widow, whom he had before learned was a little more than forty years of age. When he arrested Mr. Johnson, Rucker stated that he regretted to inform him that he was under the painful necessity of conscripting him. "I have learned," said Rucker, "from Widow _____ that you are only thirty-nine' she says that you told her so, and I feel it my duty to take you down to Col. Blake."

"Oh! ah! yes," said Mr. Johnson, "in fact sir, to tell you the truth, sir, I did lie just a little to the Widow _____ I wanted, yes — I wanted to get married — you understand, don't you Major."

"I don't understand anything about it," said Rucker, "you must go with me."

Mr. Johnson's knees smote one another, and in tremulous accents, he besought Major Rucker to permit him to send for the old family Bible. This was agreed to. In the mean time Rucker and his new levy proceeded to Col. Blake's Head Quarters. By the time they reached Knoxville, Rucker became satisfied that his follower was not less than three score years and ten. The Widower's hair dye was washed away, his false teeth had been removed, his form was bent by the immense pressure of mental anxiety.

Col. Blake wished to know why this antediluvian had been brought to him; but so complete had been the metamorphosis of the gay widower, that even Rucker blushed when he looked upon him.

The Family Bible came, and there it was written in the faded scrawl of Mr. Johnson's grand mother "Silus Jonsing baun in Bunkum, Nawth Calliny; Anny Domminy 1783!!"

Knoxville *Daily Register*, November 30, 1862.

___ Petition to Military Governor Andrew Johnson from women in Gordonsville [Smith County] to fight the Confederacy

Gordonsville Tenn. Nov [1862]
Hon. Andrew Johnson
Sir,

We the undersigned offer our services for the purpose of aiding to put down the rebellion and will be very much obliged if you will supply us with arms and if you will accept us please send them immediately. if not we will arm ourselves and bushwhack it.*

Papers of Andrew Johnson, Vol. 6, p. 45.

♦ DECEMBER ♦

1 "We skirmished right on a bed of sweet potatoes and cabbage": Sergeant George G. Sinclair's first combat

On picket duty seven miles from Nashville on the Nashville and Chattanooga railroad.

December 3, 1862

...

We had our maiden battle three days ago [December 1]. We were sent out on a foraging expedition and were assailed by some of Breckenridge's cavalry but we laid six or seven of them, they not doing us any damage in return. We are gaining

---

*Fifty-four women signed the petition, ranging in age from sixty to nine. Most were single, young women, and a number of mother-daughter and sister-sister combinations. Only a few were actually substantial property holders. See: Papers of Andrew Johnson, Vol. 6, fn. 1, p. 45. There is nothing to suggest that their petition was granted.

quite a reputation as a crack regiment and I tell you, we earn it too, for finer never turned into the field. Well on that day we were thrown out as skirmishers and we skirmished right on a bed of sweet potatoes and cabbage which were buried for winter use. We appropriated all that the whole company could carry. Our mess secured nearly a bushel and four hogsheads of cabbage. You may bet that we lived high while those lasted, they are out today. As we are out on picket, we shall try to replenish out stock of vegetable before tomarrow night

...

George G. Sinclair

Sinclair Correspondence

3 A West Tennessee Confederate Ghost
A Ghost Story.

We heard one of Gen. McCown's officers tell a hard story on yesterday. It seems that when McCown was in West Tennessee this officer was sent into a neighborhood where he was well known. He was riding in a buggy and overtook an old acquaintance and friend, named Robert Bond. Bond was on foot. The officer, after the usual salutations and inquiry after the news, asked Bond to take the buggy and drive on to the next house and await his coming that he was tired of riding, and wished to walk the intervening half mile. When the officer came up to the house the buggy was standing there and the horse tied to the gate.

The officer asked the ladies at the house what had become of Mr. Bond. They, amazed, answered that Bond had been killed in a skirmish near Corinth, and that his body had been brought home and buried on the day before the officer arrived.

He asked the ladies who had brought the buggy to the gate. They answered that there was no driver, that the horse came quietly to the gate and that one of their number had got out and tied him.

It is needless to state that the officer who made this statement discredits his own senses, but he is confident that he could not have mistaken Bond for another man, that his personal peculiarities were well known to him, but how he could have disappeared, and how a dead man could have driven off a horse and buggy, and then vanished, or why his disembodied spirit should have appeared to him when he did not even know that Bond was dead, are questions often asked by the officer referred to. He is, evidently, surely puzzled by the occurrence as were his auditors by its narration.— Knoxville *Register*.

Montgomery *Weekly Advertiser*, December 3, 1862.

4 Capture of outpost, Stones River at Stewart's Ferry

Report of Maj. D. W. Holman, C. S. Army.

CAMP NEAR LA VERGNE, TENN., December 4, 1862.

CAPT.: I have the honor to report that, with the approval of the brigadier-general commanding, I left my encampment near Stone's River about 12 o'clock last night with 50 men, a part of Capt. [J. T.] Martin's company, of my battalion, and proceeded in the direction of Stewart's Ferry, on Stone's River, 12 miles distant, for the purpose of capturing some of the enemy's pickets. By traveling obscure roads and recrossing Stone's River about 1½ miles above Stewart's Ferry, we came in between the enemy's main force at McWhirtersville [Donelson] and Stewart's Ferry. When within a quarter of a mile of the pickets, I dismounted 20 men, and sent them 300 yards ahead, and ordered them to proceed noiselessly to the place first ordering them to surrender, and, if they refused, to fire. A part of the mounted men under Capt. Martin, and the balance under Lieut.'s [T.] Banks and [A. S.] Chapman, were so disposed on either side of the road as to catch any who might attempt to make their way to the main force. Sergeant [J. M.] Critz, who commanded the squad of dismounted men, when within 15 steps of the reserve, ordered them to surrender. They refused, and one of them fired. Immediately my 20 men fired; 1 lieutenant and 2 privates were left dead upon the spot. I think the whole reserve (9 men) were either killed or wounded; but the cedar undergrowth was so very thick that we did not see them, nor could not, without carefully searching, which we did not have time to do. Three horses were killed, and we captured 6, with bridles, saddles, &c., 2 excellent Belgian guns, 1 pistol, several India rubber coats, &c. The two vedettes, who were some distance from the reserve, made their escape through the bushes, and we did not have time to pursue them. Being within 1 mile or less of a large force, I thought it but prudent to move away at once, and with as much rapidity as practicable. At sunrise

this morning I got back to my camp without the loss of a man, horse, or anything else.
...
OR, Ser. I, Vol. 20, pt. I, pp. 30–31.

8 Major-General Rosecrans order to Major-General Thomas to hire spies
Nashville, December 8, 1862
Maj.-Gen. THOMAS, Gallatin:
Hire and keep spies out over the river and in all directions. Get butternut clothing, if necessary.
W. S. ROSECRANS, Maj.-Gen.
OR, Ser. I, Vol. 20, pt. II, p. 139.

8 Excerpt from Corporal William Records,' 72nd Indiana Infantry, letter home
Castillion Springs, Tenn. Dec. 8th 1862
...Since I last wrote I have seen some of the horrors of war. On Thursday one of my mess mates, P.S. Nowlin took verry sick, and on Friday night at 22 min of one ocl'k he died — he never knew anything aft 4 P.M. Thursday. It took 3 men to hold him in his bed until 10 P.M. — Then 2 could hold him. he had to be held until 2 in the morning. B.F. Magee & I were with him unto the last. Saturday we burried him. Sunday morning we heard canonading at Hartsville and before we got our breakfast we were ordered into line, then we shoved out for Hartsville, part of the time on double quick, and part of the time on quick time. the distance is 8 miles. we got there by eleven A.M. but considerable of that time had been used up in feeling our way with Skirmishers —

The place had been guarded by one brigade of our Division. before we got there the enemy captured it and burnt the camp but we were so close that they did not get time to destroy everything. They left most of the Quarter Masters stores and wagon loads of arms. We got on the battle field just as they left. The camp was all on fire and burning. They made the prisoners wade the river as soon as the Surrender was made, and when we got there the enemy was just crossing. our artillery took position and shelled them like fury. I will now tell you the part that Elisha and I played. Elisha kept up all the time. but as I had been sick so long I was weak and had to fall out once when we were marching in line of battle. — that is the hardest way to march that I ever marched. we had to go through brush through fields over fences, through door yards, through houses, across gulches, up hills and over stone walls. after going about one mile in that way, the position of the enemy was found out. we then marched in column by the right flank. I then got up with the Co. and kept up until we got within about one mile of the scene of battle when they got to running and hollooing so that I could not keep up. but I followed on. I had had no water since we started. So by this time I was almost famished for water. Some of the boys eat snow, it being 2 in, but I was afraid it would do more harm than good. as I went along I noticed a large amount of arms stacked, but never once thought of being near a battle field, when all of a suden I came on a dead man! he was a rebel. in three steps father I came up to 2 more. one I noticed had a canteen. I shook it and found it was full of water. I was so awful thirsty that I took it off of him and drank the water. he was yet warm. After leaving them I came to where our dead lay. they were laying verry thick. they belonged mostly to the 104 Ill as that was the only regt in the whole Brigade that acted like brave men. The two Ohio Regts 106 & 108 showed the white feather. one broke without firing the other fired one round. Our men had 50 killed out right, besides many wounded. The rebels about as many in killed as near as can be ascertained. Elisha was among the detail to burry the dead. — in passing over the field, I counted 31 union men and one capt., 6 rebels and one Lieut. Making in all 39 dead that I saw. It is a horrible thing....
your affectionate bro.
W.H. Records
...
Records' Correspondence.

12 Pup Tents
We have all seen the long wagon trains that encumbers our Army on the march and we know how large a part is taken up with bulky tents that usually fail to reach us when we need them worse is rainy weather. Our movements are frequently delayed by the necessity for keeping them under our protecting wing. Morgan and Wheeler the rough riders of the Confederacy are wont to swoop down upon them at unexpected times and places. They are seldom able to carry away the wagons so the torch usually reduces them to blackened piles of scrap iron while the mules gallop away with their captors without a murmur. The grapevine has for sometime been telling us that every man

shall be his own baggage wagon and the report was confirmed today when Lieut. Dexter exhibited in camp the newly contrived "Shelter tent" which is to take [the] place of our "Sibleys" and each man is to carry for himself. It is nothing but a strip of canvas 6 × 10 feet which will cover about as much space as a dog house. We therefore call them "pup tents." We are expected to stretch them over a ridge pole and stake them to the ground on each side in the shape of the letter A, and then crawl under them on all fours. We measured Lieut. Weld of Co. E with one of the pup tents and found him too long at both ends and now we are waiting for instructions from the Government how to make him fit. We don't know whether to saw off the ends or to drive them in.

Diary of Lyman S. Widney

13 Extent of damages to one Madison County farmer's property after six months of occupation by Federal forces

I am at a loss what to do. I was well fixed here before the war, even to within the last six months but how different now. My place is a perfect waste. House burned down, fencing pretty well all burned, not an acre enclosed on the place, no hogs-about 130 killed. My cattle, except 2 milch cows, killed; 1 mule and 3 good horses taken. The planks and weather boarding and part of the roof of [the] lint room and most of the boarding of the gin house [are] gone. My gin stand broken to pieces & ruined, every cast wheel broke, saws bent, part of the thresher taken. My harness run through the cutting knife and cut in pieces about an inch long. My timber going fast. Farming implements destroyed or burnt up. Had most of them packed in [the] cellar. At least 1,000 barrels corn foraged away....

Robert H. Cartmell Diary.

15 Federal report relative to Jefferson Davis' attendance at John H. Morgan's wedding and speech in Murfreesborough

NASHVILLE, TENN., December 15, 1862–1.10 P.M.

Maj.-Gen. HALLECK:

Reports of last evening fully confirmed. Jeff. Davis attended John H. Morgan's wedding last night: was serenaded, and made a speech, in which he said Lincoln's proclamation put black and white on an equality. Urged them to fight until death, and to hold Middle Tennessee at all hazards, until Grant could be whipped. Bragg ordered all Kentucky and Tennessee exiles conscripted. Buckner, Breckinridge, and Hanson protested and threatened to resign. Jeff. took the matter in hand.

Things will be ripe soon.

W. S. ROSECRANS, Maj.-Gen.

OR, Ser. I, Vol. 20, pt. II, p. 179.

16 Slaughter house workers sought in Knoxville

LABORERS WANTED.

We are authorized by Col. Blake to say that all conscripts whom we employ at our port house will be detailed. We will pay good wages and sell each hand ten pounds of salt at ten cents per pound every Saturday night. Hands from a distance will be furnished with good house to camp in.— They should bring blankets with them.

Knoxville *Daily Register*, December 16, 1862.

17 A night at the Nashville theater; an excerpt from the diary of John Hill Fergusson, 10th Illinois Volunteer Infantry

...the morning very cold and windy N. Fancher and My Self went up town about 9 o'clock with some coffee to traid for a coffee pot we got 35 cts ... we went to the theater in the evening it was 25 cts each, the pirfurmince acted was king Henry the 2nd it was very interesting but the wind up play was better then the first it was [about] a gentleman how was aposed to wemen and brought his son up to the age of 18 in perfect ignorance of wemen he had never saw one nor even [knew] that such a thing ever existed he made a contract with a gentleman in the ciup for him and his son to live with him whare he could have an opertunity of giving his son a good education this gent in the city had a lovely dater she was to be she was to be locked up in his room when he was at liberty in the house no woman was to be seen by him only the old lady and she was as crass as 2 sticks [?] there was no danger of him falling in love with hir the girl happened to be out side and was lamenting what a pitty it was that Such a lively young man should be kept in ignorance of a woman the young man happened to rais the window and look out and for the first time in his life beheld a lovely girl in all the splendure that could adorn the human frame! He opened the door and run out but the girl got out of sight before he came out the 2 old men and old woman run after him and catched him the expected what he saw and wanted to know of his father what it was he seen he said he never seen anything in his life that looked so pritty his father told him it was a burd a kind of buzzard and take care of them they ware a queer kind of burd , they would betray him and leed him astray they took him into the house when they thought the girls door was locked up and all was safe they let the young man run around out side again he was not satisfied he wanted to hunt up the pretty burd he seen the young Lady was as anxiouis to see him as he was to see hir she had a way of opening her door from the in side so she slipped out and watched the young man running around keeping concealed behind the cornors at last he got his eye on hir again and rant to catch the burd but she run all around when he found he was not likely to catch hir he get some corn and scattered it down for hir and said hear pritty burd eat some corn she stoped running then waited some she stood and looked at him for a short time then told him she was no burd then he wanted to know what she was that looked so pritty he said the first time he saw her he felt all over he did not know how she went on to explain what she was and that wemen ware for men to love by this time the 2 old men and old woman came running out in an aful fix and no sooner a past then the ware in each others arms as tight as again there grips and fall back in there sick buts that concludes to gave it.

John Hill Fergusson Diary, Book 2.

24 Christmas Eve Dance and Executions in Confederate Murfreesboro

An Account of Two Very Different Scenes — A Ball and an Execution.

A letter from Murfreesboro', Tenn., dated the 26th ult., gives an account of two scenes of camp life — a ball and an execution. The writer says:

On Christmas Eve [1862] the officers of the First Louisiana and Second Kentucky regiments gave a ball at the Court House in Murfreesboro', which proved a magnificent affair and complete success. The beauty and fashion of this little city and many distinguished officers were present. The decorations were exceedingly handsome. Among them I noticed four large "B's" constructed of evergreens: "Beauregard and Bragg, of La.;" "Buckner and Breckinridge, of Ky." Over the windows were the names, "Pensacola," "Donelson," "Shiloh," "Santa Rosa," and "Hartsville," all en-wreathed with cedar. Conspicuous were numerous United States flags — Union down — trophies belonging to Gen. John H. Morgan, furnished for the occasion by his lady. New Year's Eve will be celebrated by another ball to be given by the officers of the 9th and 9th Kentucky regiments and Cobb's Battery. Truly the grim soldiers feel fond of laying aside their stern occupation for the smiles of fair ladies. I hope they may not experience another Waterloo; but instead, when begins the "sound of revelry by night," may the beauty and chivalry enjoy themselves without interruption from the cannon's opening roar.

In strong contrast with such scenes comes the announcement of five military executions in one day — one by hanging, the rest by shooting. The first was a spy, a traitor, and a thief, named Gray. The crime committed by the other four was desertion. It was my duty to witness the execution of one of the latter. As the brigade was being formed on three sides of a square, the clouds grew dark and heavy as if the very heavens frowned upon the bloody deed about to be enacted. The troops remained in one of the heaviest rain storms I ever remember, until the prisoner was brought in the centre of the square, riding in a wagon, followed by a hearse. After bidding a few friends adieu, he, with a firm step, without kneeling or being blindfolded, faced the firing party composed of one lieutenant, one sergeant, and fifteen men — twelve of the guns were loaded with balls and three with blank cartridges. At 12 o'clock Lieutenant B. gave the command "ready!" "aim!" "fire!" when the prisoner fell dead, pierced by eleven balls. Some of these men were arrested after an absence of six months. I would advise all deserters who may be skulking around the cities of the Confederacy, to return while Gen. Bragg offers them pardon.

Savannah [Georgia] *Republican*, January 10, 1863.

28 A tête-à-tête between enemies prior to the battle at Stones River

An Incident of the Battle of Stone's River.
Correspondence of the Nashville *Dispatch*.
Camp at Murfreesboro', Feb. 9, 1863.

I was thinking every scene of the late tragedy played by the armies of the Cumberland and Mississippi had been shown in some way or other; but there remains one to which I was an eye witness, that gives distinction to no particular character;

yet, for its novelty, (as such is generally a constituent of tragedy,) is somewhat interesting. On the 27th of December, our army arrived at Stewart's Creek, ten miles distant from Murfreesboro.' The following day being Sabbath [28th], and our General being devout, nothing was done, except to cross a few companies on the left as skirmishers, our right being watched by the enemy's, as well as ours; both extending along the creek on opposite sides. Despite of orders, our boys would occasionally shut an eye at the Confederates, who were ever ready to take the hint. This was kept up until evening, when the boys, finding they were effecting nothing at such long range, quit shooting, and concluded they would "talk it out." When the following occurred:

Federal (at the top of his voice) — Halloo! boys, what regiment?

Confederate — Eighth Confederate.

Fed. — Bully for you.

Confed. — What's your regiment?

Fed. — Eighth and twenty-first Kentucky.

Confed. — All right.

Fed. — Boys, have you got any whisky?

Confed. — Plenty of her.

Fed. — How'll you trade for coffee?

Confed. — Would like to accommodate you, but never drink it while the worm goes.

Fed. — Let's meet at the creek and have a social chat.

Confed. — Will you shoot?

Fed. — Upon the honor of a gentleman, not a man shall. Will you shoot?

Confed. — I give you as good assurance.

Fed. — Enough said, come on.

Confed. — Leave your arms.

Fed. — I have left them. Do you leave yours?

Confed. — I do.

Whereupon both parties started for the creek to a point agreed upon. Meeting almost simultaneously, we (the Federals) were, in a modulated tone, addressed in the usual unceremonious style of a soldier, by [:] Confed. — Halloo, boys! how do you make it?

Federal — Oh! bully, bully!

Confed. — This is rather an unexpected armistice.

Fed. — That's so.

Confed. — Boys what do you think of the Proclamation?

Fed. — We think it will suit a *nigger* and an Abolitionist, but not gentlemen.

Confed. — Now your heads are level.

Fed. — Boys, are you going to make a stand at Murfreesboro?

Confed. — That is a leading question; notwithstanding, I will venture to say it will be the bloodiest ten miles you ever traveled.

Thus the conversation went on for some time, until a Confederate Captain, (Miller, of Gen. Wheeler's Cavalry,) came down, requesting an exchange of papers. On being informed we had none, he said he would give us his anyhow, and wrapping a stone in the paper, threw it across. Some compliments were passed, when the Captain suggested, as it was getting late, we had better quit the conference; whereupon both parties, about twenty each, began to leave with, "Good by, boys;" "if ever I meet you in battle, I'll spare you." So we met and parted, not realizing we were enemies. My God, when will this unnatural war have an end! — when shall friend cease to seek the life of friend, and mankind once more realize the blessings of peace?

Eighth Kentucky.

Nashville *Dispatch*, February 21, 1863.

30 "From the Front."

Our Army is still in line of battle a few miles in front of the town awaiting in momentary expectancy the opening of the conflict. The advance of the Federal columns steadily continues and without doubt this morning's son will herald in the great tournament of arms. At various intervals during yesterday the sullen roar of cannon and an occasional crash of musketry threw a momentary thrill across the heart. It was only the introduction of the mighty combatants to each other. Later in the day silence reigned throughout — the precursor of the coming storm. We could not gather up news other than that our losses had been immaterial. Tomorrow there will be much to say.

Murfreesboro *Daily Rebel Banner*, December 30, 1862.

31 Kate Cumming's reflections on the old and new years

The last day of 1862 — how teeming with wonderful events has been the past year!

The South has suffered, O, how terribly! Thousands and tens of thousands of precious lives have been sacrificed to the god of war. In every state of our beloved land there has been a temple erected to the insatiate Moloch. This is not all; women and children have been left homeless, and even driven out into the pitiless storm, and even the bitterest frowns of nature have had more kindness in them than the hearts of our ruthless invaders....

How hard it is to think of all this knowing ... without feeling hate, bitter hate, toward these whom are the cause of it! We were more than mortal were it otherwise, but I trust that with it all we will leave vengeance to Him to whom it belongs.

Amid all this suffering the star of hope for our cause shines brighter and brighter, although in the West we have lost much territory. Our armies are improving every way. They are better clad and better fed than they were. We have much sickness, but nothing to what we have had.

Life in camp has improved, physically and morally. The medical department has also improved. Surgeons have to be thoroughly examined before receiving commissions. Congress has passed a law making provision for ladies (where they can be had) to take charge of domestic arrangements in hospitals.

Manufactories has arisen where before the way they were not known. Women, who thought such things impossible are making shoes and knitting socks. In every form-house the spinning-wheel and loom is heard. Fields are teeming with grain, where once grew cotton and tobacco. We have enough vessels running the blockade to keep us in tea and coffee, and cattle from Texas to keep us in beef. In fact, if the war lasts much longer, we will be the most independent people in the world.

Although we have lost many great and good men, numbers have risen to take their place. The foe have work yet before them; they have to conquer Lee, Jackson, Long street, Hill and a host of others in Virginia, with their invincible armies. Beauregard at Charleston; Hindman and Price in the far west; the ubiquitous Morgan; and last, though by no means last, the army; of Tennessee, and its veteran commanders, Johnston and Bragg. I have not forgotten noble little Vicksburg and her heroic defenders; with these and God's blessing, I trust that the time is not far distant, when dove-eyed peace will hover o'er our now distracted land.

Mr. Burgess, a member of the battery my brother is in, called this evening and left some money for Mrs. W., a Christmas donation from Mrs. Otis of Mobile. It is rumored that a battle has commenced at Murfreesboro. May God give us the victory!

Cumming, *A Journal of Hospital Life*, pp. 54–55.

DECEMBER 31, 1862–JANUARY 3, 1863 THE BATTLE OF STONES RIVER (MURFREESBORO).

1863

♦ JANUARY ♦

1 Excerpts from George F. Cram's [105th Ohio] letter to his mother

...

Yesterday I was talking with a very aged man who was a soldier in 1812. He said that when the excitement first broke out about this war the "big men" went around the country telling the people that Lincoln's robbers were coming down here for no other purpose than to set the Negroes free, incite insurrections, and pillage the country. Is it a wonder that the poor ignorant commoners deluded into this belief should rise and fight even without clothes, for the defense as they thought of their liberty, poor ignorant wretches! How much have the rebel chiefs to account for!

...

Last week our quarter master got us a lot of bacon that so rotten you could smell it all over the camp. If we could only get salt beef, a great many of the boys now sick would be well. Another man has just died, while I was writing the above. He had been sick for some time and suddenly dropped dead. My health continues pretty good for I take care of myself and keep as far from the Dr. as possible....

This morning we received news of a federal success at Murfreesboro. It gives the camp a cheerful aspect to hear good news....

Letters of George F. Cram

1 An initial report on the battle of Stones River
Battle Near Murfreesboro'.

The city was considerably excited yesterday by rumors of a sanguinary battle being in progress near Murfreesboro', between the armies of Rosecrans and Bragg, but these rumors were of such a contradictory character, as to render it impossible to arrive at anything certain in regard to the fight. It appears that the skirmishing Tuesday was simply for the purpose of securing positions which the contending parties desired to occupy. At an early hour yesterday morning, by the time it was light, it is said the battle commenced by an attack upon the Federal lines by Gen. Van Dorn, and the reports brought down represent the fight that ensued as very obstinate and bloody; but we could learn nothing as to the probable extent of the loss on either side....

Nashville *Dispatch*, January 1, 1863.

3 A skirmish at Stones River; an excerpt from the diary of Colonel John Beatty

...

Rifle pits are being dug, and I am ordered to protect the workmen. The rebels hold a strip of woods in our immediate front, and we get up a lively skirmish with them. Our men, however, appear loth to advance far enough to afford the necessary protection to the workers. Vexed at their unwillingness to venture out, I ride forward and start over a line to which I desire the skirmishers to advance, and discover, before I have gone twenty yards, that I have done a foolish thing. A hundred muskets open on line from the woods; the eyes of my own brigade and of other troops are on me, and I can't back out. I quicken the pace of my horse somewhat, and continue my perilous course. The bullets whistle like bees about my head, but I ride the whole length of the proposed skirmish line, and get back to the brigade in safety. Colonel Humphreys, of the Eighty-eighth Indiana, comes up to me, and with a tremor in his voice, which indicates much feeling, says: "My God, Colonel, never do that again!" The caution is unnecessary. I had already made up my mind not to do it again. We keep up a vigorous skirmish with the enemy for hours, losing now and then a man; but later in the day we are relieved of this duty and retire to a quieter place.

Beatty, *Citizen Soldier*, pp. 208–209.

4 Surgical operations after the Battle of Murfreesboro, excerpt from the diary of John C. Spence

...

The surgeons were quite busy dressing the wounds of soldiers brought in from the battle field. Their operations resembled a *butchers* stall-here and there a soldier laid upon a table, under the influence of chloriform, undergoing amputation of arms and legs, which were thrown in a corner of the room-and, from the manner that many of them worked at the business, it would seem that they would be better employed working on the leg of a *calf*, than a man, scarcely distinguishing a tendon from an artery.

Unfortunate for the poor soldiers who has to be the subject for these *quacks* who are sent to the army or go to learn their business. This *humanity?*

The three college buildings were used as hospitals, all the churches, several of the store rooms, and several large dwelling houses. The seats out of the churches and shelving and counters out of the store rooms. Nearly all the families had one or two wounded men in care.

Spence Diary.

12 Egalitarian embalming
Embalming the Dead — A Process Practicable to All.

The modern processes by which the bodies of officers and soldiers of the army have been embalmed and restored to their friends is not the least of the blessings which science has bestowed upon the world since the beginning of the war. The expense of this process, in most cases, places its advantages beyond the reach of people of moderate means. Those who have adopted the business as a profession, are in some cases, extortionous in their charges, particularly where officers are the subjects; and the whole matter is surrounded by professional secrecy impenetrable to persons of unscientific tastes.

A matter of so great general utility and importance should not be monopolized or turned wholly to individual emolument. It may not be out of place to give, in this connection, a simple recipe by which any physician or surgeon of ordinary capacity can embalm the dead, and preserve them from decomposition or putrefaction for a length of time to answer all practical requirements. The following was handed to me shortly after the battle of Antietam, by the Medical Director of the Ninth Army Corps:

The liquid chloride of zinc injected into the cerebral or femoral artery, will preserve bodies from decomposition or putrefaction for a great length of time.

The mode of obtaining this liquid is to take (say) one quart of hydrochloric acid to an earthen vessel, and add small pieces of zinc until reaction ceases

...

H. W. Rivers, Surgeon of Volunteers
Ninth Army Corps.

Nashville *Daily Union*, January 12, 1863.

ca. January 15, 1863 Skirmish in Scott County near the New River settlement: the battle for the bacon

A SKIRMISH

From the Richmond *Enquirer,* Jan. 20 [1863]

Capt. Thomas Butler has been the hero of quite a gallant little achievement, on the edge of Scott County, Tenn. It appeared that at the New River settlement there had recently been stationed two companies of Federal soldiers, under command of Capt. Noah Doherty, a Tennessee renegade from Anderson County. Capt. Butler, on learning of their presence, at the head of thirty men, started in search of them. On reaching the spot where they varmints were encamped, Capt. B. demanded the surrender of the whole party, which was responded to by a volley from ten or fifteen muskets. One ball grazed the Captain's lip, and trimmed his moustache in the most approved style of the tonsorial art. A brisk skirmish ensued, in which six of the Abolitionists were killed, a number wounded and several captured. The remainder took to the woods.

The fruits of this little skirmish were the capture of some fifteen or twenty horses, a like number of Belgian rifles, two or three thousand pounds of bacon, and a like amount of flour, besides the capture of a Captain and eight or ten men.

New York *Times*, January 25, 1863.

16 The sniping death of one Federal soldier in September 1862, according to the testimony of Col. E. M. McCook, given on January 16, 1863

...

Question. At what place was it that you attempted to burn the corn fields and at what time was it?

It was after we left Murfreesborough, at that place where one of the soldiers had been shot in a field. He had unbuttoned his pantaloons and sat down to relieve himself, when he was shot out of a house. I found his body lying there. I tried to burn the fields. Every person ran away from there; there were none but women left, no men.

...

We were on the march; he was one of the soldiers who were in advance and had left the column.

OR, Ser. I, Vol. 16, pt. I, pp. 328–329.

17 Brigadier General Gideon J. Pillow's report on progress of his conscript sweep

HDQRS. BUREAU OF VOLUNTEERS AND CONSCRIPTS,

Fayetteville, January 17, 1863.

Col. G. W. BRENT,

Assistant Adjutant-Gen.:

I reached here this afternoon and immediately entered upon the duty preparatory to the organization.

I expected to get everything ready for a forward movement by Wednesday morning. My purpose was first to rake Bedford County, in which there are 1,500 men liable to duty under the conscript law. I was anxious to clean out that county by one movement, and doing it at once to avoid giving alarm.

A partial movement over one portion of the county will give the alarm, and cause the conscripts to scatter and hide out.

...

I will rapidly sweep Middle Tennessee to the enemy's lines if the cavalry is furnished....

I shall, with such force as can be armed and fitted for the field, leave on Wednesday morning for the movement on Bedford.

....

GID. J. PILLOW, Brig.-Gen., C. S. Army, Chief of Bureau of Volunteers and Conscripts.

OR, Ser. IV, Vol. 2, p. 362.

19 Witnessing the whipping of a slave in Nashville; an excerpt from the diary of John Hill Fergusson, 10th Illinois Volunteer Infantry

... we had orders ... to guard a large camp of about 2000 conterbands we have to be on duty every other day.... I was sergeant [of the guard] taking in the afternoon I chanced to go up into a Large hall: whare I beheld for the first time in my life a oversear over the Neagares : flogging a great big darkey. The darky lay on [his] belley across a Mess chist with his head hanging over on the side next to the whipper his coat was pulled up to his shoulders he Lay and took upward of 100 lashes with a black snack whip the darkey never said a word he would only rais his head once in a while and Look up the whipper would turn the butt end of the whip and stack him on the head and dam him to keep his head down I had no oppertunity to see his back after the flogging but his head was cut in different places with the but of the whip I thought it rather sevear after the darkies flying from bondage and coming to us for protection.

John Hill Fergusson Diary, Book 2.

21 Boiler plate opinion in Chattanooga

We have not heard as yet of a negro police in Nashville, but from all accounts, that city is full of blackguards.

"By Lincoln we live, by Lincoln we move, and by Lincoln we have our being" is the latest prayer of thanksgiving among the Yankee lick-spittles and nigger thieves.

Chattanooga *Daily Rebel,* January 21, 1863.

21 A newspaper advertisement by W. D. Humphries, Confederate Post Ordnance Officer in Chattanooga

Powder and Lead

We need all the lead we can obtain. I will pay a liberal price for it, delivered at the Ordnance Depot, or give Powder at a fair *pro rata* of exchange. Bring it on at once, and don't disdain small quantities.

Chattanooga *Daily Rebel,* January 21, 1863.

23 Daniel Ellis' account of the murders of James Taylor, Samuel Tatum, Alfred Kite, Alexander Dugger and David Shuffield, East Tennessee Unionists seeking to escape Confederate East Tennessee.

...

When the rebels first fired, poor Taylor surrendered; they continued to shoot at him, while he begged them to treat as a prisoner, but instead of this, one of these incarnate devils ran up and soon silenced in, by shooting the top of his head off with a musket. Two of them then caught him by his feet, and pitched him violently over a large rock down a steep declivity, which bruised his body and broke his limbs in a most shocking manner; and, not yet content with this display of barbarity, they then threw great rocks upon him. They then took from his mangled person a very fine watch and a considerable sum of money. Tatum was killed nearly at the same time that Taylor was, he being first wounded in the shoulder, and then dispatched with great cruelty. The other three men ran some distance, while the rebels were shooting at them as fast as they could; at length they surrendered, and commenced imploring for mercy; but they might as well have asked for mercy from a gang of blood-thirsty tigers as to take it at the hands of these devils in human shape, for they were entirely heedless of their piteous cries and lamentations. In vain these poor supplicating prisoners told their reckless and infuriate[d] captors that they had done nothing deserving death, and were only trying to keep out of the Southern army. All their asseverations could not save them from the dreadful doom which their inflexible tormentors at once proceeded to assign them. Their hands were tied behind them, and they were taken to a bending sapling and hung. Some of the rebel soldiers took the ropes which they carried with them for the purpose of carrying forage on their horses, and tied them around the necks of their victims, while others would hold them up until the rope was tied to a limb, and them let them go. In this way all three of these poor men were hung up to torture, and suffer a thousand pangs of death; for they were hung so as not to break their necks, but rather to be choked by degrees, which was the refined and cruel mode of punishment which was resorted to by these inhuman murderers. Two of the poor fellows, before they were hung, begged hard for a time to pray; but even this privilege was not allowed them. The other one had been severely wounded in the beginning of the bloody affray, and was not able to talk. While they were suspended by their necks, and before life was extinct, they were treated with the greatest brutality, by their reckless murderers beating them with their guns. Captain Roby Brown, a citizen of Johnson County, Tennessee, and one of the home guard in that county, enjoyed himself very much at this miserable feast of blood. He had a complete frolic around them while they were struggling in all the agonies of a terrible death. He knocked them with his gun, and would then dance upon them, and turn them around violently, telling them to "face their partner." He would say to them that "he did not like to dance with any person that would not face him;" while they, with their tongues as black as ink protruding out of their mouths, and their eyes bursting from their sockets, exhibited a spectacle of horror which was enough to strike terror to the very soul of any person who was not perfectly hardened in villainy and crime, and callous to the most wretched displays of human suffering, and steeped in the deepest depths of infamy. But I can not presume to say that this most desperate and incorrigible scoundrel, Roby Brown, was in the possession of a human heart; if he was, it was entirely impervious to human feeling and to human sympathy, and was as cold and hard as the glacier rock of Mount Jura's bleakest hill-top. He may rest assured that he will receive a just recompense of reward for his terrible crimes, both in this world and in the world to come, for an avenging Nemesis will pursue him with her terrible whip of scorpions around the whole orb of his earthly existence; and when the Dim Unknown shall unlock the casket which confines his guilty soul in its tenement of clay, and hurries it to appear before the great Omnipotent in all its naked deformity, there he will receive that just retribution which in iniquitous and wicked life richly deserves, in the "everlasting fire prepared for the devil and his angels."

...

Thrilling Adventures for Daniel Ellis, pp. 107–110.

25 "...I can have the fun of shooting at Yankees...." a Texas Ranger's letter home from Middle Tennessee

Mr. Polk Childress, who in Capt. Houston's Company, Terry's Texas Rangers, wrote to his mother, Jan. 25th, from near Shelbyville, from which we take the following:

"I went all through the Murfreesboro fight and never received a scratch. One Regiment lost sixty four killed and wounded; our company three; Ellis and Burns supposed to be badly wounded, and Blair shot through the arm. Our company has only fifty men, officers and all; it is next to the smallest company in the Regiment.

I have been in the war sixteen months, and can stay that much longer if necessary, but I would like to have peace and go home; but I have never regretted coming to Tennessee, where I can have the fun of shooting at Yankees, occasionally. It would have killed me to have been compelled to lay in one of the forts on the frontier, doing nothing; here I have something to keep me alive and stirring; and I consider the good health I have had owing to the constant exercise. I have plenty of money, a good horse, six-shooter and sharpshooter.

San Antonio *Semi-Weekly News,* March 16, 1863.

26 Confederate Engineer's plans for the fortification of Chattanooga

ENGINEER'S OFFICE, Chattanooga, January 26, 1863.

Gen. J. E. JOHNSON, Cmdg. Department No. 2, Chattanooga, Tenn.:

GEN.: According to your instructions I have the honor to submitting to you a small sketch in order to fortify Chattanooga. I shall not undertake to demonstrate the utility of fortifying that place. Every one can see at once in looking at the map of the country that it is one of the most strategical points of this department. Consequently I will proceed at once the explanation of the system of fortifications I respectfully propose to your approval. My first object in locating these fortifications has been to study the probable approaches by which the enemy can attack this point. I am arrived to the conclusion that Chattanooga can be approached only from three different points: First, by the Walden's Ridge road north of the river; second, by crossing the river some distance above and coming by the way of Harrison or Cleveland; third, by crossing the river below at Battle Creek, or at Kelley's Ferry, and coming through Lookout Mountain. I propose to defend the first approach (north of the river) with the works Nos. 1, 2, 3, and 4. Each of them is located on a commanding position, and are combined together in order to concentrate their fires on any points the enemy might take on the opposite bank of the river. A more efficient defense can be made by occupying the two points marked 13 and 14, and building a pontoon bridge over the river for communication. Such bridge might be very useful, too, for other purpose. The second approach (by crossing the river below) is to be defended by the works Nos. 4, 5, 6, 7, 8, 9, and 10, all of which are located on commanding positions and arranged together in order to cross their fires. The third approach (through Lookout Mountain) is to be defended by the works Nos. 11 and 12, on the flank of Lookout Mountain, and in case of necessity assisted by the works Nos. 8, 9, and 10. All the works are to be provided with a magazine. Besides, I propose a central magazine for depot, to be put in the work No. 1. I shall speak of the armament of these works in a few days.

I have the honor to be, very respectfully, your obedient servant,

JAS. NOCQUET, Maj. and Chief Engineer, Department, No. 2.

OR, Ser. I, Vol. 52, pt. II, p. 417.

27 An 89th Illinois Volunteer Sergeant's thinking about the Emancipation Proclamation; an excerpt from George G. Sinclair's letter home, from camp in the Murfreesboro environs

...I am tempted to think a little differently for all or most of our generals have gone to Washington and to us, we have it here, find out what we are fight for whether it is altogether for the *nigger* or the *Union* and Constitution *as it was*. If the nigger is the object and Abe Lincoln's Proclamation still to be the main feature and guide for the prosecution of this unholy war against our own countrymen, then I am out of it forever and shall act conscientiously in leaving the army. There are other news too that we have started some excitement and hopes that it may be so, that was of the states of Wisconsin, Illinois, Indiana and Ohio repudiating the President's Proclamation of September 22nd 1862, their legislation refusing to raise another dollar or another man to carry on the war with and farther to recall all the troops that each of the states have in the field unless the President recalled his proclamation. I hope this may be so for them, it will give the nigger loving quality a chance to fight for the freedom of their homes having been deceived in the object of this war and swindled into enlisting to preserve the Union when in fact it was only a cloak to raise men to fight their abolition battles.

...

Sinclair Correspondence

28 Child killed playing with a pistol

Probable Fatal Accident.—We regret to learn, that a serious, if not fatal, accident occurred to a son of Mr. B. Clemons yesterday morning. It appears that a playmate of his was amusing himself with a loaded pistol, when it exploded, the ball entering little Battle's groin, inflicting a dangerous wound, from which it is feared he will not recover. Some persons must be to blame for allowing a boy so young to have possession of a pistol, either loaded or otherwise. Such things should be always kept out of reach of children.

Nashville *Dispatch*, January 28, 1863.

30 Newspaper report on the condition of the Confederate Army at Tullahoma after the Battle of Stones River

OUR ARMY IN MIDDLE TENNESSEE.

Tullahoma is a melancholy place. It is a little wayside depot, with a few squalid huts, a few framed housed and cottages, and a great many body lice-just now. It was once a famous locality for maple sugar and gin cocktails. Devilish little of both "at last advises." Camps, soldiers, and snow now predominate. The ground is covered with snow. It flies through the crevices of this tent, even as I write. A motley tent this, I tell you—made out of a Brussels carpet and a coffee sack. Four of us occupy it and pass our time in martial meditations fancy free. Lord, if the General could only hear us! However, we regard this situation as a good one because it isn't likely to bring us into a fight shortly. Fighting, since Murfreesboro, is at a discount....

That Murfreesboro business was bloody, you can yet see the traces of it. An empty sleeve now and again, or two crutches, or a face with a big patch on the side of its head. But the boys are in good spirits, never saw them better. I meet many an old friend, "Well, how goes it old boy?" says he, "Sorry you were not with us down there, but-better luck next time Jolly old fight!" For endurance, personal daring and enthusiastic onset it has not been equaled since the time the war began. Here's a health to its heroes!"

(signed) "BUSTEMENTE."

Chattanooga *Daily Rebel* January 30, 1863.

31 Guerrilla raid on railroad in the Richland Woods

GALLATIN, February [1], 1863.

Col. C. GODDARD, Assistant Adjutant-Gen.:

At dusk last evening [January 31] an outlaw by the name of Peddicord, with 40 men, tore up four or five rails in the Richland Woods, about 14 miles from here. They were attempting to burn a cattle guard on the road, when 15 men of the One hundred and twenty-ninth Illinois approached. The rebels ran. They were dressed in our overcoats. I have 350 men after them, and I expect to hear that the rebels fell off their horses and broke their necks. Fifty or more citizens collected at the place with the rebels, to look on, aid, and assist. I propose to make an example of some of them. The trains are running.

E. A. PAINE, Brig.-Gen.

OR, Ser. I, Vol. 23, pt. II, p. 33.

♦ FEBRUARY ♦

1 Just because Federal forces had occupied Nashville in February 1862 did not mean Confederate partisans had abandoned their loyalties. The spirit they showed was an irritant to the head of Federal forces in Nashville, Brigadier-General Robert B. Mitchell; it was reported his solution was to punish the Rebel families by forcing them to administer to the "confederate wounded" in Nashville. The army medical director was ordered to select "forty five of the sick and wounded Confederate soldiers and have them distributed to the three richest Nashville pro–Confederate families. Failure to do so would result in the penalty of forfeiture of their property.

Rebellion Record, pp. 41–42.

2 Attack on Fort Donelson

Nearly a year since the battle and loss of Fort Donelson to the Union, a force of some 4,000 Confederates under the leadership of Generals Wheeler, Forrest, and Wharton attacked the fortress in a fight that lasted the entire day. An official report stated: "In the battle they charged and charged again under continuous fire of shot and shell, and were finally driven back after many repulses." Another report stated: "We killed more than 100 of the enemy, and have some 100 prisoners here; with the gunboats ... we got about 200 of them. Our loss is 12 killed and about 30 wounded."

OR, Ser. I, Vol. 23, pt. II, pp. 45–46.

3 U.S. gunboats bombard Confederates surrounding Federal force at Dover

Excerpt from the Report of Lieutenant-Commander LeRoy Fitch's report of March 17, 1863

On February 3 ... [a]t 8 P.M. arrived at Dover, [Tenn.], found the garrison entirely surrounded by the enemy, and out of ammunition. The gunboats shelled and dispersed the rebels.

Navy OR, Ser. I, Vol. 24, p. 57.

4 General J. E. Johnston wrote to the Confederate Secretary of War in Richmond that:

This army is suffering from the use of fresh pork. It has no other meat. I respectfully recommend that it be permitted immediately to draw salt meat from Atlanta and fresh beef from Maj. [J. F.] Cumming, in Northern Georgia. He is salting beef. It would be better to salt the hogs which are eaten fresh here, and issue the beef fresh.

OR, Ser. I, Vol. 23, pt. II, pp. 625–626.

5 Capture of Union bushwhackers

We came into Scott County yesterday. Heavy snow storm last night. The regiment moved ... and captured 18 prisoners, all renegades under command of one Captain Early of Bradley County, who is himself among the prisoners. We first found them in a house, and they all took to their heels and made their escape in the mountains, but we followed their tracks in the snow and found them in a cave.

...

Diary of William A. Sloan, February 5, 1863.

6 The confession of a Union bushwhacker

Feb. 6.— Our company made another excursion to day and took one prisoner whom we had good reason to believe was a bushwhacker, as we found him running from a house, and it took our best horses to catch him. He denied being a bushwhacker, but a halter around his neck brought out a very humble confession. There was a strong disposition on the part of the boys to hang him, but the officer in command ... would not permit it, and as he protested that he had joined the band under coercion, and had never fired a gun, but tried to avoid going with them, and as he had the appearance of an honest, ignorant mountaineer, we therefore sent him back with the other prisoners without registering a bushwhacking charge against him.

Diary of William A. Sloan, February 6, 1863.

7 A night at the McMinnville opera, an entry from the Lucy Virginia French diary

...all day Mollie and I were preparing her dress for the concert — it was white swiss trimmed with cerise tulle, coral jewelry, a beautiful moiré antique carise sash, and velvet fushias in her bosom. She looked very, very charming indeed. The house was ... packed and everything passed of quite pleasantly. I am very annoyed, however, by some officers who sat on chairs in the aisle just "jam up" to me — who had been drinking and were very anxious for the concert to be over so they could again get some "more of the same sort." They were determined that everybody near them should know that were Cols.—talked loud and long of "my regiment" ... until they thought everybody was fully convinced of the[ir] officership and then they commenced passing coarse remarks upon the girls and wishing the bore would stop and the ball commence so that they could get brandy. I was sick with the fumes of their breath—disgusted with their conversation—and indignant at their ingratitude....

War Journal of Lucy Virginia French,
entry for February 8, 1863.

8 War's effect on charitable donations in Nashville

The passing winter will be preserved in the memory of the people of Nashville as the synonym of care, vexation, and hard-living.

...

Around hearthstones not long ago the glowing pictures of happiness and plenty, may now be seen gathered shivering, hungered children, and parents racked with anguish, straining their heart-strings to resist despair; larders always heretofore plentifully filled, now scarcely afford a single meal, and the anxious father despondingly awaits the return of uncertain to-morrow to provide a morsel for his little ones.

This is no fancy sketch.... Fearful, indeed, is the responsibility weighing upon the authors of this accursed war.... Sincerely do we pray for the return of peace with its reinstatement of industry, of trade, of commerce and their thousand attendant blessings.

Nashville *Daily Union*, February 8, 1863.

9 Standing picket at night was a dangerous business, especially when challenged by the enemy. Occasionally errors were made and a picket might be shot at by one of his own. In such a case a confrontation was inevitable, as this excerpt from a letter of George G. Sinclair [89th Illinois Volunteers] demonstrates. After a mistaken challenge the night of the 8th Sinclair decided to seek his opponent out and make amends.

"The poor devil was so scared that by morning I had made up my mind to forgive and forget it thinking myself very fortunate in getting off without a scratch. But the poor fool reminded me that I must not call him such hard names another time like that in a threatening tone as if he had the perfect right to shoot me when he pleased and me to say nothing about it. I had ought to put a ball or my bayonet through him on the spot when he threatened to shoot the second time. His remarks rather riled.... I gave him a few belts in the face to teach him manners. He was very reasonable after that. Without joking it was no laughing affair to have a man shoot at you even in the dark.... George G. Sinclair."

Sinclair Correspondence

10 Major-General J. J. Reynolds' led an expedition from Murfreesboro to Auburn, Liberty, Alexandria, Lebanon, Carthage and Gallatin on February 3–5 and captured some Confederate mail, letters written home to families of Rebel soldiers. According to General Reynolds report:

These letters breathed but one sentiment—all tired of the war, and wanted to return home and remain there. Many said they would not go any farther south, and expressed a desire to desert, but feared in that case the Argus eyes of the rebel inhabitants at home, who would watch them and report them to the conscript agents, by whom they would be seized and sent back to their regiments and to death. These letters stated most positively that deserters ... were shot in various instances, and that citizens who had guided the Federal army were hanged.

OR, Ser. I, Vol. 23, pt. II, pp. 54–57.

11 Smuggled goods in Nashville.

We ... learn ... from Col. Truesdail ... Chief of the Army Police, that ... smuggled goods captured by his detectives ... amounts to about $300,000 ... quinine alone, about $10,000 ... a heavy contraband trade has been attempted to be carried on.

Nashville *Dispatch*, February 11, 1863.

12 An Irishman in the Army of Tennessee complains about the cold in winter camp:

"The other morning Tom Moonly-one of 'ours' and as live a specimen of Erin as ever dug a ditch-came in from the trenches perfectly blue with cold. 'Ochoar! says he, 'and isn't this enough to friz the river Styx in Purgatory! Divil a drap in camp, an' myself as cowld as a goose's foot on a block of ice in Canada! I axed Liftinant Shaw for a drink, or a dollar, and he gave me nather. Sure I'll die altogether an' be buried in the woods, an' the jaybirds and whippoorwills will cover me up, and preach my funeral. Begorra! Captain, would ye give me a bit of a place to the fire?' I made room for the lamenting son of the 'Isle,' who presently became quite merry and facetious, as the flames thawed his frozen body.

Chattanooga *Daily Rebel*, February 12, 1863.

13 Mary L. Pearre, Williamson County, engages in hiding horses from Yankee foragers:

Was writing ... leisurely when in came Matt exclaiming 'Mollie! The Yanks are coming!' Hastely dropping my pen, I ran to the door expecting to see the bluecoats. It proved to be our neighbors running off their horses to hide them from the Feds. who are within 10 miles of here. About fifty horses are being hidden among our hills. Though I know there is imminent danger of all our horses being taken, yet there is much of the ludicrous in the hurry and confusion of men, women, children and horses that I cannot help laughing. I had a *nice* run through the mud assisting to catch or animals just now. Will cease writing and stand picket for the appearance of the Feds.

Diary of Mary L. Pearre

14 Unsuccessful hunt for a Union recruiting agent near Maynardsville, East Tennessee:

We are still at Maynardsville. I made a little excursion last night with two of my comrades on a hunt of a northern recruiting officer who had been very secretly recruiting in the neighborhood for some time. I had a good clew and a good guide but failed to find the man. He probably had become suspicious and crossed the Clinch River into a place of safety.

Diary of William E. Sloan

15 Metallic coffins

An Agreeable Surprise.... Three fathers came up the Cumberland river ... [to bring] back home with them the bodies of their sons who had fallen in ... the ... battle of Stones' River. They carried ... three metallic coffins.... The boat ... stopped ... at Clarksville ... and the grief-stricken fathers stepped ashore ... to their astonishment ... they saw ... their three sons, who were ... overjoyed to see the "old folks."... The meeting was a ... surprise to both parties.

Nashville *Daily Union*, February 15, 1863.

16 Excerpts from the letter of Lieutenant-General Leonidas Polk, in Shelbyville, to his wife, Frances, at their plantation home, Ashwood in Maury County concerning the promotion of his son to captain and a dress pattern for his wife:

Shelbyville, Tennessee, February 16, 1863

My beloved wife,

...You will receive this day Meck* who I send to see you on a furlough of twenty days. He will give you all the news and he will also tell you that I have relieved him from his situation as 1st Lieut. of his battery and made him assistant to the Chief of Artillery. I found that he was seriously embarrassed by the weight of responsibility ... attached to his affairs ... and though pride and vanity on my part at his advancement ... so much ahead of his years, might have prompted me to keep him where he was, especially as he had the prospect of advancement to the office of Captain might have induced me to continue him where he was, yet my duty to him as a father forbid this and I ordered him to be relieved and put into a position of equal honour and of great usefulness, and where his attainment in his particular branch would be available for the government....

He takes with him a present ... a dress pattern. I think it very pretty, and as it is all ... home spun– I hope you will value it and am sure you will wear it. The pattern I send you is with the broad stripe and I think will 'make up' very prettily....

W. P. A. Civil War Records, Vol. 3, pp. 38–39.

17 Gang turf battles in Nashville

Throwing Rocks.—The attention of the police is directed to a dangerous amusement just come into vogue among boys, white and black. A party meets almost every evening in South Nashville, composed of "The Wilson Springs Boys" and "The Cherry Street Boys," who form themselves into line of battle and pelt each other with rocks, to the imminent danger of passers-by, and to the demolition of sundry window-lights. A similar party meets on Broad street almost every day, between school hours, and serious consequences may ensue unless it is stopped. On Sunday evening about a dozen boys assembled on a lot on Market street, north of the Louisville and Nashville depot, and carried on a war of rocks until one or two passers-by narrowly escaped serious injury.

Nashville *Dispatch*, February 17, 1863.

---

*Their son William Mecklenburg Polk.

18 Affair near Moscow, excerpts from the report of Major F. M. Long, Forty-first Illinois Infantry

SIR: On the morning of the 18th instant, I was detailed to take command of 160 men ... to escort a forage train that was going out after forage.

...

While we were loading the [wagon] train, I received information that 150 of [R. V.] Richardson's rebel cavalry had made their appearance about a mile west of us.... I immediately ordered the guards in line, ready for action. When our train was loaded, I placed half the guards in front and the remainder in the rear of the train.... we started for camp, moving unmolested until within 2½ or 3 miles of camp, when I discovered a body of rebel cavalry south of the road, about 150 strong, preparing to make a dash upon the train. I sent orders to the front guards to return with all possible speed, at the same time hurrying forward with the rear guards. In consequence of the bad condition of the roads, the train was somewhat scattered, and both the front and rear guards were from a half to three-fourths of a mile from the center of the train.

In the mean time the rebels had made their dash and attacked the train in the center; the front and rear guards coming up, engaged the enemy at the same time. The engagement lasted about five minutes, when the enemy were ... in full retreat.

Our loss was 1 man wounded and 16 missing. We also lost 42 mules and 2 horses....

OR, Ser. I, Vol. 23, pt. I, p. 59.

19 Clarification of Nashville's Negro Laws relative to a slave's living arrangements

The Negro Laws. February 17, 1863

— In our brief abstract of laws for the government of slaves and their masters, we stated that the former were not permitted to live on the premises of anyone but their owner or employer *without the owner's or employer's consent*. By an act passed subsequent to that in our mind's eye, neither the owner nor employer can give such consent. In other words, slaves *must* reside upon the premises of their owner or employer, and any other person allowing them upon their premises are subject to prosecution.

Nashville *Dispatch*, February 19, 1863.

19 Guerrilla Outrage

A Guerrilla Brute. Refugees from Maury County report that a most deplorable state of affairs exist in that county. A band of rebel cavalry is scouring the country, led by one Capt. Lewis Kirk, of Lawrence county. He has forced numbers of gray-headed Union men, fifty and sixty years of age, into the rebel army, and now holds in confinement several of the oldest and most estimable citizens of the county, because they refuse to take up arms. One brave old man told him that if he would give him a chance, he would take up arms for the Federal Government. This Kirk was formerly a blacksmith, we are informed, and a noted bully in Lawrence county. He was in jail at Columbia for near three years, for murdering Mr. Westmoreland of Giles county, without provocation, and in cold blood. When the rebellion broke out, he sent word to Governor Harris that if he would get him out of jail he would join the rebel army, and he was let loose. He is now fighting for 'Southern Rights' against Lincoln's myrmidons.

Nashville *Daily Union*, February 20, 1863.

21 Thomas' Legion

The Indian Legion.— Major Thomas, commanding the Legion of Cherokee Indians, who have rendered much service to the Confederate cause in East Tennessee, was in our city yesterday. The Major is now with his aboriginal allies in the mountains on the border between this State and North Carolina, where he is in reality conciliating the tories. Let us mention a fact or two communicated to us by Major Thomas, to the credit of these dusky warriors. They excel any troops in either the Northern or Southern armies for subordination — an Indian always executes an order with religious fidelity. They scrupulously respect private property — there are no reports of depredations where they are encamped. They are the best scouts in the world, and hence the good that they have accomplished among the mountain tories and bush-whackers. A notice that Maj. Thomas' Indians are in a section of country brings in the dodgers at once, for they know that hiding out will not avail against the Cherokees. By their aid the Major has enlisted without bloodshed, a great many men in his corps of sappers and miners, who have thus been converted from mischievous tories and bush-whackers into useful employees of the Confederate Government. The Major, if the war lasts, will yet be of infinite service to the Government.— Knoxville *Register*, [February] 21st.

Weekly Columbus [Georgia] *Enquirer*, March 3, 1863.

22 Advertisement for draft substitutes in Chattanooga

"SUBSTITUTES WANTED"

Two thousand dollars each, will be paid for five, steady, able bodied men, of forty-six, to fifty-eight years of age. Apply in person or by letter.

J.M. Willy, Chattanooga, Tenn.

Chattanooga *Daily Rebel*, February 22, 1863.

23 Amusements in the Army of Tennessee at winter camp at Tullahoma

MATCHES AND OVER MATCHES

A pair of privates of the ____ Tennessee had a grudge, and one of them also [received] a newly arrived box of provision 'from home.' They resolved to fight for the latter in adjudication of the former. An hour was appointed, a vast assemblage collected, both entered the ring arranged, the combatants placed in position. Intense excitement; much gambling on the result; terrible odds. Do not be alarmed, I mean no description in detail.... The battle was fought, the victory won, the box of provisions paid over when lo, a second champion appeared, and offered to eat the entire contents for 'twenty five dollars *Confed.*, or, in default of so doing to pay down to the owner, thereof, the handsome sum of one hundred ditto.'

The wager was accepted. Bets were again offered and taken. Excitement again resumed the sway. The box ... contained the following articles of food: One turkey, two dozen eggs (boiled), one dozen biscuits, one pound of butter, six dried peach pies, one bottle of molasses, and six onions!

The wretch won his wager!

Chattanooga *Daily Rebel*, February 23, 1863.

24 Executions and small pox in Army of Tennessee winter camp in Tullahoma

...

...Tullahoma is a dull place. There is but little of interest transpiring to note. Bragg, occasionally to break the tedious monotony of a dull camp life, has a soldier for some unbecoming conduct shot. There have been several shot since we have been at this place both officers and privates. It was mostly for misbehavior or cowardice before the enemy in the late battle before Murfreesboro. So far there have been none shot in our Brigade, and I have never yet witnessed such an execution.... We also have small pox here, but then we have all become used to that, so we have but little dread of it....

Hannibal Paine Letters.

25 Excerpt from the letter of James Vascoy, 12th Indiana regiment, in Grand Junction to his parents

...[O]f our company one of them was taken up by one of his friends that come after him and took him home there was too taken up some time ago and the man got as far as Memphis and stopt to stay overnight he went to bed with seventy seven dollars and he was found dead next morning with his money taken ... o what will this world come to the wickedness of our nation is grate at this time and there must be a change before this war will close but I think that the people begins to see the one thing well fother I see the need of living in redines for death at all times I see men falling nerly evry day and if we put our trust in him he will bring us off more than conker threw him who has dyde for our sins....

Vanscoy Correspondence.

26 Nashville's Negro Control Law

Resolved That all negroes laying around loose in this city and not employed, and having run away from their masters (some who are loyal to the United States) with the expectation of being free, and, as they are not capable of self-government, and are a nuisance to the community in which they live, unless they have a master to superintend and provide for them, that all such be arrested ... and either confined in jail or made to labor on public works, or be advertised in order that their masters by paying all necessary expenses, may be reclaimed, and send them where they properly belong, and thereby rid the public of an intolerable nuisance, and show our constituents while we are in favor of a restoration of the Federal [constitution] at every sacrifice, we have no sympathy with negro worshipers, or those who would destroy our country, for the purpose of abolishing slavery, thereby placing the negro on an equality with the white race.

...

Nashville *Daily Union*,
February 27, 1863.

27 Skirmish near Bloomington, on the Hatchie River, Tenn.

Report of Brig. Gen. Alexander Asboth U.S. Army.

HDQRS. DISTRICT OF COLUMBUS, MARCH 2, 1863.

GEN.: Col. Wolfe, commanding at Fort Pillow, reports that Capt. Moore, Second Illinois Cavalry, reached, on the 27th ultimo, at daybreak, with 200 mounted [men], the principal camp of the rebel Col. [R. V.] Richardson, in the neighborhood of Bloomington, on the Hatchie. The rebels, however, started on the previous day to the southeast, leaving only 8 men to guard the camp and collect conscripts. This guard was taken, with all the property in their charge, 27 horses and mules, wagons and commissary stores, and the camp, with several large buildings and comfortable quarters, entirely destroyed.

ASBOTH, Brig.-Gen.

OR, Ser. I, Vol. 24, pt. I, p. 422.

28 A Confederate war correspondent's observations on the Army of Tennessee in winter camp at Tullahoma.

Our army is again in good fighting trim, and the ranks swell rapidly filling up by the influx of absentees. I suppose it is better clothed, equipped and fed than ever before. The country is bountifully supplied with game, but the boys are forbidden to shoot, for fear of hitting some General's aid. These sweet-smelling, kid-glovey, band-boxy, tea-cakey, ottar-of-rose exquisites, are as plentiful as gnats around a vinegar jug.... It is true they dangle a dress sword gracefully, run handsome horses in dashing stile, and smile most daintily at the ladies, yet it is no less true, they can tell the ragged, weather beaten fellow that foots it with his gun and heavy knapsack, exactly what he ought to be. You can thus very readily appreciate the field and scope of their usefulness, and the necessity of taking every precaution to protect them from the weather and disagreeable inconvenience of camp life, and to guard against the rudeness of bringing them in contact with unmannerly soldiers, and everything calculated to grate harshly on their tender sensibilities....

Chattanooga *Daily Rebel*, February 28, 1863.

♦ MARCH ♦

5 Solicitation for a Confederate Conscription Substitute

"WANTED"

A Good, sound, substitute; not subject to conscription; a stout youth of 16 preferred: for particulars enquire of Mr. Gentey, at E. T. R. Depot.

Chattanooga *Daily Rebel*, March 5, 1863.

5 "A Touching Incident,"

Last Sabbath [1st] I was wandering through the large grave-yard near this place, where sleep so many of our gallant soldiers, who have fallen by the hand of disease, I noticed three or four young ladies attired in deep mourning enter the grave-yard. They passed before several of the new made soldier's graves and knelt down over then and wept. They seemed to utter a prayer for the departed spirits of the heroic dead of martyrs, who had yielded up their lives to the defense of their country, and although they passed away in a strange land, without the hand of a kind mother or sister to soothe their dying moments an[d] minister to their last wants, their lonely grave-yard be visited and watered, with the tears of the fair daughters of the sunny South. And long after the din of battle is hushed, and peace spreads her gladsome wings over our land, these fair angels will visit the *soldier's* grave, and bedew it with their tears and plant flowers and ever greens around the last resting places of the departed heroes of the Southern soldier.

Chattanooga *Daily Rebel*, March 5, 1863.

5 Observations on Federal officers and courtesans in Murfreesboro, an excerpt from the diary of John C. Spence

...

...on the subject of officers and men, [I] will presume it may not be out of place to say a little more about them. There are among this class of gentry here women purporting to be wives of officers-but, from the conduct of many of them, leaves reason to doubt. An army is not a place for a female of proper of refined feelings When we see a woman wearing long ringlets, large ear trinkets, a flowing feather in her hat, galloping up and down over the country with officers and soldiers, having oyster suppers and wine drinking, it may be set down she does not lie at the feet of Boaz for nothing. Such we see here. Perhaps there were some that were genuine wives, that made their visits to the army. The majority were of the former description. A Lady or Gentleman can always be known in any situation they may be placed, and so may the other class be as easily distinguished. In either case, it does not require a keen observer to see the difference.

...

Spence Diary.

6 Contraband Social Life in Nashville Colored Church and Ball-Rooms.

A few days ago we devoted a paragraph to the colored population, in which we stated that the churches have of late become sadly neglected. Various reasons are assigned for this, one of which is, that the boys and girls are afraid to turn out on Sunday, because many of them have been pressed into Government service in their Sunday clothes and compelled to work in them. This might be obviated by procuring passes exempting those attending church from being pressed on Sunday. Such passes would readily be given by the Commander of the Post. But that is not the reason; there are others more cogent: namely, the bad example of negroes from the free States, and contrabands. Hundreds of these may be seen upon the streets all day Sunday, when the weather is fine; and when rainy they may be found congregated in the various lodging places, devoting the day to dissipation, debauchery, gaming, etc. A heavy responsibility rests upon our colored preachers at this time; they might and ought to be materially aided by the military, if the latter feel disposed to consider that the morals of the negro are worth preserving, and believe that religion has precisely the same effect upon them as upon white people, viz.,: in making and keeping them honest, sober, industrious, and well conducted in all respects.

The being religious and regularly attending church does not necessarily deprive them of innocent amusements — indeed, it adds to their ability to enjoy rationally the social gatherings they so much delight in — their balls and parties, which were formerly conducted in the most unobjectionable manner by our Nashville boys, but many of which have the past winter degenerated into places of assignation, drunkenness and general disorderly conduct. So low, indeed, had they become, as we are credibly informed, that few of our Nashville girls and boys would attend them

On Wednesday last [4th] we were informed that the colored gentlemen of Nashville were to give a ball on that night at the City Hotel, to which no "disreputable" contrabands of soldiers were to be admitted, and we determined at once to be there to see how things went on. The following is a copy of the neatly printed ticket:—"Cotillion Party, to be given at the City Hotel, on Wednesday, March 4th, 1863. James Thomas and K. Douglas, Managers. Music by Bill Porter's String Band. No Ladies admitted without a Gentleman. Admission, $1."

The bell had just tolled the hour of 9 P.M. as we wended our way across the Square, and in fifteen minutes thereafter we introduced ourselves to Mr. Thomas, whom we found guarding the entrance. Bill Porter had just seated himself upon his elevated seat, and while tuning his violin (a valuable one, by the way,) was informing an impatient youth that no fashionable ball commences before 9 or 10 o'clock. Bill had two assistants-a second and base, and discoursed music sweet, eloquent, and spirited, and all being in readiness for the dance Bill called out—

"Gents will please take of dar has, and put 'em in dar pockets, or somewhar else. Better put 'em in yer pockets; I see some white gentlemen here. [Bill has considerable native humor in him, which he occasionally dispenses gratuitously.]

The sets were formed, and all stood looking at Bill with eager anxiety, waiting for the command- "*First* four right, and left —*Back* to your places — *Bal* an cue —*Turn* your partners —*Swing* corners and do it good —*Ladies* chain —*Half* promenade," etc. to the end of the chapter, when Bill told them to "*Prom*enade all," but before he had well got them in motion, he called out —"*Swap* partners, an' get *better* ones," adding, "You mustn't dance all night with one lady bekas [ie., because] she's putty."

During the dance and afterward, we had an opportunity of seeing and observing nearly all in the room. There were nearly one hundred present, male and female being about equally represented; all, or nearly all, were dressed in their best, and *all* were clean. The boys were generally neatly attired; only one being clad in that extravagant style so universally adopted by negro representatives upon the stage; the one alluded to had on a neat black suit, with a full bosom ruffled shirt of the largest dimensions, extending out in front several inches, and flapping upon the right of his breast, on the left lapel of his coat he wore a white satin ribbon, of large dimensions, not less that sixteen inches in diameter. The girls wore dresses of every conceivable variety, but white skirts prevailed, with bodies (or waists , or whatever they may be called) of all shades, from drab to black, and generally of silk. Some two or three wore their hats, and one wore a wreath of artificial flowers.... the best dancer was Lizzie Beach; she was dressed in white muslin, without any ornaments but a neat pin, she is tall, graceful, and danced an infinite variety of steps-enough to astonish an Elsaler, but all in good time, and modestly executed. She had for a partner a boy in military overcoat, who seemed well up in the Terpsichorean art, but was scarcely a match for Lizzie, we would like to see them with the floor to themselves, and would expect a rich treat.

Time wore on, and several steles were danced, when Bill requested the boys to "*Treat* your partners, all you boys that's got money; and you that hasn't, run you face Them that hain't got no money, nor a good face, can try if there's a lady that'll have pity on 'em, and dance the *next* quadrille. The aristocracy then retired to supper, and the remainder kept up the dance.

The refreshment table was extremely neat, and well filled with all the delicacies the market affords, and up to the hour our leaving, there was naught but incessant mirth prevailing, echoed by the "had-had, ha-a-a-hui!"

Nashville *Dispatch*, March 6, 1863.

7 Salt rations for soldiers in Army of Tennessee ordered diverted to horses

CIRCULAR. HDQRS. ARMY OF TENNESSEE, Tullahoma, March 7, 1863.

Hereafter all the salt received in mess-beef issues by the troops of this army will be turned over to the artillery and quartermasters of their respective commands, for the use of their horses.

By command of Gen. Bragg:

OR, Ser. I, Vol. 23, pt. II, p. 665.

11 An account of Ella V. Reno and Sarah E. Bradbury, Federal soldiers

"The Romantic Story of the Female Soldiers."

In our Sunday's issue we published the fact that Ella V. Reno and Sarah E. Bradbury had been arrested in military uniform, at Murfreesboro,' and sent to Col. Truesdail. After an examination into their case, the Colonel generously provided them with comfortable female attire, and furnished them with means to reach their homes. Miss Bradbury, whose assumed name was Frank Morton, made a written statement of her life, under oath, before the Judge Advocate, from which we make the following extracts:

"I am eighteen years old, was born in Wilson county, Tennessee, and moved from there to this county about one year ago. I was raised by a stepfather, my mother having died when I was seven years old. I have no recollection of having ever seen my father. I lived seven miles from Nashville, on the old Chicken road that leads from Nashville to Lebanon.

"I have been in the service six months. I first went into the 7th Illinois cavalry, in company C. This company was the body guard of Gen. Palmer. I was induced to go into the service by my friend, Mr. H., who, by his frequent visits and manifestations of love, won my heart. I dressed myself in men's clothing and determined to follow him. I served in this company two months, making a faithful and attentive soldier; while there I became Orderly for my General, and flatter myself that I made him a good officer. During all this time my sex was never discovered. Unfortunately, my friend was captured by the rebels while out scouting the day after I went into his company, and I have never heard of him since.

"Despairing of seeing him again, and becoming attached to a young man in the 22d Illinois infantry, I joined his regiment in order that I might be the more with him. I was with him constantly, and we have passed many pleasant hours together. One day, while taking a walk with him, and thinking that I had gained his confidence, I gave him my history and disclosed my sex. This he was surprised to hear, for he had taken me for a boy, and was disposed to doubt me. Since that time he has made me frequent proposals of marriage. Circumstances proved to me that I was mistaken in my man, for I soon became satisfied that he was not a gentleman. Thus losing confidence in him, I made up my mind to return to my home. When I thought of having left home without the consent of my friends, I instantly abandoned the thought, and determined to remain in the army. Camp life agreed with me, and I never enjoyed better health in my life.

"Afterward I became a member of General Sheridan's escort, company L, 2d Kentucky cavalry. One day Colonel Barret sent me as bearer of dispatches to Col. Libott, a distance of six miles. On my return, one of my brother orderlies betrayed me to the Colonel, he becoming jealous of my reputation as an orderly, and having found out my sex a few days previous. My sex thus exposed, I was arrested and sent to Col. Truesdail in irons. May I never fall into worse hands, for I found him a gentleman in every sense of the word.

"I have made a good and faithful soldier, have

learned a good deal of human nature, and had some aspirations as a soldier, and though at the time of my arrest that my chances were good for promotion. I will try to profit by the lessons I have learned."

We strongly suspect Frank to be one who figured in Nashville some months ago. The soldiers brought a large number of girls with them — one is still here, known as Charley, and several have returned to their homes in the North.

Nashville *Dispatch*, March 11, 1863.

11 Gender incognito and the cavalry
Army Police Proceedings.
Before the Chief of Army Police, Nashville, March 10, 1863.— Two females were arrested on board a steamboat on Saturday night, dressed as soldiers, in company with a body of cavalry. They were provided with female apparel and sent to Louisville. Such martial spirits are not needed, and their presence in the army is detrimental to its best interests. In this case the Chief of Police very properly addressed a note to the officers in command of the cavalry, informing them that if these instances continued, a severe example would be made of both women and the officers encouraging them to such a course, in accordance with an order of the Commanding General.

Nashville *Dispatch*, March 11, 1863.

12 "Tornado."
We are informed that Shelbyville was visited by another hurricane on last Saturday [7th] night, which blew down the Baptist Church, the Depot, Telegraph Office, besides other buildings. One person is said to have been killed....

Fayetteville *Observer*, March 12, 1863.

12–13 Confederate wounded and prisoners of war in Nashville: excerpts from the diary of John Hill Fergusson
Thursday 12th
today has been clear and cold.... Francher & MySelf went to the depot ... but learned the train did not arive until 6 so we started back to camp on our way through the city we seen large numbers of ambulances unloading a set of secesh prisoners they ware wounded in the battle of Stone river and had been in the hospital at Murfreesboro ever since there was one hundred and 50 of them the greatest part of them ware gon on crutches some were shot in the shoulder and some in the arm but mostly in the leggs there was 70 prisoners brought in Last night from franklin
Friday 13th
this morning was a little chilly.... James Anderson & MySelf went over [to] town with John Ingle and Mr. Baker on our way to the depot we passed the large bilding whare the secesh prisoners ware they ware looking out of the windows of the 3 story & bieing* apples of off a set of Little boys they would drop down there money then the boys would throw the appals in at the window one to a time they would frequently miss the window and as the appals would fawl to the ground the soldiers would catch them: the prisoners would sing out: there that one is last that yankey has caught it. another would sing out: come Mr Yankee sling that up hear the yanky would reply: you bedamed ther was quite a crowd gathered on the side walk on the oppsit side of the street there was guards brought down and disperced the crowd and made the boys leve with there appals....

John Hill Fergusson Diary, Book 3.

14 "Chattynoogy *Rebel*"
Newsboy on the Street-"'He-yeah's yer Chattynoogy *Rebel*!
Federal Prisoner from Spring Hill†-"What's that boy?"
Boy —"*Rebel*, sir."
Fed.—"Well I guess I'll take one o' them — tried to take one 'tother day at Spring Hill — and didn't."

Chattanooga *Daily Rebel*, March 14, 1863.

15 General Bragg forbids use of negro teamsters for Army of Tennessee ordnance and ambulance trains
CIRCULAR. HDQRS. HARDEE'S CORPS, Tullahoma, March 15, 1863.
By direction of Gen. Bragg, negro teamsters will not be substituted for white drivers in ordnance and ambulance trains.
By command of Lieut.-Gen. Hardee:

OR, Ser. I, Vol. 23, pt. II, p. 698.

15 Measures by Federal forces to protect public health in Murfreesboro, an excerpt from the diary of John C. Spence

---

*begging
†Skirmish at Spring Hill, March 9, 1863

... the army were receiving large droves of beef cattle. Some of them were fine looking, other had to be killed soon, to keep them from dying. They were generally kept in lots in and about town. It took about fifty or sixty every day to supply the demand of the army and hospitals. They would drive out that number, [then] shoot them down. When butchered, it generally covered over a half acre ground, the entrails, heads and feet, left lying there — so in the course of time several acres was covered in this way, and it began to get warm weather. The smell became very offensive.

We began to be apprehensive that it would cause sickness, but as fortune would have it, the authorities took the matter in hand-dug pits, had the offensive [offal] collected up and thrown in and covered up. This caused the atmosphere to improve. Large numbers of horses were shot, such as were very poor, diseased and woarn out. Here was a fortune lost to some speculating, enterprising Yankee, in the way of sculls, horns and shin bones.

A system of street cleaning now commenced. Hands were set to work scraping up all the litter that was lying in the streets, gutters and corners, [and] hauled it out of town. Things now begin to put on a more cheerful and healthy appearance....

Spence Diary.

15 Witnessing a black religious service in Nashville

Sunday 15th

...So after traveling around until we got tiared we returned to camp: we came past whare the darkies ware holding meeting I stoped we stoped to hear them they preached as good sound toctorin as any white man: and I never heard heared abetar prayers offered up by any minister of the gospel then was offered up by them darky....

John Hill Fergusson Diary, Book 3.

16 A Confederate soldier's observations about theft in the Cleveland environs.

There is a camp of Federal troops within a mile and a half of our home, and they sometimes visit our house and the houses of other southern people in the neighborhood and carry off such articles as they like, but the worst enemies by all odds, and the ones for whom our people have the greatest dred are those who call themselves "homeguards," but who are simply organized bands of bushwhackers and robbers.

Diary of William A. Sloan, March 15, 1863.

24 Major-General Granger's idea to rid Middle Tennessee of Confederates

FRANKLIN, March 24, 1863.

Maj.-Gen. ROSECRANS:

In reply to your circular of March 21, received to-day, I would say my portion of the country is swarming with the meanest, bitterest kind of enemies. I know of no other way to report the names and numbers of active enemies than to say that everything in this neighborhood would come under that head, and that the use of a fine-tooth comb of immense size moving southward would have more effect than any other mode I can propose to get rid of their presence.

G. GRANGER, Maj.-Gen.

OR, Ser. I, Vol. 23, pt. II, p. 168.

27 Excerpts from the diary of Mary L. Pearre: "Not another pill will I swallow except opium. I rather like its effect."

Three weeks has passed since I have penned a line. Ruth, May & myself have all been ill, are now convalescent. I have been confined to my room for two weeks & have been well physicked with quinine, opium & with various powders & pills. Have no faith in M.D.'s & their stuff. Yet by dent of much persuasive eloquence aided by acute pain the prevailed upon me to be drugged to any amount. I am far from being well yet. Have forsworn any more dosing. Not another pill will I swallow except opium. I rather like its effect.

While I have been ill, time has kept the uneven tenor of its way. Various events have occurred

Brentwood, six miles from here, was surprised and taken last Wednesday by Genl. Forrest & Starnes. The attack was made just at day. Took 680 prisoners that morning, a wagon train with medicine and supplies of every kind.

About 12 o'clock the Federal calvay (from Franklin) came into collision on the Hillsboro pike two miles from here. We were victor again and captured several hundred more bluecoats. Mag says this even has caused me to get well rapidly. Perhaps so. I have been elated since.

Bob Cotton brought me a package of letters he took out of a Yankee tent. They were from a Mrs. Abbie Sears to her husband. It made my heart ache to read her tender loving wifely letters, so full of devotion & passionate longing for his return. Poor thing. Her husband is a prisoner and she as yet is unconscious of his fate. This is only an incident of war, a mere speck among its accumulated horrors. My hand trembles so I can scarcely write. I would desist could I find a better employment. Am so tired of being sick and seeing those that are sick that I have shut myself up alone though there is no fire and the room is rather damp....

How many of us have adopted the motto in all things — if you cant be — at least seem to be & go on eating "husks" as it were & holding as life's chief good the complete and final subjugation of genuine emotion & substitute in it place an artificial mode of thinking, speaking and eating.

Here I will make an extract. Truly there are two senses in which every search, every combat, may said to be closed. One where the victor grasps his prize or waves aloft his sword in the moment of triumph. The other when bleeding, mained or dying, the vanquished sinks to earth without the power to arise.

...

Am studying "Phrenology." Just began yesterday.... Am rather skeptical in regard to the science....

Diary of Mary L. Pearre.

28 A Negro teamster escapes execution by Confederates during the battle of Stones River, an excerpt from the letter of Amandus Silsby to his parents

March 28

Camp near Murfreesboro, Mar. 28

My dear father and mother:

...Gen. "Rosy" has not organized any negro regiments, I do not know whether the rebels killed all the negroes teamsters they were enabled to carry off with them. I saw them shoot two of them. I saw one of the poor fellows make his escape but Sambo thought a moment before his time was up. Seeing them coming, he tried to escape, but two of the rebels riding up, commanded him to stop! He stood trembling, while one of them asked him what he was doing there with the Federals. "I-I-I was only go'an 'long wid de a'mee" "Well come along with us, we'll soon teach you what it is to be caught among the Yankees." Shortly after they were obliged to leave Sambo, and Skedaddled from our cavalry, much to the joy of the Negro, who jumping up and down shouted "Go it Bully! Give 'em H__ll!" I was glad to get away took for it went very much against the grain to hear their boasting talk, which riled my temper considerably....

Silsby Correspondence, March 28, 1863.

◆ APRIL ◆

1 April Fool's joke played on Confederate General B. F. Cheatham near Shelbyville

April 1st (Fool's Day) passed off pleasantly, a few jokes were passed off at the expense of the unsuspecting, General Cheatham was presented with a nice Apple Toddy made not of Apple Brandy by Vinegar — by Miss Golhson.

Moorman's Memorandum.

2 Guerrilla attack on U.S. ships at Palmyra

NASHVILLE, April 3, 1863.

Gen. GARFIELD, Chief of Staff:

Col. Boone telegraphs from Clarksville as follows:

The fleet gunboat *St. Clair*, and transports *Eclipse, Luminary*, and *Lizzie Martin* were fired into at Palmyra. Gunboat and *Luminary* perhaps taken. The *Eclipse* arrived here disabled; reports the advance of rebels on this place. We will hold until re-enforced.

WM. P. BOONE.

NASHVILLE, April 3, 1863.

Gen. GARFIELD, Chief of Staff:

I have just received the following dispatch from Clarksville:

Scouts report the gunboat and *Luminary* escaped capture. The rebels are at Palmyra in force; have there a rifled 6 and smooth 12 pounder, and other caliber not ascertained. We must have the siege guns ordered for this post. Send them at once.

WM. P. BOONE.

...

OR, Ser. I, Vol. 23, pt. II, p. 205

Excerpt from a Federal soldier's diary relative to the attack at Palmyra

April 3, 1863. — We also had a small fracas on the Cumberland River yesterday. One gunboat was considerably disabled and one transport was shot through several times but did not damage her a great deal. They have all fell back on [Fort] Donelson again and they are waiting for more gunboats to guard them through to Nashville. Our cavalry has started out this morning to learn the strength of the enemy at that place. At 3 o'clock P.M. we were ordered in line for battle and threw our tents down. We were then ordered to march up to the fort. We then stacked our guns. The cannons commenced practice to shoot and elevated their pieces on the hills and they all shot excellent. We are not in the old camp again and we have everything fixed up.

Diary of Charles Schreel,
Company E, 71st Ohio Infantry

4 Confederate deserters in East Tennessee
Deserters — One Hundred and Eighty Dollars Reward.

Headquarters Camp Instruction,
Knoxvile, April 4, 1863

The Above Reward will be paid for the apprehension and confinement in jail, or delivery to me at this place, or $30 each, for the following named deserters from this camp;

BENJ. F. COOLY, deserted on the 31st March, 1863, is 30 years of age, five feet 8 inches height, complexion dark, eyes dark, hair black; resides in Roane county, Tenn.

E. P. COFFY, deserted on the 2d inst., is 27 years of age, 6 feet 2 inches height, dark complexion, dark eyes, black hair; resides in Washington county, Tenn.

L. K. SEXTON, deserted on the 2d inst., is 29 years of age, 6 feet 1 inch height, dark complexion, hazel eyes, dark hair; resided in Greene county, Tenn.

P. L. MYNATT deserted on the 2d inst., is 36 years of age, 5 feet 8 inches height, fair complexion, gray eyes, dark hair; resides in Knox county, Tenn.

ISAAC TROUT, deserted on the 3d inst., is 23 years of age, 5 feet 6 inches height, dark complexion, gray eyes, and black hair; resided in Knox county, Tenn.

McD. GUINN, deserted on the 4th inst., is 36 years of age, 6 feet high, fair complexion, blue eyes, dark hair; resided in Greene county, Tenn.

By order of L. PECK, Maj. P. A. C. S., Commanding Camp of Instruction.

Knoxville *Daily Register*, April 18, 1863.

6 U.S. Navy's Retaliation at Palmyra

Excerpt from the November 25, 1863 Report or LCDR LeRoy Fitch regarding operations in the Ohio, Cumberland, and Tennessee rivers, August 23, 1862–October 21, 1863, relative to the sack of Palmyra, April 6, 1863:

As soon as I reached Smithland and had coaled, I received a dispatch ... saying the fleet under convoy had been attacked by batteries at Palmyra, and that his vessel, the *St. Clair*, was disabled.

I got underway immediately and moved up, arriving at Palmyra the afternoon of the 6th of April. I landed opposite and sent a detachment on shore ... with orders to burn every house in the place, and not to allow the men under his command to remove or pillage a single article.

The order was carried out fully.

Just after the boats landed several stragglers broke out of their concealments and ran; he fired on them, killing one and wounding another.

I was opposed to the wanton destruction of property, but in this instance I deemed it justifiable, for it was one of the worst secession places on the river, and unarmed transports had been fired into from door and windows of the houses.

...

Navy OR, Ser. I, Vol. 23, pp. 316–317.

8 Confederate Coney-Catching near Wartrace

Gen. Liddel's command, stationed near Wartrace, Tenn., are having a good deal of sport in catching a large number of rabbits daily. An old friend of ours says that on last Friday the boys captured about four hundred of the "molly cottontails." They manage the thing well. Two or three regiments march out and surround a thicket, then cavalry men with dogs enter the thicket and put the rabbits to flight, when our boys close in with clubs, sticks, etc., making a clean sweep of the varments. Quite a Luxury, and a great saving in a commissary point of view.—Chat. *Rebel*.

Montgomery *Weekly Advertiser*, April 8, 1863.

12 Skirmish at Stewartsborough. Tennessee

Report of Col. William W. Lowe, Fifth Iowa Cavalry.

FORT DONELSON, April 13, 1863.

Yesterday one company of the Fifth Iowa Cavalry, Capt. [D. A.] Waters, of Maj. Garrid's command (now out seizing horses), had a highly successful engagement with rebels, completely routing them, killing and wounding several, capturing 17 prisoners and 25 horses, besides arms, &c. Among the prisoners are Maj. Blanton, Capt. Lealer, of Cox's regiment, and the adjutant and surgeon of Owen's battalion. This Blanton is the same who was captured during the winter by one of my scouting parties, and made his escape somewhere north of Cairo.

W. W. LOWE, Col., Cmdg.

OR, Ser. I, Vol. 23, pt. I, p. 239.

15 ".... [T]he man in the moon must hold his nose"; an excerpt from a letter home relative to the hygienic conditions of the Army of the Cumberland in Murfreesboro

Sickness in the regiment prevails to an alarming extent; average attendance at the sick call, 100, perhaps 100 more are not fit for duty. This army of 40,000 men is encamped on a space so small that it is utterly impossible to keep the camps clean. Thousands of dead horses, mules and offal of every description, literally cover the whole face of the earth inside our picket lines; and each emits a thousand stinks, and each stink different from its fellow. The weather for months has been almost one continual flood of rain, and now, as the sun comes up more nearly straight over us, and pours down his boiling rays on this vast, sweltering mass of putridity, the stinks are magnified, multiplied and etherealized until the man in the moon must hold his nose as he passed over this vast sea of filth.

McGee, *72d Indiana*, p. 118.

19 Observations on the Sabbath in Nashville
Nashville Tennessee April 19th

...John Marvin, Tim Marvin, Jos. Blackson Harvey ... & My Self went to a presbyterian church in the lower end of town heard a very good sermon the text taken from Corinthians first chapter & 21 verce the preacher prayed for the welfair of the union & the success of our army there was but very few cittizens at church about a duzin Ladies and a number of Children and some twinty five or 30 men the balance were Soldiers the church was not over one third full it is the finest and best finished church I have seen in Nashville.... we went to the Presbyterian church this evening and saw a great many young secesh lades they try to look sour at the soldiers but pleasant and smiling countenance will beat out in spite of ther teath.

John Hill Fergusson Diary, Book 3.

21 Consequences for Disloyalty in Nashville
ORDERS
Headquarters, U.S. Forces
Nashville, Tenn., April 21.
Orders.
The sympathizers with the existing rebellion in this city and vicinity, apparently considering the dictates of their political sympathies as of more power than the obligations imposed upon them by their residence and protection within the Federal lines, the General commanding of this post orders as follows:

I. All white persons over the age of eighteen years and residing switching the lines of this command, who do not within ten days from the publication of this order, subscribe to the oath of allegiance or non combatants' parole, and file with Col. John A. Martin, Provost Marshal, bonds with sufficient securities for the faithful observance of such oaths or paroles will be requested to go South of the lines of this army, by routes to be designated by the military authorities.

II. Parties who have already subscribed to proper oaths or paroles and bonds, and who have not been guilty of acts or words of treason subsequent to the taking of such obligations, are exempted from the operations of this order.

III. Forfeiture of the amount of bonds given as above, and of all other property of persons violating obligations taken in accordance with this order, together with such other punishment as may be decreed by a military commission, will follow any violation of the requirements of such oaths or paroles.

IV. All persons who are unwilling to subscribe to the obligations herein ordered, will report their names and place of residence, within ten days specified, to Col. John A. Martin, Provost Marshal.

By order of
Brig Gen. Robt. B. Mitchell
John Pratt, A. A. General

Nashville *Daily Union*, April 21, 1863.

21 The oath or exile in Nashville
Wednesday 21. An order in today's paper, ordering every white person over 18 to take the oath in 10 days or be sent South, how unhappy....

Diary of Rebecca Carter Craighead.

21 Capture of McMinnville by Federal forces
The McMinnville Raid

On Monday of last week a body of Federal cavalry from Murfreesboro dashed into McMinnville and burned the Cotton Factory, which was one of the most extensive and valuable in the South, and, beside, destroyed the Depot, Railroad Bridge, a locomotive and three box cars.

The question naturally arises, through whose carelessness was the raid permitted? Why was McMinnville left unprotected? Factories and provisions are not so plentiful in the South that we can afford to lose them in this wise. A Court of Inquiry should be held to ascertain how it is that a cavalry command can dash to the rear of Gen. Bragg's army, destroy property of inestimable value, and return to their own lines unmolested. There was — there must have been, gross negligence.

Fayetteville Observer, April 30, 1863.

23 Guerrilla depredations near Richland
HDQRS. 129TH ILLINOIS VOLUNTEERS, Richland, Tenn., April 27, 1863.

Capt. PHELPS PAINE, Assistant Adjutant-Gen.:

SIR: I have to report to the general commanding that a band of thirteen guerrillas, on the evening of the 23d instant, attacked a Union man named Thomas Nowill, at his residence, some four miles from our camp. After severely wounding him, they succeeded in capturing; took him his family without hat or coat; took him off some fifteen miles and there murdered him, literally hewing him to pieces. With them were some at least of what Capt. Peddicord used to call his "command" — Ellis Harper — Berryman, and, some say, Peter Blane. As we could not take the murderers, I sent down yesterday the fathers of Harper and Berryman. Last night, some 2 A.M., I received pretty reliable information that a band of some seventy-five rebels were moving toward Franklin, on La Fayette road. My mounted men were then out and did not return until about daylight, and then so jaded were their horses that I have not been able to ascertain any further news. Almost nightly robberies are committed in the country out from five to fifteen miles from this station. If we are expected to stop this a much larger mounted force will be indispensable; though if there were one of the companies from the tunnel sent here, so that I could send 75 or 100 into the country to watch roads, fords, and houses at night, we might possibly effect something more. If four companies at the tunnel would build some little stockades they would be quite as safe as the five now are. Should the general see fit to move any company from the tunnel here, Capt. Baird, of Company E, has asked me to get his company moved here, if be in accordance with the best interests of the service. He would be a very efficient officer in that kind of service.

Your most obedient servant,

A. J. CROPSEY, Maj. 129th, Cmdg. Regt.

OR, Ser. I. Vol. 52, pt. I, p. 305.

23 Public Health Problems in Fayetteville
Clean up. — We would respectfully refer the attention of the authorities, civil or military, or both, to the condition of the streets, allies, etc., of Fayetteville. Dead hogs, mules, and horses may be found in the corporation or vicinity, on all sides in every state of decomposition. The air is thick with incipient disease, and unless a speedy purifying is resorted to, mid summer will again find the cholera, or some other fatal epidemic in our midst. In behalf of the citizens, we ask that our town may now have a thorough cleansing. The soldiers, we have no doubt, would unite in the request.

Fayetteville Observer, April 23, 1863.

24 Provost Orders — No. 16
PROVOST MARSHAL'S OFFICE
NASHVILLE, TENN., April 24, 1863.

I. All citizens or unauthorized persons not commissioned or enlisted in the Army of the United States are prohibited from wearing the uniform, or any part thereof, of the Army. Any person violating this order will be summarily stripped of the same, and any repetition of the offence will subject the offender to arrest and punishment.

II. Officers and soldiers are prohibited from wearing badges of a rank or corps to which they do not belong. They must restrict themselves to the uniform and badges belonging to their rank or corps, under penalty of arrest.

JNO. A. MARTIN, Colonel and Provost Marshal

Nashville Daily Press, May 9, 1863.

26 Chattanooga Rebel Newspaper Report on the McMinnville Raid*

The Raid on McMinnville.

We have conversed with a gentleman just from McMinnville. He represents the outrages of the enemy in that quarter as surpassing any yet perpetrated in Middle Tennessee. His account is substantially as follows:

The enemy appeared on the Northwest side of the town at noon on Monday. — Tidings of his approach had been brought in an hour or two before, allowing the stray cavalrymen, convalescent soldiers and others a chance of escape. There was a company of Provost guardsmen present, who made a stand against the first advance for the purpose of giving our wagons, et cetera, a fair start. After a brisk skirmish of half an hour, overpow-

---

*April 20, 1863.

ering numbers forced this handful of men to disperse. Some escaped and others were captured. There being no further obstacle the Federals proceeded at once to the public square. They were mostly mounted infantry, estimated at between six and ten thousand in number.

Their first business was the destruction of the large Cotton Factory, near the railroad bridge. It is one of the most extensive, and has been also one of the most useful in the South. It was completely destroyed. They then burnt the depot buildings, and adjoining houses, and the bridges across the Barren Fork....
— Chatta. *Rebel*, 26th.

Weekly Columbus [Georgia] Enquirer, May 5, 1863.

ca. 26 Shooting at the Worsham House, Memphis

A SHOOTING AFFRAY.— A few days since Alexander Nutall, who kept a gambling house on Jefferson street, was shot by Mike Lyons, at the Worsham House, under the following circumstances: It seems that Lyons and Nutall have been enemies for some time, and every time they saw each other it was increased by one or the other making some remark. In the morning of the day of the affray took place, Nutall swore he would shoot Lyons at sight; in the evening they both met at the Worsham House and after having a few words Lyons fired, the ball taking effect in Nutall's body, from the wound of which he has since died. After he received the fatal wound, he rose and taking aim at Lyons discharged his pistol, but his hand was too unsteady, as the charge went harmlessly by. Lyons gave himself into the hands of the civil authorities and has since been discharged. Nutall was one of the many dangerous characters with which this city is now infested. It is said he was always ready for a quarrel and had shot three men.

Memphis *Bulletin*, April 28, 1863.

27 The Fortune Telling Lady on Second Street in Memphis

Madam Cora James, the only reliable clairvoyant of the day, is daily astonishing citizens of the highest rank by her wonderful clairvoyant power in revealing the past and predicting coming events, Madam James has mastered all the science embraced in this glorious gift of prophecy and invariably gives satisfaction to all who consult her, and all acknowledge the truthfulness of the revelations made to them. Clairvoyant examinations and prescriptions in all chronic disease, insanity in its various forms, rheumatic affections, nervous afflictions and all complaints peculiar to females, Madam James warrants curing. Ladies and gentlemen don't procrastinate, as this is a rare chance, but come at once. Rooms at the Bluff City house, on Second street between Madison and Monroe streets. Go up two pair of stairs.

Memphis *Bulletin*, April 27, 1863.

29 "I rose up and fired one shot and fell back." J. M. Winn, Confederate soldier, to his wife in Robertson County
Camp 15 miles East of Carthage
April 29th, 1863
Dear Priscilla:

Learning that I have an opportunity of sending you a letter I proceed to write to you, hoping very cincearingly that it may reach you in safety & find you well and doing well. These lines leave me in fine health & the boys are all well so far as I know, (of our Reg)

Thos. R. Mason I learn is getting well of his wound. I haven't been in but one battle since I came out this time, that was at Snows Hill near Smithville. I leigh under the Enemies' fire about ½ an hour, was then ordered to retreat. I rose up and fired one shot and fell back. Our company lost Lieutenant Ashbrook, wounded in the head he is getting well....

The boys see a tolerable hard time, everything is high out here. Corn is worth $10. per lb., Bacon from 25 to 35 cts. per lb. Horses are worth from 100 to 800 Dollars.

Write soon, write how you are & how you have been all the time, and if you have anything there say what it is and its name. Give all the particulars.

Winds of Change, p. 57.

29 Special Order, No. 13
Office District Provost Marshal,
District of Memphis
Memphis, Tenn.,
April 29th, 1863

I. ... If, after ten days from the date of this order any house of ill fame, kept for the purpose of prostitution and lewdness, is discovered in this District, the inmates thereof will be arrested and sent North, and their household furniture reported to the Commanding Officer for confiscation.

II. Any officer or soldier of the United States Army, who in this District should so far forget the respectability and dignity of his position, as to appear in places of the above named character, except on official duty, will, upon discovery, be reported with his name, and regiment, to the Commanding General.

III. Masters of steamboats are prohibited from bringing to this District and landing, as passengers, "prostitutes" or women of disreputable character. A violation of this order will subject the offender to arrest and fine.

The local Provost Marshals in this District will see that these orders are enforced.

MELANCTHON SMITH, Lieut. Col., and District Provost Marshal.
Approved
Headquarters District of Memphis
Memphis, Tenn., April 30th, 1863
Approved
By order of Brig. Gen J. C. Veatch.
F. W. FOX, A. A. G.

Memphis *Bulletin*, May 1, 1863.

30 The war against prostitution in Memphis

Closing Houses of Ill Fame.—It is a fact too notorious that our city at the present time is a perfect bee hive of women of ill fame. The public conveyances here become theirs by right of conquest, so much so, that a lady fears to side through the streets for fear of being classed with them. To a certain extent the steamboats plying between this and other cities North of here have not the same respectability that characterized them in former years. In fact morality, from importation of lewd women from the North, is almost at a discount. It is no common occurrence to see that class of beings walking arm and arm with men who wear the apparel of gentlemen, who are here in civil as well as military capacity, in broad daylight, to the infinite satisfaction of the women and the great annoyance to respectable people. The nuisance can be stopped, will it be? An order closing houses of ill-fame, punishing officers and soldiers for associating with the inmates of those houses and making it a heavy penalty for steamboatmen to bring lewd women down the river would no doubt have the desired effect.

Memphis *Bulletin*, April 30, 1863.

30 Favoritism in the execution of Confederate conscription in Union county

The following unique letter was handed us by Capt. Webb, of the Enrolling Office of this Department;

UNION COUNTY, April 30, 1863

To Col. Blake, Comeding Cornscripts and so fourth:

Now Sur, I beg leeve to make a few remarks. Are the cornscripts ov ower cownty liable and ordered to be arrested. And delivered over at Knocksville to who has the collection ov them. Are the cornscripts officers aloud to seez one man and send wurd to anuther to cleer out and hide hisself? And then Kernel ar we kumpelled to have rollin officers who send men and buoys ove the mountings, telling the young men not yet 18 that the C. Gov. had abanderud ages under 18, and was ketchin corncripts by weight. And by this they have actery sceered off sum who ar not 17 years old-one in particler Elber Dawl, near me wus told that ef he weighed 124 lbs, he sertinly must go into the service of the C. S., and that nite he left for Ky., and is over thar now. We has in this cownty every enrollin offiser for the very wust cort of Likninite, & every one relatives ov the Cheerman or Cownty Court Clerk & this clerk was Thornberg's 1st Lieut. & the Cheerman is no better. Can we not have these stowt young men cauld into the servis or let them run off as sum ov them will do & have men over, 45 appointed or appint ower justices ov the peas & uther persins exempt from Concript this would at once put amazingly formydable foarce ov young men into the field & leave them who now have nuthin to do offishally to attend to the enroaling clerks sheriffs justices & other exempts. I have ritten to Congress asken them to pass a kempulserry law on the cownty coarts to make up the rollin officers entirely ov the exempt whether you have the power to change the appointments I know not, but this ere you can do, put them into the army a foarce the cownty courts to make other appointments for the pressant incumbenters in moast of the cownties in East Tennessee is a burlesk on the military but I kno that we has sum very good uns if I can get an order I will arrest a phew bad men & who ar lyin out steling everything in thar reach I have extended my few disjointed remarks much further than I espceted at first yours truly

JOHN DOOLY.

We are inclined to believe that the publication

of the foregoing patriotic letter will result in important reforms in the enforcement of the Conscript act, and we accept in advance the thanks of Col. Blake for the invaluable suggestions presented.

Knoxville *Daily Register*, May 21, 1863.

◆ MAY ◆

1 Strict provision control orders issued for the Confederate Department of East Tennessee

GENERAL ORDERS, No. 8. HDQRS. DEPT. OF EAST TENNESSEE, Knoxville, May 1, 1863.

The following general order from headquarters Department of East Tennessee is republished for the information of all concerned. It will be strictly enforced:

I. The transportation of flour, bacon, corn, and oats from the Department of East Tennessee is strictly prohibited.

II. When Government supplies are purchased for shipment from the department, authority must be obtained at department headquarters for their transportation.

III. Railroad and steamboat companies will in every case require this authority to be presented before shipping such supplies.

By command of Maj. Gen. D. H. Maury:

OR, Ser. I, Vol. 23, pt. II, p. 807.

4 "...we discovered a negro woman waving a rebel flag."

As we passed a residence on Summer street yesterday, glancing in at a window, we thought we discovered a negro woman waving a rebel flag. It was a mistake, however, as we ascertained subsequently. It was a rebel flag, but it was being used in knocking down cobwebs. We trust that ultimately rebel flags and cobwebs may go together.

Nashville *Daily Press*, May 5, 1863.

7 Allegiance Registration Drive

The Oath of Allegiance.

Quite a large number of our citizens yesterday repaired to the Capitol for the purpose of renewing their allegiance to the Government. The following is the accurate list up to last evening

April 22	200	Day order was issued
23	225	2nd day
24,	280	3rd "
25,	320	4th "
27	768	5th "
28	792	6th "
29	974	7th "
30	1078	8th "
May 1	637	9th "
2	305	10th "
4	457	11th "
5	507	12th "
6	427	13th "

The total thus far is 6,520, including less than 600 paroles of honor.

Nashville *Daily Press*, May 7, 1863.

10 Observations on Federal forces in Murfreesboro, an excerpt from the diary of John C. Spence

The Federal soldiers here are taking matters quite easy, lying about in the shade eating and drinking. There is quite a mania among them in the way of remodeling their camps. They haul large quantities of cedar brush to ornament their tents, make latice frame and work the branches in. This destroys a great deal of timber. It appears they came to destroy, it matter[s] not which way.

...

But the greatest excitement here among the soldiers is buying ginger cakes, pyes and lemonade. Many add whiskey, as the effects are seen some times by their being overcome by the article. When this happens, as a punishment, the guilty will have to carry a rail on his shoulder for about two hours each day for two or three days or a headless flour barrel, with the head of the man out at the top, for this length of time. This is for getting drunk, a mode of punishment in the camps by the Yankees. They don't appear to mind it much. Some of them would be willing any time to carry rail or barrel, for a good swig of whiskey.

Some of the boys, as they call themselves, are troublesome, slipping round citizens gardens and stealing vegetables as they get of any size, onions in particular. They will go to any length to obtain a fiew onions.

Spence Diary.

10 "Quite a feather in MY cap." Capture of Confederate cavalrymen near Murfreesboro by Lt. Albert Potter, Fourth Michigan cavalry picket

Headquarters Co "H"

Camp 'Park,' Murfreesboro

Thursday May 14, 1863

Dear Sister

... I was out on Picket last Sunday [10th] and had quite a little adventure. Captured 3 Rebels and their Horses and Saddles and arms complete. Quite a feather in MY cap. Several of the rebs had been seen for 2 or 3 days back, on the road in front and they nearly all stopped at a home about a mile beyond my videttes. I thought perhaps I could nab them, so I took a Relief, mounted, and went to our outpost a little before Daylight. I then dismounted tied my horse and had seven of my men do the same, ordering the remainder to come to our support if they heard firing. We went down cautiously to the house. I sent a man to the left and right of the road, for you know, we were outside of our lines and did not know what we would come across. We got to the house about daylight, surrounded it. No one there, but, the owners, strong old sesesh, Alexander by name. Presently we saw 3 horsemen come up the road. We secreted ourselves so that if they came to the house we could surround them. They came on, my men ran out in the road in the rear of them — cried surrender. One of them, who had had his gun in his hand all the time, raised it as if to shoot. When quicker than thought my boys fired. One ball struck his hip and came out just below his belt in his abdomen. Another one struck his wrist another one struck his horse. I hollered at the men to stop firing or they would have killed him. I felt sorry for him, smart good looking, if he had not raised his gun the boys would not have fired. He died in a day or two. I expected the firing would draw more of them upon us and when the ambulance came, I took 20 men with me and went down. But no one came in sight. Since then they have kept a fire there all the time.

Potter Correspondence.

10 Baptism in the Army of Tennessee; excerpt from the letter of Third Sergeant John R. McCreight, Ninth Tennessee Infantry to his sister

...

Dear Sister,

...

There is still a great deal of religious feeling in the army here.... A great many have professed and many are inquiring the way. On last Sunday I stood on the banks of the Duck River amid a large crowd and witnessed the emersion of ten soldiers. They formed a line, took each other by the hand & marched into the River. There were a good many Ladies there to witness the scene. After they came out of the water several of the Ladies came up extended a right hand of fellowship with them. There were a great many things in camp life that tends to blunt the sympathies and affections of our hearts, but when I witnessed the above scene I could not refrain from shedding tears. On the evening of the same day in the 13 Reg T.V., the ordinance of Baptism was administered to several by sprinkling. I hope and trust that this good work will go on until the whole army becomes religious and then that long prayed for boone will come (Peace) which we all so much desire....

...

J. R. McRight

Ninth Tennessee, p 155.

11 Nashville public health inspection reminder
HEADQUARTERS UNITED STATE FORCES, INSPECOR GENERAL'S OFFICE}
Nashville, Tenn., April 26, 1863

The owners and occupants of businesses and dwelling-houses within the limits of this city, are hereby reminded of the Order published March 16th, 1863, requiring them to have the streets, alleys, and backyards adjoining their respective houses thoroughly cleaned.

A thorough inspection of the city by proper authorized persons will be had in a few days, and anyone found to have neglected to obey the Order will be severely punished.

By Order of Brig. Gen. J. D. Morgan,

Nashville *Daily Press*, May 11, 1863.

11 A visit to the Stones River battlefield; an excerpt from the diary of John Hill Fergusson, 10th Illinois Volunteer Infantry

Monday 11th

N. Fancer and MySelf went out to Murfreesboro. Left Nashvill at 12 o'clock and arrived at Murfreesboro at sundown. We had an opertunity of vewing the battle field near Murfreesboro it is mostly a fine open level country the enemy had decidetly the advantage as they occupide the timber on the South side of the field where they could conceal there forces they also had the advantage of Stones river, our forces had to advance across a large space of open country exposing there intior ran to the concealed enemy the field are yet laying thick with dead horses and buirring grounds are thick on all sides both of our dead and the rebels each party is buirred seperatly our dead is fenced around whare the grave of the enemy are laying open to the curious the smell of the country around that neighborhood is very offencive there is no incampments any way close as it would not be helthy or agreeable at this season of the year....

John Hill Fergusson Diary, Book 3.

12 An Amphibious Assault on Linden
Report of Lieutenant-Commander Phelps, U.S. Navy, commanding Tennessee Division on combined expedition to Linden, Tenn., May 12, 1863.
U.S. Gunboat *Champion*
Tennessee River, May 14, 1863
Sir:

On the 5th instant I left Paducah with the *Covington, Queen City, Argosy, Silver Cloud* and this vessel (*Champion*) and proceeded up this river, destroying on the way every kind of boat that could serve the rebels to cross the river. On the 11th we were at Cerro Gordo, and I then sent the *Covington, Argosy,* and *Silver Cloud* to Eastport, the highest navigable point at this stage of water, and myself dropped down a few miles to communicate, by previous appointment, with Lieutenant-Colonel W.K.M. Breckenridge. Along the river I heard of detachments of rebel cavalry at various points, whose occupation chiefly consisted in plundering, in carrying off Union men, and in taking conscripts. At Linden, in Perry County, Tenn., there was a rebel force of this kind posted. I arranged with Colonel Breckenridge to cross his small force and cover different points with the gunboats, places to which he could retreat if need be, while he should attempt to surprise Linden. The boats above rejoined me on the 12th, having found all quiet above, and at night I dropped down the river to the landing for Decaturville, where I found the colonel with but 55 men of his regiment, all he had with him. Some from a Michigan regiment that were to join had failed to come in. We at once took the cavalry on board, crossed it over with little noise, and the boats took their positions at intervals along the river some miles above and below. Colonel Breckenridge's movements were timed so that his arrival at Linden-12 miles from the river-should be just at daybreak, and he completely surprised the place. The rebel pickets fired upon him and dispersed. Only some 20 of the 118 rebels at muster the evening before had time to reach the rendezvous at the court-house before it was surrounded. The little party returned with Lieutenant-Colonel [W.] Frierson, 1 captain, 4 lieutenants, 1 surgeon 30 regular rebel soldiers, 10 conscripts, 50 horses, 2 transportation wagons, arms, etc. With the court-house were burned a lot of arms and supplies. Three of the enemy were killed. Our loss none; only 1 horse killed.

Colonel Breckenridge's men are Tennesseeans (First West Tennessee Cavalry Regiment), are perfectly familiar with the people and country, and are admirably calculated for this kind of service, while the colonel himself is just the man. I should be glad if General Grant would direct that he, with a battalion of his regiment, say 300 men, should operate on the Tennessee. I can easily provide for his transportation when necessary, at no cost, using flatboats, and can cooperate with him effectually for the good of the service on these waters. I have brought the prisoners to deliver at Cairo. The conscripts took the oath and went home.

...

From the best information I can gather, the rebels are concentrating their forces about Rosecrans. Van Dorn's force is reported at Spring Hill and Columbia, and the general [i.e., Van Dorn] is said to have been assassinated by a jealous surgeon on his staff. The force that was about Duck River has gone to Spring Hill. The captured colonel reports that he should have left Linden for the same destination one hour later. The rebels are concentrating, it would seem, every available man about General Rosecrans.

I left three gunboats below Duck River to watch that stream, and I have come down to take up a new boat with her some flats and light barges, in which we can transport coal over the shoals for our use. None of the boats carry coal for such voyages. What General Rosecrans is doing I have not been able to learn. Van Dorn's division lies between him and the Tennessee, cutting off communication. Till a battle has decided the fate of Middle Tennessee, I apprehend there will be no rebel movement upon this river. If the enemy is successful, he is not doubt prepared to move for the immediate possession of the river. Secessionists report that the plan is to recapture Fort Henry, and to fortify also Carollville.

I am, respectfully, your obedient servant.
S.L. Phelps, Lieutenant Commander.

Navy OR, Ser. I, Vol. 24, pp. 669–670.

Report of Lieut. Commander S. Ledyard Phelps, U.S. Navy.

CAIRO, ILL., May 15, 1863.

Following telegram just received from Paducah, May 14, 1863:

Capt. PENNOCK, U.S. Navy, Capt., Cmdg. Station, Cairo:

Am just down from Tennessee River. Have on board prisoners captured at Linden, Tenn., on the night of the 12th. Took on board gunboats 55 men and horses of First West Tennessee Cavalry, under command of Lieut. Col. William K. M. Breckenridge; landed them on the east side of the river. Sent gunboats to cover all landings above and below. Col. Breckenridge dashed across the country to Linden; surprised the rebel force more than twice his number, capturing Lieut.-Col. [W.] Frierson, 1 captain, 1 surgeon, 4 lieutenants, 30 rebel soldiers, 10 conscripts, 50 horses, 2 army wagons, arms, &c. The court-house, which was a rebel depot, was burned, with a quantity of arms and supplies. The enemy lost 3 killed. Our force, none; only 1 horse killed.

Col. Breckenridge, after his exploit, reached our vessels in safety and recrossed the river. Will send prisoners to Cairo.

S. L. PHELPS, Lieut., commanding Tennessee Division, Mississippi Squadron.

OR, Ser. I, Vol. 23, pt. I, p. 331.

16 A wedding at the Stones River battlefield
FROM MURFREESBORO.

To-day we had a novel wedding. The bridegroom was private J. N. Hamilton, of the 15th Indiana volunteers, and the bride Miss A. Bonn a volunteer nurse from Chicago. The ceremony took place on the bank of Stone river — on the very place where the 15th Indiana fought so nobly in the battle of Dec. 31st, 1862. The nuptial knot was tied by Rev. Post Chaplain at Murfreesboro.' A large circle of friend and acquaintances was present and just as the ceremony was over, and the newly married couple were receiving the well wishes and congratulations of their friend, Gens. McD. McCook and T. L. Crittenden drove up in a carriage, but too late to witness the ceremony. They were not too late however, to exact a kiss from the blushing bride. After they had received the usual amounts of wishes for their future, the whole party made a tour to that portion of the field on which Gen. Wagner's brigade fought, (the extreme left) and which Bragg said was impenetrable. The party then returned to town.

This I believe, is the first "wedding on the battlefield" of the war and also the first wedding of the kind in the army of the Cumberland.

Yours Truly,
"HOLDFAST."

Nashville *Daily Press*, May 16, 1863.

18 Prostitutes and Whisky at the 39th Ohio Volunteer Infantry Regiment's Camp Line; an excerpt from George Hovey Cadman's letter to his wife

....

We reached Memphis by six P.M. [May 12th]. The last 30 miles of Country we passed through seemed as fertile and beautiful as any thing I ever saw in England. When we arrived in Memphis our trouble began. Women and Whisky are plentiful here, and the men had been so long debarred from both that it did not take them long to raise Hell generally. Never did I see such a scene before in my life, and hope to God I never may again, for some days, in spite of all the Endeavors of the Colonel who did his utmost to preserve discipline, the Camp was one wild scene of Debauchery. One Copy [i.e., "company"] got all its men in the [Irving] Block* but three. Our men were not quite as bad as that, but the biggest part were drunk, in fact drunkenness was the order of the day, so you may form some idea of what the Camp was like, and with some Hundreds of the most Abandoned women in the world to add their evil influence, I thought the habitués of Wapping and Shadwell† were bad enough, but the Harpies of this place beat them all hollow. I shall be glad when we get our orders for Vicksburg which I expect is our ultimate Destination, for here we are nothing but prisoners. We cannot go more than 50 yards from our Camp without a pass, only in consequence of the misconduct of our Regt. We have now about 30 of our Regt. in the Guard House, for offenses committed while Drunk. Even now women come to the very Guard line with their bodies strung round with Whisky under their Clothes to sell themselves and a bottle of Liquor for a Dollar. For

---

*The military jail in Memphis.
†Notorious red-light districts in London, England.

the first few nights we could get no sleep for the cursing of the men [and] screaming of women and the firing of pistols outside our Camp....
George Hovey Cadman Correspondence.

21 "Having gone ½ miles, I looked back, and, to my surprise and indignation, saw no one following." Federal Expedition from Murfreesborough to Middleton*

Report of Maj. Gen. David S. Stanley, U.S. Army.
HDQRS. CHIEF OF CAV., DEPT. OF THE CUMBERLAND, Murfreesborough, Tenn., May 27, 1863.

GEN.: I have the honor to report, for the information of the general commanding, that, having learned that quite a force of the cavalry of the enemy was lying about carelessly at Middleton, I started on the evening of the 21st, with a portion of Gen. Turchin's division and Col. Harrison's regiment of mounted infantry, to attack them. I was furnished by Gen. Sheridan with the best guide I have ever yet followed. We marched to Salem, and thence, striking out south, marched south through fields and by roads, keeping 3 miles west of the Middleton road. I had designed to surround the rebel camp at daybreak, but the stupidity of Lieut. Lawton, Fourth Michigan Cavalry, in breaking the column, caused one and a half hours' delay.

Just as day was breaking, I ascertained we were within 2 miles of the enemy's camp, and near the place he usually posted his pickets. I then ordered a direct attack by the entire column upon the camp, and gave the order myself to gallop for the first mile, and then to go at full speed upon the rebels. I put myself with the advance guard, with Lieut. O'Connell, Fourth U.S. Cavalry, ordering him to run over the enemy's pickets, and ordered the advance.

Having gone 1½ miles, I looked back, and, to my surprise and indignation, saw no one following. At the same instant I heard shots in front. I sent one orderly after another, and finally rode as fast as my jaded horse could carry me back, and found the entire column at a walk and turned upon a by-road at direct right angle to the road we were going on. By fours, by companies, and by squadrons I turned them back, and soon arrived in the enemy's camp, to find that Lieut. O'Connell, to whom the word gallant applies, not as a compliment, but in its true old English signification, had, with his intrepid squadron,

whipped the enemy out of his three camps. The rebels, with the exception of a few men in the Eighth Georgia Regt. and some Georgians, escaped to the cedar thicket — literally *sans culottes*. An attempt at a stand was made by the fugitives 1 mile from Fosterville, but they fled upon the approach of our support.

We destroyed probably about 800 stand of arms, all the camp equipage and saddles, blankets, and clothing in all camps, some wagons, and, perhaps, captured about 300 horses. These latter have been put in the different regiments.

The incidents of the affair will be found in the accompanying reports of subordinates. The head of the column, led by Gen. Turchin, not keeping up was a serious blunder. It deprived us of at least 600 prisoners. Perhaps I am to blame for not taking more precautions, but when I lead I certainly have a right to expect every soldier in my command to keep up, and especially when I ride as sorry a nag as the one I was on that morning. However, it is a matter of the past; it was bad luck, and we shall hope for better next time.

I cannot speak in terms too high of the conduct of Lieut. O'Connell, Fourth U.S. Cavalry, and his brave squadron. He was well assisted by Lieut.'s Rendlebrock and Wood. The latter, a most promising and interesting young officer, is since dead of his wound. With such officers and men our cavalry must soon be what I know it is fast becoming a real terror to the enemy. To this squadron belongs whatever of the brilliant that may be attacked to the affair.

Maj. [W. H.] Sinclair, Capt. [J.] Hawley, and Lieut. [W. H.] Greenwood, of my staff charged gallantly with the advance guard.

Very respectfully, your obedient servant,
D. S. STANLEY, Maj.-Gen. and Chief of Cavalry.
OR, Ser. I, Vol. 23, pt. I, pp. 334–335.

28, 29 Juvenile Grand Larceny in Memphis
"A Bank Entered by a Boy and Robbed of $5,400."

One of the most daring robberies which has been committed in this city for several years took place Thursday [28th] afternoon. It was the robbery of an exchange office, the names of the owners of which are we omit for various reasons. The chief of the Police, Mr. Winters, was apprised of the facts of the

---
*Today Midland.

robbery, and yesterday [29th] he and his detectives Morrison, Johnson, Winters and Mahoney, set about hunting up the perpetrators of the deed. The only information they could obtain from the persons who lost the money was that four or five boys were seen about the outside of the exchange office a short time before they missed the money.

Detective Johnson soon made up his mind where the thief was, and accordingly after a tedious search found a boy by the name of Thomas Porter, who admitted the facts in the case and implicated Marcus Dunn, Daniel Grady, David Driscol and Frank Lavalle. He said the boys including himself, a large pile of money lying on a table in an exchange office, and all agreed it would require but little effort to get it provided the man in the office would step out for a minute. Just at that time he walked into a back room. As soon as he was out of sight, Thomas Porter, a boy not more than ten years of age, jumped over the counter and took all the money which was within his reach, $20 in silver and $5,380 in green backs. He, as soon as he got outside the room divided the money and each boy went on his way rejoicing. Chief Winters, who by the way is one of the best officers we ever knew, and the detective, whose names are given above, after capturing Thomas Porter went in search of the boy whose name he had already given, and before six o'clock yesterday afternoon all of the boys were safely lodged in the stationhouse and [most?] of the money recovered. The officers who ferreted out the little [thieves?] should receive the warmest thanks [of the bankers?] of this city ... [remainder illegible]

Memphis *Bulletin*, May 30, 1863.

♦ JUNE ♦

1 Scouts from Forrest's cavalry in the Nashville, Murfreesboro and Franklin environs and release of civilian prisoners in Franklin by Federal authorities
SPRING HILL, June 1, 1863 — 10 P.M.
Gen. BRAGG:
My scouts have just returned from Franklin, and report the enemy have released all the citizen prisoners and are under marching orders. I will move up in the morning as near Franklin as possible, and remain as near the enemy as prudent, and would like the balance of the cavalry to move up, if you think it advisable.

N. B. FORREST, Brig.-Gen., Cmdg.
OR, Ser. I, Vol. 23, pt. II, p. 856.

1 Artillery practice at Fort Negley and the State House, Nashville
...target shooting was pracktised today from 1 to 2 by the sedge guns in the fort and from the large guns at the State house the distance nearly 2 miles
John Hill Fergusson Diary, Book 3.

1 Lincoln county voters choose delegates to the Tennessee state Confederate nominating convention
Public Meeting.
At a meeting of the voters of Lincoln county assembled at the courthouse in Fayetteville, on Monday, June 1st, 1863, James D. Grizzard, Esq., was appointed Chairman, and S. H. McCord, Secretary. Whereupon a motion of Col. James B. Lamb, it was resolved,
1st. That we approve of the Convention called to assemble at Winchester on the 17th inst, for the purpose of designating a candidate for Governor and members of Congress.
2nd. That all citizens of this county who can conveniently attend at Winchester on that day, be, and they are hereby appointed delegates to represent this county in the Convention.
J. D. Grizzard, Ch'n.
S. H. McCord, Sec.
Fayetteville *Observer*, June 4, 1863.

2 General Braxton Bragg joins the Protestant Episcopal Church
Gen. Braxton Bragg has joined the Protestant Episcopal Church. He was confirmed a few days since at his quarters in Shelbyville, The Rt. Rev. Bishop Elliott, of the diocese of Georgia, officiating.
The above item, which appeared in the *Mercury* of the 15th, is not exactly correct. Gen. Bragg was not 'confirmed at his quarters.' On Tuesday evening, June 2, after evening prayer, in the church of the Holy Redeemer, Shelbyville, Tenn., Gen. Bragg received the Apostolic rite of confirmation at the hand of Bishop Elliott.
...
Chattanooga *Daily Rebel*, July 2, 1863.

2 One of Fremantle's observations on the Army of Tennessee
The soldiers on sentry at General Polk's quarters this afternoon were deficient both of shoes and stockings. These were the first barefooted soldiers I had yet seen in the Confederacy.

Lieut.-Col. Arthur James Lyon Fremantle, Liet.-Col. Coldstream Guards *Three Months in the Southern States: April–June,* p. 83.

3 Excerpts from a Texas Ranger's letter relative to the religious revival in the Army of Tennessee
Letter from the Rangers
Texas Ranger's Camp,
Sparta, Tenn., June 3d, 1863...

...it is gratifying to state, that the Lord of Hosts continues to pour out his Spirit in different portions of our army, and through the instrumentality of means to convert souls. For some weeks past, there has been considerable interest manifested in the "army of Tennessee," both at Tullahoma and Shelbyville, which has resulted in the conversion of several hundred souls, whist many more are inquiring the way of life. This blessed work is confined principally to the infantry.... The cavalry, occupying the front, and being much more scattered, and often changing locality, has not an opportunity for a united or protracted effort, and hence we cannot record the visible tokens of his presence and power in a revival....

The Christians of different denominations are waking up to the importance of this work, and agencies are being established for supplying the soldier with suitable reading. The Methodist and Presbyterian Churches, in their late spring meetings, have made arrangements for sending some of their most eminent ministers as missionaries to the different armies in the Confederacy; whilst the lower church judicatories are undertaking the work of supplying chaplains for the brigades and regiment in the service. Other denominations have doubtless taken similar action, but it has not met my eye. There has heretofore been a lamentable deficiency in chaplains, and it all doubtless owing to the early legislation of Congress on the subject ... we hope that soon every regiment will be blessed with the means of grace. The soldier appreciates the preaching of the Gospel, and it has an elevating and hallowing influence upon his heart and life, it reminds him of other days, of brighter scenes, and the loved ones at home. It cheers the heart, too, to know that he is not forgotten in prayer by those who are far away. I know that multitudes of devoted Christians every where will join us when we pray, "Lord, revive thy work in the army and navy."...

Houston *Tri-Weekly Telegraph,* June 17, 1863.

3, 24–25 Efforts by Provost Marshal for the Army of Tennessee to publish misleading information in the Chattanooga *Daily Rebel*

June 3, 1863, Tullahoma. The Provost-Marshal for the Army of Tennessee, Colonel Alexander McKinstry, sent the following communication to Franc M. Paul, the editor of the Chattanooga *Daily Rebel*:

Please publish an article conveying this idea in your first issue: "We are at a loss to comprehend why General Johnston should have sent Breckinridge's corps back to Middle Tennessee. He must be in a secure condition, either from his position or from an abundance of troops.

OR, Ser. I, Vol. 23, pt. II, p. 860.
SHELBYVILLE, TENN., June 24, 1863.
FRANCIS M. PAUL, Editor *Rebel,* Chattanooga, Tenn.:

Publish an article to this effect: "We are happy to see that re-enforcements continue to arrive for Bragg's army. Our trains to-day are loaded with troops," &c. Don't mention the names of the commanders.

ALEX. MCKINSTRY, Col. and Provost-Marshal-Gen.
SHELBYVILLE, TENN., June 25, 1863.
FRANCIS M. PAUL, Esq., Chattanooga, Tenn.:

DEAR SIR: I telegraphed to you last evening, requesting you to publish an article to the effect that we were receiving re-enforcements, &c. You will have seen by the Northern press the dilemma they have been in concerning Breckinridge, on account of your notice of his return, and you will see by this, too, how much the press can assist us, and how much they look to it for information. They now (he knowing ones) know that he is with Johnston. To save your credit with them, let me ask you to put in something to the effect that Gen. Johnston recalled him, or could not spare him-whatever may suggest itself to you-to account for his being there now. They get all of our papers. Yours being the nearest, and, of course, the latest, appears to be looked upon by them as the best information. I am frequently in the receipt of Northern papers, and will take great pleasure in sending them to you.

Yours, truly,
ALEX. MCKINSTRY, Col., &c.

OR, Ser. I, Vol. 23, pt. II, p. 885.

4 Engagement (artillery) at Franklin; Forrest repulsed*

Report of Col. John P. Baird, Eighty-fifth Indiana Infantry.

FRANKLIN, June 6, 1863. (Received 6 P.M.)

GEN.: ...The attack commenced at 3 P.M., 4th. From information derived from prisoners, I think Forrest's whole force advanced-three brigades and two regiments. Forrest was with them. They sent Armstrong's brigade to my left and Starnes' to the right, working toward Brentwood. I know Forrest was personally in command, and we took prisoners from all the regiments in Armstrong's brigade.... They would not come in range of howitzers, but drove in my pickets and little force of cavalry; had two batteries; only opened with one, but soon got range, and I had to fire on them to force them to change position; also to support my pickets. I did not fire on Thursday at a range more than average of a mile; they came to town and I shelled them out. Col. Campbell came in on my left with a brigade of cavalry, sent from Triune by Gen. Granger, and drove Armstrong back, taking 10 prisoners. Friday morning, Col. Van Derveer arrived with a brigade of infantry and battery from Triune, and assumed command of forces here at noon. Early in the morning yesterday quite a large force appeared on Columbia pike, and I fired a few shots to dislodge them; they finally fell back. Our loss is remarkably small, but am sorry to report Col. Faulkner, Seventh Kentucky Cavalry, was wounded mortally. Col. Van Derveer left at noon to-day, taking with him all the force Gen. Granger sent here, although Granger ordered him to send the cavalry.... I would like permission to burn up the town, so I can see the front ... our loss ... will not exceed 10 killed and wounded. We took 28 prisoners, and the enemy must have lost fully as many more killed and wounded. If attacked, I will fight as long as we can fire a shot....

J. P. BAIRD, Col., Cmdg.

OR, Ser. I, Vol. 23, pt. I, p. 361.

4 Gingerbread cakes and young ladies: letter from Confederate Major General S. B. Buckner to E. C. & Lizzie Lillard, Lizzie & Emma King and Sallie McClain Vs. Mrs. Buster & Others

Knoxville, Tenn., June 4, 1863

My Dear Young Ladies,

It pains me very much to learn from our brave Soldiers at Vicksburg, Who are now bravely defending the beautiful valley of the Miss from the Ruthless invader of our soil, to be informed by them that you had deprived them of their rations Such as sweet bread, more commonly called Ginger Cakes, which was prepared for them by their wives, mothers and sisters. It is with regret that I shall and do order you one and all to appear before me at these head quarters to answer the charge made against you viz.,: Sweet bread thereby trying to make yourselves Sweet at the expence of the Poor Soldiers.

Specifications

1st for eating said ginger bread without butter

2" Taking to large mouth fulls

3" Eating as much as 2 rations each without water

4" Consumg the whole 10 sacks and asking for more

Maj. Gen. S. B. Buckner, Commander Dpt. East Ten

W. P. A. Civil War Records, Vol. 2, p. 174.

4 "Sent South."

Captain John Conover, of the 8th Kansas, yesterday, accompanied the following names persons beyond the lines of this department: Mr. Nicholas C. Branch, his wife, Mrs. Bethenia Branch, and six daughters, Misses Mary A., Bethenia, Susan W., Martha A., Sallie J., and Virginia T.

Nashville *Daily Press*, June 5, 1863.

6 Concern expressed for the plight of Nashville prostitutes

"The Cyprians in Trouble."

On Thursday evening lower College street was thrown into a state of unusual excitement in consequence of an official notification received by some of the Cyprians to vacate their premises. The order required Captain H. C. Hodges, A. Q. M., to take possession of the houses occupied by Mary Combs, Mary Stratton, Lou Hulse, Maggie Seats, Jennie Rogers and two or three others, and directed the said occupants to vacate their several buildings before 12 M. on Monday, the 8th of June, 1863, and hand over the keys to Captain H. C. Hodges.

On Friday morning [5th], nearly all the hacks in town were brought in requisition, and Post Headquarters, the Capitol, and other places, were

---

*There were three official reports issued concerning this engagement. One is presented here.

besieged, with the hope of having the order countermanded. At length it was whispered around that the house could be retained if the proprietors would dismiss all their girls, and not allow soldiers to visit the places. This made matters worse for when all expected to be turned out of doors, there was a consolation in all going together; but for each girl to look out for a home for herself, to be cast among strangers, perhaps be compelled to wander all night in the streets, was more than they could bear, and the wailings and lamentations of the unfortunate creatures were pitiable in the extreme. Like other human *beings*, these *poor* girls have their loves and ties of kindred, of home, and of friends; many of them are as helpless as children, and totally unfit to take care of themselves; and there are none to give them a helping hand to reform, none to give them a helping hand to reform, none to give then shelter in time of need, none to say "daughter, you are forgiven; sin no more."...

While upon this subject, we may as well allude to the indelicate practice of soldiers riding in open carriages with these girls through the street in broad day; and would suggest that the Provost Marshal make an endeavor to put a stop to it. The girls are not to blame. The neither pay for the carriages nor induce men to ride in them. The fault lies with the men, and to them alone the military and civil authorities ought to direct their attention in suppressing this practice.

Nashville *Dispatch*, June 6, 1863.

7 Sergeant Charles Alley, 5th Iowa Cavalry attends religious services for slaves in Clarksville...

...I got leave from the captain to go up in town to go to church if there was any. Found on inquiry there was no service for "white folks" in the afternoon. But there was for "Niggers." I concluded to go to the M.E. church as it was then (3 o'clock) open. The sermon by a white minister was from Isaiah 1–19–20. "If ye be willing and obedient ye shall eat of the good of the land. But if ye refuse and rebel, ye shall be devoured by the sword for the mouth of the lord hath spoken of it." And there followed a thing—the speaker would probably call a sermon—that was enough to disgust any man. He told the congregation that the land meant Heaven. That they must not look to eat of the good things of the earth; they were not for them. That God required them to be obedient to their masters and if they were treated all their days even with the oppression and violence they must not think to resist but must be patient looking to God to reward them. What Angels the fellow would have the slaves to be, he a rebel against the just laws of his country....

Alley Diary

ca. 12 Confederates capture Union spy Pauline Cushman near Franklin

Shelbyville, June 18th

...Forrest's forces on Friday last [12th] went in pursuit of a woman to whom suspicion had been attached. She had reached the Yankee pickets in front of Franklin when they came in sight, but on they dashed, driving in the Yankees and capturing their "booty." She proved to be a Miss Cushman, a theatre actress, claiming relationship with the celebrated Charlotte, and had upon her person plans and drawings of our fortifications, and the disposition made of the latter. It is said that she was a crinoline scout for McClellan in Virginia, and performed valuable services. Her fine talents are, doubtless, occupied at present time in planning an escape from Columbia, where she is under guard.

N.

Savannah [Georgia] *Republican*, June 22, 1863.

15 Writer's block at Beersheba Springs; an excerpt from the journal of Lucy Virginia French

...I sat down in the morning to do my writing—about 9 o'clock [I] began to feel sick and at 10 was obliged to undress and go to bed. Took laudanum and brandy-lay in bed all day....

War Journal of Lucy Virginia French, June 15, 1863.

18 Advertisement for a Slave Auction in Lincoln County

EIGHT LIKELY SLAVES FOR SALE!

Pursuant to a decree of the County Court of Lincoln county, Tennessee, pronounced at its June term, 1863, in the case of Pleasant Halbert, Admr, and others—Bill of sale of Slaves—I will on Saturday, the 1st day of August next sell to the highest bidder, in the town of Fayetteville, Lincoln county, Tennessee, the following SLAVES, viz: Amanda, aged about 35 years; Martha, about 6 years; and Gordy, about one year, (these will be sold in one lot,) Ann, about 19 years; Tom, about 16 years; Andrew, about 14 years; Josephine, about 10 years; Nancy, about 8 years. The above slaves will be sold on a credit of twelve months, except the sum of 5 per cent on the amount of sale, which will be required in cash. Notes with two or more approved securities will be required of the purchaser, and a lien retained upon said Slaves until the purchase money is paid.

DANIEL J. WHITTINGTON
Clerk and Special Commissioner

    Fayetteville *Observer,* June 18, 1863.

20 A wealthy planter's son eschews being drafted in the Confederate army

My son Thomas L. Porter (a conscript) procured a substitute (Near $5,000) & got a certificate of discharge from the army.

    Diary of Nimrod Porter, June 20, 1863.

21 "I do say I never imagined people could live so." An aristocrat visits mountain folk near Beersheba Springs

...

Yesterday we rode out to see some of the "mountain people." I do say I never imagined people could live so. One house was clean — but everything seemed to be dropped just where they were done using it, and left there until they wanted to use it again. Somehow I never conceived of anything so wholly untidy and uncomfortable.... Mrs. Armfield said these people were the "aristocracy" of the mountain and she took me to see them as a curiosity. The strangest thing to me was that they showed not the slightest embarrassment, but appeared to think themselves all right, and just as good as anybody living. At Walker's we found a young soldier home on furlough and it was astonishing to see how the service had improved him, and how much better he appeared than his surroundings.

...

    War Journal of Lucy Virginia French,
    June 22, 1863.

22 Governor Isham G. Harris' Proclamation at the Confederate State Nominating Convention held in Winchester, Tennessee

PROCLAMATION BY THE GOVERNOR OF TENNESSEE.

The President of the Confederate States has made a requisition upon Tennessee for 6,000 troops for the term of six months from the 1st of August next under the provisions of an act of Congress entitled "An act to provide for local defense and special service," a copy of which is hereto appended. These troops will be mustered into the service of the Confederate States, but held for the defense of their own homes, and in no event will they be ordered beyond the limits of this State.

This force must be composed of men over forty years of age, or such as from other causes are not liable to conscription, and if not raised by volunteering by or before the 1st day of August next, must be then immediately raised by a draft upon that part of the militia between the ages of forty and fifty-five years.

As volunteers you will have the right to organize your companies, battalions, and regiments by the election of such officers, as you may prefer.

You will be permitted to remain at your homes engaged in your ordinary avocations until such emergency shall arise as to make it necessary to order you to the field.

You will be armed, and while on duty under orders will be paid and subsisted as other Confederate troops.

When the emergency which called you to the field shall have passed, you will be relieved from duty and return to your homes and ordinary pursuits your pay and subsistence being stopped until you are ordered again to the field.

Volunteer companies, battalions, or regiments of infantry or mounted men who furnish their own horses will be accepted.

If drafted from the militia you will be placed in such infantry organizations as the authorities may deem best, and will most probably be continued on duty during the entire term of service.

The muster-rolls of volunteer companies must distinctly set forth that the company is raised for local defense and special service within the State of Tennessee for the term of six months.

You will return your muster-rolls to the adjutant-general of the State immediately upon the organization of a company of not less than sixty-four privates, with such officers as are required by law.

If said companies are organized into battalions or regiments previous to being mustered into service, they will elect their field officers; but if mustered into service as companies, the President will appoint battalion or regimental officers.

The enemy has shown that he fears to meet our gallant and invincible armies in the field unless he outnumbers us two or three to one.

He has therefore resorted to a system of raids

upon unarmed neighborhoods for the purpose of devastating and pillaging the country, destroying our resources, and laying waste our homes.

Men of Tennessee! if you would resist these raids, predatory bands, and incendiaries of the enemy, organize at once and stand ready to repel or crush them.

If you would protect your private property, defend your wives and children, your personal liberty, your national independence, and your lives, organize at once and stand ready to strike for them.

Let the beardless boy and the hoary-headed father organize for the defense of their altars, their homes, and all that is dear to freemen.

Let the gallant men who have been disabled by the exposure and hardships of the camp or the casualties of bloody fields give to these new organizations the benefit of their experience and example.

Let every man who can wield a musket or draw a sword, who is so situated that he cannot swell the ranks of our Army for constant duty, organize at once for home defense and special service.

While I may justly claim, without the fear of successful contradiction, that Tennessee has already furnished to the Army of the Confederate States more troops in proportion to population than any State in the Confederacy, and in proportion to numbers engaged upon most of our battle-fields Tennessee soldiers have bled even more freely than those of other States-much as she has already done in this struggle for national independence, I am proud to know that she is able and willing to do more, and that she will persevere to the end of the struggle, however long or bloody it may be.

I therefore appeal to you by every consideration of patriotism personal interest, personal reputation, national independence, and the high character you have hitherto borne as citizens of the "Volunteer State" to rise up as one man, organize, rally to the standard of your Government, and in the majesty of your power make the invader feel that every hilltop bristles with the bayonets of freedom and every mountain pass has become a Thermopylae.

Give him a new and stronger proof of the fact that we stand as a unit, deeply solemnly, and irrevocably resolved on preserving independence at any and at every cost; that the march of the invader and the rule of despotism will be resisted at every step now and forever as long as there is a man or a boy in Tennessee who can pull a trigger, wield, a blade, or raise a finger in defiant resistance.

With this spirit prevailing our whole people, under the providence of a just God, we will at no distant day be blessed with independence, peace, and prosperity.

In testimony thereof I have hereunto signed my name and caused the greater seal of the State to be affixed, at Winchester on this the 22d day of June, A. D. 1863.

[SEAL]
ISHAM G. HARRIS,

OR, Ser. IV, Vol. 2, pp. 666–670

June 23, July 7, 1863 Middle Tennessee or Tullahoma Campaign

24 Skirmish at Middleton

HDQRS. RESERVE CORPS, In the Field, near Christiana, Tenn., June 25, 1863 — 7 A.M.

GEN.: I have just this moment heard from Gen. Mitchell. After a very stubborn resistance made by the enemy, he drove him out of Middleton yesterday evening [24th]. He is now returning here to supply his command with forage for his horses and rations for his men. He found the country about Middleton devastated, and his horses have had nothing to eat for three days. He is now within 3 miles of this place, and I have sent out forage and rations to meet him. I will send to Murfreesborough to-day for additional forage and rations for him. His command will not be fit for service before to-morrow night, and I will retain it here awaiting your orders.

G. GRANGER, Maj.-Gen., Cmdg.

OR, Ser. I, Vol. 23, pt. I, pp. 532–533.

◆ JULY ◆

2 Poetry aimed at rousing the spirits of soldiers in the Army of Tennessee

Never Give Up!

Soldiers of the Army of Tennessee, from all the Southern States of your sunny land, the nation watches you with breathless interest:

Never give up!

Never give up! though the grape shot may rattle,
 Or the full thunder cloud over you burst,

Stand like a rock, and the storm or the battle
Little shall harm you although doing their worst.
Never give up! if adversity presses,
Providence wisely has mingled the cup,
And the best counsel in all your distresses,
Is the stout-hearted watchword of never give up.

Chattanooga *Daily Rebel,* July 2, 1863

ca. 2 Guerrilla attack trains near Murfreesboro

A few days since a party of our guerrillas went around in the rear of Murfreesboro' and blew up two locomotives and trains, with torpedoes, one on the Nashville and Chattanooga, and the other on the Franklin and Nashville road. The torpedoes were placed underneath the track, with a screw percussion cap, or friction primer attached, which was so placed on the iron rail that the wheel of the car pressing over it, caused the fulminating powder to explode and ignited the magazine. We did not learn the extent of the damage.

Chattanooga *Daily Rebel,* July 5, 1863.

July 3–4, 1863 Battle of Gettysburg

July 4 Vicksburg Surrenders

7 "The Cyprians Again."

Brigadier General Granger yesterday issued an order on the previously obtained authority of General Rosecrans, for the removal of all women of ill-fame from this city, which produced a considerable agitation in the Northern part of the city. A combination of urgent reasons makes this ejectment highly proper, and we, for one, hope it may be carried out to the letter. Notification has been served on about forty of the frail sisters, who will depart on the Louisville road this morning. Notification has been served on about forty of the frail sisters, who will depart on the Louisville road this morning.

Nashville *Daily Press,* July 7, 1863.

8 Round up of prostitutes

Departed.

The commotion amongst the ladies [who] dwell in suspicious places was inconceivably great yesterday. Squads of soldiers were engaged in the laudable business of heaping furniture out of various dens, and then tumbling their disconsolate owners after. Many very affecting scenes of abdication from long occupied domiciles took place. But they were not allowed to enact them all on terra firma; a boat was chartered by the Government for the especial service of deporting the "sinful fair" to a point where they can exert less mischief, and about forty of them took passage. Where they will be sent, is not stated in the order enforcing the exodus. A variety of ruses were adopted to avoid being exiled; among them, the marriage of one of the most notorious of the cyprians to some iniquitous scamp. The Provost Marshal didn't regard the separation as wicked or unchristianlike, so he compelled the artful daughter of sin to take a berth with her suffering companions, and she is on her way to banishment. This course toward bad women will have a salutary effect upon the morale of the soldiers in this Department — at least we hope so.

Nashville *Daily Press,* July 9, 1863.

9 Report on the expatriation of Nashville prostitutes

Departure of the Cyprians.

Yesterday [8th] a large number of women of ill-fame were embarked upon three or four steamers, and transported northward. The number has been estimated at from one thousand to fourteen hundred-probably five or six hundred would near the mark. Where they are consigned to, we are not advised, but suspect the authorities of the city in which they landed will feel proud of such an acquisition to their population. We hope the commanding officer will issue an order as soon as possible, ordering off all contraband prostitutes — they contribute considerably more toward the demoralization of the army than any equal number of white women, and certainly have no more claims upon our sympathy.

Nashville *Dispatch,* July 9, 1863.

10 Black prostitutes replace white prostitutes in occupied Nashville

It is the mistaken opinion of some of our good citizens that the flight of a large number of white harlots from our midst will prove an infallible cure of the evils so justly complained of and so utterly demoralizing to the military camp and the city. But the sudden expatriation of hundreds of vicious white women will only make room for an equal number of negro strumpets.... Unless the aggravated curse of lechery ... as it exists among the negresses [*sic*] of the town, is destroyed by rigid military or civil mandates, or the indiscriminate expulsion of the guilty sex, the ejectment of the white class will turn out to have been productive of the sin it was intended to eradicate and in a hundred fold more excessive and loathsome ratio. This community has endured long enough the humiliating improprieties of negro females, publicly connived at and brought about by soldiers and others every day of their lives. We dare say no city in the country has been more shamefully abused by the conduct of its unchaste females, white and Negro [sic], than has Nashville for the past fifteen or eighteen months. It is time a summary and effectual remedy was applied where it is most needed; and we trust that, while in the humor of ridding our town of libidinous white women, General Granger will dispose of the hundreds of insolent black ones who are making our fair city a Gomorrah [sic]. In the essential work of suppressing such a glaring and hurtful evil, let there be no partiality shown — not the least."

Nashville *Daily Press*, July 10, 1863.

13 The Capture of Jackson, Tenn.

The following authentic details of the taking of Jackson, Tenn., by Col. Hatch, of the 6th Iowa volunteers, gives further particulars of that gallant affair than any we had previously received:

The 2d Iowa and 3d Michigan regiments were led by Col. Edward Hatch against the rebels, who held the place, under command of Gen. Forrest. These regiments stormed the fortifications and, after one of the sharpest cavalry fights of the war, in which the enemy's cavalry fought better than the attacking party had ever before known them to do, a complete victory was gained and the proud flag of the Union floated above the fortifications at Jackson. The enemy's cavalry were fiercely attacked by General Hatch, and his men rode them down like nine-pins, putting them completely to flight. The enemy acknowledge that they had a large superiority of numbers, and that they were whipped; this stamps the battle as a gallant affair.

...

The enemy had one hundred and seventy eight men killed and wounded, including ten commissioned officers. One hundred and fifty prisoners, regular troops, were taken; four hundred conscripts were allowed to go. Among the material captured were three hundred stand of arms.

Memphis *Bulletin*, July 21, 1863.

16 Prostitutes' progress, Cincinnati, Ohio, as well as Newport and Covington, Kentucky "The 'Frail Sisters.'" —

The Cincinnati *Gazette* of the 17th says: "The *Idahoe* came up yesterday from Nashville, bringing a cargo of one hundred and fifty of the frail sisterhood of Nashville, who had been sent North under military orders. There does not seem to be much desire on the part of our authorities to welcome such a large addition to the already overflowing numbers engaged in their peculiar profession, and the remonstrances were so urgent against their being permitted to land that that boat was taken over to the Kentucky shore; but the authorities of Newport and Covington have no greater desire for their company, and the consequence is that the poor girls are still kept on board the boat. It is said (on what authority we are unable to discover) that the military order issued in Nashville has been revoked in Washington, and that they will all be returned to Nashville again."

Nashville *Daily Union*, July 19, 1863.

16 One Army of Tennessee private's account of the retreat to Chattanooga as a result of the Tullahoma Campaign

CAMP NEAR CHATTANOOGA, TENN., July 16, 1863

...On or about the 24th of June we were then in front in Shelbyville working on the fortifications. About that time Col. Morgan's "Regiment of Cavalry" move in near the works about one-half mile from our encampment, but from the pace of work I did not get a chance to go see him, as I would have like to have done. On the night of the 26th we got orders to cook rations. About sunrise on the 27th we were formed, not knowing where we were going, to the front or rear. We struck the pike, moved by the left flank, to the rear, in retreat. This day was a hot, sultry one. As we passed through Shelbyville we saw every indication of retreat. Union families were seen peeping through windows exuberant with glee; other families of Southern sympathy were in great distress and gloom. I then thought of yourself and family, feeling as if every foot we moved would prolong you're your banishment from your once pleasant and happy home. We marched all day in the rear of the army, and night found us seven or eight miles from Shelbyville, worn-out and sick. During the night the rain fell in torrents, and the only shelter was trees. On the 28th we arrived at Tullahoma, cooked four days' rations on the 29th, and moved to the front on pickets three miles from the line of fortifications — just our brigade — the enemy showing evidence of fight. We occasionally heard a bullet pass. It seemed they were advancing, but slow and cautious. On the 30th the First Kentucky Cavalry had drawn back to our line of skirmishers, and reported the enemy in force two hundred yards from us. We remained thus until after sunset, when a report from a rifle in our front, then a volley which we didn't answer, expecting the enemy wanted to advance his lines. At dark all was quiet as death. We laid down upon our arms with sad feelings, thinking that the day of July 1st would usher us on a field of death and carnage. About 10 o'clock we are aroused from sleep and move to the rear, it having been ascertained that Rosey had evaded us by the right flank, and was endeavoring to get to the mountains before we could. We marched all night and until noon of the 2d. We halted at Alizonia, nothing unusual but the heat, and a great many cases of sunstroke. The 3d, at daylight, we moved through Winchester, stopping within two miles of town to rest in the heat of the day. Before we got seated the cavalry were skirmishing in Winchester. We pushed on, got to Cowan Station at 3 or 4 o'clock, formed line of battle, and lay without any further molestation. The 4th day of July we made an early start over the mountains, the enemy's cavalry still pushing us closely until we crossed the mountain and the Tennessee River. We were then more secure, and all the wagons safe in camp at Shell Mound Springs, which is large enough to float a large boat, and very cold. On the 5th we crossed one mountain, climbed another, and camped on the mountain thirteen miles from this place. On the 6th we got on the railroad, arriving here to learn of the fall of Vicksburg. The troops do not seem so much affected by the intelligence as would be supposed. The consolation is: the gallant conduct of the heroic garrison, and the hardships they underwent before the place surrendered, and the loss the enemy sustained there. It has cost them more than it can be worth, as it does not insure them the free navigation of the Mississippi River. Well, we are lying under the summit of old Lookout, but do not expect to remain, as we have got work to do, and the sooner the better for us. There is no doubt that the enemy will find it easier to recruit since our late reverses....

J. H. Lynn, Company E, 154th Tennessee Regiment, T. V.

How it Was, pp. 181–186.

20 Cyprians ordered back to Nashville
Don't Want Them.

It is extensively hoped in Nashville that the reported countermanding of the order by which the ill famed women of the town were deported, is without foundation. Without desiring to impose such a burden upon any other community, we would prefer that those women remain as far away as possible. Send them to Great Salt Lake city; they'd make admirable latter day saints, and old Brigham would shout gloriously at their conversion. It will require the largest fraction of a century to cure the evils they have inflicted on this community, and it can never be done if they are permitted to come back.

Nashville *Daily Press*, July 20, 1863.

21 Gangs of Memphis
Riot Among the Boys

It seems that the New York [draft] riots have set everybody crazy on the riot question — even the boys are not getting along well unless they can get up a riot on their own account. Yesterday, therefore, they undertook the game out in the neighborhood of Chelsea. Some boys from the locality known as Scotland, gathered together, and marched into Chelsean territory. This invasion roused all the wrathful fires of pride of place in the bosoms of the Chelsea boys. A call for organization was made. The boys of the invaded territory flew to arms; clubs, stones and brickbats were their principal weapons. The number, though small at first, rapidly increased until each side numbered about fifty. A regular pitched battle was fought, in which the Chelsea boys, aided by reinforcements from Pinch were victorious, the invaders being forced to evacuate. The boys composing these bands were of all ages, ranging from six to twenty years. Some ten or fifteen the boys were more or less injured by being stuck with clubs, stone, and such like missiles. Some soldiers who had watched the fight interposed, and restored quiet among the rowdies.

Memphis *Bulletin*, July 21, 1863.

26 The Sack of Beersheba*
Scenes enacted here today beggar description. Early in the morning the sack of the place began.

---

*Located in the Cumberland Mountains, Beersheba was a hotel summer spa for wealthy famialies. It stands today.

But a few of the "bushwhackers" were in — the mountain people came in crowds and with vehicles of all sorts and carried off everything they could from both hotel and cottages. Mr. Armfield seeing that the place was going, opened Dr. Harding's and Mr. Bass' cottages, just opposite, and told his negros to come and remove whatever they wanted. The negros "pitched in with a will" — and furniture and housekeeping articles changed places rapidly. Mrs. Scott's wagon was here — she had it filled, and Mr. Hadden took it down home for her, going in company with our gentlemen. Darlin' and Mr. Armfield started about 11 o'clock intending to remain over night at Mr. Scotts. In the morning Miss Jane and I went to Sunday school with the children, but no one arriving but Miss Martha Smartt and Maj. we came home without any school.... I left there ... but the scenes we witnessed were indescribable. Gaunt, Ill-looking men and slatternly, rough barefooted women stalking and racing to and fro, eager as famished wolves for prey, hauling out furniture — tearing up matting and carpets — running to and fro after entrances into inclosures, the women fully as full of avaricious thirst as the ruffainly men. Others seated on their piles of plunder, smoked and glared defiance on any one who came near them. One crone, a Mrs. Anglin, ... sat on her pile, and crooned a hymn by snatches and starts! One girl-bare-headed and barefooted took off some dress from B[isho]p Otey's. She could not wait until she reached home to try them on, but put down her bundle in a fence corner, tried one on and had a great overgrown boy hooking them up for her! Satisfying herself as to the fits — she resumed her bundle and marched on! (Speaking of fits reminds me that one of those Yankees who were up here on Tuesday [21st], fell down in a fit at the dining room door — just as he was going to breakfast. He was a frightful object — and they deluged him with water and poured brandy over his face, and beat and rubbed and shook him. They saw Jane and Mollie and one of them said "it was a d____d shame for them secesh women to be laughing at Dare." Mrs. M. asked what was the matter? They said he had a fit in consequence of his night ride, no supper, the storm, the losing of the way — the scare, etc. etc. "Why!" she exclaimed, "soldiers scared — scared into fits!" "Oh!" if you'd been there you'd been scared too — my horse jumped down a precipice 15 feet high, — etc. etc.) At Mrs. Freeliln's house they held an orgie the whole night, singing, shouting, and it is believed dancing. I heard the noise among the cottages myself, when I closed my shutters at 11 o'clock. It was a brilliant moonlight — fair and cloudless, with a light breeze blowing. Nature so serene and lovely seemed to smile upon the scene of confusion. They dragged off mattresses — fine furniture etc., into the woods, and left it, coming back for another load, and in this way many who had no conveyances managed to get away a great deal. It called up before me (on a small scale,) visions of the reign of terror and the mob of Paris shouting "to Versailles!" The difference was that blood flowed there so freely — and it would have flowed here — if resistance had been made. And not withstanding it was so serious an affair, many incidents occurred which provoked me to laughter. Miss Sue White said that one woman had a lot of books from Bishop Otey's residence — many were Latin and French books, and there were some volumes of very profound theological character, and pamphlets of Church proceedings. The woman who did not know a letter to save her life, said "she had some children who were just beginin to read and she wanted the books for them — she wanted to encourage 'em!" To crown all imagine one scene of old "Meg Merilees"* sitting on her plunder with a bucket in her hand scooping out greasy boiled cabbage and swallowing it wholesale and clawing it up in her long bony fingers and helping another who being more fastidious rather expostulated as the manner of being helped — when old Meg cried out "take woman as ye can git it — ye mustn't be so nice these times." Two women went into a regular fist fight and kept it up for an hour — clawing and clutching at each other because one had more than the other! A band would rush up and take possession of a cottage — place a guard, drive off everyone else, stating that this was theirs, and many were the scenes of contest that ensued. The men would have red curtain tassels on their hats — the women beggared description as to costume. I saw one tall, lathy, figure with a tallow face and hank hair — bare-footed, bareheaded, — a skirt of faded calico rent in several places, a body of a different material with a belt of red horse

---

*A gypsy in the poem "Meg Merilees" by John Keets.

girth, vainly endeavoring to "make the connection" between the two incongraous garments! She went off like a locomotive hither and thither leaning forward until she was half bent in her eagerness to get everywhere before somebody else! All day it was beautiful, sunshine and calm, over the white cottages nestling among the heavy green foliage — but oh! the scenes enacted around that doomed Hotel and among these birds nest dwelling place[s] of luxury and taste in rural retreats! It is that "the masses" had it all their own way on this memorable day,— the aristocrats went down for the nonce, and Democracy— Jacobinism — and Radicalism in their rudest forms reigned triumphant. It has been a memorable day this 26th, July 1863.— when "the master" went down to town "to take the oath" and become in Lincolnite parlance a "subjugated rebel," and Bersheba was sacked in his absence by a wild onset from the very people he has been building up for years! The "bushwhackers" were in in the evening, and "one Campbell" ... went to Hobb's and stole off our magnificent Morgan horse ... I have given thus but a faint and feeble as well as disconnected outline of the strange doings of Sunday. I never expected to be in a "sacked city" but I now have a "realizing sense" of what it would be — having witnessed the sacking on a small scale. And having seen something of the demoralizing effect upon the servants, and indeed upon ourselves, I can imagine what its effect would be upon an army if allowed to ravel in the license which has marked the proceedings of this day. I know of nothing which would utterly annihilate the soldier in a man so soon.

War Journal of Lucy Virginia French.

27 Federal scout Purdy to Lexington-capture of Confederate forces

Monday, July 27, 1863 — We moved out at 5:30 A.M. to Jacks Creek 5 miles distant which is a very small town on a little creek. There we took the road to Lexington, Tenn., 18 miles distant. During the forenoon the 15th Ill. Cav. was sent off on the left flank and came suddenly upon the rebels under Col. Newsome 300 strong who fled without offering resistance. We reached Lexington at 3.00 P.M. It is the capitol of Henderson County. The courthouse was burned. Soon after our arrival the rebel Col. Campbell of Brag's [sic] army with two commissioned officers and five soldiers approached our picket post thinking it was their own men. They were all captured. The citizens do not seem to like our presence in their town.

Pomerory Diaries, July 27, 1863.

29 All's fair in love and war; self defense in Knoxville

A Sad Occurrence.

On the night of the 29th inst., between the hours of 8 and 9 o'clock, a personal difficulty occurred between J. C. Cole, and Wm. A. Clark, partners in a manufacturing establishment of this city. We regret very much that circumstances lead us to make a brief statement in regard to the sad and unfortunate affair.

From what has been reported to us, it appears Mr. Cole and Clarke were devoted friends until of a recent date. Frequent attentions from Mr. Cole, to a young lady (a sister to the wife of Mr. Clarke) caused Mr. Clarke to make many threats and infringe upon the feeling of the two admirers. On the night spoken of, Mr. Cole was innocently conversing with the lady of his affections, when he discovered Mr. Clarke approaching him with a double barreled shot gun from behind a fence; seeking an opportunity to empty its deadly contents. Mr. Cole then immediately stepped a few paces from the house and commenced firing upon his assailant-several shots were fired-one taking effect in the left side of the lady, and one in the leg of Mr. Clark.

Mr. Cole at once gave himself up to the authorities, and stated he was perfectly willing to abide by the law as he was forced to act as he did in self-defense.

The affair is much to be regretted but it is hoped and believed by many that the wounded lady will recover.

Knoxville *Daily Southern Chronicle*, July 31, 1863

♦ AUGUST ♦

3 Cracking down on Confederate soldiers in Knoxville

Post Headquarters,
General Order No. 2

By virtue of the following "Special Order No. 91, Headquarters, Department of East Tennessee, (Knoxville, August 1st, 1863)" to-wit:

"VII. The Commandant of the Post will take such steps as he may deem necessary to keep the city clear of officers and soldiers improperly away from their commands, and to prevent drunkenness among both officers and men, and keep so far as possible, detailed men in the city from strolling the streets.

VIII. All orders from the Commandant of the Post relating to the city or its police, shall be respected, and he will be responsible for the general good of the city."

The following are ordered:

I. All officers and soldier coming to Knoxville, are required to report at Post Headquarters immediately on their arrival, register and have their leaves furloughed or orders [re]vised.

II. To prevent trouble and confusion, all officers on duty at this Post are requested to call at Headquarters and procure passes for themselves and those under their command.

III. The officers in charge of the Police Guards are instructed to arrest all officers found drunk in the city.

By order
John B. Major, Capt. comd'g Post.
Knoxville *Daily Southern Chronicle*,
August 4, 1863.

4 Curs Beleaguer Memphis
"Memphis and the Dogs."

Our city is a general thing, as free from vices as any city of the same extent in the land. And her citizens are equal in refinement to those of any other city east or west, north or south. But yet they seem to have a strange penchant for dogs. These roam about the streets, in the back portions of the city in packs, and as soon as the sable vial of night is thrown over the scene, these dogs set up a yelling and howling which, in truth, renders "night hideous." Not only this, they beset the way of the belated pedestrian, in such numbers, and of such formidable size as to render it almost dangerous to walk the streets after night. We wonder if there is not some way to stop their infernal howlings. We can't help dreaming of hydrophobia. And no wonder, for the last sounds we hear, when we retire to sleep, is the howling of dogs.
Memphis *Bulletin*, August 4, 1863.

7 "I may endure." Life in the Confederate army in Chattanooga

Notwithstanding, the regiment has had nothing to eat but corn bread for more than two days. They have sent us to work on fortifications. Being on guard yesterday and barefoot, I was excused and managed to get a quart of milk. I may endure.
Van Buren Oldham Diaries.

10 The irritation of war; an excerpt from the Van Buren Oldham diary

I have bought me some letter paper and intend to write whether I have any correspondence or not. I have a boil on my buttocks caused by itch[ing] from which I have been suffering sometime. It is very painful and I am excused [from duty] because of it.
Van Buren Oldham Diaries.

11 Boils, bare feet and writing in Confederate Chattanooga

Today I thought I was getting off [work] again by being excused from work on account of my boil but when I came to find out all barefoot men were excused. I have been writing the whole of the day. I can not tell at this moment what I have written.
Van Buren Oldham Diaries.

12 Oldham gets new shoes in Chattanooga

Excused again today from work. Managed to draw a pair of shoes and I am not a liar if they didn't feel awkward to my feet. I went to see ... two old women who gave me dinner. I shall never forget these old women. They have been kind to me.
Van Buren Oldham Diaries.

13 "The Frail Ones."

We learn from the *Press* that the Provost Marshal, by order of Gen. Granger, has notified all the public women of this city to report at the Provost Marshall's office on or before the 15th day of August, and that on presentation of a Surgeon's certificate and payment of five dollars, they will receive licenses. All such women found without certificate and license, after the specified date, will be arrested and incarcerated in the work house for a period of not less than thirty days.
Nashville *Dispatch*, August 13, 1863.

16 "Dog Killing."

We have observed the dog-killers to be very active in plying their vocation. Yesterday they destroyed, of these animal, not a few. We are perfectly willing that the work should go on until the last of the canine race that frequent the streets to bark at the passerby as he pursue his nightly way, shall share the fate of the howling curs "gone before." But we do protest in shooting dogs down and leaving them to load the atmosphere with such horrible stench as dogs undergoing decomposition will produce. The ordinance providing for their dogs being killed, also expressly declares that they shall be removed beyond the corporation limits. Notwithstanding all this the dog-killers leave them where they shoot them. Yesterday, down on Beal street, we saw a monstrous sized dog defunct, from the effects of leaden pills administered by the dog-killers. He was fast decaying beneath the heat of a summer sun, impregnating the atmosphere with an intolerable scent. Such things should not be. It will (if permitted to go on) produce a pestilence which will sweep, with the besom of death, every portion of our fair city.

Memphis *Bulletin*, August 16, 1863.

18 Bad humor and hunger in Confederate Chattanooga

I am in a bad humor this evening but I hardly know for what unless it be that I am hungry and can not get enough to eat. I have just eaten a slice of bacon, the first meat of the kind I have eaten in quite a number of days. It was delicious I am sure.

Van Buren Oldham Diaries.

19 Capture of guerrilla leader Dick McCann

AUGUST 19, 1863.—Skirmish at Weems' Springs, Tenn.

Report of Capt. James Clifford, First Missouri Cavalry.

NASHVILLE, TENN., August 23, 1863.

CAPT.: I have the honor to submit the following report of the expedition to Weems' Springs, Tenn.:

In compliance with your instructions from headquarters District of the Cumberland, I left camp at Nashville, Tenn., with my company (F), First Missouri Cavalry, Maj. Gen. G. Granger's escort, at daybreak on the morning of the 18th instant and proceeded to Hillsborough, Tenn., where I arrived at 1 P.M. Here, in accordance with your instructions, I was joined by Company C, Fourteenth Michigan Infantry (mounted), under command of Capt. Mackey. I left there at 9 P.M., travelling all night, and arriving within half a mile of Weems' Springs at 8 o'clock on the morning of the 19th instant.

Here I halted and gave directions to Capt. Mackey how he should maneuver his company, dividing both companies into four platoons, each under command of a commissioned officer. Every man being in readiness, I ordered the charge, which resulted in the capture of Maj. Dick McCann and 14 others, together with 27 horses, their arms and equipments. The notorious guerrilla chief was captured by Private Martin W. Culp, of my company, and first recognized as the same by Lieut. William Davis, who immediately introduced the gentleman to me. I of course had him well cared for, with the others of his command who fell into my hands. I fed my horses and rested at Weems' Springs until noon, when I started for Franklin, Tenn., where I arrived with my command soon after dark on the 19th instant. Here I turned Maj. Dick McCann and prisoners over to the provost-marshal, and rested my men and horses until the afternoon of the 22d instant, when I departed with my company for Nashville, arriving there about 8 P.M. without the loss of a single man or horse.

Too much praise cannot be bestowed on Capt. Mackey and the officers and men of his company.... having traveled 105 miles in less than twenty-four hours.

I have the honor to be, captain, very respectfully, your obedient servant,

JAMES CLIFFORD,
Capt. Co. F, First Missouri Cav.

...

OR, Ser. I, Vol. 2, pt. II, p. 638.

21 Artillery bombardment of Chattanooga

HDQRS. FIRST BRIGADE, FOURTH DIVISION,
Opposite Chattanooga, August 22, 1863.

...

Gen. GARFIELD:

...

We shelled Chattanooga, at intervals, from 10 to 5 P.M. yesterday, silencing every battery that opened on us. But few of their guns could reach us, being mostly 12-pounder howitzers and 6-pounders rifled. They opened on us with nineteen different guns. One 32-pounder rifled gun covers all on this side. Lilly made most excellent shots, dismounting guns at 2,000 yards. He threw shells directly in their embrasures....

...

...Col. FUNKHOUSER, Ninety-eighth Illinois:

I am directed by Col. Wilder to say to you that we opened fire on Chattanooga at 10.30 A.M. yesterday, and shelled the enemy's works at intervals until 5 P.M., they replying with nineteen guns, all small, except one 32-pounder rifled. They did not use them all at any one time, however. The place is well fortified; not many troops to be seen in the town or vicinity; best information puts them below here. Prisoners say it is well understood that this is only a feint, and that the real point of attack is down the river. An intelligent contraband who lives at the foot of Lookout Mountain, on this side of the river, reports troops passing all night; thinks they were cavalry. No force this side the river, except a few bushwhackers in the mountains. We are scouting the country and watching the river to-day. All quiet in town this morning.

...

ALEX. A. RICE, Capt. and Assistant Adjutant-Gen.

OR, Ser. I, Vol. 30, pt. III, pp. 122–124.

21 A description of Nashville

NASHVILLE

The City-Streets-Contrabands-Army Feeling Toward Them

Nashville must have been a quiet, shady respectable Southern City once, with a number of very handsome residences embowered in trees, or surrounded with neat gardens. It is prettily situated on the hills by the Cumberland; its public buildings, far more pretentious than the town, are very handsome and imposing, and the view from the Capitol over the hills and valleys of Tennessee, is beautiful. But at present the city is nothing but a garrison town. Everything is appropriated for the soldiers. From the windows of elegant private residences, may be seen protruding the slouched hats and cigars of our officers: guards patrol the verandahs, orderlies stand before the gateways, soldiers fill up the deserted warehouses, even the churches are turned into hospitals and the huge unfinished hotel, said to have cost $300,000 (whose owner offered his whole property, worth $5,000,000, for the use of Rebel Government,) is now crowded to the very top as barracks. Barricades still remain in some of the streets, a witness of the struggle which was expected. Soldiers are quartered in the City Hall and in the Capitol; and through the principal streets there is at all hours of the day and night an incessant rumble and tramp of army wagons, cavalry, led horses, marching infantry, scouts, orderlies, sutlers' wagons, troops of mules, officers and soldiers, and artillery, apparently with name or end.

From the Capitol, can be seen all over the country, on every hill and in the valleys, the tents of our camps.

Fortifications, earthworks and forts are going up on every side, to protect this the great garrison-town of the frontier. The Capitol itself is guarded with artillery and a stockade. This is a spacious and cool building, ornamented with exquisite native marble, and built of the beautiful shaded limestone of Tennessee. Here is going on a great deal of the military and civil business of this department.

Here come all the citizens and people from the country who want passes or who desire to take the oath of allegiance; here Gov. Johnson is carrying on his multifarious affairs; here the officers of the military Government are transacting their appropriate business, and here the Courts-martial meet.

The interior shows a most lively and motley throng at any hour.

A number of the wealthy citizens of Nashville have entirely abandoned the city, others who are Secessionists have remained in the utmost seclusion and poverty. Mrs. Polk, I understood, still occupies her house — the tomb of the Ex-President guarding the place from disturbance. Union people are fast coming in and filling the houses and places of business, so that Nashville will resume the character it had before the war fairly broke out, of a loyal and national city.

The condition of the town, however, does no credit to loyal officials. The streets even surpass those of New-York in accumulated filth, dirt and garbage, and under this tropical sun, steam with odious exhalations.

Soon Gen. Butler is anxiously called for by all who are obliged to endure the squares or streets of Nashville. Another special want is of a decent hotel. Coming from the Galt house in Louisville, perhaps the best kept house in the whole country, the contrast is forcible. I was recommended to the Sewanee House as "the only one where clean sheets are certain to be given!" That was its only recommendation. Otherwise the traveler finds bad cookery, a table like that of sixpenny restaurants, dirt, vermin, incivility, and disorder-all for $2.50 per day. The other hotels are said to be worse. If only some enterprising person would set up here a first-class hotel, he might make his fortune in three years! The travel is immense.

THE CONTRABANDS

One of the most pleasing sights in Nashville are the contrabands; a respectable, orderly, well-mannered folk, who do their work faithfully and make no disturbance. They seemed prone to work less briskly than our white laborers, but more steadily. The officer overseeing some large squads at work on the fortifications of the city assured me that they accomplished quite as much as any white laborers. The saving in pay, from the lower wages of the Negroes over white labor, amounts, I am assured by high authority, to a thousand dollars a day to the department of the Cumberland.

It is a remarkable fact that along with the occupation of the city by Union forces, the Negroes at once begun to open schools for themselves. I met companies of the neatly dressed, bright little black children going regularly to school. A bookseller says that he sold many more spelling books in a short time than he has done before for years in Nashville. The Negroes are already organized into pioneers and laborers in ROSECRANS' army, and will be shortly, into regiments of infantry on cavalry, as more come in. Every day the pathetic little bands of refugees, wearily working toward liberty, are brought within the lines from Georgia or Alabama.

The slaveholding families are anxiously considering the subject of "help" now — whether they are to be exposed to the eternally-changing households of our Northern families, or whether they can keep their servants a long time under wages. So far as I have conversed with them, there does not seem to be as much vexation at the loss of their slaves as might be expected. Those who have lands, hope that the loss of the laborers will be more than made up by the increased price of land under the new immigration which they confidently expect.

And then, even if with no higher principle all have bowed themselves to a great revolution, which they see to be inevitable.

The feeling of the army toward the Negroes, I think, has reached as sound, healthy condition-that is, it is mostly indifference, such as they might feel toward, white laborers and refugees. As soldiers, I think they would respect them for Milliken's Bend and Port Hudson have settled the opinion of the army that "Negroes will fight." How clear it is that the only path of the Negro toward a recognition of his manhood will be through blood. Nothing but hard blows will do away with the vulgar prejudice against him, as a creature without the courage or the nature of a white man.

The army, it must be remembered, has become intensely anti-rebel, and, so far, Anti-Slavery. A great challenge has passed over it during three years of war, and it has learned to hate with bitter hatred the institution which has brought such ruin and disaster upon the country. This revolution in opinion was expressed to me recently by an officer in language more terse than reverent "I was an out-and-out Breckenridge Democrat once, Sir, but now, Sir, I am an Abolitionist."...
...

New York *Times*, August 21, 1863.

23 A glimpse of life in Chattanooga prior to the Federal occupation

No shelling to day but a continued bang of musketry has been kept up between the pickets along the banks of the river. Citizens since the first gun [was] fired have been busy moving out of town. The woods and roadsides are lined with crying women and dirty babies.

Van Buren Oldham Diaries.

25 Prudence advised to Knoxville Confederates as the Federal army advanced

THE MOVEMENT IN KNOXVILLE.

The [Knoxville] *Register* of the 25th has the following:

We must caution our friends not to be agitated by the many rumors in circulation.-Let them be calm, cool and resolute during the impending crisis. We shall probably have a hot day's work in East Tennessee before long. Many seem to look for a general engagement daily, but this cannot occur. There may be heavy skirmishing during this week, but we hardly think a battle will come off before next week or the week after.

We have a gallant army in the field, under able and skillful commanders, and when they meet the enemy will give a good account of themselves.

We have not heard yet that any of the enemy have crossed either the Tennessee or Clinch rivers, though they are said to be at several different points on the other side of both these streams. Our reports represent them as being scattered from Chattanooga to Big Creek Gap, a distance of a hundred miles. Of course it will take them some time to concentrate for a general action.

Macon *Daily Telegraph*, August 27, 1863

27 Artillery duels across the Tennessee River, Chattanooga environs

The firing from across the river was renewed today and replied to by our batteries. From an eminence near camp could be seen the smoke from the guns. I have been unusually lonesome and want for something exciting, something to kill time.

Van Buren Oldham Diaries.

27 "...he died a glorious death fighting for his country without a friend to aid him." The discovery of the remains of an M. I. A. Federal soldier in the Columbia environs

...O' Lordy as we passed through here last fall a fellow by the Name of Pool a member of Co. C of our regt fell out of rank and never was heard of since until today as we passed along some of the boys discovered a grave in a peach orchard they passed along 4 miles North of here they recolected there was the last place Pool was seen some of them went over and found a small board set up at the head of the grave. With Pools name Regt and Co on [it] inquiries were made how he came by his death an old farmer told us that he was given out and could not march the rebels came on him and ordered him to surrender but he would not he raised his gun and pluged one of them through the heart he afterwards killed 2 with his baynet before he fell he died a glorious death fighting for his country without a friend to aid him

John Hill Fergusson Diary, Book 3.

28 William Garrigues Bentley, Ohio 104th Volunteer Infantry, Letter Home from Scott County, Tennessee

Chitwood's Scott Co., Tenn.

August 28th 1863

We have marched nearly 100 miles since I wrote last and are now about 70 miles from Knoxville ... we have done some big marching ... through an almost unbroken forest for 70 miles, in some places we had to march *Indian* fashion for 2 or 3 miles along foot paths ... I never saw such a variety of trees and bushes. Black, white, red & chestnut oak, chestnut, hickory, poplar, white & yellow pine, cottonwood, persimmon, chincopin, laurel, etc. We have just got to the foot of the high hills of Cumberland Mts. We have crossed several pretty steep points that are considerably above the *level*, for we have been going *up* for two days we only have 26 miles of mountains roads between here and Knoxville, now — to Jacksboro.... We will leave tonight or in the morning. Gen. Burnside is with us. He is a splendid man I think. His HeadQuarters are close to our Regiment. He looks exactly like his likeness in *Harper's,* he is a very large man, will stop and talk with a private as quick as anyone else...

Smith, Barbara Bentley and Baker, Nina Bentley, eds., *"Burning Rails as We Pleased." The Civil War Letters of William Garrigues Bentley, 104th Ohio Volunteer Infantry.*

30 The lighter side of artillery bombardment "Fooroom-Boom! Ker-gip!"

At this writing, 12 o'clock M. [Noon], the enemy are shelling the town vigorously. Our sanctum and our solitaire printer, with his 'case' and composing stick, are removed to the basement of the Bank of Tennessee [where can] be heard frantically imploring our neighbor Haskell to open his door. The voice is evidently that of a 'dry' soldier. At least we judge so from the huskiness of his throat. Possibly wants a drink. Probably won't get it, as Haskell has retired to his earthworks.

Boom! Whiz-z-z!! Goes another angry shell.

'Oh, Mr. Haskell!' goes [the] voice outside.

Fooroom-BOOM! Ker-gip!

'HASKELL! open the door!'

Crash came a shell over the roof, struck a Chattanooga hog in the side, and sent him squeaking to the happy hunting grounds.

[The] soldier couldn't stand it any longer. He broke. We can hear the retreating echoes of his footsteps. Haskell has at length opened the door and calls after him: 'What do you want?'

Reply in the dim distance: 'Oh, d__n it, you're too late. 'Spect a man to have nine lives like a cat, and get murdered for one drink?'

Drama closes. Scene shifts! Suthin' rumbles. Exeunt, at a double quick.

[A rumor was circulating in the Confederate press that the *Daily Rebel* left Chattanooga during the bombardment. According to the editor, however:]

The rumor is ... altogether incorrect. The Rebel lives. Its 'heavy bronze' has been moved to the rear, with that of the whole army, out of the way of active operations; but both of its editors, with a sufficient quantity of material and typographical force to print a daily war bulletin, remain, and will remain to the last hour. Whilst we are penning these lines, shells from the enemy's batteries are falling within our rear premises, and exploding in the street in front. If any citizen of Chattanooga has seen an evidence of a 'change of base' on our part, his imagination has led him far astray of the mark. Chattanooga maybe burnt to the ground, but the position will not be lost; and so long as our army is here to defend it, we shall share whatever befalls its gallant soldiers, many of whom are fellow comrades of war in past campaigns, and nearly all of whom are our friends and patrons.

   Chattanooga *Daily Rebel*, August 30, 1863.

31 "Divine Worship."
Nearly all the churches in the city, which have been occupied as military hospitals, are restored to their congregations. We were glad to notice yesterday that divine services were held in the Cumberland Presbyterian Church. The Sabbath School teachers of this and the McKendree Church also held meeting, yesterday morning, for the purposes of reorganization. It is hoped that the renovation of all the churches lately given up will soon be accomplished, that our Sabbath days may again present the holy appearance, and our people reinstate the religious influences which should ever distinguish a Christian land.

   Nashville *Daily Press*, August 31, 1863.

✦ SEPTEMBER ✦

1 Confederate spy's report on Federal strength in Memphis
 Twelve Miles Southeast Of Memphis, Shelby County, Tenn., September 1, 1863.
 Col. McCulloch:
 Sir: I visited Memphis yesterday and spent five hours in the city. I availed myself of the opportunity offered and gained information through a good secesh who had taken the oath. There are only about 3,000 troops in the city and only a battalion of cavalry, they having sent all their available force to Arkansas, except a garrison. The place is unfortified in two directions, and can be approached on the State line road with a few cavalry, and a small force sent up toward LaGrange and Germantown to draw their forces out, and those coming in this direction can do so at night without their knowing it, and as there are large supplies there and boats arriving from above every hour, you can destroy so effectually that it will compel them to fall back from Arkansas.

I saw two boat-loads commissary stores going down yesterday, and, as you know, to prevent desertion, the troops must have clothing and boots, and I am certain there is enough to equip 50,000 men. There are no breast-works. Come on the State-line road and 1,000 cavalry can take it now by surprising it at daylight, and if you should come you could send someone in a day or two ahead, and keep the others engaged at Germantown to prevent their coming before you had effectually destroyed all.

Such a thing would give new energy to the whole army. The streets are full of deserters. I saw a Yankee officer bring one in the barber's shop and pay his bill for a shave and hair-cut, and when once they get in there they can't get out....

I send you some Northern papers I purchased yesterday in the city. I was afraid to get any more for fear of arousing suspicion. I inclose you a letter from Mr. Jamieson, a wealthy secesh. I don't know the contents, but think it is about robbers who claim to be of your regiment, though I don't think they do. If you consider this worthy of your attention and Gen. Lee will send the cavalry, you can do the cause a great deal of good. The people are better secesh now than any of Mississippi.

...

J. A. Harral.
   OR, Ser. I, Vol. 30, pt. IV, pp. 581–582.

1 Rumors of war in the White County Cherry Creek community, a day in the life of Amanda McDowell
I have ended another tiresome day. Hear that the Yankees were at Sparta. Then heard that they were gone. Heard also that it is Purt's brother who is Capt. of the Bushwhackers. Heard that Bragg was going to fall back to Virginia. Wonder what I will hear next?

   Diary of Amanda McDowell.

3 Excerpts from the Official Report of the Capture of Knoxville and Kingston
 Headquarters Department of Ohio
 Near Loudon Bridge, Tenn.,
 Maj. Gen. W. W. Halleck
 ...
Gen. Hartsuff's corps, after the concentrating of which I notified you, moved forward. Gen. Carters' cavalry division of that corps preceded

the corps in three columns, under command of Gen Shackleford, on Loudon Bridge; one under Col. Bird, on Kingston; one under Col. Foster, on Knoxville. The last named places were taking without material opposition; but at Loudon the enemy was strongly posted. After a brisk skirmish they were driven back by Shackleford's command. They fired the bridge before they retreated, and it is now in ruins.

Col. Bird captured at Kingston a steamboat in process of construction, but nearly finished.

Col. Foster captured at Knoxville two locomotives and a number of cars, and a very considerable amount of army stores were captured....

Great praise is due to the troops ... for their patience, endurance, and courage ... we suffered no loss from the hand of the enemy, except a few wounded....

A.S. Burnside, Major-General

New York *Times*, September 20, 1863.

4 Malodorous Nashville
"The Sewerage of the City"
Partly from a want of enterprise in our municipal government, and partly through the carelessness of citizens, the sewerage of the town is frightfully defective. Until the past two or three weeks, generous floods of rain descended to purify our devoted city and save us from pestilence; but now we are in the midst of a drought, which is likely to prevail throughout this and most of the next month; and unless some plan is speedily adopted to rid our streets and premises of the contaminating filth that spreads its vomitive quintessence into ever particle of space, we shall not long have a corporal's guard on the healthy list. There is no special Board of Health, we believe, to take the lead in this matter; we once had such an institution and it gave to Nashville a world-wide reputation for cleanliness and hygeian. What say the "city fathers?" Do they ever pass along near the Maxwell house, or any other of the perfumed localities, before breakfast, or after tea, when everything is still. If they do, and inhale the delectable effluvium without being staggered and having a hurried desire to "cast up" all superfluous nourishment, they are proof against almost anything — they need not be "copper-bottomed" or "iron-clad." If we are to submit to the exhalations from dirty cellars and back premises, another month, all the good-smelling extracts ever compounded by the great Lubin* would fail to restore our nasal organs to their natural functions, nor would all of the Plantation Bitters in the country bring back our appetites. Shall we endure these unnatural sacrifices? That's the question. Shall we be stunk to death? That's another question. Are the city authorities in a condition to have the sewers cleaned and improved as necessity demands? If so, the public would delight to see them "stirring their stumps" even to the extent of making the public lend a helping hand, i.e., in looking to the neatness of their own yards and alley. If the corporation is *not* able to undertake the momentous job, it is unfortunate; and General Granger will have to step into Doctor Butler's boots and clean out Nashville on the same admirable plan that New Orleans was redeemed from disease and death. At all events, let us have a movement to this great end at once, for procrastination will render it impracticable a month or so hence. The reasons are innumerable. Action! action! action!

Nashville *Daily Press,* September 4, 1863.

4 Evicting the poor in Nashville
"Turned in the Streets." Yesterday morning an officer and twelve men went to the "big brick [building beyond] the railroad," on Market street, and in the most unceremonious manner possible, bundled men, women, and children out of doors, and their furniture and traps after them, out of windows and doors, a large amount of their earthly goods being destroyed or damaged in the hasty, removal. We presume some military necessity demanded this extraordinary proceeding, but we cannot help think that if Gen. Granger had known that many of the unfortunate inmates have large families, he would have provided them with shelter elsewhere before ordering their removal. There were, we believe, seven families in the house, with from one to six children each — say thirty children; with no prospect of shelter at 4 o'clock yesterday afternoon, but a very fair show for a cold rainy night. We thought further to be remembered that these people, though *very* poor, are honest. We trust that when this paragraph meets the eye of Gen. Granger, he will at least provide temporary shelter for such as may not have found a friend to take them in.

Nashville *Dispatch,* September 4, 1863.

---

*P. F. Lubin (1774–1853), a famous French performer.

5 Ms. Ward's cotton
"A Heroic Woman."

A day or two ago a widow lady named Ward, who resides some eight miles from the city on the Pigeon roost road, was coming to this city, with two bales of cotton, when she was stopped by three guerrillas who declared their intention to burn her cotton. The lady was not disposed to submit very tamely to this arrangement. She therefore produced a repeater, and told them that she would shoot the first man who dared to move a step toward carrying out their threat.... and they "slunk away" to their hiding place.

Memphis *Bulletin*, September 5, 1863.

7 Confederate works shelled and skirmish

HDQRS. U.S. FORCES, Opposite Chattanooga, September 8, 1863 —10 A.M.

...

GEN.: I forward several communications from different officers, which will give you some idea of the position of affairs here.

On yesterday I had the works of the enemy shelled at Chattanooga as a diversion from Gen. Wood, who is opposite in Lookout Valley. He had a sharp fight with them, driving them out of the valley. They are strongly intrenched between Lookout Mountain and the river. I shall try to shell them to-day from this side. There seem to be no camps now above Chattanooga at any point in sight.

The river is guarded by cavalry, infantry having left two days ago. Large bodies of troops have been moving to be no increase of force about the city. As near as we can learn, Cheatham's division of four brigades is here yet. What has become of Buckner? I have no information except what is contained in report of scout, marked No. 1.

I am, sir, very respectfully, your most obedient servant,

G. D. WAGNER, Brig.-Gen., Comdg.

OR, Ser. I, Vol. 30, pt. III, p. 459.

8 Confederate evacuation of Chattanooga completed

Excerpt from the October 1, 1863 report of Major-General Thomas L. Crittenden, U.S. Army, commanding 21st Army Corps, relative to Confederate evacuation of Chattanooga.

September 9.— At 2.20 A.M. received dispatch from the general commanding the army, approaching the two Reconnaissances ordered, and directing that the whole command be held in readiness to move round the point of Lookout Mountain to seize and occupy Chattanooga in the event of its being evacuated; to move with caution and not to throw my artillery around the point of Lookout Mountain till I am satisfied that the evacuation is not a ruse. Should I occupy Chattanooga, I am to order Gen. Wagner and all his force across to join me.

At 5.45 A.M. further dispatches from department headquarters, apprising me of the evacuation of Chattanooga and ordering that the whole command be pushed forward at once with five days' rations, and to make a vigorous pursuit. This latter dispatch was too late to stop the Reconnaissances ordered, but I lost no time in putting the balance of the command in motion and arrived at Chattanooga with Gen. Wood's division at 12.30 P.M., having taken peaceable possession of same.

...

OR, Ser. I, Vol. 30, pt. I, pp. 602–603

8 Action at Limestone station and skirmish at Telford's station

Excerpt from Itinerary of the Twenty-third Army Corps, August 1-September 30, 1863.

...

September 7.—.... a detachment of the One hundredth Ohio Volunteer Infantry, under Lieut.-Col. Hayes, was sent east on the East Tennessee and Virginia Railroad, to Limestone Station, where, on the 8th, they were attacked by superior forces of the enemy and compelled to surrender. Losses, 3 wounded, 17 commissioned officers and 263 enlisted men captured.

September 8.— Lieut.-Col. Hayes, One hundredth Ohio, and 300 men had a skirmish at Telford's Station with 1,500 of the enemy, under Gen. Jackson; 1 killed and 2 wounded. Thirty of the enemy killed and wounded. Fell back to Limestone Creek, to await re-enforcements. Fought the enemy, 1, 800 strong, for two hours, and then surrendered. Loss, killed, wounded, and taken prisoners, 200 men. Col. Crittenden to Sevierville.

...

OR, Ser. I, Vol. 30, pt. II, p. 578.

8 The fight against malaria in Memphis

"City Fumigation." Strangers here are frequently heard to inquire the object of the offensive fumes of tar with which the night air of Memphis is impregnated. It is the fumigation by order of the authorities to counteract the malaria and the noxious effluvia arising from the many hospitals and camps with which the city abounds, and although unpleasant to the senses, it is one of the best sanitary measures than can be levied. The dangers of night malaria cannot be exaggerated. Napoleon equally great in saving as in destroying life, always protected his troops against it. If compelled to encamp near a marsh, he kept large fires burning all night between the camps and the source of the malaria. In pitching camps in such a situation the commanding officers should, if possible, locate it to windward, not to leeward.

Memphis *Bulletin*, September 8, 1863.

9 Confederate surrender of Cumberland Gap

Excerpt from the Itinerary of the Twenty-third Army Corps, August 1-September 30, 1863.

...

September 9.—.... Rebels at Cumberland Gap, under Gen. Frazer, surrender 2,300 men, 12 pieces of artillery, including Gen. Frazer and staff. The First Brigade, Third Division, and Third Brigade, Fourth Division, there. The First Brigade, Fourth Division, to within 11 miles of Athens. Bridge at Charleston destroyed by enemy.

OR, Ser. I, Vol. 30, pt. II, p.578.

11 Newspaper Report Concerning Confederate Conscription Agents Disrobing Southern Union Women

The reader can form some idea of the joy with which the loyal men and especially the women of Tennessee will hail the arrival of Burnside and Rosecrans, when it is remembered that only a few weeks ago the rebel conscript officers were going through East Tennessee, *stripping white women while at work in the fields,* pretending they must do so to ascertain whether they were not men disguised, to avoid conscription. These women were the wives and daughters of loyal men who had been compelled to flee from their homes on account of their Union sentiments. The Nashville *Union* says of this business of stripping women:

"People of Tennessee, consider the damnable brutality of these minions of the Southern Confederacy. What think you of this handling, stripping, and inspection of the wives and the daughters of your fellow citizens for the purpose of detecting disguised Lincolnites? Shall the women of Tennessee be subjected to ruder insults by these soldiers of the licentious slaveocracy than are offered to pubic prostitutes? Are the matrons and maidens of our state to be treated as a slave dealer would treat a female slave on his auction-block?"

Milwaukee *Daily Sentinel*, September 11, 1863.

15 Union meeting in Cleveland broken up by a Confederate raid

We made an excursion to Cleveland to day, and broke up a Lincolnite meeting, which was being held by the tory citizens of Bradley County. We charged the town and took them by complete surprise, capturing a good many of them, whom we released again, though the boys took their best horses. One Lincolnite was shot through the arm with a revolver, while running, but was not [killed]....

Diary of William A. Sloan, September 15, 1863.

15 African-American cotillion in Knoxville

Colored Ball — Quite a brilliant and recherché affair came off among our Knoxville "citizens of African descent" last night at Ramsey's Hall. It was really a most admirable imitation of similar efforts at Terpsichorean amusements of the part of their Caucasian brethren. The beauty and fashion there collected was rather admirable; gay belles of every tint, from pearly white to sooty, vied with their male gallants in white kids, gorgeous dresses, and the pretty amenities of fashionable life. The music was excellent, and all went smoothly and gaily on until the small hours. The lobby glittered with envious shoulder straps, who, not being able to participate, could only admire.

Knoxville *Daily Bulletin*, September 16, 1863.

18 Looking for love in the Memphis want ads "Attention, Battalion."

Wanted, correspondence, by an amiable and interesting young lady, of marriageable age-just twenty two-of elegant style, graceful carriage, of medium hight and suggestive proportions, possessed of a happy disposition and domestic habits, with one or more gentlemen of intelligence and standing and of known respectability, with a view to love, matrimony and the consequences. All communications strictly confidential. Address, with or without *carte de visite*, Glass Box 20, Memphis, Tenn.

OLLA BEACH

P.S. No "gay or festive cusses" need apply.

Memphis *Bulletin*, September 18, 1863.

20 Murder in a Cherry Creek church, White county

Oh! what a dreadful circumstance has happened. Jeff Snodgrass fell a victim to malice, was shot at church. Oh! what wretched condition our country has got into. Who would have thought, but what a man, or woman either, would have been safe at church, but it seems that neither man nor woman was safe at Cherry Creek yesterday.

Mr. Quarles was shot and thought to be dead but was not; Jeff was killed dead, and Martha Simms had a pistol cocked at her. I never heard of such an affair all my life. It was all Dee Bradley's doings. Some say she fired the first pistol, but others that were by Jeff said that he fired first and she fired second....

Diary of Amanda McDowell.

22 Braxton Bragg's Address to the triumphant Army of Tennessee at the battle of Chickamauga, September 19–20

HDQRS. ARMY OF TENNESSEE, Field of Chickamauga, September 22, 1863.

It has pleased Almighty God to reward the valor and endurance of our troops by giving to our arms a complete victory over the enemy's superior numbers. Homage is due and is rendered unto Him who giveth not the battle to the strong.

Soldiers, after two days of severe battle, preceded by heavy and important outpost affairs, you have stormed the barricades and breastworks of the enemy, and driven before you in confusion and disorder an army largely superior in numbers, and whose constant theme was your demoralization and whose constant boast was your defeat. Your patient endurance under privations, your fortitude and your valor, displayed at all times and under all trials, have been meekly rewarded. Your commander acknowledges his obligations, and promises to you in advance the country's gratitude. But your task is not ended. We must drop a soldier's tear upon the graves of the noble men who have fallen by our sides and move forward. Much has been accomplished. More remains to be done before we can enjoy the blessings of peace and freedom.

BRAXTON BRAGG.

OR, Ser. I, Vol. 30, pt. II, p. 38.

22 The burning of Blountville

BLOUNTSVILLE, TENN., September 22, 1863.

GEN.: We met the enemy at Hall's Ford, on the Watauga, this morning at 9 o'clock, where our passage over both rivers was disputed by a heavy picket force of cavalry. After considerable skirmishing, the enemy was driven back and near to town, where we found the enemy posted in a chosen position with four pieces of artillery.

It was with difficulty that we could dislodge them after four hours' fighting. I at last effected it by a charge of the Sixty-fifth Indiana Mounted Infantry, Fifth Indiana Cavalry, and Eighth Tennessee Cavalry, which was made just before dark. Our loss is not heavy, about 6 killed and 14 wounded, mostly of the Sixty-fifth Indiana Volunteers. We captured about 50 prisoners and 1 piece of artillery.

The shells of the enemy set fire to the town, and a great portion of it was consumed. Lieut. Miller, of my staff, will communicate all further desired information of my position and the enemy's movements, and what is deemed necessary by me.

Very respectfully,

JOHN W. FOSTER

OR, Ser. I, Vol. 30, pt. II, pp. 592–593.

25 Frightened Federals

HDQRS. TWENTY-FIRST ARMY CORPS, Chattanooga, September 25, 1863.

Maj.-Gen. PALMER, Comdg. Second Division:

GEN.: The general commanding was pained when he learned this morning from the general commanding the army that soon after the picket firing commenced last evening there were many men seen to break to the rear, some reaching the city and secreting themselves. Such men, although receiving the pay and emoluments of United States soldiers, are not soldiers. This skulking and retreating at the sound of the enemy's guns will hereafter be severely punished. Division commanders will issue such orders and enforce such regulations as will at least arrest the individual guilty of such misdemeanor, and hold brigade commanders responsible for the detection and prevention of this great evil.

By command of Maj.-Gen. Crittenden:

OR, Ser. I, Vol. 30, pt. III, p. 854.

29 P. O.W. tragedy in Nashville

TERRIBLE ACCIDENT AT THE MAXWELL BARRACKS.

100 Confederate prisoners killed and Frightfully Wounded-Strange Meetings-Incidents, etc.

One of the most startling and fatal accidents

occurred in our city yesterday that we have ever been called upon to chronicle. The scene of the sad disaster, so fraught with human suffering, was the unfinished building, situated on the corner of Church and Cherry streets, known as the Maxwell House, which is used as a barracks for our soldiers. At the time of the accident, about 600 Confederate prisoners were confined there, in the upper or fifth story. At the signal for breakfast, the prisoners rushed to the head of the stairs, on their way to the dining-room, all gaiety and thoughtlessness. The rush was so sudden and their weight so great that the stairs gave way with a loud crash and 100 of the prisoners were suddenly precipitated, with a perfect avalanche of broken and scattering timbers, through two sets of flooring, to the third floor, where they landed one quivering mass of bleeding, mangled humanity. Two ... were instantly killed, and the whole of them more or less injured. Many of them were frightfully disfigured, having their legs, arms or heads broken.

The news of the accident spread rapidly through the city, and in a short time the streets in the vicinity were crowded with persons anxious to learn the extend of the terrible affair.

Guards were immediately thrown around the building to prevent the unfortunate sufferers, who were now being removed from the wreck, from ... crowds. Ambulances were hurried to the spot, and the misguided and suffering Confederates, who had braved the dangers of many a hard fought battle to be maimed for life by an accident, were taken to the prison hospital. Here they were attended by our surgeons and nurses with all the kind and tender care that could have been shown a Federal soldier wounded under the Stars and Stripes fighting for the Union. The secesh ladies also waited on them with an untiring devotion that would reflect honor on a more righteous cause. One of the injured prisoners, a mere stripling, who has been captured several times before, remarked that he "would not care half so much if he had taken his breakfast."

In another part of the building were some Union refugees, lately arrived from Northern Georgia. Upon the occurrence of the fatal accident, some of the men rushed to the rescue among the foremost. One of them found among the sufferers three of his neighbors from Georgia, who had long since left their homes for the rebel service. Another refugee found his son, who had been conscripted, and of whom he had not heard in 16 months. A third encountered a brother from Texas, from whom he had been separated eight years. Such are the sad and impressive scenes, which can scarcely be called strange in this unnatural war....

...

Nashville *Daily Press*, September 30, 1863.

29 Memphis Constabulary
Our Police Force.

We believe there are fifty policemen in the employ of the city, yet there are but two kept on the levee at any time; and while we are about town quite late — never getting home until one or two A.M.-we have not met one of the "stars" on the street for many a day. It appears to us there should be more men on the levee night and day, and that around town there should occasionally be seen one of those to whom we may properly say, "Watchman, tell us of the night!"

Memphis *Bulletin*, September 29, 1863.

30 Encounters of the squirrel kind
"The Squirrels on the Square."

A most affecting friendship is springing up between these little jokers and many of our soldiers. Like most friendships, however, it costs something. One man in a hospital gown, spends five cents every morning in pandering to their insatiable appetites. Another, whose left leg is at Corinth, is ruining himself on almonds.

Memphis *Bulletin*, September 30, 1863.

♦ OCTOBER ♦

1 Federal Medical Report relative to the Battle of Chattanooga

Report of Surg. Israel Moses, U.S. Army, Medical Director, Post of Chattanooga.

OFFICE OF MEDICAL DIRECTOR OF POST, Chattanooga, Tenn., October 1, 1863.

SIR: In obedience to orders, I repaired to this post, and, arriving September 18, reported to the commanding officer as medical director. Receiving orders from you to prepare beds for 5,000 wounded, I found scant supplies for not more than 500, and buildings capable of holding that number built by the Confederates and occupied as a hospital, with about 150 sick already in. Also a large building, two stories high, built by the

Confederates as a receiving hospital, capable of holding 150. These buildings were without doors or windows and destitute of every convenience.

A partial supply of medicines, blankets, furniture, and dressings was on hand, estimated for 1,000 men, but deficient in many articles. I selected several buildings which might be converted into hospitals.

On September 19, Saturday, an engagement took place about 7 or 8 miles distant, and was renewed with great fierceness during the forenoon of the 20th [Sunday], during which our wounded numbered over 6,000. On this and the following day [Monday], as nearly as I can estimate, 4,000 wounded officers and men were received and assigned to various buildings and private houses, hotels, and churches.

...

All the severe cases were dressed the same night they arrived, and other the next day, and all received food, of which many had been deprived for two days.

This work was performed by a corps of 43 surgeons who reported to me either by your order or as volunteers (of whom 4 were Confederate medical officers).

About three-fourths of the wounds were flesh, or of a lighter character, the other fourth being of the gravest character inflicted by musketry.

Few shell wounds or by round shot were seen, owing to the fact that little artillery was employed by the enemy.

On Monday the lighter cases were sent across the pontoon bridge, and on Tuesday others to the number of nearly 3,000. The officers who could bear transportation were sent in ambulances toward Stevenson.

On Wednesday not more than 800 of the gravest cases remained in town, and many of them have since been removed to the camp hospital.

Owing to the establishment of division hospitals there remains under my charge only Hospital No. 1, the Crutchfield Hospital, and Officers' Hospital.

Into these hospitals were received, on the evening of September 29, about 250 wounded, who were brought in from the Confederate lines.

Our hospitals are at the present time crowded beyond their capacity, and should they thus continue it would render a serious fear in my mind that our operations would be unsuccessful.

I have performed a large number of amputations and resections in the several hospitals, all of which thus far promise well.

Operations have been performed by various surgeons, in charge of hospitals and on the field, with a fair amount of success thus far.

...

The general condition of the patients is good, but our hospitals are greatly in need of bunks and mattresses, at least one-third of the grave cases being still on the floor, with only a folded blanket to lie on.

In view of the increasing risk of so many patients with suppurating wounds being crowded together, I would respectfully suggest an early provision for increased accommodations by tents with flooring....

...

I. MOSSES, Surgeon, U.S. Volunteers, Medical Director of Post.

OR, Ser. I, Vol. 30, pt. I, pp. 244–245.

3 Death of Major-General W. T. Sherman's son in Memphis

"FUNERAL OF WILLIE SHERMAN."

No better evidence can be afforded of the popularity which the gallantry and amenity of Gen. Sherman have secured, than the appearance of the mourning group who attended the remains of his little son on Sunday from the hotel to the steamer. His staff officers and the regimental officers of the 13th regulars wore mourning badges and the countenances of all present gave token how much everyone felt for the afflicted parents. Little Willie was a sergeant in fanciful appointment, of the 13th, and the roughest soldier of that regiment wept when his death was announced. The lad had shown great aptitude for military affairs accompanying the General on every occasion and taking part in all the concerns of the camp with an inquiring mind, that promised in future years a distinction rivaling the fame of his father. We tender our sympathies with those of the great number who mourn with him.

Memphis *Bulletin*, October 6, 1863.

5 "There, you d____d fool, you see what you get by leaving your door open?" Confederate bombardment of the Army of the Cumberland in Chattanooga

The enemy opened on us, at 11 A.M., from batteries located on the point of Lookout mountain, and continued to favor us with cast-iron in the shape of shell and solid shot until sunset. He did little damage, however, three men only were wounded, and these but slightly. A shell entered the door of a dog tent, near which two soldiers of the Eighteenth Ohio were standing, and buried itself in the ground, when one of the soldiers turned very coolly to the other and said, "There, you d____d fool, you see what you get by leaving your door open?"

Beatty, Citizen Soldier, pp. 350–351.

5 Sergeant Charles Alley, 5th Iowa Cavalry, on United States Colored Infantry

Today for the first time I saw colored soldiers on duty — what a change. The United States are being fast brought to reason. Thank God for that, even if the means are severe. Strange how men can talk so loudly of "liberty and equality," and yet deny their fellows all rights, not to speak of privileges at all. How grandly the war is uprooting the ideas that have been fostered by centuries of wrong. May the good time soon come when all men shall enjoy all the rights that are compatible with order, when all men shall Love God above all and their neighbors as themselves.

Alley Diary

6 Confederates burn Shelbyville

STEVENSON, October 7, 1863–4 P.M.

Brig.-Gen. GARFIELD:

Chief of Staff:

Maj.-Gen. Butterfield telegraphs me from Tullahoma this P.M. that the rebels burned Shelbyville last night and that they are now there. The damage done the railroad not yet known. I cannot learn that they have been in the vicinity of any of the bridges; they appear to have crossed the road. The cavalry within my reach, in condition or numbers, do not warrant me in dispatching them to Huntsville, where I should expect them. In the first place, one division had been ordered to take post at those points, and when it was found they had passed there, they were seasonably directed to return to them. I forbear comment until more fully advised. The pontoon bridge at Bridgeport was completed yesterday.

HOOKER, Maj.-Gen.

OR, Ser. I, Vol. 30, pt. IV, p. 160.

8 MADAME CORA JAMES

The Great Natural Clairvoyant, Physician and Life Reader, Office, Greenlaw's Block, Main St., Bet.[ween] Union and Gayoso Sts., Upstairs

Can be consulted by Ladies and Gentlemen on all things pertaining to the past, the present and the future....

...

Unlike the many who flaunt their serric powers before the public, she invariably gives satisfaction to all who may consult her, and all acknowledge the truthfulness of the revelations made to them.

As a Physician, Madame James can, in a Clairvoyant state, tell you your disease and its cause, and point out how to cure the most obstinate case. Diseases that have for years baffled all medical skill, insanity, Dropsies, Affections of the Liver, Consumption in its various forms, Nervous complaints, Rheumatic affections, inflammatory and acute Cancers, Melancholy, loss of Memory, also all complaints peculiar to females, Madame James pledges to cure, and other complaints of long standing too numerous to mention. Testimonials of persons who had nearly lost their sight and hearing and are now in perfect health, will be produced. Invalids and those who are despairing from long course of treatment by regular diplomatic Physicians, don't defer giving Madame James a call.

Memphis Bulletin, October 8, 1863.

9 Affair at the Railroad Tunnel, Cowan

HDQRS. ELEVENTH AND TWELFTH CORPS, Stevenson, Ala., October 12, 1863.

SIR: I have the honor to submit the following as the result of the investigation of the particulars attending the attack on the tunnel guard and the obstruction of the tunnel between Cowan and Tantalon, on the evening of the 9th instant:

Lieut. Robert Cairns, Twenty-eighth Kentucky Volunteers, was stationed at that time on the mountain over the tunnel with 50 men of his regiment, while guarding the track through the tunnel were 16 convalescents commanded by a sergeant. About 7 P.M. of that day, while the men of Lieut. Cairns' command were preparing their supper, they found themselves suddenly surrounded by a force of the enemy and broke and ran in all directions, hiding for the most part in the bushes.

The party on the track, it would appear, offered the only resistance made, and this consisted of a few shots, after delivering which this party also ran. The men straggled back to their post and to

Cowan early on the following morning, the 10th instant, and were continuing to arrive at 12 m., at which time it was believed that but 1 man had been captured. Lieut. Cairns reached Cowan early on that morning, but was ordered to return by Col. Given, One hundred and second Ohio Volunteers, commanding.

This much of the particulars of this affair was derived from parties to whom it had been communicated by Lieut. Cairns.

Col. Given, commanding at Cowan, on hearing the musketry on the evening of the 9th, directed 2 officers and 4 mounted men (the latter composing his entire cavalry force) to proceed in the direction of the tunnel and ascertain its cause. They were met about a mile from Cowan by one of the men who had fled from the tunnel, by whom they were told of the defeat. Col. Given then convened a council of war, following whose decision he determined to throw his force of 500 men into the defenses. He disposed them as follows: 300 men, composing a battalion of the One hundred and second Ohio, were placed in the earth-work; 150 convalescents in the stockade next the town, and the remaining 50 men, a company of the Thirty-third Indiana Volunteers, were posted in the stockade next the tunnel. Col. Given assured his different commanders that these several defenses were to be held to the last extremity.

These dispositions were completed about 9 P.M., and remained unchanged, except that a small force was thrown out about midnight on each flank until daylight.

...

R. H. HALL, Capt., and Aide-de-Camp.
OR, Ser. I, Vol. 30, pt. II, pp. 720–721.

11 Skirmish at Henderson's Mill: A Confederate staff officer's account of the skirmish at Henderson's Mill

When several miles beyond Greenville on the road to Jonesboro' Genl Jackson's advance (Genl. Jackson *Brigade* of 500) constituted our advance Guard, was fired upon just at daylight. It was within two miles of Hendersons mill-where we were going to Camp, and I was going to the front by order of Genl. Williams to halt the column there. The beautiful morning star, harbinger of coming day, was shining like a diadem on the brow of night-& we were peacefully, tho' regretfully pursuing our way-when all at once a volley of musketry into the head of the column woke up to the feast of death.

One of Genl. Jackson's Staff was captured & perhaps a few of his men killed. It was too dark to see more than 100 yards in the heavy timber in which the Enemy were concealed.

I had just reached Genl. Jackson who was again advancing his column of infantry to drive them from the woods — supposing they were East Tennessee Bushwhackers — when a furious volley was against poured into us from behind the trees not 75 yards in front. To prevent being shot from my horse, as Yankees generally shoot too high, I dismounted in an instant, but soon found myself left alone in the road under a heavy fire all the others having sought the generous protection of the neighboring trees. My horse was wild with excitement — so that I could not mount him until Rufus Todd held him for me-

As soon as our men got shelter they opened briskly upon the Enemy, & soon our artillery came up & shelled the woods. It was not yet good light. Genl. Williams immediately coming up ordered Jackson forward with Thomas Legion-(Infantry) and Carter to charge with his brigade of Cavalry —

The boys went in with a shout charging gallantly, driving the Yankees from one position to another. The General was in the front cheering the men onward-as he appreciated the critical position in which we were placed. The Enemy confidently expecting us to remain at Blue Springs, had thrown a heavy cavalry force under Col Carter (4 reg'ts of 2500 men — the same who went to Bristol and burnt Blountville,) in our rear to hold us in check until the forces on the other side could come up; therefore we must fight out or be captured: "horse, foot & dragoon," artillery & transportation, & all. Our men I say went in gallantly-drove the Enemy back, & only once gave up any ground & then a batt'n of Mounted men were driven from the woods, but were soon rallied —(the Genl. assisting) & returned to the fight. The Enemy used their artillery at first, but when we once got them started they never got time to unlimber again. The fight lasted until about 7½ A.M.-& ended by the flight of the Enemy before the impetuous charges of our boys, who never stopped but kept on, never giving the Yankees time to rally & form.

We drove them some three miles when they left the main road at double quick-taking a road to the left towards Kingsport, leaving our way open

to pursue our falling back. So we were delivered from a Yankee trap.

Thank God for the gallantry of our troops! The losses we sustained I cannot determine....

...

Our boys were very much elated with their success, & the way the Yankees "skedaddled." Thus ended the battle of Henderson's Mill — fought between Greenville & Rheatown, Tenn., on the morning of Sunday the 11th.

Diary of Edward O. Guerrant, September 10, 1863.

ca. 16–17 Resistance to Confederate conscript sweep in West Tennessee.

The Memphis *Argus* of Oct. 27th, [Tuesday] says: We learn from a gentleman recently arrived from the vicinity, that during the last week [12th-18th] a company of guerrillas entered the region of country on the Tennessee side, back and west of Fort Pillow and Island 37 for the purpose of conscripting citizens. They commenced work and although the citizens dodged them as much as they could, in a day or two Captain Mason, the leader of the guerrillas, succeeded in securing six or seven citizens of respectability, taking them from their residences without even allowing them time to provide for their families.

Matters took a turn, however, for which the conscripting gentry were entirely unprepared. A number of citizens had formed themselves into a company, with such arms as could be obtained, for the purpose of resisting the conscription....

The citizens discovered the route of the guerrillas designed taking on their exit from the neighborhood, and lay in wait for them. The company, closely guarding the conscripts, made their appearance in due time, on Friday [16th] or Saturday [17th] last, and at a point where attack was least expected (for opposition in their irruption was anticipated) they were startled by a volley from some bushes by the roadside, and the sudden appearance of a large number of men with arms in their hands.

Two or three of the guerrillas fell, and one or two others were wounded. Those who were unharmed or slightly injured, put spurs to their horses and were soon beyond the reach of bullets. In their excitement, they quite overlooked the conscripts, who, overjoyed at their deliverance, at once rejoined their friends, and all returned to the neighborhood together.

Nashville *Daily Press,* November 6, 1863.

21-November 25, 1863 Siege of Chattanooga
HDQRS. OF THE ARMY, Washington, December 6, 1863.
SIR:
...

It appears, from the Official report which have been received here, that our loss in the operations of the 27th, 28th, and 29th of October, in reopening communications on the south side of the Tennessee River from Chattanooga to Bridgeport, was 76 killed, 339 wounded, and 22 missing; total, 437. The estimated loss of the enemy was over 1,500. As soon as Gen. Grant could get up his supplies, he prepared to advance upon the enemy, who had become weakened by the detachment of Longstreet's command against Knoxville.

Gen. Sherman's army moved up the north side of the Tennessee River, and during the night of the 23d and 24th of November established pontoon bridges, and crossed to the south side between Citico Creek and the Chickamauga. On the afternoon of the 23d, Gen. Thomas' forces attacked the enemy's rifle-pits between Chattanooga and Citico Creek. The battle was renewed on the 24th along the whole line; Sherman carried the eastern end of Missionary Ridge up to the tunnel, and Thomas repelled every attempt of the enemy to regain the position which he had lost at the center, while Hooker's force in Lookout Valley crossed the mountain and drove the enemy from its northern slope.

On the 25th, the whole of Missionary Ridge from Rossville to the Chickamauga was, after a desperate struggle, most gallantly carried by our troops, and the enemy completely routed. Considering the strength of the rebel position and the difficulty of storming his intrenchments, the battle of Chattanooga must be regarded as one of the most remarkable in history. Not only did the officers and men exhibit great skill and daring in their operations on the field, but the highest praise is also due to the commanding general for his admirable dispositions for dislodging the enemy from a position apparently impregnable. Moreover, by turning his right flank and throwing him back upon Ringgold and Dalton, Sherman's forces were interposed between Bragg and Longstreet, so as to prevent any possibility of their forming a junction.

Our loss in killed, wounded, and missing is reported at about 4,000. We captured over 6,000 prisoners, besides the wounded left in our hands, 42 pieces of artillery, 5,000 or 6,000 small-arms, and a large train. The enemy's loss in killed and wounded is not known.

...

H. W. HALLECK, Gen.-in-Chief.
OR, Ser. I, Vol. 31, pt. II, pp. 11–12.

24 Let them eat fish.
MARIETTA, Ga., October 24, 1863.
THE COMMISSIONERS OF THE CONFEDERATE STATES, Sitting at Augusta:

...The infamous enemy who invades our country threatens to starve us into submission. God said: "Let the waters bring forth abundantly," and it was done. He gave to man dominion over the fish of the sea. In our rivers, lakes, and bays there is an inexhaustible supply of fish, which in our abundance we have never resorted to. It is the part of wisdom now to look to this providential supply placed beyond the reach and control of the enemy. If driven to the necessity the Army can be fed from the waters. In political economy supply and demand determine prices. The plan to diminish the price of meat for the Army is to increase the supply. As agents for the Government this becomes a legitimate question for your body. How is this to be done? The stock regions are mainly in the hands of the enemy, and in the cotton States we have not time to grow them now to meet what may become an important emergency; that is, a scant supply of meat for the Army. The most certain and ready resource, then, is to assume dominion over the fish of the sea. How is this to be done? I make the following suggestions:

First. By orders from the proper military department detail 10,000 men from the several armies, selected for their fitness for this service, such as disabled soldiers, new conscripts, and men over forty-five (if found necessary), who shall be placed under proper officers at the best fisheries to be found in the Confederacy.

Second. They are detailed as a permanent force to furnish an additional supply of meat for the Army from the waters, by all the appliances used for such purposes, to wit, traps, seines, floats and hooks, trot-lines, nets, spears, gigs, hooks, &c.

Third. The Government to furnish a supply of salt and the fish as caught to be scaled, dressed, and salted. This service can be rendered by women, either white or black, or both.

Fourth. A detail of rough carpenters should be made to make boxes and barrels, and quartermasters to superintend the transportation to depots, &c.

Fifth. Officers in attendance should make reports weekly to higher authorities.

...The object is to add to the supply of meat for the Army, thereby enabling you to control the price thereof. An experiment may show that it is economy in the Government thus to employ force enough to furnish half the meat required by the Army. It is the legitimate mode of effecting the price of what is to be bought. If this force should average ten pounds each per day it would give 100,000 pounds per day, which would be rations for an army of 200,000 men. We know that men can live on fish. We know that the supply in the rivers is abundant. We know that industry and system will get them out of the waters. It is too uncertain in the hands of individuals, hence the necessity of organizing a regular force to work at this alone by the Government. They are reliable meat growers. It develops one of the hidden resources of the Confederacy at a time when it is needed.... The supply is in the waters beyond doubt, large enough to feed the whole population of the Confederate States, and will we sit down and say we can't get out enough to feed 200,000 men? At many of the fisheries a large quantity of oil could be made-much needed now by the Army. The plan will not interfere with the field force, and its successful execution is recommended by the highest considerations. To insure success, however, I think that if the Secretary of War will give the orders and authority to Gen. Gideon J. Pillow that he will put the whole plan into operation sooner that any man in the Confederate States. He is practical and of untiring energy and industry. He knows how such things can be done.

...

S. R. COCKRILL, Nashville, Tenn.
OR, Ser. IV, Vol. 2, pp. 916–918.

29 A Slave Holder's Contempt for the Negro Exodus to Union Lines. An Extract from the Diary of Eliza Rhea Anderson Fain

...

Poor deluded, infatuated Negroes are flocking to the Northern army from the east, the west, the north and the south thinking they will free them. They are leaving homes of plenty; masters and mistresses within whose hearts are ... found the only true feeling of humanity for the African race to be found in the world (I suppose). They are cuffed, kicked and knocked by the self proclaimed philanthropists of the North. When I think of it, I feel God is letting fill up their cup of iniquity that his judgment may be more severe. I tremble for the North, the fiery indignation of the Lord of hosts seems tome to be gathering blackness every day. They know not what they do.

...

Fain Diary.

30 A Fortune Telling Lady visits Memphis

Madame Belgraves, the Renowned Fortune Teller is now making her first tour in the South, and will make but a short stay in Memphis. All who wish to avail themselves of her extraordinary powers, would do well to call soon. Her manner of telling fortunes and selecting conjugal partners has astonished the most incredulous. She may be found for a few days longer at No. 18 Madison street, up stairs.

Memphis *Bulletin*, October 30, 1863.

◆ NOVEMBER ◆

1 Hunting Conscripts

Rebels and Blood Hounds.

Editor, Bulletin: As you published an article in your journal a few days since alleging that the rebel conscripting officers were in West Tennessee and Mississippi, hunting down citizens with dogs, in order that they might be forced into the rebel ranks, and as the rebels of this city have taken particular pains to denounce the article referred to as a base lie, I simply say this much on this subject; I know that one Capt Elam in Gibson county, carries his negro dogs with him to run down loyal men, to put them in the rebel army, and this same scoundrel has voluntarily gone forward and taken the oath of allegiance to the Government, when last winter he was imprisoned for his misconduct in spouting his rebel sentiments, he was released by the recommendation of Union men of his neighborhood. Now he is hunting them down with a pack of dogs that he used to hunt negroes with. In conclusion, any rebel denying that their officers are guilty, as above charged, is a d____d liar.

CITIZEN

Memphis *Bulletin*, November 1, 1863.

2 The case of a Union wife and an adulterous Confederate husband in Middle Tennessee

Head-Quarters United States Forces
Murfreesboro, Tenn., November 2d, 1863.
Governor Andrew Johnson.

The bearer Mrs. Johnson has presented a case for my consideration, that has to many points for me. I have therefore taken the liberty to advise her to lay the case before you Excellency, believing you to be the only person in the State, competent to give her proper counsel in the matter. I have taken some pains to inquire into the case, and I learn from very reliable Union families in this place, that she is a very estimable Lady, and that what she related about her situation is substantially true. While she has always been a *true* woman, and Loyal, her husband has been a Libertine and a Rebel, and is now living in a state of *adultery* within the Rebel lines, leaving her and her little ones to suffer the anguish, that necessarily follows such transactions. I look upon it as a dreadful thing for a pure minded woman, to be under the necessity of living with either a Libertine or a Rebel, but when the two great sins, become united in one person, it becomes positively insufferable, and will certainly admit of executive interferance. Mrs Johnson can tell you the situation of the Property, and in short, the whole story better than I can. I really hope something can be done for her, although I have no interest in the matter, any more than the natural sympathy, that ought to be found in every human breast, when the innocent are wronged. I have no acquaintance with the Lady and should not have known anything about the case except by the accident of my position at this time. Believing you to feel a lively interest in all that pertains to the citizens of Tennessee, is the only excuse I have to offer for this intrusion[.]

I am Sir Very Respectfully
Your Obedient Servant
Wm. L. Utley, Col. Comd'g Post Murfreesboro Tenn–
Gov. Andrew Johnson Tennessee

Papers of Andrew Johnson, Vol. 6. pp. 447–448.

3 First Regiment of U.S.C.T. and Eighth Iowa Cavalry placed guard duty on the N&NWRR

HDQRS. DEPARTMENT OF THE CUMBERLAND,
Chattanooga, November 3, 1863.
Brig. Gen. A. C. GILLEM, Nashville:

The First Regt. Colored Troops, from Elk

River, will be ordered to report to you for duty on the Northwestern Railroad. A regiment of cavalry 1,100 strong, now marching from Louisville, will also be sent to you for guard duty. The general commanding wishes you to assist the colonel of this regiment [Eighth Iowa Cavalry] in disciplining his regiment and perfecting it in drill, as it is but recently organized. All the troops on the Northwestern Railroad are under your command while engaged on that work, and the general expects you to control them and enforce discipline. By order of Maj.-Gen. Thomas:

C. GODDARD, Assistant Adjutant-Gen.

OR, Ser. I, Vol. 31, pt. III, p. 28.

4 Skirmish at Motley's Ford, Little Tennessee River

Report of Brig. Gen. William P. Sanders, U.S. Army, commanding First Cavalry Division, Department of the Ohio, with complimentary letter from Maj. Gen. John G. Parke.

MARYVILLE, TENN., November 5, 1863.

GEN.: Lieut.-Col. Adams has just returned from the Little Tennessee with 40 prisoners, 4 commissioned officers, all captured at Motley's Ford. Col. Adams got near the river just as a regiment was crossing the river; charged them; drove them into the river, where he says at least 40 or 50 were killed or drowned in crossing, as his men were within a few yards of them while in the water. He describes the sight of the rebels in the river as most frightful; says the entire regiment of rebels lost their arms.

...

W. P. SANDERS, Brig.-Gen., Cmdg.

OR, Ser. I, Vol. 31, pt. I, p. 254.

4 Confederate Guerrillas in West Tennessee

MORE REBEL OUTRAGES IN WEST TENNESSEE. Gibson and Carroll Counties the Scene of their Operations. Diabolical Outrage upon a Soldier of 1812. Stores Broken Open, Citizens Robbed and Sickly Men Conscripted.

Editor Bulletin: As I have reliable information from the upper counties of West Tennessee, I will make a note for your valuable journal. In Gibson and Carroll counties, the rebels are having a jolly time conscripting loyal [Union] men, running them down with negro dogs, and heaping all kinds of insults on them. And as the rebels of Memphis make it a daily business to denounce the Union soldiers as thieves, cut-throats, and everything else that will covey a rebel's idea of all that is mean and low, I propose to give them a specimen of how their own saintly crew can steal, rob and plunder. They went to old may YANDELL's in Gibson, and took every horse the old man had but one worthless one; they carried off his young stock, that could be of no use to them. They then proceeded to take all the clothing that belonged to his daughters. Old man YANDELL, is an old *soldier* of 1812, and is between 75 and 80 years age. Yet these saintly disciples of liberty could rob him, and then tell him he was an old Abolition traitor, and ought to be robbed. This saintly crew then went to Milan and broke in the night into HIRAM HANSBAIR's store, carried off four or five hundred dollars in money, and all the goods they could carry. They then broke open the store of Mr. SHEPPARED, and destroyed and plundered his house. They then proceeded to old man WM. HARRIS and carried away 200 bushels of corn, 1000 bundles of fodder, and to pay for the same denounced him as a d____d *traitor* to the glorious Southern Confederacy.

They conscripted a young man in the neighborhood who was not able to carry a musket, and because his Creator had made him a sickly man, they gave him a genteel cursing and took every stitch of clothes he had, down to his shirt and pants. And still to hear these saintly rebels of Memphis talk, their soldiers never do any wrong. And there is not a day but what this crew are housed up in some back-room plotting treason and perjury, and heaping their damnable curses upon the heads of the Union officers of this city. They are called thieves, cut-throats, vagabonds, negro-stealers and every loathsome name that a rebel can think of, and let one speak of their saintly crew in disreputable terms they re ready to denounce it as a d____d lie. I say to these gentry, pull the bean out of your own eye, and you can then see *h*ow to get the mote out of your neighbors.

CITIZEN

Memphis *Bulletin*, November 4, 1863.

November 4–December 23, 1863 The Knoxville (Tennessee) Campaign.

5 Jewish Social Association
"Eureka Club."
This is an institution up by some of our German and Jewish citizens, who have therein set

an example most worthy to be imitated. The Eureka hold their meetings in a well furnished room on Cedar street, opposite the Commercial Hotel. They have here a billiard table, a suitable library, fine music, and other means of social recreation.

They not unfrequently amuse themselves with private theatricals, at which, of course, none attend but such as are complimented with tickets of invitation. Their meeting last night was devoted to the drama, and passed of delightfully. These exercises were all carried on in the German language, and, of course, "outsiders" who may have been honored with the privilege of being present, can only be impressed with the general tone and manner of the performance.

Let our natives form clubs like the Eureka. The festivities last night wound up with a dance. It was a pleasant evening, and we thank the management for an invitation.

Nashville *Daily Press*,
November 5, 1863.

5 Excerpt from the letter of R.T. Van Wyck, 150th New York Volunteer Infantry, relative to the construction of winter log shelters in the Federal camp at Normandy

Normandy, Tenn.
Nov 5th 1863
Dear Mother,
...

We have at different times been deluded with the hope that we had put aside our migratory nature and were going to be stationary for the winter; but as often disappointed and been obliged to leave partially finished houses, sometimes to occupy shanties erected by other regiments, and as often have been obliged to take up quarters upon "Terra Firma," well ventilated. As to the shanty buildings we have many different styles, differing with the materials used, (cut uniformly of one length, perhaps 12 ft by six). The fireplace and door in one end, tier of bunks for four in the other. The height of the sides not often more than four feet. If made of logs, the same every way, except some rough. In some of the fireplaces an oven is inserted which, at one encampment we occupied only a few hours, we had the satisfaction of baking delicious biscuit (so we thought in comparison with Tenn. manufacture).

...Suffice it to say while we are thus occupied our mind is employed and ... not dwelling upon the disagreeable inconveniences of this position....
...
R. T. Van Wyck

MSCC/CWRC

5 The Wages of Sin. An Extract from the Diary of Eliza Rhea Anderson Fain
...
Mr. Finley related to us a circumstance which took place of thrilling interest to the believer and one which should impress the sinner deeply. Mr. F. felt it was a solemn warning. The evening before they went to Blountville the last time the men were cooking their suppers when one of them in a light careless manner for some slight offence said to another "Go to Hell." He replied "I don't want to go by myself." Next morning they were ordered to march when a call was made for a volunteer guard to advance. The young man who had uttered the last sentence above quoted and whose name Mr. F. thought was Barnes came forward to go. They had not proceeded far when a ball struck him in the head. He reeled and fell from his horse a dead man. To the believer it is impressive showing the great importance of constant watchfulness and prayer. To the sinner it speaks in solemn tone "prepare to meet thy God." O Lord impress us deeply with the uncertainty of life and teach us to know thee.

Fain Diary.

10 SPECIAL FIELD ORDERS, No. 75, relative to the jurisdiction and authority of the chief of the secret police in East Tennessee

SPECIAL FIELD ORDERS, No. 75. HDQRS. ARMY OF THE OHIO,
November 10, 1863.

I. R. A. Crawford, of Greenville, Greene County, Tennessee, is hereby appointed chief of secret police in East Tennessee. He is fully empowered to employ under his command and order as many men as he may deem necessary for said service, and at such pay as their service may be worth in his estimation.

He is empowered to make requisitions for clothing, horses, equipments, arms, and ammunition, as well as all other necessaries that said service may require, and the same shall be furnished accordingly.

He is fully empowered to arrest and hold for examination all persons who may in anywise be in complicity with the enemy, or any person or persons suspected guilty of treasonable or disloyal conduct toward the Government and laws of the United States; also to seize from all such persons such property as he may deem necessary for the good of the service.

He is fully empowered and strictly enjoined, with the men subject to his order and command, to closely watch the movements of the enemy, and to immediately report the same to these headquarters, and to use every available means in his power to prevent any surprise of our forces by the enemy.

He is fully empowered to employ and send agents into the lines of the enemy for the purpose of finding out the strength, movements, and designs of the enemy, and to report the same to these headquarters.

...

By command of Maj.-Gen. Burnside:
OR, Ser. I, Vol. 31, pt. III, pp. 111–112.

10 Recruiting Negro soldiers in Murfreesboro

An order is out for recruiting negro soldiers at this place, and put them in [a] camp of instruction. Although the Yankees profess not to press them into service, they operate about this way-on Sunday evening a file of soldiers repair to the church door and stand as the negro men come out. They take them in possession, put them in confinement and any other they see about the streets.

They are taken through an examination, such as will make soldiers are retained, the others are let off. They want devilish looking and able bodied negros for this purpose.

When a sufficient number is obtained, [they] are put in squads under drill by some qualified Dutchman.

Passing one morning by one of the churches or barracks, a squad was being drilled by a Dutch officer, who could not speak english plainer than he should, is marching the negros up and down the room. Say to them, ["]Marsh! lep-lep (meaning left foot). No! te odder foot!-lep! lep! to odder fot you po tam fool! If you tont lep when I tells you, I'll prake mine sword over you tam wolly head! Halt! Marsh! Now, lep! lep! gis see! You got de odder foot. Take tat mit your tam nonsense ["] (strikes him with the side of his sword).

Such is about the start with them at first. In a short time they get in the way of keeping the step in marching and manouvering. To every appearance make a pretty good Yankee soldier when they are dressed in the "Loyal" blue, but whether they can be made to stand powder and led is another question....

...

Spence Diary.

12 Hog War in Cocke and Greene counties

...

HDQRS., Paint Rock, November 12, 1863.

His Excellency ZEBULON B. VANCE, Raleigh, N.C.:

DEAR BROTHER: I have raided Cocke County and a part of Greene, pretty thoroughly, and brought out safely 800 hogs and some horses and cattle.

On yesterday [11th] I started to Greeneville, but was overtaken by a courier stating that 300 Yankees had attacked Lieut. Richie and took 100 hogs from him. I immediately tacked about with 60 men and made after them. We met them, 200 strong, 5 miles of Newport, and had a brisk fight, driving the enemy back several hundred yards. We had 2 men wounded, 1 of whom is at Hawk's house, the other here. The enemy's loss, 1 captain killed and 2 men wounded. My men fought well. The wounded are of Capt. Boykin's company, South Carolina cavalry. My hogs (800) are all above the springs. Col. Mallett has ordered Capt. McRae back, and I will not let him go; it is impossible to do without him, and I wish you to lay the facts before the War Department. I am not only saving property for the Government, but threatening the enemy on his lines, and keeping him uneasy, and drawing some of his force away to watch me. Please haste to lay this matter before the authorities. The enemy went to mouth of Chucky last night. No other news excepting that heavy cannonading was heard toward Rogersville yesterday.

Your brother,
ROBT. B. VANCE, Brig.-Gen.

...

J. A. SEDDON.
OR, Ser. I, Vol. 29, pt. II, pp. 836–837.

13 Of pumpkins, hard tack and oxen steaks

Igo Ferry November Friday 13th

Last night and today [illegible] rain N. Fancher Brother James and McDaniel went out to hunt something to eat this morning as we have been rather suffering for something to eat. We have been living on about 3d rations since we have been here and begins to feel as if we can stand it no longer they went up to a little island north of Sody creek about 2½ miles north of camp where they found ... quite a number of pumkins lay all over the fields cattle as the fences were thrown down and destroyed as is customary through a country where Soldiers go these pumpkins they filled their sacks and brought them into camp

As our Cook was washing today it fell on me to get dinners and I ... then put on a kettle with some watter peeled and sliced about half a bushel of pumkins and boyled for some time and seasoned with salt while this cooking operation was going on James was out and luckily for the times [illegible] part of a box of crackars which Co. B had thrown away for bad one out of which we gathered over a pack of good pieces ... supper being ready at the usual time concisting of stewed pumkins and beef stake sliced of[f] the sholders of an ox and a little coffee. Such a fed we have not had for a month it is sertinly worth noteing down to be remembered our apitites being keen and sharp forced us to eat until we were scarcly to role over and still we have a supply on hand for tomorrow who would not rejoyce in our circumstances
...

John Hill Fergusson Diary, Book 3.

14 Day long skirmishing at Stock Creek, Blount county; the account of a member of the Twenty-Seventh Kentucky Mounted Infantry

An account from a member of the Twenty-seventh Kentucky Infantry Regiment
...

November fourteenth, early in the morning, the rebels made a dash on the pickets, and captured part of the Eleventh Kentucky cavalry. They soon began to press our lines all along the river with a heavy force—Wheeler's and Forrest's. About nine o'clock General Sanders ordered our forces to fall back. We fell back to Stock Creek, skirmishing all day. In the evening our regiment was put on picket extending from Frenche's bridge across Stock Creek on the Martin Gap road, along the creek to its mouth, where it empties into Little [Tennessee] River; a distance of about five miles.

Rebellion Record, Vol. 8, p. 315.

14 Report on Federal fortifications at Shellmound

HDQRS. SECOND BRIG., FIRST DIV., FOURTH ARMY CORPS, Shellmound, November 14, 1863.
Gen. J. J. REYNOLDS, Chief of Staff:

My fortifications are in measure complete. Since my arrival I have thrown up breast-works 1,000 yards long, 10 or 12 feet at the base, sloped off to 4 or 5 feet at the top; sufficient in height to protect the men. Have also erected a fort of great strength, of earth, sufficient for six guns, having one embrasure extra, making seven embrasures. Embankment finished off 10 feet at the top; all the work well revetted. This is all at Shellmound.
...

OR, Ser. I, Vol. 31, pt. III, p. 143.

November 18–29, 1863 Federal march to the relief of Knoxville

19 Skirmish at Meriwether's Ferry, Obion River, near Union City

NOVEMBER 19, 1863.—Skirmish at Meriwether's Ferry, near Union City, Tenn.
Report of Capt. Franklin Moore, Second Illinois Cavalry.
UNION CITY, November 20, 1863.

I have just received the following from Capt. F. Moore, whom I sent after the rebels, who went to Hickman. "We came, we saw, we conquered."

NOVEMBER 20, 1863. Col. WARING, Cmdg., Union City:

I attacked the devils at Meriwether's Ferry, at noon, yesterday. I whipped them and killed 11 men, and took Col. Sol. G. Street and 55 men; also one wagon-load of arms and some horses. My loss none, except 1 man wounded.

Yours, truly,
F. MOORE, Capt., Cmdg. Battalion

OR, Ser. I, Vol. 31, pt. I, p. 570.

19 General Braxton Bragg's solution to desertion in the Army of Tennessee

MISSION RIDGE, November 19, 1863.
Gen. J. E. JOHNSTON:

The deserters are an incumbrance to me and must be shot or they run off again. Gen. Maury consents to take them on his forts for laborers. I ask no exchange. Sherman's army just arrived.

BRAXTON BRAGG.

OR, Ser. I, Vol. 31, pt. III, p. 716.

19 Lieutenant-General James Longstreet's tactical advice to Major-General McLaws

HDQRS., November 19, 1863.

Maj.-Gen. McLAWS:

GEN.: Please impress your officers and men with the importance of making a rush when they once start to take such a position as that occupied by the enemy yesterday.

If the troops, once started, rush forward till the point is carried, the loss will be trifling; whereas if they hesitate, the enemy gets courage; or, being behind a comparatively sheltered position, will fight the harder. Besides, if the assaulting party once loses courage and falters, he will not find courage probably to make a renewed effort.

The men should be cautioned before they start at such works and told what they are to do, and the importance and great safety of doing it with a rush.

Very respectfully,

J. LONGSTREET, Lieut.-Gen.

OR, Ser. I, Vol. 31, pt. III, p. 719.

November 23–25, 1863 Battle at Chattanooga

24 Military orders compelling vaccination in Nashville; a skirmish in the battle for public health
Small Pox in Nashville

It will be seen from an order from Headquarters, published elsewhere, that in consequence of the continued spread of small pox in this city, all persons, citizens as well as soldiers, are required to have themselves vaccinated at once. For the benefit of the community, a medical officer will be in attendance daily, from 3 to 4 o'clock P.M., at the *Alderman's Room*, in the Market house, on the Public Square, and at Engine House No. 3, on Cherry street, South Nashville. Gratuitous vaccination will be afforded at these depots. The neglect or violation of this order by citizens will subject them to a fine or to be sent north of the lines.

Nashville *Dispatch*, November 24, 1863.

November 24–25, 1863 Battle of Lookout Mountain

26 Federal orders to collect and bury the dead and to collect all captured Confederate battle flags
HDQRS. DEPARTMENT OF THE CUMBERLAND, Chattanooga, Tennessee, November 26, 1863.

Maj.-Gen. GRANGER:

GEN.: The major-general commanding the department directs that you give orders to your corps to have our dead collected so that they may either be brought to this place for burial or buried upon the field. You will also cause to be counted and reported to these headquarters the number of dead rebels the parties collecting our dead may find....

GEN.: The major-general commanding directs that you collect and preserve all flags taken from the enemy, and to ascertain and report as accurately as may be the circumstances attending their capture.

Very respectfully, your obedient servant,

WM. D. WHIPPLE, Brig.-Gen. and Assistant Adjutant-Gen.

OR, Ser. I, Vol. 31, pt. III, p. 253.

27 Members of the 5th Kentucky cavalry see the elephant
Row at the Circus.

A number of soldiers belonging to the 5th Kentucky cavalry, made a charge upon the circus on Friday night [27th], creating considerable alarm. The guards stationed there interfered, and a general fight ensued, in which guns and pistols were freely used, resulting in the death of a corporal of the Provost Guard, and the wounding of one of the cavalrymen. We are informed that all the members of the company engaged in this disgraceful affair have been placed under arrest by the proper officer, and that the guilty parties will be punished as they deserve.

P.S. The name of the Corporal who was killed is Davis, an estimable young man. We also learn that one of the cavalrymen was killed and one wounded; one of the circus men was also wounded.

Nashville *Dispatch*, November 29, 1863.

November 29, 1863 Assault on Fort Sanders, Knoxville.

♦ DECEMBER ♦

3–4 Action at Wolf River Bridge, near Moscow

Report of Maj. Gen. Stephen A. Hurlbut, U.S. Army, commanding Sixteenth Army Corps, with complimentary order.

MEMPHIS, TENN., December 5, 1863.

The enemy, about 3,000 strong, with three pieces of artillery, under Lee and Chalmers, struck La Fayette and Moscow yesterday at 1 P.M. They were at Moscow by Col. E. Hatch, who, after a sharp conflict, drove them 4 miles, and again engaged them. They retreated to Mount Pleasant, and have gone this morning. We lost 4 killed and 11 wounded and 25 captured. The Sixth Illinois Cavalry lost 125 horses and equipments. Full particulars not received. Col. Hatch severely wounded. The line is open to-day. Loring's division of infantry is at Okolona, so reported. Roddey, at Courtland. Two regiments north of the river. Bell, at Trenton, with 2,500 men, looking toward Paducah.

...

S. A. HURLBUT, Major-General
MEMPHIS,
December 7, 1863.

The affair at Moscow the other day [December 4] was more spirited than I thought. The negro regiment behaved splendidly. Our loss is 7 killed and about 40 horses—10 captured. We have captured in the movement 54 prisoners; buried 30. The entire loss of the enemy cannot be less than 150. Forrest is gathering the guerrillas together at Jackson. I shall move on him from Columbus and Moscow simultaneously.

...

S. A. HURLBUT, Maj.-Gen.
GENERAL ORDERS, No. 173. HDQRS. SIXTEENTH ARMY CORPS, Memphis, Tennessee, December 17, 1863.

The recent affair at Moscow, Tennessee, [December 4] has demonstrated the fact that colored troops, properly disciplined and commanded, can and will fight well, and the general commanding corps deems it to be due to the officers and men of the Second Regt. West Tennessee Infantry, of African descent, thus publicly to return his personal thanks for their gallant and successful defense of the important position to which they had been assigned, and for the manner in which they have vindicated the wisdom of the Government in elevating the rank and file of these regiments to the position of freedmen and soldiers.

By order of Maj. Gen. S. A. Hurlbut:
OR, Ser. I, Vol. 31, pt. I, p. 577.

4 Confederate forces burn La Fayette and Grissom's Bridge; sharp skirmishing at Moscow

MOSCOW, Tennessee, December 5, 1863.
Gen. TUTTLE, LaGrange:
Courier arrived from Collierville in the night. Enemy burned La Fayette, but did not capture the post. They have fallen back on Collierville. Grissom's Bridge is burnt. I have ordered Mizner to remain at Saulsbury or Grand Junction. Negro scout I sent out last night reports the enemy camped near Mount Pleasant. I am sending out what cavalry I have here to reconnoiter. An attack is feared at Collierville. Send patrols of Seventh Illinois and Second Iowa to this point. Is there any news from Corinth? I will dispatch Gen. Hurlbut this morning.

B. H. GRIERSON, Brig.-Gen.

...

MOSCOW, December 5, 1863.
Maj.-Gen. HURLBUT:

Communication with Corinth all right. Col. Mizner has again been as far south as Ripley. All quiet on that end of the line. Forrest crossed the Hatchie at Bolivar, and reported going to Jackson. No definite information with regard to his force. Enemy have burned Grissom's Bridge and La Fayette. Scout, whom I sent out last night, reports the enemy encamped near Mount Pleasant. Rail road will be in running order from here to Corinth to-day. Fight pretty sharp here yesterday; our loss 4 or 5 killed and about 20 wounded. Hatch wounded through the right lung, but doing well this morning. Fifteen dead rebels are found on the field so far; their loss much heavier than ours. The Sixth Illinois lost heavy in horses, 30 or 40 killed. I am sending patrol to Mount Pleasant to report back to Morgan at La Fayette.

B. H. GRIERSON, Brig.-Gen.
OR. Ser. I, Vol. 31, pt. III, p. 342.

5 A January-May marriage disintegrates in Memphis

"Scan Mag."*

Some time ago a man past middle age, a widower in fact, became smitten with the charm of a young school girl of fifteen. She was young, and inexperienced, while he was well posted in the business of love, ardent and earnest. The homage of any man, no matter what his age or station, is grateful to woman as long as it is honest and pure. The Miss was flattered by his attentions, and allowed him at last to win her consent to a marriage. She was poor, while he was a worthy, industrious mechanic, just able to support a wife, and that was it.

---

*The meaning of this story title is not exactly known, although from the context of the story it may have meant something like "Scandal Magazine."

It was a January and May over again, and it is well known the wide world over, that such alliances seldom prosper. She was a giddy girl, whose bounding blood accorded illy with the sluggish flow of his enfeebled currents. She had an overweening desire for finery, and that was something her husband, with his limited resources, could not procure for her. Before they had been married a year she began to wear gay colored clothing, a fancy bonnet, dainty gaiters, etc. The husband began to suspect that there was an Ethiopian in the woodpile, and remonstrated. There was a domestic explosion at once, and mutual recriminations were exchanged freely in the shape of broomsticks, invectives, hot water, hot names and bullets [?] of wood.

On the next day the bird that the old man had caged took wings to herself and fled. The bereaved spouse took the matter most unphilosophically, and grieved disconsolately. He pined and refused to eat. He neglected his labor, and it was feared by his friends he would become distracted. At last the intelligence came that the truant wife was boarding at the house of a person who was considered no better than she ought to be. He repaired to her, and begged her to return to his home, but she refused, whereupon he appealed to the military authorities for assistance. Although it was not a case that came directly under their supervision, they were disposed to make an effort to rescue the woman from the course of ruin which she had entered upon, and restore her if possible to arms of her natural protector.

She was arrested and brought up for the purpose of adjusting the difficulty, but it was found the moral disease had become too deeply seated. She admitted her shame and gloried in it, flatly refusing to go back, and declared here intention to continue the career she had commenced. It was absolutely appalling to see this mere child of sixteen so completely transformed to a very fiend of wickedness. She sneered at the tears of her husband, and laughed at his entreaties. The officers she defied to do their worst, and at last she flounced out of the room when she was released as an incorrigible, and went down stairs in triumph. When her husband saw how completely she was lost to him and all the world, his sorrow knew no bounds. It was heart-rendering to witness it.

Memphis *Bulletin*, December 5, 1863.

7 "Some puked and heaved at an awful rate." Sick wheat flour in the 10th Illinois Volunteer Infantry in the Madisonville environs

Dec. 7th 1863, 5 ms South of Madisonville, Monday 7th Munrow Co. Maddisonville Co Seat

A little after day light orders came for our company to report to our regt and be ready to march at 9 o'clock A.M. when ariveing at camp we found that some wheat flour has been issued but our company had no time to cook it so we had to carry it along all day with the exceptions of a pint of rather thin mush we have not eat any thing today the other companys of our regt cooked and eat brackfast off the flower they drawed and all that eat of it was less or more sick some puked and heaved at an awful rate the thought at first [was] that it was poisoned but afterwards found out that it was what they call sick wheat the officers advised us not to use ours but throw it away, but we could be advised we were bound to eat it if we died in 10 minutes. So after getting into camp I devided it out to each man his share some made it in little cakes, placed them on a piece of board or rail, and sort of dried or tosted it by the fiar and some mixted it up in tin cups and scratched out a little hole in the ashes, poured it in and covered it up with hot ashes and let it cook after the manner of rosting pitatos Brother James had a tin plate which him and myself used to bake our on some of the boys became very sick and more then heaved but I was not effected so bad although I felt sick of the stomic

We marched 15 miles today and camped 5 miles South of Maddisinville a little town better looken then most of towns of the same size. Some 300 rebs cleared out as we advanced.

John Hill Fergusson Diary, Book 3.

10 Skirmish at Gatlinsburg*
Reports of Col. William J. Palmer, Fifteenth Pennsylvania Cavalry.

HDQRS. ANDERSON CAVALRY, Trotter's Bridge, December 11, 1863.

GEN.: I have the honor to report that on yesterday morning a little after daybreak I reached Gatlinburg, 15 miles from Sevierville, on the

---

*The skirmish at Gatlinburg was part of the Knoxville, Tennessee Campaign. It was most likely the only time in which Indians, most likely Cherokee, fought United States troops in Tennessee during the war.

Smoky Mountain road, with 150 men, having approached from a point on the same road 3 miles in the rear of Gatlinburg, which point I reached by a circuitous and almost impassable trail from Wear's Cove.

At the same time Lieut. Col. C. B. Lamborn, with about 50 men, reached Gatlinburg from the north by the Sevierville road, which he intersected at Trotter's Bridge, 7 miles north of Gatlinburg, by a road leading from Wear's Cove, where our forces divided.

Capt. H. McAllester, with the remainder of our force, consisting chiefly of men whose horses were unshod or unfit to travel over the rough mountain trails, had been sent the previous afternoon to Sevierville from Chandler's, 18 miles from Knoxville, where I turned off to go to Wear's Cove. His instructions were to pickets the roads out of Sevierville, preventing any one from leaving the place, in order that information of our movements might not reach the enemy.

Lieut.-Col. Lamborn and myself reached Gatlinburg from opposite directions at about the same moment, both finding pickets posted, who immediately fired, thereby alarming the enemy's camp, which we found situated on a steep wooded ridge, commanding both roads and intercepting communication between us.

It being impossible to make a dash upon them, we were obliged to dismount our men and deploy them [as] skirmishers. We drove them from their position, which was a strong one, in about an hour, but, unfortunately, the steep wooded ridge on which they had their camp jutted on to the mountain on the east, and it was impracticable to prevent the rebels on retreating from taking up this mountain where we could not reach them, and where they continued firing from behind the thick cover for several hours. They finally retreated, scattering over the ridges to the Great Smoky Mountain.

From all the information I could get, I estimate their force at about 200, of which 150 were Indians and the remainder white men, the whole under the command of Col. Thomas, an old Indian agent.

We captured their camp with 1 prisoner, 16 horses, 18 muskets, 2 boxes of ammunition, several bushels of salt, meal, dried fruit, &c., and a large quantity of blankets, old clothing, &c. A number of squaws had reached them the previous evening, and they had evidently intended remaining at Gatlinburg for the winter, as their declarations to the citizens in the vicinity proved.

We destroyed the log huts and frame buildings composing their camp, and have returned most of the horses to their loyal owners. Col. Thomas was evidently taken by surprise, as he had not time to get his hat from his quarters at the foot of the ridge, which one of our men captured.

I regret to report that two of my officers and a sergeant were wounded in the skirmish, Capt. Clark seriously in the knee. Capt. Betts received a painful flesh wound in the arm. The sergeant's wound was trivial. The loss of the enemy is not known. If any were killed they carried them off when they retreated.

Col. Thomas has most probably taken his men back to Quallatown, in North Carolina, but I have sent a scouting party out this morning to ascertain.

I very much regret that we were not more successful. We rode all night over a foot path that many of the citizens considered impracticable; and while I cannot see that we could have done better under the circumstances than we did, yet I can now see from my knowledge of the ground (which was entirely unknown to us before) how I might have captured most of the party by making certain dispositions before reaching Gatlinburg.

I start this morning for Evan's Ford, on French Broad, 9 miles from Sevierville, and between that place and Dandridge, where I learn 100 rebel cavalry crossed last night.

I am, general, yours, respectfully,
WM. J. PALMER, Col.

OR, Ser. I, Vol. 31, pt. I, pp. 438–439.

18 Incidents from the Siege of Knoxville
INTERESTING FROM KNOXVILLE.
Appearance of the City After the Siege — Depredations of the Rebels — Illness of General Burnside.

Captain H. C. Pike, Second Ohio Volunteer Corps, arrived in this city last night direct from Knoxville, which place he left on the 10th. At that date the main body of Longstreet's army was at Rogersville. Longstreet had, during his retreat lost about three thousand men in prisoners and detesters. There were swarms of fugitives from his ranks, a great many of them Georgians — the choice veterans of the Rebel army — worn out with hard service and quite disheartened. The retreating Rebels were suffering intensely for want of clothing and food, and were demoralized in an extraordinary degree by their hardships and disasters in East Tennessee.

Longstreet had abandoned his siege train consisting of six guns, and they had fallen into our hands. The carriages were burned before the guns were abandoned. General Foster arrived at Knoxville on the 10th, and assumed command. General Burnside was sick several days after the retreat of the Rebels, but was recovering, and would leave for home by way of Chattanooga. The boys of the army were very sorry to part with him, though General Foster's fame as a soldier was not unknown to them, and they had much confidence in him.

Captain Pike met two heavy supply trains between Cumberland Gap and Knoxville; the foremost was within twenty-four miles of its destination. They were loaded with coffee, sugar, salt, and hard bread. There were thirty days' supplies for Burnside's army in Knoxville when the Rebels retreated. The people of the surrounding country were destitute, the Rebel army having consumed everything eatable, and devastated the region to a deplorable extent.—*Cincinnati Gazette, Dec. 16th.*

...

Knoxville, Dec. 3, 1863.—Knoxville and its suburbs present the perspective of a wreck, the embodiment of a great disaster, a master-piece of ruin. The destruction of property wrought in and about Knoxville during the last twenty days, has not, I am informed by those experienced in other fields, been equaled during the war. Scarcely a fence is to be found in a circle of ten miles diameter round the town. Beyond our lines ruin is still in the ascendant. The Rebels, however, confined themselves to pillage indiscriminate and universal. The rifled every house within their reach. General McLaws' headquarters were at the palatial residence of Robert Armstrong, and, notwithstanding the protestations of the chivalry and promises of protection, the house was literally stripped of everything; clothing (male and female, children's and adults') was all taken. The officers broke into Mrs. Armstrong's room, in which she had been permitted to place her clothing and a few valuables, and stole everything. Her garments were sold to Rebel families in the neighborhood. Her silk dresses were torn into strips and disposed of for aprons. The General's staff and nearly a regiment go uproariously drunk upon the contents of the wine cellar, which was well stored with foreign liquors and wine from Mr. Armstrong's own vineyard. All of Mrs. Armstrong's household stores, preserves, pickles, &c., were eaten and the jars broken on the spot. The grain, sugar, coffee and family provision were of course taken. On the morning after the evacuation I found Mrs. Armstrong, whose personal beauty and refined culture seem to be equaled only by her loyalty, eating her breakfast from a fragment of a plate, with a carving knife. It was all of her abundant plate left.

The garments they had on comprise the entire wardrobe of the family. The house exhibited the marks of the conflict. One shell had entered the turret, leaving a hole two feet in diameter. Ten balls had gone through the front door and hundreds through the windows and doors. Two passed through the piano. The blood of one of the Rebel sharpshooters was still fresh on the floor of the turret, where he had been killed during the memorable fight of Wednesday, in which Sanders fell. In fact, all the marks of musketry were made in that action.

From Armstrong's I visited Hazen's paper mill, where 130 of the Rebel wounded still remained. The mill is destroyed. Fifty thousand dollars will scarcely replace the mischief here. The wounded are in every house, and are taken a good care of as is possible under the circumstances. The Rebels left but few surgeons and no medical stores whatever.

On reviewing the Rebel works around the town, it is evident that they were intended for defense as well as offense. Continuous ranges of rifle-pits encircle the town, and on every hill are redoubts and forts, several of them exceedingly strong and well built. I saw marks of some twenty-five cannon at different points.

All that I can learn from their works and conversation with those within their lines confirms my belief at the time, that their assault of Fort Sanders was their very best. Three brigades of picked men made the assault; 25,000 men stood ready to follow up the success. The attack was made after the reinforcements of Williams and two brigades of Buckner's Corps, and the most complete confidence of success was expressed, and no doubt felt by officer and men. The bloody, unexpected and decisive repulse was a terrible and disheartening blow to them. This fact is confirmed by letter of officers and men in command, found in a Rebel mail captured by us. Their loss in that assault is also confirmed at about 1300.

Upon the heels of the Fort Sanders disaster came the news of the still more terrible and decisive defeat of Bragg, and promised reinforcements to us. Upon this evening the defeated Rebel raised the siege and departed, worse off by five thousand men, than he came, and by no means add into to his military fame by his utter failure in East Tennessee. He will be content hereafter with the light borrowed from Lee, and not again attempt to shine on his own hook. During the entire siege Generals Hascall, Manson, White, Ferrero and Shackelford have been indefatigable and vigilant. General White, by his gallantry and skill during the retreat from Loudon, has won the encomiums of all.

Philadelphia *Inquirer*, December 18, 1863.

23 Skirmish with guerrillas, Mulberry Village, Lincoln County

December 23, 1863.—Skirmish at Mulberry Village, Tenn.

Report of Col. Silas Colgrove, Twenty-seventh Indiana Infantry.

Tullahoma, December 26, 1863.

I have the honor to report that, on the 23d instant, I sent a forage train out into the neighborhood of Mulberry Village, Lincoln County. The train was accompanied by a guard of 70 men, under the command of First Lieut. Porter, Company A, Twenty-seventh Indiana Volunteers. Lieut. Porter was furnished with copies of General Orders, No. 17, November 17, 1862, and General Orders, No. 30, December 30, 1862, Department of the Cumberland, and also Special Orders, No.___, of these headquarters, for instructions. At or near Mulberry Village, I am informed by Lieut. Porter, he divided his train into four detachments and sent the several detachments upon different plantations, sending an equal guard with each detachment. This, I understand, was done for the purpose of facilitating the loading of the train. It was about 7 o'clock in the evening when that portion of the train which Lieut. Porter was with finished loading and started to camp.

The lieutenant reports that while he was in house receipting for the forage a part of the train went ahead and went into camp, leaving three wagons in the rear. He started to camp with these three wagons, distance about 2 miles. He had with him 15 men as guard. When within one-half mile of camp he discovered that the foremost wagon had got about 300 yards ahead of the other two. He went forward for the purpose of halting it. When he rode up he found the wagon stopped. Two men immediately rode up to him and presented pistols at his head and demanded his surrender. With this wagon was the teamster and wagon-master of the Ninth Ohio Battery, and 2 men who had helped to load the wagons, all unarmed except Lieut. Porter. The guerrillas numbered but 4, and were armed. Lieut. Porter, the wagon-master, and 3 men were immediately mounted and taken through a gate, passing about 200 yards up a creek and then into a corn-field; from there they were hurried forward, avoiding roads, &c., until about 1 o'clock in the morning. They were halted on the bank of Elk River, about 1 mile below where the Mulberry [Creek] empties into it. A fire was built and their captors informed them that they were going to camp for the night.

Their hands were tied behind them; everything of value was taken from them. They were then drawn up in line 4 or 5 steps in front of their captors; one of them, who acted as leader, command "Ready"; the whole party immediately fired. One of the men was shot through the head and killed, as supposed, instantly; 3 were wounded. Lieut. Porter was not hit, and immediately broke and ran. He was followed and fired at by one of the party three times. He reports that he saw that he would be overtaken, and changed his course and ran to the river and threw himself over a precipice into the water. Having succeeded in getting his hands loose, he swam to the opposite shore; was fired at five or six times while he was the water. He secreted himself under the bank of the river.

His captors swam their horses across the river and made search for him, but failed to find him. He afterward made his way up the river about three fourths of a mile and swam back again. He lay in the woods the remainder of the night and the next day. On the night of the 24th, he traveled about a mile and got to a house. The party sent out by me on yesterday brought him in. He is now lying in a critical condition owing to the exposure, cold, fatigue, &c.

He reports that he would know his captors should he see them again, one of whom is believed to be a man by the name of Tulley, living near Lynchburg; another a Bowne, who is a deserter from the rebel army and has been during the fall and winter with guerrillas. A third man rode a bay stallion and is known to the citizens of Mulberry; his name I have not yet learned. The men who were shot were immediately thrown into the river, one of whom was supposed to have been killed, and one from the nature of the wounds and his appearance after the body was recovered, is supposed to have been drowned. The hands of these two men were found tied behind them when taken out of the river; the other two men succeeded in losing their hands and got of the river, one of whom has died since at the hospital at this place; wound not considered necessarily mortal.

...

OR, Ser. I. Vol. 31, pt. I, pp. 624 625.

1864

♦ JANUARY ♦

10 Sickness in the 105th Ohio
Nashville
Jan. 10, 1864

...

There is considerable sickness in the regiment now, the cold weather seems to be productive of disease when we are not sufficiently prepared against it. Small pox is alarmingly prevalent and scarcely any measures are taken to check or control it. Men just recovering are running at large over the whole regiment and those just taken down remain in their own tents, exposing their comrades, frequently several days before going to the sick house. I have been exposed several times but do not fear it. One boy in our company died with it a short time since and another is now sick. Other companies are worse, some having five or six sick ones.

...

Letters of George F. Cram

15–20 A Railroad Journey from Knoxville to Chattanooga

CHATTANOOGA, Jan. 21, 1864
LETTERS FROM THE WEST. No. 13.

Friday, Jan. 15th, was a fair day. But waiting for the train to leave Knoxville for London from 3 to 7 P.M. was not exhilarating. It started overloaded. Soldiers in box cars or platform cars, covering the tops of all the cars; one "coach," as they call it here, filled to a jam; broken windows, no light, no fire, mud several inches deep on the floor-this was the load one poor wheezy locomotive, the only one in order, jerked along at a snail's pace, accomplishing the thirty miles in from four to five hours. The moon shone kindly, and enabled the crowd to seek camping grounds or other places wherein to pass the residue of the night. We — myself and the genial Doctor of the 29th Massachusetts — providentially found a log hut temporarily occupied by old friends, (friends of week's standing are old friends in such a region as this,) and obtained the luxuries of a fire and a blanket on the floor. The 16th was spring-like indeed. But the sun rose on a strange scene. The bridge was gone, and desolated Loudon was a deserted village on the other side of the river.

On this side were groups of soldiers — weary with waiting — and the sad sight of eight or nine women, with several little children and their household furniture, beds, bread troughs, kettles, spinning-wheels, &c., who had spent the night in the open air, near the railroad track. Those were but a single lot of the many like refugees, stript of nearly everything and on the edge of starvation, striving to get north or elsewhere to better their wretched condition. There was no boat. Nobody knew when there would be a boat, and the Tennessee was falling rapidly! The prospect of getting on was gloomy enough, and how to kill time, get food and lodging, became the difficult problem. But we managed to solve it after a fashion in our mess. We had two knives and a spoon, but no plates, and the rest of our table furniture was equally meagre. Still we contrived to live better than our neighbors, and became quite the aristocracy of the four or five huts and surrounding bivouacs.

Sunday, the 17th, in temperature was a New England May Day. Gladly would we have exchanged it for a driving snow storm in New England. Rations were growing sensibly smaller, and the prospect of moving on was no brighter. We were as isolated as we should have been on a desert island in mid-ocean. Nothing to do, nothing to read, stuck in the mud, without change of clothing, we still continued to be jolly and hope for the best. Convalescents, officers on leave, reenlisted soldiers, refugees and others, in numbers sufficient to fill several boats, were waiting for the chance of a passage.

There was nothing of Sunday about our position; yet there were hours for thought and reflection. Some of these suggested by recent experiences and observations were bright and encouraging; others of an entirely different character. The devotion, generally speaking, of the rank and file to the cause constantly excited admiration. The gentlemanly bearing, intelligence and fidelity of numerous officers of all ranks were indications that our armies were in a fair degree well led. But hope and confidence were sadly weakened, only too frequently, by evidences of grossest mismanagement and incompetency. Many are the appointments not fit to be made.

Political management, bargain and corruption are doing their vile work to a lamentable degree. Boys fill places of immense responsibility, and where organization and wise integrity are most needed, there is too often confusion and culpable negligence.

Thus are the treasures of the country wasted and the lives of the people sacrificed. In many quarters and unflinching weeding process and a radical reform are demanded. There are men wearing the eagle or the star who are a daily curse to the service.

Notwithstanding these nuisances, and notwithstanding other evils patent at every step, the general impression of the state of affairs is favorable. The military crisis, if supplies can be kept up, is passed in this region. A few more blow—another short and sharp campaign—ought to annihilate the rebel forces, and drive them to their "last ditch." War is almost an unmitigated evil, and if the extent to which it is such, were half comprehended, in those parts of the land its ravages have not reached there would be no rest among the people in their eagerness to end this peculiarly cruel war by the final victories.

At 9 P.M. the sweet sound—sweeter than the music of AEotian harps—of the steam whistle broke upon the stillness of the night. Early Monday morning a wade through a mile or less of mud put us on board the "Lookout." What mattered it that she was to go sixty miles down the river after freight, left by another boat, to return again to Loudon? What mattered it that Chattanooga was not to be reached for three or four days? We were out of prison. We were in motion. Going backwards and forwards was "homeward bound." Not only we, but convalescent and furloughed soldiers, who had earned by far the better right to be rejoining kindred and friends, and to retire awhile from the front!

To an unselfish disposition it was pleasant to learn on board the boat, that those coming after us over this disjointed and rough route are to fare better than was practicable in our case. The railroad to Chattanooga is in running order. This releases the steamers for up-river work, until the bridge at Loudon is rebuilt. If therefore, the army can worry through a few weeks more, the question of adequate, even abundant supplies will be favorably settled. In our party was a noble specimen of a man, a Captain in the 8th Michigan. He was a study for days. Plain and homely in manner, no father was ever more careful of his children than he of his squad of convalescents. All with him was principle and duty. His rule was to do nothing in the army he would not do at home; so he neither drank nor swore nor gambled. We heard from others that he did not know what fear was, and had always chosen the post of danger. If justice were done to merit, his shoulders should wear the star that is given so often to far more pretension and infinitely less worth. Such instances of conscientiousness, integrity and self-respect are not rare; and when met with are a compensation for abuses which make one at times almost despondent for the country.

Among the incidents of the round-about voyage, thus far, were seeing "the boys," too eager to enjoy their furloughs to wait for the uncertain steamers, going down stream in canoes, "dug outs," pontoon and flat-boat; trading with the natives, buying chickens, hogs and other articles, for salt, coffee or greenbacks; exchanging morsels of meat with a refugee woman for candles, of which we stand in need; confiscating rails for fuel; listening to stories of fights, captures, and various adventures; having a false report, as it turned out, of a case of small pox on board, and other experiences that could belong only to this strange time of war.

Tuesday the 19th was clear and not cold. With the freight a disabled boat had left at White Creek Shoals, we started at daylight again, bound for Loudon. A brisk trade was driven at one of the landings for chickens, and half a hundred were soon waiting execution in boxes and barrels. The motley collection of passengers were orderly, and variously employed, seeking lounging places and exercising ingenuity for chances to cook, being the chief occupations. In the afternoon the sensation was that orders had come from post to post, to stop all able bodied troops in transit and look out for Morgan, who was threatening a raid. This caused some commotion, as it was supposed his object would be to get the steamers, cut communications and obtain supplies. He did not make his appearance, however, to trouble us; and we were not called upon either to fight, or surrender, or run. The general belief was that the "scare" was without reason.

Reaching Loudon about 9 P.M., we unloaded freight, and took on quite a small army of officers of all ranks, and started on the downward trip again at midnight. Wednesday, 20th, was serene and fair as anybody could desire, and specially agreeable to our crowded company. The number of passengers, the difficulty of getting food, sleep and sitting places, made the trip tedious. But such evils come to an end after patient endurance, and we arrived at Chattanooga without new adventures, at 10 o'clock, P.M.

Boston Evening Transcript, February 1, 1864

16 Confederate Cherokees in Tennessee and North Carolina
The North Carolina Cherokee Indians.—The Ashville (N.C.) *News* says:

It has seemed to have escaped the attention of the public the very important services rendered the cause of the South by the North Carolina Cherokee Indians, organized and now commanded by Col. William H. Thomas, of Jackson county. These troops have done much valuable service in the mountains of this State and Tennessee, and we are pleased to observe by General Order that they have attracted the attention of General Bragg in a marked manner. The detachment of Captain G. H. Taylor, (himself a half breed) are all Cherokee Indians. We believe that since the commencement of hostilities, the war has not developed a single Indian tory or traitor. And in connection with this creditable fact we may state another. Some two or three cases only of desertion have taken place among the Indians, and they were cases in which a youngster just ran off to see his sweetheart, or a husband to see his wife, and in both cases the offender expected to be back before he was missed. On the appearance of the truant at home, the chief immediately called his council together to deal with the matter, considered to be a disgrace to the tribe. In one or more of these cases the deserter was arrested and soundly thrashed, and in all of them they were tied securely and sent back to their command in custody of a guard composed of elder members.

Richmond [VA] *Whig*, January 16, 1864.

18 Confederate Soldiers in Yankee Uniforms
Bloody Works in Tennessee.—In its news from Longstreet's command, the Atlanta "Confederacy" has the following:

About four or five days ago a squad of our men, ten or twelve in number, captured a lot of Yankee clothing, and were in the act of draping themselves in their captured property, when they were recaptured by the Yankees, who finding them in Yanking clothing, contrary to their published orders, led them out for the purpose of shooting them. Just at this time the 4th and 7th Alabama regiments of cavalry arrived upon the spot and charged them but not in time to save our men, who were shot down in cold blood the ruthless villains escaping. A few days afterwards the regiments above alluded to caught 15 or 20 yankees and shot them in retaliation.

Fayetteville (NC) Observer, January 18, 1864

18–20 Small Pox in Knoxville
Russellville, Jan. 18.—A gentleman who left Knoxville, Tuesday, gave interesting news from that city. The small-pox was raging terribly among the Yankees and negroes, there being six hundred

cases in the city In consequence of this and the scarcity of forage, the enemy had moved up to Strawberry plains, leaving a garrison of six hundred men. Our troops moved forward on the 19th, for the purpose of driving the enemy from French broad river in East Tennessee. They met them in Chuckey river on Saturday, the enemy making a feeble resistance, and retiring on Dandridge. They were pursued by our troops. We are still pushing forward, and yesterday very heavy firing was heard in that direction. It ceased at dark.

...

Houston Daily Telegraph, February 8, 1864.

19 "Disorderly House"

Sally Park, a young woman currently reported to be no better than she should be, was escorted by a gentlemanly policeman to the presence of the recorder yesterday morning, and there required to answer to the charge of keeping a disorderly house. We leave you to imagine what the term "disorderly house" signifies, and proceed with the story. She failed to convince his honor that the charge was a base and groundless slander so he accepted a loan on behalf of the city of $10 and costs and permitted her to go her way in peace.

Memphis *Bulletin*, January 19, 1864.

20 Melton Zachary, hard-core juvenile delinquent: a social consequence of civil war

The arrest and imprisonment of this young man leaves an opening for the reformation of some of our juvenile thieves, who, during the past two years or more, have pursued their practice of stealing almost with impunity. During the examination of Mel. on the recent charges, as well as on other investigations before the Recorder, we have been astonished at the unblushing manner in which young boys acknowledge to their own complicity in burglaries, robberies, and other rascalities. Yesterday morning four boys appeared as witnesses, whose confession alone would entitle them to an apprenticeship in a house of correction until arriving at years of maturity. And there are dozens like these — children of honest and industrious parents — who are on the broad road to ruin, with the penitentiary or the gallows before them. Unfortunately, we have no house of correction for such boys, and therefore the greater necessity for parents to keep a vigilant watch over their boys, many of whom are absent from their homes the greater part of the time, night and day. Perhaps the closing of the Public Schools has much to do with the demoralization of our youth, but this will not excuse parents for their neglect of their children's morals, and especially in allowing them to roam about the city at all hours of the night. We trust the Police will continue their endeavors to break up these juvenile bands, until the evil complained of is removed.

Nashville *Dispatch*, January 20, 1864.

20 The trial of Melton Zachary "Recorder's Court."

...

Melton Zachary was charged upon three separate warrants with stealing jewelry, an overcoat, two boxes of cheese, some brown sugar, a keg of butter, a bale of rope, etc. T.T. Smiley and J.M. Brien, Esq., counsel for the defence.

The rope and sugar case was first taken up, and J. H. Adams examined. He identified the rope as a portion of the property stolen from the Northwestern railroad depot, and testified that he was agent for the owner, having receipts for it. The property was there on Saturday night, and he missed it on Sunday night. Joe Phillips testified that he and Charlie Weimar had been running their sled near the Sulphur Springs, and were returning home about eight o'clock on Saturday night, when the met Mel. under the bridge; Mel. was sitting on some boxes like the one in Court- a cheese box — with the rope alongside him. He asked Joe to take the things on their sleighs, and they refused; offered to give them a dime, and the still refused, when Mel. took up a rock and threatened to kill them, unless they consented. Witness and Charlie Weimar then put the boxes and the rope on their sleds and toted them to a black woman's house on the corner of Gay and Cherry streets, where they left them and Mel. Heard Mel. tell the woman to take care of them until he returned. Charlie Weimar corroborated Joe in every particular, and a severe cross examination by Mel.'s counsel failed to elicit anything different from their first statement. William Tomlin, recruited out of the workhouse for Col. Croft's regiment, testified that he saw Mel. at the New Theatre on Saturday; night, and that Mel. told him he had some cheese and things at the depot, and that if he would go with him, and help him get them away, he would share with him. Refusing to go, Mel. left and witness went into the theatre.

Cross examined — Was mad at Mel. because he stole a coat from the St. Cloud hotel, and only gave him a dollar for his share; they were partners, and he ought to have had half; has been imprisoned for stealing; don't deny being a thief; belongs to near Franklin. Officer Lynch testified to finding the rope and sugar in Mel's sleeping room, in the house of his mother, on Sunday night about 12 o'clock. Mel. was about going to bed when witness and Thompson got there.

On the second warrant, charging Mel. with stealing jewelry from the store of J. Well & Co. 34 Union street, one of the proprietors testified to the robbery, and identified several article produced in Court as a part of the stolen property, which in the aggregate, amounted to between $50 and $100. Charlie Talman testified that he and the other boys heard Mel. say on Saturday night, that he was going to rob the store alluded to, and they watched him. Saw Mel. take up a rock just as the clock struck 11, and throw it in the window. He then broke through Greig's alley, went around by the tin ship and returned up Union street, when he took from the window all that he could get. Gave witness a breastpin. Three other boys were watching Mel. that night-Joe Phillips, Charlie Weimar, and Tomlin. He had no spite against Mel. Officer Lynch found a portion of the jewelry in Mel's room on Sunday night, in a pocket book. Tomlin was near by, and heard the glass break; did not get any of the jewelry.

The stolen overcoat was produced in Court and identified by Tomlin as the one stolen from the St. Cloud hotel, as charged in the third warrant. The coat was sold to a negro for six dollars, of which he paid $2 down, one of which was paid to witness, and the balance was to have been paid the next day, and was paid to Mel., who refused to share it with witness. The coat was found the officer at the house designate.

The Court ordered that the prisoner give bonds in $4,000 for his appearance the next term of the Criminal Court., or in default to the be committed to jail. Counsel for defence made an earnest and eloquent appeal for a reduction of the amount of bail, but the Court would have none of it.

Nashville Dispatch, January 20, 1864.

21 Report on Confederate guerrilla activities between the Cumberland and Tennessee rivers

We have some cheering news from the Cumberland river, in the vicinity of Clarksville, through the Federal lines. Captain Bruce Phillips, formerly of the 14th Tennessee regiment, and who commanded that regiment, in the first day's fight at Gettysburg, who received authority last fall to recruit a regiment of cavalry inside the Federal lines, is now in the section of the country between the Cumberland and Tennessee rivers, doing serious damage to the foe. He has between 150 and 200 men and has been actively engaged all winter in annoying the Federal Garrisons at Clarksville and Fort Donelson, and the working parties upon the North-western railroad. Not long since he attacked several thousand of the armed negroes working on the railroad, killed and wounded a large number, and put the rest to flight. Some of them whose masters lived in Clarksville, had reached that place, and reported that their whole force had been scattered except those were killed and wounded, and that they themselves had been so badly scared that they had been running for thirty miles to get home. A few days before Christmas, Captain Phillips with fifteen men was in the immediate vicinity of Clarksville. The fact becoming known to the Federal commander at Clarksville, he dispatched a party of fifty — to capture them. Phillip's party ambuscaded them, and killed seventeen and wounded many others. Only seventeen of the party returned to Clarksville. Capt. Phillips is a daring and efficient officer, is entirely familiar with the country in which he is now operating, and will doubtless do much good.

Macon *Daily Telegraph*, January 21, 1864.

25 Public health initiative taken in Nashville by U.S. Army

General Orders, No. 5
Headquarters U.S. Forces
Nashville, Tenn., Jan 25, 1864

I.... The municipal regulations failing to keep the city effectually policed, it is hereby ordered, for the preservation of the health and lives of the citizens, and of the troops on duty at this place, that the occupant of every house daily sweep or scrape clean the pavement or sidewalk in front of his building. This will be done daily before 9 o'clock A.M. On stated days, hereafter to be announced, each occupant will clean to the middle of the street in front of his premises, collecting the sweepings into piles, to be carried away by Government wagons.

For any neglect of this regulation, a fined double that enforced by the municipal ordinance will be imposed by the Provost Marshal; and if not paid at his office within one week from notice, will be levied by sale at public auction of goods sufficient to realize the sum.

A commissioned officer is detailed to superintend the policing of the city, whose special duty it is to report any neglect or violation of this order.

By command of Brig. Gen. R. S. Granger

Nashville *Dispatch*, January 28, 1864.

26 A juvenile gang in Memphis

"Big Raid by the Mackerel Brigade."

Some of the members of this celebrated gang of pilferers and thieves made a raid on Saturday and Sunday nights, on the store of S.P.C., Clark & Co., and D.O. Gibson, north side of the square. They broke the windows and took out goods of considerable value. They broke the windows and took out goods. They levied quite a contribution on Clark's splendid stock of hats, abstracting goods to the value of one hundred dollars, besides putting him to considerable expense repairing the damage done to the windows. It is time that band of petty thieves was broken up.

Memphis *Bulletin*, January 26, 1864.

27 "A Salt and Battery"

A grocer, on Front row, had a pet joke, which he has been in the habit of getting off at least once a week for some months past. He offers to give a two hundred pound of salt to a man who will carry it the length of his store, without setting it down. He always wins the wager, for the man who carries the salt will have to set it down at last. It was a mere catch in the words of the proposition. A darkey came up with him yesterday, however. He went into the store, looking unusually green, and soon was picked out for a victim of his joke. Coffee shouldered the "Salina," and after carrying it down through the store, *hung it up on a hook*, thereby winning the sack fairly, as he never "set it down" at all. The merchant paid the forfeit, and then offered to give a monstrous cheese to the darkey if he could butt it off the top of a barrel with his head, when it was set up edgewise. The negro did not wait a second invitation, but ran a tilt at the "Western reserve" immediately. The cheese was spoilt, the centre of it being soft and decayed. The human battering ram went clear through it, and was the most damaged looking customer afterward you ever saw. He withdrew his forces in dismay.

Memphis *Bulletin*, January 27, 1864.

♦ FEBRUARY ♦

4 Paradise Lost

[From the Boston *Traveler*, Feb. 4, 1864]

"The Desolation in Tennessee."

An enterprising adventurer, who has been on a tour in Tennessee of an extensive and somewhat dangerous character, on his return to Murfreesboro, writes, under date of Jan. 30, as follows:

In years gone, and not long ago, Tennessee was a paradise. Peace and plenty smiled; law and order reigned. How is it now? After a week's journey, I sit me down to paint you a picture of what I have seen. To the East and to the West, to the North, and to the south, the sights are saddening, sickening. Government mules and horses are occupying the homes — aye, the palaces — in which her chivalric sons so often slumbered.

The monuments of her taste, the evidences of her art, characteristics of her people, are being blotted from existence. Her churches are being turned into houses of prostitution, her seminaries shelter the sick and sore, whose griefs and groans reverberate where once the flower of our youth were wont to breathe poetic passions and dance to the music of their summer's sun. Her cities, her towns and her villages are draped in mourning. Even the country, ever and always so much nearer God and nature than these, wear the black pall. Go from Memphis to Chattanooga, and it is like the march from Moscow in olden time.

The State capitol, like the Kremlin, alone remains of her former glory and greatness. Let this point (Murfreesboro') be the centre, and then make a circumference of thirty miles with me, and we will stay "a week in the womb of desolation." Whether you go on the Selma, the Shelbyville, the Manchester, or any other pike, for a distance of thirty miles either way, what do we behold? One wide, wild and dreary waste, so to speak.

The fences are all burned down; the apple, the pear and the plum trees burned in ashes long ago, the torch applied to thousands of splendid mansions, the walls of which alone remain, and even this is seldom so, and where it is, their smooth plaster is covered with vulgar epithets and immoral diatribes. John Smith and Jo Doe, Federal and Confederate warriors, have left jack knife stereotyping on the doors and casings, where these, in their fewness, are preserved. The rickets and the railings — where are they?

Where are the rose bushes and the violets? But above all, and beyond all, and dearer and more than all else — where, or where, are the once happy and contented people fled who lived and breathed and had their being here? Where are the rosy cheeked cherubs and blue eyed maidens gone? Where are the gallant young men? Where are all — where are any of them?

But where are they gone — this once happy and contented people? The young men are sleeping in their graves at Shiloh, at Corinth, at Fort Donelson, and other fields of so-called glory. The young women have died of grief or are broken hearted; the children are orphans....

Southern Banner [Athens, Georgia]
April 20, 1864.

11 Report on Juvenile Warfare at Shieldstown, Knoxville environs

Boy Soldiers.— A correspondent of the Philadelphia *Press*, writing from Blain's Cross Roads, Tenn., says: "Across a little creek is a place they called Shieldstown. The spirit of war is among the boys of six, eight, and ten years old, and the fight raged fiercely between the Shieldstowners and Knoxvillers. They used slings and Minie balls, which they used with great dexterity. They had camp fires built along in a line. Every morning each party appeared on its own side of the stream, drawn up in array, ammunition was distributed out of a bag, fifteen rounds to the man, and they commenced. Old soldiers of the 9th Corps, who have been through many a storm of shot and shell, kept at a respectable distance as they hurled their Minies with vigor. One day the Shieldstowners made a charge at the single plank that crossed the stream, the Knoxvillers ran, all except one little fellow about eight years old, who stood at the end of the plank, swearing oaths like Parrott shells, calling them cowards, and, by a vigorous discharge of Minies, repulsed the assault. The casualties amounted to bruises and cuts in all parts of the body, rather serious to look at, or to think what they might have been; but every little fellow was proud of his wound. So it went on for several days, when one bright morning, as they were drawn up in full fighting array, and only awaited signal to commence, suddenly appeared some women in rear of each; a half dozen were caught up, severely spanked, and led off. The rest were disconcerted and dispersed."

New Orleans *Daily Picayune*, February 11, 1864.

12 John Wilkes Booth in Nashville

The distinguished tragedian, J. Wilkes Booth, takes his farewell benefit to-night, his engagement closing the following evening. The entertainment will commence with Shakespeare's tragedy, "The Merchant of Venice," and close with "Catherine and Petruchio," a Shakespearean comedy. In the former, Mr. Booth appears as Shylock; in the latter as Petruchio. The pieces have been well cast, and we may expect them to be produced in the most brilliant style.

Mr. Booth came amongst us a stranger, his reputation as a rising star having preceded him, creating a general desire amongst our playgoers to get a "taste of his quality." His first night was a splendid ovation; the theater being densely packed, every foot of standing room occupied, and numbers sent away unable to get in. Nobly did he fulfill expectations, and establish himself as a favorite. Every succeeding performance has been a repetition of his successes. In no part has he failed. His genius appears equal to anything the tragic muse has produced; and the time is not too distant when he will attain the high niche of professional fame. His engagement here will not soon be forgotten by any who have attended the theatre, and the records of that establishment will transmit it to those who follow after him as the best played here during the most eventful of dramatic seasons.

We expect to see the house literally overflowing to-night. Gentlemen with ladies should make it a point to go early to be sure of seats.

Nashville *Daily Union*, February 12, 1864.

13 Robbers in Carroll County

Same robbers visited me again last night. Drew a pistol on me to make me tell where my mules were. I did not tell. They made Allen, a Negro boy tell. Bursted the door open & took the two last work mules I had. Took Allen off. I learned other names: Bill Nevel, (old Ruben Nevel's son) G. C. Smith and George Nevel. Cal Lusk and old

Byrd Lusk are the ringleaders of the gang that visits this section.

"Younger Diary."

23 Civil War Fiction set in Tennessee
WHIPPING THE WRONG WOMAN. By James T. Trowbridge

A Sketch of Chivalry of East Tennessee

We cut the subjoined game at cross purposes from Mr. Thornbridge's new novel of "Cudjo's Cave."

A brief preface will make it intelligible. When Secession was first augurated in East Tennessee, many loyal men who had been for months privately drilling that they might fight if need should be, in defense of the Union, were obliged to leave their homes and take refuge in the mountains. Among them was a well to do farmer named Stackridge, a man of some influence in the community, and one whom the confederates were especially anxious to arrest. By adroit espionage they became convinced he held communication with his family; and the more unscrupulous among them conceived the chivalrous idea of whipping Mrs. Stackridge until she revealed the hiding place of her loyal mate. Wherefore not? None of them would hesitate to whip a slave woman who rebelled, and the wife of an incorrigible "Union shrieker" could hardly expect a lighter doom.

Near to the Stackridge farm lived Widow Sprowl, a rabid secessionist, whose only son had been outlawed for some act of violence under the old government, but was welcomed to the service of the new and honored with a commission in the confederate army. He was in command in the vicinity, and sent two Germans of his company, who might be relied on for literal adherence to military orders, to pay Mrs. Stackridge the humane visit to which we have related. Now it chanced that the good woman was absent from home, having gone out to call upon a neighbor (not Mrs. Sprowl) and during her absence the captain's mother, intent upon borrowing groceries from one who, under the circumstances, would hardly refuse to lend, knocked twice at the door and, meeting no response pulled the hospitable "latch string" and entered the empty house — Her first feeling was that of resentment. What right hade Mrs. Stackridge to be absent when she came to borrow?

As she explored the pantry and closets, however, and became convinced that she was absolutely alone in a well-provisioned farm-house, her countenance lighted up with a smile.

"I can burry what I want jest exactly as well as if Mrs. Stackridge war at home," thought the widow. And she proceeded to fill her basket. She helped herself to a pan of meal, borrowing the pan as well. "I'll fetch home the pan," said she, "when I do the meal, exposing her craggy teeth with a grim smile. "If I don't before, I'm a feared Mrs. Stackridge'll haf to wait for't a considerable spell! What's in this box? Coffee. May as well take box and all. Bring back the box when I do the coffee. Wish I could find some tobacky somewhars-wonder whar they keep their tobacky?"

Now, the excellent creature did not indulge in these liberties without some apprehension that Mrs. Stackridge might return suddenly and interrupt them. Perhaps she had not followed Mr. Stackridge to the mountains. Perhaps she had only gone in to the village to buy shoes for her children, or to call on a neighbor. "If she should come back and ketch me at it, why, then I'll tell her I'm only jest a borryin,' and see what she'll do about it. The prop'ty of these yer darned Union shriekers is all gwine to be confiscated, and I reckon I may as well take my sheer when I can git it. There a paper o' black pepper, and I'll take it jest as 'tis. Thar's a jar of lump butter, — wish I could tote jar and all — have some of the lumps on a plate anyhow."

She had soon filled her basket, and was regretting that she had not brought two, or a larger one, when a handsome new tin pail hanging in the pantry caught her eye. "I bin wantin' a such a pail as that, the long while." And she proceeded to fill that also. Just as she was putting the cover on she was very much startled by hearing foot-steps at the door.

"O,' dear me! What shall I do? If it should be Mr. Stackridge? But it can't be him! If it's only Mrs. Stackridge or one o' the niggers, I'll face it out. They won't das to make a fuss, for they're Union shriekers and my son's capting in the confederate army!"

Thump, thump, thump, loud knocking at the door.

"My, it's visitors! Who can it be? She set down her pail and basket. "I'll act jes' as if I had a right here, anyhow!

She was hesitating when the string was pulled, and two strangers, stout, square built, with foreign-looking faces, carrying muskets, and dressed in confederate uniform entered. "Mrs. Stackridge:" said they in heavy Teutonic accent.

"Ye-ye-yes-"stammered the widow trying to hide the guilty basket and pail behind her skirts. "What do you want of Mrs. Stackridge?" One of the strangers said to the other, in German, indicating the plunder. "This is the woman. She is getting provisions ready to send to her husband 'in the mountains.'"

"Let us see what there is good to eat," said the other.

Mrs. Sprowl, although understanding no word that was spoken, perceived that she borrowed property formed the theme of their remarks. "Have some?" she hastened to say, with extreme politeness, as the Germans approached the provisions.

"Tank ye," finding some bread and cold meat. And as they ate with appetite, exchanging and grunting with satisfaction.

"O,' take all you want," said the widow. "You're welcome to anything there is in the house, I'm shore!"—adding, within herself, "I am so glad the soldiers have some. Now, whatever is missing will be laid to them.'"

"You da lady of da house?" said the foreigners, munching.

"Yes, help yourselves!" smiled the hospitable widow.

"You Mrs. Stackridge?" they inquired more particularly.

"Yes, take anything you like," replied the widow.

"Where your husband?"

"My husband! My poor dear husband, he has been dead these—" She checked herself, remembering that the soldiers took her for Mrs. Stackridge. If she undeceived them, then they would know she had been stealing.

"Dead?" The Germans shook their heads and smiled. "No, he was here last night, he was seen. You take dese tings to him in de mountain."

"Would you like some cheese?' said the harassed widow.

"Tank ya! Dis is better as rations."

Mrs. Sprowl returned to the pantry, in order to replace the provisions she had so generously given away and then prepared to part with the basket and pail, inviting them repeatedly to make themselves quite at home, and to take whatever they could find.

"Wait!" said they. Each had a knee on the door, and one hand full of bread and cheese. They looked up at her with broad complacent unctuous faces, smiling but resolute. And one, with his unoccupied hand, laid hold of the handle of the basket while the other detained the pail. "You will tell us where is your husband!" said they.

O, dear me, I don't know. I'm a poor lone woman and whir my husband is I can conceive, I'm shore."

"You will tell us where is your husband," insisted the men; and one of them getting up on his feet, stood before at the door. "He's on the mountains somewhere. I don't know whar, I don keer," cried the widow excited. There was something in the staid determined looks of the brothers she did not like. "He's a bad man, Mr. Stackridge is. I'm a secessionist myself, you are welcome to everything in the house — only let me go now."

"You will not go," said the soldier at the door "till you tell us. We come for dat."

On entering they had placed their muskets in the corner. The speaker took them and handed one to his comrade. And now the widow observed that out of the muzzle of each protruded the butt end of a small cowhide. Each soldier laid his gun aside and, and laying hold of the said butt end, drew out the long, taper belly and dangling lash of the whip, like a black snake by the neck.

The widow screamed. "It's all a mistake. Let me go, I ain't Mrs. Stackridge!"

Nothing so natural as that the wife of a notorious Unionist should deny her identity in sight of the whips. The soldiers looks to each other, muttered something in German, smiled, and replaced their muskets in the corner.

"You tell us where is your husband; or else we whip you. Dat is our orders." This they said in low tones, with mild looks and with a calmness which was frightful. The widow saw that she had to do with men who obeyed orders literally, and knew no mercy.

"I hain't got no husband. I ain't Mrs. Stackridge. I'm a poor lone wider, that jest came over here to burry a few things and that's all!"

"Ve unterstan. You say shust now you are Mrs. Stackridge. Now you say not—Dat make no difrinse. Ve know. You tell us where is your husband, or ve string you up." This speech was pronounced by each foreigner, a sentence each, alternatively. At the conclusion one drew a strong chord from his pocket, while the other looked with satisfaction at certain hooks in the plastering overhead, designed originally for the support of a kitchen pole, but destined for another use.

"Don't you dast to tech me!" screamed the false Mrs. Stackridge. "I am a secessionist myself, that hates the Union shriekers wus'n you do, and I've got a son that's a capting, and a poor old widder at that!"

"Dat we don't know. What we know is you tell us what we say or whip you. Dat's Captain Shprowl's orders."

"Captain Sprowl?! That's my son, my own son! If he sent you, then it's all right!"

"So we tank. All right" and the soldiers seizing her, tied her thumbs as Lysander* had taught them, passed the cords over the hook as they passed the clothes line over the cross beam the night before, and drew the shrieking woman's hands above her head precisely as they hauled up Tobey's. They then turned her skirts up over her head, and fastened them. This also had they been instructed to do by Lysander. It was, you will say, shameful; for this woman was free and white. Had she been a slave, with a different complexion, although perhaps quite as white, would it have been any less shameful? Answer, you believers in the divine rights of slave masters!

"Now you will tell?" said the phlegmatic Teutons, measuring out their whips.

"Go for my son! My son is Capting Sprowl," gasped the stifled and terror stricken widow.

"Dat trick won't do. You shpeak, or we shtrike!"

"It is true, it is true! I am Mrs. Sprowl, and my husband is dead, and my son is Capting Sprowl, and [I am] a poor lone wider and if you strike her a single blow he'll have you took and hung."

"If he is your son, den by your own son's words we whip you. He vill not hang us for dat. You vill not tell? Den we give you ten lash."

Blow upon blow, shriek upon shriek, followed. The soldiers counted the strokes aloud deliberately, conscientiously, as they gave them, "One, two, tres," &c., up to ten. There they stopped. But the screams did not stop. This punishment, which, it was sport to inflict upon a faithful old negro, which it would have been such a good joke to have bestowed on a staunch Unionist, was no sport, no joke, but altogether to thy mother, O' Lysander! Then she, who had so often wished that she too owned slaves, that when she was angry she might have them strung up and flogged, knew by fearful experience what it was to be strung up and flogged. Then she, who sympathized with her son in his desire to see every man, woman and child that loved the Union, served in this fashion, in her writhing and bleeding flesh the stings of that inhuman vengeance. Terrible thunder, for which she had only herself to thank. Robbery of her neighbor's house — the dishonest borrowing, not of these ill gotten goods only, but also of her neighbor's name — had brought her by what we call fatality to this straight. Fatality is but another name for Providence.

The soldiers waited for a lull in the shrieks, then put once more the question:

"You tell now? Where is your husband? No? Then you git ten lash more. Always ten lash until you tell."

A storm of incoherent denial, angry threats, sobs and screams was the response. One of the soldiers drew her skirts over her head again, and gave another pull at the cords that hauled up her thumbs, while the other stood off and measured his whip. Just then the door opened and Captain Sprowl looked in.

"How are you getting on, boys?" The question was accompanied by an approving smile which seemed to say, "I see you are getting on very well!"

"We whip her once. We give her ten lash. She no tell."

"Very well, Give her ten more"

The widow struggled and screamed. Had she recognized her son's voice? Muffled as she was, he did not recognize hers. Nor was it surprising that in the unusual posture that he found her he did not know her from Mrs. Starbridge. He stood in the door and smiled while the soldier laid on.

"Make it a dozen," he quietly remarked. "And smart ones to wind up with!." So it happened that, thanks to her son's presence the screeching victim got two smart ones additional.

"Now uncover her face. Ease up on her thumbs a little I'll question her myself— Good Lucifer!" exclaimed the captain, finding himself face to face with his own mother.

Twenty-two lashes and the torture of the strung-up thumbs had proved too much even for the strong nerves of Widow Sprowl. She fell down in a swoon. Lysander, furious whipped out his

---

*Lysander Sprowl.

sword, and turned upon the soldiers. They quietly stepped back, and took their guns from the corner. He would certainly have killed one of them on the spot had he not seen by the glance of their eyes that the other would, at the same instant, as certainly have killed him.

"You scoundrels have whipped my own mother!"

Captain," they calmly answered, "we opey your orders."

"Fools!"—and Lysander ground his teeth—"you should have known."

"Captain," they replied "if you don't know, how should we know? We never see dis woman pefore. We come. We find her taking provisions from da house. We say, 'She take dem to her husband in der mountains.' We say, 'You Mrs. Starkridge? She say yes to everything. We not know she lie. We not know she steal. We not say 'You somebody else.' We opey orders. We take and we whip her. You come in and say, 'Whip more' We whip more. Now you say to us 'Scoundrels!' You say 'Fools!' We say 'Captain it was your orders we opey.'"

Having by a joint effort sententious English pronounced this speech, the brothers stood stolidly awaiting the result; while the captain, still gnashing his teeth, bent over the prostrate form of his mother.

"Bring some water and throw [it on] her, you idiots!" he yelled at them. "Would you see her die?"

They looked at each other "Water? Yes, that was what was wanted. They remembered practice of the previous evening. One found a wooden pail. The other emptied the contents of the tin pail the widow had "borrowed." They went to the well. They brought water "To throw on her?" Yes that was what he said. And together they dashed a sudden drenching flood over the poor woman, and as if the swoon was another fire to be extinguished. These fellows obeyed orders literally—a merit which Lysander had failed to appreciate. He swore at them terribly. But he did not countermand his last order. Accordingly they proceeded stoically to bring more water. Lysander had got his mother's head on his knees, and she had just opened her eyes to look and her mouth to gasp, when there came another double ice cold wave, blinding, stifling, drowning her. Too much of water hadst thou, poor widow!

Lysander let fall the maternal hand, and bounded to his feet, roaring with wrath. The brothers, imperturbable, with the empty pails at their side, stared at him with mute wonder.

"Captain, dat was your orders. You say 'Pring vasser and trow on,' We pring vasser and trow on. Dat is all."

"But I didn't tell you to fetch pails full."

This sentence rushed out of Leander's soul like a rocket, culminated in a loud, explosives oath, and it was followed by a shower of fiery curses falling harmless on the heads of the unmoved Teutons. They waited patiently, until the pyrotechnic rain ceased, then answered, speaking alternately, each a sentence, as if with one mind, but with two organs.

"Captain, you hear. Last night vas de house a fire. You say "Bring vasser.' We pring a little. Den you say to us 'Tam you why in hell you shtop?' and you say, "Ven I tell you pring vasser, pring till I say shtop.' Vun time more today you say "Pring vasser, and you never say shtup. You say 'Trow on. We trow on. Vat you say we do. You say vat mean, dat is mistake for you."

The Scioto Gazette February 23, 1864.

26 Champ Ferguson captures Washington
Report of Col. Robert K. Byrd
LOUDON, February 28, 1864.

SIR: The following dispatch just received ... dated February 27:

Champ Ferguson, with 150 men, made a raid on our courier-line last night at Washington, in Rhea County, killed the provost-marshal ... and captured all the couriers from there to Sulphur Springs, killing 1 and wounding 2 others. He carried off 11 horses and 11 repeating rifles.

G. GRANGER, Maj.-Gen.

OR, Ser. I, Vol. 32, pt. I, p. 485.

♦ MARCH ♦

4 Taking the oath

A number of rebels come to Nashville daily and take the oath of amnesty. Some of them take it with "wry faces." The fact is, they are like the fellow that, on a wager, eat [sic] the crow. They can "eat crow" but d____d if they have a hankering for it!

Nashville *Daily Union*, March 4, 1864.

ca. 6 Fuerguson's and Hamilton's guerrilla bands defeat W. B. Stokes' 5th U.S. cavalry scout

Excerpt from the letter of Alvan C. Gillem to Military Governor Andrew Johnson
Nashville, March 11, 1864

Governor,

... Two of Stokes Companies were Scouting near Sparta last week, when they were attacked by Hamilton & Ferguson and twenty seven of them killed — all six of the officers and forty men escaped[.] The disaster is charged to the ignorance & cowardice of the officers — at last Stokes Regt. has been concentrated & is at Sparta....

Papers of Andrew Johnson, Vol. 6, p. 643.

ca. 6–7 Col. Fielding Hurst's 6th Tennessee Cavalry [U.S.] burns Jackson and Brownsville

Excerpt from the report of N. B. Forrest

HDQRS. FORREST'S CAVALRY DEPARTMENT, Columbus, March 10, 1864.

Col. T. M. JACK, Assistant Adjutant-Gen.

COL....

Hurst is still reported in West Tennessee, and a portion of Jackson and Brownsville have been burned by his men....

N. B. FORREST, Maj.-Gen.

OR, Ser. I, Vol.32, pt. III, p. 609.

8 "I am almost crazy with my spine, took a dose of Morphine, I am in so much pain it does not affect me." A page from the Confederate smuggler Belle Edmondson's diary

March, Tuesday 8, 1864

Cousin Mat, Frazor and Joanna went in town this morning. Joanna was to have returned this evening, did not come. We heard what the Yanks were after — old Frank the detective carried them to Felix Davis's and took him and his wife both to Memphis, they are now in the Irving Block, we did not hear the offence, only 'twas some old grudge he had against Mr. Davis. They stole a good deal from Widow Hildebrand's but she has taken the oath, and I don't care much. I pity poor Mr. & Mrs. Davis, they have been so kind to our Soldiers.

Nannie Perkins came home this morning. Joe Clayton — Memphis Light Dragoons — came on short furlough. Tate & I are going after Mrs. Clayton & Hal tomorrow. We all spent the evening in the Parlor, singing and playing. I am almost crazy with my spine, took a dose of Morphine, I am in so much pain it does not affect me-All spent day in my room sewing-Laura and Beulah in, Tip not arrived. Oh! I am so lonely, and suffering so much.

Diary of Belle Edmondson

11 U.S.S. *Peosta* bombards Confederate guerrillas near Yellow Creek on the Tennessee River

No circumstantial reports filed.

At about 1:30 P.M. the crew responded to an apparent threat to the boat and began shelling the woods near the mouth of Yellow Creek firing in all about 36 rounds. They then proceeded up the river, returning in a few hours. There, four of the crew landed and fired a small framed building located near the creek.

U.S.S. *Peosta* Daily Deck Log

17–19 Counter-insurgency operations near Beersheba Springs

On Thursday evening [17th] about 60 Rebels dashed thro' this place [Beersheba Springs] — two stopping a moments at Mr. A's — one of them was Luke Ridley, a son of the Judges! The encamped in a little grove near Mr. Dugan's at the base of the opposite mt. where their camp-fires shone all night long. About dawn [18th] this place [Beersheba Springs] was full of Yankees — flourishing their pistols and in hot haste after the Rebs. Their number was about 3 times that of the Rebs — they were principally Stokes' men — the rebs said they were Colonel Hughe's men and belonged to Carter's command. It seems they had been down to Decherd — destroyed a train, (containing only hay and forage) and were getting back to Sparta I don't know where the Yanks are from — at all events they got down the mt. unseen — and surprised the rebels at breakfast — who took off pell-mell up the opposite mt. Looking at its rugged face and rocky brow from here, as it lies nearly opposite to us one wonders how they could scale that height on horseback, but they did. As they came out on top of the mt. they made a little stand — one Yankee was wounded and has since died at McM. The rebels lost some of their saddles, blankets etc. in the melee, and one man. He was a wounded man, had been shot somewhere through the body at the R.R. and it is supposed gave out as he reached the top of the mt. and was shot down after he surrendered. He was shot through the head. Mr. Dugan found him on Friday [19th], the brought him down to the valley and buried him. He was a youth, apparently about 18 years if age — none knew who he was. Will not some mother's heart watch for him who shall come

*City of McMinnville, TN.

no more, and ache with its lonely watching. The Yankees returned soon from the pursuit — and went on to town [McMinnville] — making a great story of the affair by the time they reached there
    War Journal of Lucy Virginia French,
        entry for March 20, 1864.

12 "I have not suffered much with my spine today, though only on account of taking Morphine last night, which has made me insensible to the pain." A page from Belle Edmondson's diary
 March, Saturday 12, 1864
 Tate and Bettie went to Memphis this morning, did not succeed in getting anything through the lines, the Picket was very insulting to her. She brought me a letter, but not for myself, only my care, to Mr. Lawson in Henderson's scouts. I forwarded it to Capt. H. also a package of late papers, by Mr. Harbut, who spent the evening with us. We all sat in the Parlor, and have had a pleasant evening. Mr. Harbut vacxinated Father, Helen, Nannie and I, also Jane and Laura. I have made the skirt to my swiss Mull, and fixed me a beautiful braid pattern, and drew on the skirt ready for my work on Monday morning. I have not suffered much with my spine today, though only on account of taking Morphine last night, which has made me insensible to the pain. 11 o'clock, so I will to bed-no Beulah. Father gave me a key today....
      Diary of Belle Edmondson.

13 The Sin of Race Mixing and the Fortunes of the Confederacy. An entry from the Diary of Eliza Rhea Anderson Fain
 Have enjoyed a precious privilege today of going to the house of God and hearing from our loved minister precious truths. The North has departed from the Bible, she has set it aside for a higher power she found it confliction with her with her views on the subject of slavery. Their misguided zeal and sympathy for the poor African has entailed upon their country one of the most cruel, the most bloody, terrible wars that any people have ever known. While the South by her disregard for the commands of the high and holy one have provoked his wrath. The terrible sin of amalgamation has gone up before the great and holy one, until he has poured out upon us the fierceness of his wrath. This sin has for years been a great trouble to me. I have been so grieved at the thought of the white man enslaving his own flesh and blood — of changing the race of being whom God in his providence and for reasons known to himself seems to have set apart as servants for the descendents of Shem and Japheth. We of the South have sinned in not speaking against this sin, as we should have done. The lord is now judging us for it.
         Fain Dairy.

15 A perilous visit home for Confederate cavalrymen in the Cleveland environs
 We arrived at home this morning before daylight and found our mother and two little brothers well, but they are having a hard time on account of all the robbers plundering them. We learned from our mother at Bro. Jim called at home a few nights ago while passing with his little band of secret scouts, and he came near being captured at our own house. He was standing in [the] rear of the house talking with our mother in low tone when suddenly the enemy made a rush on the house from different directions, as if they had been lying in wait, and they filled the house, searching every room and closet for him, and at the same time plundering the house of whatever struck their fancy. On their approach Bro. Jim dropped back a few steps in the dark and then concealed himself at the corner of the garden fence where he could watch their movements. After they left our mother again came out and found Jim and had some further talk, and he said he could have easily [killed] one or two of the robbers with his revolver and them made his escape, but he feared to do so lest they take revenge by murdering the family and burning the house. He then returned to his comrades who were waiting for him some distance from the house.
 Brother Flavel and I did not wait for day light, but we fell back about three fourths of a mile into a dense forest in the hills, and concealed ourselves in a deep hollow some distance from any road, where we knew we would be safe during the day. Three of our comrades are gone to Benton to visit their people, and are to return to us in two days. The other two are Vance and Alex. Hannah (brothers) and they are with us, but to night they aim to cross the Ocoee River to visit their father and mother and their own families, while Flavel and I will visit out own home again.
    Diary of William A. Sloan, March 15, 1864.

15 A skirmish in the battle for public health in Nashville
 Dead Carcasses.
 A very wholesome order has just emanated from

Lieut. Col. Horner Provost Marshal, forbidding the practice of depositing the carcasses of dead horses and mules within the limits of the city, and requiring that all such dead animals be hauled to a point on the river bank, below the Government corals, and thrown into the river. Any soldier, citizen, or Government employee, leaving any such dead carcass within the city limits, or within one-half mile of the same, or any owner of such dead animal neglecting to have it hauled away, will be arrested and imprisoned.

Nashville *Dispatch*, March 15, 1864.

15 Zinc Coffins

W. R. Cornelius,

Government Undertaker,

Dealer in All Kinds of Metalic and Burial Cases and Zinc Coffins.

Will attend properly to the transportation of bodies, or giving any information regarding deceased Soldiers.

"BODIES EMBALMED."

Having secured the services of Dr. E. H. LEWIS, of New York, (and more recently from the Army of the Potomac,) for embalming of the dead, by Dr. Holmes AMERICAN PROCESS, acknowledged to be the best, and only true process in the United States, will have bodies embalmed when desired.

Principal Office and Ware-Rooms, No. 49 Church Street, Nashville, Tennessee.

Branch houses at Murfreesboro', Tullahoma, Wartrace, Shelbyville, Chattanooga and Stevenson, Alabama.

All communications promptly answered.

Mr. W. R. CORNELIUS is authorized to refer to me. He is a gentleman of integrity, and will perform all that he undertakes or promises.

ANDREW JOHNSON

Military Governor

Memphis *Daily Union*, March 15, 1864.

15 The fate of Confederate Cherokees

LO! THE POOR INDIAN.

A Treaty of Peace with the Cherokees of North Carolina — Thirty Prisoners, with Tuckaneeche, their Chief, take the Oath of the Great Father at Washington.

Correspondence of the New York Tribune.

Knoxville, March 15. — While riding, a day or two since out on the Marysville road, I came upon three Indians who were slowly wending their way toward Knoxville. One of the party was tall, muscular and swarthy, with the long, black and coarse hair and high cheekbones which everywhere mark the Indian. The other, a man of medium size, with only just enough of the hair and complexion of his comrade to suggest his origin, while his intelligible English grey eyes, and other features of the white race, declared him a half-breed. He wore a little grey Confederate cap, and other clothes commonly worn by the Rebel soldiers. The third and principal personage was an old man bending under the weight of eighty years, supporting himself by a long cane, which he held in both hands, while the other two respectfully waited the slower motion of their old friend.

He wore no covering on his head except a handkerchief wrapped about it like a turban. His features were intelligent, with a pleasing, thoughtful expression, but little furrowed by age. A healthy crop of grey hair covered his head. While I engaged the half-breed in conversation, the old man stood leaning on the top of his staff, and listened very inventively, though seeming to understand but imperfectly what was said. This old man, I learned, was TUCKANEECHE, the chief of the North Carolina Cherokees, who had come all the way from his mountain home n North Carolina to see the great Indian — the head of the army of the Union, in Knoxville. The visit, it may well be supposed, was not wholly a voluntary one. A number of his tribe were prisoners of war, detained here, and their liberty depending upon such arrangements and pledges as he and they might be able jointly to make with the military authorities touching their future conduct.

The Indian prisoners captured by the Fourteenth Illinois Cavalry some time since, on account of which has been sent to you, asserted that they were made to believe by the Rebel leaders that they were fighting for the old Government; and gave assurances that if their tribe and chief could be made acquainted with the true state of affairs, they would lay down their arms at once and forsake their old leader, Thomas in a body. It was with the view of coming to some understanding with these people, and, if possible, of securing their friendship, or at least their immune neutrality, that two of the prisoners were permitted to return to their village of its vicinity in the Chilhowie Mountains, in order to explain matters and bring in their chief. Meantime, the prisoners were held as so many hostages for the faithful performance of the mission. The two messengers had to proceed with the greatest caution and address, so as not to be captured while upon their delicate and difficult errand.

Upon learning the situation of his people, the old chief rose up, and, taking his staff and a small supply of food, cheerfully undertook the journey. They were over a week on the way.

Tuckaneeche was received by the big Indians in Knoxville with distinguished consideration, General Schofield, commanding the department, General Sam Carter, Provost Marshal-General, and Captain Thomas, his chief of staff, extended to him the kindness which is so well calculated to renew the memory of the ancient good will heretofore and always exercised toward their tribe by the Government at Washington. Why should they fight against their best friends? They say it was altogether a mistake, and that they can prove they hurrahed for Jeff. Davis *and the union!* If that be so, they might certainly be forgiven. Let the Indian have the benefit of his own story. Though unwilling to spoil so good a one, I must confess I do not believe more than half of it. The half-breed, with who I spoke freely, and who neither knew me, nor the motive I had for making the inquiry, stated that the Indians were "drug into the fight." He "heard old Thomas tell them, if they didn't fight for the South, there were South[ern] men enough to kill every last Injin of 'em, and they would do it too."

After a true and full explanation of affairs, and the arms, conditions and benefits of the oath of amnesty and pardon which the Great Father in Washington had offered them, they were permitted, jointly and generally to swear perpetual good will to Uncle Sam. The old chief, with a king of Hebraic signature, appended his name and title to the document. Solemnly, pledging that, for himself and his tribe, he would forever bear true faith and allegiance to the Government of the United States, and give no aid, encouragement or comfort to its enemies in any matter whatsoever. The ceremony released some thirty Cherokees from further detention as prisoners of war, but they will not return to their homes until our neighborhood is freed from the presence of Thomas and his pirate Crew. From the most trustworthy information I can obtain, Thomas' Indians have about all deserted him, and his agency for mischief is pretty much at an end. There is no doubt d that the Indians will kept their agreement if it is possible for them to do so, which is the difficult point in the case. As soon as they can be reached by Rebel agents of conscription they will either be shot, or forced into the ranks again. I learn that many of them have been thrown into prison, and that others are wandering in dens and caves of the mountains to escape the Rebel service.

Philadelphia *Inquirer*, March 28, 1864.

16 Confederate raid on N&C Railroad, near Tullahoma

Railroad Raid.

..."A band of guerrillas under Colonel (unknown,) attacked the freight train from Nashville, near Estelle Springs to-night. By displacing a rail the train was thrown off the track and burned. Capt. Beardsley of the 123d New York and seven men have just arrived here on a hand car, having been paroled after being stripped of their clothing and money, watches and jewelry. The Rebels killed three negroes who were on the train. Two of the band were killed. No losses on our side. They belonged to Roddy's command."

Nashville *Dispatch*, March 18, 1864.*

17 Wedding party at the home of Mr. Reynolds on Walden Ridge

I do not suppose that the history of the world contains such a rare case of universal *concord* being the result of such universal *discord*. The [wedding] party was composed of 1st, Rebel and Union citizens; 2d, Rebel and Union soldiers; 3rd, Rebel and Union deserters; 4th, Rebel and Union spies; 5th Rebel and Union bushwhackers.

Scarcely a harsh word was uttered during the whole night; all danced together as if nothing was wrong, and parted mutually the next morning, each party marching off separately.

Considering the great hatred existing between the different parties it is marvelous that bloodshed was not the immediate result.

Chattanooga *Gazette*, March 17, 1864

18 Carrion Road

The *Chattanooga Gazette* states that between the point of Lookout Mountain and Bridgeport, down the Valley of the Tennessee, lie twenty five miles of dead mules in one continuous string.

Daily National Intelligencer, March 18, 1864.

---

*This raid is the subject of a number of Official Reports *indicating the raid took place on the 16th.*

21 Skirmish at Reynoldsburg, Tennessee
Report of Col. Isaac R. Hawkins, Seventh Tennessee Cavalry.

UNION CITY, TENN., March 22, 1864.

GEN.: A detachment of 10 men belonging to Maj. Hardy's command, stationed at Reynoldsburg, Tenn., has just arrived, who state that on the 20th they left the major there with 50 men; that at 11 A.M. the 21st a detachment of 20 men were attacked by from 100 to 150 Confederates, and are probably all captured. That about 100 men of the battalion are somewhere south of Huntingdon; that there are only about 100 men in camp and a large amount of public stores there. I am apprehensive for the fate of the major. The fight occurred 65 miles from this place.

ISAAC R. HAWKINS, Col., Cmdg.

OR, Ser. I, Vol. 32, pt. I, p. 624.

24 Confederate attack on Union City
The Rebels Attack on Union City, Tenn.
Surrender of Four Hundred Union Troops.

Cairo, March 25. The enemy being reported in force near Union City, Tenn. yesterday morning, General Brayman, with a force of 2000 men and a battery of artillery, proceeded by railroad to within ix miles of that place, when they learned that Colonel Hawkins, with 400 of the Seventh Tennessee Cavalry, and surrendered at 11 A.M., after repulsing the Rebels, who mustered 2000 men, three times.

The enemy burned all that was combustible about the fortifications, and marched off with their prisoners....

Philadelphia *Inquirer*, March 28, 1864.

25 Civilian pursuit of Yankee thieves in Maury County

...Soldiers came to the shop & at Puse's house and presented their pistols cocked at George, make him give up his money they then commenced to rob Anderson & Jack about that time I got word of it & went to their releaf charged upon them they give back & I ordered the blacks to take them, the soldiers took to their heels [and] ran crossed the field fence runing south east until they got to the S.E. Corner of the field then they crossed the fence into Warfield's woods there Anderson & Jack overtook them with 2 double shot guns the fight ensued from behind trees 7 guns were fired, 4 pistols by the soldiers 7 & 3 guns by the boys. It terminated by the soldiers beging for quarters by giving up there money they had robed the boys of they went on to there command told they were attacked by the gurillas & one of them got his wounds dressed & put in a wagon & went on[.]

...

Diary of Nimrod Porter, March 25, 1864.

31 A Day in the Life of an Ohio soldier
March 31st 1864
My dear sister....

Maybe thee will be interested in an account of the manner that we spend our time in camp. I will try to give you some idea of my doings. Today is a pretty good sample — I was waked out of a sound *nap* at 5½ o'ck by "*drummer call*," pulled on my boots & got my traps on, said traps consisting of cartridge box, haversack and rifle. Fell into line for roll call and after the roll is called by the Orderly Sergt. open ranks and the Lt. Inspects every gun and cartridge box, then drill for a few minutes in the *Manual of Arms*, then break ranks and get breakfast. Which means in this case, a dish of fried crackers with gravy made with flour and water with a cup of strong coffee, not a bad meal when you get used to it. After breakfast comes *policing*. Then *Guard Mounting* at 8½ o'ck that takes 3 men from a Co. each day and I wasn't one of them this morning. Then we are off duty till 10 o'ck when we have Co. drill for ¼ hour, after this we have nothing to do till 12 P.M. when we have roll call again, then eat dinner. By the way, I had a rare dish for dinner viz. *Oyster Soup*. I bought a can of dove oysters for only $2.00 which made me an excellent dinner and I have some left for breakfast. This is pretty expensive you will think, but it don't happen more than once a year, for we can't get them often. At 2 o'ck we went on Battalion Drill, lasting till 3 o'ck when we came in and brushed up for Dress Parade which came off at 3½ o'ck. I can't tell you how it appears but is a *pretty* sight to anyone who has never seen a Parade.

After it is over, we get supper, *fried crackers*. I have just finished a plateful of them with sugar and I feel exactly as if I'd had my supper. We got plenty of rations now. We drew clothing today, I drew a pair of shirts, shoes & blouse and I am well provided for in the way of clothing...

I want thee to write to me often, even if I don't answer them every time in thy *name*. Be a good girl and *help* mother all thee can. I know thee will without asking.

Believe me ever, Thy Bro — W.

Bentley Letters.

♦ APRIL ♦

2 A traffic jam in Nashville

"The Railroad Bridge."

We have heard frequent complaints from all sorts of people concerning the delays to which they are subjected by keeping the bridge open unnecessarily. Yesterday we determined to watch the bridge for a short time. At ten minutes before one o'clock P.M., a solitary steamer might have been seen coming down the river [*G.P.R. James*]. The weary bridge keeper did undoubtedly see her, for immediately the draw began to move, and the flags to wave, and the passengers to halt and look frightfully hungry, wearing a diabolical smile, and the wagons and other we-*hickles* began to collect on either side. The streamer aforesaid steamed herself down to the workhouse dock, came to the left about face, hailed someone on a coal barge, and hove to for 30½ seconds, when the Captain and Pilot applied their thumbs to the tips of their noses, "smile" to the health of the bridge keeper, rang the bell, and steamed back again. Up and up she goes, one hundred anxious eyes following after her, until she reaches the water-works, and there she rests from her labors. The crowd of people increase, and the line of wagons grows longer and longer, and the locomotive becomes tired, and whistles, and blows, and puffs and sweats, but still the unfeeling Captain refuses to allow his boat to go through the bridge. Anxious inquiries are made as to *when* the boat is going to come down, but none are there to answer. On this side of the river, Front and Locust streets are crowded with all sorts of vehicles, on the other side are a train of cars waiting to cross, a train of government wagons stretching from the bridge back as far as the eye can reach, and numerous mules, horses, and things. At length, at eight minutes before two, the bridge man smells a huge mice, and the draws begins to move, slowly but steadily until she is in the proper place, when the multitude rush over, and the locomotive follows. When the wagons got over we cannot say, probably in an hour or so.

Now for a few questions: Would it not be well for the bridge keeper, for opening the bridge, to ascertain whether or not a boat wishes to pass through?

Might not the bridge be closed as soon as a boat passes, without waiting half a day to ascertain if some other boat desires to pass?

If a hack is worth a dollar and a quarter an hour, how much is a half mile train of Uncle Sam's wagons worth during the same period of time?

If fifty or one hundred wagons, with their attendants, are kept waiting one hour every day, how many dollars does Uncle Sam lose every month by these unnecessary delays?

We *paws* for a replay.

Nashville *Dispatch*, April 2, 1864.

3 "The bad conduct of our own men troubled me greatly." An entry from the Diary of Eliza Rhea Anderson Fain

Last night I lay down with a troubled heart. The bad conduct of our own men troubled me greatly. This morning as I was assisting to prepare my breakfast I was much impressed with the thought we may be reduced to great want for provisions, everything looks so dark and gloomy. The rain continues to fall, so that we cannot do anything about farming. Our horses have all been taken out of the country. The able bodied portion of most families, white and black are gone. Women and children with few boys and a few stout black men are all that's left.

Fain Diary.

6 Last notice to remove public health nuisances in Nashville

Important Notice. We are informed on authority that the mountains of dirt, ashes, filth, or what not, piled up in front of sundry houses, must be removed immediately at the expense of the owner or occupant of the house from whence it was exhumed, or the officers of the city government will indict the occupants for creating a nuisance. General Granger says he never contemplated having huge nuisances removed at the expense of Uncle Sam. We have warned you in time, reader; so look out for a notice to appear, and answer, etc., if your mud-piles are not removed this morning.

Nashville *Dispatch*, April 6, 1864.

7 Entry in Alice Williamson's Diary, Sumner County

Another (rebel) soldier was shot yesterday. The

Yankees went to jail and brought him while a citizen was standing near. He said the soldier was very poorly clad but his countenance was that of a gentleman. When the guard brought his horse to him (a broken down one from the camp) he asked what they were going to do with them. On being told to "Mount that horse and say no more..." he did so remarking that he supposed they were going to shoot him. They took him to the river to shoot him but finding some gentlemen there — Mr. H. & M. they said they had gone in a hornet's nest to shoot and went somewhere else. When they carry them out to shoot them they are given a worn out horse and tell them if they can escape they may; they say "have fine fun chasing the boy with fresh horses" I am sorry I did not commence my journal when old Payne first came; he was worse then than now.

Williamson Diary

10 Forrest announces plans to move on Fort Pillow

HDQRS. FORREST'S CAVALRY,
Jackson, Tenn.,
April 10, 1864.

Maj.-Gen. LEE, Cmdg. Cavalry:

GEN.... I move to-morrow on Fort Pillow with two brigades, the force at that point being 300 whites and 600 negroes. Grierson is reported moving up the State line road from Memphis, and I would suggest that you look well to that quarter. Col. Neely, commanding Richardson's brigade, is near Raleigh and east of Wolf River. I will return to this point by the 15th.

I am, general, with respect, your obedient servant,

N. B. FORREST,
Maj.-Gen., Cmdg.

OR, Ser. I, Vol. 32, pt. III, p. 770.

11 An interesting patient in Ward 3, Hospital 8, Nashville

While in ward 3 ... I was beckoned to, from a sick bed, whose occupant wished me to come and "rejoice with him." Upon going there he assured me with a mysterious air, that he "isn't going to tell everybody, but as I was a particular friend of his, and he had always thought *right smart* of me, he would tell me something surprising."

Upon expressing my willingness to be surprised, he confidently and joyfully assured me that though very few people knew it, yet he was "*The veritable man who killed Jeff. Davis, President of the Confederate States!*"

He waited a moment to note the effect upon me of this pleasing intelligence, when I quietly told him I didn't know before that Jeff. Davis was dead, but that if he was, and he was the one who killed him, they ought to give him a discharge and let him go home, as he has done his share of the work. Then he joyfully assured me, that "they have promised to do so, and that his papers are to be made out to-morrow." But more serious thoughts came to me then, for I saw written on his countenance, in unmistakable characters, the signature of the Death angel, marking him chosen, and though I knew not how soon his papers would be made out, was certain that before long they would be, and that he would receive a full and free discharge from all earthly toil and battle the Great Medical Director of us all!

Powers, *Pencillings*, p. 27.

12 A Gruesome Discovery in Day's Creek, Shelby County

April, Tuesday 12, 1864

...we heard there was a Yankee Negro Soldier dead on Day's Creek, so Bettie, Kate, Robert and Mary & myself started in search. We found him, and it was an awful sight, he was in the Water in full uniform, his napsack on the bank of the creek, oh! I would give anything if I had not seen it....

Diary of Belle Edmondson

12 Capture of Fort Pillow

JACKSON, TENN., April 15, 1864.

GEN.: I attacked Fort Pillow on the morning of the 12th instant with a part of Bell's and McCulloch's brigades, numbering 1,500, under Brig. Gen. James R. Chalmers. After a short fight drove the enemy, 700 strong, into the fort under the cover of their gun-boats. Demanded a surrender, which was declined by Maj. L. F. Booth, commanding U.S. forces. I stormed the fort, and after a contest of thirty minutes captured the entire garrison, killing 500 and taking 200 horses and a large amount of quartermaster's stores. The officers in the fort were killed, including Maj. Booth. I sustained a loss of 20 killed and 60 wounded. Among the wounded is the gallant Lieut. Col. Wiley M. Reed while leading the Fifth Mississippi. Over 100 citizens who had fled to the fort to escape conscription ran into the river and were drowned. The Confederate flag now floats over the fort.

N. B. FORREST, Maj.-Gen.

HDQRS. FORREST'S CAVALRY, Jackson, Tenn., April 15, 1864.

Colonel:

...

Have dispatched by telegraph of the capture of Fort Pillow.

Arrived there on the morning of the 12th and attacked the place with a portion of McCulloch's and Bell's brigades numbering about 1,500 men, and after a sharp contest captured the garrison and all of its stores. A demand was made for the surrender, which was refused. The victory was complete, and the loss of the enemy will never be known from the fact that large numbers ran into the river and were shot and drowned. The force was composed of about 500 negroes and 200 white soldiers (Tennessee Tories). The river was dyed with the blood of the slaughtered for 200 yards. There was in the fort a large number of citizens who had fled there to escape the conscript law. Most of these ran into the river and were drowned.

The approximate loss was upward of 500 killed, but few of the officers escaping.

It is hoped that these facts will demonstrate to the Northern people that negro soldiers cannot cope with Southerners. We still hold the fort.

...

I am, colonel, with respect, your obedient servant,

N. B. FORREST, Maj.-Gen., Cmdg.

OR, Ser. I, Vol. 32, pt. I, pp. 609–611.

16–May 4, 1864 Social change in Columbia, reaction to the establishment of freedmen's schools

...greate excitement about the negro schools in the Town.

Nimrod Porter Diary, April 16, 1864.

...some excitement about the negro schools in Town....

Nimrod Porter Diary, April 18, 1864.

...[Mayor] Andrews, W. J. Andrews, Wiley George, Jno. Latta, Jack Porter, St. Ledger White all in gard house for whipping the negro teacher (Cap Jordan)....

Nimrod Porter Diary, April 22, 1864.

...The Mair & others still in the gard house.

Great many contraband negroes leaving their masters.

Nimrod Porter Diary, April 25, 1864.

The Grand Jury has found true bills at the citizens Andrews & others for whipping a negro by the aldermen the military won't give up the prisoners.

Nimrod Porter Diary, May 4, 1864.

18 Libation poetry from Nashville

Whiskey is not, by official sanction, sold to civilians and officers only, *ad lib*. On the strength of this fact, our muse, awaking with our body this morning to the reality of a genuine Bourbon cocktail, inspires us with the following:

Liquid Lyric
by Uno Hoo.
Time was when *ailing* topers could
But to their *ails* add *ale*;
A combination most extreme
And always sure to fail.
But now, ambrosia's once more loose,
And Whiskey being free
(Though quite restricted in its use)
It ends are plain to see.
This prescience is no witches gift;
"Extremes will often meet";
Thus saith the ancient proverb, and
Old proverbs can't be beat.
Thus, once the whiskey market bound,
Showed up the wond'rous sight
Of all men *loose* and *aleing* hard:
'Tis now reversed-they're *tight*.
Thus is it, by the inverse rule,
In men both black and white,
When whiskey's *tight*, mankind is *loose*;
But when 'tis *loose*, they're *tight*.

Nashville *Daily Press*, April 18, 1864.

20 "Larnin's only for rich folks." Elvira Powers' visit to the Refugee Home in Nashville

Visited the Refugee Home ... this P.M.... As I entered one room, a woman was bustling about in a great passion, and picking up a few personal rags, while ordering her son to get up and they would find a place to stay where shouldn't be "set to do niggar's work!"

She was a healthy, strong woman, and had been repeatedly requested to make her own and son's bed, and assist in sweeping or cooking for the numerous inmates. Indeed, I think she had received a gentle hint that it might be as well to see that her son and herself have clean linen as often as once in two or three weeks, and that the use of a comb occasionally would not detract from personal appearance. But she had her own peculiar ideas, obtained from living under the domination of a peculiar institution, and didn't fancy being dictated to in the delicate matter of her *personelle*.

Upon entering what is called the lecture-room we saw several families and parts of families, which had within two hours arrived on the trains from Alabama or Georgia.

I found that some of these snuff-dipping, clay-colored, greasy and uncombed ladies "from Alabam and Gorgee," are as expert marksmen as any of our northern exquisites, as the deposit the "ter-baker" juice most beautifully into and around any knot-hole or crack in the floor, and while they are at a distance of several feet. It's wonderful how they do it-I am afraid I should never be able to learn.

We approach one woman who is standing by a rough board bunk, upon and around which are several children overcome by the fatigue of travelling. She, unlike the generality, is neatly dressed in a clean dark calico and sunbonnet, and wears a cheerful and intelligent look. She informs us that these are all her children-six of them, that her husband is in the Union army, only a few miles out, that he had sent for to come here, and she expects to see him in a few days. She cannot write, for she hasn't been to school a day in her life, and she says:—

"An' that thar's suthin' you people hev' up north, thet we don't. Poor folks that, hev' a chance to give thar children some larnin'; but them that owns plantations down our way don't give poor folks a chance. Larnin's only for rich folks. But my children shan't grow up to not know no more nor that father nor thar mother, ef I kin' help it. Ef this war don't close so's to make it better for poor folks down har, we'll go north. Thar's a woman what kin' write," she adds with an admiring glance to the other side of the room, "an' she's writin' a letter for me to my husband."

We glance that way, and see a youngish woman, whose entire clothing evidently consists of one garment, a dress which is colored with some kind of bark. She sits in conscious superiority, scarcely deigning to notice up, as we approach, while she is carefully managing the writing with one eye, while her head is turned half way from it, so that the ashes or coal, from the long pipe between her lips, man not fall upon the paper. Her air and manner are evidently intended to be regal, for isn't she the woman "*what kin' write!*"

At a little distance sat a hale, broad-shouldered, stalwart man, who looked as if he were able to do the work of half a dozen common men, who inquired of us, where "Hio was-if 'twas in Illinois"- and whether if he went to either of those places he would be "pressed into the service." In reply, we informed the gentleman that "Ohio was not in Illinois," but if he went to either, he would probably have to stand his chance of being drafted, together with other good loyalists — with the physicians, lawyers, editors, and ministers. He did not reply to that, but his look spoke eloquently.

"For a lodge in some vast wilderness,—
Some boundless contiguity of shade
Where war and draft not come."

Miss Ada M., the Matron of the Refugee Home, was in our room this eve, and said that she was yesterday preparing some sewing for some young Misses, who were conversing earnestly about the Yankees. Finding their ideas rather erroneous with regard to that class of people, she made a remark to the effect that she was one herself.

"Why, you aint a Yankee?" exclaimed a Miss of fifteen dropping her work in bland astonishment.

"Yes, indeed, I am," was the reply.

"Why," said the girl, with remarkably large eyes, "I've allays hearn tell that the *Yankees has horns, and one eye in the middle of their foreheads!*

Powers, *Pencillings*, pp. 54–59.

28 A Federal sham battle in Lookout Valley; an excerpt from George F. Cram's correspondence
Lookout Valley
April 29, 1864
Dear Mother
...

Yesterday afternoon we had one of the grandest performances that our regiment ever took part in, namely, a division drill and sham fight. The men all went out with thirty rounds of blank cartridges and aiming at the grounds selected for the battle, they were drawn up as follows. The 105th were thrown forward as skirmishers and formed into a double line. At proper intervals behind was the first line of battle consisting of three regiments deployed, extending the line a little over a mile. Behind this line was the second. This was drawn up in column by division, consisting of four regiments. And still behind this line were two regiments at either flank in close column. The artillery were posted on the flanks, taking positions on two small hills, covering our grand advance. First the skirmishing commenced by our regiment and continued till we had advanced about three miles and taken possession of every point. Then the enemy were supposed to be found in force, and our regiment were withdrawn and formed in line with the first line of battle. Now the fight commenced in earnest, and with the first line of battle. Now the fight commenced in earnest, and the quick rapid discharge of musketry soon filled the valley with dense smoke. The artillery firing too was executed beautifully and the booming of the canon echoed from hill to hill and thence to the grim wall of Lookout. Of course, we drove the enemy and took any amount of prisoners, with[out] any loss whatever on our side.

Genls. Thomas, Hooker, Butterfield, Brannan and Whipple were there to witness our movements. Butterfield conducted them.

...

Letters of George F. Cram

30 An editorial analyzing the causes for the reduction of workers' wages

"Reducing the Poor Man's Wages"

There are those in our country who, at all hazards, are resolved on holding on to the negro, and perpetuating slavery, even in the loyal region of East Tennessee. They know and feel that the people are sick and tired of fighting to perpetuate slavery in the Cotton States; that not one in ten of all the voters in East Tennessee have any interest in the institution; that they have seen their homes made desolate, and their loved ones slain and cruelly murdered on account of the nigger; that the spirit that actuated these outrages is showing itself as malignant as ever, under the guise of *Unionism*, and of upholding the constitution and laws, and finally, the real people see that there will be no peace in the country while the struggle is kept up to hold on to the disturbing element.

Gentlemen, with a view to carry the poor and laboring classes with them, at the ballot-box, to bolster up the institution, take the ground that if the negroes are emancipated, the competition will become so great between the negroes and the laboring classes of the whites, that poor men will have to work for nothing. This is all stuff. The emancipating of negroes will not *increase* their numbers, but *diminish* them. They are already here, and as slaves are in competition with white laborers, and really *keep down the white man's wages*. Emancipate them, and they will cease to be in competition with white laborers. Nay, more, our theory is, that in process of time they will, like the Indian tribes, become extinct.

But it is of no use to argue this question. The institution will be wiped out, and ought to be, and that section that clings to it longest will see the most trouble, and the last to get rid of the horrors of war. Men who lend themselves to help bolster up slavery now, whether they own any or not, are in their own light, and will prove to be their own tormentors.

Brownlow's Whig and Independent Journal and Rebel Ventilator, April 30, 1864.

30 Elvira Powers remarks on the progress of her contraband students at the Refugee farm

The aptness of the pupils, as a whole, is really surprising. Some have learned the alphabet, I am told, in three days, and others in a week.

It is said that all northern people who visit the school, very soon fall a victim to that fearful disease, known by the southern chivalry and northern copperheads, as "niggar on the brain." And I will confess my belief that were I to teach in this school very long, I might become so interested in some of my pupils I should sometimes forget that they were not of the same color as myself, and really believe that God did make of one blood all nations of the earth.

They present every shade of color from the blackest hue to a fairer skin than my own. It is often necessary to find out who the mother is before you know whether the person is white of black. The age [of the student body] varies from four to thirty.

The progress of some is really astonishing. One little black girl of seven years, and with wooly head, can read fluently in the Fourth Reader, and studies primary, geography, and arithmetic, who has been to school but one year. I inquired if any one taught her at home, if she had not learned how to read before that time. "Oh, no, I learned my letters when I first came to school, and I live with my aunt Mary, and she can't read. She's no kin to me, and I haven't any kin, but I call her aunt."

Perhaps she never had any, or is related to Topsey, and if questioned farther, might say she "'spects she grew." A boy about twelve, who has been to school but nine months, and who learned his letters in that time, reads in the Third Reader and studies geography. Some are truly polite. The first day of my taking charge of one of the division, a delicate featured, brown-skinned little girl of about nine years came to me and said with the sweetest voice and manner:—

"Lady will you please tell me you name?"

I did so, when she thanked me and said:—

"Miss P____ can you please hear our Third Reader this morning." It was not an idle question either, for the school is so large that now, while two of the teachers are absent, from illness, some of the classes are each day necessarily neglected. And so eager are the generality of the pupils to learn, that most of them are in two or three reading and spelling classes at the same time.

One might now not only exclaim with Galileo, "The world does move," and we move with it. For though but a little time since the negro dared to say: I think," lest the master might exclaim,— "You think, you black neggar — never you mind about that, I'll do your thinking for you." But would instead, say deferentially, with bent head and hand in his wooly hair, "Wall, massa, I'se been a studyin' about dat dar," is now learning to stand erect and confess that he does think; as well as learn to read and write.

One of the more advanced pupils told me that her father taught her to read and write before it was safe to let anyone know that he did, or that he could himself read.

Powers, *Pencillings*, pp. 61–63.

♦ MAY ♦

1 Elvira Powers' description of a black church service in Nashville

This P.M., Miss O. and myself accompanied Rev. E. P. Smith to listen to his "colored preaching," as he termed it, in the same church in which is the school for the colored children. It was a rare treat — and the first colored audience I ever saw.

Do not imagine a squalid, ragged, filthy audience; but one where silks, ribbons, velvet, broadcloth, spotless linen and beavers predominated, with a sprinkling of beautifully cared for silver, and gold-headed canes, with about the usual proportion of fops to the canes that one may find in an audience of equal size, of our own color. Some of these persons are free and own property. But one would scarcely covet some of the ladies their silks and velvets, when she learns that it is purchased with the avails of extra labor at night after the day's work "for de missus is done."

But so it is. And although the church was built some years ago with their money, yet it was held in trust by white people because "negroes cannot own property."

I have been repeatedly told that I would turn pro-slavery when I came south and saw how things really were. I do not feel any of the first symptoms as yet, but quite the contrary. Instead, I'm getting to believe that the day when the Emancipation Document was sent forth, was that of which it is said "a nation shall be born in a day," and I'm learning to think that this gospel, which is

"Writ in burnished rows of steel"

And read by

"The watch-fires of an hundred circling camps," is the "word" which "makes men free," and will forever strike the manacles from the oppressed bondsman.

One indignant white man, during the first prayer which was made by a negro preacher, and in which he asked for blessing upon the Union arms and freedom for slaves, left his seat and walked the whole length of the church, with heavy tread and with his hat on his head, while a voice called out,—

"Take your hat off!"

During the closing prayer the negro very properly prayed, "Oh Lord, wilt dou give de people good manners and teach 'em right behaviour wen dey come into de house ob de Lord!"

The sermon was the Bible-story of the death of James and the release of Peter from prison. It was told in a simple, earnest, impressive manner, to a deeply attentive, impressible audience. When he drew the picture of the angel entering the prison, and taking Peter away as easily as though "his chains were made of wax and a lighted candle was held beneath them, while the four quarternians-sixteen-soldiers were powerless to act," one old man laughed outright, a joyous, grateful laugh, others made their peculiar grunting noise which no combination of sounds will give exactly, while others shook hands and cried "Glory to God." During the singing some women had the "power" so that they passed round, embraced and shook hands.

Some joined the church, and the negro preacher told them he "hoped that wouldn't be the last of it, and they they'd be faithful and come to church; " but that some joined whom he "never could get a chance to set eyes on again, so that when they died he never culd tell WHICH PLACE THEY'D GONE TO!"

I have forgotten to note in its proper place, that upon entering the church Miss O. and myself took seats in the only unoccupied pew in the body of the church. But Rev. Mr. S. beckoned us forwarded to a side seat by the pulpit. We took our seats there, but soon a neat, elderly egress came forward and said with a coaxing smile and voice, "Young ladies go up in de altar an' set —*you* doesn't wan to set down here wid dese yere colored folks." We preferred remaining, and she urged the matter in vain. Soon an elderly mulatto man, probably a prominent member in the church, whose portly form was assisted in its waddles by a gold-headed cane, came forward and made the same request. But not being accustomed to the highest seat in the synagogue on account of our possessing a lighter color, we declined doing so until all the seats were filled and some must stand, when we did go; but upon others coming in they also were induced to take a seat in the altar.

Powers, *Pencillings*, pp. 67–68.

1 Gossip in McMinnville

...The 19th Michigan left.... The streets of Mc are said to have presented a sorry sight the morning they left. The Union feminine element which had so frantically thrown itself entirely away into Abraham's bosom, was dissolved, melted, and steeped in briny tears,-and while it took its long-lingering farewell of the shoulder straps, the darkey feminine element in the streets hung like clouds about the necks and brows of "uncle sam's boys" in the ranks and made the air melodious with their lamentations. The hard-beat of rebellion looked on unmoved by all this panorama of despair. The feminine "secesh" element was centered upon finding out how the "union element" conducted itself at Beersheba. The Col. would say but little — indeed there was but little need since they, themselves had trumpeted their own doings as soon as they returned. It seems they were much "cut" by not being invited to Mrs. A's and made a good deal of "to-do" over it — tho' some did aver that they cared nothing for the attentions of Mrs. A. or Miss Franklin' they only wanted the use of their parlor and piano, to entertain their beaux! One of the rebel sisters remarked that "Those girls never had been able to get into respectable society, and they imagined they could not make an entrée with an armed force, but they were mistaken." It seems that the Yankee beaux tried first to get the rebel ladies to accompany them but when they politely declined — the Union feminine were taken as a "dernier resort!" Funny doings. It is funny to see the "loyalty" neglected when there is a ghost of a chance to catch a "rebel" smile — but so it is, and all natural enough I suppose too. Yankee officers are men (in a measure,) and men in whatever degree that they may exist will always run themselves to death to obtain "whatsoever they can't git.... "

War Journal of Lucy Virginia French.

3 Myra Adelaide Inman's unforgettable day, a young Cleveland woman's prayers for Confederate victory

A lovely day. Will I ever, can I ever, forget this day? Never, never. Our hearts all bowed down in grief. I am sitting at the parlor window. I hear the drums beating, the bands and fifes playing and ever and anon I let my eyes wander over the once beautiful country, I behold the foes marching and their guns and bayonets glistening in their onward march to desolate our country and rout our high spirited but downtrodden friends. I have (yes, we all have) mingled many a tear with our fervent prayers to God for our success. Fifteen thousand, they say, are to march from here. Whilst thousands are going from this vicinity, and thousands are to flank our poor boys; God have mercy on their souls. If it is Thy good pleasure, let us be caused to rejoice at Thy interposition in our behalf; let our enemy be totally routed, driven back, and their baggage captured from them. Let Lee in Virginia achieve a glorious victory over Grant. Let peace soon dawn on us and we be made to rejoice and praise god for giving us victories and causing us to establish our independence. Humble the hearts of all the people in the Southern States;

cause them to feel that Thy help alone we can gain the battle and establish our independence. Oh, our Father! Give us the victory if it is Thy will. I feel that it is our sins alone that will prevent us from being the victor. Watch over and guard and protect our friends in this coming struggle. Save the souls of those whose lot is to fall on the impending battle. Sherman is marching on Gen. Johnston with an army of one hundred and fifty thousand strong. Such an army has never been mustered in these United States. We wish and tremble at the result. A few weeks will decide it. Sgt. Douglass came and told us good-bye. Thousands of cavalry have passed this morn, going on, on to kill our beloved friends.... Uncle Caswell has no hope for our success.... We finished the ironing today.

Diary of Myra Adelaide Inman.

3 Harriet Beecher Stowe's play in Nashville Theatre.—"Uncle Tom's Cabin" is to be repeated at this house this evening. Last night the house was crowded from pit to dome to witness its rendition, and, judging from the plaudits of the audience assembled, we had no doubt it would continue to draw good houses for several nights to come, Little Ella Bailey, as "Eva," was rapturously received, and made the most of her character.

Nashville *Dispatch*, May 3 1864.

5 Determining race at the Refugee School in Nashville

Day before yesterday (5th) a girl came to school who had just the look and complexion of a snuff-dipping refugee. She, also, like them, wore a dress of the same color, derived from some kind of bark. Her manner was as listless and her expression as vacant. Wishing much to know whether she could claim our superior race as her own, or whether a few drops of the black blood in her veins had procures perhaps from her father and master the fiat-"only a niggar! " I made known my curiosity to one of the teachers, with my perplexity as to how I should obtain the coveted information, without wounding her feelings.'

"Oh! You need not fear for that," was the reply, "They're used to it, and expect to be asked whether they're niggars or not."

I could not do it, however, without considerable circumlocution; and commenced by asking if she could buy herself a book, whom she lived with, &c. After some time the questions eliminated the fact that though she didn't know whether she was free, or a "refugee," her own second name, or the age,—she *did* know that she had lived most of her life in Texas, where she had always worked out of doors, had hoed corn, and ploughed-that she lived with the same people now—that her father she had never heard anything of-that he mother was black, "though not really black," and finally that she herself was a "niggard,"—which nobody else could have told her by her features or complexion.

Powers, *Pencillings*, p. 73.

7 On Nathan Bedford Forrest's Family, Brothers and pre-war Business in Memphis

Antecedents of the Rebel General Forrest and his Family.

A Knoxville correspondent of the N.Y. *Tribune* writes:

The news of the capture of Fort Pillow by Forrest, and the cowardly butchery which followed of blacks and whites alike, has produced a profound sensation here. The universal sentiment is-"let no quarter be shown to those dastardly butchers of Forrest's command while the war lasts."

These Forrests, the eldest of whom, Gen. Bedford Forrest, has by this and other atrocities obtained such a record of infamy, were all negro traders. There were four brothers-Bedford, who kept a negro pen for five years before the war on Adams street, in rear of the Episcopal Church, Memphis; John, a cripple and a gambler, who was jailor and clerk for Bedford; Bill Forrest, an extensive negro trader at Vicksburg; and Aaron Forrest, general agent to scout the country for his other brothers. They accumulated large sums of money in their nefarious trade, and Bedford won by that and other influences a natural promotion to a Brigadier. He is about 50 years of age, tall, gaunt, and sallow visaged, with a long nose, deep set black, snaky eyes, [illegible] and hair wore long. He usually wore, while in the "nigger" trade in Memphis, a stove pipe hat set on the back of his head at an angle of forty-five degrees. He was accounted mean, vindictive, cruel and unscrupulous. He had two wives-one white, the other colored (Catharine), by each of which he two children. His "patriarchal" wife, Catharine, and his white wife, had frequent quarrels or domestic jars.

The slave pen of old Bedford Forrest, on Adams street, was a perfect horror to all negroes far and near. His mode of punishing refractory slaves was to compel four of his fellow slaves to stand and hold the victim stretched out in the air, and then Bedford and his brother John would stand, one on each side, with long, heavy whips, and cut up their victims until the blood trickled to the ground. Women were often stripped naked, and with a bucket of salt water standing by, in which to dip the instruments of torture, and with a heavy leather thong, their backs were cut up, until the blisters covered the whole surface, the blood of their wounds mingling with the briny mixture to add torment to the infliction. One slave man was whipped to death by Bedford, who used a trace-chain doubled for the purpose of punishment. The slave was secretly buried, and the circumstance was only known to the slaves of the prison, who only dared to refer to the circumstance in whispers.

Such are the appropriate antecedents in the character of the monster who murdered in cold blood the gallant defenders of Fort Pillow.

Boston Herald, May 7, 1864.*

9 A Bolivar school girl's epitome of three months of socializing with Confederate soldiers

Gracious me! Is it possible that I have not written in my Journal for nearly three months! And no wonder, for I have had such glorious times with Confederate soldiers that I forgot [it] and every thing else. The dear fellows were with us a good long while during which time I was never happier. Oh, what delightful times we did have, having company all day and accompanying the soldiers to parties at night. We made a great many acquaintances among them was William Polk, a dashing young flirt (all my suspicions are formed on reports and appearances). Seargt. Major Cleburn, Adjutant Pope, and Lieut. Colonel all of the 7th Tennessee, Capt. Elliot and many other of the 14th. [I] am acquainted with Generals Forrest and Chalmers also. Almost all the respective staffs like the Generals better than all the staffs put together.

Diary of Sally Wendel Fentress.

14 Burial of a Drummer Boy at Bean Station Touching Incident.

After the battle at Bean Station, East Tennessee, the rebels were guilty of all manner of indignity toward the slain. They stripped their bodies, and shot all persons who came near the battlefield to show any attention to the dead. The body of a little drummer boy was left naked and exposed. Near by, in a humble house, there were two little girls, the oldest but sixteen, who resolved to give the body a decent burial. They took the night for their task. With hammer and nails in hand, and boards on their shoulders, they sought the place where the body of the dead drummer boy lay. From their own scanty wardrobe, they clothed the body for the grave. With their own hands they made a rude coffin, into which they reverently put the dead boy.

They dug the grave, and lowered the body into it and covered it over. The noise of the hammering brought some of the rebels to the spot. The sight was too much for them. The stillness of the night — the story so eloquently told by the heroic labors of the little girls. Not a word was spoken, no one interfered, and when the sacred rites of burial were performed, all separated, and the little drummer-boy sleeps undisturbed in his grave on the battlefield. Such tenderness and heroism deserve to run along the line of coming generations with the story of the woman who broke the alabaster box on the feet of the Savior, and with her who of her penury cast her two mites into the treasury.— Louisville *Journal*.

Fort Smith *New Era*, May 14, 1864.

17 School Outing

School Picnic.— The annual pic-nic of Mr. R. Dorman's School took place yesterday [17th] at the residence of Mr. W. F. Bang, about two miles north from Edgefield, one of the most lovely spots in this county. The scholars accompanied by their teachers, left the schoolrooms about nine o'clock, and marched in procession to the opposite end of the bridge, where carriages, buggies and wagons, were awaiting them. Soon after reaching the ground, the boys and girls assembled around a platform, on which were seated the lovely girl who was selected as the Queen of May, her Maids of Honor, and others intended to participate in the exercises, which were exceedingly interesting and instructive, and consisted of singing, [and] ad-

*As cited in PQCW.

dresses.... Not the least interesting event of the day was the presentation of Master Oscar Hill, on behalf of the scholars, of two superbly bound Bibles, one to Mr. Dorman and the other to Miss Dunham. The address was delivered in the most admirable manner, and was full of sublime sentiment. We regret our inability to publish the address entire, with the reply of Mr. Dorman, but on our return to town we found all our space occupied. The rain put a sudden stop to the general fun, and interfered somewhat with the dinner, but all were brought safely home, but the constant kind care of the teachers. We regret to say that Charlie Walker met with a painful accident on the ground, but he will probably recover from it in a few days.

Nashville *Dispatch*, May 18, 1864.

20 The poetry of unrequited love
Love in the County Jail.

Mel. Zachary is becoming desperate-desperately in love; the longer he remains in limbo the more ardent his devotion to his "dearest Mary." Read how eloquently he pleases his cause:

Nashville, May 17, 1864

Dearest Mary:— Hoping that your eyes will light on these few lines now being traced by this trembling hand, and hoping that Providence will crown my feeble efforts with at least a kind consoling word of hope. Alas! thou, the idol of my heart, the adored of my only love, truly and tenderly do I love you and I hope I am not too unworthy of being loved in return. Although in bondage, I hope I will one day be at liberty; then, I trust, I will realize my only thoughts and wishes. Yes, I will then devote my life and all I have to your welfare, and hope that ours will be the union of souls which conjoin forever, and springing from a mutual perception of everlasting bliss, our walk through life will be strewn with choicest roses, uninterrupted by the thorns of misfortune. Oh! I long to be with you, to gaze upon those bright orbs of dazzling kindness; but alas! I must stop, and call cruel Fate, and the answer I find is as follows:

Like some lone bird without a mate,
My heart is weary and desolate;
I look around, and cannot trace,
One friendly smile, or welcome face,
And in crowds I am still alone,
Because I cannot love but one.

Hoping to hear a favorable response, I remain your devoted lover,
Melville Zachary.

Nashville *Dispatch*, May 20, 1864.

21 Vendetta on White's Creek Turnpike, Nashville

Saturday [21] morning two men dressed as soldiers and reported to belong to the twelfth Tennessee, met Wm. Pearson, who was driving a wagon, a few miles out from the city on the White's Creek Turnpike, and after a few words they drew their revolvers and commenced shooting at him. Pearson left his team and endeavored to escape. Five or six shots were fired, one of which is supposed by parties who witnessed the affair, to have hit him. When last heard of he was proceeding along the pike in the direction he had started when endeavoring to escape. His friends fear that he has wandered into the woods, and has died from the effects of his wound. Pearson was a young man, and formerly lived in Grundy county, in this State. The men who attacked him stated to some parties who witnessed the shooting, that the affair had its origin in a difficulty of several years standing. Any information in regard to Pearson left at this office will be delivered to his friends.

Nashville *Dispatch*, May 23, 1864.

24 Johnson the Canadian vs. Rochester Bardwell; bare-knuckle boxing in Nashville
Great Battle in Germantown.

Considerable maneuvering and chaffering has been going on in the neighborhood of the mule pens, between the friends of J. W. Johnson, the Canadian bruiser, on the one part, and those of Lewis P. Bardwell, of Rochester, New York, on the other, concerning the respective merits of their champions. To settle the dispute amicably, we are informed that a fight was agreed upon, to take place on Tuesday, the 24th inst., in the northern part of Germantown, when and where those in the secret assembled to witness the sport, of which a looker-on gives the following account:

ROUND 1. Johnson squared off for the first blow, but Bardwell dodged him, and put in a well-directed left hander.

2. Bardwell came up in fine style, and gave his opponent some heavy blows, but struck too high.

3. Johnson tapped Bardwell's claret, which flowed freely from his sneezing apparatus.

4. Bardwell got the advantage, and kept it to the finish, notwithstanding Johnson showed himself game, and made a good fight. In the tenth round the seconds separated them, they having clinched, and the eleventh was so severe that both parties were thoroughly blown. In the 12th and 13th rounds Johnson put in some heavy licks, but in the 14th Johnson showed evident signs of weakness, Bardwell keeping cool, and getting in a few smart blows, two or three of which Johnson returned.

In the fifteenth round Johnson came up to the scratch in good style, though very tired, and put in several well directed blows, one of which peeled Bardwell's nozzle; but it was plain that the fight was up, Bardwell being quite fresh still; and length B. got the opportunity, and throwing out a stunning blow from the shoulder, knocked Johnson out of time.

Chicago Jack seconded the Canadian, and Bridgeport Jerry did the honors for Bardwell.

Nashville *Dispatch*, May 26, 1864.

28 Literature for Youngsters
"Something for the Young Folks"
We have received from F. Katzenbach, 270 Main street, a little library for little people which is for sale at his store, consisting of *Poems, for Little Folks, Tales of the Great and Brave, Stories of Animals, Christmas Stories, Stories of Natural History, the Rabbit's Bride, Tales of Adventure, Stories of Foreign Lands, Casper's Adventures, Fairy Stories, Fables in Verse and History of Birds.* These books are of convenient size for little hands, beautifully printed, handsomely bound, and illustrated plentifully with engraving. We have dipped into one or two of them, especially the fairy stories, and for a while realized the poet's wish, "Would I were a boy again." The cruel princess, the heartless magician, the cross old grandmother, the kind fairy, the brave adventurer, the lucky little fellow that blundered into fortune, how they passed before us as we knew them long, long, before we became the possessor of gray hairs and the tiresome amounts of wisdom we get with them, as a matter of course. Wisdom here is wisdom in these little books that can make young eyes sparkle and young hearts thrill with an ecstasy our nature seldom fails to impart. Those who would make the young people happy with a gift should call at Katzenbach's store. They are published by Carobs & Nichols, Boston

Memphis *Bulletin*, May 28, 1864.

♦ JUNE ♦

3 Bawdy photographs
Lewd Pictures
The display of highly colored daubs and photographs of naked women, obscene groups, etc., in the windows and upon the stands of our stationers, booksellers, and news dealers has become most noticeably common and deserving of public attention and censure. We have long been accustomed to see such, upon a larger plan, hung about the walls of grogshops, club rooms, and places visited only by the male sex, but when they are to be introduced into the street windows and compiled into albums, it is certainly carrying the thing a bit too far — altogether too far. Such pandering to vitiated taste is at least unbecoming many of those who have been guilty of the practice, and in our opinion the city ordinance, prohibiting the publication or sale of obscene books, would apply as well to the sale of obscene pictures.

Memphis *Bulletin*, June 3, 1864.

6 African Americans celebrate the second anniversary of the fall of Memphis
Grand Colored Demonstration.
Yesterday, being the anniversary of the arrival of the Federal forces at this place, our colored population thought it proper to commemorate the event by a Pic-nic which came off at Odd Fellows' Hall. We supposed at one time, when looking out upon the streets, that there had been an eclipse of the sun, (or some other strange phenomenon,) which by some miscalculation of the astronomers had been set at a wrong date, but as the black mass neared the spot where we were standing, we discovered our error, as it turned to be a procession of the "culled persuasion."

Memphis *Bulletin*, June 7, 1864.

7 Protests concerning Provost Marshall's shooting dogs
How Much Lower?
We have had to chronicle many a case of downright dishonesty and theft, but never in the course of our journalistic career have we put before the public the quintessence of meanness which we

are called upon not to expose. According to late military orders, owners of dogs were compelled to put muzzles upon their canine pets, and all dogs found running the streets without the same would be shot by the Provost Guard, whose duty it was to execute the order. The order in many cases has been complied with and so now we hear complaints almost every hour in the day made by parties who have had the muzzles stolen off their dogs. The wretch [who would] remove the safeguard of poor old [Fido?] after having been placed there by his master, should himself be muzzled, and allowed to walk the streets in no other way.

Memphis Bulletin, June 7, 1864.

7 Nimrod Porter's dream

I dreamed a dream last night & another the night before, I think unfavorable to the South. Something verry [strange] a going on, I saw father and mother, Grandmother & 2 little boys in my sleep last night. [T]hey [were] in my room very cordially I was glad to see them. (What is the interpretation)

Diary of Nimrod Porter, June 7, 1864.

11 General Paine's anti-guerrilla campaign in Lincoln county; an excerpt from the letter of Captain Henry Newton Comey, 2nd Massachusetts Infantry

Tullahoma, Tenn.

June 11, 1864

Dear Sister,

Yours of the 6th containing ten dollars was received last Wednesday. It was delayed on the way somewhat, however it was thankfully received....

There's not much of interest transpiring at present. General Paine returned this week from his foray into Lincoln County, having killed nineteen guerrillas and bushwhackers and among them two leaders. General Paine burned several still houses (houses where whiskey is made) and several other houses, all told the people of Lincoln County that if the bushwhackers and guerrillas who were robbing and molesting the rail road were not stopped within fifteen days he would burn the whole country. His measures are having quite a salutary effect on the citizens of Lincoln and the adjoining counties. They have recently held a meeting in which all guerrillas are denounced and it was decided that guerrillas henceforth should not be allowed in the counties. The guerrilla leaders retaliated with a message in which they threatened General Paine. They said if General Paine should kill certain men in the county that they kill and burn all the union men.

...

Henry

Comey Correspondence, pp. 171–172.

13 Retaliation, the Federal army's strategy for suppressing guerrillas in Lincoln County; an excerpt from the letter of Captain Henry Newton Comey, 2nd Massachusetts Infantry

2nd Mass. Inf. 1st Div. 20th Corps. Army Tullahoma, Tenn., June 13, 1864

Dear Father,

Yours of the second inst. contained ten dollars came to hand last night....

...

...Maj. Gen Milroy's Headquarters is here now. General Paine is also here yet. General Paine is a terror to guerrillas because he is shooting every little while. He sentenced a man to be shot for keeping a still house and I suppose it was because this man has been guilty of harboring guerrillas for wherever there is whiskey there will be guerrillas. Their courage is mostly whiskey courage. I happened to be at the Generals headquarters and heard that man beg for his life. Some of the guerrillas die game, will not beg at all. They bushwhack for plunder, not that they care anything for the Southern Confederacy. Last Thursday a scouting party went to Hillsboro and shot C. C. Brewer, formerly Clerk of this county. A man formerly of good standing, he was a captain in the rebel army, but left the army and went to bushwhacking. The way of the transgressor is hard. Heretofore the bushwhackers of this vicinity thought that the U.S. Government would not dare to would not dare to execute any of them for fear they would retaliate, but they now see that all such ideas are flawed. It is surprising to see the effect of General Paine's course upon some of the rebels in this vicinity. All at once they are getting to be very strong Union loyalists, to all appearances. When the General wants to get information he sends out into the country to some old farmer who he knows has such information and orders him to report at such an hour. It is needless to add that his order is obeyed and the man, whoever he may be, is very careful not to be behind time. Stokes

Regiment of Tennessee Cavalry is here now and it is said that his men had rather kill than eat.

...

H. N. Comey
> Comey Correspondence, pp. 172–173.

13 Skirmish at Collierville
No circumstantial reports filed.
WHITE'S STATION, June 13, 1864.

Information is just received that some 2,000 of our men have reached the vicinity of Collierville, fighting their way. The effective force of my cavalry is getting ready to hurry to their assistance, and if you will authorize it, I will load a train now here with infantry and send it in conjunction with the cavalry.

S. D. STURGIS, Brig.-Gen.
> OR, Ser. I, Vol. 39, pt. I, p. 89.

14 Bringing in the Sheaves; Tennessee Presbyterians Return to the Fold

TENNESSEE PRESBYTERIANS RETURNING TO LOYALTY.— The Nashville correspondent of the New York *Times* says that the Unionism of Tennessee is beginning to pronounce itself ecclesiastically. An initiatory movement has taken place on the part of one religious body at least, toward a resumption of former time-honored associations. The Presbytery of Nashville, in August, 1861, in an evil hour and hot haste, broke asunder the bonds which till then had bound its churches to the Old School General Assembly. They piously resolved to join the General Assembly of the Confederate States, provided such body should have not only a "name," but a "local habitation." The stress and constant crisis of Southern affairs have made such General Assembly as yet little better than "airy nothing;" nor has the most piercing eye, in the finest "frenzy rolling," been able to body it forth in any substantial form and proportions. No meeting of the Presbytery has been held since Donelson fell.

The churches of the body were drooping, woe-begone, without coherence, without vitality, formless and void. It was found that its only hope of resuscitation was to undo the evil it had done, and renew fealty to man and to God, by renewing its former connection. A meeting of Presbytery was called accordingly, in proper form. The churches, some twelve or fifteen, were notified, with scrupulous care. The majority refused to appear by their representatives, but a constitutional quorum was present. The meeting was duly organized according to Presbyterial forms; and the former action, swinging the Presbytery off into the deadly embrace of rebeldom, was solemnly and decisively rescinded. The Presbytery now stands where it always stood, until the poisonous breath of secession blowing upon it, withered its beauty and sapped its vital strength. It will be sure to revive now. Returning loyalty and good faith is a potent remedy for a "mind diseased" as well as a body; the cause of the malady in either case being-rebellion.

> *New Haven Daily Palladium*, June 14, 1864.

15 Entry from Alice Williamson's Diary, Sumner County

In all the doings of the Yanks their fiendish acts today will balance them all. They brought a man in today and hung him up by the thumbs to make him tell where he came from: he told them but they would not believe him. He fainted three times. They took him down at three o'clock to shoot him I have not heard whether they did so or not. They would neither give him food nor water though he begged for the latter often. This was done by order of "the Nicklen."

> *Williamson Diary*

16 Nashville émigré assistance union
Nashville Refugee Aid Society.

This Society met yesterday, according to adjournment, Vice President Root in the Chair. Mr. Carey, chairman of the Committee on Constitution, reported one, which, after a few amendments were made thereto, was adopted. As the Constitution provides for an Executive Committee of nine, Madames Scovel and Maginess were added to that committee to make up the number. Rev. Mr. Ingraham, chairman of the committee appointed to draw up a report of the business of the Society from its formation, made a partial report, which will be complete by the next meeting. The Society then adjourned to Wednesday next, at P.M.

> Nashville *Dispatch*, June 16, 1864.

18 Bigamy in Nashville
"A Case of Bigamy."

A case of bigamy was yesterday laid before W. D. Robertson, Esq., the defendants being Isaac M. McIver and Margaret Flasher, who were married by the Rev. Dr. Good lit on the 13th of the present month, and arrested under a charge of bigamy on the 16th. The prosecutor is John Flasher. James L. Smith, Esq., appeared for the prosecution, and T. T. Smiley and Robot. Cantrell, Esq., for the defense. Both Flasher and McCarver belong to company G, first Tennessee Light Artillery.

McCarver is a young man, perhaps twenty-five years old, with an open, honest countenance, and prepossessing appearance, tall in stature, and genteel in dress and demeanor. Margaret Flasher is short and stout, much older than her new husband, and without any personal attractions; she appeared in court dressed in white, with red and blue trimmings on her white undersleeves; a surplice waist, with black ribbon trimming, a gaudy breastpin securing the ends of the ribbon in front. In her hand she held a paper fan, with the letters of the alphabet printed upon the upper end, one letter in each fold. On her lap rested a large silk handkerchief, in color purple, yellow and white, and the picture is completed by the reader fancying her reclining upon the lap and shoulder of her young husband, the pair talking sweet love to each other. After waiting one hour, the trial began, both parties agreeing to try both cases together, McCarver for violating section 4832 of the Code, and Margaret Flasher for a violation of 4839 of the Code.

John J. Rush was the first witness. He testified that he was acquainted with Mrs. Flasher; he also knew John Flasher, knew them in Memphis; has known them about three years or more; they have been living together as man and wife. (Objected to by counsel for the defense and allowed.) Witness had heard Mrs. Flasher declare that she was marries to John Flasher. (Objected to by defence, and allowed.) Was acquainted with Margaret before she was married; they were married the fall before the war commenced, and came here to Nashville together, as man and wife; they always lived quietly and peaceably together; they lived together in camp and she did his cooking while in camp, until an order was issued rejecting females from camps when John Flasher procured a house for his wife and she went to live in it, her husband going to see her frequently. Cross examined by Mr. Cantrel-They were married at Grant's brickyard near Memphis, in the neighborhood of three years ago; witness had lived in the house with them, both at Memphis and in this city; was not present at the marriage, but is well acquainted with the man who married them; cannot swear they were married, not having witnessed the ceremony; can hardly swear to what he sees at times.

Mr. Smith here introduced the license and the certificate of marriage, and called the attention of the Court to the fact that the defendant Margaret was therein described as Margaret Flasher, her husband's name John Weatherspoon — Was present at the marriage of the two defendants by the Rev. Dr. Goodlett; she answered to the name of Margaret Flasher; knows Dr. Goodlett too be a minister of the Gospel.

Another witness testified to the same effect.

The first witness was re-called, and testified that Margaret was generally known in camp as John Flasher's wife.

Mr. Hines belongs to the same company; Mrs. Flasher was generally understood to be the wife of Mr. Flasher. McCarver enlisted early in February.

Mr. Williams belongs to the same company, knows the defendant; he belongs to the same company also. Mrs. Flasher passed as the wife of Flasher.

Mr. Davis testified to the same facts; never knew they were not married.

The evidence from the prosecution here closed, Mr. Smith stating his case clearly and briefly. Mr. Cantrel followed, arguing that no other marriage had been proven than that between the two defendants, and that therefore they ought to be acquitted. Mr. Temple followed, on the same ride, taking the same ground, and Mr. Smith closed the argument, all displaying much ingenuity and industry. The Court adjudged the defendants guilty, and required them to give bond of $1000 each for the appearance at the Criminal Court in default, to be committed to jail.

Nashville *Dispatch*, June 18, 1864.

19 Military conditions in and around Tullahoma, excerpt from a letter from Major-General Robert Huston Milroy to his wife in Rensselaer, Indiana

Tullahoma Tenn
June 19th 1864
My Dear Mary,
...I arrived here on the 7th inst.... This town is but a little larger than Rensselaer. It has been a town of 3000 inhabitants before the war, but it was the headquarters of the rebel army for some time after the battle of Murfreesboro and was the head qrs of our army a while and has been occu-

pied by troops so much that ... it is badly used up. A large portion of it has been burnt at different times and is a very cheerless place. The timber has been cleared away for a mile around the town and the country is tolerably level.... My command is scattered all along the R.R. 150 miles between Nashville and Chatenooga and is stationary.... I like General Paine who commands the Brigade whose head quarters is at this place, very much.... He has had about 200 guerrillas shot since he has been stationed here. It is not often that his men bring any in that they capture, when they do and Paine ascertains them to be gurillas beyond a doubt he orders them quietly walked outside of the pickets and shot, and no report is made of the matter and nothing is said about it. Two of them have been shot that way since I come here. I would not have known anything of it had I not happened on their dead bodies in riding out. This course has struck terror into the people of sucesh proclivities and they have all become intensely loyal. The Union Citizens are greatly pleased with Paines course and say he is the only man among the Union Generals who has done things right. No treatment of the Rebs is too severe and bloody for the Union citizens who have suffered so much.... A brigade of Tennessee Cavalry have been here temporarily for ten days for scouting purposes. They have been going most of the time and have killed about fifty gurillas. They are a wild, half civilized set of devils, but few of them can read or write. Most of the officers and nearly all the men get drunk-they have no discipline and do about as they please. They fight pretty well, but rob, plunder and steal like a band of robbers, drunken parties of them fired on my pickets last night half a dozen times, and the pickets returned fire but no one was hurt. They are camped around outside of the pickets and waited in town after dark to get some whiskey and could not get in. Beard is my officer of out posts was up with the pickets till two o'clock trying to get some of the wild devils killed and come very near getting shot himself. They have been ordered away from here and I have no control of them. I am glad they are to leave in the morning.... I am horribly sick of this dull monotinous life and would much rather be at home.... Write to your Husband Truly

R. H. Milroy.

Papers of General Robert Huston Milroy, pp. 358–360.

21 Bushwhackers vs. Brigadier General E. L. Paine in Middle Tennessee

Brig.-Gen. E. L. Paine is settling the bushwhackers who have been unsettling Middle Tennessee so long, had having killed about 75 last week. He had nine shot on the public square in Lynchburg, Lincoln county, and several in Fayetteville. Among the number that had been killed was one Massey, who is said is a Brigadier-General C. S. A. He superintended all the guerrilla operations in Middle Tennessee. General Paine told the citizens if they wanted to fight the Government to go and join the rebel army under Joe Johnston. He further told them if they staid inside the Federal lines they might think secesh, feel secesh, die hating the government, and go to h__l hating it, but they should neither talk treason nor act it. If they did, he told them he would make them houseless, homeless and lifeless, as he had determined to kill every bushwhacker that he caught. The 5th, 10th and 12th Tennessee cavalry were with Gen. Paine, and did the hands-on for the bushwhacking rebs. The 5th still remember the "calf killer" massacre, and are avenging it terribly.

Chattanooga Daily Gazette, June 21, 1864.

24 "The Negroes About Town."

The city is again filled with vagabond negroes —Thieves, prostitutes, and loafers. The civil authorities find it impossible to keep them within the bounds of common decency. What has become of the negro camp? Many negroes might be hired out, were it not that the rules are rather too stringent. It seems to us unreasonable to expect a man to give bonds to keep a negro a year, and pay good wages for that length of time, when he cannot tell whether the servant is worth what she eats; or whether she would remain with him a year, or whether she would do anything, if she did remain, but eat and sleep.

Nashville *Dispatch*, June 24, 1864.

25 A boar attack

Root Hog or Die.

On Line street, in the vicinity of College street, there perambulates a large and hungry-looking specimen of the genus porcine, feminine gender. In the same locality lives a feminine negro, the maternal ancestor of sundry little nigs, who amuse themselves by playing on the street. Yesterday the party of the first party took a fancy to the rear part of the smallest specimen of the party of the second part. The little nig was pushed down-the hog seized him and ran, mother, children and friends running, following in the chase. Away they go, the hog holding on to the little nigger, and the excitement running high, until at length a white man seized an axe with which he gave the hog a terrible blow upon the head. A grunt of pain followed, and the little nig fell, his anxious mother picking him up, and washing his dirty face with tears of joy at his deliverance from the jaws of the enemy.

Nashville *Dispatch*, June 25, 1864,

25 Hiring workers in Bedford county, an outcome of the transition from slave to free labor

Shelbyville Tenn. June 25th 1864

Gov Andrew Johnson

I write to you this morning to ask some information & to obtain some action on your part if you are authorised to act in the premises. There is now in and around this place, a Number of Negroes that have left their former masters, many of whom are without work, and the services of all are required, in the growing crops & the harvest that is not matured—

The trouble is that there is no one here authorized to act in such cases, and persons fear to hire the Negroes as many of them belong to persons in this vicinity & trouble might grow out of it, under existing laws. It would be better for the Community for the Negroes to have work for them they can get provisions honestly & if they cannot git work they must eat & will eat.

There is a gentlem[an] here by the name of (Horner A F) who rented off and he has done all he could do to avoid difficulties about Negroes, & he finds from whom he could hire Negroes he would pay them from 20 to 26 dollars per month & the same difficulty arises with them[.]

If you have the authority if you will appoint someone here to take charge of the contrabands and hire them out, or if you will authorize A F Horner to hire the hands he wants I will pledge my word for it, that he will not interfere with any negro that is at home, nor will he try to get one to quit his home as there is plenty here that have been here for 5 to 10 months to do all my house & will not do anything that is not strictly honest[.] he is from Ohio and an acquaintance of my wife & has been here for about 12 months & intends to make this his home & is one of the most active energetic & business men of my acquaintance, & I feel a strong desire to keep such men with us[.]

You will please examine the orders & grant the request if you have the power [.]

Very Respectfully Thos. H. Coldwell

Papers of Andrew Johnson, Vol. 6, pp. 755-756.

29 Excerpt from a Bolivar school girl's diary relative to a skirmish in Bolivar

During this long delay we have seen trouble and joys rise and fall successively. General Forrest's entrance into our little village flushed [us] with victory. His retreat causing sadness to fall upon every body's spirit. He was in the yard during the whole skirmish. Bullets were whizzing above and below us, burying themselves in and burrowing the ground. One shattered a paling near where Ma was standing. Houses, twenty three in number were burnt the stores were sacked, the merchants' chests were blown and hammered to pieces. The Confederates went South, and lately have had a large battle. It was a victory, but oh so dearly bought. Of Company E Captain Tate, Charly, Neely and Billie Hardy killed. Dashiell Perkins wounded. Adjutant Poe was killed. These were all that I knew. Charly Neely's death was indeed a sad one. Idolized by his family, he was a gallant soldier, noble boy and a constant Christian.

Diary of Sally Wendel Fentress, June 29, 1864.

• JULY •

2 Suspension of civil government in Memphis, SPECIAL ORDERS, NO. 70

Headquarters District of West Tennessee

Memphis, Tenn., July 2 1864

I.-The utter failure of the Municipal Government of Memphis for the past two years to discharge its proper functions, the disloyal character of that Government, it's want of sympathy for the Government of the United States, and its indisposition to co-operate with the Military authorities, have long been felt as evils which the public welfare require to be abated. They have grown from bad to worse, until a further toleration of them will not comport with the sense of duty of the Commanding General. The city of Memphis is under Martial Law, and the Municipal Government existing since the armed traitors were driven from the city has been only by sufferance of the Military authorities of the United States.

Therefore, under the authority of General Orders No. 100, dated War Department, Adjutant General's Office, April 24th, 1863,

It is ordered that the functions of the Municipal Government of Memphis be and they are hereby suspended until further orders. The present incumbents are forbidden to perform any official acts, or exercise any authority whatever, and persons supposed to be elected officers of the city, an election held on June 30th, 1864, will not qualify. That the interests and business of the city may not be interrupted, the following appointments of City Officers are made:

[list of names follows]

Who will be fully respected in the exercise of the duties assigned them and all records, papers, monies, and property in any manner pertaining to the offices, government and interests of the city of Memphis, will be immediately turned over by the present holders thereof to the officers above appointed to succeed them. Said officers will be duly sworn to the faithful discharge of their duties, and will be required to give bonds to the U.S. in the sums at present prescribed by law and the City Ordinances for such officers respectively.

The Officers herein named and appointed will constitute a board, which shall discharge the duties heretofore devolving upon the Board of Aldermen; and the acting Mayor shall be Chairman thereof and their acts, resolution and ordinances shall be valid, and of full force and effect, until revoked by the Commanding General of the District of West Tennessee, or superior military authority.

By order of Major Gen'l C. C. Washburn

Memphis *Bulletin*, July 2, 1864.

2 Smuggling in Memphis; tricks of the trade

A dead mule belonging to a Memphis citizen was being hauled out of the lines the other day, when a bayonet thrust revealed the fact that the carcass contained 60,000 percussion caps, a quantity of ammunition, and other contraband articles, which some Rebel sympathizer had taken this means of smuggling.

Nashville *Dispatch*, July 2, 1864.

2 One-half price Yankee-ice
Northern Ice.

Riddleburger & Co. have been selling pure northern ice at little more than one half the price demanded by others. This caused an unusual demand upon his stock, which has run out, but will soon be replenished, the military authorities having, in the most generous manner, promised to aid in furnishing transportation for all he may be able to purchase, in order that the public may receive a bountiful supply of this necessary article. We hope our portly friend will be able to carry out his views.

Nashville *Dispatch*, July 2, 1864.

3 Removing Street Filth in Memphis
"Cleaning the Streets, etc."
Mayor's Office
Memphis, July 3, 1864

Pursuant to orders from the Mayor General Commanding District of West Tennessee, the owners or lessees of all houses, sheds, enclosures or vacant lots in the city of Memphis, are hereby notified to immediately remove all grass, weeds, and rubbish from the sidewalks and gutters fronting their premises, and to fill all holes in their lots or ground in which water may collect.

Flatboats must be kept free from stagnant water, or removed without the city.

On Monday, July 18, 1864, and on each succeeding Monday, the loose dirt in front of each home or lot shall be cleaned by the owner or lessee thereof to the middle of the street, and piles made of the dirt near the edge of the gutters, when it will be the carted away at the expense of the city.

The police force, the street commissioner and wharf master are charged with this enforcement of this regulation, and they will arrest and carry before the recorder of the city all delinquents for such fine or other proceedings as the offense may deem it.

T.H. Harrison, Lieut. Col. and Acting Mayor

Memphis *Bulletin*, July 10, 1864.

3 Report of Murder and a Lover's Revenge in Overton county

From the Nashville *Times*.

Extraordinary and Thrilling Narrative.

Romance of the War in Tennessee — A Young Woman Shoots a Guerrilla to Avenge the Murder of her Lover.

The following simple and unvarnished story has hardly a parallel in the pages of fiction.-Its strict truth is beyond question:

Near Murfreesboro, June 28, 1864.

To the Editor of the *Times*:

The original of the following letter is in my possession. The events so graphically narrated transpired in Overton county, Tenn. I knew Dr. Sadler from a small boy. The man who killed him for no personal grudge, but on account of his sentiments. I have no personal acquaintance with the young lady, but have the highest authority for stating that she is a pure, high minded girl, the daughter of a plain farmer in moderate circumstances. It only remains to state that Peteet was killed January the 30th [1864] and Gordenhire February 4, 1864, so that the vengeance they invoked has overtaken all three of the murder of M. G. Sadler.

John W. Bowen.

Martin's Creek, April 30, 1864.

Major Cliff: According to promise I now attempt to give you a statement of the reasons why I killed Turner, and a brief history of the affair. Dr. Sadler had, for two years previous to his death, seemed equally as near and as dear to me as a brother, and for several months nearer than any person-my parents not excepted. If he had not, I never would have done what I did-promise to be his.

The men who killed him had threatened his life often because he was Union man; they said he should not live, and after taking the oath they arrested him, but Lieut. Oakley released him at Pa's Gate. He stayed at Pa's till bed time, and I warned him of the danger he was in, told him I had heard his life threatened that day, and that I felt confident he would be killed if he did not leave the neighborhood and stay off until these men became reconciled. He promised to go; said he had some business in Carthage and would leave. He promised us he would leave the neighborhood that night, or by daylight next morning, and we felt assured he had gone. But for some unaccountable reason he did not leave. About 4 o'clock P.M. next day news came to me at Mr. Johnson's, where I had gone with my brother, that Dr. Sadler was killed. I had met Poteet, Gordenhire and Turner on the road and told my brother there that they were searching for Dr. Sadler to kill him. Sure enough they went to the house where he was and strange to me, after his warning, he permitted them to come in. They met him, apparently perfectly friendly, and said they had come to get some brandy from Mr. Yelton, which they obtained, and immediately after drinking all three drew their pistols and commenced firing at Sadler. He drew his, but it was snatched away from him; he then drew his knife, which was also taken from him.

He then ran round the house and up a stair-way, escaping out of their sight. They followed, however, and searched till they found him, and brought him down and laid him on a bed, mortally wounded. He requested some of his people to send for Dr. Dillin to dress his wounds. It is strange to me why, but Sadler's friends had all left the room, when Turner went up and put his pistol against his temple, and shot him through the head. They all rejoiced like demons, and stood by till he made his last struggle. They then pulled his eyes open and asked in a loud voice, if he were dead. They then took his horse and saddle, and pistols, and robbed him of all his money, and otherwise insulted and abused his remains.

Now, for this, I resolved to have revenge. Peteet and Gordenhire being dead, I determined to kill Turner, and to seek an early opportunity of doing it. But I kept my resolution to myself, knowing that I would be prevented. I went prepared, but never could get to see him.

On the Thursday before I killed him, I learned he was preparing to leave for Louisiana, and I determined he should not escape if I could prevent it. I arose that morning, and fixed my pistols so that they would be sure fire, and determined to hunt all that day. Then sitting down I wrote a few lines so that if I fell, my friends might know where to look for my remains. I took my knitting, as if I were going to spend the day with a neighbor living on the road towards Turner's. It rained very severely, making the roads muddy, so that I became fatigued and concluded to go back and ride the next day, or Saturday. But Ma rode my horse on Saturday, and left me to keep house. We had company Sunday, A.M., so that I could not leave, but the company left about noon, and I started again in search of Turner. I went to his house about two and a half miles from Pa's. I found no one at home, and therefore sat down to await his return. After waiting perhaps, one-and-a-half-hours, a man came to see Turner, and not finding him, he said he supposed he and his wife had gone to Mrs. Christian's, his sister-in-law, who lived about one-half mile distant.

I concluded to go there and see, fearing the man would tell him I was waiting and he would escape me. I found him there, and a number of other persons, including his wife, and father and mother. Most of them left when I entered the house I asked Mrs. Christian if Turner were gone.

She pointed to him at the gate, just leaving. I looked at the clock and it was 4½ o'clock P.M. I then walked out into the yard, and as Turner was starting called to him to stop. He turned I fired at the distance of about 12 paces, and missed. I fired again as quick as possible, and hit him in the back of the head, and he fell on his face and knees I fired again and hit him in the back, and he fell upon his right side. I fired twice before, only one of these shots taking effect. By this time I was in five steps of him, and stood and watched him till he was dead. I then turned round and walked toward the house and met Mrs. Christian and her sister coming out. They asked me what I did that for. My response was, "You know what that man did the 13th of December last — murdered a dear friend of mine. I have been determined to do this deed ever since, and I shall never regret it." They said no more to me, but commenced blowing a horn. I got my horse out and started home, where I shall stay or leave when I choose, going where I please and saying what I please.

Chattanooga Daily Gazette, July 3, 1864.

4 The 4th of July in Columbia

The cannon was heard in Town of Columbia celebrating the day ... a great many negro men[,] women & children with there flags & flag poles[.] [A] dinner was prepared for many at White's Spring but the black ladies was marched to the Table[.] [T]he soldiers pitched in & devoured it & so the blacks was quite unlucky (they got none). In the evening the soldier was sent all over Town& pressed & captured all the able bodied negro men that could be gathered, several hundred, to gone somewhere to work....

Nimrod Porter Diary, July 4, 1864.

7 Railroad Guards

An Act of Retaliation.

It will be seen by an order from Gen. Washburn, elsewhere in our columns, that in view of the recent attacks upon railroad trains running between this city and Saulsbury, by Confederate soldiers and guerrillas, he has been forced to the necessity of taking stringent measures for the suppression of such acts in the future. The order provides for the arrest of forty of the most prominent and bitter "secesh," residents in and between Memphis and LaGrange, who are to be placed in squads of twenty in the most conspicuous positions on the train running to and from this city each day, so that those giving aid and comfort to rebels may, in case of further attacks, be made to suffer as well as innocent citizens and Federal soldiers. This course will be persisted in until such attacks on the part of the enemy are stopped with the assurance that they will not be resumed. The order states that several citizens of Memphis who have publicly applauded thus murderous business, will be awarded the most prominent and dangerous positions on the cars, and that quarters will be provided for them at White's Station, where they will receive proper care and treatment. No fair minded person will for a moment dispute the justice of this order, which is only calculated to put a stop to a barbarous system of warfare on the defenders of the Union by lawless, unorganized parties of guerrillas infesting the line of railroad from this city; it is a proper retaliation, and will no doubt net prolific of good results to all concerned. It is high time that such steps were adopted. The execution of this order is entrusted to Brig. Gen. Hatch, commanding the cavalry division.

Memphis *Bulletin,* July 7, 1864.

8 Methodology for Identifying a Soldier's Corpse

Dr. Josiah Curtis, well remembered as an intelligent physician and former resident of our city, is exercising the office of medical director at Knoxville, Tennessee, department of Ohio. In a copy of Parson Brownlow's paper, the doctor has sent a printed copy of a circular well calculated to aid in the identification of bodies of soldiers after death. It seems to us it would be a good regulation for general adoption in the army. It is as follows:

Upon the death of a soldier in this military department — whether in hospital or in the field — the chaplain, wherever one if on duty, and in all other cases the surgeon, is instructed, whenever practicable, to cause the name, rank, company, regiment, date and cause of death, last place of residence, and any other items deemed of importance relating to the deceased, to be legibly written upon white paper, with ink, and to place this record in a bottle, to be well corked, and deposited in the coffin, at the foot of the body, before burial.

Lowell Daily Citizen and News,
(Lowell, MA,) July 8, 1864.

8 Murderers hanged
Execution

Robert T. Gossett and Oliver [Obed] C. Crossland were executed on Friday [8th] under sentence for killing Depew and others in October last.

Nashville *Dispatch*, July 10, 1864.

9 Public health and private pets
Concerning Dogs.

In another column is an order from Lieut. Col. Harris relative to dogs. The owners of canines are required to have them muzzled immediately, in default of which they will be subject, on conviction before the Recorder, to a fine of not less than five nor more than fifty dollars for the first offense, and five dollars for each hour thereafter that the order may be violated.

The police are required to have all dogs running at large within the city, and not carefully muzzled, killed and removed at the expense of the city.

In view of the fact that a number of mad dogs have been running about of late, this is an important order, and should be strictly observed.

Memphis *Bulletin*, July 9, 1864.

9 Increase in locomotive sentries
More Conscripts for the Train Guard.

...

A force of some fifteen or twenty of those arrested were sent out on the train this morning, according to the order. It is thought that this course will insure the trains running between this city and LaGrange from all danger of attacks from guerrillas in [the] future. We shall see.

Memphis *Bulletin*, July 9, 1864.

9 Fresh Vegetables from the Sanitary Commission
FRESH PROVISIONS FOR THE ARMY

The Sanitary Committee on Wednesday sent to the army one thousand one hundred and fifty barrels of fresh vegetables and eight thousand heads of cabbage.

A dreadful accident — but happily unattended with direct loss of life — occurred on the Nashville and Chattanooga Railroad on the 30th ultima. Three trains left Chattanooga at nearly the same time, the first being a long one, a number of the cars containing wounded soldiers who were being conveyed, to Nashville. While descending a very steep grade near Cowan, Tennessee, the engineer lost control over the second train, which dashed madly into the first one, burling the locomotives and cars of both trains down the mountain. Nearly all the passengers, among whom were three ladies, were wounded, but, strange to say, not one person was killed outright.

Daily National Intelligencer, (Washington, DC) July 9, 1864.

10 Domestic thievery in Nashville
"Hall-Thieves."

Citizens should keep their hall-doors locked, as hall-thieves are being heard from in every portion of the city. They assume the character of beggars, going from house to house, and stealing what ever they can lay their hands on without discovery. Night seems to be the favorite time for plying their nefarious trade, and hat racks are made the objects of special attention. It is said that there is an organized band of these characters, of both sexes and colors, with a head or chief, who, Fagin-like, receives and disposes of their booty. If so, the police shall devote a little attention to the matter and, endeavor to break it up at once, by bringing the offenders to justice.

Nashville *Dispatch*, July 10, 1864.

ca. July 10 Champ Ferguson captures 500 U.S. Army horses near Kingston

No circumstantial reports filed.

Report of Capt. Robert Morrow, Assistant Adjutant-Gen., U.S. Army.

HDQRS. DEPARTMENT OF THE OHIO, Knoxville, Tenn., July 15, 1864.

GEN.:

...

The commanding officer at Kingston, Tenn., reports that guerrillas, under Champ Ferguson, drove off a few days since 500 U.S. horses that Capt. Fry was pasturing within a few miles of that place, and that the mounted force available was inadequate to their pursuit and recapture. Gen. Ammen reports that orders have been given and that efforts will be made to recover the stock and punish the raiders....

I have the honor to be, very respectfully,

R. MORROW, Capt. and Assistant Adjutant-Gen.

OR, Ser. I, Vol. 39, pt. I, p. 234.

11 A Cuckold's Revenge in Nashville
Recorder's Court.

...

Calvin Brown had a wife.— He had a wife, some four months ago, until Eli Pickett, by his superior attractions, secured her affections, and lured her from Cal. to himself, about a month ago. Three weeks ago last Saturday night [June 18], while Eli was slumbering in the arms of the faithless Dinah, somebody stole two female dresses and Eli's pants, containing a key and ninety cents. As the thief passed around the porch by Eli's window, the latter thought he saw Cal.'s physiognomy at his window; fearing to die at that moment, Eli allowed the thief to depart in peace, and the next morning he called in the aid of the Civic and military police to have Cal. arrested, for stealing his breeches and threatening his life. Both failed to nab Cal, who was not seen again until last Saturday [9th], when Eli met him on Cedar street, and pistol in hand, demanded that Cal. should accompany him to the office of Provost Marshal. Cal. proved an alibi in the larceny case, and a good character and quiet demeanor in that charging him with disorderly conduct; he was there for discharged, while Eli had to pay a fine of $5.

Nashville *Dispatch*, July 12, 1864.

13 Hideous rape of Mrs. Annie Mason
A Brutal Outrage.

A Mrs. Annie Mason, residing in the vicinity of Court Square, while passing through a by street in the southeastern part of the city, early last evening on her way to make arrangements for the renting of a residence in that quarter, was met and confronted by two men each with a canteen of whisky, who invited her to drink, and on her refusing, and attempting to pass, seized and forcibly carried her into a grove, some distance off, robbed her of all the money she had, tore her clothing almost entirely from her person, bound her to a tree in an upright position, and then commenced the hellish work of violating her person, repeating it a number of times, and quelling her cries by blows and curses. Between each act of violation the person of the unfortunate woman, those fiends in human form sat nearby, drinking and cursing in the most heartless and indifferent manner. Towards midnight they departed leaving their victim, still tied to the tree, and insensible. She remained in this condition all night, and early this morning was discovered nearly dead, by a woman passing near the scene of the outrage, who gave notice to the military authorities by whom she was removed to one of the hospitals, and tenderly cared for. On regaining her consciousness, she made a deposition, which led to the arrest of one Hugh Burns, who she immediately identified as one of the parties. He denied any complicity in the affair, but was sent to the Irving Block to await the result of further investigate. The other ruffian is still at large, but as careful description of him is in the possession of the authorities, and he will in all probability, be speedily arrested. Mrs. Mason, at the hour of this writing, was in a helpless condition from the injuries sustained. And her death was momentarily expected she is about 30 years of age, a widow, and has one child, a girl aged about eight years. She has always born an exemplary character. It is hoped that the ruffians who so inhumanly abused her, will meet with the severest punishment that can be meted out to them.

Memphis *Bulletin*, July 13, 1864.

16 A Denizen of the Deep in Nashville
Mammoth Sea Turtle

Major Gunklen, the enterprising proprietor of the St. Nicholas, introduced into his establishment, on Saturday last [16th], a large green sea turtle, weighing three hundred and twenty-five pounds. The "animal" was alive and kicking and during the day received numerous visitors. We heard a stranger remark as he was surveying the monster that he "didn't think a craft of that size would ever get over the shoals at the present state of water." We couldn't see it, ourselves, as we discovered that the sea-fowl, while promenading across the floor, was drawing *four* feet *large!*— in fact, feet of elephantine proportions. Turtle — to thee we smile, when you are slaughtered and made into soup.

Nashville *Daily Press*, July 18, 1864.

18 Advertisement for Swayne's Bowel Cordial
Summer Complaint or Looseness, Diarrheea and Dysentery.

Cholera Infantum, Gripping Pains. Cramps or Spasms.

Swayne's Bowel Cordial. Let no family be without this medicine during the summer months: In case of a sudden attack in the night — Cholera Morbus, Colic, Pains, Vomiting, Sick Stomack. In adults or children it will give immediate relief. Prepared by Dr. Swayne & Son, Philadelphia. Sold by W. J. & C. W. Smith, Cor. Church and Vine Sts., Nashville.

Nashville *Daily Press*, July 18, 1864.

✦ AUGUST ✦

1 Guerrilla attack at Silver Springs, Wilson County

"Attacked by Guerrillas — Narrow Escape"

Dr. Wm. Reynolds, of this city, went to Wilson county several days ago, to purchase some mules. He bought them, eleven in number, and on Monday last [1st] while on his way to this city, he was halted by seven guerrillas who demanded the mules and a negro, whom he had along, driving them. Situated as he was, he had to submit to their demands. The visitors then retired with the spoils, and the Doctor started on his journey to this city, but before proceeding far he was overtaken by two of the same party, who, with drawn pistols demanded his horse and ... money.... He told them he had but very little which was in a belt around his body. The guerrillas threatened to shoot him if he did not deliver it instantly. The Doctor put his hand behind him as if in the act of taking off his belt, but instead ... drew a pistol and fired, killing one of the men on the spot. The other then commenced to fire upon him, and he continued to return the shots, both firing several times when the guerrilla skedaddled, and the Doctor, glad of his escape from his clutches, made quick tracks this way, saving his money and his horse. The Doctor's coat shows that the skirmish was rather dangerous; two balls entered his coat sleeve, and another through the coat just above the shoulder. The affair occurred in the neighborhood of Silver Spring where other robberies have recently been committed.

Nashville *Daily Press*, August 3, 1864.

3 "...I talked a few minutes when him and six of his men came to the door with pistols cocked, and asked me where I was from and what was my business there." Dispersal of guerrillas in Spencer, Van Buren County

Liberty Tennessee Aught. 5th/1864

Governor Johnson,

Sir I hereby Send you a report of what I have done Since I last reported. On the 3d of this Month I received news of Capt. Carter and Champ Ferguson Combining forces and moving in the direction of Tracy city with the intention of attacking it. I immediately Started with fifteen men in pursuit of him after traveling Some Sixty miles I reached Spencer. I there arrested a man who Seemed to know where Carter was, and informed me that he had returned from his attack on Tracy City. He informed me that Carter and his men was then at Hemlock Hollow, which is Twelve miles from Spencer on the Chattanooga Road. I then set my plan to get him. My self and Vannatta disguised ourselves and Started in the advance. Some four miles from Spencer where I stopt to enquaire after talking a few minutes telling them I was a Southern Soldier and wanted to find Capt Carter, I talked a few minutes when him and Six of his men came to the door with pistols cocked, and asked me where I was from and what was my business there. I told him that I was from Lebanon and then gave him an introduction to Mr. Smith was Vannatta and told him we wished to Join him. He then remarked to me to go to the Stable and feed our horses and have dinner As I was unsaddling expecting to have a good time my men came in view of the house[.] Carters men discovered them, and it was not more than twenty steps to a Swampy thicket where it was impossible or a horst to go through I dismounted my men and pushed through but Succeeded only in hitting one, I captured all their horses and equipment also a large amount of goods that he had captured at Tracy City. I then searched the house and premises where I found about five wagon loads of arms and ammunition which I had piled and burned for want of transportation[.] The arms was principally Enfield Rifles, unserviceable and all loaded which made it dangerous when they were burnd If you will permit those fifteen men to remain with me I will insure that Carter will never mount himself or make another raid[.]

Your Obedient Servt Joseph H. Blackburn, Comdg. Detchmt

Papers of Andrew Johnson, Vol. 7, pp. 76–77.

4 Report on Miscegenation in Nashville

About three months ago, Mr. William Scruggs, who resides ... fourteen miles from town on the Hillsboro Pike, hired a refugee named Nash to work upon his farm. When the work was finished, Nash was paid off and discharged. He loitered about the place until Tuesday evening last [August 2], when he and one of Mr. Scrugg's negro girls disappeared. Mr. Scruggs came to town yesterday morning, and with the aid of a police officer, succeeded in finding the two in bed, in a house on the alley between Church and Union streets in the rear of the Maxwell house, or Barracks No. 1. The woman was taken in charge by Mr. William Thillet, a friend of Mr. Scruggs, and the two of them had taken shelter from the rain in the saloon of P. B. Coleman, when three soldiers came along, in company with a negro boy, who pointed the girl out to the soldiers, and the later immediately took possession of the girl, told her she was free, and at liberty to go where she pleased. The matter was laid before the military authorities who declined to inquire into the subject, or to have anything to do with it.

Nashville *Dispatch,* August 4, 1864.

7 The negro philanthropic fair in Memphis
Fair by Colored People

A fair was held at Barrett's Hall, on Main street, near Union, on four evenings last week, for some charitable purpose, but the colored people in this city. The enterprise was successful beyond all anticipations and everything passed of quietly and pleasantly.

Memphis *Bulletin*, August 7, 1864.

8 The nature of counter-insurgency missions and contraband conditions in the Tullahoma environs, an excerpt from a letter from Major-General R. H. Milroy to his wife in Rensslaer, Indiana

Tullahoma Tenn.
Aug 8th 1864
My Dear Mary,

I recd yours of the 29th ult. and 30th some days ago and was glad to learn that you were all well. I am still socializing here. My most important enjoyment is sending out after gurillas that are committing depredations in the country. I have one Regt of Tennessee Cavalry here that are splendid gorilla hunters. They are well acquainted with the country and there is a deadly hatred between them and the gurillas, caused by out rages committed by the latter upon the families or friends of the former. The most of my Tennessee troops are refugees who have been driven from their homes, and all have wrongs to avenge so they take no prisoners. This suits me exactly and they know it so I never see any guerrilla prisoners and frequently hear of them being killed and see their horses and arms. A great many negroes both male and female run away from their masters and come here and at other points along the R. R. and hire to Qr Masters, rail road repairers and wood contractors and I have daily application from them to send for their children that they could not get away with them and they are afraid to go back for them. I have turned this branch of the business over to Col. Dunn. He is an abolitionist and takes pains to give all the help he can to those poor creatures in getting their families together.

...
Your Husband Truly,
R. H. Milroy

Papers of General Milroy, pp. 372–374.

12 "Fishing at White's Creek"

An interesting party of fishers, consisting of His Honor the Mayor, Councilmen Saben and Rust, Captain Puckett, Deputy Marshal Steele, Superintendent Chumbly, and several others, left town early yesterday morning for White's creek, for the purpose of enjoying a day's recreation among the finny tribes.

Arrived at the bridge after a pleasant drive of an hour, the party debarked from their vehicles, selects some of the best feeding places, and went at the business before them with all the zest which the pure air, the cool spring water, and the inspiriting fluid contained in the demijohn, imparted to them.

After fishing an hour or two, the darkies announced dinner, and all the fishers repaired at once to the green spot on which was spread a substantial repast of trout, and butter and toast, drum and bacon, perch and crackers, and whisky, with all the *et caters* necessary to tickle the palate and promote digestion.

Dinner over, all hands again went to the river to fish, but on looking over the huge pile already caught, and bearing in mind the angler's maxim, never to take from the river more than you need for present use, they concluded to "smile" to their good luck; the which having been gone through with, they "smiled" to "the day and all who honored it," and then "smiled" to a safe return, when seats were taken, whips cracked, an off they go at full speed for home, reaching here before seven o'clock in perfect order, and bringing with them an abundance of fish, among the lot a splendid six-pound trout of beautiful proportions.

Nashville *Dispatch*, August 13, 1864.

14 U.S. Ship Manufacturing in Nashville
UNITED STATES SHIP YARD
Nashville

Very few of our citizens are aware that we have

a shipyard doing a large business within a pistol shot of the Public Square, yet such is the fact. Even those who may have become aware that ship carpenter work is being executed here, are perhaps utterly in the dark as to the amount of business done and the magnitude of the contemplated improvements. It seems to us that but about six weeks ago we first saw a few men at work on some barges on the Edgefield side of the river, north of the railroad bridge. Since that time we have daily noted the improvements going on, and on Saturday last we determined to stroll over the grounds to see what was going on.

Accordingly, we sought Captain John W. Clark, under whose charge the ship yard is being constructed and the government work done, and by his permission walked over the yard, and through the offices, and barracks, and workshop, and other places, and took a few notes of what we saw for the reader's benefit.

The ground selected for the shipyard is about nine acres, fronting on the river, and extending north from the railroad about two hundred and fifty yards, which is nearly all fenced in, by a substantial plank fence. There are four main entrances to the yard, each gate way surmounted by a sentry-box.

On the southeastern corner a house is being erected for the storage of tools, while upon the northeastern corner will be located the straggles, barn, etc. After passing the tool-house, we come to the office, in which Mr. Arthur Clark presides as Chief Clark, and adjoining the office are the officers' mess room sleeping rooms, kitchen, storeroom, etc., etc.

To the north of these buildings, one is being erected 123 feet long by forty feet wide, intended for workshops, store-room, etc. A blacksmith's shop will be fitted up on the first floor, and carpenters, moulders, etc. will find splendid accommodations to carry on their avocations on the second floor. This will be a great relief to the men who are now working in a small place under canvas.

Farther northward, and near the bank of the river, are the barracks, erected with a view alike to the health and comfort of the men. These are superior to any we have seen, the light and ventilation being much better than most others. No. 1 is occupied by mechanics, and No. 2 by the laborers, the negro quarters being some twenty yards east from there. Between the barracks is a well constructed kitchen, large enough to provide food for two or three hundred men, store room or pantry attached. On the eastern end of the barracks are dining rooms for the men occupying them; and to the west, detached from the barracks by a few feet, are wash rooms, with a large tank between them, from which they will be supplied with an abundance of water, which is thrown up from the river by a force pump.

In a few days, as soon as a sufficient number of hands can be obtained, Capt. Clark intends to commence the construction of a "way" on which to haul steamers, and barges needing repairs. Several boats and barges have already been repaired at the yard, and the *Mattie Cobler* is now undergoing a thorough overhauling as well as some of the larger barges.

In the workshops we saw a very fine skip in course of construction for the ferry at the foot of Spring street, and a jolly boat refitted and painted.

There are nearly two hundred hands employed in the yard, and several teams employed in hauling lumber.

Mr. Robert Cull is the General Superintendent, to whom, as well as to Capt. Clark, much credit is due for the amount of work already done, and the admirable manner in which everything is kept. Indeed, it is just what might be expected of man of energy and character like Capt. Clark.

Nashville *Dispatch* August 14, 1864.

15 "Meeting of Colored Citizens"

The meeting of the colored citizens of this vicinity, yesterday at Fort Gilliem, was very largely attended. The procession which passed through the streets was very large, composed in part of a great number of hacks, filled with well dressed people. The Band of the Tenth Tennessee favored them on their route to the grave with some spirited and excellent music. So far as we noticed, the behavior of the persons in the procession was orderly, and quiet, and void of offense to all except those who believe in the divine right of the peculiar institutions. The assemblage at the grove was immense.

Mrs. Langston [of Oberlin, Ohio], the appointed orator of the day, was, unfortunately, unable to attend, but some colored speaker, whose name we did not hear, is said to have made a patriotic and truly excellent discourse, which was listened to with profound attention.

Some excellent and appropriate remarks were made by Gen. Chetlain and Col. B.D. Mussey. Altogether, the affair was highly creditable to the colored people. They manifested a devotion to the Government which many white people in this city would do well to imitate. Had the miserable Legislature and Governor of Tennessee manifested a tithe of honesty, good breeding, good sense, and patriotism in 1861, which the colored people showed yesterday, Tennessee would not have called upon to mourn the death of 40,000 of her citizens.

Nashville (*Daily Press* &) *Times*, August 16, 1864.

16 Pornography in Memphis
Bawdy Books and Pictures.

The attention of the police is called to the fact that there are a number of persons going about the city peddling obscene books and pictures. Yesterday we noticed two of these gentry doing a big trade, one in a store on Main street and the other on the levee, and at various times we have heard of others. They are said to be from New Orleans and up the river, and spend a goodly portion of their time upon steamboats. A sharp lookout should be kept for these gentry, and they should be punished severely if caught. Memphis is not so utterly depraved that she cannot be made worse.

Memphis *Bulletin*, August 16, 1864.

16–19 A Confederate soldier's visit home in the midst of civil chaos in Bradley County

Aug. 16.—At home once more. I arrived at home this morning at two o'clock and found the family well, which consists of our Dear Pa and Ma and two little brothers, Wisner and Nevins. They are having a lonely time here with the enemy around them, and have a hard time to live, as they are robbed by the vandals every time they are known to have anything on hand to eat. I only remained with them a few minutes, and then continued with my company on a scout through the mountains. We crossed Ocoee River at Haskins' Ford, and moved down the north side of the river to the Helderbrand Ford on the old Federal Road, and encamped. Thirty men of the Ninth Tenn. Battalion are here on picket duty. There is only three miles from my home, yet I dare not go home to stop over night for fear of the prowling enemy hid about the neighborhood. All of our men who can do so in safety are visiting their homes.

Aug. 17.—I went home and spent several hours with the family. Took dinner with them, and then returned across Ocoee river, and stayed all night at Mr. W. Higgins' near Benton. Our cavalry division is camped on Hiwassee River, on Savannah Farm.

Aug. 18.—I went into Benton and found several of our boys from the regiment, and we scouted round the country generally, visiting friends. I returned to Ocoee River and stayed with the 9th Battalion pickets.

Aug. 19—I went home this morning, but returned to the pickets immediately. A part of the cavalry has been to Cleveland and destroyed the railroad. A courier reported about noon that the entire corps under Wheeler moved off in the direction of Riceville yesterday. By some mistake they failed to call in the 9th Battalion pickets, and we were therefore left behind. We all started together, and crossed the Hiwassee at Columbus a little before sunset; went down the river to Knox's Ferry, and took the road to Athens.

Diary of William E. Sloan.

17 Dr. Coleman's Cure.

A large proportion of the human race suffer more or less from venereal diseases, or their complaints. The taint once acquired is often said to lurk in the blood, and manifests itself through succeeding generations. The great fault of the age immediately preceding this, was that this frightful class of disease were combated only in their symptoms, which being once subdued, the patient was declared cured, through the deadly virus is still unexpunged from the system. Fortunately for humanity, a better state of things has been inaugurated, and the increased knowledge acquired by the foremost in the ranks of medical practitioners, enables them to strike at the very root of the disorder. Prominent among them is Dr. Coleman, who had devoted the labor of his life to the discovery of the means of totally eradicating the venereal taint, and leaving the patient as free as before infection. That he has succeeded, his thousands of former patients testify; that he will still succeed, his large present practice plainly proves. Dr. Coleman is one among the very few specialists now practicing, who are able to what they promise—work a perfect cure. He can do this, and that in a safe and speedy manner, without danger or exposure. His office is located on Cherry street, between Cedar and Deaderick. Visit him, all ye who are afflicted. You cannot afford to remain away.

Nashville *Dispatch*, August 17, 1864.

20 Skirmish with guerrillas and mutilations at Pine Bluff, near the Great Western Furnace

AUGUST 20, 1864. Skirmish at Pine Bluff, Tenn.

Report of Lieut. Col. Elijah C. Brott, Eighty-third Illinois Infantry. HDQRS. U.S. FORCES, Fort Donelson, Tenn., August 25, 1864.

COL.: I have the honor to make the following report of a skirmish between a portion of rebel Gen. Woodward's command, numbering 110 men, and Capt. William W. Turnbull, Company B, Eighty-third Illinois Volunteer Infantry, and eleven men of his company: On the morning of the 17th instant Capt. Turnbull received orders from these headquarters to proceed with his company as guard to telegraph repairers on line leading to Smithland, Ky. On the morning of the 20th, near the Great Western Furnace, a distance of about fifteen miles from the fort, a citizen reported to the captain six guerrillas. The captain learning by going across the rebels would be obliged to travel three miles while the captain would reach the same place in traveling one mile, hoping thereby to capture the six guerrillas, the captain, with eleven men, started in pursuit; but on reaching said place the guerrillas had preceded him a very few minutes. The captain and men followed nearly to the Tennessee River, a distance of six or eight miles from his camp. Came from them 1 horse and 1 gun. The captain then concluded to return to camp, and when but a short distance on his return he was met by 110 men of Woodward's command, who fired into the captain and party at a distance of about twenty yards, the captain returning the fire. The rebels then charged on and overpowered them, killing the captain and 7 men, horribly mutilating their bodies, their heads and faces terribly beaten, and from two to four bullets in each. One man being wounded and left on the field was carried by ladies to the house of a citizen. While lying on a couch a second party came up. One of the fields seeing the wounded soldier fired his pistol at him three times and killed him. Two men escaped and reached the fort in safety, and 2 more taken prisoners. A detachment consisting of Company B, mounted infantry, and Battery C, Second Illinois Light Artillery, Capt. James P. Flood commanding, found the bodies on the ground where the fight had occurred, gathered for burial by the citizens. The body of Capt. Turnbull was found some distance from the scene of strife, he, it seems, having fallen back and defended himself until overpowered and killed.

All of which is respectfully submitted.

I am, your obedient servant,

E. C. BROTT, Lieut.-Col., Cmdg. Post.

OR Ser. I. Vol. 39. pt. I, p. 468.

20 Capture of Confederate soldiers by U.S. C. T. in Meigs County

We arrived at Athens before daylight. Our regiment is gone down on Tennessee River to Meigs County. I learn that a good many of them were captured by some Yankees who were stationed on the river cutting timber, and Col. McKenzie has taken the remainder of the regiment and the First Tenn. And gone in pursuit. The men who were captured had gone home, and had appointed a place to meet before returning to the regiment. The Yankees (who were mostly niggers) found out their place of meeting, and waylaid and captured them as they arrived. I came on with the cavalry division via Sweetwater, toward Little Tenn. River.

Diary of William E. Sloan.

28 "Wild Steer in the City"

On Sunday evening last, a drove of cattle belonging to the Government was passing through the city. Amongst the lot was a large, long-horned steer, which broke loose from the drove, and as wild as a young buffalo on the plains, proceeded through the streets, seeking whom he might devour. On Market Street, near the Medical College, he made a rush at Miss Parrish, Mrs. Jones and her daughter, who were walking through that thoroughfare. Mrs. Jones and Miss Parrish made their escape by getting on the College wall, when the steer ran towards Miss Jones, knocked her down, and tore her clothing considerably; she endeavored to extricate herself from the reach of the furious animal, but as she rose from the ground, the steer would again gore her, which he repeated, until the lady, perfectly exhausted, fell down in an insensible condition; the raving animal then left her, and proceeded on his course towards Sladetown, where he attacked a negro man, and gored him until life was extinct. He then took after another negro, and he made his escape by running round a tree, managing to manoeuver as to keep the horns of the beast from reaching him. As droves of cattle pass through the city daily, it is well for people to be on their guard, and parents should be particularly careful that their children should be kept out of the way.

Nashville *Daily Press and Times*, August 30, 1864.

✦ SEPTEMBER ✦

1 Shaveless Sundays in Memphis
A Change in the Programme.

Sunday was a day of general dissatisfaction to a good many of our citizens, who forgot to get their face cleaned on Saturday instead of Sunday, and on account of the new order, the barbers got on Saturday evening, a great many of our young men (as well as old) were disappointed, and had to go to church hairy and unshaved, but next Sunday we hope to see everybody with a smiling and clean face; and to have this we would advise all those in want of a shave to call on our fellow barbers on Saturday between the hours of 6 A.M. and 12 P.M. They intend to accommodate every customer that will call on them that day, and they are very happy to be put on equal footing with other white men on the Sabbath, and hope it may continue this way. We were told by a good many of our German barbers, that last Sunday was the first time in ten years that they had a chance to go to church in the forenoon, they are all (with the exception of one or two) very glad, and thank Mayor Harris for the favor he has done them, and hope he will act to their wish in the future. Last fall the barbers requested the Board of Mayor and Aldermen to do them his favor, but they would not be bothered with the poor barbers of Memphis, and laid the petition, which was signed by most every barber (white and negro) on the table.

Rally to get yourself shaved on Saturday, and give our barbers a day of rest, and think of the third commandment where it says: "Thou shalt keep the Sabbath." Do not tempt a man to perform on Sunday morning.

Memphis *Bulletin*, September 1, 1864.

2 Skirmishes at and near Union City, Tennessee
SEPTEMBER 2, 1864.-Skirmishes at and near Union City, Tenn.
Report of Col. James N. McArthur, Fourth U.S. Colored Heavy Artillery.

COLUMBUS, KY., September 3, 1864.
I sent yesterday morning Lieut. Murray, with seventy men of the Seventh Tennessee Cavalry, to Moscow, with orders to find the enemy and engage him, if possible. He was joined by Capt. Berry with his command, and at Union City Lieut. Murray came up with Capt. Churchill and Col. Dawson's command and dispersed them, killing 6 and capturing 11 men. At the same time Capt. Berry was two miles west of Union City, he came upon Capt. Campbell's command, killing 2 and capturing 1 wounded man, 1 Government horse, guns, pistols, &c. Campbell's command fired into Lieut. Murray's detachment a few hours afterward from the brush. Lieut. Murray just arrived. Our loss, in all, 1 horse. He reports a rebel force of 300 at McLemoresville, Tenn.

JAMES N. MCARTHUR, Col. Fourth U.S. Colored Artillery (Heavy), Cmdg. Post.

OR, Ser. I, Vol. 39, pt. I, p. 493.

3 "I am unarmed and in your power, but you have mistaken your man; you can kill me, but you can't make me *draw off my own shirt*." Federal atrocity at New Market
From the *Christian Observer*.
Savage and Fiendish Atrocity.

The following communication to the Attorney General of the District of East Tennessee, contains an account of the most diabolical and savage acts of malignant cruelty of which we have seen a record since the commencement of the present war. Language fails us to express the abhorrence and detestation which every one, not lost to humanity, must feel for the vile and cowardly miscreants who, instead of meeting their victim singly in open day, decoy him from home in the dead hour of night, and inflict upon him their worse than murderous revenge, simply because he had dared to preach the gospel.

Bristol, Tenn., Sept. 3d, 1864
To J. G. Wallace, Esq., Attorney of the District of East Tennessee:

Sir — In compliance with your request, I proceed to make a brief statement of the facts connected with my being driven from my church, my home and family at New Market, East Tennessee.

After bed time, August 3d, 1864, Captain James Crawford, Lieut. Wm. O. Sizemore, of Hawkins county, and others, (all, perhaps, of the Federal army) entered my house and searched for "guns, swords, pistols and concealed rebels." They found none, for none such were there, nor had there been. Before leaving my house they asked my position in regard to the war. I told them that my sympathies were with the South; whereupon, they gave me two orders, accompanied with much profanity: 1st, "To go to hell and preach for the devil;" 2d, "Never again to preach at New Market." I made no answer — I uttered not one offensive word. My conclusion was, however, that duty forbade me to comply with either order. I therefore attended to my ministerial duties as usual, until the morning of August 18th, I met Lieutenant Sizemore in the street, and he inquired if I had preached since I received the above orders. I answered him I had; whereupon, as he turned away, he remarked, "All right — we'll send you to Knoxville." I remarked, mildly, "I thought it all right, or I would not have preached." That night, just after we had retired to rest, a man in the garb of a Federal soldier came to my door, and decoyed me off under the pretense of my being called to a neighbor's house. I dressed and went forth with this man, and soon met three other soldiers, viz: Lieutenant Sizemore, Bill Owens and a third man, unknown to me. — The three conducted me towards the depot. Now, for the first time, I suspected that *I was arrested*, and was *en route* for Knoxville. They were so bitter and so disgustingly profane that I asked but one question — "Where do you wish me to go?" and made one remark expressive of surprise at being thus snatched from my home at night.

We passed out of town about a half a mile from my house, when Sizemore, who superintended the whole affair, asked me, "Are you a rebel?" I replied to this effect: "I am a sympathizer with the South; I can't deny it without lying, and I won't falsify my word." — He replied. "*That's enough — halt.*" In obedience to his orders, I drew off my coat. The other two men did the same. He then ordered me *to draw off my shirt* — (had not put on my vest and cravat). This I declined doing. The order was repeated with a terrible threat, and a revolver drawn upon me. I replied, "I can't do it — that is an indignity which I will not consent to place upon myself." The order was again repeated, with curses and threats, and the pistol at my breast. I remarked, "I am unarmed and in your power, but you have mistaken your man; you can kill me, but you can't make me *draw off my own shirt.*" By Sizemore's orders, the other two drew off my shirt, and each taking hold of a hand, they began inflicting, the one upon my naked back, and the other upon my naked breast, a most severe whipping with hickories prepared for the occasion. They wore out three sets of switches or withs, and, during the time, Sizemore, by threats and commands, increased the severity and rapidity of the blows; and also himself broke off a limb from a tree nearby; the limb had several prongs, and was longer than his body, and with this limb in both hands he exerted himself violently until he had worn it to a mere club. Here I pleaded with them to desist, but in vain; asked them to shoot me and thus end my misery, assuring them that I had no fears of death. But the club still fell heavily and fast upon my bruised, bleeding, lacerated body. It became insufferable; I tried to avoid the strokes, when a blow upon the head brought me to the ground. As I lay there, they lashed me with fresh switches; and once upon my feet again, was knocked down the second time by Sizemore — several blows from the fist of one of them having failed to knock me down. One large scar over each eye I must wear to the grave, and how many others upon my back, breast and arms may be scars for life, I know not. They left me, and with difficulty I put my shirt partly on and got back to my house; sent for Dr. Blackburn, who washed and bound up my wounds, ordered the free use of aperients and the frequent bathing of my body in a solution of muriate of ammonia. He treated my case in accordance with this prescription until the day I fled from my home.

A day or two after I was beaten as just described, rumored threats were current on the streets to the effect that a like fate awaited any man who visited me, or manifested any sympathy for me in my sufferings. Personal threats were made against Rev. Isaac N. Caldwell and others, among the best and most quiet and inoffensive men of my congregation. Again fresh threats are heard — threats of scourging and death in case we did not fly the country. These threats were understood to have been made by the same parties who so misused me. We are now out of the Federal lines, but our families and friends may ere this have fallen victims to the fiendish rage of such men as Sizemore, Owen & Co.

Very respectfully,
Geo. E. Eagleton.

Richmond [VA] *Whig*, October 7, 1864

4 Confederate Major General John H. Morgan killed in Greeneville.

HDQRS. FORCES EAST TENNESSEE, September 5, 1864.

Lieut. O. C. FRENCH, Brig.-Gen. Gillem's Staff:

LIEUT.: In answer to your communication relative to the killing and surrender of the late Gen. John H. Morgan I must say I know but little. I was with Gen. M. when he left Mrs. Williams' house. He handed me one of his pistols, and said that he wished me to assist him in making his escape. I told him it was almost useless, as we were entirely surrounded. He replied, saying that we must do it if possible. We were concealed in a clump of bushes, when a soldier rode up to the fence, wearing a brown jeans jacket. We naturally supposing him a Confederate soldier came out of the bushes, Gen. M. stepping at the same time through the fence. The soldier demanded a surrender, much to our surprise. Capt. Wilcox, of the Federal army, with some other soldiers, rode up. I, with Mr. Johnson, hastened toward him, looking back in the direction of Gen. M., hearing cries, "kill him!" "kill him!" from every quarter except Capt. W., who received my surrender very gentlemanly; but before I reached Capt. W. I saw Gen. M. throw up his hands exclaiming, "Oh God!" I saw nothing more of him until he was brought to the street dead. I am satisfied that Johnson and myself were both fired on after we surrender, but by men so far from us that it must have been impossible for them to know that we were prisoners.... If Gen. M. surrendered before he was shot I do not know it.

I am, lieutenant, very respectfully, your obedient servant,

J. T. ROGERS, Capt. and A. A. A. and I. G., late Gen. John H. Morgan's Staff.

OR, Ser. I, Vol. 39, pt. 1, p. 492.

4 Ailments, grasshoppers and army worms in Carroll County

This is a very clear war day. I was taken yesterday with itching and burning. Last night suffered very much with cramp in my stomach and breast and quite unwell today. It is what is called St. Anthony's fire. It is very bad. The grasshoppers have been destructive this summer. The army worm has been quite destructive to grass and weeds since the first of Aug. Some of the worms are dark, ashy color, dim stripes; others a shiny black with pale yellowish stripes from ¼ inch in length to 1¼ inch.

Younger Diary

4 Skirmish near Campbell's station

Struck railroad again at Campbell's Station, and destroyed several miles. Passed one stockade which the artillery worked on awhile, but without effect. The enemy advanced in the evening, and after a short skirmish he retired. We left the railroad again and moved to Cambellton [sic].*

Diary of William A. Sloan, September 4, 1864

8 Lady Godiva's Nashville carriage-ride
Disgusting Sight

On Thursday [8th] afternoon last, at about six o'clock, the good citizens of Cherry 'street, from Cedar to Broad, as well, doubtless, many others, were treated to a sight so loathsome, abominable and insufferably disgusting, that it would be allowed no mention in our columns, were it not to call forth the effective arm of our corporation law and authorities to prevent the repetition of a similar occurrence. A fleshy, (truth will not permit us to say *fair*) *fille de joie*, whose sense of modesty seemed wholly to have been merged in the large development of her physical charms, entirely nude from her waist heavenward, in an open hack, drove rapidly up Cherry street. She was attired in a deep red dress, a jaunty hat trimmed with red, and reminded us of (we intended to quote Shakespeare about Patience sitting on a monument, but "in order to suit the times: we will say) she reminded us of a conflict of arms in the ocean of blood. As she passed the Maxwell Barracks, the hundreds of soldiers both in and near it, set up a lusty and continuous shout of admiration and she was carried past the Post Office building on an enthusiasm so wild and hearty that it can, as the novelists say, "better be imagined than described." We have somewhere seen the expression "there is a pleasure in being mad, which none but madmen feel." There may be a pleasure to these frail daughters of humanity in thus airing in the grateful evening air, but it is a pleasure we would fain believed shared in by none other than themselves. Against such indecency we enter the grave and indignant protest of ourselves, and in the name of our good citizens, and for the sake of our pure women, we

---

*Campbellsville.

earnestly hope our city authorities will promptly and rigidly see that this disgraceful and degrading spectacle shall never again stain the fair name of our good city, we think that the women who thus exposes to, and pollutes the public view with her disgusting nudeness, should be fined and punished to the full extent of the law.— We think the hack driver who engages in such a business, would have his licensee taken from him, his horses and carriage confiscated, himself fined to the fullest extent, and, as a just finale to the whole affair, be sent to work for ninety days.

Nashville *Daily Press*, September 10, 1864.

11 "I am sure that I hit one of them because as soon as I shot at him, he fell." Daniel C. Miller's account of a fight with and surrender to Confederates after defending Blockhouse No. 6 on the N&C line

Murfreesboro, Tenn.
Sept. 11, 1864
Dear parents,

Arrived safe and sound in Murfreesboro today. We were all in the blockhouse on Aug. 31 when at 7:00 o'clock we saw about 50 men on horseback about ½ mile behind our house marching to the railroad. Then a fellow named Martin Stimmel and I went to see what they were doing and saw them start to tear up the railroad ties—we each fired 5 or 6 shots and they fired after four or five ties were torn up. As we turned to go back to our blockhouse their pistols shots rang out and we had to jump back. When we got back we saw 6,000 around our house about 1000 yards, so that we couldn't do very much with them. 8 or 10 of us went to the railroad bridge which they were trying to set afire and we made them jump. Several fell and we could see them as they raised their hands before they fell. I am sure that I hit one of them because as soon as I shot at him, he fell. This was about noon—then five men came with a white flag and they wanted us to give up the blockhouse or they would put cannon on it-which later did happen. We said we wouldn't give it up and they left. In five minutes we saw that they had a 12 lb. Cannon brought out of the woods and they put it behind a little rise where we couldn't do anything to them and it was too far for our rifles. Then came shell after shell over our blockhouse— two of them it a beam and shattered it. They shot at us six times and only hit twice—then our Sergeant put up a white flag and they quit. You should have seen the Rebels coming out of the woods from every angle. They plundered out house and we had to stand in ranks. We burned our rifles (or twisted) so that they couldn't use them. They made us go with them for two days and two nights about 40–50 miles....

Miller Correspondence.

20 Skirmish between guerrillas and U.S.C.T. in Robertson County

"Colored Troops After Guerrillas."

"Old Robertson" is famous for good whisky and bad guerrillas. On last Tuesday [20th] a party of five bushwhackers caught a young man near Springfield, and robbed him of all his valuables. Colonel Downey, of the United States Colored Troops, stationed at Springfield, heard of the robbery and immediately sent out a squad of his men, who came upon the guerrillas about ten miles from Springfield, towards the Kentucky line. The colored chivalry immediately opened fire on the rebels, and stiffened three of them as cold as a lump of ice. The other two, squealing with fright, looked over their shoulders, and with hair standing on end, eyes as wide as saucers, cheeks as pale as their dirty shirts, and chattering teeth, fled as if the everlasting devil was after them. The guerrillas made as good time as ever a Tennessee race-horse did. Of course the soldiers had to give up the chase, as there was no use trying to compete with Jeff. Davis's chivalry in a foot-race.

Nashville *Daily Times and True Union*,
September 20, 1864.

22 Confederate attack repulsed at Bull's Gap

BULL'S GAP, TENN., September 22, 1864—3.50 P.M.

Gen. BURBRIDGE:

The enemy attacked the forces at this place this morning, and were repulsed. They are now visible on our flank. It is Gen. Ammen's and my opinion that all their available force is here.

ALVAN C. GILLEM, Brig.-Gen.

OR, Ser. I, Vol. 39, pt. II, p. 440.

23 Sorrow of one young woman upon learning of Major-General John H. Morgan's death

...I cut me out a pair of drawers & made them this eve. *This night our dear & only brother left this world of sorrow to dwell in realms of eternal bliss. Gently & softly the sad news came of Gen. Morgan's*

death, tempered from a thunder bolt to a mournful regret that our southern Marion had fallen. Killed in Mrs. Williams' garden at Greeneville, Tenn. A woman by the name of Mary Henderson rode 13 miles in the night and reported where he was....
                                    Diary of Myra Adelaide Inman

25 "I had the worst case of venarial Diseases." A confidential endorsement of Dr. John White by Sergeant F. B. Chapman, Battery "C" 1st Tennessee Artillery

State of Tennessee Fort Negley
Near Nashville September 25th 1864
To the atharities of the war department Dear sires

Whereas the Draft or enrolment is to take affect in this State in a short time from this present day, I do hereby Recommend that Dr John White a colard man who is the best Botanic Doctor know known of and is the most usful Doctor that is in the city of Nashville For the soldiers for the fact is well know that he cures more cases of venarial Diseases than all Doctors in this place. and I know of upwards of one hundred soldiers that has been unfit for dotty for months and all attention played to them by our army Drs. That could be and still the soldier would pain away when almost redy to go to his grave but ah he would hear of his noble Dr John White the colored man. he would go to this Dram in a short time the soldier joined his Respected Command and well reported for Doty. and hear is my own case. I had the worst case of venarial Diseases. I suffered almost Death and I had the best Drs. in this city and still I was sinking fast. when I herd of this colored Doctor I had given up all hopes of ever getting well tho I Concluded to try the Colored Dr. I was taken to him. he went to work with me and I know I am sound and as good a soldier as in the fort and there is a half Dosen more cases of the same sort in my Company and if Dr John is not put in the armey he will soon have my comerads all well and ready for doty as well as hundred of other soldiers. So this being the onley Doctor in this city that is a sirtan cure for venereal Diseases of all kinds I do theirfor hope that Dr. John White as above named will be excused from all Drafts or enrolments that may Be ordered or allow him the power to furnish a substitute in order that he may be left at this post for the benefit of the soldiers at this on Doty. I am gentlemen.

very respectfully your umble survant Sergt F B Chapman
Battery "C" 1st Tenn art
Papers of Andrew Johnson, Vol. 7, pp. 189–190.

30 The Barbers' Ball
"Barber's Cotillon Party."
Barbers from time immemorial have been celebrated for their convival mood, and many of the most attractive pages of Gil Blas, Don Quixote, and the Arabian Nights owe their zest to the liveliness of some devil-may-care barber, who would tell jokes and play off pranks in spite of every obstacle. The Nashville barbers possess this flow of spirits to the fullest extent, and have an association which is social and jovial, as well as benevolent and self-protecting. On last night they held a select grand banquet and cotillon party in the Court House, which would have done credit to any association. Frank Parrish, by the way, who has travelled all over Europe, and shaved all the Generals, both Reb and Union, who ever stopped at the St. Cloud, is the President of the association. The music was truly excellent, the colored banjoist, violinists, and guitarists of this city being well known here and at all the noted watering places round about. The affair was conducted with great decorum and propriety. Long life to the Knights of the Razor, who perfume our locks and polish our faces!
                    Nashville *Daily Times and True Union*,
                                            September 30, 1864.

30 Massacre of Home Guards near Fayetteville by Blackwell bushwhackers and murder near Shelbyville
Guerrilla Operations in Tennessee.
Nashville, Tenn., Oct. 6.
The Rebel Capt. Blackwell on the 30th ult. surprised and captured some guards numbering thirty-two, at Shelbyville, Tenn., and burned the railroad depot, and a lot of arms and munitions of war. Ten of the Federal prisoners were shot by Blackwell near Fayetteville. The balance were delivered to Forrest. Six of the latter escaped, and had reached Shelbyville. One hundred and fifty rebels, under Duval McNairy, attacked Lieut. Blizzard, of the Fifth Tennessee Cavalry, in charge of a large drove of cattle from Johnsonville, within fifteen miles of Nashville. The federal guards numbered sixty, half of whom were killed, wounded or captured. The balance escaped and

arrived here safely. There was a stampede of the cattle, and large numbers are straying through the country.

New York *Times*, October 7, 1864.

♦ OCTOBER ♦

1 Surrender of block-houses at Carter's Creek
Report of Lieut. Albert Kramer, Sixty-eighth New York Infantry, Assistant Inspector of Block-Houses.

OFFICE OF ASSISTANT INSPECTOR OF BLOCK-HOUSE, Columbia, Tenn., October 3, 1864.

I have the honor herewith to submit my report of damages to fortifications in my section during the recent raid of Gen. Forrest.

On Saturday, 1 P.M., came Gen. Forrest and staff with flag of truce of Block-house No. 5, which was in command of Second Lieut. E. Nixon, Company E, Seventh Pennsylvania Cavalry, and demanded a surrender of the block-house with garrison, which demand Second Lieut. E. F. Nixon complied with without firing a gun. Lieut. Nixon, who was in command of Block-houses Nos. 3, 4, and 5, ordered the sergeants in command to surrender. Sergt. A. Frohn, Company L, Seventh Pennsylvania Cavalry, in command of Block-house No. 4, Bridge No. 4, and Sergt. W. Rhinemiller, Company M, Seventh Pennsylvania Cavalry, was in command of Block-house No. 3, Bridge No. 3. Sergt. W. Rhinemiller refused three times to comply. Lieut. E. F. Nixon then threatened to place him in arrest; he also fired on the flag. Lieut. E. F. Nixon rode with Forrest's adjutant to First Lieut. J. F. Long, Company B, Seventh Pennsylvania Cavalry, commanding Block-house No. 6, Bridge No. 5, and tried to induce him to surrender, which [he] refused to do, and ordered Lieut. Nixon, with the adjutant of Gen. Forrest, away from his block-house. First Lieut. Long fought him from 2 P.M. until 12 m.; killed 10 rebels and wounded several; but they succeeded in destroying his bridge; his command and block-house were uninjured. During the truce, the rebels under cover of the railroad bank, succeeded in firing the bridge with turpentine; one end was burned, and the whole fell in. Block-houses Nos. 3, 4, and 5 are burned to the ground; also Bridges Nos. 3 and 4. It is learned Carter's Creek Station, the water-tank, and saw-mill, and the railroad destroyed from there to Spring Hill. Rumor says Lieut. Nixon surrendered for a bribe of $10,000. The rebels had no artillery, and his three block-houses were double cased up to the top log of the loop-holes. The garrisons of the three block-houses and water-tanks and saw-mill were taken prisoners, except 1 man escaped. Block-houses No. 3 was garrisoned with thirty-two men, Block-house No. 4 with twenty-two men, Block-house No. 5 with thirty-one men. Thirty men garrisoned the water-tank and saw-mill. Altogether 115 men captured. Rumor says they have all been paroled, and arriving this day at Franklin. Sunday morning at 8 our pickets were driven in at Duck River bridge, but we succeeded in driving them off without any damage to the works, or loss of life. Sunday morning our pickets were attacked on four different roads, Pulaski, Bigbyville, Mount Pleasant, and Hampshire. Fights and skirmishes continued until 6 o'clock in the evening, when the enemy withdrew in the direction of Mount Pleasant, and encamped on Gen. Pillow's plantation, moving next morning in the direction of Waynesborough. Forrest's force is reported at 2,500 men. The railroad is open from here to Pulaski. These are the whole facts as far as I have been able to ascertain. Will report further information as soon as I get it. Have no laborers nor carpenters to build these three blockhouses. Please inform me what I shall do.

Very respectfully, your obedient servant,

A. KRAMER,

First Lieut., 68th New York Regt., Asst. Insp. of Block-Houses.

OR, Ser. I, Vol. 39, pt. I, pp. 507–508.

1 Legal Defense for Gambling
A Model Counsel.

Gabriel and Ned, "brack gemmen," staked $50 aside on a game of "seven up." Office Smith came upon them, like the unwelcome guest, and lodged them in jail. A lawyer undertook their defense, and mustered for the occasion all the eloquence and rhetoric of which he was master. In the course of his argument he held that gambling was only a slight offense, and too trifling to demand punishment. He considered it trifling, in fact, and so innocent, he occasionally indulged in it himself, and had tried his luck only the night before. At this the Court smiled, the City Attorney laughed. The eloquent counsel had make a good hit, and, in appreciation thereof, the accused were released on paying the trifling fine of $10 each and cost. It was quietly suggested to our reporter that the legal gentleman was considerably more than "half primed."

Memphis *Bulletin*, October 1, 1864.

1, 4 Guerrilla warfare and retribution near the Wolf River

"Attack by Guerrillas — An Act of Retaliation — Seven Houses Burned."

A few soldiers watering their horses in Wolf river on Saturday afternoon [1st], when attacked by guerrillas concealed in the woods on the opposite side, and three of them [were] wounded. A detachment was rushed forward, but failing to find the enemy, returned. We learn from "True Blue" living on the other side, that the guerrillas were four in number. They were seen to go toward the river early in the afternoon, and return after the firing was heard. Residents recognized them as belonging to a company of thieves and cut-throats led by and infamous scoundrel named Gamrels. One is named Hall. He is a deserter from the 8th Iowa Infantry. Another was recognized as one Davis, a resident of this county. Several weeks since a Federal soldier was killed by some of the gang. Information reaching headquarters on Tuesday [4th], that the gang was harbored and that some of them lived in the above vicinity, it was ordered as an act of retaliation, that the houses there be burned. Accordingly a detachment of cavalry was sent over the same afternoon. They went to work with a will, and in a short time laid several houses in ruins. The scene of the destruction was about half a mile from the river. Among those burned out were Mrs. Harris, Tom Sellers, and one Jones.

Memphis *Bulletin*, October 6, 1864.

2 Skirmish near Columbia

Excerpt from the Report of Nathan Bedford Forrest on his North Alabama, Middle Tennessee Raid relating to skirmishing at Columbia, October 2, 1864.

...

On the morning of the 2d I proceeded toward Columbia, eight miles distant from where I encamped the previous night. Six miles from town I ordered Col. Wheeler to advance and drive in the enemy's pickets. I followed close upon his rear with my whole command. Col. Bell's brigade was ordered to move upon the northern part of town, Gen. Lyon was ordered to throw his brigade on the west, but south of Mount Pleasant pike. The reasons that prevented my storming and capturing Pulaski now existed with redoubled force, for I had not a single piece of artillery, and only half of the troops I had with me at Pulaski. Not intending to make a formidable assault I did not press the enemy. My object in making this demonstration was to take observations for future operations. Satisfying myself of the strength and position of the forts and fortifications, I returned toward Mount Pleasant, at which place I camped during the night.

...

Nathan Bedford Forrest, Major-General

OR, Ser. I, Vol. 39, pt. I, p. 547.

4 Dr. Coleman's Cure for a Solitary Habit Onanism or Self Abuse

How many parents have seen the reason of a gifted son go to ruin; have seen him fade away from their homes, their hearts, and their hearths, like a shadow of evening from the hills, and have turned in tears to the tomb to which he has gone down, in the bloom of beauty and the morning of existence, without once suspecting that the darling hope of their declining years was a victim to a solitary habit, which alas, is so common among the young. Let those thus afflicted call on DOCTOR COLEMAN, No. 64 North Cherry street, or address him by letter. Post Office Box 502, Nashville, Tenn.

Nashville *Daily Press*, October 4, 1864.

5 Attack on a Federal Cattle Drive
Rebels About–Cattle Drove Attacked

Lieut. Blizzard of the 4th Tennessee Cavalry, who was in charge of a force detailed to bring a large drove of cattle to this city from Johnsonville, reports that on yesterday he was attacked by about one hundred and fifty rebels within fifteen miles of this city (Nashville). His force consisted of about sixty men, one half of whom were killed or wounded and captured, the others making their escape and arriving here in safety. A general stampede occurred among the cattle, and a large number of them are straying through the country. Lieut. B. was fired upon twice, and his horse fell down with him....

Nashville *Daily Press*, October 6, 1864.

8 A visit to the State Penitentiary in Nashville
Visited the Penitentiary....

Found it would be impossible to visit the military prison without a pass, with which we had neglected to provide ourselves. Were obliged to wait some little time for some one to accompany us, and in the meantime two ladies and a gentleman from the north, made a welcome addition to our part.

While waiting at the door, saw a party of about fifty Butternuts marched up close to the door, two by two, by a captain. They were halted and rations of bread and meat were dealt out, the first they had to eat in twenty-four hours. They were deserters, some from Forrest's forces. Saw a paper signed by two of them saying they were very anxious to be employed here by Government. They were marched away, and those wishing to go, will be sent north.

"We have in that yard about three hundred bushwackers and guerrillas," said the communicative guard.

"Ah, and what do you do with those?"

"Well, we just stretch their necks for them a little," said he, with a self-satisfied smile, and with a motion of the hand and neck as if in imagination he saw one in that very interesting situation.

"Just as you did Mosely the other day," we said.

"Yes, ho! He was a splendid looking fellow, fine features, well formed, black hair and whiskers, and straight as an indian!"

This Mosely was a guerrilla, who used to lay in wait by roadsides and kill the drivers of stray Government teams, burn the wagons, sell the horses or mules, and pocket the proceeds. He was hung a few days since.

There are now about one hundred and six in the Penitentiary property, six or seven for life, and "the best men they have," and five or six are given the limit of the law short of that, which is twenty-one years.

We passed into the prison yard, the door was barred behind us, and we made the round of the workshops. First we entered the rooms where the native cedar was made into little fanciful pails and cups, in which the red cedar was dove-tailed into the white in wavy and curious patterns. I purchased one of these only about three inches in height. Various things for use such as pails, tubs, bureaus, tables, stands, large chests-nice for furs- and wardrobes are also manufactured from this beautiful red color.

It seems so strange to look at the men and know that they must work on in silence, hour after hour, day after day, and year after year with a bar upon their lips. Of course to a woman it seems such a terrible punishment to keep one's tongue still. Isn't it horrible? I should thing one's tongue would cleave to the roof of the mouth after a little.

Then we went to into the tobacco factory and saw "the weed," from the time when the leaves are rolled and tied, to the pressing of the same, and the baking, to that when it is turned out "ter-backer," — a delicious cud for certain animals who are blessed with two feet, but which those with four never permit to pass their dainty lips.

"How is it about the health of those who work here all the time?" was the query.

"Good," the overseer replied emphatically. "I was but sixteen when I first engaged in the business-was slender and weakly, but in a year's time was strong and well."

This does not prove, however, that he might not be just as well, if a carpenter or machinist, and his labor have been of some befit to the world, instead of the reverse. Wanted to lower his self-respect a little by telling him so, but didn't.

We saw also the narrow cells where they sleep. One cell was only occupied, by a maniac. He was chained by the foot, and standing in the open door with hands behind him. We were cautioned not to go within a certain distance. His position indicated that his hands were folded or carefully crossed, but we found afterward that he held a club in his right hand. He watched us in silence with lowering eyebrows and hanging head, apparently measuring the distance between himself and us, with his small, black, malignant eye.

"Cannot I speak to him" inquired one of the ladies.

"Yes, you can, but I wouldn't advise you to," said our attendant. "You'd likely be sorry for it if you do. He never speaks to anyone unless spoken to, but that easily angers him."

It seems that for years he was a captain on the Mississippi River, where he acted on the proverb that drowned men tell no tales with those whose purses he thought worth his care. He afterward became a highway robber on land. His term of fifteen years expired about a week since, and they have been trying to get him transferred to the Insane Asylum, but the officers of said institution object to receiving him on account of being made insane while here. He has been so dangerous that he has been chained constantly for four years. They dare not go near enough for him to get hold of one, and his foot is pushed within his reach. Kindness they say only makes him worse-treating those worst who show him favors.

Powers, *Pencillings*. pp.101–106

10 Elvira Powers pays a visit with Mrs. ex-President James K. Polk

Called this morning on Mrs. James K. Polk to obtain some leaves and flowers for souvernirs of the place, to arrange on paper for a Sanitary Fair. Received very cordially by Mrs. P., who accompanied me to the grounds and cut the leaves and blossoms for me herself. She also presented a find photograph of the place, taken from Vine Street, and showing the tomb of the ex-president.

Mrs. Polk has not entered society since the death of her husband. In person she is perhaps a trifle above the medium height, slender, with high forehead and delicate features, and bears marks of taste and refinement. Think she has passed through the ordeal of her former position with a true sense of its real worth in comparison with Christian duties and deeds of philanthropy.

Powers, *Pencillings*.

10 Affair at South Tunnel, Gallatin

Report of Capt. Benjamin S. Nicklin, Thirteenth Indiana Battery.

HDQRS. U.S. FORCES, Gallatin, Tenn., October 10, 1864.

I have the honor to forward you the following statement regarding the attack on the colored troops at the tunnel: About 3.30 o'clock this P.M. two soldiers of the Fortieth U.S. Colored Infantry came to these headquarters with report that Harper and his band had attacked them at the tunnel, and that they (being only two) could not resist them, and started for this [place], pressing two horses in on the road. The negroes stated that the rebels were tearing the track up, burning ties, &c. I immediately sent (3.45) Capt. Cleveland, of First Tennessee Mounted Infantry, with forty men, to scene. At 5 o'clock this evening I sent Lieut. Gable and fifteen men of the One hundred and first Colored Regt. up the railroad to the tunnel and Buck Lodge to remain until I could hear from you. Not expecting to hear from the cavalry until to-morrow I gave them orders to pursue and kill every one of the scoundrels they caught, and hearing from the conductor or baggage man of the down train that he saw 6 dead bodies — 4 soldiers and 2 railroad hands — lying near the track, some of them with the heads cut open with an ax, and only seven men at the tunnel, I ordered Lieut. Gable to remain as stated, and to-night at 7 o'clock I sent six of my batterymen armed, on a hand-car, up to the tunnel, with orders to the sergeant to investigate fully and report to me to-night. I am now waiting on them to return, which will be 11 or 12 o'clock to-night. I will then finish this report in time to send it you by the 1 o'clock train to-night.

While waiting for them I would call your attention to the fact that the country above us is full of guerrillas. Governor Johnson's proclamation enrolling the citizens is sending them to the guerrillas and to the rebel army. This county has not even the germ of loyalty in it, and while the rebels and guerrillas are advised of every movement of our side we can learn nothing of them until too late. Men that talk loud, both here and at Nashville, of their devotion to the Union, never do an act for its support, but, if their negroes are to be believed, when they are at home stigmatize all as Yankees, and chuckle over the way they get around the Federal authorities. I have a long list of names, together with witnesses and charges, that I will forward you as soon as I get it completed, showing how the citizens of this and Wilson County act, and if I am here next week will try and arrest some of them. If there was one more full company of mounted [men] here than there is, the county could be kept quiet, because if every man who furnished them anything was dealt with severely they would soon learn to fear us as much as they pretend to fear the rebels or guerrillas, and when they learned that lesson they could and would give us information. There is not force enough at this point-there is only sixty cavalry (Tennessee mounted infantry) and my battery that are at all reliable; eighteen of the cavalry are on picket duty every day, and fifteen of the artillery as patrol, and leaves but few men for scouting purposes. One company more, either infantry or mounted, with what we have would do, for we could always have enough men to scout within fifteen to twenty miles of the post. The guards on the railroad are negroes, and recruits at that.

Twelve o'clock at night. — My couriers have not returned from up the road yet, but I learn from the conductor on this train that Harper and his band killed 5 of the colored soldiers and split their heads open, set fire to the wood pile, but the coming of the cavalry we went up started them. If I learn anything further I will write you.

Yours, very respectfully,

BEN. S. NICKLIN, Capt. Thirteenth Indiana Battery, Cmdg. Post.

OR, Ser. I, Vol. 39, pt. I, p. 843.

10 Licensed prostitution established in Memphis by U.S. Army

City Medical Inspection Department

Mayor's Office, Memphis, Tenn., September 30, 1864

PRIVATE CIRCULAR

All women of the town, in the City of Memphis and vicinity whether living in boarding-houses, singly or as kept mistresses, rare notified that they must hereafter be registered and take out weekly certificates.

Women who can show that they are living privately with a responsible citizen of good character will be exempted from the weekly medical inspection by calling weekly, between 2 and 5 o'clock P.M., and paying the regular hospital fee. No woman residing in a boarding-house will be registered as a KEPT woman.

All other than such kept women, whether practicing prostitution regularly or occasionally, are ordered to call on the City Medical Inspectors at the private office, second story over the confectionery store on corner of Main and Union streets, entrance through the stores, or at No. 21 Union street, on any afternoon between two and four o'clock before the 10th of October, and receive a medical certificate, for which two dollars and fifty cents will be charged.

Or women can receive the medical certificate at their homes by requesting the Medical Inspector to visit them, and paying one dollar extra for the visit. A note directed to lock-box 201, post-office, giving the street and number, will be attended to.

In receiving the medical certificate a ticket of registry must be called for personally at the Mayor's office, for which ten dollars will be charged.

The money received goes to the support of the private female wards in the new City Hospital, on the corner of Exchange street and Front Row, into which registered women are admitted at any time for any disease upon showing their weekly certificate, are afforded all the privacy and comfort of a home, and nursed by an experienced matron and female nurses, free from any cost or charge whatever.

"Street walking," soliciting, stopping or talking with men on the streets; buggy or horseback riding for pleasure through the City in daylight; wearing a showy, flash or immodest dress in public; any language or conduct in public which attracts attention; visiting the public squares, the New Memphis theatre, or other resort of LADIES, are prohibited and forbidden.

Good conduct will ensure relief from detective or police visits, exposure or loss, and a violation of the orders will inevitably incur punishment.

Any woman of the town, public or private, found in the City or vicinity after the 10th day of October, 1864, without her certificate of registry and medical exemption certificate, will be arrested by the police and punished.

This circular is intended for the information of women only, and must not be shown or given to men.

By order of the Mayor: John B. Gray

City Medical Insp. Dep't.

The Medical and Surgical History of the War of the Rebellion, Vol. 1, pt. 3, p. 895.

11 Skirmish near Fort Donelson involving the Fourth Colored Artillery (U.S.C.T.) CLARKSVILLE, October 11, 1864.

Maj. B. H. POLK, Assistant Adjutant-Gen.:

Capt. Flood reports that Lieut.-Col. Weaver and ninety colored troops from Pine Bluff were attacked to-day five miles from [Fort] Donelson by 200 rebels. The rebels were handsomely whipped, with the loss of Lieut.-Col. Sorey, and about 25 men killed and wounded.

Our loss, 1 lieutenant and 3 men killed and 9 wounded.

A. A. SMITH, Col. Eighty-third Illinois, Cmdg. Post.

OR, Ser. I, Vol. 39, pt. III, p. 218.

18 A female cavalryman

Soldier Gal.

Sarah, alias John Williams, a private in the 2d Kentucky cavalry, was sent to the to the Post prison, to be held until further orders. This gay "soldier gal" has served for three years, and her sex never discovered, (so report saith,) until the present time. She is a veteran and deserves promotion.

Nashville *Dispatch*, October 18, 1864.

29 A religious revival in the Cherry Creek community

...There is a big meeting going on not far from Mr. Hampton's and his little son went one night and someone stole his mule bridle and saddle. Mr. Hampton does not believe in the way they carry on their big meetings, and I agree with him. I do not think I am an enemy to religion. I do not want to be, but I do not think if anything in the world requires calmness and deliberation, that is that thing. I think there are hundreds, especially the young, that are carried away by the excitement and understand nothing at all of the doctrines of religion.

Diary of Amanda McDowell.

29 Skirmish near Fort Donelson.
CLARKSVILLE, October 29, 1864.

Capt. THOMAS C. WILLIAMS, Acting Assistant Adjutant-Gen.:

Lieut.-Col. Brott, of Fort Donelson, reports that a part [of] Forrest's force, with three pieces of artillery, sank a steamer and barge loaded with army clothing at Fort Heiman this morning. Capt. Cutler, with twenty-five mounted infantry, attacked and drove across the river sixty of Col. Malone's Confederate cavalry to-day, killed 2, wounded 8.

A. A. SMITH,
Col. Eighty-third Illinois.

OR, Ser. I, Vol. 39, pt. III, p. 509.

♦ NOVEMBER ♦

19 Difficulty in the Nashville Red Light District

Battle in Smoky

A number of soldiers belonging to the third Tennessee cavalry got into Smoky yesterday afternoon, and raised considerable excitement. One or two of them were arrested by the military police, but they were unable to cope with a whole regiment, armed and using their weapons freely. One soldier got his head so badly smashed that his life is despaired of; the police officers made a narrow escape, and were finally compelled to beat a retreat through the back door of one of the houses the soldiers were firing into. As length, having driven the "enemy" from the field, the soldiers quieted down for a time. It appears plain to us that such disgraceful conduct might easily be avoided if officers would remain with their companies, and insist upon good discipline. If this cannot be done, soldiers ought to be disarmed before they are allowed to run wild through the streets.

Nashville *Dispatch*, November 20, 1864.

22 A Boy Commits Murder
Juvenile Precocity

Last night Coroner Coleman was called upon to hold an inquest upon the body of John Phillips, aged 14 years, who was killed about 7 o'clock last night by Oliver Morton, aged 12 years, a son of Dr. Morton. From what we can learn on the subject, some person had stolen some cigars from the Commercial Hotel, and John Phillips accused Oliver of taking them, calling him a "d____d thieving son of a ____," at which Oliver drew his pistol, and shot John, the ball taking effect in the lower part of the breast bone, passing through the lungs, and lodging in the back, causing death in a few minutes. A verdict in accordance with the above facts was rendered.

Nashville *Dispatch*, November 23, 1864.

25 Altercation between the 9th Pennsylvania Regulars and 4th Michigan Volunteers on Smoky Row

Serious Affray on Smoky.

Persons of a nervous disposition, living in the vicinity of the Louisville depot, were badly scared Friday night at hearing several vollies of musketry and small arms fired in the direction of Smoky. Their fears pictured Hood with his whole army attacking Nashville, and we are told as an undoubted fact that several hastened with trembling fingers to do up their slender sock of valuables, and were cogitating as to the kind of bed-room the coal cellar would make. None laughed louder, nor called "fool" longer than the scary individuals in question, when the real cause of the reports was understood. We understand that several members of the 13th United States Infantry (Regulars), and the 9th Pennsylvania and 4th Michigan volunteers got into an altercation near Mat. Carson's house, in reference to the respective fighting abilities of volunteers and regulars. Getting excited over their debate, pistols were drawn, and the regulars retreated into Carson's domicile, which was immediately attached and carried by the volunteers. Evacuating their first line of defences, the regulars fell back in good order, and up to their next line of defence at Dutch Lize's. Matters were beginning to look rather squally, when the guard made their appearance, and speedily arrested nearly all of the parties concerned. Up to this time over a hundred shots had been fired, and the two houses were almost riddled. Strange to say, in spite of the prodigious waste of gunpowder, no one was hurt, though one woman rather narrowly escaped, having part of her shoe cut off by a ball. The guard, not satisfied with the arrests they had made, seized every man they found in the neighborhood, and marched them off to the guard house. Some twenty were thus picked up, many of them estimable citizens, who had to spend the long, dreary night in their cheerless domicile, until nine o'clock, when the Recorder set them at liberty. We learn that four of the ringleaders in the affray escaped from the guard house, and have not yet been recaptured.

Nashville *Dispatch*, November 27, 1864

28 Revival and Murder in a Cherry Creek Church

I hardly know where to begin at to write this time. We all got so frightened on Monday night that we hardly know ourselves yet. I reckon I had better begin at the beginning and write it all down if I can think of it. On Monday evening [28th] the meeting was still going on at the church, but it was very muddy and disagreeable and I did not want to go much, for I knew there would be no preaching at all, only singing (and poor at that) and shouting and crying, but some of the girls wanted to go and I went with them as [sister] Mary would not. Pat and Fayette [Amanda's brother] and William and others of the boys went; Lucetta, Margaret, Carrie, Celete, Nannie and myself were all the girls that went. When we got there, there were several Federal soldiers there, but it was a common thing and no one seemed to care anything about them. But they got information some way that those renegade Rebels that prowl about up the river were going to come and attack them that night. Some of the congregation had heard it but did not believe it. Fayette told the boys that he did not think there was any danger if they would keep a good lookout. Pat told them to look sharp. They went out after the congregation gathered and ordered all the stragglers into the house and told Pat to let no one pass out, and they went off and hid their horses and put Charles Burgess out to watch. And they would come in the house some but were out most of the time. I saw Pat keeping the door, but thought Mr. Hickman had ordered it. Two or three professed, and from the time the first one professed there was such a noise that nothing was distinct. Some shouting, some laughing, some praying, some crying, some singing and all crowded as close round the altar as was possible to get, and at least two thirds of the crowd were between the window and door and the pulpit. I with others got near the altar as possible in order to see, and also to assist in the singing. They pressed on me so that I perched myself on the edge of the pulpit. (There was no one on it but little boys.) Lucetta sat up there with me. Carrie and the others were near on a bench. Most of the people were up on the benches. In the midst of the noise a shot was heard at the window and in an instant another. I jumped from my seat, in order to get out of the way of the bullets, for I saw flashes and heard the shots faster than I could count them, unless I had been more composed than I was. Someone pushed me down off the bench I was standing on the right of the women, for everyone in the house nearly were down as near the floor as they could get by this time. I tried to find room for my feet on the floor but could not and had to remain on my knees on someone for ever so long. There was so much noise and confusion that I could not distinguish anything, and I could not imagine what was up. I had to pull Celete down to keep her from being hit; she was so frightened that she was standing on top of a bench screaming with all her power, and making no effort to keep out of danger. I tried to pull her and Cetta both down and make them hush, but they were so frightened they could not understand me. It is no use saying what I thought about it. But I thought when I saw so many shots fired right toward the crowd that they were surely firing at the people just to see how many they could kill, and I had a strong notion of going round there and asking them what they meant, but I could not get out and then I had my hands full trying to take care of the girls, and then I thought I might get shot before I could get around there. The instant the firing ceased I started to hunt the boys and see what was the matter, for I had never thought of the Rebels. I had to get Carrie to hold Cette, and told the girls to say together. The whole house was in an uproar, the soldiers swearing and roaring and the women screaming. The first person I found was Hamp Clark. I asked him what it meant, he said they were shooting at "them boys"; but I did not still take the hint, for some of the Rebels had on blue Yankee clothes and I thought they were Yankees. I pushed round through the crowd asking everyone I met for Fayette and Pat. I found out that there was man killed and got to him as quick as I could and there were two soldiers sitting on the benches, and one of them had the dead man's feet up on the benches, and one of them had the dead man's feet up in his lap. I asked him if the man was dead. He said, "I don't know. I thought I would tie his feet together." I examined him and saw he was a stranger to me. The man's indifference about who it was that was dead made me know that it was not a personal enemy quarrel, and the thought flashed over me that they were Rebels. I asked him and he said, "Yes." I met Sam Stone, and he said, "Don't be scared. I don't think Fayette is badly hurt." I asked him in Fayette was shot; he said, "Yes." I then asked if it was done on purpose; he said he reckoned not. I found Fayette lying in the altar where he had sat down on the mourners' bench and fallen over and P. Cameron had caught him. I asked him if he was badly hurt, and if it was done on purpose. He said "No" both times. He then told me to go and get leave to carry him home. I didn't know where to go, but there was a man standing on a bench walking and swearing at a great rate and I made my way, to him and he said, "Yes, of course, take him home." Then Fayette came to himself and spoke to the man and told him they had been in the war together and to call him "Benson." The man seemed slow about recognizing him, but told us we could go. I ran back to where the girls were and got them not out of the house but in the middle of the floor and went all over the house as fast as I could, hunting for Pat, but could not find him. We got Fayette to wait and lie down on the writing bench. I thought it would be dangerous to start. But every little bit he would get frenzied and want to start anyhow, but one soldier advised us not to go. I met several of the [Confederate] soldiers and tried to talk to them. I found only one that had any civility about him. I found Emma Williams, when I first started out, lying on the floor, and asked if she was shot. She said she did not know and, I, knowing her as I did, did not expect there was anything the matter and sure enough there was not, but Ann Gooch was wounded in the thigh and lower part of the abdomen, one bullet making four holes. And the boy that I saw was badly hurt, but I did not get to see either of them again. Some of the women fainted and looked like they never would come to. At last the soldiers went out and got on their horses and came back to the door swearing about the Yankees' horses and wanting someone to go and show them where they were. Several of us told them that they were in the yard when we came in. One man swore that was a dead man in the yard under the window. I got a candle and looked but could not find one. And there was no one there. At last they told the congregation to get away from there. Jim Cooper told me he saw Pat go out at the door. And a soldier told me that me some men ran and he shot at them and heard a man holler. I felt uneasy but thought I would get them all started with Fayette and if he did not come to us in the lane, I would get some one to help me hunt him, but he came to us before we got far. Fayette got home very well by one walking on each side of him, but was out of his mind off and on all night. It was Sam Potete that was killed, and the man was taking off his spurs in order to get his boots off, so I have heard since. They did take his boots off and held me up and called to know who they would fit, took his coat and hat too, but dropped the hat. P. Camron asked leave to take him away, but they said, "Let him lie there," and he lay there all night, but they carried the wounded to Mrs. McGhee's. Fayette says he had got up on a bench to try to get them to quit shooting, and a man snapped a pistol at his breast and them pressed to his head and fired. He is not certain but thinks it was Benson and that he did it on purpose but don't want it known.

Diary of Amanda McDowell.

30 Battle of Franklin

As [we] marched through an open field to the rampart of blood and death, the Federal batteries begin to open and move down.... "Forward, men," is repeated all along the line. A sheet of fire is poured down into our very faces.... "Forward, men!" The air loaded with death dealing missiles. Never ... did men fight against such ... odds....

"Forward, men!" And the blood spurts in a perfect jet from the dead and wounded. The earth is red with blood.... The death angel shrieks and laughs.... I had made up my mind to die—[it] felt glorious. We pressed forward.... Cleaborne's division was charging.... I passed on until I got to their [Yankees] works and got over on their side. But in fifty yards of where I was, the scene.... seemed like hell itself.... Dead soldiers filled the entrenchment.... It was a grand holocaust of death.

Sam Watkins, Co. "Aytch," pp. 219–222.

General Hood has betrayed us. This is not the kind of fighting he promised us at Tuscumbia and Florence, Ala. when we started into Tenn.

This was not a "fight with equal numbers and choice of the ground" by no means.

And the wails and cries of widows and orphans made at Franklin, Tenn. Nov 30th 1864 will heat up the fires of the bottomless pit to burn the soul of Gen J B Hood for Murdering their husbands and fathers at that place that day. It can't be called anything but cold blooded Murder.

Diary of Capt. Samuel T. Foster,
Granbury Texas Brigade

Account of Isham Green Harris, Confederate Governor of Tennessee.

HEADQUARTERS, ARMY OF TENNESSEE, NEAR NASHVILLE, December 5, 1864, VIA BARTOW, AND MOBILE, December 10, 1864:

We pursued and overtook the enemy at Franklin, where he had thrown up one line of breastworks and commenced two others.

The enemy evidently intended to hold permanently the line of Franklin and Murfreesborough.

We attacked him in position about 4 o'clock P.M. and successfully carried their two outer lines.

At dark we had reached and stood upon the outer edge of their interior and last line of works while the fight continued until 11 o'clock.

We held our position during the night, expecting to renew the fight in the morning, but unfortunately under cover of the darkness, about 12 o'clock, the enemy had retired, leaving killed and wounded on the field.

We were unable to use our artillery on account of the presence of the women and children in the town.

We massed about 100 pieces of artillery that night [and] opened on the enemy at daylight, expecting the non-combatants to have gotten out before day.

We have lost an unusual large proportion of officers.

Generals [Patrick Ronayne] Cleburne, [Hiram Bronson] Granbury, [William Wirt] Adams, [Otho French] Strahl, and [States Rights] Gist were killed.

Generals [John Calvin] Brown, [William Andrew] Quarles, [John carpenter] Carter and [Thomas Moore] Scott were wounded.

We have captured about 1,300 prisoners and picked up on the battlefield about 6,000 stands of arms.

We have also captured a large number of colors.

We have also captured four locomotives and trains and are running the Tennessee and Alabama railroad.

Other trains are cut off, which we hope soon to have in our possession.

About 5,000 of the enemy are cut off at Murfreesborough.

The Army is in fine health and excellent spirits, and confident of success.

The people are delighted and enthusiastic at our advance.

SOR, Ser. I, Vol. 7, pp. 677–678.

The fighting at Franklin from a Confederate Private's Point of View, John M. Copley Forty-ninth Tennessee Infantry:

We were now ordered to fix bayonets, fire, and charge the first line of works. They received us with a volley of musketry, but all opposition was inadequate to check our columns in the slightest degree, and with one prolonged and loud cheer we carried the first line of works at the very points of the Federal bayonets. They stood their ground until we mounted the top of their works, but as we went over, part of their line of battle broke and fled, while the remainder lay down flat on their faces in the ditch to save themselves, and were either killed or captured; but few of those who fled succeeded in reaching their main line. Our lines of infantry swept over their works, annihilating nearly everything before us.... It appeared as if our troops had received an electric shock, which aroused their enthusiasm to its highest pitch, and the air resounded with loud shouts from our whole army....

After taking this line of works, we made a momentary halt in order to reform our front line ...

we now pressed closely at the heels of their retiring line, to storm the second. Their batteries immediately opened upon us with a perfect hailstorm of grape and canister, and when within a short distance of their main line, we encountered the *abatis*, or *bois d'arc* hedge, and also the line of *cheval-de-frise*; here the battery of thirty-six guns a little to our right, and that of twelve guns on our left, all double charged with grape and canister ... sent a tremendous deluge of shot and shell through our ranks, and these seconded by ... the infantry behind the works, and also another battery of six guns directly in our front, made the scene of carnage and destruction fearful to behold.

This hurricane of combustibles now burst forth in its height of fury, leaving ruin and desolation in its pathway, and nothing could be heard above the din of musketry and the roar of cannon, which was incessant. They fired on friend and foe, for we so closely pressed the retreating line in our front that had they waited for their own men to enter the works we would have gone over with them, and carried all before us. Whenever the dense smoke, in some degree, was cleared away by the flash and blaze from the guns, great masses of our infantry could be seen struggling to get over those ingeniously wrought obstructions, who were being slain by hundreds and piled in almost countless numbers. In the confusion which here ensued, numbers of our forces were thrown farther to the left and near the pike, forming a confused body of soldiers who were totally oblivious to all sense of order, thus giving the battery of thirty-six cannon on our right, the one of six pieces in our front, and that of twelve to our left, full play upon them. The firing of these guns was so rapid that it was impossible to discover any interval between their discharges.

The slaughtering of human life could be seen down the line as far as the Columbia and Franklin pike, and where the works crossed the pike the destruction was indescribable. Along that portion of the works in front of the batteries on the right, our troops were killed by whole platoons; our front line of battle seemed to have been cut down by the first discharge, for in many places they were lying on their faces in almost as good order as if they had lain down on purpose; but no such order prevailed amongst the dead who fell in making the attempt to surmount the *cheval-de-frise*, for hanging on the long spikes of this obstruction could be seen the mangled and torn remains of many of our soldiers who had been pierced by hundreds of minie balls and grape shot.... As the great clouds of smoke had to some extent vanished and I could look around me, I saw to my surprise I was left alone in the ditch ... and not a living man could be seen standing on my right; neither could one be seen for some distance on my left. They had all been swept away by that mighty tempest of grape and canister and rolling waves of fire and lead.... When the pistols were emptied.... I reloaded my gun, and turned towards the embrasure of the cannon, which was a few feet on my right, and tried my best to shoot the artillerymen ... before I could shoot, a cannon would run out and fire, forcing me to take refuge away from it. After getting my face blistered and eyebrows burned off, I abandoned that dangerous place by getting back away from the blaze of these guns.

Streams of blood ran here and there over the entire battle ground, in little branches, and one could have walked upon dead and wounded men from one end of the column to the other; the ditch was full of dead men and we had to stand and sit upon them, — the bottom of it, from side to side, was covered with blood to the depth of the shoe soles.

...

South of the Columbia and Franklin pike our troops were in some degree successful in capturing part of the line of works; the Federals who survived this onslaught took refuge behind the works on the north side of the pike, in our front. Our numbers were too weak on that portion of the line to charge the position in our front with any hope of success; however, they succeeded in reaching ... the residence and in the yard of Mr. Carter his son was killed dead. He had not been at home for two or three years, and as he passed through the yard and stopped at the door his sister ran and caught him by the hand and attempted to throw her arms around his neck, when a Federal soldier, who had taken refuge in the house, ran up and shot him through the body, killing him dead in the arms of his sister....

...

As the firing from the enemy in our front began somewhat to abate, sixteen of our soldiers, who were in the ditch some twenty or thirty feet on my left, sprang up and ran out of the ditch, attempting to escape; a whole volley of musketry was fired at them, killing the last one to a man....

...Captain Williams then requested some one to hand him a white handkerchief, but not one could be found. One of our soldiers who was fortunate enough to have on a white shirt, tore off a large piece and handed it to him. The captain tied this on the end of a ramrod, and hoisted it over our heads so it could be seen by the Federals. A Federal officer ordered the troops in our front to cease firing, which they did. He came up to the works ... and said: "Throw down your arms, boys, and come over."...

Copley, Sketch, pp. 49–61.

◆ DECEMBER ◆

3 First Action at Bell's Mill, U.S. N, capture and recapture of U.S.S. *Prairie State* & *Prima Donna*, and dispersal of Confederate artillery

Excerpt from the Report of LCDR Le Roy Fitch aboard the U.S.S. *Moose* at Nashville on December 4, 1864:

...

...about 9 P.M. [December 3], I received intelligence that the enemy's left wing had struck the river and had batteries planted at Bell's Mills, about 4 miles below Nashville by land but 18 by river, and that they had captured two steamers. [I ordered the tin clads and gunboats: *Neosho, Carondolet, Moose, Brilliant, Fairplay, Reindeer,* and *Silver Lake* to the bend.]

...

I directed Acting Master Miller [of the *Carondolet*] to run below the lower batteries, giving them grape and canister, then round to and come back and fight them upstream

...

The boats moved down perfectly quiet, with no lights visible, and were not seen by the enemy until the *Carondolet* opened fire on their lower battery and encampment.

...

As soon as the *Carondolet* opened fire the enemy poured a heavy volley of musketry into the boats along the entire line, and also opened on us with their upper battery of four guns. About this time the *Fairplay* had stopped to keep from running into the *Carondolet*, and the smoke from the guns and smokestacks, combined with our steam, settled around us so very thick in this bend that I could see nothing nor could the pilots see where we were running; so, finding myself nearly in contact with the *Fairplay*, I was also forced to stop, and after the *Carondolet* and *Fairplay* had passed below the bend I found myself still in the smoke and in a rather bad position, as the batteries were then firing directly into me and so far on my port quarter that we could not bring our guns to bear. I therefore directed the pilots to back up, as it was clear above and below it was intensely thick. I was afraid by this time the *Carondolet* and *Fairplay* had passed the lower battery, rounded to, and were again moving up, which would make our chances for colliding very great. I therefore decided to back up again, about the upper battery, as I could not remain where I was long enough for the smoke to lift; and, as the rebels were now giving this boat their entire attention, made it also dangerous to attempt to round to. In backing up above the batteries, I necessarily moved slowly, but the pilots.... handled the vessel so magnificently that we were able to keep our guns working on them so rapidly that in a great measure they were kept silent.

When I got above the battery where I could use the port broadside and bow guns, they soon ceased firing, as the *Reindeer* had by this time got above their guns, rounded to, and was in a good position to assist this vessel in case she was disabled.... I concluded to wait till daylight, knowing that the *Carondolet* and *Fairplay*, which were below the lower battery, would keep everything quiet and take care of the captured steamers.

The musketry along the bank and on the hillside was for a time very annoying, but we soon drove them off. The firing from their battery for a time was very rapid, but ... most of their shell and all their grape passed entirely over us.... The river at this point is not over 75 or 80 yards wide, and part of the time we were directly under their guns. Two percussion shells struck this boat in the hull ... above the water line ... one struck in the wheel, but none of them did much damage. One ... came ... close to the magazine, but did not explode. Another struck us fair.... but was turned from it course by striking one of the deck beams; it also did not explode.... The *Silver Lake* ... kept the musketry silent along the bank above.

In the morning, very early, we again moved down, the *Neosho* having this time joined us, but saw nothing of the enemy; the batteries were removed.... Between 8 and 9 A.M. I met the *Carondolet* and *Fairplay*, with the transports ... all was clear below, I returned to Nashville with the gunboats and transports.

...

The numbers of rounds fired were as follows: *Carondolet*, 26; *Fairplay*, 37; *Moose*, 59; *Reindeer*, 19; *Silver Lake*, 6.

...

Navy OR, Ser. I, Vol. 26, pp. 640–643.

6 Second Action at Bell's Mill, Cumberland River, U.S. N.

Excerpt from the December 17, 1864 Report of Lieutenant-Commander Fitch:

We then went down abreast of the lower battery ... here I stopped and used grape and canister against the enemy, and at the same time ... receiving a concentrated fire ... but this was the best position I could get to use the canister. I could not hurt them from above nor from below, owing to the shape of the river and the natural protection they had chosen behind the ... hills. I had also ... faith in the endurance of the *Neosho* and therefore chose this position as the most favorable ... to ... use canister and grape at from 20 to 30 yards range. Our fire was ... deliberate, but soon had the effect to scatter the enemy's sharpshooters and infantry, but owing to the elevated position of the batteries, we could do but little injury. The enemy's fire was terrific.... I lay in this position about two and a half hours, and finding that the enemy's shot and shell were cutting away the ... pilot house and letting it down so as to hide the fighting pilot house, and obstruct our sight, I steamed on up the river ... and met the fleet under convoy. Seeing that it would be impossible to get the transports below the batteries with losing several, I sent them back to Nashville ... I then cleared ... the ... deck and went down the second time, taking the *Carondolet*. I had her made fast to the bank above with instructions not to open till I went down and drew the enemy's fire, which would show their position.... We passed against just after dark, but were saluted with two guns as we passed and them could get no more responses.

...

...I desire to bring to your favorable notice John Ditzenback, quartermaster on the *Neosho*. During the engagement of the forenoon of the 6th instant all our flag and signal staffs on the *Neosho* were shot away and the flag lay over the wheelhouse. As soon as we had passed the upper battery, and while yet under fire of the enemy's artillery and musketry, Pilot John H. Ferrel ... and John Ditzenback, quartermaster on board of that vessel, went out of the pilot house and, taking the flag from where it lay, tied it up to the stump of the main signal staff, which was the highest mast we had remaining.

Navy OR, Ser. I, Vol. 26, pp. 649–652.

7 Reconnaissance and engagement, Wilkinson's pike near Murfreesborough, a.k.a., "Battle of the Cedars"

Report of Major-General LOVELL H. ROUSSEAU, on activities December 5–8, 1864.

HDQRS. DISTRICT OF TENNESSEE, Murfreesborough, December 12, 1864.

Dispatches from Gen. Thomas of the 5th and 8th instant received last night. Railroad train to Stevenson for supplies will take this dispatch to be forwarded. Wires down between this and Stevenson. On the 8th instant I dispatched by courier by way of Gallatin reporting operations her on the 4th instant. The enemy attacked the block-house at Overall's Creek, fired seventy-four shots, doing no damage. I sent three regiments, under Gen. Milroy, to its relief. The enemy (Bates' division) were routed and driven off. We took some prisoners, near thirty, but no guns. Loss of the enemy unknown, as night closed in before the fight was over. Our troops, new and old, behaved admirably. We withdrew at night. The next evening [6th] Bate returned, skirmished with and drove in our pickets, and threatened the fortress; pretty heavy skirmishing till the 7th, when the enemy moved around on the Wilkinson pike, northwest of the fortress. He was re-enforced by Forrest with 2,500 cavalry and two division of infantry. On the evening of the 6th he made a breast-work of logs and rails on Wilkinson's pike, from which he was driven on the 7th by Gen. Milroy with seven regiments of the garrison here; a pretty severe engagement, lasting perhaps three-quarters of an hour. The rout was complete, infantry and cavalry running in every direction. The fight was well conducted by Maj.-Gen. Milroy, and the troops behaved most gallantly. We took 207 prisoners, including 18 commissioned officers, 2 pieces (12-pounder Napoleons) of artillery, which were at once placed in position in the fortifications, and 1 stand of colors belonging to the First and Third Florida. Our loss in the fight at

Overall's Creek was 5 killed and 49 wounded, and on Wilkinson's pike more fully in my dispatch of the 8th, which may not have reached you. I am subsisting off the country, which I think I can do. Before the fight on the Wilkinson pike, Buford's division of cavalry took possession of about one-half of the town of Murfreesborough, shelling it vigorously and destroying many of the houses. With a section of artillery and a small force of infantry, I drove them, wounding and killing 30 and taking 25 prisoners. A captain of artillery left his boots, letters, sponges, staff buckets, on the ground. We lost one man wounded. The enemy's cavalry all around, but I think in small bodies. We forage without molestation. No enemy near here that I know of. Cheatham reported coming this way through Triune. All right here, and will endeavor to keep it so.

LOVELL H. ROUSSEAU, Maj.-Gen.

OR, Ser. I, Vol. 45, pt. I, pp. 614–615.

14–15 Third Naval engagement at Bell's Mill Bend, Cumberland River below Nashville

Excerpt from the December 17, 1864 Report of Lieutenant-Commander Le Roy Fitch:

About 10 P.M. of the 14th I received a note from headquarters.... At daylight I got under way with the following boats ... *Neosho, Carondolet, Moose, Reindeer, Fairplay, Brilliant* and *Silver Lake*, for the purpose of attracting the attention of the batteries while our troops were moving to the rear. I sent the *Neosho*, Acting Volunteer Lieutenant Samuel Howard, on down to go below the batteries, feel their strength, and then return.

The *Neosho* was only to engage them to attract their attention. Acting Volunteer Lieutenant Howard then returned to where I was, just above their works, and reported but four guns in position. These I could easily have silenced and driven off, but our army had not yet advanced sufficiently to insure their capture. I therefore maneuvered around above them till in the afternoon, when our cavalry had reached the desired position in the rear; the *Neosho* and *Carondolet* then moved down again and the rebels.... Our object having been ... carried out, the *Neosho* and *Carondolet* then moved on to opposite Bell's Mills, took position, and tied up to the right bank to assist our cavalry that was at the time considerably annoyed by a rebel battery of four guns situated on the side of a hill back from the river about half a mile. A few rounds of shell and shrapnel from our heavy guns, together with the firing from one of our land batteries planted on a hill above us, soon silenced the rebels and scattered the supporting column....

It was ... getting dark very fast, and not knowing the exact position our forces had taken the firing on our part ceased.... where they remained until daylight next morning (15th), when we again dropped down and found our forces in entire and undisputed possession of the field. Having accomplished all that I could ... I returned ... to Nashville.... Having made the desired reconnoissance as far up as Stone's River and finding all quiet, Acting Volunteer Lieutenant Glassford returned during the night....

Navy OR, Ser. I, Vol. 26, pp. 650–651.

15 Irony

Slaughtering and Sausage Making.

Yesterday we paid a visit to the slaughter house of Jenkins & Brother, and were agreeable surprised and delighted with our visit. The establishment is under the direction of Mr. Peter Craiger, who keeps it in superb order; among his assistants are Uncle Phil. Coleman, who has been butchering here for the last forty years, and Aunt Esther, who has dressed more tripe during the past thirty five years than would be required to carpet Davidson county. The most interesting operations to be witnessed here is the manufacture of sausages. Craiger puts in the machine the requisite amount of salt, pepper, sage, etc., and about 150 pounds of meat in lumps from half a pound to a pound; he puts the machine in motion, and in six minutes the meat is ready to be forced into its enclosure. This last operation is performed by hand, and yards of sausages are thrown out in a remarkably short space of time, to the astonishment of those inexperienced in such matters. A visit to this establishment is well worth the time required.

Nashville *Dispatch*, December 16, 1864.

15–16 Battle of Nashville

Nashville, Tenn., 15th. The army commenced moving today with Stedman's corps on the left, the 4th corps next, then A. J. Smith's corps. The cavalry moved to the right, and the 23d corps was held in reserve. Reconnoitering lasted until meridian, when at 12½ o'clock the order to advance was given, and the whole column moved onward. The rebels expected Thomas would attempt to turn their left flank, and prepared works to receive our forces. To keep up the delusion, Stedman was ordered to skirmish heavily on the rebel's left. While Stedman was maneuvering the rebels were massing their right, and we concentrating the 16th and 23d corps and Wilson's cavalry on our right. The result was that when the bugles sounded the advance, our right wing advanced rapidly between the left of the rebels and the Cumberland River, completely doubling up a rebel division posted to blockade the river. A battery was taken here and sent to the rear.

The rebels by this time perceived that our attack on the right was a feint, and Hood soon attempted to atone for his mistake, but was too late.... The hill where the rebels were posted was taken with little loss.

In an hour or so the rebels presented a strong front, and our progress for a moment was checked. It was now visible that the contest was about to commence. Another diversion on our left was made to enable our right to get into position and strengthen themselves ready for a charge. In front of the 4th corps and about one mile beyond the rebels had a strong line of works defended by a heavy line of skirmishers.

Wood ordered a charge, and with promptness and decision the men leaped over the breastworks and advanced. In less than twenty minutes our force had possession of the rebel works, and the banners of the 4th corps were planted upon them. Our men ... without orders pushed forward and reached the second line of rebel works by most strenuous exertions, capturing some prisoners, which with those captured previously, amounted to over one thousand.

The second line of intrenchments ... was located on the verge of a hill, a mile beyond the skirmish line. These intrenchments were built with great skill. Some time elapsed before our men got in position to advance. Our cavalry had advanced meanwhile until its right wing rested on the hills six miles beyond Nashville....

The corps of Schofield and Smith were in position directly parallel on the left. Our skirmishers advanced to Hillsboro' pike, sheltering themselves behind the fences on the north side, while the 4th corps formed right angles, the front division lying directly across the Hillsboro' pike, and the remainder being to the left....

At half-past three all was ready for the charge on the second line of the rebel works. The position was a strong one, and to reach which our forces had to ascend hills to an elevation of 15 degrees, without any protection. Our forces were massed and hurled with irresistible force against the rebel lines. At ten minutes before 5 the charge commenced. The 1st and 2d divisions of the 4th corps moved west, and the 3d division, at right angles with it, moved south. On the right of the fourth corps was the corps of A. J. Smith. The 1st and 2d divisions of the 4th corps had the hardest part of the task. They had to move in exposed positions to the rebel works in front, and these works were more formidable and stronger than elsewhere. Under a heavy fire of grape, canister and musketry, our men moved steadily forward....

After advancing within one hundred and fifty yards of the works the rebel fire became very severe. Our troops never wavered, but with shouts along the line they advanced and were almost immediately upon the intrenchments. The distance yet to be passed did not exceed one hundred yards, and reinforcements were in sight coming up, yet the rebels evinced no signs of retreating, and discharged volley after volley into our ranks at a distance of twenty-five yards. A few of our men had now reached the works and were using the bayonet when some few of the rebels fled, followed by others, and soon all broke and fled in the wildest confusion. Their artillerists attempted to secure four 12-pounder Napoleon guns, but succeeded in getting only one off the field. The other three fell into our hands, together with two caissons and a large lot of small arms. We also captured in this charge about 400 prisoners. Prisoners reported that Hood told them they could hold their position against any Yankee force which could be brought against them. Our losses did not exceed 100 killed and wounded.

Smith's and Schofield's corps had in the meantime advanced half a mile to the south of Hillsboro' pike, capturing a whole battery of six guns. This makes the total of artillery captured today-five guns being taken on the extreme left by the 15th Ohio-amount to 18 guns. Several battle flags were also taken. The rebel loss in killed and wounded was not less than 600, while ours was about 300.

The rebels have taken up another line, and may defend it tomorrow if they do not retreat tonight.

The colored troops behaved splendidly, and lost severely. Col. Schaffer's colored regiment and the

17th colored regiment lost nearly all their officers....

The gunboat fleet were engaged down the river, about fourteen miles from the city, shelling the rebel left. The headquarters of Chalmers was captured with fifteen wagons and all his books, papers, valuables, &c. These are now at our headquarters.

The Provost Marshall General says about 550 prisoners have reached the city up to 9 P.M. The total number of prisoners captured will not fall short of 1200.

Boston Evening Transcript, December 19, 1864.

16–17 Fancy Women visit the Nashville battlefield

Seeing the Elephant.

Two of the fancy women of College street went out on Friday [16th] to see the fight. By some means their carriage got outside of the picket lines and inside the rebel lines before they were aware of the fact. Seeing Rebel soldiers about, they ordered the hackman to "bout ship" and put for town, but before he could do so, the carriage was surrounded by Rebel cavalry, who took the establishment in charge, believing the occupants were spies. They were sent to the rear and placed under guard, where they remained until the retreat commenced, and then they were ordered to move southward, another nymph du pave having in the meantime been picked up and placed in the same hack. At length the horses gave out-they could no longer draw the load through the mud; so three cavalrymen were ordered to take them in charge. The women protested, and begged consideration for their laces and valuable silk dresses, but without avail. They were compelled to evacuate the carriage and mount in front or behind the riders as each preferred, and thus they entered Franklin, literally covered with mud. They were placed under guard at a hotel, and closely questioned by an officer, who seemed at a loss to know what to do with them, whether to send them south as spies, or send them adrift. At length, on Saturday [17th], the Federal cavalry came thundering along, and the women were left in their room. On Sunday night they arrived here, one of them riding behind a Federal guard, and the other two riding an old mule, and thus they were landed at the door of the Provost Marshal's office, who, after taking evidence of their identity, discharged them.

Nashville *Dispatch*, December 22, 1864.

29 Adolescent War Games in Edgefield and at the Capitol

JUVENILE HEROES.—Since the battle before Nashville, some of our boys have been practicing war in their own way. A few days ago, about a dozen of them agreed for a fight in Edgefield. After deciding who should represent the Federals and who the Rebels, the former took possession of the hill, and the latter went below. After waiting sometime for Hood to attack the Federals, Thomas ordered a charge upon the Rebel forces. Down the hill they rushed at full speed, each armed with a stick, when the Johnnies dropped, and the Feds, being unable to stop their headlong career, dashed into the Rebel lines, and by the time they had recovered themselves, three of them were taken prisoners, but the army being then too small to cope with the Rebel army, they were allowed to fight again. Thus the fight went on, with success to one or the other, until we were too far off to distinguish the position of the contending forces. Yesterday some juveniles dug entrenchments near the Capitol, sent out scouts, reconnoitered the neighborhood, were driven back, fired their arrows into the advancing foe, rushed out again to rescue their lost ammunition, back again to their breastworks, and thus continued, working like Trojans, for an hour or more, until their mammas called them in.

Nashville *Dispatch*, December 29, 1864.

1865

♦ JANUARY ♦

1 Emancipation Day parade in occupied Memphis

The pageant of our colored population yesterday was susceptible of a similar duplex aspect. There may have been some ludicrous things, some foolish things some absurd things about the procession yesterday. Men who are so fearful of the bugaboo of negro social equality and amalgamation-so apprehensive of the blacks surpassing the whites in intellectual and industrial pursuits that they fear to deal justice to the negro, and cannot see that the true interest of Tennessee lies in wiping out the effete institution of slavery, encouraging the emigration hither of free white labor and frankly, according with the policy of Government and the will of the nation, doubtless saw such to ridicule in the exhibition of the humble callings pursued by the blacks, their parade of school children, and their display of benevolent organizations, as well as their speeches, prayers and singing.

The man who looked ... to ascertain ... their law abiding character, their loyalty to the Union, their wish to educate their children, their profound gratitude to God, saw more than laughable or absurd incidents. He saw a race rising from ignorant, imbruted chattelism to manhood. He saw them ... not thirsting for revenge ... not dreaming of lying in idleness, but with prayers ... hymns ... cheers for Lincoln, expressions of intense regard for Union soldiers, and ... exhorting each other to manful lives and honest labor.

Memphis *Bulletin*, January 2, 1865.

3 Confederate foraging in the White County Cherry Creek community, an entry in the journal of Amanda McDowell

Rebels again. I am sorry for the farmers on Cherry Creek tonight, for if all accounts are true, their corn and fodder will go up tonight. Mrs. Mansel came up here tonight to save her mare. Mr. Hickman met a great many, and one took his gloves off his hands, and they pressed Mrs. Simms' team and some meat and Mr. Cooper's team also and some come up after Will Snodgrass' horses and were going to take Mr. Hickman's wagon, some come to Hickman's and called for supper and feed for their horses, and [said] they were Rebels and were going to camp on the creek, that they were from Kentucky and would be passing till after midnight. They were all well dressed and mounted which corroborated their tale of being just from Ky. for they always come back from there in a good fix, unless they are pursued too closely, and they have to be hard run to prevent their taking time to get what they want if they find it. Mrs. Mansel was at Mr. Hickman's and feared they would take her mare.

Diary of Amanda McDowell.

6 Expedition, Edgefield to N&CRR, Nolensville, Triune, Murfreesborough, Beard's Mill to Lebanon, Shelbyville, Fayetteville, Pulaski — mopping up after Hood's retreat

No circumstantial reports filed.

SPECIAL ORDERS, NO. 6. HDQRS. SIXTH DIV., CAVALRY CORPS, MILITARY DIVISION OF THE MISSISSIPPI, Edgefield, Tenn., January 6, 1865.

I. Col. Mix, commanding Eighth Michigan Cavalry, will march with his regiment to-morrow at daylight, crossing the river by the pontoon bridge [or by the railroad bridge, if most convenient]. He will divide his command into two nearly equal bodies — one wing moving by the roads to the right of the Nashville and Chattanooga Railroad, via Nolensville and Triune, to Murfreesborough; the other by the turnpike to Beard's Mill, and thence, if parties of the enemy are heard of in that direction, to Lebanon, concentrating afterward with the right wing at Murfreesborough. At Murfreesborough the command will draw rations and being they divided into two equal detachments as before, will move by such roads as Col. Mix may think to afford the best opportunities for affecting a thorough patrol of the country to Shelbyville, the two wings concentrating at that point. From Shelbyville the command, dividing into two equal bodies as before, will move to Fayetteville, concentrating at that point, and from there to Pulaski, where the whole division will presently concentrate. The object of the expedition is to pick up the many stragglers from the rebel army who are understood to be lurking in the country, particularly a regiment of Tennessee cavalry under command of Lieut.-Col. Withers, which is understood to be scattered through the counties of Davidson, Williamson, Wilson, and Rutherford. The strong probability is that wherever found the enemy will be in inferior force, and they will be, therefore, promptly and vigorously attacked and pressed; but no force of less than one-half the regiment will be detached to operate independently. Col. Mix will command the left wing, moving by Beard's Mill. The officer commanding the right wing will be furnished with a copy of this order. The wagon of the regiment will be left to follow with the remainder of the division. Special pains will be taken by all officers to preserve the condition of the horses. The general commanding expects that no trooper will become dismounted on this expedition.

When the rations of the command fail provisions will be seized in the country, memorandum receipts being given. Indiscriminate pillage is forbidden. If any complaints of this character reach these headquarters, the general commanding will hold the officer of the regiment responsible.

By command of Brig.-Gen. Johnson:

> OR, Ser. I, Vol. 45, pt. II, pp. 526–527, and Memphis *Bulletin*, January 6, 1865.

6 Complaints about excesses of Captain Worthman's Union home guards in the Shelbyville environs

HDQRS. POST OF MURFREESBOROUGH, Murfreesborough, Tenn., January 6, 1865.

Maj. JOHN O. CRAVENS, Assistant Adjutant-Gen., Tullahoma, Tenn.:

MAJ.: I have the honor to report that complaints are almost daily brought to me of the conduct of certain men who style themselves "home guards," said to be organized at Shelbyville by one Capt. Worthman. These men go about the country and, without warrant, take from the citizens horses and mules and forage, without giving receipts or vouchers; enter houses, order their meals, search trunks and bureau drawers; all, I suppose, in the name of the Government of the United States. I am told that a perfect reign of terror exists at and in the vicinity of Shelbyville. I am further informed that the said Capt. Worthman, in less than three days, paroled about 150 rebel deserters, on his own authority and contrary to positive orders from department headquarters. I shall send a party to examine and collect evidence, and, if circumstances warrant, to arrest all the offending parties, when I will make a full report. A few days since Lieut. Sheets, acting assistant adjutant-general, arrested and sent to Tullahoma a man who represented himself as belonging to the Fifth Tennessee Cavalry, furloughed by his captain and surgeon; unfortunately, the names of the men-the captain and surgeon-were not taken.

H. P. VAN CLEVE, Brig.-Gen., Cmdg. Post.

> OR, Ser. I. Vol. 45. pt. II, p. 528.

7 "You will assure yourself that they are dead before leaving them...." General Robert H. Milroy's orders to Captain William H. Lewis, Co. A, 42nd Missouri Volunteers, to recover property stolen from Union loyalists by Confederate bushwhackers

Sir: You will proceed to the residences of the persons herein named and deal with them in accordance with the following instructions. In all cases where the residences of the persons are ordered to be destroyed you will observe the following previous to setting them on fire. You will first search their houses and premises to see if they have any articles belonging to the U.S. Govt or that are contraband of war, which you will bring away in case any are found. Also all or any of the following articles that may found belonging to aforesaid persons.

First All horses, hogs, sheep, cattle, and any other animals or articles of whatever description may be valuable to the U.S. Govt especially those that are valuable to the Quartermaster, Commissary and Hospital Department.

Second All stoves and stove pipes of whatever description and all kitchen utensils, Queens ware, beds, bedding, knives, forks & etc also all chairs, sofas, sociable lounges and everything of the character of household furniture

Third All windows, sash, glass, looking glasses, carpets, & etc

Fourth Every article of household furniture which you do not bring with you must be destroyed or burned with the house

Fifth All barns, stables, smoke houses, or any other outbuildings of any description whatsoever of any building or article that could possibly be of any benefit or comfort to Rebels or Bushwhackers their friend or any person aiding, abetting, or sympathizing with Rebels Bushwhackers " etc which could be used for subsistence for a man or beast will be destroyed or burned.

Sixth All animal forage or other articles bought in by you will be turned over to Lieut. J. W. Raymond AAQm on this Staff to be subject to the order of Maj Genl Milroy to be disposed of as he may think proper, taking a receipt therefore from Lieut. Raymond.

Seventh The train accompanying will be subject to your orders, together with all the persons connected with it, whether soldiers or civilians and you will cause any of them who may be guilty of committing depredations upon Loyal citizens or their property to be arrested an you will not yourself or suffer those under your Command to commit any trespass, or do any damage to persons or property except those specified in this order.

Eighth You will burn the houses of the following named persons, take any of the articles named above that they may have, together with all forage grains belonging to them that you can bring away which may be useful to the U.S. govt for military purposes or otherwise and will give no receipt of any kind whatsoever. Joseph How, Dist. 11, ½ mile south of Hillsboro one mile west of the Hillsboro and Winchester road. [Seven names are included in this section]

Ninth The following person will be shot in addition to suffering in the manner prescribed in Paragraph # 8. [Four names appear in this section of the order.]

Tenth The following named person have committed murder and if caught will be hung to the first tree in front of their door and be allowed to hang there for an indefinite period. You will assure yourself that they are dead before leaving them also if their residence they will be stripped of everything as per the above instructions and then burned [Four names appear in this section of the order]

If Willis Taylor is caught he will be turned over to Moses Pittman and he will be allowed to kill him.

Fire & Blood, pp. 117–121.

12 "...the brown semi-liquidity which, at the present moment, is so abundant a 'product' in our city streets, was known by the classic appellation of 'Lollypop.'"

In ancient times, before the war ... the brown semi-liquidity which, at the present moment, is so abundant a "product" in our city streets, was known by the classic appellation of "Lollypop." Certain vain believers in the unlimited progress of the human race, among other Utopian speculations, imagined that when the streets were founded up and graveled, lollypop would cease to be a Southern product, so far as Memphis was concerned. Experience ... has refused this ... notion. It looked fair to presume that when the streets were raised in the center, so that the water falling ... would naturally flow to the gutter. As the centrifugal is opposed by the centripetal, so the progress of liquids to the gutters is opposed by an ingenious resource resorted to by the directors of street regulations in Memphis. Some weeks ago, each householder and property owner in the city was ordered to clean the dirt out of their gutters. This was done in lines along each side of the street. There it now lies, obstructing the flow of water from the center to the gutter, thus favoring the production of "lollypop." This product is an excellent renewed stock of the material from whence, next summer, the dust will arise, that forms so useful a defense against the heated rays of the ... sun....

Memphis *Bulletin*, January 12, 1865

12 Report of George E. Cooper, Surgeon, U.S. Army Medical Director, relative to amassing, transportation and treatment of wounded Confederates left behind during Hood's retreat

Report of Army of the Cumberland

HDQRS. DEPARTMENT OF THE CUMBERLAND, MEDICAL DIRECTOR'S OFFICE, January 12, 1865.

Bvt. Brig. Gen. W. HOFFMAN, U.S. Army, Commissary-Gen. of Prisoners:

SIR: The information you have received concerning the collecting together the wounded rebel prisoners at Columbia and Pulaski, Tenn., and to which you refer in the communication of the 2d instant, and which has been referred to me, is correct. In consequence of these towns being on the line of Hood's retreat, many of the prisoners who had been wounded at Franklin and were being carried to the rear were left there. These were augmented in number by the wounded brought in from the rear guard of the rebel army. As soon as it was learned that wounded rebels in any number were at Columbia and Pulaski Surg. O. Q. Herrick, superintendent of transportation of sick and wounded, was directed to have them removed to Nashville as soon as the railroad would be opened. On December 19, 1864, Surgeon Brinton, U.S. Volunteers, superintendent and director U.S. general hospitals at Nashville, was ordered by telegram to designate and set aside for the reception of the rebel wounded a hospital of capacity sufficient for the whole number, and directions were at the same time sent prohibiting the entrance of visitors. On the same day a telegram was sent to the superintendent of sick and wounded to scour the country from Brentwood Heights to Spring Hill and bring into Franklin and Nashville such as would bear transportation. On the 22d of December, 1864, Surgeon Herrick was telegraphed to remove to Nashville, as soon as the road would be opened, all the rebel wounded at Columbia, as well as to collect all from the surrounding country and bring them in. On the 28th ultimo Surgeon Herrick received similar instructions regarding the wounded rebels at Pulaski. On the 30th of December, 1864, Surgeon Brinton, superintendent of hospitals at Nashville, was directed to make use of such of the rebel surgeons as he might require in the treatment of the rebel wounded, being informed at the same time that, previous to putting them on duty, it was absolutely necessary for them to be put upon their written parole by the provost-marshal-general Department of the Cumberland. From all this it may be observed that everything was done in order to have the rebels properly cared for, both as sick men and prisoners of war. As soon as the Tennessee and Alabama Railroad shall be opened every wounded rebel in our possession whose life will not be endangered by so doing will be brought to Nashville, and not only those in the hospitals but those, too, who are scattered in the farm-houses through the country.

Respectfully, your obedient servant,

GEO. E. COOPER, Surgeon, U.S. Army, Medical Director.

OR, Ser. II, Vol. 8, p. 56.

13 Military Governor Andrew Johnson announces the adoption of an amendment to the state constitution abolishing slavery in Tennessee

NASHVILLE, TENN., January 13, 1865.

Hon. A. LINCOLN, President of the United States:

The convention composed of more than 500 delegates from all parts of the State have unanimously adopted an amendment to the constitution forever abolishing slavery in this State and denying the power of the Legislature passing any law creating property in man. Thank God that the tyrant's rod has been broken.

This amendment is to be submitted to the people for ratification on the birthday of the Father of his Country, when, without some reverse of arms, the State will be redeemed and the foul blot of slavery erased from her escutcheon. I hope that Tennessee will not be included in the bill now before Congress and be made an exception if the bill passes.

All is now working well, and if Tennessee is now let alone will soon resume all functions of a State according to the genius and theory of the Government.

ANDREW JOHNSON, Military Governor.

OR, Ser. III, Vol. 4. p. 1050.

14 Abolition and guerrilla eradication called for by State Convention

TENNESSEE STATE CONVENTION.

Slavery Declared Forever Abolished — Parson Brownlow Nominated for Governor.

Cincinnati, Saturday, Jan. 14.

The [Cincinnati] *Commercial* has a special dispatch from Nashville, which says:

"The Tennessee State Convention have unanimously passed a resolution declaring slavery forever abolished, and prohibiting it throughout the State.

The convention also passed a resolution prohibiting the Legislature from recognizing property in man, and forbidding it from requiring compensation to be made to the owners of slaves.

A resolution was also accepted abrogating the declaration of State independence, and the military league made with the Confederate states in 1861; also abrogating all the laws and ordinances passed in pursuance hereof;

All the officers appointed by the acting Governor since his accession to office were confirmed.

The proposition of the convention are to be submitted to the people for ratification on the 22d of February, and on the 4th of March an election is to be held for Governor and members of the Legislature.

Nearly three hundred delegates participated in

the proceedings of the convention, and the greatest harmony and good feeling prevailed.

Parson Brownlow is the unanimous choice of the convention for Governor."

Nashville, Saturday, Jan. 14.

The Tennessee Union State Convention, in its session to-day, nominated Parson W. G. Brownlow for Governor by acclamation.

A delegate asked if he would accept, whereupon he responded in the following language:

Gentlemen: I settle the controversy by assuring you that I will accept. (Applause.) I cannot be expected to do anything more, and I certainly ought to do no less than tender to you, as a convention, my sincere and unfeigned thanks for the honor and distinction you have conferred upon me. I will not speak to you at length now, gentlemen, but what I lack in speaking. If the people should ratify the nomination made by you, I will try to make up in deeds and acts; and, God being my help, if you will send up a Legislature to reorganize the militia and pass other necessary business, will put an end to this internal system of guerrilla fighting in the Sate, in East, Middle and West Tennessee, if we have to shoot every man concerned in such business. [Loud and long continued applause, amid which the Parson retired.]

The convention are nominating members of the Legislature to-night.

...

New York *Times*, January 15, 1865.

15 Notification of the death of Peter L. Critz
Tupelo Station, Miss.
January 15, 1865
Mr. A. Critz — Sir:

It is with much regret that I seat myself this afternoon to announce to you the death of your son, Peter L. Critz. He was killed at Franklin, Tennessee, while charging the enemy's works. We had taken one line of works and were fighting with bayonets the second line, and Peter was on top of the works when he was shot. He had in his pocket a very fine pipe with his name engraved on it which he said he was saving for his Father. He was shot through the pipe, through the heart, and through the neck, and never did a more gallant officer fall by the ruthless hand of the invader.

Peter was in command of our company when killed. We lost all of our company there except myself and James Reynolds. Reynolds lost his right arm, and I was wounded in the left leg with two balls. I am now almost well. We all feel at a loss without Peter. We had elected him Captain of our company. He has left a great many warm friends in the regiment to mourn (his) loss. None of his things were saved on account of none of his company being there to see it. One of the infirmary corps told me that he buried Peter and Mrs. Koemegay's son together and that they were buried decently. We lost a great many good men there. Our brigade now numbers only one hundred and fifteen men. We went into the fight with five hundred men.

I would have written sooner, but this is the first opportunity I have had of getting a letter off. I will close now.

Yours most respectfully,
R. G. Phillips, Co. B 24th Mississippi Regt. Brantley's Brigade

Peter L. Critz Correspondence.

17 Report on skirmishes with Confederates during the December 10–29, 1864 Expedition from East Tennessee into Southwestern Virginia

KNOXVILLE, January 17, 1865.
Lieut. Col. G. M. BASCOM:

Col. Kirk, Third North Carolina Mounted Infantry, has come in. Capt. Kirk wounded, two men killed, three men wounded. He had several skirmishes, in which he was infirmly successful, killing over 100 of Palmer's men and the guerrillas, and wounding a large number; he captured 32 prisoners and 56 horses. He did not penetrate into North Carolina beyond Warm Springs.

DAVIS TILLSON, Brig.-Gen.

OR, Ser. I, Vol. 45, pt. II, pp. 609–610.

18 Unpaid bill in Memphis; the carnal adventure of a Confederate deserter at Montgomery's bordello

T. B. Johnson, a recent Confederate deserter, found himself at the Recorder's Court. Maggie Montgomery "a lady of easy virtue" testified that Johnson had called at her house on a recent occasion, drank wine, and shared her bed, and departed without paying her claim for services rendered. She claimed that inasmuch as houses of the stamp kept by her are licensed by the city, it is the duty of the city to prevent and punish imposition on the keepers of said housed, as practiced by the defendant, and she therefore looked for redress....
His honor, however, failed to see the case in that

light, and informed the exasperated nymph that it was not within his jurisdiction.

That being the case Ms. Montgomery preferred charges of drunkenness and disorderly conduct against Johnson. The judge fined him $18.00, and he was happy to have an end to the affair. It was rumored also that Johnson had not paid the hack who took him to and from Montgomery's bordello.

Memphis *Bulletin*, January 18, 1865.

27 Explosion of steamer transport *Eclipse* at Johnsonville, and loss of 27 killed, 78 injured,

PADUCAH, KY., January 27, 1865.

Governor O. P. MORTON, Indianapolis, Ind.:

The steamer *Eclipse* blew up at Johnsonville at 6 A.M. this day, Ninth Indiana Battery, Capt. Brown, on board. Sixty-eight men injured, more or less; ten died. They have arrived at this post. I am doing all I can for them. If you can render any assistance, please do so for the wounded.

S. MEREDITH, Brig.-Gen.

OR, Ser. I, Vol. 49, pt. I, p. 600.

WASHINGTON CITY, October 15, 1865.

Bvt. Maj. Gen. M. C. MEIGS, Quartermaster-Gen. U.S. Army:

...

...The steamer *Eclipse*, destroyed at Johnsonville, Tenn., January 27, 1865, by the explosion of her boilers, and resulting in the loss of 27 soldiers killed and 78 more or less injured, which is believed to have been occasioned by the use, in an emergency, of an unsafe boat.

...

OR. Ser. I, Vol. 52, pt. I, Supplement, p. 714

28 Action at Athens

Jan 30 1865, Athens Tenn

To Brig Gen Johnson Mil Gov

On Saturday [28th] the rebels numbering over three hundred attacked this place & we repulsed them with thirteen killed & thirty five badly wounded[.] our loss five slightly wounded[.] The rebels captured twenty five our men including Maj John McCaughey & they took him some twenty five miles from here & killed him this morning by shooting him five times[.] they also killed Maj Devine[.]

Papers of Andrew Johnson, Vol. 7, p. 447.*

29 Guerrillas obstruct trains from Cleveland to Charleston

CHARLESTON, January 29, 1865.

Maj. S. B. MOE:

I go now with both trains flagging against train No. 2 from Knoxville. If I can get operator at Athens I will notify you, otherwise will send dispatches by courier. The guerrillas obstructed the track between every train near Cleveland, but did not show themselves.

C. H. GROSVENOR.

OR, Ser. I, Vol. 49, pt. I, p. 610.

◆ **FEBRUARY** ◆

1 Skirmish in McLemore's Cove, Tenn.

Report of Lieut. Col. George A. Gowin, Sixth Tennessee Mounted Infantry.

RINGGOLD, February 2, 1865.

After leaving camp yesterday morning I learned that Gatewood was in McLemore's Cove with seventy-five men. I therefore marched up the cove road, I being upon his rear during the evening without letting him know that I was there. I waited for him to camp. About 10 o'clock at night I attacked his camp and made a smash of him, killing a number, capturing several horses, guns &c. I took no prisoners. I was attacked by a squad of bushwhackers to-day. We killed two. I have lost no men, nor had any wounded.

G. A. GOWIN, Lieut.-Col., Cmdg. Sixth Tennessee Mounted Infantry.

OR, Ser. I, Vol. 49, pt. I, p. 33.

1 Circular Order relative to the organization of home guard companies in South-central Middle Tennessee and Northern Alabama for the purposes of exterminating bushwhackers

CIRCULAR

HEADQUARTERS DEFENCES N. & C. R. R.

TULLAHOMA, TENN. Feb. 1st, 1865

To the people of Coffee, Lincoln, Bedford, Franklin, Marshall, Grundy, Warren and Cannon Counties State of Tennessee, and of Jackson county, Alabama

It is ordered that all the male residents from the age of fourteen (14) years without regard to age,

---

*The author of this note is not identified.

infirmity or occupation is required in every neighborhood in said Counties shall, within ten (10) days after receiving this order, organize themselves into HOME GUARD COMPANIES of convenient size, from forty (40) to one hundred and fifty (150), according to the population and convenience of each neighborhood, for the purpose of *exterminating and driving out all Bushwhackers, Horse Thieves and other lawless Men, and restoring law and order*.

Every male resident of said Counties over fourteen (14) years without regard to age, infirmity or occupation, is required to enroll his name in the Company of his neighborhoods within five (5) days after the organization of the Company, on pain of being considered disloyal and treated accordingly.

Those incapacitated from age, disease, or being cripples, can give their influence, counsel, advice, send information, &c., &c. Only those able for active field duty will be expected to turn out when they hear of Bushwhackers, Guerrillas of Thieves in their neighborhood, or when ordered to do so by their officers, (unless expressly named.)

Each Company will organize by enrolling their names and selecting some men of *well known loyalty* as Captain, who must be confirmed by the Maj. Gen. Commanding, and furnished with instructions before he will be empowered to act. The Captain to appoint one first, and one second Lieutenants, five sergeants and eight corporals, and five members to constitute a company court for the trial of all crimes and offenses committed by members of the company. Each company to continue its organization so long as it shall be deemed necessary for the peace and safety of the neighborhood. Each neighborhood failing or refusing to organize a company within ten days after receiving or hearing of this order will be considered *disloyal*, and treated accordingly. The time having come for all men to take sides, and either show themselves the active friends of the Union and of law and order, or openly join the enemy, inaction on the part of any one will be no longer tolerated. The location, names of officers, and strength of each company, to be promptly reported to these Headquarters when organized, that measures to their arming may be taken, and instructions given.

By Command of MAJ. GEN'L MILROY

Papers of General Milroy

2 Letter from Miss Rhoda Inman in Hamilton County to Confederate soldier John G. Carter

Knowing of your extreme anxiety to hear from home I hasten to respond in Sister's stead, to two letters received from you a few minutes ago.

Before proceeding farther, I will relieve your anxiety by telling you that she is well, and staying at Ms Cannon's. Mrs. Cannon complained of feeling very lonely and will have Sister to spend a portion of her time with her. Sister has been out there about a month.

The children are all well, Little Rhoda is walking and is a very sweet, sprightly child. Sister has written to you by flag of truce, but from what you say they have not had the good luck to reach you. It may be several days before we have a change to send your letters out to her therefore determined myself to write you immediately. Your brother Peyton was taken through here a prisoner about three weeks ago (Christmas Day, 1864), he was looking very well and was in fine health, your father and Mr. Shadden went out the depot to see him. Mag Shadden has gone to Cincinnati, Ohio, to school.

Sister has received five letters from you since she left Georgia. Johnnie is here with us. He is an excellent child and talks of you a good deal, says frequently when he gets up in the morning, that he dreamed of pa last night.

Annie has gone to school to Miss Nannie Kennedy four or five months since she came home. She is not going now. Mr. Blount is teaching here and has a very large school.

Sister had no difficulty in getting good winter shoes for the children. Sister asked Annie what message she would like to send you, and childlike, her new calico dresses were uppermost. She would like to tell you about her four new calico dresses. Jimmy is extremely proud of his new book.

We had some very kind officers boarding with us last summer. Your father's family are all well. I know sister will write you soon.

I remain

Affectionately yours,

Rhoda Inman

W. P. A. Civil War Records, Vol. 2, pp. 1–2.

2 "There is no salvation except by blood." Excerpt from the Diary of Major-General R. H. Milroy relative to fighting guerrillas in Middle Tennessee

Thursday, February 2, 1865
Tullahoma, Tenn

[I] started Lieutenant. Col. Stauber of the 42nd Mo. V. I. with an expedition of 300 men today to evangelize the country between Elk and Tenn Rivers in Guerrilian Mo. style-that is by *fire and blood*. I have by experience become a firm believer in the doctrine that "There is no salvation except by blood." There is nothing like it for the poisen which brought on the bushwhacking, robbing, thieving, etc.

I find fire and blood properly administered to be perfect balance.

Papers of General Milroy, pp. 8–9.

3 Editorial Extolling Citizens to Enlist to Defend Against Guerillas

We have already recorded the death of Majors Divine and McCaughey, two of East Tennessee's most worthy sons, at the hands of the gang of guerillas who were in Athens a few days ago, and who are even now threatening our line of communication towards Knoxville. Although they were officers of the Federal army they were inhumanly murdered after being captured. These atrocious acts have aroused a volume of indignation among our loyal population which will not be satisfied until ample vengeance shall be visited on the heads of any and all of those roving desperadoes who may fall into our hands, and open every rebel sympathizer who shall be convicted of having aided them in any way whatever. The Government should take steps to retaliate on these fiends. It is bound to do so. Major McCaughey, in addition to being one of the purest men in the State, and one of its most thoroughly loyal and patriotic citizens, was an officer of a twelve months battalion. *It was because he was loyal and an officer, that he was inhumanly butchered.* We call upon the military to note this fact, and to make such an example of some guerrillas who may be captured as shall insure the safely of other officers who may fall into their hands. Let the military remember that if they would protect themselves they must vindicate the memory of the old patriot, John McCaughey. We have a word for Tennesseans on this subject. Quite a number so State troops have recently been raised, and are now being equipped. Some call them Home Guards, but they are not. They are soldiers and as such they have a reputation at stake. They are not only United States solders; but they are East Tennessee solders. East Tennessee has already furnished her thousands of troops, and none of her regiments has ever turned its back to traitors in a disgraceful manner. No man has yet had occasion to be ashamed to acknowledge that he belonged to an East Tennessee regiment. So far there is not a single spot to blemish the escutcheon of East Tennessee. Shall there be now? No, no-a thousand times, no! Then let every officer and man belonging to the troops now being raised in this Division of the State resolve to excel-if that could be done-in desperate courage and unceasing vigilance their friends and neighbors who enlisted before them. Let there be discipline, and when he enemy shall be prowling through [last line missing]

Chattanooga *Daily Gazette*, February 3, 1865.

5 Skirmish near McMinnville

FEBRUARY 5, 1865.-Skirmish near McMinnville, Tenn.

Report of Capt. Howard N. Woley, Forty-second Missouri Infantry. FEBRUARY 5, 1865.

I have the honor to report to you the history of our engagement with some of the Southern chivalry. They were supposed to be the notorious Perdham, together with some other bands of desperadoes, as their combined numbers were full 100. We followed them all day, or until about 3 P.M., when we came on their camp in the mountains. They had picked their position and had made a good selection, and were it not for their condition they might have held their position for a while. They were posted along a gulch running south to the brow of a hill. They were also in line along the hill. As Capt. Lewis came up in the advance they poured a heavy fire into our advance as we ascend the hill where they were posted. Most of our officers being in the front, Capt. M. M. Floyd, of the Fifth Tennessee Cavalry, was severely wounded, also two soldiers belonging to the same regiment. The boys of the Forty-second were uninjured, except by slight scratches and bullet holes in their clothes. The rebels left so rapidly that it was impossible for us, on worn-out horses, to overtake them. On examination we found two dead horses, and from indications two men were killed or severely wounded and taken off the field by their comrades. Capt. Lewis says he can hold the country and scatter the rebels all through. He thinks a few more of the Forty-second would be acceptable, as the home guards will not all do to tie to. We go to McMinnville from here.

By order of Capt. Lewis, commanding scout.
Your obedient servant,
H. N. WOLEY, Capt.

OR, Ser. I, Vol. 49, pt. I, p. 34.

10 Affair near Triune, or Trouble at the Guerrillas' Ball

FEBRUARY 10, 1865.—Affair near Triune, Tenn.
Report of Capt. Robert H. Clinton, Tenth Tennessee Infantry.

NASHVILLE, TENN., February 12, 1865.

MAJ.: I have the honor to make the following report:

In obedience to orders received from Maj.-Gen. Rousseau, commanding military district, I proceeded on the 9th of February at 6 P.M. with a force of thirty-five men belonging to the Fourteenth Tennessee Cavalry (of Capt. J. L. Poston' company) to the house of one Charles Luster, thirty miles south of Nashville, at which place, according to information, there was to be a ball at which some twenty guerrillas were to be present. Nine miles from this City, on the Nolensville pike, I searched the house of a widow named Patterson, whose son is a bushwhacker and said to be the leader of a gang infesting that immediate neighborhood. I found one man in bed. The guide knowing nothing of him, I did not think it necessary to arrest him. In searching the house the men found two shotguns, one Derringer pistol, and one carbine. I ordered them to be destroyed. They were loaded and ready for use. I then proceeded on the march passing through Triune at 11.30 P.M., arriving at Luster's house at 12.40 A.M. A quarter of a mile from the house I halted the command and dismounted, leaving ten men to hold the horses; with the other twenty-five I proceeded across the fields, and when within fifty yards of the house I divided the command, sending twelve men under Capt. Poston to the left. With the other thirteen I went to the right with orders to form a circle around the house upon reaching it. When within about twenty steps of the house I discovered some eight or ten negroes around a fire. One of them ran from the fire to the house to give the alarm, halloing, "The soldiers are coming!" I had previously given orders for the men not to fire unless we were fired on.

Notwithstanding that the negro had given the alarm we were so close to the house that they had not time to make their escape before we had it surrounded. They were commanded to come out. As soon as that command was given someone in the house fired upon two men who were trying to force open the back door, powder burning the face of one man and wounding the other slightly on the hand. Our men, seeing them rush out of the house, breaking through our lines, fired upon those who were trying to make their escape, and I learned the next morning that four of them were killed on the spot, and one wounded died subsequently. By morning all the dead were conveyed away, only one being found, and he was discovered on an adjacent hill a quarter of a mile from the house. I believe that the citizens had the dead and wounded conveyed away in order to conceal the fact of there having been guerrillas at the party. One McCrairy supposed to be loyal, informs us that there were certainly five guerrillas there, or at least strange men that he knows nothing of. If any innocent person was hurt, all I can say is, it was from their being in bad company. My having been ordered there to capture a party of guerrillas and finding so large a crowd of men there who fired upon us first, it was but natural that we should return the fire, and if any innocent person was hurt I cannot think that it is my fault, having obeyed the orders I received, and performed my duty. On the road back on the night of the 10th about two miles this side of Triune in turning a hill we encountered a band of seven mounted guerrillas about 600 yards off. We gave chase and at one time nearly overtook them, but, they being on fresh horses and ours completely jaded, after a chase of four miles I abandoned them and returned to Nashville. I brought in four prisoners, but upon investigation I turned two of them loose, retaining the other one of whom, E. F. Haynes, being charged with guerrillaing and pointing out Union men and urging upon Hood's men to burn their horses and hang them; the other, Albert Rutledge, being charged as accessory to the murder of a Union man named Hibbs. In conversing with the citizens I found but very little Union sentiment, a disregard for their oaths and a disposition to harbor and protect the guerrillas, and especially so in the case of the Widow Patterson, nine miles from Nashville, who has a son marauding in her neighborhood.

I have the honor, major, to be, very respectfully, your obedient servant,

R. H. CLINTON, Capt., Tenth Tennessee Infantry.

OR, Ser. I. Vol. 49. pt. I, pp. 38–39.

12 Major-General R. H. Milroy's solution for guerrilla activity in the Tullahoma area, an excerpt from a letter to his wife in Rensselaer, Indiana

Tullahoma, Tenn
Feb 12th 1865

...I have no news to write of any interest to write about except brutal Murders by bushwhackers which is an almost daily occurance in some direction around us, but the history of these atrocities would be too long and would shock you. But I have fell on a plan to stir up the people against these monsters and to pitch in and help us clean the country out. Blood and fire is the medicine I use. I shoot the men who are friendly with and harbour the bushwhackers and burn their houses. By spreading death and fire in a neighborhood where the bushwhackers have friends, the survivors come rushing in demanding in terror "What shall we do to be saved?" I tell them to organize companies-get guns-horse clubs or anything else and rush out after the bushwhackers-kill or capture them and being them in and we will be their friends and protect them-and they are doing it splendidly-They know where the hiding places and paths of the bushwhackers are and I have got up a war of extermination between the people and the bushwhackers or am fast getting it up. The people have heretofore been natural and the bushwhackers could go where they pleased among them. But this state of affairs is fast changing. I was about to hang two notorious Bushwhackers on last Friday by a public execution. They had been captured by some new green Wisconsin troops and brought in alive. They had recently brutally murdered two negroes after whiping them nearly to death mostly because they had been working for the Yankees. I had the gallows erected near town, had them taken out and up on the scaffold [with] a thousand soldiers and people around to see them hung, and they were making speeches and bidding good buy when a dispatch arrived from Gen. Rousseau to try them by military commission first before hanging them. This was a great dissappointment, especially to my Missouri troops, who are the greatest enemies to bushwhackers I have ever met. I can easily prove the villians guilty and will have the pleasure of hanging them yet....

...

Your Husband Truly,
R. H. Milroy

Papers of General Milroy, pp. 495–496.

15 Editorial applauding white officers and negro troops

Officers Commanding Negroes.

Some of our most refined citizens have so great a horror for white officers who stoop to command negro regiments or brigades, that they say they can't treat them with respect. Let us look into this matter, and reason a little about the case. These officers are officers of the United States army, and are only doing their duty by obeying their superiors — Our Government has resolved on arming and fighting the negroes, and in or judgment negroes are good enough to fight rebels with. And as the fight is about the negro, it is proper that he should take a hand.

But, for years past — forty years of the time we can recollect — monied men of the South have bought up droves of negroes — put them in irons — and driven them through here to the States of Alabama, Mississippi, and Louisiana, with the lordly owners on the horses, with large stock, driving whips in hand, occasionally used upon such negroes as would lag behind. In many instances they have traveled on with the drove in carriages, and on springs, with select mulatto girls, to take care of them during their absence from home! In many instances, when they have sold these girls for the money they have sold their own *offsprings* and *relatives!*

When these traders have been successful and made fortunes, man and families have taken them into their houses, treated with great deference, and recognized them as fit associates, who now turn up their noses in derision at an officer who will consent to command negroes! What inconsistent creatures we are!

Brownlow's Whig and Independent Journal and Rebel Ventilator, February 15, 1865.

16 Assault on the Federal garrisons at Athens and Sweet Water, Tenn

FEBRUARY 16, 1865.-Attacks upon the garrisons of Athens and Sweet Water, Tenn.

REPORTS.

No. 1.— Gen. Robert E. Lee, C. S. Army commanding Army of Northern Virginia.

No. 2.— Brig. Gen. John C. Vaughn, C. S. Army.

No. 1.

Report of Gen. Robert E. Lee, C. S. Army, commanding Army of Northern Virginia.

HDQRS. ARMY OF NORTHERN VIRGINIA, February 24, 1865.

Gen. Echols reports that detachments of Vaughn's cavalry struck the railroad beyond Knoxville at Sweet Water and Athens, capturing the garrison at both places. Sixty men of Second Ohio Regiment, with horses and equipments, were taken.

R. E. LEE.

No. 2.

Reports of Brig. Gen. John C. Vaughn, C. S. Army.

BRISTOL, February 20, 1865.

A small force from my command struck the railroad at Athens, west of Knoxville, capturing the garrison, which has caused two regiments to be sent below from this force above Knoxville.

J. C. VAUGHN, Brig.-Gen.

OR, Ser. I, Vol. 49, pt. I, p. 47.

22 Depredations committed by Federal soldiers in McMinnville; an excerpt from the journal of Lucy Virginia French

...some Yanks came — wanting milk — they said. I met them at the back door — spoke pleasantly but held the door knob in my hand. I saw they were preparing to come in but I did not invite them and bolting the door, directed them to Mammy's house to get the milk. They went— dreadfully dissatisfied and grumbled to the servants that I had not asked them to come in the house. They were gentlemen, had been raised— never had been in any place before but what they were asked in the house, if they had been officers she would have asked them in — if they had been secesh etc. etc. etc., until Mammy and Puss said they thought both were born fools. The servants told them I never asked soldiers in the house — soldiers did not expect it and have no right to expect it — they usually come to get something and if I had it I gave it and they went away — if they expected to be invited in they most[ly] come with some friend to introduce them etc. etc. Finally they commenced about killing chickens...— then they wanted milk which was brought — then walnuts — these also were furnished — some wanted bread and this was handed over also — then they went off after examining all the outhouses, etc. carefully — for what I do not know. Just as dinner was on the table and we sitting down to it here they came again — whiz! Bang! Went the rocks everywhere. They were after the chickens, and they carried them off in triumph. Not all satisfied however, for they came back 3 times after more but failed to catch them. Mammy was so mad she was fit to fly and Puss was quite as much exasperated.

War Journal of Lucy Virginia French, February 26, 1865.

24 Capture of Confederate navy officers attempting commando attacks upon Tennessee River shipping

HDQRS. DISTRICT OF EAST TENNESSEE AND FOURTH DIVISION, TWENTY-THIRD ARMY CORPS, Knoxville, Tenn., February 25, 1865 — 7.15 P.M. [Received 27th.]

Maj. S. HOFFMAN, Asst. Adjt. Gen., Department of the Cumberland, Nashville:

Two officers in the uniform of and claiming to belong to the Confederate navy were captured yesterday near Loudon. They state they were of a party sent from Richmond to destroy the bridges and steamboats on the Tennessee River. The balance of the party made their escape and are still at large.

DAVIS TILLSON, Brig.-Gen., U.S. Volunteers, Cmdg. District and Division.

HDQRS. DISTRICT OF EAST TENNESSEE AND FOURTH DIVISION, TWENTY-THIRD ARMY CORPS, Knoxville, Tenn., February 25, 1865.

Maj. Gen. JAMES B. STEEDMAN, Chattanooga:

Two officers in the uniform of and claiming to belong to the Confederate navy were captured yesterday near Loudon. They state they were of a party sent to capture and destroy the steam-boats on the river. The remainder of the party made their escape and are still at large; they may attempt to carry out their plan. I respectfully suggest that guards on the boats be increased and cautioned to exercise unusual vigilance.

DAVIS TILLSON, Brig.-Gen., U.S. Volunteers, Cmdg. District and Division.

OR, Ser. I, Vol. 49, pt. I, p. 769.

♦ MARCH ♦

1 Major-General R. H. Milroy's secret

...My brother Jim come out her about ten days ago to get a cotton farm. There is a large amount of Cole Oil region in Tennessee. I put Jim [on it], after getting all he could lease. He has already ... with a few others leased a large amount of valuable lands which will be immensely valuable some day and he is going ahead and will probably have the most valuable oil possessions in the U.S. I am a secret partner with him but keep this a secret as it was not alowed of army officers....

...

Papers of General Milroy, p. 498.

5 Rebel Riverine Commando Team Captured

Acting Rear-Admiral S. P. Lee, Commanding the Mississippi Squadron, General Orders No. 48.

On last Sunday morning, [5th] Captain Chapman, a pilot on the steamboat *Chickamauga,* being at his home at Chapman's Landing on the Tennessee River, 4 miles below Kingston, noticed that the rebel women of his neighborhood were moving around the country rather more than usual. These proceedings attracted his attention, because they are an infallible indication of some rebel movement being on foot. Thinking that perhaps some rebels from the army had returned to their homes, he took his gun and started out to see what was up. He went down toward the river, and had not gone off his own place before he made a startling discovery. Hauled close in to the shore, and concealed by brush from the view of any one passing up or down the river, was a large yawl, without any occupants, but heavily loaded with several boxes and various packages. Captain Chapman was within 20 feet of the boat before he discovered it. Immediately suspecting the state of affairs, he looked around to see if the owners of the boat were near, but could see no one. In a moment or two more his attention was attracted by hearing a gun cap snap. Without making any display of his having discovered the boat, he returned to his own house and then he started off to find some citizens to aid him. Gathering six of them together, he returned to the neighborhood where the boat was fastened. Here he discovered nine men on a hill about a half mile from where the boat had landed. Disposing his little force so as to get between them and their boat, he made a bold show of what men he had, and issuing orders to imaginary troops, called upon the rebels to lay down their arms and surrender. Their guns and ammunition having been wet by the recent heavy rains, and believing that a superior force was around them, they immediately complied; one of them however, after laying down his gun, jumped down the hill and disappeared. After laying down their arms they were ordered to march off a few yards, when their guns were secured. The whole party then proceeded to the boat. On the road the rebels asked where the rest of their captors were, and upon being informed that the seven present-on an old man, and one a mere boy-were the only force, the expressed great chagrin that, after having run hundreds of miles through the Federal pickets, they should at last be capture by "tories." On arriving at the boat it was thoroughly inspected, but its load was treated with the greatest care, no one even desiring to touch the various articles of which it was composed. The boat itself was a regular-built yawl, 30 feet long, 3 feet deep, and 6 feet wide at the bottom, flaring out considerably. It is calculated to carry 40 men, and hold between 3 and 4 tons. It had "No. 3" painted on the sides. There were six oars in the boat, and were said by those who handled them to be of the very best make. Each oar is 16 feet long and was muffled. Each man in the party had a fine Enfield musket and a regular navy cutlass. One of the cutlasses was shown to us; including the handle, it is 23 inches in length, and the blade is nearly two inches wide. On the handle are the letters "C. S. N." The boxes found in the boat are 1½ feet wide and 2 feet long, each containing a torpedo. A large number of fireballs, made by soaking balls of cotton in turpentine, were also found, but the most dangerous article of all was a sort of hand grenade and fireball combined. It was 6 inches in diameter and 10 inches long, and appears to have been made by winding cotton around some sort of an infernal machine. At one end is a cap so that the affair would burst on striking any hard substance, and, as if to make the assurance doubly sure, a fuze was inserted at the lower end, so that it might be lighted and would burn for some time before exploding. A network of copper wire kept the cotton in shape, and wooden handles 2 feet long were fixed in it, for the purpose of throwing the machine for some distance. As if the cotton itself was not inflammable enough, it had been dipped in some gummy preparation to make it burn fiercer. After examining everything, the prisoners were sent with a strong guard, to Kingston. After they started, Captain Chapman went over the fields to find the fellow that had escaped, and fortunately caught him within a short distance of where his companions had surrendered. The steamer *Lookout* came along about this time, and she took the yawl in tow, and the prisoners being placed on board, she went on to Kingston, where the Holston, received the precious boat and started with it for Knoxville.

One of the men captured had been keeping a diary, and from that and their conversation we learn somewhat of their plans and proceedings, though the former appear almost too rash and reckless for belief. It seems that the boat was built in Richmond, and its crew was composed of picked men from what the rebels term the Confederate States Navy. Leaving Richmond on the 3d of January last, they came to Bristol by rail, and went from there to the salt works, where the boat was placed on the waters of the Holston River. Their progress down the Holston was delayed by the low water, so that they were compelled to lay by for several days. They first passed the Federal pickets at Kingsport. We have heard that in passing under the bridge at Knoxville, they attempted to set fire to it, but were frightened off by the sentinels. They themselves say that their instructions were to commit no depredations until they got below Kingston. In passing under the bridge at Loudon they were hailed by the sentinels, but on replying that they were a trading boat, they were allowed to go on. After passing Loudon they stopped, and two of the chief officers went ashore and were captured by some of our forces, who came across them in some way. After waiting for these officers till they felt certain that they were captured, the boat under command of a Lieutenant Wharton, went on until they were finally discovered at Kingston. As to their plans, they may or may not be what they stated them to be, but they were certainly dangerous. After passing Kingston they were to burn every steamer that they could, and they had evidently intended to begin at the place where they were discovered, as it was but a short distance from Chapman's Landing, at which place the steamers are in a habit of stopping to wood. Proceeding down the river, on arriving at Chattanooga, they were to fire all the boats at the landing and depots along Water street. Next, sawmills and the shipyard were to be set on fire. It was supposed that by this time the burning boats and warehouses of the river front would attract the greater portion of the citizens and military to that locality, while they, landing at the foot of Seventh street and coming into the western end of town, would fire the warehouses and depots.

Among the items of news which they communicated was one to the effect that Lee's army was to leave Richmond about the 1st of March and retreat in the direction of East Tennessee. The operations of these men were expected to clear away some of the obstructions to such an advance and render the march of the rebel army into Georgia comparatively easy. Fortunately for the residents of Chattanooga and the preservation of the vast amount of Government property in the shape of steamers depots, and quartermaster and subsistence stores stored about the city, the affair was discovered, and all the parties actively concerned in it arrested. It is to be hoped that if these raiders are found guilty of all the infernal plots with which they have been charged, that they will meet with speedy justice. The fate of Andrews, the Union soldier who, in 1862, attempted to burn the bridges on the Western & Atlantic Railroad, should be taken as a precedent.

Navy OR, Ser. I, Vol. 27, pp. 87–89.

8 Ennui brought about by reports about guerrilla activity in West Tennessee

According to the Memphis *Bulletin*, there appears to be no end of guerrilla outrages coming under the purview of the local editor. We are tired of copying them.

New Orleans *Times*, March 8, 1865.

9–10 Guerrilla activity near Memphis
Killing, Robbing and Whipping.

The Memphis *Bulletin* of the 9th and 10th has the following pleasant record:

AN ATTROCIOIUS MURDER — THE VICTIM STRIPPED.

A very inoffensive young man, named Allender, who lives near the State Line Road, was out shooting on last Tuesday with a small shot gun, when he was met by guerrillas, who ordered him to give up his gun. He refused, saying that as it was for only firing small shot, it would be useless to them. The guerrillas advanced to take the gun, when

Allender prevented it, threatening to shoot if any one assailed him. At this two of the guerrillas drew their revolvers and shot him dead. They then rifled his pocked, and stripping the body, carried off the clothes.-*Memphis Bulletin, 9th*.

GUERRILLA OUTRAGE—*Two Southern Men Hung.*—Two men who had been into Memphis with teams and colored drivers, to sell cotton, were, on Tuesday, going out on the Hernando road, and when a few miles from the city, they were met by guerrillas, who charged them with being Union men. The imputation was denied, but this did not satisfy the guerrillas, who robbed them of a considerable sum of money whipped the negro drivers in a most inhuman manner, and finally hung the two cotton sellers, whose names were White and Johnson. From one of these murdered men the guerrillas took over three hundred dollars.-*Memphis Bulletin, 9th*.

COTTON BUYER HUNG.—A man named George Sterling, who lived outside the line on the Raleigh road, and has been accustomed to purchase cotton and bring it into Memphis, was caught on last Wednesday by guerrillas, who robbed him of $500, and then hung him.-*Ib*.

WHIPPING AND HANGING.—*A Bloody Fight.*—Two men, names Robert Jackson and Wm. Flood, own farms on the Hernando road, ten or eleven miles from the city, and had both been reported guerrillas when the occasion offered. Some misunderstanding recently occurred between them and this led to a collision on Wednesday. They fought with bowie knives, and the contest was of the most desperate and sanguinary character. One of the men was almost literally hacked to pieces, and lived but a few minutes. The other still lives, but is dangerously wounded., *Ib., 10th*.

DARING ROBBERIES—*Increase of Crime.*—A man named Flannegan, an employee on the steamer Fanny, was going through Shelby street last Wednesday night, and a short distance from the Gayoso House was assailed by two men, one of whom sprang from behind a post and the other from an alley. Having no warning, he was unable to defend himself, and being knocked down, he was, while insensible, robbed of one hundred and twenty dollars. The desperadoes escaped before Flannegan recovered his senses.

A man named John Dunn was going up the wharf last Wednesday night, when two men met and asked him the time of night. Mr. Dunn pulled out his watch to give the desired information, when one of the rascals grabbed it and started to run. Dunn called loudly for the watch, and ran after the escaping thief, but the accomplice tripped him up, and they escaped before he regained his perpendicular.

The house of Mrs. Richards, on Poplar street, was entered by two burglars early on Wednesday evening. They asked her whether she had any money, and getting no satisfactory answer, the rummaged her house and found fifteen dollars. Mrs. Richards screamed for help, but one of the rascals seized had compelled her by threats to keep quiet, until, having secured her watch and a lot of clothing, they escaped.

William Watson was going through Beal street near the market on Monday night, when he was knocked down and robbed of sixty dollars.

...

New Orleans *Times*, March 15, 1865.

10 Return of religious animosities between the Presbyterian and Episcopal congregations in Bolivar

To-day was the day appointed by our President [Jefferson Davis] as a day of fasting and prayer. I for one observed it, though perhaps not with the right spirit. All the animosity which formerly existed (but which we had hoped had completely died out) between the Presbyterian and Episcopalian churches seems with the last few days to have been revived. Everybody is talking of *the* church some think one some the other. Everybody is commenting on a book which the Episcopalian Minister is circulating by the name of "A Presbyterian Minister in search of *The* Church" which our pastor pronounced (also any good sensed person) a collection of falsehoods to deceive the ignorant. There is a class of young ladies who intend being confirmed, and this book is given preparatory to confirmation. How wrong to cultivate feeling so injurious to the cause of Christ and so unchristian like in their bearing, instead of cultivating feelings of goodwill toward all men in imitation of our gentle Jesus. The apple of discord has now been thrown among us. Father is divided against Son, Mother against daughter, all ties of Christian affection completely and perhaps forever surrendered.... Yankees reported in eight miles of town this morning. At LaGrange this evening, also at Salisbury, I believe.

Diary of Sally Wendel Fentress, March 10, 1865.

10 Guerrilla Outrages in Tennessee

The Memphis *Bulletin* of the 4th prefaces another half column of guerrilla items with these remarks:

Very few persons have any idea of the reign of terror that exists just outside our army lines. The numberless rages, murders, robberies and conscriptions that daily occur are not, in most cases, known in the city until some days after they happen.

New Orleans *Times*, March 10, 1865.

13 The case of the unwed widow and the recovery of an unfaithful husband in Memphis

A Boarding House Incident.- It is reported that among the ladies of Memphis who object to being considered the keepers of boarding houses, but for a liberal compensation take a few respectable ladies had gentlemen as members of families, is a widow with some pretensions to good looks and with very stylish notions. This attractive lady has as a member of her family, a handsome and carefully gotten up gentleman, who had resigned his commission from the army, and devoted himself to social enjoyment. It was rumored that he and the widow were about to marry, and everybody thought it was a very suitable match, except that the lady had been quite secesh, and the gentleman being from the northwest was supposed to be a little of an abolitionist. Thus matters stood, when on last Monday [13th] night the widow and her admirer, having paid a visit to the Vincent's for supper, returned home in the best of spirits. How long they sat in conversation, no one knows, but some time after midnight a good looking, but plainly dressed lady, who had come down the river on the steamer *Belle Memphis*, and had, it appears, been some time prospecting in the widow's premises, knocked at the widow's chamber. How she got in the house no one knows. Perhaps she bribed the servants; but, somehow, in she got and knocked at the widow's door until it was opened, when in she sprang, just as an exit was made from a window. The widow says it was a cat that jumped out. However this may be, the strange lady found, safe in his bed, her husband, for it turned out that she was the wife of the Northern gentleman whom the widow was supposed to marry. The next morning the husband and wife left Memphis without bidding adieu to the widow, who has very little to say about the matter.-Memphis *Bulletin*, 18th

New Orleans *Times*, March 28, 1865.

22 The death and funeral of a slave in the French household in McMinnville

...on Wednesday morning, the 22nd at about 7 o'clock, poor Martha passed away from earth — I trust into a heavenly rest. I felt very badly on that day — the winds roared and raved everywhere — shook the windows, and drove the smoke down the chimneys. I had a fire made in the front bed-room, where I staid with the children after we got Martha laid out, and all the house clean and quiet. I made wreaths to put over her of white peach blooms and hyacinths and arbor-vitae. She looked very natural. That evening Mollie came and how glad I was to see her! I had been feeling so sick, and lonely and depressed all day. M. had heard in the evening that Martha was dead, and came right off as soon as school was out, walking three miles and crossing the river on horseback behind a negro — to get here. I was so grateful to her. That night there was a room full of negros to sit up — I sent them in refreshments about midnight — coffee, cordial, bread, fresh peaches, etc. They were very quiet and orderly, no noise except when some one slipped out for wood to replenish the fire — and the sound of the hymns the sung all thro' the night. I could not help feeling sorry for the negros — times are so changed with them from what they were before this war. Their merry-makings then were so numerous and so characteristic — as also were peculiar ways of conducting all these things, which were characteristic — and so picturesque — if I may use the term. In a few years these things will pass away — be merged in Yankee customs — in accordance with, and obedience to that old Puritanic spirit which will never permit anybody to speak, act, or thing but just as it thinks, speaks and acts. Let us of the South be not boastful that we are a separate and different people — but grateful. On the next morning — Thursday — about 10 o'clock she was dressed in a white dotted swiss — a Sunday dress I had given her last spring-with wreaths placed around her, and white hyacinths on her bosom and her hands which were bound with white ribbon. No church member could be found to sing and pray as is customary among them — so I read a portion of the burial services as well as I could — standing at the head of her coffins, and Mollie who stood by me sang a hymn — "When I can read my title clear." There were none but women at the burial, except Mr. R., and old Uncle Moss whose wagon took the coffin to the grave. The [negro] men were here at night, when they could steal in, but in day time most of them were in hiding. All went from here by Mammy and myself— neither of us being well. Mollie did not return...

War Journal of Lucy Virginia French, March 27, 1865.

25 "The Negro Celebration": Nashville's African-American community demonstrates its support for the constitutional abolition of slavery in Tennessee

The negroes, old and young, of every hue, shade and color, turned out yesterday to ratify the amendment to the State constitution abolishing slavery in Tennessee. The procession formed on Capitol Hill, at about 10 o'clock, and came down Cedar street with streaming banners, headed by a brass band, discoursing sweet strains to the slow and measured march of the "regenerated contrabands." A dense cloud of dust enveloped the procession and it was only visible at intervals. As they passed up College street, we caught a glimpse of the motley throng. The soldiers were in the van, followed by the "Order of the Sons of Relief," wearing "yaller regalias." Next came the "free American citizens of African descent," in their Sunday clothes, followed by the female portion of the colored procession. The juvenile darkies brought up the rear of this moving panorama, and at intervals the air resounded with shouts of glory from the enthusiastic crowd. The Marshals of the day were mounted, and highly decorated with all the colors of the rainbow. Among the devices or mottos born aloft, we noted the following:

"Will Tennessee be among the first or last to allow her sable sons the elective franchise?"

"United we stand, divided we fall."

"Nashville Order of Sons of Relief."

"We ask not social, but political equality."

"We can forget and forgive the wrongs of the past."

"We aspire to elevation through industry, economy, education and christianity."

After marching through the principal streets of the city, the procession wended its way to Walnut Grove, in the western environs of the city, where they were addressed by several able orators. The principal theme of the different speakers was the elective franchise, which right they emphatically claimed, and would petition the Legislature for it at its first session. If it was not granted by that body, they would thunder at the doors of the Capitol until their voices were heard, and the political equality of their race established.

The procession called to mind the familiar old melody of "Old Joe kicking up behind and before, and the yellow gal is kicking up behind old Joe."

Nashville *Dispatch*, March 25, 1865.

29 "The 'Forty Thieves.'"

This gang of juvenile thieves are still operating in our city. Yesterday several of them were engaged in selling oranges and lemons, with a basket on their arms. They resort to every petty species of merchandising to avert suspicion, and under the cover of their traffic, succeed in robbing their victims. We are informed that a portion of the gang left for Huntsville and Chattanooga yesterday morning to prosecute their labors in a more "congenial clime." Some five or six of them have been arrested here, and convicted. This may tend to disperse the band, as the police and citizens are on the alert for them. Their debut in Nashville has proved very unsuccessful, and there is no prospect of their keeping out of the clutches of our police if they remain. Under these circumstances we would suggest to "the boys" that they procure a pass from the Provost Marshal and return to Louisville. They may be sufficiently skilled in the art of picking pockets and stealing calico, for that city, but they are sadly deficient in the necessary requisites for their business in such a city as this. Stealing has been reduced to a science here, and the most proficient of the calling are "gobbled" daily. It is folly of the "forty thieves" or any other thieves to enter into competition with the experts of this place, Dick Turpin and Sixteen String Jack,* if they were living, would starve to death in less than a week in this city, if they were not assassinated before they got fairly under way.

Nashville *Dispatch*, March 29, 1865.

---

*Dick Turpin and John Rann, also known as Sixteen String Jack, were highwaymen during the 1700s. Dick Turpin plied his trade in England and was hanged in 1739. Sixteen String Jack, so named for the eight strings with tassels at each knee of his breeches, terrorized Scotland until his hanging in 1774. Thanks to Kassandra Hassler, TSL&A Reference Department.

♦ APRIL ♦

1 "These bushmen have been troubling the Southern citizens very much."

The boys came down today. Kyle, Nick Mc, Sam Fain and Mr. Pinkerton. They were out on a scout Friday night in Caney Valley-were fired on by bushmen. All escaped unhurt. I feel so thankful when a kind Providence directs the balls aimed at them in another direction. These bushmen have been troubling the Southern citizens very much. I fear they may be permitted to go on by the Federal Government until our men shall become desperate and turn upon the Union folks with a feeling of desperation. They have been restrained by our Government and female influence. Women of the South have generally urged our Soldiers to do right but they are beginning to feel entreaty will be useless.

Fain Diary.

2 Mourning for the Confederacy in McMinnville

Little or no change that we know of in the status of our country's fortunes in the past few days. We received some papers yesterday ... but beyond the rumor of an engagement said to have taken place between Joe Johnston and a portion of Sherman's forces at Bentonville N.C. in which the Richmond papers claim a victory for Johnston and all the Yankee press [claim] the same for Sherman.... The North is jubilant a the fact (as they regard it,) that the rebellion is at its last gasp — in desperate and final throes — that this Campaign is to finish it, and the subjugated South is to bow at their feet entreating Peace and Pardon on any terms. And God knows it looks that way — our cause seems hopeless enough. We know that God can help us, if it be His will-that He can and perhaps may lead us in a way we have not known — and we still must trust Him thro all things. For my own part I fear we must go down. I cannot see any small clouds like unto a man's hand upon our horizon, indicating that France will see that her true interests in Mexico lie in befriending us — nor do I dare to hope that Lee, great and glorious as he is, can with his little band oppose the two veteran armies under Sherman and Grant. I long — oh! intensely to see Sherman punished — overwhelmed — annihilated in his arrogance, cruelty and assumption — yet I may not see it. The great and good Lee may go down before these arrant pretenders — and if he should it will be a bitter day for us all — God knows. I have built so much upon the success of the South — it was not wise — it was perhaps wrong too,-yet it was my last hope of Independence politically and on independence personally. We all lay our plans, and generally our plans come to nought. Strange that we should (as it would deem,) so generally set up our will in opposition to His, whose weak children we are! Ho! Our Father make us wiser, in submitting all our ways to Thine! Amen and Amen!...

War Journal of Lucy Virginia French.

5 "They killed old Dr. Simon.... " an entry from the journal of Amanda McDowell

The Rebels have been cutting up again. They killed old Dr. Simon, an old free negro, or mulatto rather. A very respectable and intelligent old man considering the estimation in which darkies are held, but so far as we know perfectly harmless and innocent of anything that could be imputed to him as a crime. I tremble for the men that are still left, for some who have never thought of danger will perhaps be the next to fall. I wish we were safe out of the country, but perhaps a safe place would be hard to find.

Diary of Amanda McDowell.

5 The Fate of the Confederacy and the Faith of a Confederate woman in East Tennessee

Mysterious it is to me why God permitted such a sad calamity to befall our South. Why He permitted the noblest blood of the South to be sacrificed for the bondage of the noble race. Many a bitter tear and sad regret has the termination of this unhappy ending caused me. — unjust as I would deem it, if I did not believe God had decreed it thus.

Diary of Myra Adelaide Inman.

5 Bushmen Plunder Mrs. Fain's Home. An Extract from the Diary of Eliza Rhea Anderson Fain

We still live thanks to our Heavenly Father. This has been a day of intense feeling with us all. This morning about 5 o'clock we were again visited by a set of outlaws such as I have never seen and hope it is the will of my God I shall never look upon such another. I had awakened Dicky to make his fire, heard them coming and said to Lizzie they are upon us get up, I was soon dressed excepting shoes and stockings. They demanded the opening of the door. I opened and Mr. William Sizemore stood before. He said "Good Morning Mrs. Fain, I am here and I intend to tear you up and burn your house down." After saying this he gave orders for them to go ahead. I told him to wait until I could say something to him. I then told him if he began the work retribution would surely take place. He replied "My family are out from here now and I do not care a d__n" and such a scene ensued for about half or three-quarters of an hour I have never witnessed. Doors bursted open, and my house literally full of robbers. They took my silver spoons 7 large, five plated teaspoons, 12 small silver teaspoons and a silver dessert spoon — all the mean in my smokehouse and many other things and last but not least my old horse George with Dickie's saddle.

...

Fain Diary.

6, 7, 12 Reaction, Denial and Despondency in Knoxville. Confederate Lizzie Welcker's reaction to the sudden end of the war

April 6, 1865, The "niggers" are all — men, women and children — out today with the 'star spangled banner' celebrating their freedom.... When — when —*when* will we be delivered?

April 7, 1865. The "news" today is that Gen. Lee has surrendered! L-a-u-g-h!!! I feel certain (although we can't know where Gen L is) that he is in the *right* [sic] place and that he and his gallant soldiers will "act well their parts"— God bless! God revere them all!

April 12, 1865.... Altho I feel dreadfully — my brain seems paralysed — I can but hope that "things are not what they seem."

Lizzie Welcker Diary.

8 A new hat for a Bolivar school girl

...I'm going to get a new hat this month, for the first time in three years. That is a Summer hat, got a winter hat last Winter and I am really ashamed to think of the cost, however it was $15.00, about one of the cheapest. Received a letter from Brother Jimmie a day or two ago. He is again in bad health, unfit for field service....

Diary of Sally Wendel Fentress.

13 Eliza Fain Learns of Lee's Surrender

...We finished [washing] about 3 o'clock. After getting through I came to the house and found Lucy ... with a Chattanooga paper containing the account of Gen. Lee's surrender with his army. It may be true but I do not believe and even were I to believe this it does not for one moment shake my confidence in my God as to the position which the South shall occupy amongst the nations of earth when this struggle shall cease....

Fain Diary.

16 Observing Lincoln's death in Pulaski

GENERAL ORDERS, No. 51. HDQRS. 6TH DIV., CAVALRY CORPS, MILITARY DIVISION OF THE MISSISSIPPI, Pulaski, Tenn., April 16, 1865.

In honor to the memory of Abraham Lincoln, sixteenth President of the United States, of whose death official notice has been received, the general commanding directs that on to-morrow all drills and other duties except those which are indispensable, such as picket and interior guard, be suspended throughout this command; that religious services be held in every regiment having a chaplain; that the public offices, all stores, shops and other places of business and amusement at this post be closed, and that the day be scarcely observed, both by citizens and soldiers, in a manner becoming the mournful occasion. The provost-marshal and the officer of the day for the post are enjoined to see that this order is duly observed. This order to be read at the head of every regiment and detached company in the command at the dress parade of this day.

E. T. WELLS, Assistant Adjutant-Gen.

OR, Ser. I, Vol. 49, pt. II, p. 368.

17 General Orders, No. 44, pertaining to public mourning for Abraham Lincoln in Memphis

GENERAL ORDERS, No. 44. HDQRS. DISTRICT OF WEST TENNESSEE, Memphis, Tenn., April 17, 1865.

The nation mourns the untimely and violent death of the late President of the United States, Abraham Lincoln, and the late Secretary of State, William H. Seward. All officers of this command will wear the usual badge of mourning upon the left arm for thirty days from the date of this order. As a mark of respect to the illustrious dead the public buildings of the city and all places of military business will be closed this day from sunrise to sunset. The funeral gun will be fired at every half hour, beginning at sunrise to sunset.

By order of Maj. Gen. C. C. Washburn:
OR, Ser. I, Vol. 49, pt. II, p. 389.

17 Commencement of mopping up against Confederate guerrillas in East Tennessee
HDQRS. DEPARTMENT OF THE CUMBERLAND, Nashville, April 17, 1865.
Brig. Gen. DAVIS TILLSON, Greeneville, East Tenn.:
(To be forwarded.)
On receipt of this make disposition of your force so as to hold East Tennessee against roving bands of guerrillas. Gen. Stanley has been ordered to this place with his corps. Communicate with Gen. Stoneman as soon as you can, and inform him that I wish him to dispose his entire force to the best advantage to preserve order in East Tennessee and Western North Carolina and to put down guerrillas, as in a short time there will be no formidable force east of the Savannah River. We have Selma and Mobile.
GEO. H. THOMAS, Maj.-Gen., U.S. Army, Cmdg.
OR, Ser. I, Vol. 49, pt. II, p. 381.

17 General Orders No. 45, commencement of mopping up operations in West Tennessee
GENERAL ORDERS, No. 45. HDQRS. DISTRICT OF WEST TENNESSEE, Memphis, Tenn., April 17, 1865.
The fall of Richmond and the capture of the principal rebel army and all the fortified places in the so-called Confederacy east of the Mississippi River, the utter and hopeless prostration of the rebel power, make it apparent that all further fighting on the part of Confederate soldiers within this military district must be from a spirit of pure malice and revenge of for purposes of robbery and plunder, and not in any hope of accomplishing any public good to any State or government. Those who now continue to fight after the liberal terms that have been offered can only be regarded as guerrillas and murderers. There are some small parties of such men roving about West Tennessee, keeping the citizens in a state of excitement and alarm, and who claim when captured to be treated as prisoners of war. All such are notified that if captured within the limits of this military district after the 25th instant they will not be treated as prisoners of war, but will be held for trail as felons and common enemies of mankind. Persons found bearing arms without competent Federal authority will be subject to the provisions of this order. This order is not intended to discourage any from laying down their arms and receiving the amnesty of the President, but to declare that such as are in West Tennessee and do not do it, but continue in open hostility, shall not be exchanged or allowed to take the oath of amnesty after their capture, but shall be tried and punished in accordance with their deserts.
By order of Maj. Gen. C. C. Washburn:
WM. H. MORGAN, Maj. and Assistant Adjutant-Gen.
OR, Ser. I, Vol. 49, pt. II, p. 389.

17 "For truly secession has been the greatest tyrant that ever reigned over this country." News of the fall of the Confederacy reaches Amanda McDowell
The girls keep my ink and things carried off so that I cannot get to write when I want to. There is some great news. I have been looking for a grand smash up for sometime, things have been so still. And [I] guess from all accounts that the great Southern Confederacy is about "gone up for ninety days" as the boys say. The news is (and it is corroborated and told over by every new arrival from Nashville) that Lee, his whole army, Petersburg, Richmond, and some say Davis himself is taken. The latter item is hardly true, but the rest is true, I expect. Some are already rejoicing over the downfall of their oppressors. For truly secession has been the greatest tyrant that ever reigned over this country. For my own part, I try not to rejoice at any one's downfall, but so far as I think will be for the good of their own souls. But I do rejoice in the prospect for peace. Some thing it will certainly be made. I fear we are going to be disappointed by will live in hope. Newton Camron got home yesterday. He has been in prison, but was exchanged and made tracks for home. A year or two ago he felt awfully disgraced because P. came home from the Southern army. I wonder how his pulse beats on the subject now.
Diary of Amanda McDowell.

18 "The enemy were concealed behind some houses, and waited until the patrol got to within 100 yards of them, when they charged." The last

Civil War military action in Tennessee, near Germantown

APRIL 18, 1865.—Skirmish near Germantown, Tenn.

Report of Capt. George W. Smith, Eleventh New York Cavalry.

HDQRS. DETACHMENT ELEVENTH NEW YORK CAVALRY, Germantown, Tenn., April 19, 1865.

CAPT.: I have the honor to report that yesterday as the patrol was marching from Germantown to Collierville it was attacked by a force of the enemy about six miles from Germantown. The force of the enemy is variously estimated from 60 to 100 strong, while the patrol was but eighteen strong, under Lieut. John H. Mills, D Company, this regiment. The enemy were concealed behind some houses, and waited until the patrol got to within 100 yards of them, when they charged. Lieut. Mills drew his men in line, but, after delivering a volley with their carbines, found he would be overpowered be a far superior force, and ordered his men to fall back to the camp at Germantown. He was closely pursued by a well-mounted portion of the enemy to within about two miles of this place (Germantown). The attacking party are supposed to be a part of Ford's command. Those of our men who fell from their horses, or were poorly mounted, were shot. Those who were killed or wounded were robbed of everything, they (the rebels) even taking the boots from some of the dead....

I have just received a telegraph from Maj. Morgan, in which he, by order of Gen. Washburn, directs that no patrols will be sent less than fifty men. I have but 190 men available for duty. Out of that my picket, thirty-two men daily; my scouting parties, thirty men daily, and all the camp duties, have to be taken, leaving me no force at all with which to operate to any advantage. I know of fifty men who are mounted on horses which are serviceable, that are in the camp at the headquarters of the regiment at Memphis. If I can have those men and 100 dismounted men for camp duties, I can operate against these guerrillas to advantage, as I have reliable information concerning their haunts.

Hoping that my request for a few more men may meet your approbation and that it may be complied with at your earliest practicable convenience, I have the honor to be, very respectfully, your obedient servant,

G. W. SMITH, Capt., Cmdg. Detachment Eleventh New York Cavalry.

...

OR, Ser. I, Vol. 49, pt. I, pp. 512–513.

18–22 Anti-insurgent patrols, Fulton and Van Buren's landings, Tipton County, along Hatchie River to Brownsville, and Randolph, execution of guerrilla leader

SPECIAL ORDERS, No. 102. HDQRS. DISTRICT OF WEST TENNESSEE, Memphis, Tenn., April 18, 1865.

For the purpose of capturing Quantrill and his band of about sixty men now operating on the Hatchie River, and Mat Luxton, with his band of about twenty, now operating in the same region, and other enemies, the following troops, will be sent out, viz.,: Two hundred and fifty cavalry on the steamer *John Raine*, upon which they will embark at 5 P.M. to-day; 350 cavalry on barges in charge of steamers *Raine* and *Cleona* at same hour. The steamers will proceed up the river and land the troops on the barges at Randolph, and will then proceed immediately to Fulton and land the troops on the steamer. The steamer will then return to Fulton. The troops landed at Fulton will dash forward to Ripley and Brownsville, and will send a party to Brownsville Landing same night, where they will meet the steam-boats of the expedition. Two hundred of the troops landed at Randolph will dash forward to Covington, and will scour the country and reach Brownsville Landing same night. One hundred and fifty cavalry will dash forward, via Portersville or Beaverdam, to Brownsville Landing, and pursue, destroy, and kill all guerrillas they may find. The steamers *Cleona*, *Dove*, and *Pocahontas* will proceed to-night at 5 o'clock up the Mississippi and Hatchie rivers, each with fifty cavalry and fifty infantry on board, and will form a junction with the rest of the command at Brownsville Landing. From that point the commander of the expedition will move as the object of the expedition may require, and will return to Memphis overland or by boat and barges as may be thought best. The cavalry will take three days' rations, and two days' rations of forage will be placed on one of the Hatchie boats, and three days' rations for the men. All commanding officers are enjoined to maintain the strictest discipline and allow no marauding or ill treatment of citizens, but citizens must be required to give information in regard to guerrilla whereabouts so far as they know, or they will be regarded as harboring and encouraging them.

By order of Maj. Gen. C. C. Washburn:

OR, Ser. I, Vol. 49, pt. II, p. 406.

Report of James Fitzpatrick, Acting Master, commanding U.S.S. *Siren*, Off Randolph, Tenn., April; 22, 1865

...

April 19 an expedition under command of Brigadier general Osband started for Brownsville, Tenn., in three columns; one from this place, one by way of Hatchee River, and one from Fulton, Tenn.

They returned this afternoon, having been successful in capturing 1 colonel, 1 major, 4 captains, 2 lieutenants, and 12 men, and killing General Shelby's adjutant. One of the men captured is the fellow that has been passing for Luxton. General Osband hung him from a cottonwood tree at this place this evening; his body is still hanging from the tree.

He confessed to burning the *St. Paul* and to killing one man on board of her. His proper name is Wilcox. His father lives in Memphis, Tenn.

The steamers *Anna, Everton,* and *Sylph* were not burned by the guerrillas. They came out of Hatchee River this afternoon.

Very respectfully, your obedient servant,

JAMES FITZPATRICK, Acting Master, U.S. S. *Siren*.

Navy OR, Ser. I, Vol. 27, p. 149.

19 News of the end of the war reaches an incredulous Madison County farmer

...Mart.... says it is not so that Lee has been captured, on the contrary formed a junction with Johns[t]on & ruined Sherman. There was a paper in town yesterday, the Cairo *Eagle*, in mourning for the death of Lincoln & Seward, said to be assassinated about the 15th by Booth an actor.... Dr. Brown stopped here ... said he saw a paper in town. The Memphis paper states that Johns[t]on ... surrendered ... Kirby Smith ... surrendered ... and Forrest was on his way to Vicksburg to surrender....

I gave these items as [a] sample of what [the] papers contain, not a word of truth in them.

Robert H. Cartmell Diary.

19 Guerrilla attack on railroad train near Morristown and civilian accountability

No circumstantial reports filed.

KNOXVILLE, April 20, 1865.

Maj. Gen. G. H. THOMAS:

The guerrillas threw a train off the track at midnight last night near Morristown, burned thirteen cars and injured the engine. The train was not guarded. The wreck is cleared and trains are all in motion. Trains hereafter will be guarded, and rebel citizens, of which there are none other from New Market to Morristown, held accountable for outrages.

D. S. STANLEY, Maj.-Gen.

OR, Ser. I, Vol. 49, pt. II, p. 414.

23 News of the assassination of Lincoln reaches Lucy Virginia French

A great tragedy has been enacted, since my last writing, in the assassination of Lincoln and Seward. The first we heard of it was on last Thursday evening. I was out in the front yard clipping some cedars when the Col. came to the door — he had just come up from the garden, in his shirtsleeves — and he said very quietly, "Well, Lincoln's dead!" I had not the smallest idea it was true. Mrs. Myers sent Billy out to tell us. The Col. went in town directly to learn the particulars. The story then ran that Lincoln and Johnson had been at the theatre together — a man had rushed up and stabbed both — killing Lincoln and mortally wounding Johnson, and the assassin had himself been killed on the instant. That was all anybody knew. Next day, in addition, comes the report that Seward had his throat cut also — then I didn't believe any of the story. Thursday, however, a courier came from Tulahoma and Mollie came up from Woodbury. The story then ran that Lincoln and Mrs. L. went to the theatre — Mr. L. was shot in the head in his box by Wilkes Booth a son of Booth, the actor, and that he escaped on a fleet horse. The same evening Seward's room was entered — his two sons were murdered and he himself had his throat cut from ear to ear. Andy Johnson and Gen. Grant were included in the conspiracy, but they escaped, and Andy was inaugurated next day — Thus goes the rumor, and we've heard nothing more of any account. There was intense excitement in Nashville — some 10 men killed for rejoicing over Lincoln's death. Gen. Milroy, at Tullahoma also had some of his soldiers shot for the same, it is said. We are told that about 30 citizens of Nashville were arrested because they implicated Andy in the assassination of "Honest Abe." Some person in Murfreesboro took the crape from their doors, which had been placed there by military order — the houses were entered and the furniture destroyed or carried off. In town here many put mourning on their doors — both parties, but no such order was issued. The soldiers, however, exerted themselves to draw citizens into some expression of joy over the tragedy — so that they would have a pretext for ill using them. I feel that it is dreadful,-a tragedy solemn even to awfulness.

War Journal of Lucy Virginia French.

28 The end of the war is accepted by a Madison County farmer

Lizzie came from school this evening says there is news in town. The substance as she gives it, is that there is to be no more fighting & peace is to be made. If true it would be glorious news, even considering the future is no easy one....

Robert H. Cartmell Diary.

Bibliography

Books, Periodicals and Publications

Abbott, Martin, ed. "The South As Seen by a Tennessee Unionist in 1865: Letters of H.M. Watterson." *Tennessee Historical Quarterly* 18 (1959): 148–161.

Allardice, Bruce S. "In Search of General William Henry Caroll [1811–1866]." *West Tennessee Historical Society Papers* 48 (1994): 60–72. Carroll of Memphis was a brigadier general in Tennessee's Confederate army.

Allen, David C., ed. *Winds of Change: Robertson County, Tennessee in the Civil War*. Nashville: Land Yacht, 2000.

Alley, Charles. *Civil War Diary of Lieut. Charles Alley, Company "C," 5th Iowa Cavalry*. TSL&A, typescript.

Andersen, Mary Ann, ed. *The Civil War Diary of Allen Morgan Geer: Twentieth Regiment, Illinois Volunteers*. Denver, CO: R.C. Appleman, 1977.

Anecdotes, Poetry, and Incidents of the War: North and South, 1860–1865, New York: Publication Office, Bible House, 1867.

Angle, Paul M., ed. *Three Years in the Army of the Cumberland: The Letters and Diary of Major James A. Connelly*. Bloomington: Indiana University Press, 1959, rpt. 1987 by Vesta Angle.

Armiensto, Ferdinand L.S. *Life of Pauline Cushman, the Celebrated Union Spy and Scout*. New York: United States Book Co., 186[?].

Armour, Robert. *The Attack Upon and Defense of Fort Sanders, Knoxville, Tennessee, November 29, 1863: An Eyewitness Account*. Knoxville: Fine Arts, 1991.

Arnold, James R. *Chickamauga, 1863: The River of Death*. Osprey Military Campaign Series, no. 17. London: Osprey, 1992.

Ash, Stephen V. "Sharks in an Angry Sea: Civilian Resistance and Guerilla Warfare in Occupied Middle Tennessee, 1862–1865." *Tennessee Historical Quarterly* 45 no. 3 (1986): 217–229.

_____. *When the Yankees Came: Conflict and Chaos in the Occupied South, 1861–1865*. Chapel Hill: University of North Carolina Press, 1995.

Atkins, Jonathan M. "Politicians, Parties, and Slavery: The Second Party System and the Decision for Disunion in Tennessee." *Tennessee Historical Quarterly* 55, no. 1 (1996): 20–39.

Bailey, Fred Arthur, *Class and Tennessee's Confederate Generation*. The Fred W. Morrison Series in Southern Studies. Chapel Hill: University of North Carolina Press, 1987, 45–76.

Bakeless, John. *Spies of the Confederacy*. Philadelphia, PA: Lippincott, 1970.

Balen, Penny. "After the Smoke Cleared." Thesis, University of Colorado, 1991. Study of Battle of Franklin.

Banks, Robert W. *The Battle of Franklin, November 30, 1864, the Bloodiest Engagement of the War Between the States*. New York: Neale, 1908.

Barber, Flavel C. *Holding the Line: The Third Tennessee Infantry, 1861–1864*, ed. Robert H. Ferrell. Kent, Ohio: Kent State University Press, 1994.

Barnes, James. *David G. Farragut*. Beacon Biographies of Eminent Americans. Boston: Small, Maynard, 1899.

Barrington, Ben. "'Old Straight' Alexander Peter Stewart, 1821–1908." *Courier* 22, no. 1 (1983): 4–5. Confederate general, professor at Cumberland University, Nashville.

Bates, Walter Lynn. "Southern Unionists: A Socio-Economic Examination of the Third East Tennessee Volunteer Infantry Regiment, U.S.A." *Tennessee Historical Quarterly* 50, no. 4 (1991): 226–239.

"The Battles for Chattanooga," *Civil War Times Illustrated* (Special Supplement), August 1971, 4–50.

The Battle of Franklin, Tennessee, November 30, 1864: A Monograph. New York: Scribners, 1897.

The Battle of Stones River. N.p.: Eastern Acorn, 1987.

Baumgardner, James L. "Abraham Lincoln, Andrew Johnson, and the Federal Patronage: An Attempt to Save Tennessee for the Union?" *East Tennessee Historical Society Publications* 45 (1973): 51–60.

Baxter, Colin F. "Baxter Bean, Civil War Dentist: An East Tennessean's Victorian Tragedy." *JETH* 67 (1995): 34–57.

Beard, William E. *The Battle of Nashville; Including an Outline of the Stirring Events Occurring in One of the Most Notable Movements of the Civil War—Hood's In-*

vasion of Tennessee. Nashville: Marshall and Bruce, 1913.

———. "The Pathfinder of the Seas." *Tennessee Historical Quarterly* 5 (1946): 320–327.

Bearss, Edwin C. "Cavalry Operations in the Battles of Stones River." *Tennessee Historical Quarterly* 19 (1960): 23–53, 110–144.

———. "A Confederate Private at Fort Donelson, 1862." *AHR* 31 (1925-26): 477–484.

———. "The Construction of Fort Henry and Fort Donelson." *West Tennessee Historical Society Papers* 21 (1967): 24–47.

———. "The Fall of Fort Henry, Tennessee." *West Tennessee Historical Society Papers* 17 (1963): 85–107.

———. *Forrest at Brice's Cross Roads and in North Mississippi in 1864*. Dayton, OH: Press of Morningside Bookshop, 1979.

———. "General John Hunt Morgan's Second Kentucky Raid (December, 1862)." Part 2: "Morgan Attacks Elizabethtown." *Register of the Kentucky History Society* 70 (April 1972): 177–188. Part 3: "Morgan Begins His Return to Middle Tennessee." *Register of the Kentucky History Society* 70 (October 1972): 426–438.

———. "The Ironclads at Fort Donelson." Part 1: "The Ironclads Sail for the Cumberland." *Register of the Kentucky History Society* 74 (1976): 1–9. Part 2: "The Confederates Prepare for the Ironclads." *Register of the Kentucky History Society* 74 (1976): 73–84. Part 3: "The Ironclads Fail." *Register of the Kentucky History Society* 74 (1976): 167–191.

———. "Unconditional Surrender: The Fall of Fort Donelson." *Tennessee Historical Quarterly* 21 (1962): 47–65, 140–161.

Beasley, Gaylon Neil. *True Tales of Tipton: Historical Accounts of Tipton County, Tennessee*. ovington: Tipton County Historical Society, 1981.

Beaty, Janice. *Seeker of Seaways: A Life of Matthew Fontaine Maury, Pioneer Oceanographer*. New York: Pantheon, 1966.

Beatty, John. *Citizen Soldier: Or Memoirs of a Volunteer*. Cincinnati: Dispatch Baldwin & Co., 1979.

Bejach, Lois D. "The Battle of Moscow, Tennessee." *West Tennessee Historical Society Papers* 27 (1973): 108–112.

———. "The Journal of a Civil War 'Commando': DeWitt Clinton Fort." *West Tennessee Historical Society Papers* 2 (1948): 5–32.

Bejach, Wilena Roberts. "Civil War Letters of a Mother and Son." *West Tennessee Historical Society Papers* 4 (1950): 50–71.

Belz, Herman. "The Etheridge Conspiracy of 1863: A Projected Conservative Coup." *Journal of Southern History* 36, no. 4 (1970): 549–67.

Bentley H. Blair. "Morale as a Factor in the Confederate Failure at Island Number Ten." *West Tennessee Historical Society Papers* 31 (1977): 117–131.

Bentz, Charles, and Yong W. Kim, eds. *The Sevierville Hill Site: A Civil War Union Encampment on the Southern Heights of Knoxville, Tennessee*. Tennessee Anthropological Association Miscellaneous Paper no. 17. Knoxville: Tennessee Anthropological Association, 1993.

Berry, Sue, and Martha Fuqua, eds. *Homespun Tales: The Battle of Franklin*. Franklin Pioneer's Corner Association, 1989.

Bevens, William E. *Reminiscences of a Private: William E. Bevens of the First Arkansas Infantry, C. S.A.*, intro. and ed. by Daniel L. Sutherland, Fayetteville: University of Arkansas Press, 1992.

Bible, Donahue. *Broken Vessels: The Story of the Hanging of the "Pottertown" Bridge—Burners, November—December, 1861*. Mohawk, TN: Dodson Creek, 1996.

Bickham, William D. *Rosecrans' Campaign with the Fourteenth Army Corps; or, The Army of the Cumberland: A Narrative of Personal Observations, with Official Reports of the Battle of Stones River*. Cincinnati, OH: Moore, Wilstach, Keys and Co., 1863.

Biel, John G., ed. "The Battle of Shiloh: From the Letters and Diary of Joseph Dimmitt Thompson." *Tennessee Historical Quarterly* 17 (1958): 250–274.

Billings, John D. *Hard Tack and Coffee, or the Unwritten Story of Army Life*. np: 1887.

Black, Robert C. *The Railroads of the Confederacy*. Chapel Hill: University of North Carolina Press, 1952.

Black, Roy W., Sr., ed. "William J. Rogers' Memorandum Book." *West Tennessee Historical Society Papers* 9 (1955): 59–92.

Blair, William Alan. *A Politician Goes to War: The Civil War Letters of John White Geary*. University Park: Pennsylvania State University Press, 1995.

Blakely, Arch Fredric. *General John H. Winder, C.S.A.* Gainesville: University of Florida Press, 1990.

Blankenship, Gary R. "Fielding Hurst, Tennessee Story: A Study of a West Tennessee Unionist of the American Civil War." Thesis, University of Memphis, 1977.

Blevins, Jerry. *Sequatchie Valley Soldiers in the Civil War: Bledsoe, Grundy, Mario and Sequatchie Counties in Tennessee and Jackson County in Alabama*. Huntsville, AL: The author, 1990.

Bodnia, George, ed. "Fort Pillow 'Massacre': Observations of a Minnesotan [Charles Robinson]." *Minnesota History* 43 (Spring 1973): 186–190.

Bogle, Robert V. "Defeat through Default: Confederate Naval Strategy for the Upper Mississippi River and Its Tributaries, 1861–1862." *Tennessee Historical Quarterly* 27 (1968): 62–71.

Bohrnstedt, Jennifer Cain, ed. *Soldiering With Sherman: Civil War Letters of George F. Cram*. DeKalb, IL: Northern Illinois University Press, 2000.

Bokum, Hermann. *The Testimony of a Refugee from East Tennessee*. Philadelphia, PA: Privately printed, 1863.

Boldrick, Charles C. "Father Abram J. Ryan, the Poet: Priest of the Confederacy." *FCHQ* 46 (1972): 201–218.

Booth, Louise. *The Beleaguered Forty—First Tennessee*. Villa-Park, CA: D.R. Booth Associates, 1996.

———. *Waiting for the Moment: Civil War Home Front:*

Indiana, Northern Alabama, Middle Tennessee Campaign. Villa Park, CA: The author, 1983.

Born, Kathryn. "The Unionist Movement in Eastern Tennessee during the Civil War and Reconstruction Period." Thesis, University of Wisconsin, 1933.

Bowers, John. *Chickamauga and Chattanooga: The Battles that Doomed the Confederacy.* New York: HarperCollins, 1994.

Bowman, Larry G., and Jack B. Scroggs, eds. "Diary of a Confederate Soldier." *Military Review* 62, no. 2 (1982): 20–34.

Bowman, S.M., and R.B. Irwin. *Sherman and His Campaigns: A Military Biography.* Cincinnati: C.F. Vent, 1865.

Boynton, Henry V. *Was General Thomas Slow at Nashville? With a Description of the Greatest Cavalry Movement of the War and General James H. Wilson's Cavalry Operations in Tennessee, Alabama, and Georgia.* New York: Harper, 1896.

Bradford, Ned, ed. *Battles and Leaders of the Civil War.* New York: Hawthorne, 1956.

Bradley, Kersy, and Martin H. Bradley, eds. "A Soldier's Report: The Battle on Missionary Ridge and Lookout Mountain." *Journal of the Lancaster County Historical Society* 92, no. 1 (1989 – 90): 15–17.

Bradley, Michael R. *With Blood and Fire: Life Behind Union Lines in Middle Tennessee, 1863–1865.* Shippensburg, PA: Burd Street, 2003.

Braly, Mary Gramling. "If I Had a Thousand Lives." *Tennessee Historical Magazine* (series 2) 1 (1930-31): 261–269.

Branch, Mary Polk. *Memoirs of a Southern Woman "Within the Lines," and a Genealogical Record.* Chicago: Joseph G. Branch, 1912.

Brandt, Robert S. "Lighting and Rain in Middle Tennessee: The Campaign of June-July 1863." *Tennessee Historical Quarterly* 52, no. (1993): 15–169. Col. John T. Wilder's "Lightning Brigade" of the U.S. Army and General Rosecrans maneuvered Bragg out of Middle Tennessee.

Branham, Lowell. "The Battle of Chickamauga." *Tennessee Valley Perspective* 4, no. 2 (1973): 10–16.

Brents, John A. *The Patriots and Guerillas of East Tennessee and Kentucky. The Suffering of the Patriots. Also the Experience of the Author as an Officer in the Union Army. Including Sketches of Noted Guerillas and Distinguished Patriots.* New York: The author, 1863.

Brewer, Richard J. "The Tullahoma Campaign: Operational Insights." Thesis, U.S. Army Command and General Staff College, Fort Leavenworth, KS, 1991.

Brooks, Donn Patton. "East Tennessee Forgotten Soldiers: The 43rd Tennessee Infantry Regiment, Confederate States of American." Thesis, Southwest Texas State University, 1991.

Brooksher, William R. "Betwixt Wind and Water." *Civil War Times Illustrated* 32, no. 5 (1993): 64–83.

Brooksher, William, and David Snider. "Bold Cavalry Raid: Ride Down the Sequatchie Valley." *Civil War Times Illustrated* 22 (1983): 32–39.

Brown, Campbell H. "Carter's East Tennessee Reid, the Sailor on Horseback Who Raided His Own Backyard." *Tennessee Historical Quarterly* 22 (1963): 66–82.

Brown, Dee. "Morgan's Christmas Raid." *Tennessee Historical Quarterly* 34 (1975): 99.

Brown, Dee Alexander. *The Bold Cavaliers. Morgan's 2nd Kentucky Cavalry Raiders.* Philadelphia, PA: Lippincott, 1959.

Brown, Leonard E. "Fortress Rosecrans: A History, 1865–1990." *Tennessee Historical Quarterly* 50, no. 3 (1991): 135–141. Earthen fort near Murfreesboro in Rutherford County.

Brown, Norman D., ed. *One of Cleburne's Command: The Civil War Reminiscences and Diary of Capt. Samuel T. Foster, Granbury's Texas Brigade, C.S.A.* Austin: University of Texas Press, 1980.

Brown, Russell K. *To the Manner Born: The Life of General William H. T. Walker.* Athens University of Georgia Press, 1994.

Brownlow, William G. *Americanism Contrasted with Foreignism, Romanism, and Bogus Democracy, in the Light of Reason, History, and Scripture; in Which Certain Demagogues in Tennessee, and Elsewhere, Are Shown up in Their True Colors.* Nashville: The author, 1856.

_____. *Brownlow, the Patriot and Martyr, Showing His Faith and Works, As Reported by Himself.* Philadelphia, PA: Weir, 1862.

_____. *The Great Iron Wheel Examined; or Its False Spokes Extracted, and an Exhibition of Elder Graves, Its Builder. In a Series of Chapters.* Nashville. The author, 1856.

_____. *Helps to the Study of Presbyterianism; or, an Unsophisticated Exposition of Calvinism, with Hopkinsian Modifications and Policy, with a View to a More Easy Interpretation of the Same. To Which Is Added a Brief Account of the Life and Travels of the Author; Interspersed with Anecdotes.* Knoxville: T.F.S. Heiskell, 1834.

_____. *Ought American Slavery to Be Perpetuated? A Debate between Rev. W.G. Brownlow and Rev. A. Pryne. Held at Philadelphia, September, 1858.* Philadelphia, PA: The authors, 1858; rpt. Miami: Mnemosyne, 1969. Rpt., Black Heritage Library Collection. Freeport, NY: Books for Libraries 1971.

_____. *A Political Register, Setting Forth the Principles of the Whig and Locofoco Parties in the United States, with the Life and Public Services of Henry Clay. Also an appendix Personal to the Author; and a General Index.* Jonesborough *Whig,* 1844.

_____. *Portrait and Biography of Parson Brownlow, the Tennessee Patriot.* Indianapolis: Asher, 1862.

_____. *A Sermon on Slavery: A Vindication of the Methodist Church, South: Her Position Stated. Delivered in Temperance Hall, in Knoxville on Sabbath, August 9th, 1857, to the Delegates and Others in Attendance at the Southern Commercial Convention.* Knoxville: Kinsloe and Rice, 1857.

_____. *Sketches of the Rise, Progress, and Decline of Secession; with a Narrative of Personal Adventures among the Rebels.* Philadelphia: G.W. Childs, 1862. Rpt., American Scene Series, intro. Thomas B. Alexander. New York: Da Capo, 1968.

Bryan, Charles F., Jr. "The Civil War in East Tennessee: A Social Political, and Economic Study." Diss., University of Tennessee, 1978.

_____. A Gathering of Tories: The East Tennessee Convention of 1861." *Tennessee Historical Quarterly* 39, no. 1 (1980), 27–48.

_____. "Nashville Under Federal Occupation of East Tennessee, 1861–63." East Tennessee Historical Society *Publications* 60 (1988): 3–22.

Bryant, William O. *Cahaba Prison and the Sultana Disaster.* Tuscaloosa.: University of Alabama Press, 1990.

Buck, Irving A. *Cleburne and His Command.* New York: Neale, 1908. Rpt., forward Bell I. Wiley, Jackson, TN: McCowat-Mercer, 1959.

Bucy, Carole. *Tennessee: The Civil War Years.* Nashville: Tennessee 200, 1996.

Burnette, Otto C. "East Tennessee Opposes Secession." Thesis, University of Wisconsin-Madison, 1993.

Burns, Amanda McDowell, and Lela M. Blankenship. *Fiddles in the Cumberlands.* New York: Smith, 1943.

Burrage, H.S. "Retreat from Lenoir and Siege of Knoxville." *Atlantic Monthly* 18 (1866): 21–30.

Burt, Jesse C., Jr. "The Captive City: Part I. Terror Wore a Blue Coat," Nashville *Tennessean Magazine*, March 24, 1957, 29–32.

_____. "Sherman's Logistics and Andrew Johnson." *Tennessee Historical Quarterly* 15 (1956): 195–215.

Cabanis, Jim, ed. *Civil War Journal and Letters of Sergeant Washington Ives.* Tallahassee, FL: J.R. Cabanis, 1987.

Caldwell, Andrew Jackson. "Matthew Fontaine Maury." *Tennessee Historical Magazine* (series 2) 1 (1930-31): 276–278.

The Campaigns for Fort Donelson: A Review of the Encounter, with Vignettes of the Men Who Fought and Articles on the Surrounding Action. Conshoshocken, PA: Eastern Acorn, 1992.

Campbell, Carl E. *A Civil War Letter from the 16th Tennessee Infantry Regiment, C.S.A.* Nashville: Carl E. Campbell, 1996.

_____. *McKenzie's Fighting Fifth: Reports and Rosters of the 5th Tennessee Cavalry Regiment, C.S.A.* Nashville: Carl E. Campbell, 1996.

Campbell, Henry. *Three Years in the Saddle. A Journal of Events, Facts, and Incidents connected with the 19th Ind. Battery.* [Typescript copy from Chickamauga National Military Park Library, Fort Oglethorpe, GA.]

Campbell, James B. "East Tennessee During the Federal Occupation, 1863–1865." East Tennessee Historical Society *Publications* 19 (1947): 64–80.

Cannon, Newton. *The Reminiscences of Newton Cannon,* ed. Campbell Brown; intro. Stanley F. Horn. Franklin, TN: Franklin L. Carter House, 1963.

Cannon, Robert K. *Volunteers for Union and Liberty: History of the 5th Tennessee Cavalry Infantry, U.S.A. 1862–1865.* Knoxville: Bohemian Brigade, 1995.

Carnes, F.G. "'We Can Hold Our Ground': Calvin Smith's Diary [April 16 – May 27, 1863]. *Civil War Times Illustrated* 24 [25] (April 1985): 24–31. Smith was 1st Lt., Co. D, 31st Tenn. Regiment., C.S.A.

Carter, Rosalie. "Captain Tod Carter, Confederate States Army." *Williamson County [TN] Historical Society Journal* 9 (1978). Died in Battle of Franklin.

_____. *Captain Tod Carter of the Confederate States Army: A Biographical Portrait.* Franklin: The author, 1978.

_____. *Tragedy at the Carter House at Franklin, Tennessee.* Franklin: The author, 1976.

Carter, W.R. *History of the First Regiment of Tennessee Volunteer Cavalry.* Johnson City, TN: Overmountain, 1992.

Cartwright, Thomas Y. "Better Confederates Did Not Live: Black Southerners in Nathan Bedford Forrest's Commands." *Journal of Confederate History* 11 (1994): 94–120.

Castel, Albert. "Fort Pillow: Victory or Massacre?" *American History Illustrated* 9, no. 1 (1974): 46–48.

_____. "The War Album of Henry Dwight, Part IV." *Civil War Times Illustrated*, Vol. XIX, No. 3 (1980): 32–36.

Catton, Bruce. "The Army of the Cumberland: A Panoramic Show with W.D.T. Travis' Panorama." *AH* 19 (1967): 40–49.

_____. "The Miracle on Missionary Ridge." *AH* 20 (1969): 60–72.

Chavanne Rose N. *David Glasgow Farragut, Midshipman.* New York: Coward-McCann, 1941.

Chester, William W. "The Diary of Captain Elisha Tompkin Hollis." *West Tennessee Historical Society Papers* 39 (1985): 83–118. Hollis was a Confederate officer from Weakley County. Diary includes 1864–65.

Christie, Amos. "Deaths and Disabilities in the Provisional Armies of Tennessee." *Tennessee Historical Quarterly* 43, no. 2 (1984): 132–154.

Cimprich, John Vincent, Jr. "Dr. Fitch's Report on the Ft. Pillow Massacre." *Tennessee Historical Quarterly* 44 (1985): 27–39.

_____. "Military Governor Johnson and Tennessee Blacks, 1862–65." *Tennessee Historical Quarterly* 39, no. 4 (1980): 459–470.

Cimprich, John, and Mainfort, Robert C., Jr. "The Fort Pillow Massacre: A Statistical Note." *Journal of American History* 76, no. 3 (1989): 830–837.

_____. "Fort Pillow Revisited: New Evidence About an Old Controversy." *Civil War History* 28, no. 4 (1982): 293–306.

Clark, Carroll Henderson. *Sixteenth Tennessee Regiment, Confederate States of American.* Spencer, TN: n.p., 1990. Articles from the *McMinnville (Tenn.) Southern Standard.*

Clark, Darius. *The Civil War Diary of Darius Clark of White County, Tennessee, Company G, 16th Infantry, C.S.A.* Huntsville, AL: J.J. Betterton, 1980.

Clark, Reuben G. *Valleys of the Shadow: The Memoir of*

Confederate Captain Reuben G. Clark, Company I, 59th Tennessee Mounted Infantry. Knoxville: University of Tennessee Press, 1994.

Clark, Sam L., ed. "A Confederate Officer Visits Richmond." *Tennessee Historical Quarterly* 11 (1952): 86–91.

Clark, Sam L., and H.D. Riley, Jr., eds. "Outline and the Organization of the Medical Department of the Confederate Army and Department of Tennessee, by S.H. Stout." *Tennessee Historical Quarterly,* 16 (1957): 55–82.

Cleaves, Freeman. *Rock of Chickamauga, the Life of General George H. Thomas.* Norman: University of Oklahoma Press, 1948.

Clemmer, Gregg S. *Valor in Gray: The Recipients of the Confederate Medal of Honor,* Staunton, VA: Hearthside, 1996.

Cleveland, Charlotte, and Robert Daniel, eds. "The Diary of a Confederate Quartermaster." *Tennessee Historical Quarterly* 11 (1952): 78–85.

Coffman, Edward M., ed. "Memoirs of Hylan B. Lyon, Brigadier General, C.S.A." *Tennessee Historical Quarterly* 11 (1959): 35–53.

Comey, Lyman Richard, ed. *A Legacy of Valor: The Memoirs and Letters of Captain Henry Newton Comey, 2nd Massachusetts Infantry.* Knoxville: University of Tennessee Press, 2004.

Commager, Henry S. *Atlas to Accompany the Official Records of the Union and Confederate Armies, 1891–95,* new ed., New York: T. Yosseloff, 1958.

Confederate States of America, House of Representatives, Special Committee on the Recent Military Disasters. *Report of the Special Committee, on the Recent Military Disasters at Forts Henry and Donelson, and the Evacuation of Nashville.* Richmond VA: *Enquirer,* 1862. In CSA, *Official Reports of Battles,* Confederate Imprints Collection Series. New York: Arno, 1972.

Conklin, Forrest. "Footnotes on the Death of John Hunt Morgan." *Tennessee Historical Quarterly* 35, no. 4 (1976): 376–388.

_____, ed. "'Parson' Brownlow on the Impeachment of Judge Humphreys and Other Matters in Washington, D.C., June, 1862." *East Tennessee Historical Society Publications* 56–57 (1984-85): 120–31. Humphreys was a federal district judge.

Connell, Moody K. *Rebel Scouts: The Last Ride Home: A True Story.* Cleveland, TN: The author, 1995.

Cooling, Benjamin Franklin III. "The Battle of Dover, February 3, 1863." *Tennessee Historical Quarterly* 22 (1963): 143–151.

Cosby, Helen Louise. "Union Sentiment in Tennessee during the Civil War Period." Thesis, George Peabody College, 1929.

Cox, Douglas E. *Joint Operations During the Campaign of 1862 on the Tennessee and Cumberland Rivers.* Carlisle Barracks, PA: U.S. Army War College, 1989.

Cozzens, Peter. *No Better Place to Die: The Battle of Stones River.* Urbana: University of Illinois Press, 1990.

Crisp, James Allen. "The Religious Awakening in the Army of Tennessee." Thesis, Duke University, 1964.

Cromie, Alice. *A Tour Guide to the Civil War.* 3rd ed. Nashville: Rutledge Hill, 1990.

Crow, Vernon H. *Storm in the Mountains: Thomas's Confederate Legion of Cherokee Indians and Mountaineers.* Cherokee, NC: Press of the Museum of the Cherokee Indian, 1982.

Cumming, Kate. *A Journal of Hospital Life in the Confederate Army of Tennessee from the Battle of Shiloh to the End of the War: with Sketches of Life and Character, and Brief Notices of Current Events During that Period,* Louisville, KY: John P. Morton and Co., 1866.

Cunningham, H.H. "Confederate General Hospitals: Establishment and Organization." *Journal of Southern History* 20 (1954): 376–394.

Current, Richard Nelson. *Lincolns Loyalists: Union Soldiers from the Confederacy.* Boston, MA: Northeastern University Press, 1992.

Curry, William L. *Raid of the Confederate Cavalry through Central Tennessee in October 1863, Commanded by General Joseph Wheeler.* Birmingham AL: Linn-Henley Research Center, Birmingham Public Library Press, 1987.

Daniel, John S., Jr. "Special Warfare in Middle Tennessee and Surrounding Areas, 1861–62." Thesis, University of Tennessee, 1971.

Daniel, Larry J., and Lynn N. Brock. *Island No. 10: Struggles for the Mississippi Valley.* Tuscaloosa, AL: University of Alabama Press, 1996.

Dargan, Elizabeth Paisley, ed. *The Civil War Diary of Martha, Wife of Dr. Charles C. Abernathy of Pulaski, Tennessee.* Beltsville, MD: Professional, 1994.

Davis, C., and Davis Swenton, eds. *Blue Grass Confederate: The Headquarters Diary of Edward O. Guerrant.* Baton Rouge: LSU Press, 1999.

Davis, James D. *History of the City of Memphis, Being a Compilation of the Most Important Historical Documents and Historical Events Connected With the Purchase of Its Territory, Laying Off of the City and Early Settlement.* Memphis, 1873.

Directory of Civil War Monuments and Memorials in Tennessee. Nashville: Civil War Centennial Comm., 1963.

Drake, Edwin L., ed. *The Annals of the Army of Tennessee and Early Western History, Including a Chronological Summary of Battles and Engagements in the Western Armies of the Confederacy.* Nashville: A.D. Haynes, 1878.

Durham, Walter T. "The Battle of Nashville." *Journal of Confederate History* 1, no. 1 (1988): 118–151.

Dyer, John P. "Some Aspects of Cavalry Operations in the Army of Tennessee." *JSH* 8 (1942): 210–25.

Eisterhold, John A. "Fort Heiman: Forgotten Fortress." *West Tennessee Historical Society Papers* 28 (1974): 43–54.

Ellis, Daniel. *Thrilling Adventures of Daniel Ellis, the Great Union Guide of East Tennessee, for a Period of Nearly Four Years during the Great Southern Rebellion. Written by Himself. Containing a Short Biography of the Author.* New York: Harper, 1867; rpt., Black Heritage Library Collection, Freeport, NY: Books for Libraries, 1972.

Fink, Harold S. "The East Tennessee Campaign and the Battle of Knoxville in 1863." East Tennessee Historical Society *Publications* 29 (1957): 79–117.

Fink, Paul M. "The Lighter Side of History." East Tennessee Historical Society *Publications* 39 (1967): 26–41.

Fisher, Noel C. "The Other War: Guerilla Warfare and Pacification in East Tennessee, 1861–1865." Thesis, Ohio State University, 1987.

Fitch, John. *Annals of the Cumberland: Comprising Biographies, Descriptions of Departments, Accounts of Expeditions, Skirmishes, and Battles; Also Its Police Record of Spies, Smugglers, and Prominent Rebel Emissaries. Together with Anecdotes, Incidents, Poetry, Reminiscences, etc., and Official Reports of the Battle of Stone River.* Philadelphia, PA: Lippincott, 1863. Rev. 5th ed., 1864.

Fleming, Doris, ed. "Letters from a Canadian Recruit in the Union Army." *Tennessee Historical Quarterly* 16 (1957): 159–66.

Fleming, James R. *Band of Brothers: Company C, 9th Tennessee Infantry.* Shippensburg, PA: White Mane, 1996.

_____. *The Ninth Tennessee Infantry: A Roster.* Shippensburg, PA: White Mane, 1996.

Frank, Joseph Allan, and George A. Reaves. *"Seeing the Elephant": Raw Recruits at the Battle of Shiloh.* New York: Greenwood, 1989.

Frantz, Mabel Goode. *Full Many a Name: The Story of Sam Davis, Scout and Spy, C.S.A.* Jackson, TN: McCowatt-Mercer, 1961.

Freemon, Frank R., M.D. "The Medical Support System for the Confederate Army of Tennessee During the Georgia Campaign, May–September 1864." *Tennessee Historical Quarterly* 52, no. 1 (1993): 44–55.

Fremantle, Arthur James Lyon, Lieut. Col. Coldstream Guards. *Three Months in the Southern States: April, June, 1863.* Mobile: S. H. Goetzel, 1864.

Fuchs, Richard L. *An Unerring Fire: The Massacre at Fort Pillow.* Rutherford, NJ: Farleigh Dickinson University Press, 1994.

Funk, Arville L., ed. "A Hoosier Regiment at Chattanooga." *Tennessee Historical Quarterly* 22 (1963): 280–287.

Gaines, W. Craig. *The Confederate Cherokees: John Drew's Regiment of Mounted Rifles.* Baton Rouge: Louisiana State University Press, 1989.

Galbraith, Loretta, and William Galbraith, eds. *A Lost Heroine of the Confederacy: The Diaries and Letters of Belle Edmondson.* Jackson: University Press of Mississippi, 1990.

Gibbons, Tony. *Warships and Naval Battles of the Civil War.* New York: Gallery, 1989.

Gildrie, Richard P. "Guerilla Warfare in the Lower Cumberland River Valley, 1862–1865." *Tennessee Historical Quarterly* 49, no. 3 (1990): 161–176.

Gist, W.W. "The Battle of Franklin, the Key to the Last Campaign in the West." *Tennessee Historical Magazine* 6 (1920): 213–265.

Gordon, Ralph C. "Hospital Trains of the Army of the Cumberland." *Tennessee Historical Quarterly* 51, no. 3 (1992): 147–156.

Graber, H.W. *A Terry Texas Ranger: The Life Record of H.W. Graber.* Austin, TX: State House Press, 1987.

Grant, Nicholas B. *The Life of a Common Soldier, 1862–1865.* Adamsville: J. Gillis, 1990.

Groce, William Todd. "Mountain Rebels: East Tennessee Confederates and the Civil War, 1860–70." Diss., University of Tennessee, 1993.

Guide to the Civil War in Tennessee. 3rd rev. ed. Nashville: Civil War Centennial Commission of Tennessee, 1977.

Hale, Johnathan D. *Champ Ferguson: A Sketch of the War in East Tennessee Detailing Some of the Awful Murders on the Border Describing One of the Leading Spirits of the Rebellion.* Cincinnati: n.p., 1862.

Harrison, Lowell. "The Diary of an 'Average' Confederate Soldier." *Tennessee Historical Quarterly* 29 (1970): 256–271.

Hay, Thomas Robson. "The Battle of Spring Hill." *Tennessee Historical Magazine* 7 (1921): 74–91.

Holden, John A. "Journey of a Confederate Mother." West Tennessee Historical Society *Papers* 19 (1965): 36–57.

Hooper, Ernest W. "Memphis, Tennessee: Federal Occupation and Reconstruction 1862–1870." Ph.D. dissertation, University of North Carolina, 1957.

Horick, Randy. "Tennesseans and the Crisis of the Union, 1859–1860." Thesis, Vanderbilt University, 1982.

House, Ellen Renshaw. *A Very Violent Rebel: The Civil War Diary of Ellen Renshaw House.* Knoxville: University of Tennessee Press, 1996.

Hugh, Ronald K. "Fort Pillow Massacre: The Aftermath of Paducah [Kentucky]. *Journal of Illinois State History Society* 66 (Spring 1973): 62–70.

Hughes, Michael Anderson. "The Struggle for Chattanooga, 1862–1863." Diss., University of Arkansas, 1991.

Inman, Myra Adelaide, "The Diary of Myra Adelaide Inman of Cleveland, Tennessee, During the War Between the States. 1859–1865." 1940. Typescript, TSLA.

Johnson, Andrew. *Papers of Andrew Johnson*, Vols. 4–6, Knoxville: University of Tennessee Press, 1976–1983.

Johnson, Leland R. "Civil War Defenses in Tennessee." *The Tennessee Valley Historical Review* (Summer 1972), 20–26.

Jones, James B. "Sam Davis, Boy Hero of the Confederacy." *Courier* 30, no. 2 (1992): 4–5.

Jones, James B., Jr. "A Brave, Vigilant, and Energetic Officer.'" *North & South Magazine*, vol. 11, no. 3 [2009].

_____. "Chatham Roberdeau Wheat: Soldier of Fortune and Confederate Martyr." *The Courier*, June 1999.

———. "The Civil War in Tennessee: New Perspectives on Familiar Materials." *Tennessee Historical Quarterly* 62, (2003): 166–187.

———. *A Documentary Guide to the Civil War on the Tennessee Cumberland Plateau*, May 1999 (self-published).

———. "Negley's Raid, June 2–9, 1862." *The Courier*, vol. XLI, no. 1 (2003): 4–6.

———. "'The Reign of Terror of the Safety Committee Has Passed Away Forever.' A History of Committees of Safety and Vigilance in West and Middle Tennessee, 1860–1862." West Tennessee Historical Society *Papers*, Vol. LXIII (2009): 1–29.

———. "The Struggle for Public Health in Civil War Tennessee Cities." West Tennessee Historical Society *Papers*, Vol. LXI (2007): 62–108.

———. "A Tale of Two Cities: The Hidden Battle Against Venereal Disease in Civil War Nashville and Memphis." *Civil War History* 31 (September 1985): 270–276.

Jones, James P., ed. "The Yankees' Jeff Davis in Tennessee." *Tennessee Historical Quarterly* 19 (1960): 166–171.

Judd, Cameron. *The Bridge Burners: A True Adventure of East Tennessee's Underground Civil War.* Vol. 1 Limestone: Nolichucky, 1995.

Lapointe, Patricia M. "Military Hospitals in Memphis, 1861–1865." *Tennessee Historical Quarterly* 42, no. 4 (1983): 325–342.

Long, E.B., *The Civil War Day by Day: An Almanac, 1861–1865*, fwd. by Bruce Catton. Garden City, NY: Doubleday, 1971

Lovett, Bobby L. "Blacks in the Battle of Nashville, December 15–16, 1864." *Tennessee State University Facility Journal* (1976): 39–46.

———. "The West Tennessee Colored Troops in Civil War Combat." West Tennessee Historical Society *Papers* 34 (1980): 53–70.

Madaus, MacLeod, and Xavier Donald. *The Rebellion in Tennessee.* Washington, D.C.: McGill, Witheraw, 1862.

"MAGGIE! Maggie Lindsley's Journal: Nashville, Tennessee, 1864; Washington, D. C. 1865. Including Letters written to her in 1862 from Professor Benjamin Silliman of Yale College, Privately Printed, 1977.

Mainfort, Robert C., Jr. "A Folk Art Map of Fort Pillow." West Tennessee Historical Society *Papers* 40 (1986): 73–81.

———, and Patricia E. Coats. "Soldiering at Fort Pillow, 1862–1864." An Excerpt from the Civil War Memoirs of Addison Sleeth. West Tennessee Historical Society *Papers* 36 (1982): 72–90.

McGehee, C. Stuart. "The Property and Faith of the City: Secession in Chattanooga." East Tennessee Historical Society *Publications* 60 (1988): 23–38.

McGlone, John. "Tennessee." *Journal of Confederate History* 10 (1994): 116–132.

McKee, James W., Jr. "Felix K. Zollicoffer: Confederate Defender of East Tennessee." East Tennessee Historical Society *Publications* 43 (1971): 34–58; 44 (1972): 17–40.

McKee, John Miller. *The Great Panic: Being Incidents Connected with Two Weeks of the War in Tennessee.* Nashville: Elder-Sherbourne, 1977.

Melia, Tamara Moser. "James B. McPherson and the Civil Ideals of the Old Army." Diss., Southern Illinois University, 1987.

Meriwether, Elizabeth Avery, *Recollections of 92 Years: 1824–1916*, Nashville: Tennessee Historical Commission, 1958.

Merrill, James., ed. "'Nothing to Eat but Raw Bacon': Letters from a War Correspondent 1862." *Tennessee Historical Quarterly* 17 (1958): 141–155.

Merrill, James M. *Battle Flags South: The Story of Civil War Navies on the Western Waters.* Rutherford, NJ: Farleigh Dickinson University Press, 1970.

———. "Capt. Andrew Hull Foote and the Civil War on Tennessee Waters." *Tennessee Historical Quarterly* 30 (1971): 83–93.

Miles, Jim. *Paths to Victory: A History and Tour Guide of the Stones River, Chickamauga, Chattanooga, Knoxville, and Nashville campaigns.* Nashville: Rutledge Hill, 1991.

Milligan, J.D. *Gunboats Down the Mississippi.* Annapolis: U.S. Naval Institute, 1965.

Miner, Mike. "The Hanging of Sam Davis: The Last Days of a Tennessee Hero." *Military Images* 11, no. 2 (1989): 12–14.

Mitchell, Enoch L., ed. "Letters of a Confederate Surgeon in the Army of Tennessee to His Wife." *Tennessee Historical Quarterly* 4 (1945): 341–353.

Moon, Anna Mary, ed. "Civil War Memoirs of Mrs. Adeline Deaderick." *Tennessee Historical Quarterly* 7 (1948): 52–71.

———. "A Southern Woman, in 1897, Remembers the Civil War." East Tennessee Historical Society *Publications* 21 (1949): 111–115.

Moore, Frank, ed. *The Rebellion Record: A Diary of American Events, with Documents, Narratives, Illustrative Events, Poetry*, 11 Vols., New York: D. Van Nostrand, Publisher, 1867–1868.

Newcomb, Mary A. *Four Years of Personal Reminiscences of the War: Four Years of Personal Experience in the War.* Chicago H. S. Mills, 1893.

Newcomer, Lee N. "The Battle of Memphis, 1862." West Tennessee Historical Society *Papers,* 12 (1958): 41–57.

Noe, Kenneth William. "Southwest Virginia, the Virginia and Tennessee Railroad, and the Union, 1861–1865." Diss., University of Illinois, 1990.

Nott, Charles C. *Sketches of the War: A Series of Letters to the North Moore Street School of New York.* New York: T. Evans, 1863, rpt. Paris, TN, Guild Bindery, n.d.

Partain, Robert. "A Confederate Sergeant's Report to His Wife during the Bombardment of Fort Pillow." *Tennessee Historical Quarterly* 15 (1956): 243–252.

_____. "A Confederate Sergeant's Report to His Wife during the Campaign from Tullahoma to Dalton." *Tennessee Historical Quarterly* 12 (1953): 291–308.

Pennington, Edgar Legare. "The Battle at Sewanee." *Tennessee Historical Quarterly* 9 (1950): 217–243.

Phisterer, Fred. *Statistical Record of the Armies of the United States.* New York: Charles Scribner's Sons, 1883; rpt. 1989, Wilmington, NC: Broadfoot.

Pittard, Mabel Baxter. "The Coleman Scouts." Thesis, Middle Tennessee State University, 1953.

Potter, Jerry O'Neil. *The Sultana Tragedy: America's Greatest Maritime Disaster.* Gretna, LA: Pelican, 1992.

Powers, Elvira J. *Hospital Pencillings [sic]; Being a Diary While in Jefferson General Hospital, Jeffersonville, Ind., and Others at Nashville, Tennessee, As Matron and Visitor.* Edward L. Mitchel, 24 Congress Street, Boston, 1866.

Prouty, Fred M., and Stephen Rogers. "Fort Wright. National Register of Historic Places Nomination Form." Original copy filed at the Tennessee Historical Commission, Nashville.

Quenzel, Carrol H. "A Billy Yank's Impressions of the South." *Tennessee Historical Quarterly* 12 (1953): 99–105.

Quintard, Charles Todd. *Dr. Quintard, Chaplain C.S.A. and Second Bishop of Tennessee"; Being His Story of the War (1861–1865),* ed. Arthur Howell Noll. Sewanee: University of the South Press, 1905.

Rable, George C. "Anatomy of a Unionist: Andrew Johnson in the Crisis." *Tennessee Historical Quarterly* 32, no. 4 (1973): 332–354.

Ramsdell, Charles W. *Behind the Lines in the Southern Confederacy,* ed. Wendell H. Stephenson. Baton Rouge: Louisiana State University Press, 1944; rpt. Westport, CT: Greenwood, 1944.

Report of the Adjutant General of the State of Tennessee of the Military Forces of the State, From 1861 to 1866. Nashville: 1866.

Rogers, Jesse Littleton. *The Civil War Battles of Chickamauga and Chattanooga.* Chattanooga: Andrews, 1942.

Rosecrans, William Starke. *Report on the Battle of Murfreesboro, Tennessee.* Washington, D.C.: GPO, 1863.

Rosser, R.W., and McGlone, John, eds. *Confederate Chronicles of Tennessee.* Vol. 2. Somerville: Tennessee Division of Sons of Confederate Veterans, 1988.

Rutherford, Phillip. "A Battle Above the Clouds." *Civil War Times Illustrated* 28, no. 5 (1989): 30–39. Lookout Mountain, Chattanooga.

Sensing, Thurman. *Champ Ferguson, Confederate Guerrilla.* Nashville: Vanderbilt University Press, 1942.

Shanks, W.F.G. "Chattanooga and How We Held It." *Harper's New Monthly Magazine,* January 1868, 137–149.

Siburt, James T. "Colonel John M. Hughs: Brigade Commander and Confederate Guerilla." *Tennessee Historical Quarterly* 51, no. 2 (1992): 87–95.

Simkins, Francis Butler, and James W. Patton. *The Women of the Confederacy.* Richmond, VA: Garrett and Massie, 1936; rpt. 1971.

Smith, Barbara Bentley, and Nina Bentley Baker, eds. *"Burning Rails as We Pleased": The Civil War Letters of William Garrigues Bentley, 104th Ohio Volunteer Infantry.* Jefferson, NC: McFarland, 2004.

Smith, Ophia D. "The Incorrigible 'Miss Ginger.'" West Tennessee Historical Society *Papers* 9 (1955): 93–118.

Smith, Samuel D. "Military Sites Archaeology in Tennessee." *Tennessee Historical Quarterly* LIX (3): 140–157.

Smith, Samuel D., and Benjamin C. Nance. *A Survey of Civil War Military Sites in Tennessee.* Tennessee Division of Environment and Conservation, Division of Archaeology, Research Series No. 14, 2003.

_____, Fred M. Prouty and Benjamin C. Nance. *A Survey of Civil War Period Military Sites in Middle Tennessee.* Division of Archaeology Report of Investigations no. 7, Nashville: Tennessee Department of Conservation, 1990.

Spence, John C. *A Diary of the Civil War.* Murfreesboro: Rutherford County Historical Society, 1993.

Stevens, John K. "Hostages to Hunger: Nutritional Night Blindness in Confederate Armies." *Tennessee Historical Quarterly* 48, no. 3 (1989): 131–143.

Stevenson, Alexander F. *The Battle of Stone's River near Murfreesboro, Tenn., December 30, 1862, to January 3, 1863.* Boston: James R. Osgood, 1884.

Sullivan, David M. "Tennessee's Confederate Marines: Memphis Detachment." *Tennessee Historical Quarterly* 45, no. 2 (1986): 152–168.

Suppiger, Joseph E. "From Chickamauga to Chattanooga: The Battlefield Account of Sergeant John M. Kane." East Tennessee Historical Society *Publications* 45 (1973): 99–108.

Supplement to the Official Records of the Union and Confederate Armies. Wilmington, NC: Broadfoot, 1994.

Taylor, Martha S. *Shiloh, Again! The Story of Stones River and the Battle of Murfreesboro, Tennessee.* Huntsville, AL: The author, 1989.

Tennessee, Records of East Tennessee, Civil War Records, Vols. 1–2, East Tennessee, Middle Tennessee and West Tennessee. Prepared by the Historical Records Survey Transcription Unit, Division of Women's and Professional Projects Works Progress Administration, Mrs. John Trotwood Moore, State Librarian and Archivist, Sponsor, T. Marshall Jones, State Director, Mrs. Penelope Johnson Allen, State Supervisor, Mrs. Margaret H. Richardson, District Supervisor, Nashville, Tennessee, The Historical Records Survey, June 1, 1939.

_____, Records of Middle Tennessee, Civil War Records, Vol. 3, Prepared by the Historical Records Survey Transcription Unit, Division of Women's and Professional Projects Works Progress Administration, Mrs. John Trotwood Moore, State Librarian and Archivist, Sponsor, T. Marshall Jones, State Director, Mrs. Penelope Johnson Allen, State Supervisor, Mrs.

Margaret H. Richardson, District Supervisor, Nashville, Tennessee, The Historical Records Survey, June 1, 1939.

———, Records of West Tennessee, Civil War Records, Vol. 3, Prepared by the Historical Records Survey Transcription Unit, Division of Women's and Professional Projects Works Progress Administration, Mrs. John Trotwood Moore, State Librarian and Archivist, Sponsor, T. Marshall Jones, State Director, Mrs. Penelope Johnson Allen, State Supervisor, Mrs. Margaret H. Richardson, District Supervisor, Nashville, Tennessee, The Historical Records Survey, June 1, 1939.

Tennessee Civil War Centennial Commission. *Guide to the Civil War in Tennessee.* Nashville: Tennessee Dept. of Conservation, 1960.

Tennessee Historical Commission, *Tennessee Historical Markers*, 8th ed. Nashville: Tennessee Historical Commission, 1996.

Tennesseans in the Civil War: A Military History of Confederate Union Units with Available Rosters of Personnel. 2 Vols. Nashville: Civil War Centennial Commission, 1964–65.

Thornton, J. Mills, III. "The Ethic of Subsistence and the Origins of Southern Secession." *Tennessee Historical Quarterly* 48, no. 2 (1989): 67–85.

Thruston, Gates P. *Personal Recollections of the Battle in the Rear at Stones River, Tennessee.* Nashville: Brandon, 1906.

Tower, R. Lockwood. *A Carolinian Goes to War: The Civil War Narrative of Arthur Middleton Manugault, Brigadier General, C.S.A.* Columbia: University of South Carolina Press, 1983.

Trent, Henry Gibson, Jr. "The Battle of Knoxville." Thesis, Southern Methodist University, 1950.

Trimble, Sarah Ridley, ed. "Behind the Lines in Middle Tennessee, 1863–1865: The Journal of Bettie Ridley Blackmore." *Tennessee Historical Quarterly* 12 (1953): 48–80.

Trudeau, Noah Andre. "Fields Without Honor: Two Affairs in Tennessee." *Civil War Times Illustrated* 31, no. 3 (1992): 42–49.

Tucker, Glenn. *The Battles for Chattanooga.* Conshohocken, Pa.: Eastern Acorn, 1992.

Ullirch, Dieter C., and Elizabeth Kitts, eds. *The Civil War Diaries of Van Buren Oldham, Company G, Ninth Tennessee Volunteer Infantry, C.S.A.* Martin, TN: np, 1999.

Underwood, Betsy Swint. "War Seen Through a Teen-Ager's Eyes." *Tennessee Historical Quarterly* 20 (1961): 177–187.

United States Surgeon General's Office. *The Medical and Surgical History of the War of the Rebellion*, Vol. 1, pt. 3, ed. Charles Smartt. Washington, D.C.: GPO, 1888.

War of the Rebellion. *Official Records of the Union and Confederate Armies in the War of the Rebellion.* 128 vols. Washington, D.C.: GPO, 1880–1901.

———. *Official Records of the Union and Confederate Navies in the War of the Rebellion.* 26 vols. Washington, D.C.: GPO, 1894–1922.

White, Robert H. *Messages of the Governors of Tennessee, 1857–1869*, Vol. 5. Nashville: Tennessee Historical Commission, 1959.

Whiteaker, Larry H. "Champ Ferguson's Civil War." *Tennessee: State of the Nation*, ed. Larry H. Whiteaker and W. Calvin Dickinson, New York: American Heritage, 1994.

Whitley, Edith Johns Rucker. *Sam Davis, Hero of the Confederacy, 1842–1863, Coleman's Scouts.* Nashville: Blue and Gray, 1971.

Wiley, Bell I. "The Common Soldier." *Tennessee Valley Perspective* 3, no. 2 (1972): 16–21.

———. *The Life of Billy Yank and The Life of Johnny Reb.* 2 Vols. Garden City, NY: Doubleday, 1971.

———. *The Life of Billy Yank the Common Soldier of the Union.* Indianapolis: Bobbs-Merrill, 1952. Rpt. in *The Common Soldier in the Civil War.* 2 Vols. in 1. New York: Grosset, 1958.

———. *The Life of Johnny Reb: The Common Soldier of the Confederacy.* Indianapolis: Bobs-Merrill, 1952; Rpt. In *The Common Soldier in the Civil War.* 2 Vols. in 1. New York: Grosset, 1958.

———. *The Plain People of the Confederacy.* Baton Rouge: Louisiana State University Press, 1943; rpt. Gloucester, MA: P. Smith, 1971.

Wingfield, Marshall. *General A.P. Stewart, His Life and Letters.* Memphis: West Tennessee Historical Society, 1954.

Worthington, Thomas. *Shiloh; or, The Tennessee Campaign of 1862: Written Especially for the Army of the Tennessee in 1862.* Washington, D.C.: M'Gill and Witherow, 1872.

Wright, Marcus Joseph, comp. *Tennessee in the War, 1861–1865; Lists of Military Organizations and Officers from Tennessee in Both the Confederate and Union Armies; General and Staff Officers of the Provisional Army of Tennessee, Appointed by Governor Isham G. Harris.* New York: A. Lee, 1908.

Young, Agatha. *The Women and the Crisis: Women of the North In the Civil War.* New York: McDowell, Obolensky, 1959.

Zornow, William Frank. "State Aid for Indigent Soldiers and Their Families in Tennessee, 1861–1865." *Tennessee Historical Quarterly* 13 (1954): 297–300.

Web Sites

American Civil War Home Page. http://sunsite.utk.edu/civil—war/warweb.html.

Barber, Gershom M. http://monumentsoftware.com/album/GM_1.htm; http://www.geocities.com/srhackettbr/barber.htm.

Betts, Vicki. http://www.uttyl.edu/vbetts. An excellent source by Dr. Betts at the Library at the University of Texas at Tyler. A wide variety of newspaper reports on many aspects of the Civil War in many states.

Bits of Blue and Grey: An American Civil War Notebook. http://www.bitsofblueandgray.com/.

Civil War Love Letters. http://spec.lib.vt.edu/cwlove/ruse.html.

Civil War Memories. http://my.dmci.net/~bmacd/default.htm.

Civil War Rosters. http://www.geocities.com/Area51/Lair/3680/cw/cw-tn.html.

Civil War Round Table, Knoxville. http://www.korrnet.org/kcwrt/history/hb-text.htm.

Court-Martial Case Files, RG 153. http://www.nara.gov/publications/prologue/crtmar.html. File MM1367, entry 15, Court-Martial Case Files, RG 153.

Critz, Peter L. Correspondence. As cited in http://www.tennessee.civilwarsourcebook.com from http://www.franklin-stfb.org.

Cruikshank, Robert. Letters. www.ehistory.com.

Feagle, Josiah. Correspondence. http://home.att.net.

Hackworth, William Collection. http://www.ehistory.com/uscw/library/letters/index.cfm.

Hansford, Willis, Correspondence. http://civilwargazette.wordpress.com/2007/11/27/frank-i-willis-of-the-51st-new-york-infantry-company-a/.

Harrison, Absolom A. Correspondence. http://www.civilwarhome.com.

Lyons, Jim, Historical Newspapers: Serving You 1972–1997. http://www.jimlyons.com.

Marchant Peter, Captain. Letters of Captain 47th Tennessee Infantry. http://www.geocities.com/bsdunagan/letters.htm.

McCord, James A. Correspondence. http://civilwargazette.wordpress.com/2006/12/04/soldier-letter-30th-georgia-details-battle/.

Miller Family Papers. Center for Archival Collections, Miller Family Papers. http://www.bgsu.edu.

Morris, William R. "The Tennessee River Voyages of U.S.S. *Peosta*." In *Timberclads to Turtlebacks: A Glossary of Civil War Ship Types*. np: Butternut Bivouac, nd. http://www.hardinhistory.com.

Motlow State Community College/Civil War Research Center. http://cwrc.org/Index.html.

Parker, Raymond R., ed. and comp. *Civil War Diary and Letters of David Humphrey Blair*. http://netnow.micron.net/~rbparker/diary.

Plante Trevor K. *The Shady Side of the Family Tree*. http://www.nara.gov.

Potter, Henry Albert, Correspondence. http://freepages.genealogy.rootsweb.com/~mruddy/letters.htm.

Randall, James M. Diary. http://www.ehistory.com/uscw/library/letters/randall/09.cfm.

Richardson, William, Letter. http://www.indianainthecivilwar.com/letters.htm.

Ritter, John A. Correspondence. http://gwillritter.tripod.com.

Seibert John C. Correspondence. http://www.indianainthecivilwar.com.

Slagg, Alexander, Correspondence. Ed. by Jon S. Berndt. http://www.hal-pc.org/~jsb/page15.html.

Smith Family Letters: Virginia Polytechnic Institute and State University, Blacksburg, Virginia 24062-9001. http://freepages.geneaology.rootsweb.com.

Southern History. http://www.SouthernHistory.net. A good site for Civil War history, emphasizing but not limited to Tennessee Civil War history.

Staunton *Spectator*. http://valley.vcdh.virginia.edu.

Tennessee and the Civil War. http://www.tngenweb.org/civilwar/.

Tennessee Civil War Home Page. http://members.aol.com/jweaver303/tn/tncwhp.htm.

Tennessee Civil War National Heritage Area. http://histpres.mtsu.edu/tncivwar/.

Tennessee in the Civil War. http://www.history-sites.com/mb/cw/tncwmb/.

Thompson, Sarah E. Papers. http://scriptorium.lib.duke.edu/thompson/.

Underwood, Albert, Correspondence and Diary. http://dcwi.com/~dave/underwood1.html.

University of North Carolina Chapel Hill Libraries. Documenting the American South, Academic Affairs Library, Electronic editions. http://docsouth.unc.edu and http://www.lib.unc.edu/mss/inv/c/. Including Carney, Kate. Diary April 15, 1861–July 31, 1862. Electronic Edition. http://docsouth.unc.edu, http://www.lib.unc.edu/mss/inv/c/Carney,Kate_S.html. Copley John M. *A Sketch of the Battle of Franklin, Tenn.: With Reminiscences of Camp Douglas*. Austin, TX: Eugene von Boeckmann, 1893. http://docsouth.unc.edu/fpn/copley/menu.html. Edmondson, Belle. Diary: January–November 1864 (transcript). Electronic Edition. http://docsouth.unc.edu/fpn/edmondson/menu.html. Kimberly Family. Personal Correspondence, 1862–1864. Electronic Edition. http://docsouth.unc.edu/imls/kimberly/kimberly.html. Lenoir Family Papers. Personal Correspondence, 1861–1865. Electronic Edition. http://docsouth.unc.edu/imls/lenoir/menu.html.

Ward, John, Correspondence. As cited in: http://www.Tennessee.civilwarsourcebook.com from: http://www.franklin-stfb.org.

Williamson, Alice, Journal. http://scriptorium.lib.duke.edu.

Metropolitan Nashville Davidson County Archives

Nashville Daily Gazette, January 5, 1861–March 18, 1864.

Nashville Daily Press and Times, August 11, 1863–August 30, 1864

Nashville Daily Union, April 17, 1862–December 10, 1864

Stones River National Battlefield Collection

Diary of Lyman S. Widney, Sergeant Major, 34th Illinois Infantry, May 25, 1864–September 25, 1864.

Diary of William M. Woodcock, 9th Kentucky Infantry.
George G. Sinclair Collection: Letters by 1st Sergeant George Sinclair to Francis E. Anderson Sinclair, his wife, September 6, 1862 to July 17, 1863.
Letters of James Jones, 57th Indiana Infantry.

Special Collections

Corbit Special Collections, University Archives, University of Tennessee at Martin.
Frank M. Gurnsey Collection, Special Collections of the Mississippi Valley Collection, University of Memphis.
John Watkins Collection, University of Tennessee Library Special Collections Division, University of Tennessee at Knoxville.
Wilder Collection, University of Chattanooga, Memphis; University of Tennessee at Martin,

Tennessee State Library and Archives Collections

Microfilm

Civil War Collection, 1861–1865, mfm. 824.
Diary of Nimrod Porter, mfm. 229.
Diary of Rebecca Carter Craighead, mfm. 661.
Diary of William E. Sloan, mfm. 154.
George Hovey Cadman Letters, 1857–1864, mfm. 824.
Hamilton-Williams Family Papers, mfm. 1303.
Harris, Ed. R., and wife, letters. Re: Death of Capt. John Harris, mfm. 824–830.
Joel Shoffner Collection, mfm. 824.
Journal of Bradford Nichol, Rutledge Battery, mfm. 1627.
Robert H. Cartmell papers, mfm. 1076.
Simon Perkins, Jr., Papers, mfm. 1527.
William Mark Eames Papers, mfm. 1302.
Zeboim Cartter Patten Diaries, 1860–1863, mfm. 119.

Manuscripts

Civil War Collection, Confederate Collection, Box 8, folder 23.
Civil War Collection, Correspondence by Jane Smith Washington, Letter, December 18, 1864, accession no. 74-74.
Confederate Collection, Box 9, Letters, Folder 21, Harris, Ed. R., and wife, letters. Re: Death of Capt. John Harris, mfm. 824-3, accession no. 1379, Box 9, folder 22.
Confederate Collection, mfm. 824-3, accession no. 1576, Box 11, folder 11.
Diary of Sally Wendel Fentress, accession no. 82-106.
Frederick Bradford Papers, 1830–1896, accession no. 68.202.
Lacy, Andrew Jackson, 1862–1863. Confederate Collection, Box C 28, folder 17, letters.
Letter from Tennessee Blackburn to John W. Blackburn, October 2, 1863; Letter from John W. Blackburn to R.J.D. Baugh, October 18, 1863. Confederate Collection, V-K-I, Box 2, folder 4.
Lucy Virginia Smith French Diaries, accession no. 89-200, 73–25.
Record Group 21, Records of the Southern Claims Commission.
Record Group 23, Civil War Collection, Confederate and Federal.
Talbot-Fentress Family Papers, 1817–1953.

Period Newspapers, Microfilm Collection

Chattanooga *Daily Gazette*
Chattanooga *Daily Rebel*
Clarksville Chronicle
[Humboldt] *Soldier's Budget*
Knoxville *Daily Bulletin*
Knoxville *Daily Register*
Knoxville *Daily Southern Chronicle*
[Knoxville] Holston *Journal*
Knoxville *Tri-Weekly Whig and Rebel Ventilator*
Memphis *Daily Appeal*
Memphis *Daily Bulletin*
Memphis *Weekly Appeal*
Murfreesboro *Daily Rebel Banner*
Nashville *Daily Patriot*
Nashville *Daily Press and Times*
Nashville *Daily Union*
Nashville *Union and American*
Trenton *Standard*

Middle Tennessee State University Microfilm Collection

New York *Times*

Index

abolition 3, 11, 13, 16, 37, 71, 73, 121, 124, 156–157, 163, 225, 252–253, 263, 264
apples 37
Army of Tennessee 135, 169, 156–157; desertion 180; negro teamsters 361
Army of the Cumberland 5, 74, 75, 135, 136, 140, 147, 171, 180, 251
atrocity 229–230

barbers 229, 233
bare knuckle boxing 212–213
Battle Creek 88–90, 88
Beauregard, P.G.T. 5
Bedford County 76, 102, 144, 218, 254
Beersheba Springs 152, 153, 157–159
bigamy 215–216
black powder, shortage of 35
blood hounds 77, 84, 176
Blount County 180
Blountville: burning of 169
Bolivar 95, 96, 113, 182, 211, 218, 262, 266
Booth, John Wilkes 193
Bradley County 128, 168, 227
Bragg, Braxton 4, 5
bridges 46, 48, 50, 53, 68, 95, 99, 101, 166, 168, 188, 203, 225, 226, 232, 234, 259, 260, 261
Buell, Don Carlos 5
Bull's Gap 232
Burnside, Ambrose 6

Camp Jackson 31
Campbell County 77
Cannon County 254
Carney, Kate 84–85, 93

Carroll County 59, 168, 193, 231, 232–23
Carter County 45, 50
Cartmell, Robert H. 10, 22–23, 23, 30, 51, 56
Cedar Creek 38
Charleston, SC 4
Chattanooga 5, 27, 63, 108, 112, 125, 132, 133, 136, 161–162, 164, 167, 169, 170–171, 181, 206–207, 222, 256; artillery duels 163–164; Battle at Chattanooga 181; Battle of Lookout Mountain 181; Confederate bombardment 171–172; "cracker line" 6; evacuation 167; extortion, 63; Federal bombardment 161–162; hospital 104–106; Huyett Battery 33; morale 154–155; plans for fortification 126–127; Siege of Chattanooga 174–175; Tories 51; *see also* Cumming, Kate; Oldham, Van Buren; price inflation
Cherokee Indians 84, 131, 183–184, 189, 200–201
Chickamauga 5
churches 10, 12, 13, 27, 29, 36, 66, 74, 75, 87, 92, 104, 114, 134–135, 136, 140, 149, 150, 152, 158, 162, 165, 179, 192, 200–209, 210, 215, 240–241, 262
Clarksville 15, 46, 54, 56, 61–62, 78, 98–99, 152
Cleveland 137, 168, 199, 209–210, 232–233, 265
Cocke County 179
Coffee County 254
coffins 130, 200; *see also* embalming

Coleman, Dr. 227–228, 235
Columbia 102, 164, 205, 221, 234, 235
Colyar, A.S. 48
combat incidents 41, 51, 58, 60, 69, 75, 102, 112, 131, 146, 151, 167, 171, 172, 181–182, 237–238, 244, 245, 246, 254, 257; battles 6, 7, 76, 79, 86–87, 120–121, 121, 127, 155, 170, 181, 241–244, 245, 246–248; captures 75, 87, 117, 140–141, 144, 156, 161, 165–166, 204–205, 228, 259, 260–261; skirmishes 2, 48, 50–51, 76–77, 77–78, 92–93, 100–101, 101, 107–108, 109, 117, 118, 121, 123, 124, 132–133, 139, 154, 157, 161, 163, 169, 173, 177, 180, 183–184, 184, 186–187, 202, 206, 207, 215, 228, 229, 231, 232, 235, 236, 238, 239, 245, 247, 254, 256, 268
Confederate guerrillas in East Tennessee 267
C.S. Navy 86, 259, 260–261; *see also* U.S. Navy
conscription 52–53, 55, 78, 93, 101, 104 112, 114, 115, 116, 133, 143, 153, 168, 174, 176, 201, 204, 263; *see also* substitutes
contraband 6, 134, 162
Corinth, Mississippi 4
County Courts 34
Cuckold's Revenge 222–223
Cumberland Army 120, 140, 147, 148, 171, 251
Cumberland Department (District) 157, 161, 163, 176, 181, 186, 251, 252, 259, 267
Cumberland Gap 88, 96, 103, 105, 168, 185

Cumberland Mountains 19, 29, 71, 76, 78, 90, 157, 164
Cumberland Plateau 7, 93, 111
Cumberland River 4, 5, 6, 57, 58, 61, 64, 130, 138, 139, 162, 191, 245, 246, 247
Cumming, Kate 103, 104, 105, 106, 121–122
Cushman, Pauline 152

Daniel, Dumpy 22
Davidson County 21, 55, 212, 246
Davis, Tillson 253, 259, 267
Davis, Jefferson C. 5, 9, 15, 27, 34, 36, 37, 56, 57, 81, 119, 201, 204, 232, 262, 267
Decatur and Nashville Railroad 95
dogs 57, 77, 84, 99, 100, 139, 160, 160–161, 176, 177, 213–214, 222
Driver, William 68–69; see also Old Glory

education 7, 9, 27, 78, 205, 208, 211–212
Emancipation Proclamation 127
embalming 123–124
"The Extornioner" 63; see also price inflation

Fain, Anderson Eliza Ray 13, 17, 175–176, 178, 199, 203, 265, 265–266, 266
Fayetteville 30, 59, 136 141, 233
female soldiers 135–136, 136, 238–239, 135–136
Foote, A. H. 4
Forrest, Nathan B. 100–101, 204, 204–205, 210–211; at Battle of the Cedars, Murfreesboro 245–246; see also Rousseau, Lovell H.
Fort Donelson 4, 5, 57, 63–66, 67–68, 128, 238
Fort Henry 4
Fort Pillow 5, 24, 80–81, 85, 86, 133, 137, 174, 204–205, 210, 211
Fort Sumter 4
Franklin 5, 6, 40, 241–244, 150–151, 152, 241–244, 253
Franklin County 254
Free Negroes 103, 226–227
French, Lucy Virginia 128–129, 152, 153, 157–159, 259, 260–264, 270

Gallatin 118, 127, 129, 237, 245,
Gibson County 176

Giles County 131
Grant, Ulysses S. 4
Greene County 38, 39, 104, 139, 178
Greenville 38, 114, 178
Grundy County 212, 254
guerrillas (a.k.a., bushmen, bushwhackers, partisans) 1, 7, 38, 77, 84, 92–93, 93–94, 94–95, 98, 99, 102, 103, 105, 109, 111, 112, 127, 128, 131, 133, 137, 138, 141, 155, 158, 159, 161, 162, 165, 167, 173, 174, 177, 182, 186–187, 191, 197–198, 201, 214, 217, 221, 222, 224, 225, 228, 232, 233, 235, 236, 237, 250, 251, 252, 253, 254, 255, 256, 257, 258, 265, 265–266

Hamilton County 48, 255
Hancock County 38
Hardima County 95
Harris, "Blood Hound" 84
Harris, Isham G. 4, 10, 13, 26, 34, 67, 76, 101, 153–154, 242
Hawkins County 38, 229
Henderson County 159
Henry County 63
hospitals 204
Hood, John Bell 6, 239, 242, 247, 248, 249, 251–252, 257
Humphrys County 57

inflation see price inflation
insanity 25
Island No. 10 5
Island No. 37 174

Jackson, Andrew 3, 94
Jackson, Charles H. 82
Jackson, R. F. 82
Jackson County 115
Jackson (Madison County) 9, 10, 15, 19–20, 22, 23, 44, 56, 87, 101, 112, 115, 155, 156, 159, 182, 198, 204, 205
Jews 9, 42, 49, 50 112, 177–178
Johnson, Mrs. Andrew 79
Johnson County 40–41, 125, 189
Johnston, Albert Sidney 4, 5, 58
juvenile crime 1, 7, 43–44, 45–46, 70, 82–83, 108–109, 130, 148–149, 190–191, 192, 193, 239, 248

Knox County 50, 139
Knoxville 5, 6, 11, 12, 16, 18, 29, 29–30, 34, 39, 39–40, 41, 42, 44, 49, 52, 54, 54–55, 62, 78, 84, 91, 96, 103, 110, 112, 115, 116, 119, 144, 151, 159, 159–160, 163, 165–166, 168, 177, 180, 181, 184–186, 185, 187, 187–189, 189–190, 193, 207, 221, 214, 232, 236, 248, 258, 260, 266; Special Orders No. 8 144

Lawrence County 131
Lexington 159
Lincoln County 30, 149, 186, 214, 217, 254; slave auction 152
Longstreet, James 5

Madison County 99, 119, 269, 270; County Court 2, 30, 57
Madisonville 183
Marshall County 254
Mason, Mrs. Annie 233
Maury County 28, 103, 130, 131, 202
McCann, Dick 161
McDowell, Amanda 16, 111, 165, 169, 240–241, 249–250, 263, 267; summation of the war 267
McEwin, Mrs. 19
McMinnville 128–129, 140, 141, 209, 256–257, 259, 263–264, 265
McNairy County 59
Meigs County 228
Memphis 26, 26, 45; armament production 92; Battle of 5, 86; cannon factory and foundry 42, 86–87; Committee of Public Safety (Vigilance Committee) 10, 11, 12, 13, 15, 20, 28, 35; dogs, 99; gender confusion, 38, 48, 110; juvenile crime 9, 70, 82, 108, 148, 190–19, 192; prostitution 7, 33, 36, 44, 70, 87–88, 142–143, 147–148, 213, 238; women 1, 7, 9, 10, 12, 16, 17, 20, 24, 25, 26, 28–29, 30, 32, 37, 38, 41, 43–44, 45, 46, 49–50, 54, 61, 82, 83, 91, 108, 110, 120, 142, 143, 147, 155, 158, 182, 183, 211, 213, 238, 263
Memphis General Orders: No. 7 90; No. 12 92; No. 44 266; No. 45 267; No. 61 92; No. 70 218–219; No. 100 219; No. 173 182
Memphis Special Orders: No. 5 90; No. 6 92; No. 9 90; No. 10 90–91; No. 12 92; No. 21 92; No. 70 218–219; No. 102 268

Middle Tennessee Campaign 154
Military and Financial Board 35
miscegenation 46, 199, 224–225
Mississippi River 4
Missouri Compromise Line (1828) 3
Monroe County 84
morphine 39, 137, 199; *see also* opiates
Mulberry Village 186; *see also* Lincoln County
murder 1, 9, 10, 125–126, 131, 141, 144, 169, 199, 211, 219, 221, 222, 233–234, 239, 240–241, 242, 251, 256, 257, 258, 261–262, 263, 267, 269
Murfreesboro (Murfreesborough) 5, 11, 12, 14, 15, 19, 26, 31, 33, 35–39, 41–51, 53–54, 55, 56, 63, 67–70, 75, 80–82, 85–88, 90–95, 98, 99, 107, 108–111, 113, 114, 119–124, 126, 127, 129, 132, 133–138, 140, 144–145, 147, 148–149, 153, 155, 157, 160–161, 166–169, 170–172, 174, 176, 179, 182–183, 190–192, 204, 210, 213, 214, 216, 218–219, 221–223, 225, 227, 229, 232, 235–236, 238, 242, 245, 246, 249, 253–254, 256, 262–263, 266, 270

Nashville 3–7, 10, 12–19, 21, 22, 25, 26, 29, 34, 36–39, 43, 46–50, 52–53, 55, 56, 58, 59, 63, 66–70, 75, 77, 78, 80, 81–86, 91, 94, 95, 102, 103, 111, 112, 114, 116–118, 125, 127–132, 134, 135–136, 140, 141, 144, 145, 149, 151–152, 155–157, 162, 166, 169–170, 178–179, 181, 187, 190–197, 199–200, 203–206, 210, 212–213, 215–219, 222–229, 231–232, 235–240, 244–245, 248, 252–253, 264; Battle of 246–247
Nashville Refugee Aid Society 215
negroes 11, 13, 15, 17, 18, 22, 24, 37, 46, 55, 57, 59, 62, 63–64, 73, 82, 85, 91, 92, 96, 97, 98, 100, 103, 104, 105, 122, 125, 131, 132, 134, 136, 138, 144, 155, 156, 158, 163, 175–176, 177, 179, 182, 189, 191, 192, 193, 196, 201, 204, 205, 207, 208–209, 210–211, 217–218, 221, 224, 225, 226–227, 228, 229, 237, 238, 249, 257, 258, 262, 263, 264; *see also* contraband
nullification 3

Oath of Allegiance 40, 75, 78 90–91, 92, 93, 96, 103, 135, 140, 144, 146, 162, 165, 197, 200, 201, 220, 267, 90–91
Old Glory 68–69; *see also* Driver, William
Oldham, Van Buren 160, 161, 163, 164
opiates 54, 111, 198; *see also* morphine
Overton County 219–221

Paris 61, 62, 63, 151
Palmyra 138–139
Perry County 146
Pickett County 41
Pillow, Gideon J. 17–18, 20, 23–24, 25, 26, 35, 44–45, 63, 64, 65, 66, 96–98, 124, 175, 234
Pillow Guards 20–21
Pine Bluff 228
Pittsburg Landing, Battle of 5
Plum Run Bend 5
poetry 154–155, 205, 212
Polk, Mrs. James 70
poor 15, 19, 20, 23, 25, 42, 44–45, 54, 55, 63, 83, 88, 93, 94, 122, 166, 205, 206, 207
Pope, John 5
Prentise Guards 20–21
price inflation 1, 27, 29, 37–38, 42, 43, 44–45, 48, 54, 56, 63, 115–116, 125, 163, 175, 219
public health 1, 137–138, 141, 145, 181, 182, 191–192, 199–200, 203, 222; *see also* smallpox; vaccination
Purdy 159

rape 233
recruitment 99, 157
refugees 1, 87, 66, 102, 131, 151, 163, 170, 187, 188, 189, 205–208, 210, 215, 224, 225, 263
religion 10, 12, 13, 26, 32, 33, 35–36, 39, 45, 55, 75, 79, 87, 91, 101, 104, 114, 134, 136, 137, 140, 149, 150, 165, 211, 215, 239, 240–241, 262; *see also* churches; Jews
Republicans, black 4
Reynoldsburg 202
Rhea County 197
Richardson, R.V. 7, 131, 133
Roane County 46, 139

Robertson County 45, 142, 232
Rousseau, Lovell H.: at Battle of the Cedars, Murfreesboro 245–246; *see also* Forrest, Nathan Bedford

sausage making 246
Schofield, John M. 6
Scott County 144, 128, 154
sea turtle 223
secession, secessionists 3, 4, 5, 9, 10, 11, 12, 13, 14, 15, 16, 17, 19, 21, 22, 26, 27, 30, 46, 55, 59, 75, 78, 91, 102, 106, 110, 139, 146, 162, 194, 195, 196, 215, 267
Secret Police 178
secret unionist societies 27
Sevier County 48
Sewanee Coal Company 48
Shelby County 41, 42, 46, 126, 65, 204, 211
Shelbyville 136, 152, 233–234
Shiloh, Battle of 6; *see also* Pittsburg Landing
ship building 225–226
slaves, slavery 3, 4, 6, 7, 13, 15, 19, 28, 30, 34, 37, 55–56, 57, 62, 66–67, 69, 79, 95–96, 97, 98, 105, 124–125, 131, 132, 152–153, 163, 168, 175, 176, 194, 196, 197, 199, 207, 208, 211–212, 217–218, 250, 252, 263–264; *see also* Lincoln County
smallpox 181, 182; *see also* public health; vaccination
Smith County 117
smuggling 129, 219
Special Orders 90, 91, 92, 142–143, 228, 268–269
Spence, John C. 12, 15, 19, 56, 85, 123, 133, 136–137, 144, 179
Spencer 224
spies 7, 20, 36, 47, 57, 71, 118, 120, 152, 165, 201, 248
State Penitentiary 236–237
Stones River, Battle of 5, 121
Stowe, Harriet Beecher 210
Strawberry Plains 21, 48
strike 55
substitutes 112, 116, 132, 133, 153, 233; *see also* conscription
Sullivan County 29
Sumner County 203, 214
Swayne's Bowel Cordial 223

Tennessee Baptist: Bible binding 45; firearm cleansing 45
Tennessee State Convention 252–253

Texas Rangers 43, 46
Thomas, George H. 5
Tipton County 21, 268
traffic jam 203
Triune (Trouble at the Guerrillas' Ball) 257–258
Tullahoma Campaign 5, 154; *see also* Middle Tennessee Campaign

"Uncle Tom's Cabin" 210
Union City 21–22, 23, 24, 31, 32, 60, 180, 202, 229
Union County 143
Unionists 21, 24–25, 27, 38, 39, 40, 48–49, 50–51, 125–126, 195, 196
United States Colored Troops (USCT) 176–177, 232
U.S. Navy 5, 42, 51, 60, 70, 75, 86–87, 129, 139, 146–147, 198, 244–246, 259, 260–261, 269; *see also* C.S. Navy

vaccination 181; *see also* public health; smallpox
"Vampires" 43, 44; *see also* price inflation
Van Buren County 225
volunteers 11, 14, 15, 17, 18, 23, 24, 25, 31, 34, 39, 41, 52, 53, 54, 56, 69, 84, 94, 100, 101, 102, 104, 106, 119, 124–125, 127, 129, 141, 145–146, 148, 153, 154, 157, 164, 167, 169, 171, 172, 173, 178, 183, 182, 186, 228, 239, 240, 246, 250, 252, 259

wager 132, 192
wages 7, 15, 37, 55, 98, 112, 119, 163, 207, 217
Wallace, Lew 5
Warren County 254
Washington County 112, 139
Weakly County 59
White, Dr. John 233
White County 16, 110, 165, 169, 249
White's Creek: fishing trip 225; Turnpike 212
wild steer 228–229
Williamson County 130
Wilson County 135, 224, 237
Wolf River 181–182
women 10, 12, 14, 19–20, 21, 22, 40, 80, 90, 111, 231–232, 232, 238, 240, 248, 260, 263, 265, 266

Yankee ice 219

zinc coffins 130, 200; *see also* embalming